Studies in the Social and
Cultural Foundations of Language No. 17

Rethinking linguistic relativity

Linguistic relativity is the claim, associated especially with the names of
Humboldt, Sapir, and Whorf, that culture, through language, affects the
way in which we think, and especially our classification of the experienced
world. This book re-examines ideas about linguistic relativity in the light
of new evidence and changes in theoretical climate. Parts I and II address
the classical issues in the relation between thought and language, and the
extent of linguistic and cultural universals. Parts III and IV show how
changes in our understanding of meaning require that we look at how
context enters into interpretation, and how context is constituted in social
interaction, reflecting properties of larger social wholes. The editors have
provided a substantial introduction which summarizes changes in
thinking about the Sapir–Whorf hypothesis in the light of developments
in anthropology, linguistics, and cognitive science; and also introductions
to each section which will be of especial use to students.

Studies in the Social and Cultural Foundations of Language

The aim of this series is to develop theoretical perspectives on the essential social and cultural character of language by methodological and empirical emphasis on the occurrence of language in its communicative and interactional settings, on the socioculturally grounded "meanings" and "functions" of linguistic forms, and on the social scientific study of language use across cultures. It will thus explicate the essentially ethnographic nature of linguistic data, whether spontaneously occurring or experimentally induced, whether normative or variational, whether synchronic or diachronic. Works appearing in the series will make substantive and theoretical contributions to the debate over the sociocultural–functional and structural–formal nature of language, and will represent the concerns of scholars in the sociology and anthropology of language, anthropological linguistics, sociolinguistics, and socio-culturally informed psycholinguistics.

RETHINKING
LINGUISTIC RELATIVITY

Edited by

JOHN J. GUMPERZ

Professor Emeritus, University of California, Berkeley

and

STEPHEN C. LEVINSON

*Director, Max Planck Institute for Psycholinguistics
and Cognitive Anthropology Research Group, Nijmegen*

CAMBRIDGE
UNIVERSITY PRESS

Published by the Press Syndicate of the University of Cambridge
The Pitt Building, Trumpington Street, Cambridge CB2 1RP
40 West 20th Street, New York, NY 10011-4211, USA
10 Stamford Road, Oakleigh, Melbourne 3166, Australia

First published 1996

Printed in Great Britain at the University Press, Cambridge

A catalogue record for this book is available from the British Library

Library of Congress cataloguing in publication data

Rethinking linguistic relativity/edited by John J. Gumperz and
Stephen C. Levinson
p. cm.–(Studies in the social and cultural foundations of
language, no. 17)
Includes indexes.
ISBN 0 521 44433 0 (hardback). –
ISBN 0 521 44890 5 (paperback)
1. Sapir–Whorf hypothesis. 2. Thought and thinking.
3. Language and culture. I. Gumperz, John Joseph, 1922–
II. Levinson, Stephen C. III. Series.
P35.R465 1996
401–dc20
95–38476 CIP
ISBN 0 521 44433 0 hardback
ISBN 0 521 44890 5 paperback

CONTENTS

CONTRIBUTORS

Melissa Bowerman
Max Planck Institute for Psycholinguistics, Nijmegen

Pascal Boyer
Dynamique du langage, M.R.A.S.H., Lyon

Herbert H. Clark
Department of Psychology, Stanford University

Elsa Gomez-Imbert
Centre National de la Recherche Scientifique, Paris

John J. Gumperz
Professor Emeritus, University of California at Berkeley

William F. Hanks
Department of Anthropology, University of Chicago

John B. Haviland
Dept. of Linguistics and Anthropology, Reed College, Portland, Oregon

Paul Kay
Department of Linguistics, University of California at Berkeley

Charles M. Keller
Department of Anthropology, University of Illinois at Urbana-Champaign

Janet Dixon Keller
Department of Anthropology, University of Illinois at Urbana-Champaign

Stephen C. Levinson
Director, Max Planck Institute for Psycholinguistics and Cognitive Anthropology Research Group, Nijmegen

John A. Lucy
Department of Anthropology, University of Pennsylvania

Elinor Ochs
Department of TESL/Applied Linguistics, University of California at Los Angeles

Dan I. Slobin
Department of Psychology, University of California at Berkeley

ACKNOWLEDGMENTS

This volume arises from a conference entitled "Rethinking linguistic relativity," Wenner-Gren Symposium 112, held in Ocho Rios, Jamaica, in May 1991. The participants were Niyi Akkinaso, Talal Assad, Norine Berenz, Melissa Bowerman, Pascal Boyer, Herbert Clark, Elsa Gomez-Imbert, John Gumperz, William Hanks, John Haviland, Paul Kay, Janet Keller, Jean Lave, Stephen Levinson, John Lucy, Elinor Ochs, Seidel Silverman, Dan Slobin, Len Talmy, Pamela Wright. The book is not a direct record of the proceedings, for which see Gumperz & Levinson (1991). Rather, it pursues selectively just some of the themes raised at the conference, and the papers have been extensively revised for publication in the light of animated discussion. Thus, although not all the participants are represented in the volume directly, their contributions have no doubt been woven into the fabric of the book. We would like to thank them all. We have in addition had the benefit of further discussions with some of them, especially Melissa Bowerman, John Haviland, Paul Kay, John Lucy, and Dan Slobin. In addition, we owe an especial debt to Seidel Silverman, who, on behalf of the Wenner-Gren Foundation, encouraged the original idea, and was deeply involved in the planning of the conference. We are also indebted to the staff of the foundation for further detailed planning and organization.

Reference

Gumperz, J. J. & Levinson, S. C. 1991. Rethinking linguistic relativity. *Current Anthropology*, 32(5), 6130.5–23.

INTRODUCTION: LINGUISTIC RELATIVITY RE-EXAMINED

JOHN J. GUMPERZ AND STEPHEN C. LEVINSON

Quelle est l'influence réciproque des opinions du peuple sur le langage et du langage sur les opinions?
The theme of the 1757 Prize Essay Competition of the Berlin Academy.[1]

1 Language, thinking, and reality

Every student of language or society should be familiar with the essential idea of linguistic relativity, the idea that culture, *through* language, affects the way we think, especially perhaps our classification of the experienced world. Much of our experience seems to support some such idea, for example the phenomenology of struggling with a second language, where we find that the summit of competence is forever over the next horizon, the obvious absence of definitive or even accurate translation (let alone the ludicrous failure of phrasebooks), even the wreck of diplomatic efforts on linguistic and rhetorical rocks.

On the other hand, there is a strand of robust common sense that insists that a stone is a stone whatever you call it, that the world is a recalcitrant reality that imposes its structure on our thinking and our speaking and that the veil of linguistic difference can be ripped aside with relative ease. Plenty of subjective experiences and objective facts can be marshalled to support this view: the delight of foreign friendships, our ability to "read" the military or economic strategies of alien rivals, the very existence of comparative sciences of language, psychology, and society.[2]

These two opposing strands of "common sense" have surfaced in academic controversies and intellectual positions over many centuries of Western thought. If St. Augustine (354–430) took the view that language is a mere nomenclature for antecedently existing concepts, Roger Bacon (1220–92) insisted, despite strong views on the universal basis of grammar, that the mismatch between semantic fields in different languages made accurate translation impossible (Kelly 1979: 9).[3] The Port Royal grammarians of the seventeenth century found universal logic thinly disguised behind linguistic difference, while the German romantics

1

in a tradition leading through to Humboldt in the nineteenth century found a unique *Weltanschauung*, "world view," in each language. The first half of our own century was characterized by the presumption of radical linguistic and cultural difference reflecting profound cognitive differences, a presumption to be found in anthropology, linguistics and behaviourist psychologies, not to mention philosophical emphasis on meaning as use. The second half of the century has been dominated by the rise of the cognitive sciences, with their treatment of mind as inbuilt capacities for information processing, and their associated universalist and rationalist presuppositions. St. Augustine would probably recognize the faint echoes of his views in much modern theorizing about how children acquire language through prior knowledge of the structure of the world.

There is surely some spiral ascent in the swing of this pendulum. Nevertheless it is important to appreciate how little real scientific progress there has been in the study of lexical or morphosyntactic meaning – most progress in linguistics has been in the study of syntax and sound systems, together with rather general ideas about how the meaning of phrases might be composed out of the meaning of their constituents. Thus there is still much more opinion (often ill-informed) than solid fact in modern attitudes to "linguistic relativity."

There are three terms in the relation: language, thought, and culture. Each of these are global cover terms, not notions of any precision. When one tries to make anything definite out of the idea of linguistic relativity, one inevitably has to focus on particular aspects of each of these terms in the relation.[4] This book will show how each can be differently construed and, as a consequence, the relation reconsidered. In addition the connecting links can be variously conceived. Thus by the end of the book the reader will find that the aspects of language and thinking that are focused on are selective, but also that the very relation between culture and community has become complex. Readers will find the original idea of linguistic relativity still live, but functioning in a way that differs from how it was originally conceived.

2 Linguistic relativity re-examined

The original idea, variously attributable to Humboldt, Boas, Sapir, Whorf, was that the semantic structures of different languages might be fundamentally incommensurable, with consequences for the way in which speakers of specific languages might think and act. On this view, language, thought, and culture are deeply interlocked, so that each language might be claimed to have associated with it a distinctive world-view.[5]

These ideas captured the imagination of a generation of anthropologists, psychologists, and linguists, as well as members of the general public. They had deep implications for the way anthropologists should conduct their business, suggesting that translational difficulties might lie at the heart of their discipline.[6] However, the ideas seemed entirely and abruptly discredited by the rise of the cognitive sciences in the 1960s, which favoured a strong emphasis on the commonality of human cognition and its basis in human genetic endowment. This emphasis was strengthened by developments within linguistic anthropology, with the discovery of significant semantic universals in color terms, the structure of ethnobotanical nomenclature, and (arguably) kinship terms.

However, there has been a recent change of intellectual climate in psychology, linguistics, and other disciplines surrounding anthropology, as well as within linguistic anthropology, towards an intermediate position, in which more attention is paid to linguistic and cultural difference, such diversity being viewed within the context of what we have learned about universals (features shared by all languages and cultures). New work in developmental psychology, while acknowledging underlying universal bases, emphasizes the importance of the socio-cultural context of human development. Within sociolinguistics and linguistic anthropology there has also been increasing attention to meaning and discourse, and concomitantly a growing appreciation of how interpretive differences can be rooted as much in the systematic uses of language as in its structure.[7]

2.1 The "classical" hypothesis: some historical background

Speculation about the relation between language, culture, and thought can probably be traced back to the dawn of philosophy. We cannot here give an adequate history of the ideas, which has yet to be written from the current perspective, and would in any case connect closely to the entire treatment of epistemology and ontology in two millennia of speculations about language and mind. Many early classical and medieval controversies centered on issues of translation, which have always played a central role in Christian thinking.[8] Speculations about the origin of language in the course of human cognitive and cultural development, and debate about whether language presupposes or instead makes available abstract symbolic thought, also have a long history, with celebrated controversies in the eighteenth century.[9] The process of conquest and colonialism also brought forth from its beginning many ruminations on the role of language in perceived cultural superiority.[10] Thus in a number of arenas, theological, philosophical, legal, and colonial, there have been for centuries well-rehearsed debates about the mutual dependence or independence of language and thought, and about the relation between social systems and that interdependence.

Special conditions reinvigorated the debate in the first half of this century in America.[11] Suffice it to say here that the phrase *linguistic relativity* achieved notoriety through its use by Whorf, and that the basis of Whorf's ideas can be lineally traced through Sapir to Boas, or alternatively through (German-trained) Whitney and other early American linguists, and thus to Wilhelm von Humboldt (1767–1835), the great German educator, linguist, and philosopher.[12] From there the conventional history has it that the trail leads to Herder and the German romantics, and on back to Leibniz in opposition to the enlightenment ideas of Universal Grammar and words as mere nomenclature for pre-existing concepts.[13] The lineage is both stepwise and direct: e.g. Sapir wrote a master's thesis on a comparison between Herder and Humboldt, while Boas of course embodied the transatlantic migration of the German tradition.[14]

However, this potted history is now known to be at least partially misleading, because Humboldt also directly absorbed French eighteenth-century ideas, some of which, by the close of the century, almost sketched his own program (Aarsleff 1988).[15] Those ideas were transmitted through multiple channels to America, directly (e.g. in the person of Duponceau, an early student of Amerindian languages), and indirectly through Humboldt's correspondence in the 1820s and 1830s with Pickering, Duponceau, and others,[16] through publication of Humboldt's works in translation as early as 1885, and via Steinthal's writings to Whitney by 1867.[17]

An additional source of these ideas is the growth of early twentieth-century structuralism.[18] For example, the Saussurean notion of *valeur*, wherein an expression picks up distinctive meaning through its opposition to other expressions, has the implication that the content of linguistic expressions depends on the system in which they are embedded, rather than in the first instance on their denotation.[19] Since no two linguistic systems or subsystems are ever identical, as is easily shown by comparison of semantic fields from English vs. French, linguistic relativity more or less follows. This form of linguistic relativism is historically tied to the cultural relativism immanent in Durkheim's later sociological ideas, which still (despite protestations to the contrary) dominate anthropological ideas. Anthropologists, as indeed do many field linguists, take these kind of structuralist ideas as a *methodological presupposition*: "strive to understand the native ideas in the context of the entire local system of ideas, leaving comparison to be made between *systems*, not between isolated words or traits across systems." It is hard to quarrel with this as a methodological stance, but it is a reasonable charge that subscribers to this doctrine have mistaken methodological prescription for theory: the result of comparison between systems may be a robust finding of universal principles governing individual traits.

The essential point here is that the ideas we associate today so especially with Whorf and Sapir have a long and distinguished lineage on the one hand, while perhaps being no more than one of two opposing perennial strands of thought, universalism vs. relativism, on the other. Nevertheless, they crystallized in a particular fashion in American intellectual life of the 1940s.[20] The idea of a close link between linguistic and conceptual categories took on a new meaning in the context of three further background assumptions characteristic of the first half of the century. One was the presumption of a (sometimes tempered) empiricist epistemology, that is, the view that all knowledge is acquired primarily through experience. The other was the structuralist assumption that language forms a system of oppositions, such that formal distinctions directly reflect meaning distinctions.[21] The third was the idea of an unconscious mental life, and thus the possibility of linguistic effects beyond conscious awareness. It was the conjunction of these background ideas together with the specific formulation of the "linguistic relativity" hypothesis, that gave that hypothesis its particular character in the history of ideas.

Sapir may have originated the phrase,[22] but the *locus classicus* (though by no means the most careful statement) of the concept of linguistic relativity is the popular articles by Whorf (1940a–b, reprinted 1956: 207–33), where the following oft-quoted passages may be found which illustrate all the central themes.

Epistemology

We dissect nature along lines laid down by our native languages. The categories and types that we isolate from the world of phenomena we do not find there because they stare every observer in the face; on the contrary, the world is presented in a kaleidoscopic flux of impressions which has to be organized by our minds – and this means largely by the linguistic systems of our minds.

(1956: 213)

Structuralism

Pattern-symbolic expressions [i.e. linguistic notations of inherent linguistic patterning] are exact, as mathematics is, but are not quantitative. They do not refer ultimately to number and dimension, as mathematics does, but to pattern and structure.   (1956: 226)

Quantity and number play little role in the realm of pattern, where there are no variables but, instead, abrupt alternations from one configuration to another. The mathematical sciences require exact measurement, but what linguistics requires is, rather, exact "patternment."   (1956: 230–1)[23]

Unconscious thought

[T]he phenomena of language are to its own speakers largely of a background character and so are outside the critical consciousness and control of the speaker.

(1956: 211)

Linguistic relativity

The phenomena of language are background phenomena, of which the talkers are unaware or, at most, dimly aware...These automatic, involuntary patterns of language are not the same for all men but are specific for each language and constitute the formalized side of the language, or its "grammar"...

From this fact proceeds what I have called the "linguistic relativity principle," which means, in informal terms, that users of markedly different grammars are pointed by their grammars toward different types of observations and different evaluations of externally similar acts of observation, and hence are not equivalent as observers, but must arrive at somewhat different views of the world.

(1956: 221)

Or in alternative formulation:

We are thus introduced to a new principle of relativity, which holds that all observers are not led by the same physical evidence to the same picture of the universe, unless their linguistic backgrounds are similar, or can in some way be calibrated.

(1956: 214)

The boldness of Whorf's formulation prompted a succession of empirical studies in America in the 1950s and early 1960s aimed at elucidating and testing what now became known as the Sapir–Whorf hypothesis.[24] Anthropological and linguistic studies by Trager, Hoijer, Lee, Casagrande, and others have been well reviewed elsewhere (see Lucy 1992a: ch. 3; and this volume).[25] These studies hardly touched on cognition, but in the same period a few psychologists (notably Lenneberg, Brown, Stefflre) did try to investigate the relation between lexical coding and memory, especially in the domain of color, and found some significant correlations (again see Lucy 1992a: ch. 5). This line of work culminated, however, in the celebrated demonstration by Berlin & Kay (1969) of the language-independent saliency of "basic colors," which was taken as a decisive anti-relativist finding, and effectively terminated this tradition of investigations into the Sapir–Whorf hypothesis.[26] There followed a period in which Whorf's own views in particular became the butt of extensive criticism.[27]

It is clear from this background that the "Sapir–Whorf" hypothesis in its classical form arose from deep historical roots but in a particular intellectual climate. Even though (it has been closely argued by Lucy 1992a) the original hypothesis has never been thoroughly tested, the intellectual milieu had by the 1960s entirely changed. Instead of empiricism, we now have rationalistic assumptions. Instead of the basic tenets of structuralism, in which each linguistic or social system must be understood first in internal terms before comparison is possible, modern comparative work (especially in linguistics) tends to presume that one can isolate particular aspects or traits of a system (e.g. aspect or subjecthood) for comparison. The justification, such as it is, is that we now have the outlines of a universal structure for language and perhaps cognition, which provides the terms for comparison. It is true that the assumption of unconscious processes continues, but now the emphasis is on the unconscious nature of nearly all systematic information processing, so that the distinctive character of Whorf's habitual thought has been submerged.[28]

In this changed intellectual climate, and in the light of the much greater knowledge that we now have about both language and mental processing, it would be pointless to attempt to revive ideas about linguistic relativity in their original form. Nevertheless, there have been a whole range of recent intellectual shifts that make the ground more fertile for some of the original seeds to grow into new saplings. It is the purpose of this volume to explore the implications of some of these shifts in a number of different disciplines for our overall view of the relations between language, thinking, and society.

2.2 The idea behind the present volume

This volume explores one chain of reasoning that is prompted by these recent changes in ideas. The line of argument runs in the following way.

Linguistic relativity is a theory primarily about the nature of meaning, the classic view focusing on the lexical and grammatical coding of language-specific distinctions. In this theory, two languages may "code" the same state of affairs utilizing semantic concepts or distinctions peculiar to each language; as a result the two linguistic descriptions reflect different construals of the same bit of reality. These semantic distinctions are held to reflect cultural distinctions and at the same time to influence cognitive categorizations, an issue re-examined in part I below.

Assuming that there is such a link between linguistic structure and conceptual categories, the possibility of conceptual relativity would seem at first sight to depend on whether linguistic codings are significantly different across languages. Very little, however, is actually known about substantive semantic or conceptual universals. It is true that there are demonstrations of universal semantic principles in a few domains like color terminology, ethnobiological taxonomies, perhaps also in systems of kinship terminology. However, these demonstrations carry no necessary general implications, and the same holds for studies of grammatical meaning. These issues are discussed in part II below.

Yet, on further reflection, distinctive linguistic (grammatical or lexical) codings are not the only ways in which "meanings" or interpretations can vary systematically across cultures. This is brought out by recent developments in the theory of meaning. These developments show that "meaning" is not fully encapsulated in lexicon and grammar, which provide only schematic constraints on what the speaker will be taken to have meant in a particular utterance. These ideas are quite general across the different theories and frameworks which typify modern linguistics. For example, the same point is made in very different ways in formal semantic theories like Discourse Representation Theory[29] or Situation Semantics,[30] where contextual determination of interpretation is one of the main issues driving development away from classical truth-conditional theories. Equally, in different varieties of pragmatic theory, from Relevance Theory[31] to more conservative Gricean theories,[32] current work is addressed to explaining how almost vacuous or semantically general expressions can have determinate interpretations in particular contexts.

These changes in the theory of meaning have been prompted quite largely by the phenomena of deixis, the existence in all natural languages of a plethora of (indexical or deictic) expressions that only refer relative to a context: if you find a note on the ground that says "See you here in ten minutes from now," you will be puzzled about who *you* denotes, where the place *here* refers to, and when the countdown from *now* began. The semantics of these expressions is designed to fix a reference only when given a context by the situation of utterance. But these are simple examples. The kind of contextual information that is actually needed turns out to be deeply embedded in practices of speaking, the local conduct of social life, and the social distribution of shared under-standings. All this is the subject of part III of this book.

A large part of the burden of interpretation is thus shifted from theories of context-free lexical and grammatical meaning to theories of use in context. Some important principles of the use of language may plausibly be argued to be universal (e.g. Grice's "maxims of conversa-tion" or the turn-taking and repair systems of conversation, or even some principles of interactional politeness). Yet others seem much more clearly culture-specific. For example, the ethnography of speaking has shown how diverse can be the principles governing the production and interpretation of utterances in specific speech events – court proceed-ings, formal greetings, religious rituals, councils, and the like. Recent work, however, shows that we cannot always think of speech events as antecedently constructed, forming the frame or context for interpreta-tion. Sometimes, through modulation of the verbal interaction itself, these contextual frames can be invoked, so that utterances can carry with them, or project, the context in which they should be interpreted. These are subtle, culture-specific, processes, learnt within the social networks that utilize them.

In that case, aspects of meaning and interpretation are determined by culture-specific activities and practices. Those activities and practices are interconnected in turn with the larger socio-political systems that govern, and are in turn partly constituted by, them: particular divisions of labor and social networks provide differential access to such activities and the associated patterns of language use. All these issues are the focus of part IV, the final part of the book.

This book therefore spans a large terrain, from the classic Whorfian issues of the relation of grammar to thought on the one hand to consideration of language use in sociolinguistic perspective on the other. One key idea that supports this span is the notion of indexicality, conceived not just in terms of the contextual dependence of deictic items, but also in the broader Peircean sense, as a broad relationship between interpreters, signals, and the context of interpretation.[33] Indexicality necessarily anchors meaning and interpretation to the context of language use and thus to wider social organization. Issues of linguistic relativity are in this way directly related to the variable cultural structuring of contexts.

Another idea is more latent in the book. If new theories of language make possible new connections between meaning and context, there are also new, if still incipient, ideas about the nature of thinking and context. One line of thought explores the idea of "technologies of the intellect": by externalizing thoughts or representing them, we are able to manipulate them in quite different ways. Goody (1977) has argued that literacy makes available multidimensional scanning of what is essentially a linear medium (consider a table of figures, which can be examined from the perspective of either its columns or its rows). Another line of investigation explores how we solve intellectual tasks by embedding them in practical activities: for example, a trucker may estimate loads in a way quite distinct from the way an architect estimates spaces (Scribner 1992, Lave 1988).[34] Finally, and most relevantly perhaps, verbal interaction may be seen in the same light: as a means of externalizing thinking that allows joint solutions to many problems, including the very determination of the meaning of utterances (see Clark, this volume). These approaches have in common the idea that thinking does not proceed just according to rules and exceptions, but also by more flexible on-the-spot solutions using general principles suited to the context. These ideas are referred to in a number of the papers in this volume under the rubrics of "practice," "habitus," "strategy," and so on.[35]

Viewed in these ways, the issue of linguistic relativity shifts significantly. From an "inner circle" of links between grammar, categories, and culture as internalized by the individual, the focus shifts to include an "outer circle" of communication and its relation on the one hand to interaction in social settings and on the other hand to individual patterns of cognition which are partly contextually attuned, and even perhaps acquired primarily through patterns of communication, in turn enabling it. Perhaps this wider perspective will help to build a bridge across the Durkheimian division that we have inherited between the psychological and social sciences.

2.3 The structure of the book

The chapters in this volume explore this series of interlocked issues. The book falls roughly into two halves: the first two sections address the classical issues of the relation between thought and language, and the extent of linguistic and cultural universals. The second two sections show how changes in our understanding of meaning require that we look at how context enters into interpretation, and how context is constituted in social interaction, and reflects properties of larger social wholes.

Part I contributes some fresh ideas about the relation of language to cognition. It seems that, despite much recent skepticism, there are indeed important language-specific effects on cognitive processing. Such claims must be hedged in various ways: perhaps the effects are confined to the process of speaking itself, not all ways of putting things imply ways of thinking, and not all thought is in a form related to language at all. Nevertheless, the debate makes it clear that we can no longer view the idea of "linguistic determinism" as a pure anachronism, not worthy of serious attention.

Part II is concerned with universals in language and culture – do these severely restrict the scope for linguistic and conceptual diversity? It seems that in some semantic domains (e.g. spatial description) where universals are expected, they nevertheless prove hard to specify or indeed to find. Yet in other conceptual domains where they are least expected (like religious ideas), they may in the end be rather self-evident. This unsettles our confidence that we know *a priori* how to apportion the explanation of behavior between the psychic unity of mankind and the divisive variation of culture. Nor in any case would the existence of enormously rich universals rule out extensive cultural difference at every level.

Part III explores how context and background assumptions enter into the determination of meaning and interpretation. Starting from the clear case of indexicals, the arguments tend to show that understanding is grounded in shared practice and mutual assumptions. Interpretive diversity can thus be generated independently of difference at the level of grammar and lexicon. The scope of linguistic relativity, thus construed as a question of differentiated meaning-systems, is now enormously widened.

Part IV takes up this idea, and explores its consequences for how we conceive of "language" and "culture." If meaning resides in interpretive practices, and these are located in the social networks one is socialized in, then the "culture-" and "language-" bearing units are not nations, ethnic groups or the like – they are not units at all, but rather networks of interacting individuals, which can be thought of in either more or less inclusive ways.

We end up then with a reconstrual of all the terms in the classic relation of language, thought, and culture.

2.4 Taking stock: some emergent ideas and future prospects

A number of important themes emerge from the volume. First, there are diverse sources of difference and incommensurability across languages and varieties. Whorf emphasized the grammatical, because he felt the unconscious repetitive, coercive patterning on the grammatical level would be reflected in a regimentation of thinking. But in this volume many other levels of linguistic patterning are considered. It is argued that the lexical level can also have deep cognitive effects, by requiring distinctions to be noticed and memorized at the time of experience, in case the need arises for later description. Recent work shows that these effects can be demonstrated and replicated across different languages and cultures.[36]

Yet there are also levels of patterning beyond the grammatical and lexical, best appreciated by switching the perspective from the language producer to the language interpreter. Here there are different patterns of interpretation, which can be invoked by complex constellations of cues across linguistic and paralinguistic levels. Here we find "transpositions" to contexts distinct from, but functionally similar to, the context of speaking. Here too we find markers of stance, or attitude, through which social relationships are signalled, and subtle contextualization cues that invoke the type of activity (banter, argument, excuse-giving, etc.) within which the utterance is to be assessed.

Thus we are led into the study of the on-line complexities of utterance comprehension, and come to appreciate the miraculous co-ordination of perspectives that is required for satisfactory communication. Serious studies of interactive discourse post-date Sapir or Whorf, of course, if only because practical recording methods were not then available. These studies show recurrent patterning on the discourse level, which may be connected to patterning at the grammatical level (e.g. through the grammaticalization of particular expressive techniques). Some of the ideas that emerge have distinct parallels to Whorf's ideas: much of the cueing of context is done through repetitive, subliminal, and subtle cues, not accessible to introspection, and which can differ systematically across cultures and social networks. Whorf was keen to establish the relation between, on the one hand, construing reality in a certain way as required by the language one speaks, and, on the other, acting in certain ways (recollect his example of the gasoline drums marked "empty," suggesting the absence of danger and prompting carelessness with naked flame). In a similar way, utilizing interpretative strategies of particular sorts can be shown to have demonstrable consequences – these become particularly salient when speaker and addressee do not share them, and systematic miscommunication results.[37]

Another set of interesting ideas that emerge is the deconstruction of the notion of "culture" or "community." Communication relies on shared meanings and strategies of interpretation. However, this common ground is distributed in a complex way through social networks. Such networks may constitute effective "sub-cultures," nested communities within communities; but they can also cross-cut linguistic and social boundaries of all sorts, creating regional and even global patterns of shared, similar communicative strategies in specialist networks.

All of these ideas have to be set within the context of the ever-increasing set of universal cognitive constraints that are being discovered. But the sources of meaning-difference are many, and what, seen in grammatical perspective, may seem like little discrepancies can have large and pervasive communicative effects.[38] Thus neither the study of sameness nor that of difference limits the interest of the other.

Given the complexity of the issues raised, the reader will find here no new overall theory. Rather, the aims are much more modest, to introduce the reader to newly discovered, arguably relevant phenomena, to place the constellation of notions associated with linguistic relativity in the context of current theory, and thereby to enrich the original hypothesis. Nevertheless, much of the range of Whorf's interests, from semantic diversity, to cognitive processes, to the nature of culture and the constitution of society, are here reflected.

Notes

1 The prize was won two years later by J. D. Michaelis with the essay "Beantwortung der Frage von dem Einfluss der Meinungen eines Volcks in seine Sprache, und der Sprache in die Meinungen" ("A dissertation on the influence of opinions on language and of language on opinions's). See Cloeren (1988: 11).

2 Compare Boas's endorsement of Bastian's assessment of "the appalling monotony of the fundamental ideas of mankind all over the globe" (quoted Brown 1991: 55).

3 In general, in the Western tradition, from classical antiquity through the Renaissance to the present day, the view that language reflects antecedent

cognitive categories has generally been in the ascendant The deep influence of Aristotle's categories and Boethius's translations, together with his own views, are no doubt part of the explanation (see Marenbon 1988: ch. 3). On the other hand, the question whether the "modes of being, thinking and signifying" are necessarily in parallel, or whether the categories might be mismatched across reality, cognition, and language was a point of active medieval disputation (see Marenbon 1987: 136ff.). Outside the Western tradition, one may find views reminiscent of "linguistic relativity" in, for example, early Indian philosophy, where the word was in some doctrines taken to be an arbitrary conceptual construction, and determinative of cognition and conceptual categories (see Staal 1976: 121–3).

4　A point already made by Hamann in 1760; see Cloeren (1988: 11–12).

5　This aspect of the Humboldtian tradition and the Sapir–Whorf hypothesis is not fully developed in this volume. See Hill (1988) and Hill & Mannheim (1992) for recent reviews of the relevant anthropological literature.

6　Despite this, the theory of translation has not played a central role in twentieth-century thinking on the subject. See however Jakobson (1966) and Steiner (1975), and Quine's (1960) celebrated thesis of the indeterminacy of translation. There is now a burgeoning practical field of translation studies; see, e.g., Baker (1992).

7　A point made decades ago by Hymes (1964, 1972).

8　See, e.g., Kelly (1979), Steiner (1975).

9　See, e.g., Berlin (1993: ch. 6) for references; Cloeren (1988), Aarsleff (1974).

10　See, e.g. Pagden (1982) for a survey of European ideas about the American Indian, in which controversies about language difference play no small part: language was presumed to mirror social development, and the Spanish champions of the Indians like Las Casas were keen to show that the Indian languages had a systematic grammar, while their detractors tried to establish that they lacked abstractions fundamental for intellectual and spiritual development.

11　Hymes's reader (1964: Pt. III) collects together exemplary papers from this tradition, and is still the best source for the student.

12　Whorf himself paints, beyond Sapir and Boas, a different pedigree (1956: 73–8). On the Humboldtian heritage see Aarsleff (1988), Heeschen (1977, 1987), Trabant (1990), Gipper (1972), and references below. Ironically, Humboldtian scholarship seems peculiarly afflicted with the woes of translation (Kelly 1979: 27).

13　See G. Steiner (1975: 74) who cites Leibniz's 1697 tract "On the amelioration and correction of German." A now largely forgotten mid eighteenth-century intellectual figure, Johann Georg Hamann, himself the teacher of Herder, preadumbrates many of Humboldt's views (Berlin 1993). Herder's own role is now controversial: Aarsleff (1982, 1988) has challenged any connection between Herder and Humboldt's views, while Mueller-Vollmer (1990: 9ff.) ridicules this account of intellectual history: "Humboldt is made out to be a kind of German-speaking French ideologue rather than a student and follower of Herder, Kant or Fichte." A convincing case for a long-running and distinctively German tradition of "linguistic relativists" is made by Cloeren (1988). Such ideas were so much in the air that in 1757 the Berlin Academy offered a prize on the theme (see quote at head of this introduction). See also Penn (1972).

14 For this, and many further interesting details, see Hymes & Fought (1975), Koerner (1992).

15 In turn the enlightenment discussion was fed by sixteenth- and seventeenth-century Spanish thought prompted by encounters with New World peoples (see Pagden 1982). For the apparent paradox of the German lack of colonial experience on the one hand and their interest in these issues on the other, there was already an answer suggested by British critics of imperial cruelties in the 1830s: the Germans had no motive to belittle the intellectual achievements of distant peoples (see Boening 1990).

16 See Aarsleff (1988: lxiff).

17 See Koerner (1992: 174).

18 On the origins of structuralism, see Koerner (1975), Engler (1975), Hymes & Fought (1975).

19 Mueller-Vollmer (1990) claims that Herder, and especially Humboldt, actually prefigured the Saussurean concept of the sign, and it is this that distinguishes the German intellectual tradition from the eighteenth-century French one. He quotes an early Humboldt text thus: "The sensory signification of those units into which certain portions of our thinking are united in order to be opposed as parts to other parts of a larger whole...is what may be called language in the widest sense of the word" (1990: 17). On the Humboldtian, and more generally Gerrnan, origins of structuralism see Koerner (1975).

20 The background to that convergence is well described in Lucy (1992a: ch. 2).

21 Perhaps especially clear in European Saussurean structuralism (for example through Saussure's metaphor of a linguistic system simultaneously dividing form and meaning like scissors cutting a sheet of paper). The surprisingly independent nature of American structuralism is described by Hymes & Fought (1975: 916ff.) who state that there is no evidence that, e.g., Sapir was aware of Saussure's work.

22 Koerner (1992: 181) (but the phrase was current in contemporary German philosophy at the turn of the century – see, e.g., Cloeren's 1988: 206–7 discussion of the ideas of Runze). We make no attempt here to characterize or compare Boas's or Sapir's views with those of Whorf – a concise summary may be found in Lucy (1992a: chs. 1 & 2). See also Jakobson (1944).

23 Whorf's views on the structure of language are much better articulated elsewhere; e.g. "it is not words mumbled, but RAPPORT between words, which enables them to work together at all to any semantic result" (1956: 67). See especially the article "Grammatical categories" ([1945] 1956: 87–101) and the surprisingly "modern" scheme for a typology of languages (1956: 125–33).

24 There has always been considerable disagreement about what Whorf "really meant." Some (e.g. Lucy 1922a) think this can be spelt out as a clear, testable doctrine; others (e.g. Schultz 1990) hold that there has been a systematic suppression of Whorf's mystical views and a failure to recognize that the texts through their very ambiguities and implicit implications articulate a protest against "epistemological monomania."

25 See also selected papers in Hymes (1964: pt. III).

26 This was not necessarily the intention of that work, which was merely to establish perceptual constraints on linguistic coding. In fact Kay & Kempton (1984) demonstrated that differential linguistic coding of colors does indeed effect perceptual judgments.

27 See e.g. Rosch (1977), on the general theory, and Malotki (1983) on Whorf's Hopi data. Many critiques have only a tenuous relation to ideas that Whorf

himself advanced, as in the case of "the great Eskimo vocabulary hoax" (Pullum 1991, see Martin 1986 for a more sober view). See also Lucy (1985, 1992a: ch. 2).

28 But see Silverstein's (1981) insistence that we have differential conscious access to different aspects of grammatical structure, a point taken up in some of the papers in this volume. Jakobson (1944) pointed out that the linguist's own categories of analysis are likely to reflect encodings in his own language.

29 Kamp (1981).

30 Barwise & Perry (1983).

31 Sperber & Wilson (1986).

32 See Levinson (1983: ch. 3), Horn (1989).

33 There is an enormous literature on the notion of indexicality, but useful reference can be made to Jarvella & Klein (1982) for the notions current in much linguistics, philosophy, and psychology, and to Mertz & Parmentier (1985) for the related but distinct Peircean notions, especially in linguistic anthropology.

34 Yet another line of thought investigates how a single task can be solved by distribution over a co-ordinated team: for example, the piloting of a ship involves single seamen each following highly specific procedures (Hutchins 1990).

35 Bourdieu (1976, 1990a: ch. 3, 1990b: ch. 3), Scribner (1992), and Lave (1988) have been influential in purveying these ideas in anthropology. Some of these ideas come originally from the work of Vygotsky; for a compendium of recent views on the implications for language, thought, and culture, see Wertsch (1985).

36 See e.g. Brown & Levinson (1993), Pederson (1995).

37 See Gumperz (1992), Young (1994).

38 See Young (1994) for an illustration of how ideologies of interpersonal relations, grammar, and contextualization strategies interact in communication, and tend to reinforce stereotypes.

References

Aarsleff, H. 1974. The tradition of Condillac: the problem of the origin of language in the eighteenth century and the debate in the Berlin Academy before Herder. In D. Hymes (ed.), *Studies in the history of linguistics: traditions and paradigms* (pp. 93–156). Bloomington: Indiana University Press.

1982. *From Locke to Saussure. Essays on the study of language and intellectual history.* Minneapolis: University of Minnesota Press.

1988. Introduction. In von Humboldt (1988): vii–lxvi.

Baker, M. 1992. *In other words*. London: Routledge.

Barwise, J. & Perry, J. 1983. *Situations and attitudes*. Cambridge, MA: MIT Press.

Berlin, B. & Kay, P. 1969. *Basic color terms: their universality and evolution.* Berkeley: University of California Press.

Berlin, I. 1993. *The magus of the North*. London: John Murray.

Boening, J .1990. Herder and the White Man's burden. In W. Koepke (ed.), *Johann Gotttried Herder: language, history and the enlightenment* (pp. 236–45). Columbia, SC: Camden House.

Bourdieu, P. 1977. *Outline of a theory of practice.* Tr. R. Nice. Cambridge University Press.

1990a. *The logic of practice.* Stanford University Press.

1990b. *In other words.* Stanford University Press.

Brown, D. E. 1991. *Human universals*. New York: McGraw-Hill.
Brown, P. & Levinson, S. C. 1993. *Linguistic and non-linguistic coding of spatial arrays: explorations in Mayan cognition*. Working Paper No. 24. Nijmegen: Cognitive Anthropology Research Group.
Cloeren, H. J. *Language and thought. German approaches to analytic philosophy in the eighteenth and nineteenth centuries*. Berlin: de Gruyter.
Engler, R. 1975. European structuralism: Saussure. In T. Sebeok (ed.), *Current trends in linguistics*, vol. XIII (part II): *Historiography of linguistics*, ed. H. Aarsleff, R. Austerlitz, D. Hymes, & E. Stankiewics (pp. 829–86). The Hague: Mouton.
Gipper, H. 1972. *Gibt es ein sprachliches Relativitätsprinzip? Untersuchungen zur Sapir–Whorf Hypothese*. Frankfurt/Main: Fischer.
Goody, J. 1977. *The domestication of the savage mind*. Cambridge University Press.
Gumperz, J. J. 1992. Interviewing in intercultural settings. In P. Drew & J. Heritage (eds.), *Talk at work* (pp. 302–30). Cambridge University Press.
Gumperz, J. J. & Levinson, S. C. 1992. Rethinking linguistic relativity. *Current Anthropology*, 32(5), 613–22.
Heeschen, V. 1977. Weltansicht – Reflexionen über einen Begriff Wilhelm von Humboldts. *Historia Linguistica,* 4(1), 159–90.
    1987. Schematismus: Wilhelm von Humboldt und Schleiermacher. In H. Aarsleff, L. G. Kelly, & H.-J. Niederehe (eds.), *Papers in the history of linguistics* (pp. 465–77). Amsterdam: Benjamins.
Hill, J. 1988. Language, culture and world view. In F. Newmeyer (ed.) *Linguistics: the Cambridge Survey*, vol. IV: *Language: the cultural context* (pp. 14–36). Cambridge University Press.
Hill, J. & Mannheim, B. 1992. Language and world view. *Annual Review of Anthropology*, 21, 381–406.
Horn, L. R. 1989. *A natural history of negation*. University of Chicago Press.
Humboldt, W. von. 1988 [1836]. *On language: the diversity of human language-structure and its influence on the mental development of mankind*. Tr. Peter Heath. Cambridge University Press.
Hutchins, E. 1990. The technology of team navigation. In J. Galegher, R. E. Kraut, & C. Egido (eds.), *Intellectual teamwork* (pp. 191–220). Hillsdale, NJ: Lawrence Erlbaum.
Hymes, D. 1972. Models of the interaction of language and social life. In J. J. Gumperz & D. Hymes (eds.), *Directions in sociolinguistics: the ethnography of communication* (pp. 35–71). New York: Holt, Rinehart, & Winston.
    (ed.) 1964. *Language in culture and society: a reader in linguistics and anthropology*. New York: Harper & Row.
Hymes, D. & Fought, J. 1975. American structuralism. In T. Sebeok (ed.), *Current trends in linguistics*, vol. XIII (part II): *Historiography of linguistics*, ed. H. Aarsleff, R. Austerlitz, D. Hymes, & E. Stankiewics (pp. 903–1176). The Hague: Mouton.
Jakobson, R. 1944. Franz Boas' approach to language. *IJAL*, 10(2), 188–95.
    1966. On linguistic aspects of translation. In R. A. Brower (ed.), *On translation* (pp. 232–9). New York: Oxford University Press.
Jarvella, R. & Klein, W. (eds.) 1982. *Speech, place and action: studies in deixis and related topics*. New York: Wiley.
Kamp, H. 1981. A theory of truth and semantic representation. In J. Groenendijk, T. M. V. Janssen, & M. Stokhof (eds.), *Truth, the*

interpretation and information. selected papers from the 3rd Amsterdam Colloquium (pp. 1–42). Dordrecht: Foris.

Kay, P. & Kempton, W. 1984. What is the Sapir–Whorf hypothesis? *American Anthropologist*, 86, 65–79.

Kelly, L. 1979. *The true interpreter*. Oxford: Basil Blackwell.

Koerner, E. F. K. 1975. European structuralism: early beginnings. In T. Sebeok (ed.), *Current trends in linguistics*, vol. XIII (part II): *Historiography of linguistics*, ed. H. Aarsleff, R. Austerlitz, D. Hymes, & E. Stankiewics (pp. 717–827). The Hague: Mouton.

1992. The Sapir–Whorf hypothesis: a preliminary history and bibliographical essay. *Journal of Linguistic Anthropology*, 2(2), 173–98.

Lave, J. 1988. *Cognition in practice*. Cambridge University Press.

Lee, B. 1985. The semiotic mediation of ontology. In Mertz & Parmentier (1985): 99–130.

Levinson, S. C. 1983. *Pragmatics*. Cambridge University Press.

Lucy, J. 1985. Whorf's view of the linguistic mediation of thought. In Mertz & Parmentier (1985): 73–98.

1992a. *Language diversity and thought. a reformulation of the linguistic relativity hypothesis*. Cambridge University Press.

1992b. *Grammatical categories and cognition: a case study of the linguistic relatively hypothesis*. Cambridge University Press.

Malotki, E. 1983. *Hopi time: a linguistic analysis of the temporal categories in the Hopi language*. Berlin: Mouton.

Marenbon, J. 1987. *Later medieval philosophy*. London: Routledge.

1988. *Early medieval philosophy*. London: Routledge.

Martin, L. 1986. Eskimo words for snow: a case study in the genesis and decay of an anthropological example. *American Anthropologist*, 88(2), 418–23.

Mertz, E. & Parmentier, R. (eds.) 1985. *Semiotic mediation: sociocultural and psychological perspectives*. New York: Academic Press.

Mueller-Vollmer, K. 1990. From sign to signification: the Herder–Humboldt controversy. In W. Koepke (ed.), *Johann Gottfried Herder. language, history and the enlightenment* (pp. 9–24). Columbia, SC: Camden House.

Pagden, A. 1982. *The fall of natural man: the American Indian and the origins of comparative ethnology*. Cambridge University Press.

Pederson, E. 1995. Language as context, language as means: spatial cognition and habitual language use. *Cognitive Linguistics*, 6(1), 33–62.

Penn, J. M. 1972. *Linguistic relativity vs. innate ideas: the origins of the Sapir–Whorf hypothesis in German thought*. The Hague: Mouton.

Pullum, G. 1991. *The great eskimo vocabulary hoax and other irreverent essays on the study of language*. University of Chicago Press.

Quine, W. O. 1960. *Word and object*. Cambridge, MA: MIT Press.

Rosch, E. 1977. Linguistic relativity. In P. N. Johnson-Laird & P. C. Wason (eds.), *Thinking: readings in cognitive science* (pp. 501–22). Cambridge University Press.

Schultz, E. 1990. *Dialogue at the margins. Whorf, Bakhtin and linguistic relativity*. Madison: University of Wisconsin Press.

Scribner, S. 1992. Mind in action: a functional approach to thinking, and the cognitive consequences of literacy. *Quarterly Newsletter of the Laboratory of Comparative Human Cognition*, 14(4), 83–157.

Silverstein, M. 1981. *The limits of awareness*. Working Papers in Sociolinguistics, No. 84. Austin: Southwestern Educational Laboratory.

Sperber, D. & Wilson, D. 1986. *Relevance*. Oxford: Basil Blackwell.

Staal, J. F. 1976. Sanskrit philosophy of language. In H. Parret (ed.), *History of linguistic thought and contemporary linguistics* (pp. 102–36). Berlin: de Gruyter.

Steiner, G. 1975. *After Babel: aspects of language and translation*. Oxford University Press.

Trabant, J. 1990. *Traditionen Humboldts*. Frankfurt: Suhrkamp.

Urban, G. 1991. *A discourse-centered approach to culture: native South American myths and rituals*. Austin: University of Texas Press.

Wertsch, J. (ed.) 1985. *Culture, communication and cognition*. Cambridge University Press.

Whorf, B. L. 1940a. Science and linguistics. *Technol. Rev.*, 42, 229–31, 247–8.

   1940b. Linguistics as an exact science. *Technol. Rev.*, 43, 61–3, 80–3.

   1956. *Language, thought and reality: selected writings of Benjamin Lee Whorf*, ed. J. B. Carroll. Cambridge, MA: MIT Press.

Young, L. 1994. *Cross-talk and culture in Sino-American communication*. Cambridge University Press.

PART I

LINGUISTIC DETERMINISM: THE INTERFACE BETWEEN LANGUAGE AND THOUGHT

INTRODUCTION TO PART I

JOHN J. GUMPERZ AND STEPHEN C. LEVINSON

Language is the formative organ of thought. Intellectual activity, entirely mental, entirely internal, and to some extent passing without trace, becomes through sound, externalized in speech and perceptible to the senses. Thought and language are therefore one and inseparable from each other.

Humboldt ([1836] 1988: 54)

Human beings do not live in the objective world alone, . . . The fact of the matter is that the "real world" is to a large extent unconsciously built up on the language habits of the group ... We see and hear and otherwise experience very largely as we do because the language habits of our community predispose certain choices of interpretation.

Edward Sapir, quoted at the head of Whorf
"The relation of habitual thought and behavior to language." (1956: 134)

1 The very idea: causal links between language and thinking

Might the language we speak effect the way we think? Generations of thinkers have been intrigued by this idea. Aarsleff (1988: xviii) summarized Humboldt's influential views thus: "Humboldt's entire view of the nature of language is founded on the conviction that thinking and speaking, thought and language form so close a union that we must think of them as being identical, in spite of the fact that we can separate them artificially. Owing to this identity, access to one of the two will open nearly equal access to the other."[1]

Whorf, as we saw in the introduction, brought to the idea a new and heady mix of an empiricist epistemology, an insistence on the underlying systematicity of language as a structured semantical system, and an emphasis on the unconscious influence of language on habitual thought:[2]

Actually, thinking is most mysterious, and by far the greatest light upon it that we have is thrown by the study of language. This study shows that the forms of a person's thoughts are controlled by inexorable laws of pattern of which he is unconscious. These patterns are the unperceived intricate systematizations of his own language – shown readily enough by a candid comparison and contrast with other languages, especially those of a different linguistic family. His thinking itself is in a language – in English, in Sanskrit, in Chinese. And every language is a vast pattern-system, different from others, in which are culturally ordained the

21

forms and categories by which the personality not only communicates, but also analyzes nature, notices or neglects types of relationship and phenomena, channels his reasoning, and builds the house of his consciousness.

(Whorf 1956: 252)

The phrase "linguistic determinism" has come to stand for these views that there is a causal influence from linguistic patterning to cognition.[3] Despite phrases like "linguistic conditioning," "linguistic legislation," "inexorable control," etc., Whorf's own considered position seems to have been that language influences unconscious habitual thought, rather than limiting thought potential (see Lucy 1992a: 129ff., Kay & Kempton 1984: 76–7).[4] Thus the phrase "linguistic determinism" should be understood to imply that there is *at least some* causal influence from language categories to non-verbal cognition; it was not intended to denote an exclusive causal vector in one direction – probably no proponent has held the view that what cannot be said cannot be thought.[5]

The idea that language could determine (however weakly) the nature of our thinking nowadays carries more than a faint whiff of anachronism; rather it seems to belong to an altogether different age, prior to the serious study of mind as an information processing device.[6] That device, in the predominant metaphor of our time, is instantiated in "wetware," whose properties are in turn dictated by the genetic code of the species. Although those properties are only dimly understood, still it is generally presumed, as Fodor (1983) has influentially put it, that the mind is "modular," composed of subsystems specialized to the automatic unconscious processing of particular kinds of information, visual, auditory, haptic, and so on. Since we can, for example, talk about what we see, the output of these specialized systems must, it seems, be available to some central information processing system, where "thinking," in the sense of ratiocination and deliberation, occurs. This picture (a close analogy of course to the computers of the day) of a single generalized central processor with specialized input/output devices is beginning to give way to a more complex version: each specialized input/output device is itself a system of modules, while "central processes" may themselves be differentiated into different "languages of thought" (propositional, imagistic, and so on)[7] – a view that the paper by Keller & Keller in this section addresses. Nevertheless the essentials of the Fodorean view are very generally held.

Thus, on this widespread view, we can expect thinking in all essentials to have universal properties, to be couched in an inner language structurally the same for all members of the species, and to be quite unrelated to the facts of linguistic diversity (see, e.g., Fodor 1983). The tenor of the anti-Whorfian assumptions can be gauged from the following quotations: "For the vocabulary of the language, in and of its self, to be a moulder of thought, lexical dissections and categorizations of nature would have to be almost accidentally formed, rather as though some Johnny Appleseed had scattered named categories capriciously over the earth" (Rosch 1977: 519); "Whorf's hypothesis [of linguistic determinism] has engendered much confusion, and many circular arguments. Its converse often seems more plausible" (Wason & Johnson-Laird 1977: 411), and "there is no evidence for the strong version of the hypothesis – that language imposes upon its speakers a particular way of thinking about the world" (p. 442); "The discussions that assume that language determines thought carry on only by a collective suspension of disbelief" (Pinker 1994: 58).

In short, many authors find the thesis of linguistic determinism wildly adventurous or even ridiculous. On the other hand, others have recently claimed to find it sober and plausible (amongst them Steiner 1975, Lee 1991, Lucy 1992a, b, together with some other contributors to this volume). It is therefore useful to attempt to clarify the issues by dissecting the relativity hypothesis into its component parts, and in particular by isolating the "determinism" hypothesis from other linked ideas. Clearly, the hypothesis of linguistic relativity relies on the presumption of linguistic difference. Thus the discovery of universals may have a bearing on that hypothesis.[8] But the hypothesis that linguistic categories might determine aspects of non-linguistic thinking is quite independent of facts about linguistic difference.[9] Let us therefore spell out the nexus of interlinked hypotheses (where the numbers [1] and [2] refer to the premises and the number [3] to an implied conclusion).[10]

[1] *Linguistic difference*
Languages differ substantially in their semantic structure: both the intensions (the senses) and extensions (the denotations) of lexical and morpho-syntactic categories may differ across languages (and may do so independently).[11]

[2] *Linguistic determinism*
Linguistic categorizations, implicit or explicit, may determine or co-determine or influence aspects of non-linguistic categorization, memory, perception or thinking in general.

This is often said to have a "strong" and a "weak" form: under the strong claim, linguistically uncoded concepts would be unattainable; under the weak form, concepts which happen to be linguistically coded would be facilitated or favored (e.g. would be more accessible, easier to remember, or the default coding for non-linguistic cognition).[12]

The mechanisms whereby semantic distinctions may have an influence on cognition can be left open; a prior task is to show that there is indeed some correlation. Whorf himself of course held the view that the unconscious "compulsive patterning" of grammatical oppositions would play a special role in habitual unreflective patterns of thought.[13]

Linguistic relativity
Given that:
(1) differences exist in linguistic categories across languages;
(2) linguistic categories determine aspects of individuals' thinking;
then:
(3) aspects of individuals' thinking differ across linguistic communities according to the language they speak.

Note that the conclusion here will hold even under the weakest versions of (1) and (2). Thus if there is *at least some* aspect of semantic structure that is not universal, *and at least some* cognitive effect of such distinctive semantic properties, then there must be *at least some* systematic cognitive variation in line with linguistic difference. That would seem, as Lucy (1992a: 3) puts it, to be as trivially true as the strongest version of linguistic relativity (that one's semantic inventory of concepts provides one's total vocabulary of thoughts) is trivially false.[14] Thus the central problem is to illuminate the degrees of language difference, and the ways in which semantics and cognitive categories and processes interact.

Now notice that modern views complicate this picture by apparently subscribing to various aspects of these propositions while robustly denying the conclusion in the syllogism above. For example, a common modern stance is:

(1′) languages differ in semantic structure, but only at a molecular level – at an atomic level, the conceptual "atoms" (e.g. "male," "adult," etc.) are identical, and are merely assembled into some culture-specific notion like "uncle";[15]
(2′) "determinism" between semantic categories and conceptual categories is in a sense trivially complete, since they are one and the same – the meanings of words are expressed in a "language" that is identical to the "language of thought." However, the directionality of the determinism runs from universal cognition to linguistic semantics (Jackendoff 1983, Lakoff 1987, Hale & Keyser 1987).

Thus although the identity of linguistic and conceptual categories in (2′) alone might be thought to entail linguistic relativity, it is in fact usually associated with some claim (often implicit) like that in (1′), allowing subscribers to presume that the "language of thought" (alias: system of semantic representations) is universal. Then the conclusion in

(3) no longer follows. In schematic form we may now oppose the two views thus:

The Whorfian syllogism

(1) Different languages utilize different semantic representation systems which are informationally non-equivalent[16] (at least in the sense that they employ different lexical concepts);
(2) semantic representations determine aspects of conceptual representations;
therefore
(3) users of different languages utilize different conceptual representations.

The anti-Whorfian syllogism

(1′) Different languages utilize the same semantic representation system (if not at the molecular then at least at the atomic level of semantic primes);
(2′) universal conceptual representations determine semantic systems, indeed THE semantic representation system just is identical to THE propositional conceptual system (the innate "language of thought");
therefore
(3′) users of different languages utilize the identical conceptual representation system.

Despite the fact that the doctrines appear diametrically opposed,[17] they are nevertheless, on suitable interpretations, *entirely compatible*, as long as one subscribes to the distinction between atomic and molecular levels of semantic representation. Then, on an atomic level, semantic representations, and their corresponding conceptual representations, are drawn from a universal language of thought, while on the molecular level there are language-specific combinations of universal atomic primitives, which make up lexical meanings (and meanings associated with morpho-syntactic distinctions) and which may have specific conceptual effects.

Most semantic analysts in practice work with an assumption of such "semantic decomposition" of linguistic expressions.[18] But it is worth pointing out that there are in fact fundamental problems with that assumption which have long been recognized (Kempson 1977; Fodor 1975; Fodor, Fodor & Garrett 1975; Putnam 1988: 5ff.), and some of those who subscribe enthusiastically to (2′) might lose some of their enthusiasm if they realized that without (1′), (2′) implies the strongest version of linguistic relativity.[19]

Let us take stock. Proposition (1) is evidently true, in the sense that languages clearly employ distinct lexical meanings. (1′) may or may not be tenable, but is in tact compatible with (1). Likewise (2) and (2') are compatible if we make a distinction between atomic and molecular concepts: the inventory of concepts in the language of thought could determine the range of possible lexical concepts, but such lexical concepts once selected could in turn determine the concepts we employ when solving non-linguistic problems. (3) would be the conclusion from (1) and (2). All thus hinges on (2). Is it even remotely plausible?

Although the thesis of linguistic determinism seems at first sight to have an anachronistic flavor, it can easily be brought to bear on modern theorizing in a way that makes it look anything but silly. First, note that there is considerable psychological evidence that our working memory is restricted to about half a dozen chunks of information, but is indifferent to the underlying complexity of those chunks (Miller 1956, Simon 1986). Thus mental operations are facilitated by grouping elementary concepts into larger chunks. And this is just what lexical items do for us. Thus there is every reason to think that such chunks might play an important role in our thinking (Fodor, Fodor & Garrett 1975; Fodor 1992: 389).[20]

Now consider Levelt's (1989) theory of speech production, a synthesis of a large amount of current theory, fact, and speculation. In this theory, the thought-stream is coded in language essentially by matching chunks of conceptual structure with lexical specifications of meaning, further lexical information then driving grammatical and phonological encoding. In order for this encoding process to begin, the speaker must regiment the conceptual structure so that it matches semantic specifications in the lexicon: if there is no match, the thoughts cannot be coded. This regimentation process might be called "thinking for speaking" (see Slobin's chapter below) and must consist of habits learnt during language acquisition.[21]

Within such a framework, it is quite easy to show that in certain respects and for certain phenomena linguistic determinism *beyond* thinking-for-speaking is not only plausible, but must be correct. The reasoning can be exemplified as follows. Consider a language that has no words for '*in front*,' '*behind*,' '*left*,' '*right*,' and so on, preferring instead to designate all such relations, however microscopic in scale, in terms of notions like 'North,' 'South,' 'East,' 'West,' etc. Now a speaker of such a language cannot remember arrays of objects in the same way as you or I, in terms of their relative location from a particular viewing angle. If I think of the visual array currently in front of me, I think of it as, say, "boy in front of tree, dog to left of tree." Later I can so describe it. But that will not do for the speaker of the language with 'North'/'South'/ 'East'/'West' notions: remembering the array in terms of notions like 'front' and 'left' will not allow him to reconstruct the cardinal directions. So if he remembers it that way, he will not be able to describe it later;

while if he remembers the array in a way congruent with the linguistic coding (in terms of 'North' and 'East,' etc.), then he will be able to code it linguistically. So it seems *prima facie* quite clear that the speaker of such a language and I simply MUST code our experiences differently for memory in order to speak our different languages. In short, thinking in a special way for speaking will not be enough: we must mentally encode experiences in such a way that we can describe them later, in the terms required by our language.

There are in fact just such languages that require the use of cardinal directions (Levinson 1992, Haviland 1993; and chapters 6 & 9 of this volume). Furthermore, this *prima facie* argument about the cognitive consequences of speaking such different languages can be backed up by empirical investigation: it turns out that in non-linguistic tasks speakers of languages that use 'North'/'South'/'East'/'West' systems instead of 'front'/ 'back'/'left'/'right' systems do indeed remember spatial arrays differently, in ways that can be demonstrated experimentally and observationally (see Levinson 1992, Haviland 1993, Brown & Levinson 1993).

Is this a peculiar case? One needs to think afresh to assess the possibilities. From the perspective of speech production, there are three different kinds of ways in which a particular language might determine how we think.[22] First, the grammatical or lexical categories may force a specific way of thinking at the time of speaking (the "regimentation" of thoughts described above). Second, such thinking-for-speaking may itself require the coding of situations in specific forms at the time that they are experienced. This is clearly so in the North/South/East/West case above. It is also clearly so in many other cases: for example, obligatory coding of number in languages with plural marking will require noticing for all possible referents whether or not they are singletons-some languages without plural marking will let one say in effect "I saw bird on the lawn," but in English I must say either a *bird* or *birds* and must therefore have remembered how many relevant birds there were (see Lucy 1992b, and ch. 1 below); or in systems of honorifics based on relative age, I must have ascertained before speaking whether the referent is senior or junior to me; or in systems of aspect requiring distinctions between perfective and imperfective, I must attend to the exact nature of event-overlap (see Slobin, ch. 3 below). These are language-specific distinctions that seem to require noticing special properties of the world so that one is ready to encode them linguistically should the need arise. Such examples suggest that those theorists who reluctantly subscribe to a relativity in thinking-for-speaking, will have also to subscribe to a consequent relativity in thinking at the time at which events are experienced. Thirdly, one may also go on to consider the consequences, or after-effects, of thinking-for-speaking in a particular way. There may for example be memory effects:

it may be easier to remember aspects of events that have been coded for speaking during prior verbalization (hence we may indulge in speaking-for-thinking). Since some languages will enforce particular codings (e.g. in systems of aspect, honorifics, number-marking, etc.), they may ensure that their speakers recall certain features of situations better than others.

At the time of writing, there has been little systematic investigation of any of these possible cognitive effects of semantic categories peculiar to, and recurrent in, specific languages.[23] Meanwhile, the chapters in this section explore the thesis of the linguistic determinism of thought from a variety of theoretical and empirical angles. Two of them (those by Kay, and Keller & Keller) are downright skeptical of any such thesis or of its importance, for very different reasons. Two of them are much more sympathetic: one of these (by Slobin) is skeptical of any effects beyond the moment of speaking, the other (by Lucy) assumes that such effects can be empirically demonstrated.

2 The chapters

The chapter by Lucy introduces many of the themes of this volume beyond the issue of the linguistic determinism of thought; for example, he considers narrow vs. wide construals of linguistic relativity, and the different ways in which structure and usage are intertwined. He also provides a useful summary of earlier relevant work.

First, he makes the important point that attitudes to notions of linguistic relativity depend crucially on opinions about the nature of thought without language (see the Kellers' chapter below, and also Weiskrantz 1988). If language is thought of simply as a sort of late evolutionary appendage, a mere transducer or input–output device, with cognition essentially independent, then linguistic relativity will not even be entertained. There is no doubt that a great deal of thinking in the cognitive sciences goes in this direction. If, on the other hand, language is viewed as a uniquely arbitrary symbolic system, which is transformative of internal mental operations, being largely responsible for the specific features of cognition unique to humans, then linguistic relativity has to be taken seriously. For the very arbitrariness of language implies (a) diversity across human groups, (b) cultural transmission.

Lucy goes on to review the existing work on the classic version of the linguistic relativity hypothesis, which holds that the structural diversity of languages implies semantic incommensurability, which is in turn linked to cognitive difference (see also Lucy 1992a for monographic treatment). He points out that there has been very little serious empirical work that meets certain minimal requirements: (a) contrastive linguistic analysis of two or more languages, where (b) a grammatical or major lexical pattern is investigated, and where (c) there are language-independent explorations of relevant aspects of cognition. Previous work on linguistic relativity by anthropological linguists has failed to tie linguistic difference into cognition, while the work of psychologists has failed to pay serious attention to linguistic difference, and recent universalist trends have discouraged interest in the whole problem. He outlines his work, more fully described in Lucy (1992b) (see also the work of Levinson 1992; in press (a), (b); and colleagues; and part II below).

Lucy then turns to consider a broader perspective on linguistic relativity that takes into account a relativity in *use* of language (a perspective championed originally by Hymes 1964). He raises the point that differences in use may be caused by structural differences, which are themselves then in turn considerably amplified through use, a thesis given exemplification by the work of Slobin (see ch. 3 below). He goes on to classify different kinds of function according to a Jakobsonian scheme ("referential," "expressive," "metalinguistic," etc.), and discusses how on each of these levels different patterns of use might engender both cultural and cognitive differences. For example, the elaboration of referential functions involved in schooling seems to have transformative effects in traditional societies. Finally, he reminds us that many authors, including other contributors to this volume, have held that these functional differences may feed back into the elaboration of structural differences, so that, for example, an "elaborated code" (Bernstein 1964) or elite mode of talk and style of conceptual analysis may control access to social strata and contribute to an ideological set of cognitive predispositions. Lucy's paper therefore bridges the current section and the last section of this book, where the relation of differences of use to the structure of speech communities is discussed.

The chapter by Slobin focuses directly on the classic issue of "linguistic determinism": can we argue that a particular language determines the way we think? Slobin recasts the problem in some fundamentally new ways. First, he advocates abandoning the original terms of discussion: let us talk not in terms of static wholes like "language" and "thought," but in terms of the relation between grammatical categories and the on-line process of converting thoughts into words – *thinking for speaking*. Secondly, from this perspective, he suggests that the conservative Boasian view that languages selectively encode features of shared perception may be too weak: grammatical categories may force the encoding of features that have to be actively construed or constructed. Thirdly, he argues that during the process of thinking for speaking our attention is directed by obligatory grammatical categories to certain perceptual features or to certain ways of construing scenes, with the result that the structural features of a language are projected into a specific rhetorical or narrative style. This projection from the grammar into features of discourse is not strictly determinative: speakers may and do on occasion use the full resources of the language to express features that the grammar does not require. In that respect, he rejects a strong version of determinism, which he associates with Whorf (but cf. Lucy 1992a: 40ff.). Nevertheless, as a general rule, features of a scene that the grammar does not code through obligatory categories are often left unsaid, and presumably may actually not be attended to during the process of thinking for speaking.

Slobin tests these claims on the basis of a comparative study of children's narrative retellings in several languages, elicited by means of a picture-story book without words. The narratives produced show that on the whole, speakers do adopt a rhetorical style in line with the language, so that, for example, if a language (like Hebrew or German) makes no contrast between a perfective and imperfective aspect, then two events that would be so distinguished in other languages are *not* distinguished in any other way either, for example, by repetition of the predicate to indicate durativity. However, the exceptions are important: sometimes speakers do make the contrasts that are not encouraged by grammatical means. This allows Slobin to explore the gradual acquisition by children of a rhetorical style in line with the grammar of the language, suggesting that they gradually learn to selectively attend and disattend to construals of a scene during the particular mental process of thinking for speaking.

Kay casts a skeptical eye on the thesis of linguistic relativity. He asks what kind of inference about the nature of thought we can make from the use of certain expressions: we call the familiar tool a "screwdriver," but the German word glosses as 'screw-puller' – Kay is not inclined to conclude that the tool is conceived differently from this evidence alone, but suggests that other scholars may be so inclined. Such scholars, he argues, should consider the fact that within the same language we often find two or more expressions that offer contrastive ways of construing the same facts. He offers four such cases, where English expressions seem to presuppose completely incompatible schemata for the very same situation. In one of these cases, he argues that the hedges *strictly speaking* and *technically speaking* presuppose incompatible views about the nature of reference. In another he argues that the different perspectives encoded in *John bought the car from Harry* and *Harry sold the car to John* require, given the systematic patterns of English grammar, seeing just one party as the agent or active party in the exchange. These different schemata within a language can hardly be indicative of essential conceptual patterns, as they are mutually conflicting. Further, they make comparison between languages complex: Whorf's contrasts between English and Hopi often select just one English construal of the situation, ignoring another which parallels the Hopi one.

Thus Kay challenges the thesis of linguistic relativity with a *reductio ad absurdum*: if one argues from the conceptual schemata encoded in the expressions of language to ways of thinking typical of its speakers, one must concede that speakers of a single language hold incompatible, inconsistent conceptualizations of the world. It is preferable instead to think of languages as offering us a *variety* of different conceptualizations which speakers may choose between, thus decoupling linguistic schematizations from thinking. Not all languages offer the same variety, but the import of that mismatch is not clear. Kay's cautionary remarks show that the would-be relativist must consider the full range of alternative expressions in any language, and consider how to make the argument from linguistic encoding to patterns of thinking given that full range. Two ideas are relevant here: one is the notion of "conventional perspective" introduced by Clark in part III, and another is Whorf's insistence that it is only the repetitive use of a predominant linguistic pattern that one might expect to influence "habitual thought."

As suggested by Lucy, another way to conceive of the problem of linguistic determinism is to think about thought without language. Most theorists subscribe to the idea that there is a kind of propositional thought closely bound up with language; some hold that this kind of thought determines the nature of semantic representations, while a minority may hold that the causal influence is in reverse. But what is there left if we subtract this kind of cognition?

Whorf's version of the thesis of linguistic determinism was formulated in an era when the psychological sciences conceived of thinking as a unified kind of process. Today, the prevailing assumption is of the "modularity of mind" (to use Fodor's [1983] phrase), wherein it is assumed that there are many distinct "modules" or information processors, each specialized to certain kinds of information: thus there may be visual processors, specialized processors of linguistic signals, specialized devices controlling motor movements, etc. These modules govern the processing of perception and motor output; perhaps the corresponding thinking is similarly divided. Keller & Keller subscribe to this widely held modern view, citing phylogenetic, ontogenetic, and neurophysiological evidence in its favour. Even some theories of linguistic semantics point to the priority of imagistic ways of thinking. What, they ask, remains of the thesis of linguistic determinism given such a view?

Keller & Keller focus on the kind of thinking involved in productive activity. Ethnographic observations of an American blacksmith confirm that production is guided by image not by the propositional forms of information that are thought to lie behind linguistic meaning. Thus even when linguistic input is used in design, the words seem to tie into a non-propositional way of thinking. The study of such verbal interaction, for example, between smith and client, seems to show that complex information is successfully and efficiently conveyed through the use of expressions that are propositionally vague, but serve to evoke relatively precise mental images.

Keller & Keller conclude that there seem to be distinct kinds of thought, quite largely independent, so that at most the thesis of linguistic determinism would be a thesis about the relation of language to just that part of the cognitive system specialized to propositional representations. At the very least, the whole thesis of linguistic relativity needs to be reconstrued in a modular theory of mind.

Notes

1 Humboldt's views here probably had in part a French origin, as mentioned in the introduction, cf. e.g.: "If speech is a thought that manifests itself, it must also be true that thought is interior and hidden speech" (Antoine de Rivarol, 1784, piscours sur l'universalité de la langue française, quoted in Aarsleff 1988: xliv).
2 For a careful explication and clarification (indeed extension) of Whorf's ideas here, see Lucy (1992a: ch. 2).
3 A prior thing to establish, one might think, is whether indeed there *are* any substantial cross-cultural differences in cognition. Anthropologists on the whole tacitly seem to suppose that there are, and then concern themselves with what exactly constitutes the difference between "us" and "them," finding it, for example, in mythic thought (Lévi-Strauss 1966), or literacy (Goody 1977), or levels of psychic development (Hallpike 1979). There is a discipline charged with this task, cross-cultural psychology (see Triandis & Berry 1980), but curiously this has played hardly any role in the linguistic relativity debate (but see Cole & Scribner 1977).
4 Cf. Schultz (1990: 10–15) who argues that some of the more extreme statements have been systematically excluded from the Whorfian canon.
5 Searle's (1969: 19–20) principle of expressibility comes close: "anything that can be meant [communicatively intended], can be said." The contrapositive is "anything that cannot be said cannot be meant."
6 For the history of the rise of the cognitive sciences, see Gardner (1985), Hirst (1988).
7 See, e.g., Jackendoff (1992).
8 The relation of universals to relativity is discussed by Gellner (1988) in an interesting way: he holds that relativity is essentially the claim that there is NOT just one world "out there," a doctrine that science has proved to be false, on the other hand science is a peculiar mode of thought that has occurred just once in cultural traditions, and is by no means universal. Universals of thought and relativity are thus on this account orthogonal issues.
9 In fact some research on the hypothesis of linguistic determinism has been conducted by the intra-language study of whether having linguistic labels for denotata makes them more easily or accurately memorable (e.g. Brown & Lenneberg 1954).

10 For another attempt to spell out the Whorfian syllogism, see Kay & Kempton (1984) (drawing on earlier distillations by Eric Lenneberg and Roger Brown). For a detailed discussion of the relation between conceptual structure and linguistic categories in contemporary linguistics and philosophy, see Levinson (in press [a]).

11 For example, *our* concept of "fish" and *their* concept of "fish" could be identical, but the extension of theirs could be larger (they might think porpoises are fish); or the extension of their term X and our term "planets" might be identical, while the intensions are contrastive (e.g. their intension of X might be "wandering star").

12 The "strong" form, though, is almost certainly a straw man, since it is unclear that anyone ever held it, despite the fact that the "weak" form is "not the one usually given, and is certainly not what most anthropology students are taught as 'The Sapir–Whorf hypothesis'" (Kay & Kempton 1984: 77). The latter authors point out that Whorf definitely presumed a level of language-independent cognition (see also documentation in Lucy 1992a: 38–45). Some commentators on Whorf claim that Whorf's own position on the "strong" vs. "weak" determinacy issue was equivocal (Schultz 1990: 14–15). Still, there is little doubt that much anti-Whorf sentiment (e.g. Pinker 1994: ch. 3, Pullum 1991) is directed at a mythical target.

13 We can take this in part to be a concomitant of the behaviorist era in which he was writing. Some modern sympathizers hold on to some notion of habituation as a causal mechanism in linguistic determinism (Lucy 1992b); see also the more guarded views of Slobin (this volume). We sketch below a different possible argument: if one is to speak a language which makes certain distinctions obligatory, one simply *must* have categorized experience in appropriate ways (i.e., have noticed how states or events were structured on the relevant parameters).

14 That some effects of linguistic coding on conceptualization are to be found is not denied by the strongest opponents of the determinacy hypothesis – see e.g. Fodor (1992: 389), Pinker (1994: 65).

15 Explicitly advanced by Katz & Fodor (1963), still adopted by e.g. Jackendoff (1990: 37ff.), despite the difficulties spelt out in, e.g., Kempson (1977: 96ff.).

16 Thus sentences of the one language may be said to be *untranslatable* into sentences of the other, in the sense that information may simply be lacking: consider the question whether "You are right" in English should be translated with a *tu* or a *vous* in French.

17 They are of course opposed in intention: the anti-Whorfian hypothesis, with some adjustments (e.g. the conclusion exchanged for the first premise), is intended to explain semantic universals (see, e.g., Clark & Clark 1977):

(1′) users of different languages utilize the identical conceptual system;
(2′) the conceptual system (the innate "language of thought") determines the semantic representation system;
therefore
(3′) speakers of different languages utilize the same or similar semantic representation systems, hence there are significant semantic universals.

18 They know, of course, that for most purposes such an analysis is equivalent to one employing unanalyzable primitives with their "components" spelt out by meaning postulates (see e.g. Lyons 1982: 93f.; for different views about the psychological plausibility of these two solutions see Chierchia & McConnell-Ginet 1990: ch. 8, and Bierwisch & Schreuder 1993).

19 True, one might still escape the relativist conclusion, by desperately adopting (1″) instead of (1) (as Fodor 1975 does):

(1″) evolution foresaw our need for notions like *logarithm, symphony, laser, hologram*, etc., and so provided the relevant underlying concepts as unanalyzable conceptual wholes (and so on for every other apparently culture-specific notion).

This looks like an obvious *reductio ad absurdum*; for discussion, see e.g. Putnam (1988: ch. 1), and Sterelny (1990).

20 Curiously, many commentators think this could not be the kind of thing Whorf had in mind: "the argument for an important linguistic relativity evaporates under scrutiny. The only respect in which language clearly and obviously does influence thought turns out to be rather banal: language provides us with most of our concepts" (Devitt & Sterelny 1987: 178); "most of the experiments have tested banal 'weak' versions of the Whorfian hypothesis, namely that words can have some effect on memory or categorization. Some of the experiments have worked, but that is hardly surprising" (Pinker 1994: 65). The concessions hardly seem banal!

21 Many nativists find this kind of linguistic determinism quite acceptable, e.g. Pinker (1989: 360) states "Whorf was surely wrong when he said that one's language determines how one conceptualizes reality in general. But he was probably correct in a much weaker sense: one's language does determine how one must conceptualize reality when one has to talk about it." But it may not be possible to clearly distinguish thinking for speaking from just plain thinking – see below.

22 These paragraphs owe much to seminar discussions at the Max Planck Institute for Psycholinguistics with Pim Levelt, Dan Slobin, and John Lucy.

23 The existing body of research is very small: see Kay & Kempton (1984), the review in Lucy (1992a), Lucy's own studies in Lucy (1992b), and the work of the Cognitive Anthropology Research group at the Max Planck Institute for Psycholinguistics, exemplified in, e.g., Brown & Levinson (1993).

References

Aarsleff, H. 1988. Introduction. In von Humboldt (1988): vii–lxvi.

Bernstein, B. 1973. *Class, codes and control*, vol. I. St. Albans: Paladin.

Bierwisch, M. & Schreuder, R. 1993. From concepts to lexical items. In W. J. M. Levelt (ed.), *Lexical access in speech production* (pp. 23–60). Oxford: Basil Blackwell.

Brown, P. & Levinson, S. 1993. *Explorations in Mayan cognition*. Working Paper No. 24. Nijmegen: Cognitive Anthropology Research Group.

Brown, R. & Lenneberg, E. 1954. A study in language and cognition. *Journal of Abnormal and Social Psychology*, 49, 454–62.

Chierchia, G. & McConnell-Ginet, S. 1990. *Meaning and grammar: an introduction to semantics*. Cambridge, MA: MIT Press.

Clark, E. & Clark, H. 1977. *Psychology and language*. New York: Harcourt Brace.

Cole, M. & Scribner, S. 1977. Cross-cultural studies of memory and cognition. In R. V. Kail & J. W. Hagen (eds.), *Perspectives on the development of memory and cognition* (pp. 239–72). Hillsdale, NJ: Lawrence Erlbaum.

Devitt, M. & Sterelny, K. 1987. *Language and reality: an introduction to the philosophy of language*. Oxford: Basil Blackwell.

Fodor, J. A. 1975. *The language of thought*. Cambridge, MA: Harvard University Press.

1983. *The modularity of mind*. Cambridge, MA: MIT Press.

1992. How there could be a private language. Extract from Fodor (1975), reprinted in B. Beakley & P. Ludlow (eds.), *The philosophy of mind* (pp. 385–91). Cambridge, MA: MIT Press.

Fodor, J. D., Fodor, J. A. & Garrett, M. 1975. The unreality of semantic representations. *Linguistics Inquiry*, 4, 515–31.

Gardner, H. 1985. *The mind's new science*. New York: Basic Books.

Gellner, E. 1988. Relativism and universals. In M. Hollis & S. Lukes (eds.), *Rationality and relativism* (pp. 181–21). Oxford: Basil Blackwell.

Goody, J. 1977. *The domestication of the savage mind*. Cambridge University Press.

Hale, K. & Keyser, J. 1987. *A view from the middle*. Lexicon Project Working Papers No. 10. Cambridge, MA: MIT Center for Cognitive Science.

Hallpike, C. R. 1979. *Foundations of primitive thought*. Oxford: Clarendon Press.

Haviland, J. B. 1993. Anchoring, iconicity and orientation in Guugu Yimithirr pointing gestures. *Journal of Linguistic Anthropology*, 3(1), 3–45.

Hirst, W. (ed.) 1988. *The making of cognitive science: essays in honor of George A. Miller*. Cambridge University Press.

Humboldt, W. von. 1988 [1836]. *On language: the diversity of human language-structure and its influence on the mental development of mankind*. Tr. Peter Heath. Cambridge University Press.

Hymes, D. 1964. *Language in culture and society: a reader in linguistics and anthropology*. New York: Harper & Row.

1974. *Foundations in sociolinguistics: an ethnographic approach*. Philadelphia: University of Pennsylvania Press.

Jackendoff, R. 1983. *Semantics and cognition*. Cambridge, MA: MIT Press.

1987. *Consciousness and the computational mind*. Cambridge, MA: MIT Press.

1990. *Semantic structure*. Cambridge, MA: MIT Press.

1992. *Languages of the mind*. Cambridge, MA: MIT Press.

Katz, J. & Fodor, J. 1963. The structure of a semantic theory. *Language*, 39, 170–210.

Kay, P. & Kempton, W. 1984. What is the Sapir–Whorf hypothesis? *American Anthropologist*, 86, 65–79.

Kempson, R. 1977. *Semantic theory*. Cambridge University Press.

Lakoff, G. 1987. *Women, fire and dangerous things: what categories reveal about the mind*. University of Chicago Press.

Lee, P. 1991. The Whorf theory complex: a critical reassessment of the ideas of Benjamin Lee Whorf. Ph.D. dissertation, Churchlands: University of Western Australia.

Levelt, W. J. M. 1989. *Speaking: from intention to articulation*. Cambridge, MA: MIT Press.

Lévi-Strauss, C. 1966. *The savage mind*. London: Weidenfeld & Nicholson.

Levinson, S. C. 1992. Activity type and language. In P. Drew & J. Heritage (eds.), *Talk at work* (pp. 66–100). Cambridge University Press.

in press (a) From outer to inner space: linguistic categories and non-linguistic thinking. In J. Nuyts & E. Pederson (eds.), *The relationship between linguistic and conceptual representation*. Cambridge University Press.

in press (b) Frames of reference and Molyneaux's question: cross-linguistic evidence. To appear in P. Bloom, M. Peterson, L. Nadel, & M. Garrett (eds.), *Language and space*. Cambridge, MA: MIT Press.

Lucy, J. 1992a. *Language diversity and thought: a reformulation of the linguistic relativity hypothesis*. Cambridge University Press.

1992b. *Grammatical categories and cognition: a case study of the linguistic relativity hypothesis*: Cambridge University Press.

(ed.) 1993 *Reflexive language: reported speech and metapragmatics*. Cambridge University Press.

Lyons, J. 1981. *Language, meaning and context*. London: Fontana.

Miller, G. A. 1956. The magical number seven, plus or minus two. *Psychological Review*, 63(2), 81–97.

Pinker, S. 1989. *Learnability and cognition: the acquisition of argument structure*. Cambridge, MA: MIT Press.

1994. *The language instinct*. New York: William Morrow.

Pullman, G. 1991. *The great eskimo vocabulary hoax and other irreverent essays on the study of language*. University of Chicago Press.

Putnam, H. 1988. *Representation and reality*. Cambridge, MA: MIT Press.

Rosch, E. 1977. Linguistic relativity. In P. N. Johnson-Laird & P. C. Wason (eds.), *Thinking: readings in cognitive science* (pp. 501–22). Cambridge University Press.

Schulz, E. 1990. *Dialogue at the margins. Whorf, Bakhtin and linguistic relativity*. Madison: University of Wisconsin Press.

Searle, J. 1969. *Speech acts: an essay in the philosophy of language*. Cambridge University Press.

Simon, H. A. 1986. The parameters of human memory. In F. Klix & H. Hagendorf (eds.), *Human memory and cognitive capabilities* (pp. 299–310). Amsterdam: North-Holland.

Steiner, G. 1975. *After Babel: aspects of language and translation*. Oxford University Press.

Sterelny, K. 1990. *The representational theory of mind*. Oxford: Basil Blackwell.

Triandis, H. C. & Berry, J. W. (eds.) 1980. *Handbook of cross-cultural psychology*. Boston: Allyn & Bacon.

Wason, P. & Johnson-Laird, P. N. (eds.) 1977. *Thinking*. Cambridge University Press.

Weiskrantz, L. 1988. *Thought without language*. Oxford: Fondation Fyssen & Oxford University Press.

Whorf, B. L. 1956. *Language, thought and reality: selected writings of Benjamin Lee Whorf*, ed. J. B. Carroll. Cambridge, MA: MIT Press.

2

THE SCOPE OF LINGUISTIC RELATIVITY: AN ANALYSIS AND REVIEW OF EMPIRICAL RESEARCH

JOHN A. LUCY

1 Introduction

The possibility that the language we speak influences the way we think has excited both popular and scientific imagination in the West for well over a century (Lucy 1985a, Aarsleff 1982). Rigorous demonstration of such influences would have profound implications not only for the scientific understanding of human life but also for the conduct of research and public policy. Yet this intense interest and manifest significance have not led to a commensurate volume and quality of empirical research. We still know little about the connections between particular language patterns and mental life – let alone how they operate or how significant they are.

On the one hand, a mere handful of empirical studies address the linguistic relativity proposal directly and nearly all are conceptually flawed in very fundamental ways. Common defects in existing research include working within a single language, privileging the categories of one language or culture in comparative studies, dealing with a relatively marginal aspect of language (e.g. a small set of lexical items), and failing to provide direct evidence regarding individual cognition. On the other hand, both speculation and research have focused rather narrowly on possible links between particular language structures and some measure of cognitive outcome and have ignored two important facets of the problem that must be treated in any full account. A full account must identify the properties of natural language which make diversity possible and give it a crucial role in cultural life. These properties and their consequences will form the cornerstone of any theory about the processes (or mechanisms) underlying the language-thought linkage and indicate exactly where diversity should have effects. A full account must also examine to what extent culturally specific patterns of use – both beliefs and practices – mediate the impact of language structure on thought or have their own direct effects independent of structural type. Understanding the cultural uses of language is essential not only for assessing the particular significance of given structural effects both within and

37

across cultures but also for assessing the general significance of language in social and psychological life. In short, empirical research on the linguistic relativity proposal must rectify the existing conceptual problems while expanding the scope of inquiry to include questions about underlying mechanism and cultural significance.

The present chapter reviews existing empirical research on linguistic relativity within such a broadened framework. The first section briefly sketches the implications of having a natural language or not. The discussion indicates that languages are distinctive, in contrast to other semiotic forms, in having a central symbolic component, and that this property both enables language diversity and holds specific implications for the relation of language and thought. The second section reviews in detail empirical research aimed at assessing the implications of having one language as opposed to another, that is, the classic linguistic relativity proposal that structural differences among languages in their categories of meaning have an impact on thought. The discussion indicates some of the reasons for the paucity of empirical research, analyzes the contributions and limitations of previous work, and describes my own recent efforts to improve research in this area. The third section outlines the significance of diversity in the discursive (or cultural) functions of language for actions in and conceptions of the world. The discussion clarifies the role of patterns of use in mediating structural relativity, suggests that variation in usage might have effects in its own right, and provides a framework for and examples of research suggestive of such effects for both the referential and expressive qualities of language. A fourth and final section discusses how linguistic structure and discursive function interact dialectically in conjunction with language ideologies and how such interactions create problems for the research process itself.

2 Semiotic relativity

Attempts to address the question of the significance of language differences for thought must begin with a consideration of the general role and significance of language in human life. Biologists and psychologists have long speculated on the very diverse worlds available to various species by virtue of the disparate sensory stimuli to which they are sensitive and the different neural capacities for organizing, storing, and manipulating such sensory input. As the only species with language, the human perspective on the world may differ not only in terms of such physical characteristics, but also as a function of the availability and use of this qualitatively different *semiotic* form. That is, in the human case, it is important to ask whether the use of the semiotic form we call language in and of itself fundamentally alters the vision of the world held by humans in contrast to other species. We can call this the hypothesis of *semiotic relativity*. Although research on the general role of language in human life and thought cannot be reviewed here, it is essential to introduce this perspective into the discussion because the evaluation of the linguistic relativity issue depends greatly on the position one first takes on the implications of having a language at all versus not having one, and then on what features of natural language are regarded as most relevant to thought.

One common view stresses the continuities of human psychology and social organization with that of other species and sees the transformative power of language as very limited. If there are differences in thought between humans and other species, they stem directly from neuro-cognitive differences in the brain, not from the system of symbolic signs which they make possible. Those adopting this perspective tend to see experience as a direct function of perception and cognition operating without language, to regard speech itself as a biological phenomenon with a specific localizable organic base, and to view language as a mere encoding of prior experience so that it may be relayed to others. A large amount of research in the social sciences, especially within the cognitive sciences, operates as if language had such an unproblematic "mapping" relationship to perception, cognition, emotion, social interaction, etc.

Another view, the one adopted here, is that the human sciences are fundamentally distinct from the physical and life sciences precisely because they attempt to encompass a new order of regularity closely associated with the use of the symbolic medium of natural language. This new medium not only adds a new level of regularity, it also transforms existing levels. Thus, where biologists operate with units such as individual organism and social group, the human sciences also explore questions of self and culture, the nature of reflective consciousness, and the significance of historically developed systems of meaning. All of the latter depend centrally on language. Further, the cultural creation of new technologies can neutralize the limits in our biological inheritance by augmenting our perceptual, intellectual, and physical powers, and this, in turn, makes our symbolic world relatively more important. Overall, the new order of diversity and regularity characterizing human life requires new approaches to supplement those of the other sciences.

Ultimately, then, an evaluation of the role of language-in-general in human thought constitutes a necessary component of any research on linguistic relativity. Such research must be informed by a semiotic perspective, that is, a perspective which clarifies the distinctive qualities of natural language in contrast to other semiotic forms and the relationship of those qualities to psychological and social life. From such a semiotic point of view, the distinguishing feature of natural language is its central *symbolic* component. The more specific distinguishing characteristics of human language inventoried in various accounts (e.g. Hockett 1958) all ultimately depend on or stem directly from this feature. Following Peirce (1932; see also Benveniste [1939] 1971 and Piaget 1973), a *symbolic* sign involves a sign vehicle which stands for some object *only* by virtue of being so taken to stand for it by an interpretant. In other words, the sign–object relationship is established conventionally in a social group rather than motivated by a "natural" connection as in the case of *icons*, where relations of resemblance obtain between the sign vehicle and its object, or *indices*, where relations of co-presence obtain between the sign vehicle and its object. The signal systems characteristic of other species always depend on iconic or indexical linkages of sign vehicle and object for their effectiveness even when also conventionalized to some degree. Human groups also continue to signal by means of icons and indices, so the presence of symbolic signs does not eliminate the presence or significance of the other sign types. Indeed, language itself as a discursive semiotic is also always both iconic and indexical – and these dimensions of language have been the focus of increasing research attention in recent years.

Because they rely on cultural convention for their effectiveness, languages are essentially social rather than personal, objective rather than subjective. This allows language to be a medium for the *socialization* or *objectification* of individual activities – including thought – to the extent that the activities depend on that medium. At the heart of this conventional system lies the symbolic component of language, the part that establishes sign–object relations *purely* on the basis of convention. This central symbolic component makes language an especially *flexible* signaling mode and makes possible the vast formal and functional *diversity* we see across language communities. Finally, because the language sign need not resemble its object or depend on its co-presence, speech can encompass any imaginable object including itself, thus providing the opportunity for *metasemiotic commentary* not only on all naturally based signals but also on itself, a *reflexive capacity* which underlies its potential to create system-internal and -external equivalences. Collectively, these semiotic properties (socialization/objectification, flexibility/diversity, and metasemiotic/reflexive capacity) which all stem from the symbolic dimension of language are the most interesting properties when comparing language with other sign modalities. A linguistic relativity proposal is a natural by-product of such a semiotic perspective. It asks about the significance of the socializing power of the diversity of language forms and functions, especially with regard to providing a vehicle for metacommentary on our actions. Indeed, it is the self-reflexive capacity of language which underlies our ability to pose the question, to investigate it, and to transcend it at least analytically, if not habitually (Lucy 1993).

3 Linguistic (or structural) relativity

There are a great many natural languages and they differ in substantial and often surprising ways (Boas [1911] 1966, Sapir [1921] 1949c). In actuality, no person speaks "language-in-general" but always a particular language with its own characteristic structure of meaning. Any investigation of the relation between language and thought must cope with this structural diversity of natural languages by asking whether and to what extent the characteristics of specific languages have an impact on the thought or behavior of those who speak them. We can, following traditional usage, call this the hypothesis of *linguistic relativity* as long as we understand that by the term *linguistic* we mean the formal *structure* of semantic and pragmatic categories available for reference and predication. Where there is a potential for ambiguity in this review, the term *structural relativity* will be used in place of *linguistic relativity*.

3.1 Paucity of research

Despite the long tradition of thought and speculation about the implications of structural diversity among languages, there is little actual empirical research and most of it is poorly done. If we restrict ourselves to studies that compare at least two languages and the modes of thought associated with them, there have been only half a dozen studies in the last fifty years (Lucy 1992b). This situation is remarkable given the intense interest in the linguistic relativity issue. In such a context, it makes little sense to speak of the linguistic relativity proposal as having been empirically decided one way or the other at the present time.

The main impediment to research in this area has been the widespread, if tacit, acceptance of certain limiting assumptions about the relationship between language and thought generally. Since the late 1950s, mainstream psychological, linguistic, and cognitive science research on this issue has been guided by three closely linked assumptions which derive ultimately from deep-seated cultural orientations but which received renewed impetus from Piagetian developmental psychology and Chomskian generative linguistics (Piaget [1954] 1967, Inhelder & Piaget 1958, Chomsky 1972). First, there has been an assumption that basic cognitive processes are universal. Any variability in performance across populations is ascribed to mere differences in content. Second, these traditions have assumed that thought shapes language. Thus, when interesting correspondences emerge between cognitive performance and a given language (e.g. English), they are routinely interpreted as having been determined by cognition. Third, these traditions assume that all languages must be fundamentally alike. This assumption may follow from the first two or may be independently posited. Since, by assumption, languages do not vary significantly, there is little reason to investigate their diverse forms.

One might expect a critique of this presumptive universalism from anthropologists and comparative linguists who are, as groups, less willing to discount linguistic diversity. Yet few are prepared to engage directly in the discourses of the other fields and many are reluctant to challenge the universality of cognitive processes given historical experience with evolutionary and racial interpretations of purported differences in mentality. By contrast, ideological universalism is ethically well received – its sometimes disastrous effects in our own century notwithstanding. Unable to mount a sophisticated critique of the notion of "basic cognitive processes" itself, or to challenge effectively the "mere content" view of cultural and linguistic differences, the aforementioned assumptions persist along with their chilling effects on research, public policy, and respect for other languages and cultures.

3.2 Review of existing research

Although concern with linguistic relativity has had a long history in the West, contemporary empirical research begins with the work of Benjamin Lee Whorf (1956a, b, Lucy 1985b, 1992b). Nearly all subsequent research has been stimulated by his work and takes it as a point of departure. This subsequent work can be divided into two broad groups: research done by anthropological linguists and research done by psycholinguists.

3.2.1 Whorf

Whorf conceived of his research as part of the larger anthropological project of documenting and understanding languages and cultures different from our own (cf. Fishman 1982). His predecessors Franz Boas ([1911] 1966) and Edward Sapir ([1924] 1949a, [1929] 1949d, [1931] 1964) speculated about the impact of language on thought, but Whorf was the first to try to demonstrate actual correspondences between the structural features of languages and specific modes of thought.

In his research Whorf (esp. 1956a) compared the formal meaning structures of *two languages* and then traced connections between such meaning structures and *habitual thought* as manifest in various cultural beliefs and institutions. For example, he showed that the Hopi and English languages encoded what we call "time" differently and that this corresponded to distinct cultural orientations towards temporal notions. Specifically, Whorf argued that speakers of English treat cyclic experiences of various sorts (e.g. the passage of a day or a year) in the same grammatical frame used for ordinary object nouns. Thus, English speakers are led to treat these cycles as object-like – they can be measured and counted just like tangible objects. English also treats objects as if they each have a form and a substance. Since the cyclic words get put into this object frame, English speakers are led to ask what is the substance associated with a day, a year, and so forth. Whorf argues that our global, abstract notion of "time" as a continuous, homogeneous formless something can be seen to arise to fill in the blank in this linguistic analogy. The Hopi by contrast do not treat these cycles as objects but as recurrent events. Thus, although they have, as Whorf acknowledged, words for what we would recognize as temporal cycles (e.g. days, years, etc.), their formal structuration in the grammar does not give rise to the abstract notion of "time" that we have. (Critics of Whorf's Hopi data [e.g. Malotki 1983] have managed to miss completely his point about structuration.) In Whorf's view, grouping referents and concepts as formally "the same" for the purposes of speech has led speakers to group those referents and concepts as substantively "the same" for action generally, as evidenced by related cultural patterns of belief and behavior.

Notice finally that there is an additional element to Whorf's formulation beyond language and thought: a *reality* against which the two linguistic patterns are tacitly compared but which was not itself seriously analyzed or explicated by him. The cyclic events and subjective experience of duration that he refers to are never fully analyzed. The practical consequences of this neglect are mitigated somewhat because he did not privilege either of the two languages but rather played them off against each other to establish his comparison. Herein lies the nucleus of a procedure for establishing a neutral basis for the comparison of language–reality relationships, a nucleus that has yet to be fully exploited. In short Whorf laid out the basic design of an approach to empirical research on linguistic relativity.

3.2.2 The anthropological linguists

Other anthropological linguists who subsequently explored Whorf's proposals continued to link grammatical structures to broad cultural patterns. However, on the whole these studies examined a single grammatical form in a single exotic language and thereby effectively abandoned the effort to analyze a widespread grammatical pattern or to make systematic cross-linguistic comparisons. So, for example, in a classic study, Harry Hoijer (1953) examined a category concerned with motion in the Navajo verb and then sought evidence of parallels in the "motion" motifs in Navajo myths and nomadic history. It remains unclear in studies of this sort how significant the grammatical pattern is in Navajo and how distinctive it is in comparison to other languages – especially those spoken by culturally similar groups. Further, since there was no actual comparison of languages, the issue of a common reality (e.g., what counts as "motion") against which they could be assessed is not explicitly raised. More recent work on "motion" in Navajo language and culture (e.g. Witherspoon 1977), whatever its other merits, suffers from the same difficulties.

Research in the anthropological tradition also typically did not provide clear evidence for a non-linguistic correlate with grammatical patterns. Cultural analyses were either nonexistent or dominated by the use of linguistic materials as, for example, in the use of myth texts by Hoijer. In several cases, a purported relation between language and culture would turn out, under scrutiny, to be a relation between the grammatical structure of a language and the lexical structure of the same language (e.g. Mathiot 1964). An adequate study of the relation between language and thought should, by contrast, provide clear evidence of a correlation of language system with a pattern of non-linguistic belief and behavior – individual or institutional. This is not to say that vocabulary items do not reflect non-linguistic culture or that discourse using language does not provide important evidence about cultural beliefs, but only that, from a methodological point of view, such materials cannot be persuasive by themselves in showing broader effects of language. Much of the otherwise excellent recent anthropological work (which will be discussed further below) focusing on the creative play of grammatical categories in discourse or linking language structure to "linguistic ideologies" suffers from a similar lingua-centrism.

In sum, by contrast with Whorf's formulation, the anthropological case studies have developed a truncated approach to the relativity problem. Thought has been assessed by reference to linguistic materials, the comparative dimension has been eliminated, and the tacit framework guiding the analyses has been an English-based view of reality. Only the linguistic analyses have had any depth to them as each author explored the interconnected meanings implicit in the structure of an exotic language and, in more recent years, expanded the focus to the complex uses of language in cultural action.

3.2.3 The comparative psycholinguists
Psychologists exploring Whorf's proposals abandoned his focus on large-scale structural patterning in languages and focused instead on small sets of lexical items or, rarely, on specific features of grammar. In either case, they usually worked with only a single language, most often English. These researchers also criticized Whorf for not assessing individual

cognition and attempted to develop techniques for doing so. These studies can be divided into two groups: those looking at lexicon and those looking at grammar.

3.2.3.1 Research on lexicons

Most psycholinguists working in this area shifted completely away from the sort of grammatical data central to Whorf's work and focused on lexical items – especially terms for colors. The meanings of these lexical items were established not by grammatical analysis but by reference to their typical denotational values – the "objects" they refer to. So, for example, American subjects were asked to list their color terms and then, subsequently, to show which of a set of color samples they applied to. Ironically, then, *lexical content* which had served to represent non-linguistic "culture" for some anthropological linguists now served to represent "language" for these psycholinguists. Needless to say, a half-dozen color terms is a rather poor representative of "language."

In the most famous of these studies, Brown & Lenneberg (1954) tried to show that certain colors were more codable than others in English – that is, subjects assigned them shorter names and tended to agree more on the application of those names to color samples. The more codable colors were recognized and remembered more readily than other colors. As one of the few rigorous studies purporting to show a cognitive effect in a field dominated by speculation, this work had enormous influence on subsequent research.

Yet notice how different this research is from Whorf's. The shift to studying codability (i.e., intersubject agreement in lexical denotation) was undertaken to simplify the research process, but it fundamentally altered the terms of the problem. First, the only "linguistic" variable remaining in the later studies in this tradition was the "code efficiency" of a set of lexical items used as labels for stimuli. Only stimulus input (a color) and behavioral output (correct or incorrect memory) were actually relevant. No evidence was presented that these forms constituted a distinctive, grammatically integrated set in the language. Second, this approach explicitly relied on a Western scientific characterization of reality (i.e., the color space). Because the conceptualization of language forms was in terms of an independently known and defined reality based on European languages, the whole approach undermined *in principle* the possibility of discovering genuinely different linguistic approaches to reality. Third, the tradition initially omitted any comparison of languages. Typically only one language received serious analysis and sometimes there was no linguistic analysis at all! (Some might count the work of Lenneberg & Roberts 1956 and Stefflre, Morely, & Castillo 1966 as exceptions to these generalizations.)

Extensions of the early color work by anthropologists Berlin, Kay, their collaborators, and critics (Berlin & Kay 1969, Kay & McDaniel 1978, Heider 1972, Lucy & Shweder 1979, 1988) generated the first broad multilanguage comparative framework to actually be applied to the relativity question and one comparative case study by Heider (1972) of the relation of language and thought. However, this comparative work still retained the lexical orientation and fundamentally Western conception of "color" characteristic of the earlier era. Rather than working from a comparatively induced typology of patterns of language–world relationships, it showed instead the distribution of languages relative to a fixed set of parameters drawn from the Western European scientific tradition.

So despite its comparative orientation, it actually washed out linguistic differences and suggested that languages merely "reflect" or "map" reality. Whereas Whorf begins with the language structure and asks what it suggests about the implicit construal of reality, these studies begin with *our* reality as a given and ask how other languages handle it. Inevitably, this latter approach leads to a conceptualization of language as a mere dependent variable, as a device for coding a pre-given reality.

Some examples of what is lost in this approach to language semantics through a highly controlled denotational task may be helpful. Zuni, a language of the American Southwest, exhibits two terms that we might translate as 'yellow' (Newman 1954). Closer analysis reveals that one term is verbal and refers to things that become yellow by ripening or aging whereas the other is adjectival and refers to things that have had yellow substances applied to them. The customary approach would select one term as "basic" (eliminating the other "nonbasic" term from further consideration) and ignore the aspect of its meaning (i.e., manner of becoming colored) for which there is no English equivalent. Hanunóo, a language of the Philippines, has four terms that seem to refer to what we call *white, black, green,* and *red* but which under further analysis turn out to mean roughly 'lightness, darkness, wetness, and dryness' (Conkin 1955). These terms can then be used to discriminate color chips but this hardly reflects their central meaning. Turning to English, we have many words that have color reference as a central part of their meaning, but which also involve other meanings (Lucy 1992b). Consider for example *blond, brunette, bay, sorrel, palomino, appaloosa, maroon, scarlet,* etc. In fact, if we look broadly across a wide array of languages, we would conclude that the real *linguistic* regularity is that terms with color-relevant meaning routinely seem to combine these meanings with plant and animal referents or with other textural and light qualities (Lucy in press). The emergence of terms specialized for reference to color in some languages is of course interesting, but can hardly be taken as the standard for what terms of other languages "really mean," nor should it lead us to ignore the semantic regularities in our own terms with such reference (Lucy in press).

An approach that carries an array of color stimuli around the world and asks people for the words that effectively discriminate among them (and do nothing else) will wash out all these linguistic patterns. It will inevitably confirm that pure color terms are a universal part of language with much the same sense as our own specialized terms since any variation that is observed will by definition lie *within* the Western-defined domain. The research procedure itself precludes any alternative finding. Notice too that radically different languages will tend to look deficient by comparison with our own to the extent that much of their descriptive vocabulary is eliminated from consideration. Although this research was important in highlighting the need for a comparative metalanguage of description, it did not, in the end, provide an adequate framework for the purposes of assessing relativity.

The Brown & Lenneberg study also inaugurated a tradition of assessing thought by presenting individual subjects with experimentally controlled memory tasks rather than by analyzing naturally occurring patterns of everyday belief and behavior. This use of experiments provided more control over some of the variables affecting performance but was accompanied by a shift of the research emphasis away from Whorf's concern with *habitual* thought and behavior and towards a concern with *potential* thought and behavior. So, in the cognitive realm, as in the linguistic realm discussed above, the search for methodological rigor led to a fundamental reformulation of the problem. The considerable gains in control were offset by the ambiguous status of the experiments as representations of habitual behavior, that is, as culturally valid representations of thought.

3.2.3.2 Research on grammar

Through the 1970s only a few of these psychological studies explored (rather inconclusively) the cognitive significance of grammatical patterns or systematically compared two or more languages (e.g. Carroll & Casagrande 1958). Those researchers who did so retained the preference for experimental assessment of individual behavior characteristic of the psycholinguistics tradition. Unfortunately, their linguistic analyses also showed exactly the same weaknesses as the anthropological studies cited above in that no attempt was made to relate the categories at issue to other categories in the language or to similar categories in other languages. Thus, each study only described a single categorical distinction in a single language even when behavioral data were collected on two or three language groups. In each case, the tacit metalanguage for linguistic characterization was "reality" (a world of objects) as construed in or viewed from English.

More recently Alfred Bloom (1981) and others (Au 1983, Liu 1985) have explored the relation between certain types of counterfactual markers in Chinese and English and speakers' facility with hypothetical reasoning. Bloom used an experimental design where he presented stories to English and Chinese speakers with the Chinese receiving translations of English texts. English speakers did better at the counterfactual reasoning tasks, and Bloom then generalized to the utility of systematic marking of counterfactuals to sustain theoretical, specifically scientific, modes of thought. However, since the stimulus materials were not absolutely identical in the two cases, his approach led to a number of ambiguities. Critics raised questions about whether certain of the Chinese sentences really meant what he claimed they meant. These disputes quickly degenerated into an unresolvable battle over the accuracy and fairness of the Chinese translation of the English constructions (see review in Lucy 1992b). There is no way to resolve such disputes except by appeal to what speakers would actually typically say about a concrete situation; but this could not be tested since the counterfactual stories by definition did not correspond to any observable events.

Further, a close reading of Bloom's original materials reveals that the various linguistic devices he describes do not form a structural set in grammatical terms but can only be identified by reference to their common use in a certain discourse mode. Further, the differences in how much counterfactual discourse the two groups engage in and how they value it seem much more telling than any structural differences. Despite the ambiguity of Bloom's results, his approach was especially significant in that experimental work and cultural analysis were brought together for the first time.

3.3 *Towards a new approach*

From this brief survey of previous empirical research we can abstract the requirements for an improved approach to research on the cognitive implications of structural diversity among languages. Such research should be comparative in that it should deal with two or more languages. It should deal with a significant language variable such as one or more central grammatical categories rather than a relatively minor vocabulary set. It should assess the cognitive performance of individual speakers aside from explicitly verbal contexts and try to establish that any cognitive patterns that are detected also characterize everyday behavior outside of the assessment situation. Finally, studies that deal with referential categories, that is with categories which denote objects and relations in the world, rather than with categories having to do solely with language-internal relations, will provide a variety of advantages for empirical research in terms of developing comparative frames and cognitive assessment procedures.

Over the past several years I have developed a systematic approach to the investigation of the relation between such diversity in language and thought with the aim of filling the gaps in our knowledge and methodology (Lucy 1992b). The research aims to be absolutely explicit about what features of language are significant for thought and how they are significant. These studies combine careful comparison of well-defined aspects of grammar with rigorous demonstration of highly distinctive patterns of perception, classification, or memory.

My first major empirical research using this approach (Lucy 1992a) explored the ways structural differences between American English and Yucatec Maya might affect the cognition of speakers of those languages. The research shows that these two languages encode objects in quite different ways and that these differences affect the nonverbal cognitive performance of adult speakers. Specifically, the research focused on the relationship between grammatical number marking and patterns of memory and classification in tasks involving objects and pictures. Since a great many languages in Asia and the Americas share the Yucatec pattern (Lyons 1977) and most European languages share the English pattern, these differences hold important implications for a broad array of languages.

English and Yucatec differ in their number marking patterns. First, the two languages contrast in the way they signal plural. English speakers *obligatorily* signal plural for a *large number* of lexical nouns whereas Yucatec speakers *optionally* signal plural for a comparatively *small number* of lexical nouns. Specifically, English speakers mark plural for nouns referring to animate entities and ordinary objects but not for amorphous substances (e.g. *sugar, mud*, etc.). Yucatec speakers sometimes mark plural for animate entities (although it is not obligatory even when referring to multiple referents) and only occasionally mark it for any other type of referent.

In nonverbal experimental tasks involving complex pictures, Americans and Mayans were sensitive to the number of various types of objects in accordance with the patterns in their grammar. The pictures showed scenes of everyday Yucatecan village life and contained different numbers of referents of the various types. Speakers performed tasks which involved remembering the pictures (recall and recognition) and sorting them on the basis of similarity. In remembering and classifying, English speakers were sensitive to number for animate entities and objects but not for substances. By contrast, Yucatec speakers were sensitive to number only for animate entities. Note in this experiment that the two groups had very similar patterns of response for the animate and substance referents where the two languages roughly agree in structure, but that they differed with respect to ordinary object referents, that is, where the grammars of the two languages are in maximal contrast. So the group difference is not one of absolute level of performance, but rather of different qualitative responses. Neither group's performance can rightly be regarded as superior or inferior – just different.

Second, the two languages contrast in the way they treat numerals and this contrast derives from a deep underlying difference between the two languages. English numerals directly modify their associated nouns (e.g. *one candle*) whereas Yucatec numerals must be accompanied by a special form usually referred to as a *numeral classifier* which typically provides crucial information about the shape or material properties of the referent of the noun (e.g. *'un-tz'íit* kib', 'one **long thin** candle'). Numeral classifiers are a well-known grammatical type and occur in a wide variety of languages throughout the world, perhaps most notably in the languages of Asia – Chinese, Japanese, Thai, etc. In my view, the classifiers reflect the fact that *all lexical nouns in Yucatec are semantically unspecified as to essential quantifications unit*. In the case of nouns with concrete reference, it is almost as if they referred to unformed substances. So, for example, the semantic sense of the Yucatec word *kib'* in the example cited above is better glossed as 'wax' (i.e., 'one **long thin** wax') – even though when occurring alone without a numeral modifier it usually refers to objects with the form and function that we call "candle." Once one understands the substance focus of such nouns it becomes obvious that one must specify a unit (i.e., provide a classifier) when counting (i.e., 'one wax' would not make sense). By contrast, many concrete nouns in English include the notion of 'unit' or 'form' as part of their basic meaning – so when we count these nouns, we can simply use the numeral directly without any classifier (e.g. *one candle*). Where our pattern is like the Maya, we use the functional equivalent of a classifier ourselves: *a cube of sugar*.

In experimental tasks involving classifying triads of certain test objects (i.e., "Is item X more like A or more like B?"), English speakers showed a relative preference for shape-based classifications whereas Mayan speakers showed a relative preference for material-based classifications – results in line with the expectations based on the underlying lexical structures of the two languages. So, for example, speakers were shown a small cardboard box of the type used for holding cassette tapes and asked whether it was more like a small plastic box of roughly the same size and shape or more like a small piece of cardboard about the size of a half-dollar. English speakers consistently matched on the basis of shape and chose the box. Yucatec speakers consistently matched on the basis of material and chose the small piece of cardboard. The same sorts of preferences also emerged in other more indirect tests. Also, once again, both patterns of classification are reasonable and neither can rightly be described as superior to the other.

Notice that this research begins with a linguistic comparison which places both languages on an equal footing. It locates and then examines in detail a pervasive and semantically significant lexico-grammatical contrast, one patently relevant to a wide array of other languages. It does not attempt to work within a single language, nor take English as the standard for assessing other languages, nor focus on a minor or rarely occurring category. It then asks about the possible implications of the linguistic patterns for the interpretation of experience generally. These implications are then converted into specific qualitative predictions about the nonverbal performance of individual speakers of the languages – both where they will be similar and where they will be different. These predictions are then tested with an array of simple tasks using materials designed to maximize real-world interpretability. The research does not simply look for language effects in other verbal behaviors, nor does it frame the assessment in terms of deficits, accuracy, or a hierarchy of complexity, nor does it undertake the assessment without serious consideration of the cultural context. In short, although much remains to be done especially with regard to tracing broader cultural ramifications of these patterns, the study articulates an approach to research in this area that remedies many of the deficiencies of earlier work.

In current research I am extending this work to new grammatical categories, exploring the ontogeny of these patterns in childhood, and tracing links between the linguistic forms and traditional Maya cosmology. For example, one of the more exciting side benefits of establishing an adult contrast of the sort just described is that it can be used as a diagnostic for the onset of language effects during cognitive development. In collaboration with Suzanne Gaskins (Lucy 1989), I have recently completed pilot research on the developmental course of the language–thought connection. Comparing Mayan and American children, it appears that young children in both groups favor shape over material as a basis of classification but that a pronounced change occurs by the age of eight. No child under the age of seven favored material as a basis of classification. In the Mayan case, there is a shift from the age of eight onward to classifying on the basis of material just as do Mayan adults. In the English case, the early shape preference weakens at the age of seven with the emergence of wide variability in individual response pattern. This variability is consistent both with the English grammatical pattern (which splits its lexicon) and with the observed variability in the adult English sample. However, it is also overtly similar to the pattern for young children in both groups and further work will be necessary to adequately characterize the English population and distinguish it from the shape-preference characteristic of younger children. Pooling all ages from three to twelve, the Maya were more likely to classify on the basis of material than were the Americans for ten out of the twelve triads. This pilot research not only further substantiates the original work, it also gives us some insight into when these grammatical patterns begin to play a shaping role in cognition. Recent work by Imai & Gentner (1993) using similar materials on Japanese, another classifier language, found similar material preferences – at least for some object-type referents – and increased sensitivity to material-based alternatives as early as the age of two in language-learning contexts – in contrast to English-speaking children. These results suggest that the original findings may generalize to other languages.

4 Discursive (or functional) relativity

There is more to language than its structure of reference and predication. There is another dimension of language variation that deserves our attention. Even within a single language, there is always diversity in the ways it is used. These differences in usage may be associated with subgroups in the language community (social *dialects* – e.g. class-characteristic modes of speech) or with differences in contexts of speaking (functional *registers* – e.g. formal discourse) (Halliday 1978). There are further differences in patterns of usage when we compare diverse linguistic communities (Hymes 1974, Gumperz 1982, Gumperz & Hymes 1972). Any investigation of the relation between language and thought must also cope with this level of functional diversity in natural languages. The question is whether patterns of use have an impact on thought either directly or by virtue of amplifying or channeling any effects due to linguistic structure. We can call this the hypothesis of *discursive relativity*, a relativity stemming from diversity in the *functional* (or goal-oriented) configuration of language means in the course of (inter)action.

4.1 Early formulations

Although there has been a long history of concern with language functions within anthropology (e.g. Malinowski 1923), anthropological linguist Dell Hymes (1961, 1966) was one of the first to argue that any claims about linguistic relativity of the structural sort are dependent on certain commonalities in the cultural uses or functions of language. Thus, proposals about structural relativity require assuming a loose isofunctionality across languages of the everyday use of speech to accomplish acts of descriptive reference. There is now a significant body of research indicating that there is in fact substantial cultural diversity in the uses and valuations of language.

Similar arguments have been made for the intellectual effects of variation of usage *within* a single language. For example, there have been broad claims by psychologist Lev Vygotsky (1978, 1987) and others for the significance of literacy, formal education, and technical–scientific language for thought. Likewise sociologist Basil Bernstein (1971) has argued that class-characteristic differences in the use of what he called elaborated and restricted codes within a single language community relate to facility with certain types of thought. Both of these approaches deal primarily with the appropriation for cognitive ends of linguistic structures associated with the referential function of language. In such cases, the various effects of language structure on habitual thought are either simply amplified by more intensive application or ideologically reshaped via purification and elaboration to achieve certain cultural goals more effectively. Such discursive practices simultaneously embody and sustain cultural goals, hence the dual relevance of ethnographic description and interactive analysis in examining them.

Nonreferential functions of language (e.g. social, expressive, aesthetic, etc.) have received much less attention. The focus on reference-and-predication makes some sense given that this appears to be the dominant function of language from a semiotic–structural point of view. However, there is no necessary reason why linkages between other functions of language and human thought could not also be investigated. Further, there may well be linkages to other aspects of individual functioning such as emotion, self-concept, etc. Although there are marked differences among languages in their pragmatic or expressive qualities, it is by no means obvious how to approach their study in a systematic way. Most existing research on language use or discourse consists of case studies with uncertain generalizability and, even when explicitly addressed to the relation of language and culture, remains heavily language-centered – lacking substantive analysis of broader psychological or social correlates. The balance of this section will be limited to indicating one possible approach to a comparatively grounded typology of functions and then providing examples of the sort of issues which might be explored.

4.2 Towards a new formulation

An overarching framework for characterizing these various forms of functional relativity and investigating their effects simply does not yet exist. By way of illustration of what such a framework might look like, let us take with some modification Roman Jakobson's (1960) well-known typology of the semiotic functions of language. (For other uses and elaborations of Jakobson's scheme, see Hymes 1974 and Silverstein 1985a.)

Jakobson's typology is anchored in the components of the speech situation. He describes three functions which will be regarded here as primary. The first, and central, function of language is the *referential* or *cognitive* function which has to do with referring to and/or predicating about something in the context. Centered on the third-person pronominal forms, it receives formal recognition in the indicative mood. Diversity in the referential function lies at the center of traditional concerns about linguistic relativity. The referential function deals with the general context, hence variability in this sphere corresponds to a potential variability in the construal of reality. The traditional question of linguistic relativity, viewed in this fashion, has to do with the relation of the structure of the referential function to speakers' conceptions of reality.

The other two primary functions have to do with the nonreferential or, to use Sapir's ([1933] 1949b) term, expressive functions of language. First, the *emotive* function focuses on language's capacity to index speakers' attitudes and feelings towards what is spoken about. Centered on the first-person pronouns, it receives formal recognition in interjections and the conditional mood. Second, the *conative* function has to do with language's capacity to affect addressees and get them to act. Centered on the second-person pronominal forms, it receives formal recognition in vocatives and the imperative mood. Anthropological linguists have long been concerned with the differing pragmatic or expressive values of language forms, but with the exception of Hymes's work mentioned above and my own work (Lucy 1989), they have rarely formulated the concern in terms of a possible relativity.

Jakobson cites two further functions both of which are *reflexive* in that they refer to or index language form and use itself. The first is the *metalingual* function which corresponds to forms which communicate about the code structure of language (e.g. in glossing): it uses a language-internal sequence to build an equation. We can easily imagine a different metalingual apparatus and consequent differences in the understandings and control over language. In recent years, the implications of relativity of this sort for thought have been of central concern to some anthropological linguists, most notably Michael Silverstein (1979, 1981; cf. Lucy 1993) and others interested in linguistic ideology (e.g. Hill 1985 and Rumsey 1990).

The second reflexive function is the *poetic* function which corresponds to forms which communicate about the message form itself: it uses an equation (parallelism) to build a sequence. Here there is a long history of concern about the different sensibility implicated in different languages in their poetic forms. More broadly, the poetic function of language is implicated in all language use in the regular structuring of meanings into utterances and texts. These, of course, differ substantially across languages. Several anthropological linguists, notably Paul Friedrich (1986), have argued for some years now that the significant locus of relativity is in the poetic or aesthetic realm – that is, when discourse foregrounds this function (see also Sherzer 1987b, 1990; Urban 1991; Caton 1990).

This semiotic typology needs further refinement and formal grounding. It must also be brought into correspondence with other typologies of language function which focus on the psychological or social function-ality of language (e.g. that of Michael Halliday 1973, 1978) and with a consideration of the functional impact of different mediational means (e.g. writing, see Goody & Watt 1968, Cole & Scribner 1981). It may eventually be possible to encompass within a unified theory the significant effects that arise from the variable forms of these other functions of language on analogy with the referential function (see Silverstein 1979).

4.3 Empirical research on functional differences

In the present context, it will only be possible to provide examples of how languages do vary discursively in ways that are relevant for both the psychological functioning of individual speakers and cultural interactions more broadly. One example each will be given for referential uses, expressive uses, and, in the context of a discussion of the interaction of linguistic structure and discursive function, reflexive uses.

4.3.1 Referential uses of language

Let us turn first to differences in the referential uses of language. Lev Vygotsky (1978, 1987; see also Lucy 1988, 1989; Lucy & Wertsch 1987) provides analysis of one type of variation in the use of language, that which arises from formal schooling. By school age, children have developed an array of conceptual representations which approximate adult forms in their outward aspect. Yet outward appearances can be misleading and Vygotsky claims that children of this age still lack true or "scientific" concepts, that is, *concepts which are subject to conscious awareness, are under voluntary control, and form part of an organized system*. In a sense, to develop further children now have to engage in a highly reflexive activity, namely, bringing the process of conceptualiza-tion itself under voluntary conceptual control. This involves placing their spontaneous concepts into a hierarchical system of relationships with other concepts.

However, from his studies of the cognitive abilities of Russian peasants, Vygotsky had come to believe that true scientific concepts did not develop of their own accord but only under the influence of formal schooling – that is, within a specific institutional structure. Scientific concepts are acquired ready-made in the school context as children learn them by *explicit verbal definition and use, that is, within a context of conscious voluntary manipulation of the linguistic code structure.*

Once encountered, scientific concepts begin to interact with the children's own spontaneous concepts. Spontaneous concepts provide the concrete materials with which to enter into and comprehend the more abstract discourse of schooling; the scientific concepts encountered in the school context provide the framework for organizing and bringing under conscious voluntary control the child's existing spontaneous concepts. Scientific concepts grow downward to find concrete content; spontaneous concepts grow upward to find abstract, systematic form. The interaction between spontaneous and scientific concepts generates the final phase of development wherein children gain conscious control over their own concepts and thinking. Thus, this final phase of development depends for its emergence on the specific verbal practices associated with formal schooling. In essence, a new functional demand from the social arena promotes a major structural reorganization of individual thought. This development depends on the socially and historically specific practices associated with schooling. Schooled children become aware that word meanings relate to one another as elements of structured systems and derive a portion of their meaning from their place in such systems. Once cognizant of this aspect of language, children can exploit more of the latent power of language as an instrument of thought (cf. Sapir [1921] 1949c).

Others have made proposals similar to Vygotsky's and over the last two decades it has become increasingly common to view schooling as inculcating specialized uses of language. However, little of this research has explored exactly which language practices affect cognition. This is of tremendous importance because what is called schooling need not be the same everywhere and some practices other than formal schooling may have similar effects. Available cross-cultural research comparing a range of schooled and unschooled populations by Michael Cole and others (Sharp, Cole, & Lave 1979; Scribner & Cole 1973; see Rogoff 1981) suggests that many of the effects of schooling derive from specific training in certain skills such as the use of two-dimensional representations, the organization and memory of disconnected information, and intensified use of the decontextual and reflexive qualities of natural language. The various sorts of institutions called "schools" may embody these characteristics to a greater or lesser degree (see the work of Stigler &

Perry 1988 who compare the diverse styles of mathematics instruction in Japanese, Chinese, and American schools).

This work on schooling converges with various lines of research in anthropology, psychology, sociology, and education which have attempted to articulate the implications of characteristic patterns of language use in certain class or ethnic groups for their school performance (Labov 1975, Bernstein 1971, Heath 1983, Hymes 1980, Bourdieu 1984), the significance of various forms of literacy for patterns of thought (Goody & Watt 1968, Greenfield 1972, Goody 1977, Olson 1977, Cole & Scribner 1981, Street 1984, Cook-Gumperz 1986), and the importance of language socialization practices for the inculcation of cultural world-view (Ochs & Schieffelin 1984; Schieffelin & Ochs 1986a, b; Ochs 1988; Miller 1986; Miller & Sperry 1987,1989). The latter body of research is especially important because it reveals vividly the cultural and subcultural diversity of language practices. Unfortunately, very little of this research actually attempts to demonstrate cognitive effects. Among the aspects of language use which vary and which might be relevant to cognition are semi-formalized patterns of presentation and dispute, training children to recite long texts, prompting a child what to say, expanding children's utterances, using leading questions, announcing activities/events for a child, verbal teasing and joking, and using a simplified lexicon and grammar. For example, routine challenges to arguments might be internalized by the child and used to examine his or her own thought; teasing might promote reflexive awareness of the problematic relation of language and reality. In both these cases everyday practice may promote the sort of voluntary, reflexive attention to language categories that Vygotsky argued was central in schooled discourse.

4.3.2 Expressive uses of language

Variability in the structures of the expressive function of language have also been studied but again not with an eye towards their constitutive role in individual functioning. One particularly vivid example is provided by Michelle Rosaldo's (1973) discussion of the public oratory of the Ilongot, a people of the Philippines. Ilongot oratory is used in public meetings by opposed parties who must find their way towards an agreement without the aid of a judge or arbitrator. The highly public nature of these speech events compels speakers to appeal somewhat more explicitly to social norms and ideals of order than would be common in private disputes in an attempt to find truth or establish the right course of action when these are far from clear. The oratory makes extensive use of a culturally recognized mode of speech which Rosaldo translates as 'crooked speech.' Crooked speech allows a man to hide behind his words or distance himself from them; it achieves indirection and disguise of intent.

Aesthetically, the speech is felt to be artful, witty, and charming. Formally, it is characterized by iambic stresses, phonological elaboration, metaphor, repetition, and puns. It contrasts with 'straight' speech which is used for everyday life.

Rosaldo then discusses how this mode of oratory is disrupted by the encounter with alternative ideals drawn from the wider Philippine sphere, a sphere now heavily influenced by speech norms of the West. Some speakers now adopt 'straight speech' as their ideal for oratory. This straight speech involves a more active body posture, appeals to external authorities, disparagement of indirection, imposition of new forms of organization on the interaction, and substitution of new metaphors. Although it might seem that these are just substitutes of new oratorical conventions for old, Rosaldo argues that there is an important difference.

... the idea of 'crooked' language is not, for traditional Ilongots, one of deviousness or deception; rather it seems to be linked to the feeling that men are equal, individual, and difficult to understand ... there is no simple path to truth, justice, or understanding;
... linguistic elaboration, and a reflective interest in rhetoric, belongs to societies in which no one can command another's interest or attention, let alone enforce his compliance. In such societies, rhetoric may be a kind of 'courtship' ..., or it may, as in the Ilongot case, be an acknowledgement of the real differences among individuals and the elusiveness of human truth. The contrasting attitude, which prefers a plain and simple style, will be associated with any social order which recognizes an ultimate and knowable authority – be it god, or science, or the army.

It remains to be seen whether Rosaldo's suspicions about the linkage of complex, indirect rhetoric with an egalitarian ethos tolerant of difference (versus simple, direct speech with an authoritarian ethos not so tolerant) will appear in other societies and whether it will generalize to non-linguistic beliefs and behaviors. What is crucial here is that the proposed linguistic effect has little to do with direct referential content – it is not that the Ilongots have lexico-grammatical forms specifically referring to an egalitarian self. Rather, the effect is due to an implicit ethos embodied in the very way language is used – Ilongots use a variety of lexico-grammatical resources in a way that implies (or presupposes) an egalitarian view of others. In short, the expressive values of speech are rather consciously deployed in a way that both reflects and constitutes a certain attitude towards social reality. Indeed, conscious valuation of the style implicates a reflexive poetic evaluation that must also be grasped in any treatment of psychological effects.

It is worth emphasizing that this Ilongot example is by no means exhaustive of the range of possibilities. We know that the opportunities for expression in language vary in many ways. We can mention, by way of further example, pronoun systems which indicate differing relationships of power and solidarity (e.g. widespread Indo-European pronominal alternates of the *tu/vous* type: Brown & Gilman 1960), systematic cultural shaping of expressive differences between men's and women's speech ([Ochs] Keenan 1974, Sherzer 1987a), subtlety of modes of indirection in making requests (Ervin-Tripp 1976), and different verbal norms for the expression of emotions (e.g. anger: Miller & Sperry 1987). In short, the rich product of the ethnographic study of language has yet to be brought seriously to play in direct consideration of the relativity of experience associated with the diversity of functions and uses of language.

5 Ideology and the dialectic of linguistic structure and discursive function

In the specific examples just given, we did not need to make reference to particular lexical or grammatical structures of the languages involved; and it may well be that there are many usage effects which arise independently of (or across) particular linguistic structures. More generally, of course, language structure and discourse functionality do not exist in isolation from one another, and the two may interact in important ways. Discourse patterns can influence the impact of structural patterns by altering the frequency of use of certain forms or by channeling them in certain directions. In time, the systematic use of a given form in one context will alter its structural value in the language generally. A given context of use can even give rise, via emphasis on a specific semiotic function, to a specific structural element. Inversely, certain structural facts may facilitate the emergence of particular uses of language, or come to shape the discourses dependent on them, in characteristic ways. We have virtually no empirical research addressing this issue, but theory and research will eventually have to deal directly with the interplay between specific cognitive and cultural uses of language and particular structural–functional configurations (cf. Lucy & Wertsch 1987, Lucy 1989, Bloom 1981).

Typically, such interactions of structure and function are mediated by certain ideologies of language which reflexively structure discursive practice (Silverstein 1979, 1985b). These ideologies add another dimension to the interaction of structure and use as speakers bring their reflective understanding of language to bear on intensionalizing and regimenting their practice and as these reflections are themselves influenced by the matrix language. Working out the details of such interactions of structure, function, and ideology remains an enormous untackled problem. One example, one with purported intellectual consequences, will have to serve here to illustrate the complex issues involved as particular language structures, social patterns of language use, and ideologies of language converge historically to produce a characteristic culture of language. (For other case studies, see Silverstein 1985b and Banfield 1978.)

An example of ideologically mediated structural-functional interplay in the referential domain appears in the intellectualization or rationalization of the standard language (i.e., the language of public life and the workplace) in the West as analyzed by Bohuslav Havránek ([1932] 1964). The functional goal of intellectualization of language forms is to make possible precise, rigorous, and, if necessary, abstract statements capable of expressing a certain complexity of thought. Such language forms may be required for legal, bureaucratic, or technical purposes and reach their fullest elaboration as a functional type in scientific discourse wherein lexical items approximate concepts and sentences approximate logical judgments. In such a case, we must recognize that the decision to use language as an aid to thought and action in this way is itself a cultural achievement and not something to be taken as given. Although the primary rationale for such forms of speech lies in the practical need for standardization in a large and complex social formation, an important secondary rationale lies precisely in the perceived advantages of such speech forms in supporting more precise, "accurate" thinking.

The intellectualization of the standard language manifests itself in the lexicon not only by a simple expansion of the vocabulary but also by changes in the structural relations among words. In order to provide unequivocal words, special distinctions, and abstract summarizing terms, new words must be created or old words adapted – words to express relationships such as existence, possibility, necessity, relations of causality, finality, parallelism, and the like (e.g. *unsubstantiated*). This entails a specialization of word formative patterns to express abstracted concrete events by a variety of forms such as substance of quality, verbal nouns, verbal adjectives, participial expressions, etc.

Intellectualization also affects the grammatical structure of the language. This is manifested in a preference for nominal groupings brought about by combining nouns with attributes or by nominal predication using empty verbs, a preference for the normalized sentence with clear formal differentiation of the subject and predicate, and a desire to achieve parallelism between the grammatical form and underlying logical structure – for instance by the expanded use of the passive voice. Finally, there is a preference for a tightly knit and integrated structure of sentences and compound sentences with an elaborate hierarchy of superordination and subordination expressing different relations of causality, finality, parallelism, and the like; this tendency also manifests itself in a certain specialization of conjunctions.

This intellectualized or rationalized language sacrifices everyday intelligibility for accuracy. General intelligibility and clarity cannot be the gauge of the accuracy of expression of a mathematical work or a legal document. Where everyday language achieves definiteness of reference by a combination of language conventions and appeal to situation, this rationalized language seeks to achieve a definiteness solely by use of an elaborate set of decontextualized conventional forms, that is, forms defined and codified so as to be generally valid rather than situationally contingent. Ultimately, speakers will require elaborate training or formal schooling in these conventions in order to be able to understand the code and use it to achieve the goals it was designed for. Socially disadvantaged speakers who lack the presupposed language skills, for example those from lower-class strata or minority language communities, may be closed out of certain occupational spheres. Indeed, socially advantaged speakers who control these language patterns may have privileged access to such spheres despite real deficiencies in qualifications in other respects.

Such an ideology can become widespread or even dominant in a culture generally by being valued and therefore analogically extended outside of the sphere(s) in which it first developed. This, again, is a cultural achievement and not necessary. Such a characteristic or dominant linguistic ideology will embody a culturally and historically specific world-view which may appear arbitrary, admirable, or foolish from the outside. Thus Bloom (1981) reports Chinese speakers' reluctance to accept or participate in the theoretical, context-independent mode of discourse characteristic of the West which they regard as amoral in some contexts. In a similar vein Carol Cohn (1987) has critically analyzed the dehumanizing implications of this intellectualized mode of discourse within nuclear strategic war-planning groups in the US and Pierre Bourdieu (1984) has made similar observations about the Western intellectual tradition generally. Bloom, Cohn, Bourdieu, and others have noted that although this mode of rationalized, decontextualized discourse achieves certain advantages in terms of scientific theory construction, it brings concomitant disadvantages insofar as it separates speakers from sensitivity to actual situations. Such an alienation from concrete realities can result in failed ethical engagement and moral action in the world. The crucial point in this, of course, is that this mode of orientation to the world is now richly embodied in the lexical and grammatical structure of the language itself – especially in the standard language of the dominant class strata. And as Whorf (1956b) noted long ago, speakers will, quite predictably, take the elements of their language as "natural" and "given" in the world. In a sense, then, we can say this linguistic ideology has been "naturalized" in our linguistic culture.

Finally, a given discursive practice which ideologically regiments language structure to certain ends can spread beyond the original linguistic and cultural milieu in which it developed. In the case of

Ilongot oratory discussed above, the Western ideology of language, with its discursive emphasis on the isomorphism of language form and thought, may come into conflict with another ideology and may come to displace it. In the case of Chinese use of counterfactuals, Bloom (1981) reports that certain existing grammatical forms have now been reinterpreted, others applied more systematically, and still others recruited to new functions to achieve "clarity" from the new point of view. What is telling in this latter case as one reads the contending points of view in the literature disputing or defending Bloom's results is that native Chinese speakers with different degrees of exposure to Western languages and discursive practices now disagree fundamentally about what the Chinese language is (or was) "really like."

In still more extreme cases, specific syntactic patterns associated with a given discursive norm can be imported into a distinct linguistic community and directly promulgated by an influential elite to produce a new structural–functional register. For example, in Thai, "syntactic reform" modeled on Sanskrit, Latin, and English aimed to produce a grammar which was more "logical" and capable of being precise and unambiguous regardless of context (Diller 1993: esp. pp. 396ff.). Verb conjugations and case markings were created out of periphrastic constructions, normative word order was defined along with an across-the-board passive, previously ubiquitous noun and pronoun deletion were discouraged (with important sociolinguistic consequences), new lexical items were added, new modes of address were established, etc. This elite register has since been promulgated through written grammars, the school system, and by elite usage as correct or proper Thai. The cognitive effects of such transformations for Thai speakers can only be guessed at without specific study, but the potential effects of discursive ideology on language structure should be clear. Ironically, one upshot of this wholesale ideological transformation of the grammar is that Western scholars can now "discover" that Thai (i.e., in its formalized "high" register) fits comfortably into the discursive and even structural patterns expected on the basis of research with the more familiar European languages.

These examples of Western formal schooling, Ilongot public oratory, and modern technical language involve focused manipulations of language for social, intellectual, aesthetic, or political ends and these manipulations each depend in turn on accepting a certain ideology of language at several degrees of generality. Yet such an ideology of language itself arises initially in a discourse which draws on the available language forms and usages in a powerful and intimate way. That is, our very understanding of language as a cultural phenomenon may draw in important ways on the structures and uses characteristic of our own language. Indeed, a number of observers have suggested that our formulation of the linguistic relativity problem itself bears the traces of our own linguistic structures and dominant ideological perspective on the nature of discursive interaction (Lucy 1985a, Rumsey 1990, Reddy 1979). It is this reflexive aspect of the linguistic relativity problem which makes it one of the more profoundly difficult and important methodological problems for all the human disciplines (Lucy 1993).

6 Summary

Natural language adds a dimension to human life not present in other species and may give rise to a semiotic relativity. The distinctive semiotic property of natural language is its symbolic component. Language retains the iconic and indexical properties characteristic of other signalling systems, but they are transformed by their conjunction with the symbolic aspect to create a communicative medium of extraordinary flexibility and diversity with implications for both the social objectification of thought and the emergence of reflective awareness. These are the aspects of natural language which will be most relevant to tracing its potential implications for thought, belief, and behavior.

The traditional linguistic relativity proposal is concerned with the implications for thought of the use of diverse natural languages. To date, despite the manifest importance of the problem, there has been very little empirical research at all, and not much of what exists has been adequately formulated. These problems stem from both disciplinary differences and broader cultural attitudes. Adequate investigation of the proposal must be comparative, deal with significant language structures and actual speakers, and come to grips with the problem of developing a comparative metalanguage. A few studies meeting these standards now exist.

More recent research on language use (or functioning) suggests the possibility of another form of relativity, a discursive relativity, centering on the cultural deployment of specialized speech modes. Although there is a growing body of research on language use, it has not been systematically evaluated in terms of its implications for thought. Such an evaluation would have to meet the same standards of adequacy already mentioned for structural relativity, but would, additionally, have to develop a typology of language functions within which a comparison could be made. Existing typologies suggest that research attention needs to be broadened beyond the traditional preoccupation with the referential capacity of language and its intellectual consequences to include an examination of the potential effects of diversity in the expressive uses of language on personal and social functioning. Some existing theory and research (e.g. on formal schooling and political oratory) can be profitably reinterpreted within this framework.

Finally, structural and functional factors may interact with one another. The existence of a certain structure of meaning may facilitate the emergence of certain specialized uses of language; a given discourse mode may amplify or channel existing structural meanings or create a new level of structural order. In such interactions, various ideologies of language may play a pivotal role in the essentialization and regimentation of both structure and use, and both language categories and cultural requirements for speaking may, in turn, shape the available linguistic ideologies. Finally, such ideologies may spread beyond their original cultural or subcultural niche to influence substantially different linguistic and discursive systems. These interactive problems have been little studied to date – at least with regard to their broader cultural and psychological consequences.

Because of the linguistic relativity he saw, Whorf placed the science of language at the center of all efforts to advance human understanding. However, from an empirical point of view, we have done little in the last half century to expand on his insights. However, when we join his work with a fuller semiotic analysis, with more recent research on the discursive (or functional) diversity among languages, and with a consideration of the role of linguistic ideologies in shaping their interaction, we can articulate more clearly the scope and complexity of the problem he identified. An adequate understanding of the dynamic interaction between language, culture, and self will depend on exploring the full scope of linguistic relativity.

Acknowledgments

The original version of this chapter was presented under the title "Empirical research and linguistic relativity" at a Wenner-Gren Conference on Re-thinking Linguistic Relativity, Ocho Rios, Jamaica, 3–11 May 1991. Slightly modified versions were presented to colloquia at Vassar College, the Philadelphia Anthropological Society, the University of Illinois (Urbana-Champaign), and Duke University. I thank the participants in all these events for their comments and questions. The final revision profited from comments on the written draft by Balthasar Bickel, Suzanne Gaskins, John Gumperz, Steve Levinson, and an anonymous reviewer. The chapter owes a general debt to Michael Silverstein.

References

Aarsleff, H. 1982. *From Locke to Saussure: essays on the study of language and intellectual history*. Minneapolis: University of Minnesota Press.
Au, T. 1983. Chinese and English counterfactuals: the Sapir–Whorf hypothesis revisited. *Cognition*, 15, 155–87.
Banfield, A. 1978. Where epistemology, style, and grammar meet literary history: the development of represented speech and thought. *New Literary History*, 9, 415–54.

Benveniste, E. 1971 [19391. The nature of the linguistic sign. In Benveniste, *Problems in general linguistics*. Tr. M. Meek (pp. 43–8). Coral Gables, FL: University of Miami.

Berlin, B. & Kay, P. 1969. *Basic color terms: their universality and evolution*. Berkeley: University of California Press.

Bernstein, B. 1971. *Class, codes and control*, vol. I: Theoretical studies toward a sociology of language. London: Routledge & Kegan Paul.

Bloom, A. 1981. *The linguistic shaping of thought: a study in the impact of language on thinking in China and the West*. Hillsdale, NJ: Lawrence Erlbaum.

Boas, F. 1966 [1911]. Introduction. In F. Boas (ed.), *Handbook of American Indian languages* (reprint ed. P. Holder) (pp. 1–79). Lincoln: University of Nebraska Press.

Bourdieu, P. 1984 [1979]. *Distinction: a social critique of the judgement of taste*. Tr. R. Nice. Cambridge, MA: Harvard University Press.

Brown, R. & Gilman, A. (1960). The pronouns of power and solidarity. In T. Sebeok (ed.), *Style in language* (pp. 253–76). Cambridge, MA: MIT Press.

Brown, R. & Lenneberg, E. 1954. A study in language and cognition. *Journal of Abnormal and Social Psychology*, 49, 454–62.

Carroll, J. & Casagrande, J. 1958. The function of language classifications in behavior. In E. Maccoby, T. Newcomb, & E. Hartley (eds.), *Readings in social psychology* (pp. 18–31). New York: Henry Holt.

Caton, S. 1990. *"Peaks of Yemen I summon." Poetry as cultural practice in a North Yemeni tribe*. Berkeley: University of California Press.

Chomsky, N. 1972. *Language and mind* (enlarged edn.). New York: Harcourt, Brace, Jovanovich.

Cohn, C. 1987. Sex and death in the rational world of defense intellectuals. *Signs*, 12, 687–718.

Cole, M. & Scribner, S. 1981. *The psychology of literacy*. Cambridge, MA: Harvard University Press.

Conklin, H. 1955. Hanunóo color categories. *Southwest Journal of Anthropology*, 11, 339–44.

Cook-Gumperz, J. (ed.) 1986. *The social construction of literacy*. Cambridge University Press.

Diller, A. 1993. Diglossic grammaticality in Thai. In W. Foley (ed.), *The role of theory in language description* (pp. 393–420). Berlin: Mouton de Gruyter.

Ervin-Tripp, S. 1976. Is Sybil there? The structure of American English directives. *Language in Society*, 5, 25–66.

Fishman, J. 1982. Whorfianism of the third kind: ethnolinguistic diversity as a worldwide societal asset. (The Whorfian hypothesis: varieties of validation, confirmation, and disconfirmation II). *Language in Society*, 11, 1–14.

Friedrich, P. 1986. *The language parallax: linguistic relativism and poetic indeterminacy*. Austin: University of Texas Press.

Goody, J. 1977. *The domestication of the savage mind*. Cambridge University Press.

Goody, J. & Watt, I. 1968. The consequences of literacy. In J. Goody (ed.), *Literacy in traditional societies* (pp. 27–68). Cambridge University Press.

Greenfield, P. 1972. Oral or written language: the consequences for cognitive development in Africa, the United States, and England. *Language and Speech*, 15, 169–78.

Gumperz, J. J. 1982. *Discourse strategies*. Cambridge University Press.

Gumperz, J. J. & Hymes, D. (eds.) 1972. *Directions in sociolinguistics: the ethnography of communication*. New York: Holt, Rinehart, & Winston.

Halliday, M. 1973. *Explorations in the functions of language*. New York: Elsevier.
1978. *Language as social semiotic: the social interpretation of language and meaning*. Baltimore: University Park.

Havránek, B. 1964 [1932]. The functional differentiation of the standard language. In P. Garvin (ed. and tr.), *A Prague School reader on esthetics, literary structure, and style* (pp. 3–16). Washington, DC: Georgetown University Press.

Heath, S. 1983. *Ways with words: language, life, and work in communities and classrooms*. Cambridge University Press.

Heider, E. 1972. Universals in color naming and memory. *Journal of Experimental Psychology*, 93, 10–20.

Hill, J. 1985. The grammar of consciousness and the consciousness of grammar. *American Ethnologist*, 12, 725–37.

Hockett, C. 1958. *A course in modern linguistics*. New York: Macmillan.

Hoijer, H. 1953. The relation of language to culture. In A. L. Kroeber (ed.), *Anthropology today* (pp. 554–73). University of Chicago Press.

Hymes, D. 1961. On typology of cognitive styles in language (with examples from Chinookan). *Anthropological Linguistics*, 3, 22–54.
1966. Two types of linguistic relativity (with examples from Amerindian ethnography). In W. Bright (ed.), *Sociolinguistics, Proceedings of the UCLA sociolinguistics conference, 1964* (pp. 114–67). The Hague: Mouton.
1974. *Foundations in sociolinguistics: an ethnographic approach*. Philadelphia: University of Pennsylvania Press.
1980. Speech and language: on the origins and foundations of inequality among speakers. In Hymes, *Language and education: essays in educational ethnolinguistics* (pp. 19–61). Washington, DC: Center for Applied Linguistics.

Imai, M. & Gentner, D. 1993. Linguistic relativity vs. universal ontology: cross-linguistic studies of the object/substance distinction. Paper presented to the Twenty-ninth Meeting of the Chicago Linguistic Society.

Inhelder, B. & Piaget, J. 1958. *The growth of logical thinking from childhood to adolescence*. New York: Basic Books.

Kay, P. & McDaniel, C. K. 1978. The linguistic significance of the meanings of Basic Color Terms. *Language*, 54, 610–46.

Jakobson, R. 1960. Concluding statement: linguistics and poetics. In T. A. Sebeok (ed.), *Style in language* (pp. 350–77). Cambridge, MA: MIT Press.

Labov, W. 1975. Academic ignorance and black intelligence. In M. Maehr & W. Stallings (eds.), *Culture, child, and school: sociocultural influences on learning* (pp. 63–81). Monterey, CA: Brooks/Cole.

Lenneberg, E. & Roberts, J. 1956. The language of experience: a study in methodology. *International Journal of American Indian Linguistics*, 22 (2, part 2, memoir 13).

Liu, L. 1985. Reasoning counterfactually in Chinese: are there any obstacles? *Cognition*, 21, 239–70.

Lucy, J. 1985a. The historical relativity of the linguistic relativity hypothesis. *Quarterly Newsletter of the Laboratory of Comparative Human Cognition*, 7, 103–8.
1985b. Whorf's view of the linguistic mediation of thought. In E. Mertz & R. Parmentier (eds.), *Semiotic mediation: sociocultural and psychological perspectives* (pp. 73–97). New York: Academic Press.

1988. The role of language in the development of representation: a comparison of the views of Piaget and Vygotsky. *Quarterly Newsletter of the Laboratory of Comparative Human Cognition*, 10(4), 99–103.

1989. *Vygotsky and the culture of language*. Paper read at the Biennial Meeting of the Society for Research in Child Development, Kansas City, MO.

1992a. *Grammatical categories and cognition: a case study of the linguistic relativity hypothesis*. Cambridge University Press.

1992b. *Language diversity and thought: a reformulation of the linguistic relativity hypothesis*. Cambridge University Press.

1993. Reflexive language and the human disciplines. In J. Lucy (ed.), *Reflexive language: reported speech and metapragmatics* (pp. 1–32). Cambridge University Press.

in press. The linguistics of "color." In C.L. Hardin & L. Maffi (eds.), *Color categories in thought and language*. Cambridge University Press.

Lucy, J. & Shweder, R. 1979. Whorf and his critics: linguistic and nonlinguistic influences on color memory. *American Anthropologist*, 81, 581–615.

1988. The effect of incidental conversation on memory for focal colors. *American Anthropologist*, 90, 923–31.

Lucy, J. & Wertsch, J. 1987. Vygotsky and Whorf: a comparative analysis. In M. Hickmann (ed.), *Social and functional approaches to language and thought* (pp. 67–86). Cambridge University Press.

Lyons, J. 1977. *Semantics*. 2 vols. Cambridge University Press.

Mahnowski, B. 1923. The problem of meaning in primitive languages. In C. Ogden & I. Richards (eds.), *The meaning of meaning* (pp. 296–336). New York: Harcourt, Brace, & World.

Malotki, E. 1983. *Hopi time: a linguistic analysis of the temporal categories in the Hopi language*. Berlin: Mouton.

Mathiot, M. 1964. Noun classes and folk taxonomy in Papago. In D. Hymes (ed.), *Language in culture and society: a reader in linguistics and anthropology* (pp. 154–61). New York: Harper & Row.

Miller, P. 1986. Teasing as language socialization and verbal play in a white, working-class community. In B. Schieffelin & E. Ochs (eds.), *Language socialization across cultures* (pp. 199–212). Cambridge University Press.

Miller, P. & Sperry, L. 1987. The socialization of anger and aggression. *Merrill Palmer Quarterly*, 33, 1–31.

1989. Early talk about the past: the origins of conversational stories of personal experience. *Journal of Child Language*, 15, 293–315.

Newman, S. 1954. Semantic problems in grammatical systems and lexemes: a search for method. In H. Hoijer (ed.), *Language in culture* (pp. 82–91). University of Chicago Press.

Ochs E. 1988. *Culture and language development: language acquisition and language socialization in a Samoan village*. Cambridge University Press.

[Ochs] Keenan, E. 1974. Norm-makers, norm-breakers: uses of speech by men and women in a Malagasy community. In R. Bauman & J. Sherzer (eds.), *Explorations in the ethnography of speaking* (pp. 125–43). Cambridge University Press.

Ochs, E. & Schieffelin, B. 1984. Language acquisition and socialization: three developmental stories and their implications. In R. Shweder & R. LeVine (eds.), *Culture theory: essays on mind, self, and emotion* (pp. 276–320). Cambridge University Press.

Olson, D. 1977. From utterance to text: the bias of language in speech and writing. *Harvard Educational Review*, 47, 257–81.

Peirce, C. S. 1932. *Collected papers of C. S. Peirce*, vol. II. Cambridge, MA: Harvard University Press.

Piaget, J. 1967 [1954]. Language and thought from the genetic point of view. In J. Piaget, *Six psychological studies*, ed. D. Elkind. Tr. A. Tenzer (pp. 88–99). New York: Random House.

1973. *Main trends in inter-disciplinary research*. New York: Harper & Row.

Reddy, M. 1979. The conduit metaphor: a case of frame conflict in our language about language. In A. Ortony (ed.), *Metaphor and thought* (pp. 284–324). Cambridge University Press.

Rogoff, B. 1981. Schooling and the development of cognitive skills. In H. Triandis & A. Heron (eds.), *Handbook of cross-cultural psychology*, vol. IV (pp. 233–94). Rockleigh, NJ: Allyn & Bacon.

Rosaldo, M. 1973. I have nothing to hide: the language of Ilongot oratory. *Language in Society*, 2, 193–223.

Rumsey, A. 1990. Wording, meaning, and linguistic ideology. *American Anthropologist*, 92, 346–61.

Sapir, E. 1949a [1924]. The grammarian and his language. In *The selected writings of Edward Sapir in language, culture, and personality*, ed. D. G. Mandelbaum (pp. 150–9). Berkeley: University of California Press.

1949b [1933]. Language. In *The selected writings of Edward Sapir in language, culture, and personality*, ed. D. G. Mandelbaum (pp. 7–32). Berkeley: University of California Press.

1949c [1921]. *Language: an introduction to the study of speech*. New York: Harcourt, Brace, & Company.

1949d [1929]. The status of linguistics as a science. In *The selected writings of Edward Sapir in language, culture, and personality*, ed. D. G. Mandelbaum (pp. 160–6). Berkeley: University of California Press.

1964 [1931]. Conceptual categories in primitive languages. In D. Hymes (ed.), *Language in culture and society: a reader in linguistics and anthropology* (p. 128). New York: Harper & Row.

Schieffelin, B. & Ochs, E. 1986a. Language socialization. *Annual Review of Anthropology*, 15, 163–246.

(eds.) 1986b. *Language socialization across cultures*. Cambridge University Press.

Scribner, S. & Cole, M. 1973. Cognitive consequences of formal and informal education. *Science*, 182, 553–9.

Sharp, D., Cole, M. & Lave, C. 1979. Education and cognitive development: the evidence from experimental research. *Monographs of the Society for Research in Child Development*, 44 (1–2, serial no. 178).

Sherzer, J. 1987a. A diversity of voices: men's and women's speech in ethnographic perspective. In S. Philips, S. Steele, & C. Tanz (eds.), *Language, culture, gender, and sex in comparative perspective* (pp. 95–120). New York: Cambridge University Press.

1987b. A discourse-centered approach to language and culture. *American Anthropologist*, 89, 295–309.

1990. *Verbal art in San Blas, Kuna culture through its discourse*. Cambridge University Press.

Silverstein, M. 1979. Language structure and linguistic ideology. In P. Clyne, W. Hanks, & C. Hofbauer (eds.), *The elements: a parasession on linguistic units and levels* (pp. 193–247). Chicago Linguistic Society.

1981. The limits of awareness. *Sociolinguistics Working Paper No. 84*. Austin, TX: Southwestern Educational Laboratory.

1985a. The culture of language in Chinookan narrative texts; or, On saying that ...in Chinook. In J. Nichols & A. Woodbury (eds.), *Grammar inside and outside the clause: some approaches to theory from the field* (pp. 132–71). Cambridge University Press.

1985b. Language and the culture of gender: at the intersection of structure, usage, and ideology. In E. Mertz & R. Parmentier (eds.), *Semiotic mediation: sociocultural and psychological perspectives* (pp. 219–59). Orlando, FL: Academic Press.

Stefflre, V., Morley, L. & Castillo Vales, V. 1966. Language and cognition in Yucatan: a cross-cultural replication. *Journal of Personality and Social Psychology*, 4, 112–15.

Stigler, J. & Perry, M. 1988. Mathematics learning in Japanese, Chinese, and American classrooms. In G. Saxe & M. Gearhart (eds.), *Children's mathematics* (pp. 27–54). San Francisco: Jossey-Bass.

Street, B. 1984. *Literacy in theory and practice*. Cambridge University Press.

Urban, G. 1991. *A discourse-centered approach to culture: native South American myths and rituals*. Austin: University of Texas Press.

Vygotsky, L. S. 1978 [1930–4]. *Mind in society. the development of higher psychological processes*, ed. and tr. M. Cole, V. John-Steiner, S. Scribner, & E. Souberman. Cambridge, MA: Harvard University Press.

1987 [1934]. *Thought and language* (rev. edn. A. Kozulin). Cambridge, MA: MIT Press.

Witherspoon, G. 1977. *Language and art in the Navajo universe*. Ann Arbor: University of Michigan Press.

Whorf, B. 1956a [1939]. The relation of habitual thought and behavior to language. In *Language, thought, and reality: selected writings of Benjamin Lee Whorf*, ed. J. B. Carroll (pp. 134–59). Cambridge, MA: MIT Press.

1956b [1940]. Science and linguistics. In *Language, thought, and reality: selected writings of Benjamin Lee Whorf*, ed. J. B. Carroll (pp. 207–19). Cambridge, MA: MIT Press.

3

FROM "THOUGHT AND LANGUAGE" TO "THINKING FOR SPEAKING"

DAN I. SLOBIN

Language is the formative organ of thought...
Thought and language are... one and inseparable from each other.
Wilhelm von Humboldt ([1836] 1988: 54)

[T]he true difference between languages is not in what may or may not be expressed but in what must or must not be conveyed by the speakers
Roman Jakobson (1959: 142)

Early in the last century, Wilhelm von Humboldt provided the *Leitmotif* for the study of linguistic relativity and determinism. The title of his great work on language clearly points to the central theme: *The diversity of human language-structure and its influence on the mental development of mankind* ([1836] 1988).[1] Languages differ from one another; thought and language are inseparable; therefore each speech community embodies a distinct world-view. The two critical terms here are **thought** and **language**, with broad-ranging definitions of each. For example, in von Humboldt's terms: "There resides in every language a characteristic **world-view**. As the individual sound stands between man and the object, so the entire language steps in between him and the nature that operates, both inwardly and outwardly, upon him... Man lives primarily with objects, [but]... he actually does so exclusively as language presents them to him" ([1836] 1988: 60).

In this century the argument is most often associated with Benjamin Lee Whorf. For example, in one of his strongest statements, he proposed: "Users of markedly different grammars are pointed by their grammars towards different types of observations and different evaluations of externally similar acts of observation, and hence are not equivalent as observers but must arrive at somewhat different views of the world" ([1940a] 1956: 221).

This doctrine of linguistic determinism, along with the facts of linguistic relativity, has clear implications not only for adult mental behavior, but also for the roles of language and thought in human development. It follows from the doctrine that children who learn different languages end up with different conceptual structures, and that these differences have pervasive cognitive effects. As Whorf put it:

"[E]very language is a vast pattern-system, different from others, in which are culturally ordained the forms and categories by which the personality not only communicates, but also analyzes nature, notices or neglects types of relationship and phenomena, channels his reasoning, and builds the house of his consciousness" ([1942] 1956: 252)

In this chapter I propose to replace **thought** and **language** with a related but rather different pair of terms: **thinking** and **speaking**. The consequences of this shift from names of abstract entities to names of activities is to draw attention to the kinds of mental processes that occur during the act of formulating an utterance. Further, I want to focus attention just on those parts of utterances that are required by the grammatical organization of the language. Here I am following a tradition in anthropological linguistics that has taken a less deterministic approach in the face of linguistic diversity, as exemplified by the thinking of Franz Boas. Roman Jakobson, in an article on "Boas' view of grammatical meaning," singles out Boas's observation that the set of obligatory grammatical categories of a language "determines those aspects of each experience that **must** be expressed" (Boas 1938: 127). Von Humboldt's grand endeavor is thereby pared down to the issues of **obligatoriness** and **expression**. Whatever else language may do in human thought and action, it surely directs us to **attend** – while speaking – to the dimensions of experience that are enshrined in grammatical categories.

Boas, in his 1911 introduction to the *Handbook of American Indian languages,* catalogued a great diversity of obligatory grammatical categories across languages. For example, he discussed the English sentence, *The man is sick,* and noted that in Siouan one would have to indicate, grammatically, whether the man is moving or at rest; in Kwakiutl one would have to indicate whether the man in question is visible or non-visible to the speaker, and near to speaker, hearer, or a third person; whereas in Eskimo one would simply say 'man sick,' with no obligatory indication of definiteness, tense, visibility, or location. To remove Boas's examples from the realm of the exotic, note that in Spanish one has to indicate whether the man is temporarily or chronically sick; that in many European languages one cannot indicate definiteness apart from gender; and so on. What Boas made of such diversity, however, is different from the suggestions of von Humboldt and Whorf:

The few examples that I have given here illustrate that many of the categories which we are inclined to consider as essential may be absent in foreign languages, and that other categories may occur as substitutes.

When we consider for a moment what this implies, it will be recognized that in each language only a part of the complete concept that we have in mind is expressed, and that each language has a peculiar tendency to select this or that aspect of the mental image which is conveyed by the expression of the thought.

(Boas [1911] 1966: 38–9)

While von Humboldt and Whorf held that concepts have no existence independent of language, Boas suggests that there is a "complete concept," existing in the mind in the form of a "mental image." The obligatory grammatical categories of each language apparently sample from a universal form of mental representation, independent of any particular language. On this view, the task of the child language learner is to determine which "aspects of the mental image" are realized in the form of grammatical marking in the native language. The mental image is given prelinguistically, and language acquisition consists of learning which features to attend to.

Was Boas right? What would a "complete concept" or "mental image" be like? Consider the two pictures presented in figures 3.1 and 3.2. These come from the middle of a picture storybook without words (Mayer 1969). My collaborators and I have given this book to children and adults in a number of languages and the present chapter is based on some of our results. For now, simply **look** at the two pictures. They present a pair of events that you can understand immediately, probably without talking to yourself at all: something happens to a boy and something happens to a dog; an owl and some bees or wasps are involved; the location is among trees. Consider the events of the second picture. What grammatical categories are implicit? Compare two languages of our crosslinguistic study, English and Spanish. As an English-speaker, it will be evident to you that the activity of the dog is **durative**, or extended in time, in

Fig. 3.1

Fig. 3.2

comparison with the activity of the boy. In narrative mode, you might say: "The boy **fell** from the tree and the dog **was running** away from the bees." English marks **progressive aspect** on the verb, and it seems that this aspect corresponds to an obvious temporal component of the "complete concept" or "mental image." If you are a Spanish-speaker, you, too, will recognize the durativity of running, because Spanish also has progressive aspect, as well as imperfective aspect. Yet you might also note that the falling of the boy is **punctual** or **completed**, since Spanish makes a contrast between perfective and imperfective aspect. However, what if you speak a language that has no grammatical marking of perfective/imperfective or of progressive, such as German or Hebrew – to pick two more languages from our crosslinguistic study based on these pictures. Boas would presumably have suggested that you are aware of the differences in temporal contour between falling and running, but simply have no need to mark them grammatically in your language.

So far so good – but let us probe the second picture a bit further. Consider the owl as an observer. In an English narrative one might say: "The owl saw that the boy fell"; or: "The owl saw that the dog was running." The distinction between *fell* and *was running*, I have suggested, seems to be clearly "in" the picture. But what about the **owl's seeing**? Note that, in both cases, in English we say "The owl **saw**." Yet seeing must have different temporal contours too. Indeed, in Spanish the seeing is perfective (PFV) in the first instance, imperfective (IPFV) in the second:

(1) a. *El buho vio   que el niño   se cayó.*
the owl saw-PFV that the boy fell-PFV

   b. *El buho veía   que el perro corría.*
the owl saw-IPFV that the dog ran-IPFV

This will be evident to Spanish-speaking readers, as it is to Spanish-speaking preschoolers in our study – in fact, these two sentences come from a story told by a five-year-old. Yet do English-speakers sense that seeing can be perfective or imperfective? Is this part of our Boasian "mental image" or "complete concept"? I rather doubt it.

Let me take you one step further, this time into a less familiar linguistic terrain. Suppose you have seen only the second picture, and have been asked to describe it as a past event. Descriptions in English and Spanish would probably be the same as in the situation in which both pictures are presented. However, this is not the case in Turkish – another language in our sample – because in that language you are obliged to choose between two past-tense inflections, one for **witnessed** and one for **non-witnessed** events. If the second picture were to be presented alone, we would witness the dog running, but we could only **infer** that the boy had fallen at an earlier point in time. As a consequence, different past tenses would appear on the two verbs:

(2) a. *Köpek kaç-ıyor-du*
    dog   run-PROG-WITNESSED.PAST
    'The dog was running.'

   b. *Çocuk düş-müş.*
    boy   fall-NONWITNESSED.PAST
    'The boy (apparently) fell.'

Turkish preschoolers are careful to make such distinctions. In English one could say, of course, something like: "**It seems** that the boy fell" or "**Apparently** the boy fell." We **do** have available **optional** lexical means for expressing notions that lie outside of the set of obligatory grammatical distinctions in a language. Nevertheless, I think we would be hard-pressed to claim that everything about this picture that **could** be grammatically encoded in all of the languages of the world is implicitly present when we look at the picture.

The Turkish evidential inflections also demonstrate that much of grammar does not deal with mental images or perceivable reality at all. Rather, much of grammar marks distinctions that are relevant to **discourse**. When I speak Turkish, I must qualify my past-tense statements by telling you something about the source of my evidence. Furthermore, when I present a situation to you in **any** language, I take a grammaticized

point of view. For example, in English I might say, "The bees are chasing the dog" or "The dog is being chased by the bees." Neither of these viewpoints – active or passive – is in the percept. Active and passive constructions serve to organize the flow of information in connected discourse. Thus, even within a single language, grammar provides a set of **options** for schematizing experience for the purposes of verbal expression. Any utterance is multiply determined by what I have seen or experienced, my communicative purpose in telling you about it, and the distinctions that are embodied in my grammar.[2]

The world does not present "events" and "situations" to be encoded in language. Rather, experiences are filtered through language into verbalized events. A "verbalized event" is constructed on-line, in the process of speaking. Von Humboldt and Whorf and Boas were right in suggesting that the obligatory grammatical categories of a language play a role in this construction. The purpose of the research presented here is to demonstrate that, by the age of three or four, children acquiring different types of languages are influenced by such categories in verbalizing the events depicted in our storybook.

In making this claim, I wish to present a new version of the von Humboldt–Whorf position on linguistic relativity and determinism. Recall that those theorists were concerned to relate **language** to **world-view** or **habitual thought**. The classic position thus seeks to relate two **static** entities: language and thought. Language is the totality of structures described by linguists. But what is "thought" or "world-view"? The hypothesis has always run into trouble in attempts to determine the mental structures that underlie perception, reasoning, and habitual behavior – as measured **outside** of the contexts of verbal behavior. (Chapters in this volume, once again, point to the difficulties involved in trying to systematically formulate and test such proposals.) I have a more cautious, but more manageable formulation – one that seeks to relate two **dynamic** entities: **thinking** and **speaking**. There is a special kind of thinking that is intimately tied to language – namely, the thinking that is carried out, on-line, in the process of speaking.[3] I believe that this is the sort of relation that Boas had in mind when he wrote about selecting aspects of mental images that are "conveyed by the **expression** of the thought." In a later formulation, he explicitly pointed to the role of communication: "In language, the experience **to be communicated** is classified from a number of distinct aspects" (1938: 127) [emphasis added]. Whorf, by contrast, clearly intended more. In the passage from 1942 quoted above, he says "not only communicates, but also ... "

Boas was probably wrong, though, in supposing that all speakers, within and between languages, have a common "complete concept"; he was right, however, in suggesting that any utterance is a selective schematization of a concept – a schematization that is, in some way, dependent on the grammaticized meanings of the speaker's particular language, recruited for purposes of verbal expression.

The reader may have noticed that I have not yet mentioned the name Edward Sapir, which usually appears in references to the "Whorf–Sapir hypothesis." Sapir sometimes took the strong view associated with Whorf, but sometimes he suggested the more cautious version that guides my own research. For example, in an early formulation, Sapir, like Boas, pointed to the role of language in the **expression** of thought: "[The forms of each language] establish a definite relational feeling or attitude towards all possible contents of expression and, through them, towards all possible contents of experience, **in so far, of course, as experience is capable of expression in linguistic terms**" ([1924] 1958:152) [emphasis added].

In my own formulation: the expression of experience in linguistic terms constitutes **thinking for speaking** – a special form of thought that is mobilized for communication. Whatever effects grammar may or may not have outside of the act of speaking, the sort of mental activity that goes on while formulating utterances is not trivial or obvious, and deserves our attention. We encounter the contents of the mind in a special way when they are being accessed for **use**. That is, the activity of thinking takes on a particular quality when it is employed in the activity of speaking. In the evanescent time frame of constructing utterances in discourse one fits one's thoughts into available linguistic frames. "Thinking for speaking" involves picking those characteristics of objects and events that (a) fit some conceptualization of the event, and (b) are readily encodable in the language.[4] **I propose that, in acquiring a native language, the child learns particular ways of thinking for speaking**.

How can this proposal be investigated? One way is to compare the ways in which speakers of different languages depict the same events in words. This approach is well known to students of translation, and there is a large and fascinating literature showing that translations of the same text cannot help but add or remove nuances in accord with the characteristics of the given language (e.g. Brislin 1976, Maslov 1985, Nida 1964, Snell-Hornby 1988, Toury 1986). Informally, we have already encountered these issues in considering various descriptions of the two storybook pictures in several languages, and in Boas's American Indian translations of *The man is sick*. However, my major concern is with the possible cognitive effects of linguistic diversity in the course of child language development, where the method of comparative translation cannot be generally applied, because one cannot ask monolingual children to carry out translations of a text. However, we can ask children in different countries to tell stories about the same sequence of pictures and see if their stories differ consistently, depending on the language that they are speaking. This is the method we have been using in Berkeley, in collaboration with researchers in a number of countries, using the picture storybook, *Frog, where are you?* (Mayer 1969). For the purposes of the present argument, I compare children's descriptions of several scenes in several languages, focusing on expressions of temporal and spatial relations. The languages are English, German, Spanish, and Hebrew, and the ages sampled are preschool (three–five years), school-age (nine years), and adult. Our findings suggest that even preschoolers give evidence of language-specific patterns of thinking for speaking, and that such patterns have implications for the development of **rhetorical style** in each of the languages.[5]

1 Rhetorical style

When one has read many of these stories in various languages, one begins to get a feeling for typical characteristics of style in each language. This can be made clear even by comparing translations into English. Consider the two pictures that we have already examined, along with the seven following pictures in the storybook: after the boy falls from the tree, he accidentally gets entangled in the antlers of a deer, with the result that the boy and dog fall into some water. The two following segments are representative of five-year-olds' narratives. One is in English, and the other is an English translation of a Spanish story, using the progressive to correspond to the original imperfective, which has no English equivalent, in order to render the version suitable in English:

(3) a. **First version:** The boy looked in a hole in the tree. An owl came out that threw the boy. And the dog, the wasps were chasing him. The boy hid behind a rock and the owl flew away. A deer that was behind the boy when he climbed . . . And he slipped on top of the- the deer, while the deer was running. The dog went first. He threw them down where there was a river. Then he fell.

b. **Second version:** And the boy looked in the tree. And then the boy fell out, and the owl was flying, and the dog was being chased by the bees. And then the boy got up on some rocks, and the owl flew away. And the boy was calling for his frog on the rocks. And a deer . . . the boy got caught on the deer's antlers. And then the deer carried him over a cliff and threw him over the cliff into a pond. And the boy and the dog fell, and they splashed in some water.

We can be reasonably sure that the mental images, and understanding of the events, are roughly the same for these two children. Yet, to the practiced eye, it is evident that the first version is Spanish and the second English. What are some of the salient characteristics of these two languages, as reflected in our narratives?[6]

The two versions are similar in their treatments of movement through time. Both narratives mark some events as being in progress. In the first, compare: *threw* vs. *was running*; in the second, *fell* vs. *was flying*. (Recall that these past progressives in the translated version were really past imperfectives in the Spanish original.) English and Spanish both have aspectual marking of durativity, and five-year-olds note this distinction. As we will see later, this feature is lacking in German and Hebrew narratives.

The two versions differ, however, in their treatment of location and movement through space. In the first version, trajectories are not highly elaborated: *threw the boy, slipped on top of the deer, threw down*. The second version depicts more detailed trajectories: *fell out, carried over a cliff, threw over the cliff into a pond, splashed in some water*. By contrast, the first version has relative clauses that depict static locative configurations, which are lacking in the second: *a deer that was behind the boy, where there was a river*. In terms of syntactic complexity, although the second version has no relative clauses, it has passive constructions, *was being chased, got caught*.

These cues are sufficient to identify the first version as Spanish and the second as English. The linguistic characteristics of these two narrative segments are typical of our preschool narratives in the two languages. In brief, where English allows for elaborated trajectories of motion, Spanish has simple verbs of change of location, supplemented by more elaborated descriptions of static locations of objects. With regard to the syntax of non-canonical clauses. Spanish preschoolers make frequent use of relative clauses, and English-speaking preschoolers make frequent use of passives – but for different purposes, of course. Spanish relative clauses fill in locative and circumstantial detail in cases where English may not have need for such detail, as discussed below with some additional examples. English passives perform the same narrative function as Spanish word-order variation. I have given a left dislocation in the Spanish version: *the dog, the wasps were chasing him*. This was really a standard object-fronting word order in Spanish

(4) *Le*   *perseguían al*   *perro las avispas.*
    CLITIC.PRO chased   OBJECT + the dog   the wasps

This corresponds in function to the English passive, *the dog was being chased by the bees*. Preschoolers in both languages can manipulate word order to topicalize a patient, although the construction types differ.

I want to argue that these systematic contrasts between Spanish and English reflect different patterns of thinking for speaking – different on-line organization of the flow of information and attention to the particular details that receive linguistic expression. These patterns hold up in quantitative analysis of our narratives, and show striking contrasts with languages of different types.

2 Temporal description

Consider, again, the scene in which the boy falls from the tree and the bees chase the dog. Here we have two simultaneous events, one PUNCTUAL, COMPLETED, and the other NON-PUNCTUAL, DURATIVE. As we have seen, English allows for an opposition between an aspectually neutral verb form and a progressive, with the neutral form taking on a default punctual value, given the lexical meaning of the verb *fall*. The description in our five-year-old's example is typical:

(5) The boy fell out... and the dog was being chased by the bees.

Such aspectual contrasts are available at even younger ages. The earliest example in our data for this scene is given by a child of 3;8 (3 years 8 months):

(6) He's [dog] **running** through there, and he [boy] **fell** off.

In Spanish, the preferred version is to mark the punctuality of falling by use of a perfective verb form, contrasting it either with an imperfective or a gerundive expression, as in the following five-year-old's examples:

(7) a. Se   **cayó** *el niño y le*   *perseguían al perro las avispas.*
      'The boy **fell-PFV** and the wasps **chased-IPFV** the dog.'

   b. Se *cayó ... y el perro salió corriendo.*
      'He **fell-PFV**... and the dog **came-out-PFV** running.'

As in English, this aspectual contrast is marked by the youngest children in our sample. Our earliest Spanish example comes from a child of 3;4:

(8) *Se* **cayó**...   *El perro está corriendo.*
    'He **fell-PFV**... The dog is **running**.'

Spanish, by providing a perfective, in addition to imperfective and progressive, thus makes it possible to grammatically mark both poles of the durative–nondurative distinction, whereas the English progressive provides explicit marking only of the durative pole.[7]

German and Hebrew lack distinctive marking of either pole of the aspectual contrast. Hebrew has no grammaticized aspect at all. Verbs are simply inflected for past, present, or future tense. German has a simple past and a perfect. Neither language has grammatical marking of either progressive or imperfective. One would assume that German- and Hebrew-speakers must be aware, in some non-linguistic sense, that the temporal contours of the two events differ. In Boas's terms, their mental images should include such a basic contrast. Yet, the obligatory grammatical categories of German and Hebrew do not require speakers to **attend to** this contrast. This is evident in the narratives in these two languages: speakers generally do not distinguish the two events grammatically, but rather tend to use the same tense for both verbs. The following examples from five-year-olds are typical:

(9) **German**:
> *Der Junge fällt vom Baurn runter . . . und die Bienen gehen hinter dem Hund her.*
> 'The boy **falls** down from the tree . . . and the bees **go** after the dog.'

(10) **Hebrew**:
> *Hu nafal ve hakelev barax.*
> 'He **fell** and the dog **ran-away**.'

These examples are from five-year-olds, but it is important to note that the language-specific patterns hold across all the ages sampled, from three to nine, and for adults. In German and Hebrew the tendency is to maintain the same tense-aspect form for both clauses, while in Spanish and English the tendency is to differentiate the two. The trend is summarized numerically in table 3.1.

Consider these figures in the light of thinking for speaking. If the figures for Hebrew and German were uniformly 100%, and for English and Spanish 0%, we could only conclude that speakers strictly adhere to the formal contrasts provided by their language, and it would not be possible to separate thinking from speaking. Critical evidence, however, comes from deviations from these extremes, indicating that other options are possible.

Some Hebrew speakers try to contrast the two events by presenting the first in the past tense and the second in the present, thereby recruiting a tense difference to mark the aspectual contrast COMPLETED–ONGOING. For example:

(11) **Hebrew** (5-year-old):
> *Hayeled nafal . . . ve hakelev boreax.*
> 'The boy **fell** . . . and the dog **runs-away**.'

Table 3.1. *Percentage of narrators using same tense/aspect form for "fall" and "run" clauses in fig. 3.1*

	Preschool (3–5)	School (9)	Adult	OVERALL
Hebrew	71	100	63	78
German	54	80	78	71
English	26	22	33	27
Spanish	23	18	0	21

Note that this option is used about one-third of the time by preschoolers and adults, while school-age children (nine-year-olds) follow the language most tenaciously in not attempting any aspectual distinction. (It is worth noting, in passing, that nine-year-olds' stories, across languages, tend to be the most stereotyped and consistent with native language patterns. This may well be an effect of schooling.)

German presents a similar picture to Hebrew. There are some attempts to mark the verbs differently, especially in preschool narratives. The first event is sometimes put in the perfect, thereby closing it off as a resultant state with regard to the second event in the present tense. For example:

(12) **German** (5-year-old):
   *Der **ist** vom Baum **runtergefallen** und der Hund **läuft** schnell weg.*
   'He **has fallen** down from the tree and the dog **runs** away quickly.'

It is interesting that the tendency in German is to mark the first event as completed, rather than to elaborate the second as ongoing. Only two narrators in our total sample of forty-eight made any attempt to mark the second event as protracted in time:

(13) a. **German** (9-year-old):
   Er rannte schneller und immer schneller.
   'He ran faster and ever faster.'

   b. **German** (adult):
   Der Hund rennt rennt rennt.
   'The dog runs runs runs.'

In fact, throughout the narratives, it is generally the case that when German speakers choose to take an aspectual perspective, they tend to orient to some marking of **boundedness**. It is intriguing that, in the history of German, there have been various attempts to grammaticize notions of boundedness or terminative aspect. English, by contrast, has gone in a different historical direction among the Germanic languages, grammaticizing the progressive. And we find that our English-speaking narratives tend to mark durativity more than termination in their descriptions. The relations between diachrony and child language would require a separate paper. However, it is worth noting that persistence of a grammaticized notion over time in the history of a language provides another sort of critical evidence that grammatical distinctions may train children to attend to particular "contents of expression," to use Sapir's term. That is to say, speakers – and hence languages – become accustomed to maintaining grammatical marking of particular semantic features, as shown in ample diachronic evidence of renovation of grammatical markers within a given semantic domain.

To return to the fates of the boy and the dog: it is important for my argument that the figures in table 3.1 are not all 100s and 0s. If this were the case, one could only conclude, with Whorf ([1940b] 1956: 213–14), that:

We cut nature up, organize it into concepts, and ascribe significances as we do, largely because we are parties to an agreement to organize it in this way – an agreement that holds throughout our speech community and is codified in the patterns of our language. The agreement is, of course, an implicit and unstated one, **but its terms are absolutely obligatory** [Whorfs emphasis], we cannot talk at all except by subscribing to the organization and classification of data which the agreement decrees.

The deviations from the overall tendencies of each language type show that the "agreement" is not totally obligatory: it is, indeed, possible to try to mark aspectual notions like TERMINATIVE and DURATIVE if they are not part of the regular system of verb morphology in one's language, as in German and Hebrew. On the other, the occasional **lack** of aspectual distinctions between the two clauses in Spanish and English shows that one is not compelled to make use of the full array of distinctions available in verbal morphology. However, what is most striking in table 3.1 is the finding **that speakers so rarely make use of options that differ from the norm**. Overall, Hebrew and German speakers **attempt** to elaborate aspectual distinctions about one-quarter of the time, while Spanish and English speakers **fail** to mark aspectual distinctions about one quarter of the time. Such tendencies appear repeatedly, throughout our cross-linguistic study of narrative, clearly pointing to different types of thinking for speaking. Speakers of all ages, across languages, certainly know, in some non-linguistic sense, that the boy's falling is punctual and completed with regard to the simultaneous, ongoing chasing and running of bees and dog. Yet they generally do not seem to be inclined to express any more of this knowledge linguistically than fits the available distinctions in the language. It is striking that children as young as three already show the "selective attention" favored by their particular native language.

In comparing languages in terms of grammatical **aspect**, as in the examples presented above, we find differences in terms of the number and kinds of distinctions that are marked. The four languages we have considered can be put on a continuum with regard to richness of aspectual inflection:

Grammatical aspect
Hebrew: none.
German: perfect
English: perfect, progressive
Spanish: perfect, progressive, imperfective/perfective

When dealing with a continuum of this sort, we ask whether there is any sort of "compensation" for missing grammatical categories in a language, or whether they are generally ignored in thinking for speaking. Our data – across a number of story episodes and languages – suggest that categories that are not grammaticized in the native language are generally ignored, whereas those that **are** grammaticized are all expressed by children as young as three.

3 Spatial description

Languages differ from one another not only in the presence or absence of a grammatical category, but also in the ways in which they allocate grammatical resources to common semantic domains. Again, it will be most useful to begin with a comparison between English and Spanish. These two languages represent opposite poles of a typological distinction with regard to the verbal expression of change of location. That is, they differ critically in lexicalization patterns for verbs of motion. Consider one of the sentences we encountered earlier in an English five-year-old's story:

(14) And then the deer **carried** him **over a cliff** and **threw** him **over the cliff into a pond**.

As Leonard Talmy (1985) has shown in detailed analyses of lexicalization patterns, the verb in English encodes some **change of location** in a particular **manner** – *throw, carry, run*, etc. – leaving it to particles and prepositions to encode directionality. English allows for quite elaborated use of such means to specify path with a single verb root. The following sentence sounds quite normal to native speakers:

(15) The bird flew **down from out of** the hole in the tree

The verb simply specifies motion in a particular manner, and the associated elements specify the trajectory: *down-from-out-of.*

Spanish verbs of motion encode either directionality – *entrar*, 'enter'; *salir*, 'exit'; *subir*, 'ascend'; *bajar*, 'descend', etc.; or manner – *volar*, 'fly'; *correr*, 'run'. However, one cannot compactly express manner and directionality in compound expressions as in English, because the grammar generally does not allow for the accumulation of path expressions. The closest Spanish approximation to (15) would be something like:

(16) *El pájaro salió del agujero del árbol volando hacia abajo.*
     'The bird exited of the hole of the tree flying towards below.'

Note that Spanish prepositions, by contrast to English, provide minimal locative specification: *de* occurs twice in example (16). In *del agujero*, 'of the hole,' it receives the meaning 'out-of' from the associated verb *salir*, 'exit,' while in *del árbol*, 'of the tree,' it receives the meaning 'in' from general world knowledge about relations between holes and trees. When world knowledge is not sufficient, the Spanish-speaker is often required to provide a static "sketch" of the relevant components of the scene, so that the appropriate trajectory can be inferred. This accounts, in part, for the flowering of relative clauses in Spanish. For example, in English one might say:

(17) The boy put the frog down into a jar.

A Spanish-speaker might say:

(18) *El niño metió la rana en el frasco que había abajo.*
'The boy inserted the frog *en* [= in/on] the jar that was below.'

The verb *meter*, 'insert,' implies that the proposition *en* is to be interpreted as 'in'; and the relative clause, *que había abajo*, 'that was below,' implies the directionality of insertion. Thus in Spanish the trajectory 'down-into' must be inferred from a combination of path-verb and a static description of the location of the goal – the jar – while in English the static location of the goal – located in the jar – must be inferred from the path-description, *down into*.

This is a systematic difference between the two languages. English tends to assert trajectories, leaving resultant locative states to be inferred; Spanish tends to assert locations and directions, leaving trajectories to be inferred. This systematic difference has effects on the grammar of discourse. One effect, already mentioned, is the Spanish use of locative relative clauses. Another effect is in the use of Spanish participles, which are frequent at the youngest ages. There are even clauses in which the only lexical verb is a participle. For example, where English-speakers tend to say "The boy climbed the tree," leaving the boy's end-state implicit, Spanish speakers often say the untranslatable *El niño está subido en el árbol* 'the boy is climb-PART in the tree.'

(19) **English: assert trajectory, imply end-state.**
The boy climbed the tree.

(20) **Spanish: assert end-state, imply trajectory.**
El niño está subido en el árbol.
'the boy is climb-PART *en* [= in/on] the tree.'
[= the boy is in a state of having climbed the tree]

The languages incline towards different patterns in what is asserted and what is implied. Thus, at many points in our narratives, English-speakers assert actions, implying results, whereas Spanish-speakers assert results, implying actions. These differences come to have an effect on overall **rhetorical style**. Thus the obligatory grammatical morphemes of a language may do more than simply direct attention-while-speaking to their semantic content. This directed attention may have consequences for what is said and unsaid in any particular language. In this case, English-speaking narrators devote somewhat more narrative attention to descriptions of processes, while Spanish-speaking narrators tend to provide more descriptions of states. (In making this proposal, however, let me underline that I am talking about thinking for speaking **only**. I am making no claims about how millions of Spanish- and English-speakers conceive of life or act in the world.)

In our small sample of narratives to the *Frog, where are you?* picturebook, there are some suggestive differences by age and language with respect to the sorts of issues of location and motion that we have been examining. The analysis of verbs of motion can be enriched by adding German and Hebrew, since German patterns itself like English – with undirected verbs of motion and a rich and differentiated collection of locative particles and prepositions – and Hebrew patterns itself like Spanish – with directional verbs and a small collection of polysemous prepositions.

There are three episodes in the story in which a character falls or is thrown downward. We have seen two of them – the fall from the tree and the fall from the cliff; and here we add a third, in which the dog falls from a window. The analysis includes all of the verbs used to describe these scenes (mainly versions of "fall" and "throw") in English, German, Spanish, and Hebrew. At issue is whether the verb occurred alone or with some kind of locative addition – a particle or prepositional phrase indicating downward direction, source, or goal of motion. Table 3.2 presents the data for three-, five-, and nine-year-olds, giving the percentages of such descriptions that had a bare verb with no locative elaboration.

First consider the three-year-olds. It is already evident that English and German form one group, and Spanish and Hebrew another. Recall that, in comparing languages according to **aspect**, it was English and Spanish

Table 3.2. *Percentages of downward motion descriptions with bare verb*

	Age		
	Three	Five	Nine
English	4	27	13
German	15	2	0
Spanish	68	37	54
Hebrew	68	72	45

that formed one group, and German and Hebrew another. It is clear that, for psycholinguistic purposes, typological differences between languages must be considered separately for each semantic domain. The ways in which a language deals with issues of time may be quite different from its treatment of space, which casts some doubt on the grand overall conceptions of language and world-view proposed by von Humboldt and Whorf.

Table 3.2 shows that English and German three-year-olds hardly ever use a verb of motion without some locative elaboration, whereas Spanish and Hebrew three-year-olds use bare verbs of motion about two-thirds of the time. This clear difference in narrative strategy holds up across age as well. Although there are different developmental patterns, at each of the three ages the contrast between the two types of languages is maintained.[8]

The most interesting developmental pattern is seen in Spanish. Here there appears to be a U-shaped curve, with some five-year-olds providing relatively more locative elaboration than either three- or nine-year-olds. Some children of this age seem to be groping for more detailed description of trajectories, using English/German construction types that are redundant in Spanish; for example:

(21) a. *Se cayó* **dentro de** *un agujero.*
     '(He) fell **inside of** a hole.' [5 yrs.]
     [= Se cayó *en* un agujero '(He) fell *en* a hole.']

   b. *Se cayó* **encima del** *agua.*
     '(He) fell **on top of** the water.' [5 yrs.]
     [= Se cayó *al* agua. '(He) fell *a* the water.']

And some five-year-olds add a locative adverb, *abajo* 'down' or 'downward,' as in:

(21) c. *Le tiró abajo.*
     '(He) threw him **down(ward)**.' [5 yrs.]

These can be looked upon as attempts to **compensate** for an apparent gap in Spanish grammar. Yet they are different from the attempts at compensation that we encountered with regard to verbal aspect. There we found a few rare instances of German and Hebrew attempts to **add** distinctions of punctuality or durativity that are not marked grammatically in the language. Here, however, we have attempts to be more explicit, using tools that are part of the grammar. Again, we see that thinking for speaking is not a Whorfian straightjacket.

Interestingly, these attempts disappear after the age of five in Spanish. They seem to be replaced by the use of extended static locative descriptions, which make it possible to infer trajectories from the combination of a motion verb and the description of a scene. That is, the

Spanish child learns to allocate information in accordance with the "rhetorical typology" of the language. The following nine-year-old's example is typical:

(22) *El ciervo le llevó hasta un sitio, donde debajo había un río.*
     Entonces el ciervo tiró al perro y al niño al río.
     Y después, cayeron.
     'The deer took him until a place, where below there was a river.
     Then the deer threw the dog and the boy to the river.
     And then, they fell.'

The four languages also fall into two types on the basis of relative use of such locative description. Table 3.3 summarizes the use of elaborated locative narration of the fall from the cliff.

First compare English and Spanish: it is evident that this pattern of extended locative elaboration develops between the ages of five and nine in Spanish, but not in English. Comparable narrations by English nine-year-olds present compact phrases with verbs of motion and associated indications of path, but with no scene-setting descriptions, such as:

(23) a. So the deer ran away with him and dropped him off a cliff in the water. And they fell in the water.

     b. And the deer ran with the boy on his antlers. So the dog was chasing the deer, and the deer just stopped, and the boy and the dog fell off a cliff into a swamp.

German nine-year-olds are strikingly similar to English-speaking Americans, with little static scene-setting and compact verbal constructions that sketch out a trajectory; for example:

(24) *Der Hirsch nahm den Jungen auf sein Geweih und schmiß ihn*
     den Abhang hinunter genau ins Wasser.
     'The deer took the boy on his antlers and hurled him
     down from the cliff right into the water.'

Table 3.3. *Percentage of narrators providing extended locative elaboration in describing the fall from the cliff*

	Age	
	Five	Nine
English	8	8
German	0	17
Spanish	8	42
Hebrew	0	42

Finally, to complete the picture, nine-year-old Israelis are strikingly similar to Spaniards, as can be seen from the following Hebrew example:

(25) *Ve ha'ayil nivhal ve hu hitxil laruts. Ve hakelev rats axarav,*
ve hu higia lemacok she mitaxat haya bitsa, ve hu atsar,
ve hayeled ve hakelev naflu labitsa beyaxad.
'And the deer was startled, and he began to run. And the dog ran after him, and he reached a cliff that had a swamp underneath, and he stopped, and the boy and the dog fell to the swamp together.'

To return to the overall theme once again, the contrast between these two types of languages seems to have important consequences with regard to thinking for speaking. In this instance, the unavailability of a particular grammatical device – a system of locative particles related to verbs – has rather large potential consequences for narrative organization. Spanish- and Hebrew-speaking children develop procedures of scene-setting in which a vaguely specified change of location becomes interpretable in context. One grammatical device which serves this function is relative clauses, and we find that Spanish- and Hebrew-speakers use relative clauses far more frequently than English- and German-speakers. This is already evident at the age of three, indicating early development of a narrative style in which description and qualification are important (Berman & Slobin 1994).

4 Learning to think for speaking

One must, of course, be cautious in making large generalizations from a rather small sample of stories told about a single picturebook in several countries. Within this framework, however, it is encouraging to find that the patterns we have found in Spain seem to hold up in comparable data gathered by Aura Bocaz in Chile and Argentina (Slobin & Bocaz 1988), and that the English patterns are repeated in several different American samples. Much more needs to be done even with the *Frog, where are you?* picturebook in the remaining languages in our sample, not to mention necessary additions of other genres and languages.[9]

I am convinced, however, that the events of this little picture book are experienced differently by speakers of different languages – **in the process of making a verbalized story out of them**. For example, there is nothing in the pictures themselves that leads English speakers to verbally express whether an event is in progress, or Spanish speakers to note whether it has been completed; to encourage Germanic speakers to formulate elaborate descriptions of trajectories; to make Hebrew speakers indifferent to conceiving of events as durative or bounded in time. (And, if we were to go on to examine our Russian and Turkish stories, we would find an indifference to indicating the **definiteness** of story participants – a category readily marked by our English, German, Spanish, and Hebrew narrators.) I suggest that, in acquiring each of these languages, children are guided by the set of grammaticized distinctions in the language to attend to such features of events while speaking.[10]

5 First-language thinking in second-language speaking

There is something dissatisfying in limiting ourselves to evidence that is so bound up with the acquisition and use of native languages. I have also suggested that the stability of grammaticized categories in historical language change can be taken as evidence of the cognitive importance of those categories for speakers. In conclusion, I would like to point to another type of evidence that seems to support my proposal that the ways one learns a language as a child constrain one's sensitivity to what Sapir called "the possible contents of experience as experienced in linguistic terms."

Consider the small collection of linguistically encoded perspectives that we have been examining: temporal contours of events marked by aspectual forms, movement and trajectories in space (and also indication of definiteness of participants mentioned in connected discourse). These are precisely the sorts of things that make it so hard to master the grammar of a second language. For example, it is very hard for English-speakers to grasp the Spanish perfective/imperfective distinction that is lacking in our native language. In fact, we seem never to master this system fully in Spanish. By contrast, we have little difficulty in figuring out how to use the Spanish progressive and perfect, or the Spanish definite and indefinite articles – since we have already learned how to make decisions about the linguistic expression of these notions in English. Yet there is nothing inherently easy or hard about **any** of these Spanish distinctions. For example, native French speakers have no trouble with the Spanish imperfective, since they have a similar category in French; but the progressive and perfect pose problems to them, since these are not French ways of looking at events. Turkish speakers have difficulty with definite and indefinite articles in learning to speak Spanish, English, and German, since there are no definite articles in Turkish. German speakers of English use the progressive where they should use simple present, although Turks do not make this error in English, since Turkish uses progressive aspect and German does not. Spanish learners of English object that we make too many obscure distinctions with our large collection of locative prepositions and particles. And so on. In brief, each native language has trained its speakers to pay different kinds of attention to events and experiences when talking about them. This training is carried out in childhood and is exceptionally resistant to restructuring in adult second-language acquisition.

Much of value for the thinking for speaking hypothesis could be learned from a systematic study of those systems in particular second languages that speakers of particular first languages find especially difficult to master. Suggestive data of precisely this sort come from a European Science Foundation project, "Second language acquisition by adult immigrants" (Perdue 1993). Two examples, one from the domain of time and the other from the domain of space, are instructive.

Consider Italian- and Punjabi-speaking immigrants to Britain (Bhardwaj, Dietrich, & Noyau 1988). Italian and English are both "tense-prominent" languages – that is, every finite clause must be grammatically marked as to its deictic relation to the moment of speaking. Italian immigrants readily acquire English past-tense forms. This makes it possible for them to construct narratives from a situationally external perspective, relating a succession of past events as seen from the present, as is done in Italian. These speakers make far more frequent use of tense-marking than of the English progressive aspect. Punjabi, by contrast, is an "aspect-prominent" language, and Punjabi immigrants make heavy use of the English progressive to narrate events "from within," from the perspective of the protagonist, in analogous fashion to the narrative use of the Punjabi imperfective.

In the domain of space the influence of Punjabi on learners' early organization of English is striking (Becker, Carroll, & Kelly 1988). In Punjabi, spatial locations are regions named by nouns, analogous to English expressions such as on *the top* of the pile and at *the back* of the *house*. Punjabi learners of English often treat prepositions as nouns, producing forms such as put *the on* please, put *the down* chair, and pull *the up* (1988: 69). English relational terms have apparently been reanalyzed as names of locations. In addition, Punjabi focuses on states as the results of processes (somewhat like the Spanish use of participles discussed above). This pattern also transfers to English. For example, a newspaper lying on a table is referred to as *put in the table* by a Punjabi-speaker. The investigators suggest that "he imagines that the newspaper was put there by someone. In Punjabi one says exactly the same thing" (1988: 73).

The European Science Foundation team concludes:

The influence of the lexico-grammatical systems of both the SL [source language] and the TL [target language] can be observed in the acquisition process. The picture which emerges is quite a simple one – an adult acquirer tries to discover in the TL a system that is similar to that of his SL, and if he does not discover any, he tries to construct one; but since it is the TL material he has to use the outcome is invariably a hybrid which is an autonomous system (often consisting of loosely or tightly integrated sub-systems) which partakes of some features of both the "parent" systems but is identical to neither. (Bhardwaj et al. 1988: 86)

I propose that the grammaticized categories that are most susceptible to SL influence have something important in common: **they cannot be experienced directly in our perceptual, sensorimotor, and practical dealings with the world**. To be sure, all human beings experience sequences of events that have particular temporal contours, put objects in locations, and so on. Indeed, animals do the same. However, only language requires us to **categorize** events as ongoing or completed, objects as at rest or as at the end point of a trajectory, and so forth. Other categories seem to be less dependent on purely verbal categorization. I would imagine, for example, that if your language lacked a plural marker, you would not have insurmountable difficulty in learning to mark the category of plurality in a second language, since this concept is evident to the non-linguistic mind and eye. Or if your language lacked an instrumental marker it should not be difficult to learn to add a grammatical inflection to nouns that name objects manipulated as instruments. Plurality and manipulation are notions that are obvious to the senses.[11] Yet there is nothing in everyday sensorimotor interactions with the world that changes when you describe an event as "She **went** to work" or "She **has gone** to work," or when you refer to the same object in successive utterances as "**a** car" and "**the** car." Distinctions of aspect, definiteness, voice, and the like, are, *par excellence*, distinctions that can only be learned through language, and have no other use except to be expressed in language. They are not categories of thought in general, but categories of thinking for speaking. It seems that once our minds have been trained in taking particular points of view for the purposes of speaking, it is exceptionally difficult for us to be retrained.

It is interesting that Wilhelm von Humboldt anticipated these questions as well. He wrote:

To learn a foreign language should therefore be to acquire a new standpoint in the world-view hitherto possessed, and in fact to a certain extent this is so, since every language contains the whole conceptual fabric and mode of presentation of a portion of mankind. But because we always carry over, more or less, our own world-view, and even our own language-view, this outcome is not purely and completely experienced. ([1836] 1988: 60)

6 Conclusion

In sum, we can only talk and understand one another in terms of a particular language. The language or languages that we learn in childhood are not neutral coding systems of an objective reality. Rather, each one is a subjective orientation to the world of human experience, and this orientation **affects the ways in which we think while we are speaking**.

Acknowledgments

An earlier version of this chapter was published as Slobin, D. I. (1991). Learning to think for speaking: native language, cognition, and rhetorical style. *Pragmatics*, 1, 7–26. The original study (A crosslinguistic investigation of the development of temporality in narrative) was designed by Dan I. Slobin, in collaboration with Ruth A. Berman, Tel Aviv University, Israel, using a method developed by Michael Bamberg (1987). The data were gathered, analyzed, and discussed in collaboration with: Ayhan Aksu Koç (Boğaziçi Universitesi, Istanbul), Michael Bamberg (Clark University), Aura Bocaz (Universidad de Santiago, Chile), Lisa Dasinger (University of California, Berkeley), Esther Dromi (Tel Aviv University), Jane Edwards (University of California, Berkeley), Aylin Küntay (University of California, Berkeley), Virginia Marchman (University of Wisconsin-Madison), Yonni Neeman (Tel Aviv University), Tanya Renner (University of Hawaii), Eugenia Sebastián (Universidad Autónoma, Madrid), Christiane von Stutterheim (Universität Heidelberg), and Cecile Toupin (University of California, Berkeley). The study was supported by the US–Israel Binational Science Foundation (Grant 2732/82, to R. A. Berman and D. I. Slobin), the Linguistics Program of the National Science Foundation (Grant BNS-8520008, to D. I. Slobin), the Sloan Foundation Program in Cognitive Science (Institute of Cognitive Studies, University of California, Berkeley), the Max Planck Institute for Psycholinguistics (Nijmegen, The Netherlands), and the Institute of Human Development (University of California, Berkeley). Additional Spanish data were gathered in Chile and Argentina, from adults and children aged 3–11, by Aura Bocaz, with support from Grant H2643-8712 from Universidad de Chile. Turkish data were gathered with support from Boğaziçi University to Ayhan Aksu-Koç and from Mellon Funds administered by the Center for Middle East Studies (University of California, Berkeley) to Dan I. Slobin and Aylin Küntay.

Notes

1 *Über die Verschiedenheit des menschlichen Sprachbaues und ihren Einfluß auf die geistige Entwickelung des Menschengeschlechts.*
2 These facts pose problems for any acquisition theory, because the child must initially be sensitive to **potentially grammaticizable** distinctions. This problem goes beyond the goals of the present chapter. For discussion of these issues see Bowerman (1989), Pinker (1989), Talmy (1987), Slobin (1985).
3 My preferred formulation of a modified Whorfian hypothesis was offered by Charles Hockett: "The impact of an inherited linguistic pattern on activities is, in general, **least** important in the most practical contexts and most important in such 'purely verbal' goings-on as storytelling, religion, and philosophizing" (1954: 122). I would extend the definition of these "purely verbal goings-on" to all acts of speaking.
4 For the purposes of this chapter, "readily encodable in the language" is limited to closed-class grammatical morphemes – specifically, tense/aspect inflections, verb particles, and prepositions. Traditionally, the hypothesis of linguistic relativity and determinism has been most clearly stated with regard to obligatory distinctions as well as to the number of options provided by a language within a domain. For example, tense is obligatory in English but modality is optional. Nevertheless, the language provides a

small set of grammaticized modalities, with rigorous grammatical specification of their use (*would, should, can,* etc.). English and Spanish both have a closed-class set of locative prepositions, but the Spanish set is much smaller and consists of prepositions with more general meanings than in English. Languages also have "semi-open" sets of lexical items that are grammatically significant, such as verbs of aspectual phase (*start, finish, keep on,* etc.). Grammatical factors such as these should all have consequences for thinking for speaking.

5 The study was planned together with Dr. Ruth A. Berman of Tel-Aviv University in Israel (Berman & Slobin 1994). The full study now includes ten languages, with ten or more narrators in each age group: **English**: ages 3, 4, 5, 9, adult (Lisa Dasinger, Cecile Toupin: University of California, Berkeley; Virginia Marchman: University of Wisconsin-Madison; Tanya Renner: University of Hawaii). **Finnish**: ages 3, 4, 5, 9, adult (Lisa Dasinger: University of California, Berkeley). **German**: ages 3, 5, 9, adult (Michael Bamberg: Clark University; Christiane von Stutterheim: Universität Heidelberg). **Hebrew**: ages 3, 4, 5, 7, 9, 11, adult (Ruth Berman, Yonni Neeman: Tel-Aviv University). **Icelandic**: ages 3, 4, 5, 9, adult (Hrafnhildur Ragnarsdottir: Reykjavik). **Japanese**: ages 3, 4, 5, 7, 9, adult (Keiko Nakamura: University of California, Berkeley). **Mandarin**: ages 3, 4, 5, 7, 9, adult (Guo Jiansheng: University of California, Berkeley). **Russian**: ages 4, 5, 6, 7, 9, 10, adult (Yana Anilovich: University of California, Berkeley). **Spanish**: ages 3, 4, 5, 7, 9, adult (Eugenia Scbastián: Universidad Autónoma Madrid; Aura Bocaz (Chile, Argentina): Universidad de Chile, Santiago). **Turkish**: ages 3, 4, 5, 7, 9, adult (Ayhan Aksu-Koç: Boğaziçi Universitesi, Istanbul, Aylin Küntay, University of California, Berkeley).

6 The original Spanish of the first version is as follows: *El niño miró por un agujero del árbol. Salió un loro que le tiró al niño. Y le perseguían al perro las avispas. El niño se escondió detrás de una piedra y se voló el buho. Un ciervo que estaba detrás al niño como se subió . . . Y se tropezó encima de la- del ciervo, mientras el ciervo corría. Primero iba el perro. Le tiraron abajo en donde un río. Luego se cayó sentado.* [The last word is omitted from the translation because it has no natural English equivalent. The narrator is apparently trying to convey the idea that the boy fell/landed in a seated posture.]

7 It should also be noted that the Spanish perfective/imperfective distinction is **obligatory**: every past-tense verb must be marked as one or the other. Progressive, by contrast, is optional in both languages; that is, one may choose not to mark a verb as progressive. However, because English does not have any other means of inflectionally marking durativity, the progressive is used more frequently in English than in Spanish.

8 Differences between English and Spanish in narrative strategy are also reflected in literary fiction. In a recent study (Slobin 1996) of novels written in the two languages, the following differences were attested, parallel to findings from the study of elicited narratives: authors writing in English make more frequent reference to source and goal in association with verbs of motion; they also provide more information about manner of movement. Translations of English novels into Spanish omit some details of both path and manner of movement, whereas translations from Spanish into English preserve such information.

9 Our data consist entirely of elicited productions. Studies of comprehension and memory also would be pertinent. Further, it should be noted that the frog

stories are essentially monologues. As suggested by several participants in the conference on "rethinking linguistic relativity," crosslinguistic studies of interpersonal discourse would add dimensions of cultural relativity in the exchange of information and in negotiation of the content and flow of discourse. Thinking for speaking, then, is one component of an approach to communication that is situated in the particularities of languages and cultures.

10 It is through listening, of course, that children's attention is first drawn to the fact that certain notions are grammatically marked in the ambient language. This suggests that, once the grammar has been acquired, there may be related effects of "speaking for remembering," "listening for understanding," and "listening for remembering." That is, the form in which one produces information may influence how that information is stored and later accessed, and the form in which one receives information from others may influence how it is understood and stored. Leonard Talmy (personal communication) characterizes all of these listener-oriented counterparts to thinking for speaking as "thinking from hearing." He proposes, however, that the influence of grammar may be washed out on the receptive end, since the form of an utterance **underdetermines** its interpretation. That is, the hearer uses all available information (grammatical, lexical, contextual, world knowledge) to arrive at a conceptualization of the speaker's communicative intent. For example, imagine listeners to the various styles of narrating the fall from the cliff. Once the listener has established that the boy fell from the deer's head over a cliff into some water, the differences between the English-style and Spanish-style versions may no longer play a role. One possible way to study the influence of grammar at the receptive end would to be to do memory experiments with fluent adult bilinguals. If one thinks for speaking in Language A (either as speaker or hearer) and later recalls the content in Language B, are the grammaticized concepts of Language A in any way still present in the recall? (Moshe Anisfeld (p.c.) has suggested memory experiments with monolinguals speaking various languages, comparing a speaker's form of encoding with later memory for grammatically relevant details of the content.)

11 You may have difficulty remembering to use these markers on every occasion – as Chinese speakers of English do not always mark the plural, to take one possible example. But this is a matter of **automatizing** attention, which may be difficult in adulthood. What I am proposing is that some grammaticized categories may be obvious on non-linguistic grounds. For such categories, the problem in second-language learning is not to make the proper conceptual distinction, but to treat it as obligatory.

References

Bamberg, M. G. W. 1987. *The acquisition of narrative: learning to use language.* Berlin: Mouton de Gruyter.

Becker, A., Carroll, M., & Kelly, A. 1988. *Final report of second-language acquisition by adult immigrants: an additional activity of the European Science Foundation,* vol. IV: *Reference to space.* Strasbourg & Heidelberg.

Berman, R. A. & Slobin, D. I. 1994. *Relating events in narrative: a crosslinguistic developmental study.* Hillsdale, NJ: Lawrence Erlbaum.

Bhardwaj, M., Dietrich, R., & Noyau, C. 1988. *Final report of second-language acquisition by adult immigrants: an additional activity of the European Science Foundation,* vol. V: *Temporality.* Strasbourg, Paris, Heidelberg, & London.

Boas, F. 1911. Introduction to *Handbook of American Indian languages*. Bulletin 40, Part I, Bureau of American Ethnology. Washington, DC: Government Printing Office. (Reprinted in F. Boas 1966. *Introduction to Handbook of American Indian languages*/J. W. Powell, *Indian linguistic families of America North of Mexico*, ed. P. Holder. Lincoln: University of Nebraska Press.)
    1938. Language. In F. Boas, *General anthropology* (pp. 124–45). New York: Heath.
Bowerman, M. 1989. Learning a semantic system: what role do cognitive predispositions play? In M. L. Rice & R. L. Schieffelbusch (eds.), *The teachability of language* (pp. 133–69). Baltimore: Paul H. Brookes.
Brislin, R. W. (ed.) 1976. *Translation: applications and research*. New York: Gardner Press.
Hockett, C. F. 1954. Chinese vs. English: an exploration of the Whorfian thesis. In H. Hoijer (ed.), *Language in culture*. University of Chicago Press.
Humboldt, W. von. 1836. *Über die Verschiedenheit des menschlichen Sprachbaues und ihren Einfluß auf die geistige Entwickelung des Menschengeschlechts* (Abhandlungen der Akademie der Wissenschaften zu Berlin). Berlin: Dümmlers Verlag. (Reprinted: 1960. Bonn: Dümmlers Verlag; English translation by P. Heath. 1988. *On language: the diversity of human language-structure and its influence on the mental development of mankind*. Cambridge University Press.)
Jakobson, R. 1959. Boas' view of grammatical meaning. *American Anthropologist*, 61, 139–45.
Maslov, Yu. S. (ed.) 1985. *Voprosy sopostavitel'noj aspektologii*. Leningrad: Izd-vo Leningradskogo Universiteta. (English translation by J. Forsyth 1985. *Contrastive studies in verbal aspect in Russian, English, French and German*. Heidelberg: Julius Groos Verlag.)
Mayer, M. 1969. *Frog, where are you?* New York: Dial Press.
Nida, E. A. 1964. *Toward a science of translating, with special reference to principles and procedures involved in Bible translating*. Leiden: E. J. Brill.
Perdue, C. (ed.) 1993. *Adult language acquisition. cross-linguistic perspectives*, vol. II: *The results*. Cambridge University Press.
Pinker, S. 1989. *Learnability and cognition: the acquisition of argument structure*. Cambridge, MA: MIT Press.
Sapir, E. 1924. The grammarian and his language. *American Mercury*, 1, 149–55. (Reprinted in 1958, *Selected writings of Edward Sapir in language, culture and personality*, ed. D. G. Mandelbaum. Berkeley/Los Angeles: University of California Press.)
Slobin, D. I. 1985. Crosslinguistic evidence for the Language-Making Capacity. In D. I. Slobin (ed.), *The crosslinguistic study of language acquisition*, vol. II: *The data* (pp. 1157–256). Hillsdale, NJ: Lawrence Erlbaum.
    1996. Two ways to travel: verbs of motion in English and Spanish. In M. Shibatani & S. A. Thompson (eds.), *Essays in syntax and semantics*. Oxford University Press.
Slobin, D. I. & Bocaz, A. 1988. Learning to talk about movement through time and space: the development of narrative abilities in Spanish and English. *Lenguas Modernas* (Universidad de Chile), 15, 5–24. (Circulated as Berkeley Cognitive Science Report 55, Institute of Cognitive Studies, University of California, Berkeley, January 1989.)
Snell-Hornby, M. 1988. *Translation studies: an integrated approach*. Amsterdam: John Benjamins.

Talmy, L. 1985. Lexicalization patterns: semantic structure in lexical forms. In T. Shopen (ed.), *Language typology and syntactic description*, vol. III: *Grammatical categories and the lexicon* (pp. 56–149). Cambridge University Press.
　1987. The relation of grammar to cognition. In B. Rudzka-Ostyn (ed.), *Topics on cognitive linguistics* (pp. 165–206). Amsterdam: John Benjamins.
Toury, G. 1986. Translation: a cultural–semiotic perspective. In T. A. Sebeok (ed.), *Encyclopedic dictionary of semiotics*, vol. II (pp. 1111–24). Berlin: Mouton de Gruyter.
Whorf, B. L. 1940a. Linguistics as an exact science. *Technology Review*, 43, 61–3, 80–3. (Reprinted in 1956, *Language, thought, and reality: selected writings of Benjamin Lee Whorf*, ed. J. B. Carroll (pp. 220–32). Cambridge, MA: MIT Press.)
　1940b. Science and linguistics. *Technology Review*, 42(6), 229–31, 247–8. (Reprinted in 1956, *Language thought, and reality: selected writings of Benjamin Lee Whorf*, ed. J. B. Carroll (pp. 207–19). Cambridge, MA: MIT Press.)
　1954. Language, mind, and reality. *Theosophist* (Madras, India), January, April. (Reprinted in 1956, *Language, thought, and reality: selected writings of Benjamin Lee Whorf*, ed. J. B. Carroll (pp. 246–70). Cambridge, MA: MIT Press.)

4

INTRA-SPEAKER RELATIVITY

PAUL KAY

1 Introduction

Linguistic relativity, so-called, takes on a new and reduced significance when we realize that the kinds of differences *between* languages which are routinely taken as evidence in favor of the Whorfian view commonly occur *within* languages.

In lecturing once on lexical semantics,[1] I wished to make the point that it is dangerous to jump from the observation that two languages provide different ways of talking about a given subject matter to the conclusion that the speakers of those languages *think* of that subject matter in distinct ways. That is, the speakers of the distinct languages may or may not think about the subject matter differently, but the fact that they talk about it differently constitutes no proof. To make this point I remarked to a Brazilian audience that I had been surprised to notice that the off-ramps on limited-access highways in Brazil are marked with the word *entrada* plus the name of a locality, while those in the US may be marked with the word *exit* plus the name of the locality. Thus, *Entrada São Jose* versus *San Jose Exit*. Such an observation, I remarked, might lead a Whorfian dealing with two very different cultures to spin a tale about how members of the cultures speaking these languages had distinct conceptions of the nature of road systems, while it is perfectly obvious, I innocently observed, that Brazilians and North Americans have exactly the same understanding of freeways. The example was received with enthusiasm, but for some of those in attendance failed to make the intended point. Several expressed the idea that this example had revealed to them that Brazilians and North Americans in fact conceptualize highways in distinct manners and went on to offer ingenious characterizations of the conflicting Brazilian and North American conceptualizations of road systems, based entirely on the observation regarding *entrada* versus *exit*.

I had earlier in the lecture attempted to make the same point with the following example. In English one speaks of a *screwdriver*, in German one speaks of a *schraubenzieher* ('screw puller'), and in French of a *tournevise* ('screw turner'). Furthermore, in two mutually intelligible dialects of

Montagnais, this implement is named by polymorphemic words that have the respective analyses 'screw.in.instrumental suffix' (English style) and 'screw.out.instrumental suffix' (German style).[2] I had thought it self-evident that German, English and French cultures are similar enough in regard to things such as screwdrivers that it would be folly to infer differences in thought or cultural conceptualization from such differences in naming. I also thought it a plausible conjecture that the naming differences between the two mutually intelligible dialects of Montagnais, both of whose speakers presumably acquired screwdrivers at the same time and fitted them into the same cultural matrix, probably did not represent differences in the internal cognitive representations of screwdrivers on the part of their respective speakers.

However, the failure of the *entrada/exit* example, the one I had thought would be most convincing because the audience was, on the whole, familiar with both of the languages and cultures in question, caused me to wonder if there is any way to persuade the committed Whorfian that the leap from observed differences in semantics to corresponding differences in thought is a leap of faith, not an inductive generalization. To date my experience has been that no number of such cautionary examples, in which one observes linguistic differences between speakers of languages that *presumably* do not differ culturally with regard to the domain in question, will persuade the committed Whorfian. He or she can, and reliably does, reply that there may well be a corresponding cultural difference. After all, no proof has been offered that there isn't any.[3]

In the present paper, I will therefore attempt to argue the same point with a different kind of data. Instead of considering cases of distinct languages which provide their speakers with contrasting ways of talking about the same stuff within a historical context in which it seems *a priori* unlikely that the speakers conceptualize the stuff differently, I will consider cases in which a single language provides each of its speakers with distinct ways of talking about the same stuff. I will attempt to show that the same kinds of contrasting semantic perspectives that can, loosely speaking, be taken on a subject by different languages can be taken on that subject within the idiolect of a single speaker of a single language. If contrasting fashions of speaking justify a verdict in favor of the linguistic relativity of thought in the first case, they must justify the same verdict in the second case. If linguistic relativity causes the speakers of different languages to inhabit different worlds, then linguistic relativity causes the monolingual speaker of a single language to inhabit different worlds, whatever that may mean.

The next section contrasts hedging expressions in English from the point of view of the differing schematizations of the world of their denotata which they appear to presuppose.

2 *Loosely speaking* and *strictly speaking* versus *technically*

Among the hedging expressions of English studied by Lakoff (1972) and Kay (1983) are the expressions *loosely speaking, strictly speaking* and *technically*. The first two represent a coherent tacit theory of how words refer to objects. The third also presupposes a coherent theory about how words refer to objects, but it is an entirely different theory. These different notions of how words refer to things nevertheless coexist in the mind of each speaker of English. Linguistic relativity is *within* each of us (if it is anywhere). Consider the example (taken from Kay 1983):

(1) Loosely speaking the first human beings lived in Kenya.

An utterance of this sentence might occur as the reply of an anthropologist to a lay person's question regarding "where the first human beings lived." The anthropologist's use of *loosely speaking* might be occasioned by a large number of communicative problems. First, believing in gradualism in the evolution of species, the anthropologist might think that the locution "the first human beings" is, strictly speaking, incoherent. Aside from this problem, our anthropologist may think that it is only proper to speak of the first human beings *known to science*, as there may be earlier hominid populations of which we have found no record. Thirdly, *Kenya* may be felt to be only an approximate geographic location for the first hominids. Fourthly, the speaker may worry about the appropriateness of using the modern political label *Kenya* to denote a geographical region that probably was not named Kenya, or anything else, at the time. One could go on. Moreover, the speaker may be troubled by all or any of this list of worries at the time of utterance.

So what does *loosely speaking* mean? I suggest that *loosely speaking*, and its cousin, *strictly speaking*, are both based on a schematization of language and its use in which there are facts in the world and words in the language, along with rules for combining the latter. Words have inherent fit, because of their meanings or senses, to certain facts, and the rules of language may be carefully or carelessly followed. If we select our words carefully so that each word exactly fits the facts it is supposed to fit and closely obey the rules of the language, we are speaking strictly. Otherwise, we speak loosely.

This picture of the relation of language to the world is, I have argued, a tacit, folk version of the Fregean theory of language, particularly Frege's theory of reference, according to which a word refers via its intension or sense (*Sinn*).

There is another theory of reference, associated with the philosophers Saul Kripke (1972) and Hillary Putnam (1975), among others, in which there is no role for the concept of intension or sense of a word at all.

Words refer on this theory in a two-stage process. There is an original act of ostention – the prototype is that of giving a person a name – and then through a series of (assumed) causal events, the association of the thing and the name gets passed along from speaker to speaker. Thus *Sylvia* means 'the person originally baptized *Sylvia*' and *gold* means 'the stuff originally baptized *gold*.' In using a word like *gold*, we rely, according to Putnam, on a linguistic division of labor according to which certain experts have kept alive the diagnostic flame, which can ascertain whether or not some presented token is really the stuff that was originally baptized *gold*. So when I say to you, 'This is gold,' we both count on there existing someone in a jewelry store or the Bureau of Standards who can make a hard decision for us if it comes to that. Meanwhile, on this theory *gold* means 'the stuff originally so baptized and which can be diagnosed by an expert should the need arise.'

This elegant philosophical theory of reference seems rather like a conscious version of the folk theory of reference that underlies *technically*, or *technically speaking*. Thus, a sentence like (2a) or (3a) sounds highly peculiar, in comparison to the corresponding (b) version, precisely because we can not imagine any set of experts relevant to the usage of the expressions *bug* and *flip one's lid*.

(2) a. *Technically that's a bug
    b. Technically that's an insect

(3) a. *Technically he flipped his lid
    b. Technically he experienced a psychotic break

Opinions about what sets of experts exist and what they have stipulated about the use of words enter into such judgments and may cause inter-individual variation. Thus, for those disposed to appeal to the fact that economic botanists have given a technical definition to *weed* (a plant that volunteers in disturbed soil), the following example is acceptable.

(4) Technically (even though a valuable plant) sunflowers are weeds

Just as the Frege versus the Kripke–Putnam theories may be opposed in conscious philosophical debate, so application of the schemata underlying *strictly speaking* and *technically* produces differing judgments of truth in the use of ordinary language when applied to the same state of affairs. For example, if it is accepted as uncontroversial that Sacco and Vanzetti were unjustly convicted, (5) is true and (6) is false.

(5) Technically Sacco and Vanzetti were murderers

(6) Strictly speaking Sacco and Vanzetti were murderers

The two folk theories differ in their truth consequences when applied to a given set of facts, under a uniform set of background beliefs. Each individual speaker of English whose lexicon comprehends both the expressions in question subscribes, if that is the word, to both of these "theories." Such " differing views of reality," when observed to obtain in different languages, are the stuff that Whorfian dreams are made on.[4] If one takes the existence of such conflicting schemata, when they appear in different languages, to provide evidence for linguistic relativity, then what will one say when they coexist in the mind of a single speaker? Linguistic relativity, so-called, seems to be as much an intra-individual matter as an inter-cultural one. If "linguistic relativity" so reconstructed is, however, a language-internal phenomenon as much as a cross-linguistic one, then its consequences for inter-cultural communication, and so on, may be less dire than often supposed.

We turn now from strictly lexical examples to some which involve grammar as well.

3 *Buy, sell, pay*, and *cost*

It has been argued by Fillmore (1977) that underlying a long list of lexical items, including *buy, sell, cost, pay, price, goods*, and so on, there is, for English speakers, a single conceptual schema or frame according to which at one time there is a participant, the "buyer," who has some money and wants some goods and another participant, the "seller," who has some goods and wants some money; at a second time goods and money change hands; and at a third time the buyer has the goods and the seller the money.

Independent of these particular facts about the linguistically encoded notion of a commercial event, there is in English a small set of very general perspectivizations of event types. Each such perspectivization of an event assigns to every participant in the frame (equivalently: every argument of the predicate) a "thematic" role. The thematic roles are reflected directly in the grammar of English sentences, via a set of linking constructions or rules which assign to each theta-role a grammatical function. For example, when one participant is thematically schematized as agent and another as patient or theme, in a transitive sentence the former is expressed as subject and the latter as direct object, while in the corresponding passive sentence, the agent participant is either expressed in an oblique *by*-phrase or is left unexpressed. (A patient/theme phrase in a passive sentence involving an agent [expressed or unexpressed] may or may not be the subject, depending on additional factors.) Some of these possibilities are illustrated by the following examples.

(7) Sidney (Agent) tossed a coin (Patient/Theme)

(8) A coin (Pat/Th) was tossed (by Sidney [Ag])

(9) Sidney (Ag) tossed a coin (Pat/Th) to Sybil (Recipient)

(10) A coin (Pat/Th) was tossed to Sybil (Rec) (by Sidney [Ag])

(11) Sidney (Ag) tossed Sybil (Rec) a coin (Pat/Th)

(12) Sybil (Rec) was tossed a coin (Pat/Th) (by Sydney [Ag])

(13) A coin (Pat/Th) was tossed Sybil (Rec) (by Sidney [Ag]) [British English only]

In the active sentences (7, 9, 11) the agent (Sidney) is subject and the theme or patient (the coin) is direct object. In the passive sentences (8, 10, 12, 13) the agent (Sidney) is expressed, if at all, in the optional *by*-phrase and either the patient/theme (coin) or the recipient (Sybil) is expressed as the subject. In these examples Sidney is always schematized as agent, Sybil as recipient and the coin as theme or patient. That is, a given framal participant always appears in the same semantic role. The different grammatical functions played by the noun phrases *Sidney*, *Sybil*, and *a coin* in (7)–(13) are therefore accounted for by differing assignments of theta-roles to grammatical functions. Hence, varying grammatical expression of framal participants may arise where framal participants are uniformly mapped onto thematic roles but thematic roles are differentially linked to grammatical functions by linking processes such as transitive, passive, oblique goal expression, and extra-object ("dative shift") constructions. These are not the cases in which we are primarily interested here, but their existence has to be established to serve as background for the cases we are interested in.[5]

There is another way in which a given framal participant may receive varying grammatical expression and this phenomenon is relevant to the issue of intra-speaker relativity. Here, mapping of thematic roles to grammatical functions is not at issue; rather the variation arises in the mapping of framal participants to thematic roles. Let us suppose that in some commercial event we wish to talk about Sidney is the seller, Sybil is the buyer, an armadillo constitutes the goods, and $50 is the money. Then, depending on whether we employ the verb *buy*, *sell*, or *pay*, we can say any of the following.

(14) a. Sidney sold the armadillo to Sybil for $50
　　 b. The armadillo was sold to Sybil for $50 (by Sidney)

(15) a. Sybil bought the armadillo from Sidney for $50
　　 b. The armadillo was bought (by Sybil) from Sidney for $50

(16) a. Sybil paid Sidney $50 for the armadillo
　　 b. $50 was paid to Sidney (by Sybil) for the armadillo

In (14) Sidney is the agent of *sell*; in (15) Sybil is the agent of *buy*. In (15) the armadillo is the patient/theme of *buy*, while in (16) $50 is the patient/ theme of *pay* and *Sidney* is a goal. The differences in grammar *within* each of examples (14), (15), and (16) are due to differential assignment of grammatical functions to thematic roles, but the differences in grammar *across* examples (14), (15), and (16) are due to **differential assignment of thematic roles to framal participants** by the verbs *buy*, *sell*, and *pay*.

Despite the fact, discussed in note 5, that thematic roles other than agents participate in the alternation transitive-subject/passive-*by*-phrase, we can be sure that in (14)–(16) we are dealing exclusively with agents in these grammatical functions. When the complement-taking main verb *have* subcategorizes for a nominal direct object and a non-finite verbal complement whose subject is controlled by the direct object of *have*, the verbal complement may appear either as a bare stem infinitive, as in (17), or as a gerundive phrase, as in (18).

(17) Sybil had Sidney choke the armadillo

(18) Sybil had Sidney choking the armadillo

In the bare stem infinitive case (17), both the matrix subject and the controlled subject of the verbal complement must be agents. Thus, (19a) is bad because the upstairs subject is not an agent and (20a) is bad because the downstairs (controlled) subject is not an agent.

(19) a. *His anger had Sidney choke the armadillo
    b. His anger had Sidney choking the armadillo

(20) a. *Sybil had the leash choke the armadillo
    b. Sybil had the leash choking the armadillo[6]

Applying this test to the verbs *buy*, *sell*, and *pay*, we see that each of them takes an agent as subject.

(21) Sybil had Sidney buy the armadillo for $50

(22) Sybil had Sidney sell the armadillo for $50

(23) Sybil had Sidney pay $50 for the armadillo

So we are satisfied that *buy*, *sell*, and *pay*, take agent subjects in active sentences (and agent *by*-phrases in passive sentences).

Now what does all this have to do with relativity? Each speaker of English can perspectivize a commercial event either in a way that takes the buyer as the agent, or in one of two ways that take the seller as the agent. When the seller is perspectivized as the agent, the goods are perspectivized as the patient/theme, as in (14). Moreover, when the buyer is perspectivized as the agent, either the goods, as in (15), or the money, as in (16), may be perspectivized as the patient/theme.

Further, there is another theta-perspective which can be imposed on the same scene, by the verb *cost*, and this perspective has no agent in it at all.

(24) The armadillo cost Sidney $50

(25) *$50 was cost(ed) Sidney by the armadillo

(26) *Sidney was cost(ed) $50 by the armadillo

(27) *Smiley had the armadillo cost $50

(28) Smiley had the armadillo costing $50

Thus, the semantics of English, as evidenced by the syntax of English, allows each speaker to take a variety of perspectives on every separate instance of the commercial event frame. A commercial event scene can be perspectivized with the buyer as agent (*buy*, *pay*), the seller as agent (*sell*), or no agent (*cost*). Just as *loosely speaking* and *technically* allow each speaker of English to take mutually opposed semantic perspectives on an act of referring, so the alternations among *buy*, *sell*, *pay*, and *cost* allow a single speaker to take a variety of semantic perspectives on each commercial event. Once again we see that the same kind of variation in semantic perspectivization that might be thought, when it is observed cross-linguistically, to indicate differences in world-view between the speakers of the languages in question, may exist within the semantic repertoire of a single speaker of a single language.

It might be argued, in fact has been, that the approach I have sketched to the semantics underlying the grammar of *buy*, *sell*, *pay*, and *cost* in terms of different theta-perspectives is not necessary or correct. One alternative view is that theta-roles are here, as elsewhere, unnecessary: the subcategorizational difference between, for example, *buy* and *sell* being simply that there is a content frame of "buyer" which is added to the commercial event frame in the first case and one of "seller" that is added to the commercial event frame in the second case. The essence of this argument is that there is a buying frame (possibly involving comparative shopping, etc.) and a selling frame (possibly involving advertising, or whatever) independently of the commercial event frame and that somehow these additional, superimposed frames determine the syntactic properties of the participants in the commercial event scene when unified with it, without necessitating recourse to the theoretical device of "thematic role."

However, it is hard to see how such an approach could explain in a non-circular way such alternations as *lend* and *borrow*: is it plausible to speak of a borrowing frame and an independent lending frame? What might count as evidence for such a claim? And it is difficult to envision how any such move could be extended to take care of alternations between varying theta-schematizations of a single morphological unit, such as *rent* versus *rent* or *lease* versus *lease*, as illustrated in the following.

(29) a. Sidney rented the apartment to Sybil
    b. The apartment was rented to Sybil (by Sidney)

(30) a. Sybil rented the apartment from Sidney
    b. The apartment was rented from Sidney (by Sybil)

(31) a. Sidney leased the apartment to Sybil
    b. The apartment was leased to Sybil (by Sidney)

(32) a. Sybil leased the apartment from Sidney
    b. The apartment was leased from Sidney (by Sybil)

There appears to be no escape from positing a multiplicity of semantic theta-perspectivizations to account for the variable syntax of the several verbs that attach to the commercial event frame. The grammar of commercial events in English seems to show that there is no monolithic world-view regarding these events, but rather that the language of each speaker allows him or her to take a variety of semantic perspectives on such events. Whorf said that the fact that English can treat *day* as a pluralizable count noun in an expression like *in ten days* indicates that English speakers, unlike Hopi speakers, who must say the equivalent of *on the tenth day*, using an unpluralizable (mass?) noun, *think* about days differently than the Hopi do (1956: 139). Yet Whorf failed to notice, it seems, that each individual English speaker can do it *either* way. If there is an important gulf of relativity that intervenes between the English and the Hopi speaker, does this same gulf intervene between the English speaker and himself?[7] The same question, I have suggested, can be asked about English speakers' grammar and thought about commercial events. Such events can be perspectivized in English in at least three different ways which involve an agent (*buy*, *sell*, *pay*) and at least one which does not involve an agent (*cost*).

4 *Spray, load* & co.

It might be objected to the preceding examples, regarding commercial events, that, after all, commercial events are relatively culture-specific institutions and a truly convincing example of intra-speaker relativity would have to involve a semantic domain or domains which might be presumed to be culturally universal. Such examples are not in fact hard to find. The first that comes to mind is the well known "*spray/load*" or "goal advancement" alternation illustrated in

(33) a. He loaded the dry hay onto the truck
    b. He loaded the truck with the dry hay

(34) a. She sprayed the leftover paint onto the wall
    b. She sprayed the wall with the leftover paint

There have been attempts to treat this alternation as akin to that between active and passive: that is, one in which the thematic roles remain the same and the grammatical functions to which they are assigned vary.[8] It has recently been suggested that none of these attempts has been successful,[9] and that we need to consider the alternations displayed between the (a) and (b) versions of examples such as (33) and (34), not as of the same kind as the active–passive alternation, where thematic roles are uniformly assigned to framal participants and variably linked to grammatical function, but rather like the alternation between *buy* and *sell*, *rent* and *rent*, or *lease* and *lease*, where the linking of grammatical functions with thematic roles remains constant but the assignment of thematic roles to framal participants varies. That is, I will defend the position that in (33) and (34) the direct objects are patients in *both* (a) and (b) versions, not patients in the (b) sentences and goals in the (a) sentences.

The first argument for this analysis is that in a sentence like (35a), which employs a verb that does not participate in the alternation, taking only the so-called goal-advanced valence but not the oblique goal valence,

(35) a. Sybil filled the truck with hay
     b. *Sybil filled hay onto the truck

it appears unquestionable that *the truck* realizes a patient role and *Sybil* an agent role. This fits with the appearance of *the truck* as subject in (non-dative) passives such as (36), the appearance of *Sybil* as the optional *by*-oblique in the passive (36) and the appearance of *Sybil* as controller of the subject of the *have* complement in bare infinitive form in (37).

(36) The truck was filled with hay (by Sybil)

(37) Sidney had Sybil fill the truck with hay

We note that *load*, which participates in the alternation while *fill* does not, behaves in these contexts just as *fill* does:

(38) a. The truck was loaded with hay (by Sybil)
     b. Sidney had Sybil load the truck with hay

On the other hand, a verb like *heave*, which treats *the truck* as goal in a sentence like (39a) (compare [33a]) allows the goal *truck* neither as transitive object (39b) nor passive subject (39c).

(39) a. Sybil heaved hay onto the truck
     b. *Sybil heaved the truck with hay
     c. *The truck was heaved with hay (by Sybil)
     d. *Sydney had Sybil heave the truck with hay

So, even though the truck is framally a receptacle (hence theta-perspectivizable as a location or goal) *the truck* behaves in (33) with the verb *load* just as it behaves in (35)–(37) with the verb *fill*, that is, as a patient.

A second argument for viewing the so-called *spray/load* alternation as a variation in assignment of thematic roles to participants, rather than as a variation in assignment of grammatical functions to thematic roles, is the following. A sentence like (33a), but not (33b), seems an appropriate answer to a question like "What happened to the hay?" while a sentence like (33b), but not (33a), seems an appropriate answer to a question like "What happened to the truck?" Similarly for the sentences in (34a, b). The reason for this seems to be that an essential part of the notion of patient consists in the idea of undergoing a change of state. In the (a) ("goal advanced") versions of these examples, the perspective taken on the event involves a change being wrought in the receptacle (truck or wall). In the (b) (oblique goal) versions, our impression is that the moved stuff, the hay or paint, is what is viewed as affected in the event. To the extent that such direct semantic intuitions and our feelings about what sentences can serve naturally as answers to what kind of questions can be counted as reliable data, these observations argue further for treatment of this alternation as one of theta-schematization rather than one of grammatical function linking.

A third argument for considering "goal advancement" to be a matter of theta-schematization rather than grammatical linking is the relative rarity of the alternation. In an unpublished study of the English verbs that occur in either the goal advanced or oblique valences, Rappaport & Levin (1985) found thirty-four verbs which participate in the alternation but an additional ninety-seven verbs which take only one of the two alternate subsategorization types. Since we are forced to posit the separate theta-schematizations to account for the ninety-seven non-alternating cases (69 percent), we get the alternative-theta-schematization analysis for free in the relatively few cases of verbs (31 percent) that do participate in the alternation.[10] Hence to posit an additional linking rule for the latter set is unmotivated as far as theoretical economy is concerned. Combined with the two preceding arguments, showing first that a linking solution will provide some possibly insurmountable technical problems and secondly that a linking solution violates our direct semantic intuitions and the testimony of our intuitions about natural question–answer pairs, this final argument, that the grammar of English will have to provide the separate theta-schematizations anyway to take care of the non-alternating verbs, appears decisive.

If the foregoing account of the goal advancement alternation in English is correct, each speaker of English is equipped with two opposed ways of talking about a certain subclass of events (apparently determined by the lexical verbs) in which someone moves some stuff to some receiving object.[11] This is presumably a type of event that can arise anywhere and that each language will consequently have to provide at least one way of talking about. In many languages there are in fact two ways: in one the moved stuff is treated as the affected thing and in the other the receptacle is treated as the affected thing. If two different ways of talking about an event amount to two different ways of thinking about that event or of understanding it, then each individual speaker of English is supplied by that language with two distinct ways of thinking about or understanding an event of this class. Yet this kind of varying "conceptualization" of a given type of event is exactly the sort of variability in "conceptualization" that Whorfians are wont to point to when the different "conceptualizations" belong to two different languages. Recall Whorf on *days* in Hopi and English. Again we see that following the terminological and theoretical practices of the committed relativist leads to the discovery of linguistic relativity internal to the isolated, monolingual speaker.

5 *Fear* versus *frighten*

There are a number of sets of predicators, verbal or adjectival, such as *fear* and *frighten*, *like* and *please*, *strike* and *notice*, in which the participant who undergoes the experience (of fear, liking, realization, etc.) may appear either as the subject of the transitive sentence (and the optional *by*-phrase of the corresponding passive): *fear*, *like*, *notice*, or as the object of the transitive sentence: *frighten*, *please*, *strike*.

(40) a. Sidney fears bears
     b. Bears are feared by Sidney
     c. Bears frighten Sidney
     d. Sidney is frightened by bears

(41) a. Sybil suddenly noticed that Sidney was weird
     b. That Sidney was weird was suddenly noticed by Sybil
     c. It was suddenly noticed by Sybil that Sidney was weird
     d. It struck Sybil suddenly that Sidney was weird
     e. That Sidney was weird suddenly struck Sybil
     f. Sybil was struck by it suddenly that Sidney was weird

In some earlier versions of transformational grammar these alternations were talked about in terms of a common deep structure underlying pairs of verbs like *fear* and *frighten* plus a transformation that interchanges subject and object before the lexical verb is inserted. There were a variety of technical problems involved with this transformation, which were never solved satisfactorily. Fillmore (1968), in introducing the notion of "deep case," which has now become the notion of semantic, thematic, or "theta"-role, suggested that these alternations, like several of those considered previously, not be treated as resulting from the assignment of distinct grammatical functions to semantically uniform objects[12] but as representing the assignment of distinct semantic perspectives to a single semantic scene. In particular, he posited not two but three distinct semantic roles: Experiencer, Content, and Stimulus. On this view, the *fear* examples (40a, b) and the *notice* examples (41a, b, c) have Experiencers as subjects and passive *by*-phrases and have Content arguments as objects and passive subjects, while the *frighten* examples (40c, d) and the *strike* examples (41d, e, f) have Stimulus arguments as active subjects and passive *by*-phrases and Experiencers as active objects and passive subjects. One argument Fillmore gave for this view is that all three roles can occur in a single clause.

(42) The bear frightened Sidney with its big claws

Here is another case in which an observed syntactic alternation is attributable, not to the mechanism that links grammatical functions to semantic roles, but to an alternation in how (syntactically linked) semantic roles are assigned by different lexical items to a constant predicate or frame. Again, the relevance to relativity is that the language provides the English speaker with alternate ways of perspectivizing an occasion of a bear and Sidney coming into contact with the result that Sidney experiences fright. In one case we can view the bear as the *content* of the fright experience; in the other as the *stimulus* of that experience. In the first case *the bear* denotes an object in the world; in the second *the bear* denotes an object in the internal representational world of Sidney. If English contained only predicates of the Stimulus-Experiencer (*frighten*, *please*, *strike*) type and an "exotic" language contained only predicates of the Experiencer–Content (*fear*, *like*, *notice*) type, the Whorfian might be strongly tempted to find here evidence for different world-views: say, one in which humans are viewed as passive recipients of sense impressions versus one in which humans actively construct the world they live in. Again we notice that English – and of course not only English – allows its speakers to talk *as if* they were committed to either of these "world-views." We are led to question thereby what actual psychological content is contained in the term *world-view*. I do not claim that world-view is a concept totally devoid of reference. I do wish to suggest that it is a concept whose unexamined application is not likely to help the anthropologist clarify the matters to which it is applied until its content has been subjected to more careful scrutiny.

6 Conclusion

We have considered cases in which different lexicalizations in a language can express two different kinds of semantic difference. In cases like the *strictly speaking/technically* contrast, the different lexicalizations represent different fundamental framings of the denotata. Thus, different truth judgments for the same situation arise depending on these variations in semantic framing, as we saw in examples (5) and (6).

In the other cases, we get differences in semantic perspective but not differences in truth judgments. Thus (14)–(16) don't say exactly the same thing, but they do have the same truth conditions. Both kinds of difference in semantic schematization have been advanced by the proponents of linguistic relativity as evidence that the languages of different peoples force them to actually experience reality in distinct ways. I have pointed out (perhaps too often) that each of these sets of opposed schematizations occurs within English.[13]

Do these observations on meaning in languages have anything useful to do with an understanding of cultures more generally? Well maybe not, but also maybe so. If we look upon the ensemble of primary lexical schemata plus theta-schematizations as a *repertoire*, rather than as a globally coherent system, perhaps we will find something useful for our understanding of cultures: that a culture does not provide its holders with a unified theory of the world – a "world-view" – any more than a language does. Rather, a culture consists in a large array of schemata for representing events and states in the world. Some of these conflict with others. Yet the conflict causes no problem to the culture's users because people do not *believe* the items of their culture, they *use* them as occasions permit and require. Accordingly, a culture is like a conceptual tool box, containing tools for making sense of the world. It is not the sort of thing that is itself supposed to make sense, any more than all the contents of a tool box need to be usable on each job.[14] One may fasten two boards either with screws or with nails. Similarly, on a particular occasion of speaking, one may schematize an event of reference either Frege-style, with *strictly speaking*, or Kripke–Putnam-style, with *technically*. The speaker who uses, say, *strictly speaking*, does not *ipso facto* make a philosophical commitment in support of Frege against Kripke and Putnam. Cultures do not have to comprise globally consistent world-views, because people never have to employ all of their culture at once. The potential conflicts cause no more trouble to actual people than does the fact that you can either nail two boards together or screw them together, but not both at the same time. If anthropologists had not assumed that the peoples they went out to study had "world-views," would they have found them? I don't pretend to know the answer to this question, but it seems worth asking.

What about linguistic and cultural relativity? Probably most languages contain many ways of schematizing most events or states. However, there is of course no guarantee that every language contains exactly the same range as every other. There might exist a kind of "relativity" here. There is the further problem of which schematizations are obligatory under which circumstances in different languages. It is a familiar problem of the translator's, for example, that it is relatively easy to render in the target language everything that was said in the original text, the problem is to render all *and only* what was said in the original text. This problem arises immediately and trivially, for example, in translating into a European language a text produced in a language that lacks obligatory tense, pluralization, etc., or in translating, say, an English or French text into a language that has a rich system of obligatory evidentials. The grammar insists on coding in the source language certain distinctions that, if coded in the translation, will often, for reasons of Gricean manner and relevance, imbue these details with undue importance. That is why translating will probably always remain an art and why there is much, I believe, to be learned about linguistic relativity from professional translators. In pursuing a deeper understanding of linguistic relativity, we might do well to remain aware, as every translator must be, of the large amount of alternative schematizing of a given event there is available within each language and hence within each speaker of that language.

Notes

1 I do not imagine that my personal experiences are of interest to the reader, but the anecdote about to be recounted is relevant to the argument of the paper.
2 I am indebted to Gerry McNulty for the observations on Montagnais.
3 Indeed, at the Ocho Rios conference John Lucy suggested, in response to this set of examples, that each ought properly to serve as the basis of an experimental undertaking to determine whether or not the linguistic difference is matched, *à la* Whorf, by a non-linguistic cognitive difference.
4 The type of situation illustrated in examples (5) and (6), in which there is a single, uncontroversial state of affairs at issue, is not to be confused with situations involving contrasting modalities, such as the following:

(a) Probably, it's false that they were guilty; possibly, it's true.

In examples like (a), what permits coherence is precisely that the different modal operators introduce contrasting states of affairs (distinct possible worlds), while in the case of (5) and (6) there is a unique and uncontested state of affairs at issue.

An attack on the point made by examples (5) and (6) which claimed that the former involves some kind of quotation would take on itself the burden of either (a) acknowledging that the notion of quotation in question applies equally to the ordinary use of proper names and natural kind terms or (b) explaining why this kind of quotation would characterize *technically* but not proper names and natural kind terms.

5 Other pairs of thematic roles participate in the active-passive alternation. In the following examples there are no agents and, in the first four of the six, no patients or themes.

(a) Sidney fears bears
(b) Bears are feared by Sidney
(c) Bears frighten Sidney
(d) Sidney is frightened by bears
(e) Sybil contracted malaria
(f) Malaria was contracted by Sybil

6 We know that it is correct to express the second constraint in terms of the downstairs subject – rather than the upstairs object, with which it corefers – because of examples like

(a) *Sybil had Sidney fall off the couch,

in which the complement verb doesn't allow its subject to express an agent. A verb like *choke* can, of course, take either agentive or non-agentive subjects, but a verb like *fall* accepts only a non-agentive subject. Thus, in (a) the sentence is only acceptable if, for example, Sybil is thought of as a stage director and Sidney's descent represents not real falling but an actor's deliberate simulation.

Actually, when the downstairs VP is passive, only agent (not, e.g., experiencer) *by*-phrases are possible.

(a) i *The tyrant had the executions seen (by the prisoners)
    ii The tyrant had the executions witnessed (by the prisoners),

demonstrating that the downstairs part of the constraint is more accurately stated as requiring an agent argument, rather than an agent subject *per se*.

7 Similarly, Whorf made a considerable fuss about SAE (Standard Average European) speakers' conceptually dividing up time into past, present, and future. But (as pointed out by Chomsky in lectures) Whorf apparently failed to notice that, although past, present, and future are doubtless important notional categories for Europeans in dealing with time, such a three-way contrast is not presented in the morphology or syntax of the English verb. Grammatically, past and present (or non-past) form a paradigmatic opposition in the morphology of English finite (main or auxiliary) verbs, whereas futurity is expressed uniquely in the modal system: *She sees* [present] *him, She saw* [past] *him, She will* [future] *see him*. The morpho-syntax of English verbal expressions does not present a three-way opposition between past, present, and future, however frequently a corresponding conceptual opposition may arise in the thought of speakers of English. A native Hopi-speaking linguist would find nothing in the grammar of English to correspond to the English speaker's exotic conceptual division of time into past, present, and future.

8 Although I will not argue the point here, I believe there is good evidence that the linking constructions, which provide the alternations between, e.g., transitive and passive or between oblique-goal and "dative" or "extra-object" valences (="subcategorization frames"), may provide additional semantic information, that is, that attached to these grammatical alternations there are differences in (perhaps non-truth-conditional) meaning. If this is correct the individual speaker of English is provided by the linking constructions with

further resources, beyond those arising from the opposing theta-schematizations, for communicating a variety of conceptualizations of a given commercial event scene.

English provides each speaker with an astonishing number of different ways of talking about a single commercial event scene. If one assumes that to each different way of talking about a thing there corresponds a distinct way of thinking about that thing, an undocumented but popular assumption among relativists, then *within* the English of an individual speaker there is probably as much relativity in how one can "think about" or "understand" commercial events as there is *between* speakers of any two languages in the world. And there is no reason to suppose that there is anything particularly special about English in this regard beyond the practical but irrelevant fact that any reader of this chapter knows it.

9 For discussion, see, for example, Ackerman (1989).

10 I am indebted to Adele Goldberg for this observation and for calling the Rappaport & Levin study to my attention. Of the ninety-seven verbs taking only one valence type, the *fill* type outnumbered the *heave* type seventy-seven to twenty.

11 Also *from* such an object:

(a) empty the tub of the dirty water
(b) empty the dirty water from the tub.

12 Or, as this was conceived at the time, as alternate "surface" representations of a single "deep" structure.

13 The list of examples could be extended indefinitely, for example by noticing that European languages, famous among anthropologists for their "linear" schematization of time, contain many lexical sets presupposing the "exotic" circular theory of time: days of the week, names of the seasons, months of the year.

Similarly, the "Chinese" version of the linear-space-to-linear-time metaphor, in which events move towards the speaker rather than the speaker moving through a landscape of events, is also represented in English. In the supposedly Chinese version, since the events are moving towards us, their direction imparts the metaphorical image of front to the earlier and back to the later event: hence past (earlier) events are talked of as in front of future (later) events. In English, this is not the most usual image, but its presence can be felt by noting that, for example, we can say

(a) Christmas precedes New Year,

although we say, according to our more usual image,

(b) Christmas is behind us, but New Year is still ahead of us.

Christmas is in front of New Year in (a) and behind in New Year in (b). English permits either perspective and, I am told, so does Chinese.

14 Charles Fillmore has used the image of a grammar as a set of tools for constructing texts.

References

Ackerman, F. 1989. Morpho-lexical relatedness in "spray/load" verb clusters: a Hungarian perspective. Ms., Department of Linguistics, University of California, San Diego.

Fillmore, C. J. 1968. *The case for case.* In E. Bach & R. Harms (eds.), *Universals in linguistic theory* (pp. 1–90). New York: Holt.
  1977. Topics in lexical semantics. In P. Cole (ed.), *Current issues in linguistic theory* (pp. 76–183). Bloomington: University of Indiana Press.
Kay, P. 1983. Linguistic competence and folk theories of language: two English hedges. In *Proceedings of the Ninth Annual Meeting of the Berkeley Linguistics Society* (pp. 128–37). Berkeley Linguistics Society.
Kripke, S. 1972. Naming and necessity. In D. Davidson & G. Harman (eds.), *Semantics of natural language.* Dordrecht: Reidel.
Lakoff, G. 1972. Hedges: a study in meaning criteria and the logic of fuzzy concepts. In *Papers for the Eighth Regional Meeting, Chicago Linguistics Society* (pp. 236–87). Chicago Linguistics Society.
Putnam, H. 1975. *Philosophical papers*, vol. II: *Mind, language and reality.* Cambridge University Press.
Rappaport, M. & Levin, B. 1985. A case study in lexical analysis: the locative alternation. Ms. Bar Ilan University and MIT.
Whorf, B. L. 1956. *Language, thought and reality: selected writings of Benjamin Lee Whorf*, ed. J. B. Carroll. Cambridge, MA: MIT Press.

5

IMAGING IN IRON, OR THOUGHT IS NOT INNER SPEECH

CHARLES M. KELLER AND JANET DIXON KELLER

Thinking is most mysterious, and by far the greatest light upon it that we have is thrown by the study of language. This study shows that the forms of a person's thoughts are controlled by inexorable laws of pattern of which he is unconscious. These patterns are the unperceived intricate systematization of his own language... His thinking itself is in a language – in English, in Sanskrit, in Chinese.   Whorf (1956: 252)

The linguistic relativity hypothesis in this strong form implies linguistic determinism: all thought is verbal or governed by patterns codified in the language one speaks. In what follows we argue that this position cannot be maintained. Mental activity occurs in diverse modes. Language, imagery, sensorimotor representation, and emotion are among the forms in which ideas can be constructed, manipulated, and revised. Each of these cognitive modalities is a distinct system involving multiple information-processing components operating independently as well as interactively. The extent to which these complex systems, in turn, interpenetrate one another is an open question, and one we will address in part herein. Independent forms of information processing must be integrated in perception and conceptualization in a variety of ways. However, there is no reason to assume that language dominates the integrative processes or to assume that imagery, sensorimotor or other cognitive representations are rooted in linguistic patterns. A variety of different kinds of evidence for multiple modes of mental activity lead us to suggest that thought is more complex than can adequately be accounted for by a relativistic position that entails linguistic determinism. We leave open the question of the influence of language in structuring thought for expression in linguistic form, a question effectively addressed by other authors in this volume.

First of all, we note that evolutionarily vision and visual imagery are prior to language. Binocular stereoscopic vision is an ancient feature in the primate lineage and non-human primates have the capacity to generate and manipulate visual images (Wynn 1989). There is no reason to assume that this mode of information processing changes radically with the emergence of linguistically facile humans. The same is true of sensorimotor representation which is obviously prior to linguistic representation in evolutionary terms. On analogy with the ontogenetic arguments of Vygotsky that some forms of thinking remain independent of speech even into adulthood (Lucy 1988), we suggest that, even after the appearance of language in evolution, alternate forms of conceptual representation remain structurally and functionally independent.

Secondly, research with aphasic patients demonstrates that localized trauma to the brain frequently results in selective disabilities. Localized lesions which result in linguistic disabilities do not necessarily impair visual, motor or emotive representation, suggesting these capacities involve discrete information-processing systems.

Thirdly, developmental evidence also argues for distinct information-processing systems with independent maturational sequences. The visual cortex is one of the first areas of the human cortex to attain a mature and relatively stable number of synaptic connections in ontogenetic development. The human being is born with an immature brain. One indication of this immaturity is the number of established synaptic connections. Distinct regions of the adult brain are characterized by distinctive, typical frequencies of synaptic connections. While particular connections are formed or dissipate throughout life, the absolute number remains relatively constant once maturity is reached. By about the age of two the regions of the brain associated with visual perception and image generation have developed a normal adult number of synaptic links (Greenough, Black, & Wallace 1987). The frontal regions of the brain, perhaps involved in planning tasks, by contrast, take ten to fourteen years to reach this level of synaptic complexity (1987). This developmental evidence suggests that if there is a primacy in the relations between cognitive processing modes in a normal individual, visual competence would be instrumental in the development of higher cognitive processing. Sensorimotor areas of the brain also appear to develop early as indicated by measures of cortical thickness reflecting the density of synaptic connections (1987). The timing of the development of synaptic linkages in the temporal lobes primarily associated with language is yet to be established. Our hypothesis is that this development will come considerably later than visual or sensorimotor development. Yet in the absence of neurophysiological measures, scholars, quite different in their theoretical positions, have distinguished linguistic and practical intelligence and have noted the influences of each form of intelligence on the other. The importance of object manipulation and motor activity for the normal process of language acquisition has been noted. In addition, language provides an impetus for development of practical intelligence beyond the earliest stages (Bruner 1966, Vygotsky 1978, Piaget 1955). While cognitive development appears to be a process involving increasing potential for convergence and integratlon of discrete forms of information, the fundamental independence of the mental faculties persists into adulthood.

Our fourth argument is derived from recent research in lexical semantics. Lakoff (1987), Johnson (1987), and Lakoff & Johnson (1980) have recently indicated that skeletal image schemata are crucial elements of categorization and lexical semantics. Lakoff analytically opposes propositional to imaginative models (1987: 117) and argues for an experientialist basis to abstract, propositional reasoning which is rooted in visual images (1987: 267). In *The body in the mind*, Johnson (1987) argues for a model of abstract reasoning based on schematic images derived from bodily representations (motor and motor-based visual schemata). Hunn (1985), in a somewhat different vein, argues for an activity signature (a representation of practical utility) as a basic conceptual component of biological categories. Hunn is not specific about the cognitive form of this activity signature which may be a complex integration of different sorts of information. However, his discussions indicate that visual and motor elements are crucial entailments. These accounts of meaning reverse the relations of cognitive priority hypothesized by Sapir and Whorf and mandate a dynamic approach to word meaning and thought more generally, involving interactive, modular components.

Comparative research focusing on linguistic and visual representations of spatial relations (Jackendoff 1989, Talmy 1983) provides further support for the independence of visual and linguistic processing systems. Grammatical indicators of spatial qualities and relations, such as prepositions and perhaps numeral classifiers, provide the means for distinguishing a limited inventory of schematic arrangements of points, axes, and trajectories. This creates a grammatically codified "skeletal conceptual microcosm" (Talmy 1983: 227) which structures and limits the expression of spatial information in language. These limited, primarily topological arrangements appear to be correlated with a subset of primitive units of the visual locational system (Jackendoff 1991). However, it is the visual elements which appear to motivate the linguistic distinctions, not the reverse. Further, despite the overlap in this subset of basic elements, in the linguistic and visual systems, higher-order conceptual representations are constructed independently in each system and significantly involve nonoverlapping sets of conceptual distinctions. The higher-order representations which emerge in each mode are noncomparable and facilitate distinct human activities.

There is further evidence for functional specificity of the distinct representational forms. Pinker & Bloom (1990) point out that the information which language is designed to convey is a well-defined set.

"Grammar is a notoriously poor medium for conveying subtle patterns of emotion," they argue. "Facial expressions and tones of voice are more informative. And although grammars provide devices for conveying rough topological information ... and coarse metric contrasts ..., they are of very little help in conveying precise Euclidean relations: a picture is worth a thousand words" (1991: 715).

The same argument has been made by Anthony F. C. Wallace in his industrial ethnography, *Rockdale*, wherein he argues:

The machinist thought with his hands and eyes and when he wished to learn to communicate he made a drawing or a model; the manufacturer and manager thought with his larynx, as it were, and when he wished to learn or communicate, did so with words, in conversation or in writing. The machinists had dirty hands from working with tools; the manager had cramped hands from writing.

(1978: 212)

Here Wallace is arguing for the primacy of imagery and activity in the thought associated with productive activity. This is echoed by Ferguson, a historian of technology, in his discussion of the thought processes involved in engineering design: "Many features and qualities of the objects that a technologist thinks about cannot be reduced to unambiguous verbal descriptions; they are dealt with in his mind by a visual, nonverbal process" (1977: 827).

Within cognitive science too it has frequently been argued that a distinction needs to be made between declarative knowledge, that which is readily articulated in linguistic form, and skill, ineffable performative patterns and representations (Anderson 1982, Dougherty & Keller 1982, Gatewood 1985, Kolers & Smythe 1979). In his discussions of imagery Kosslyn (1981) develops a version of such an argument: "Images make explicit information about relative shapes/positions and appearances. Thus when these sorts of information are required in order to make a judgement, imagery will often be used." Kosslyn argues further that "imagery is most likely to be used when relatively subtle comparisons are required, for example in deciding which is smaller, a hamster or a mouse. Both are propositionally SMALL but imagery can make finer distinctions" (1981). In the production of (novel) tangible items such fine distinctions essential to the thought process are beyond referential possibilities encoded by general purpose labels (Dougherty & Keller 1982). Skillful production, particularly of novel material items, creates precisely those conditions under which generation and manipulation of images is requisite.

While some decisions in design and production may depend upon scientific calculations, the nonscientific component of design is primary. "It rests largely on the nonverbal thought and nonverbal reasoning of the designer, who thinks with pictures" (Ferguson 1977: 828). Anthony F. C.

Wallace makes the same point in his discussion of "Thinking about machinery":

> The work of the mechanician was, in large part, intellectual work. This was true in spite of the fact that he dealt with tangible objects and physical processes, not with symbols, and that some of what he did was done with dirty hands. The thinking of the mechanician in designing, building and repairing tools and machinery had to be primarily visual and tactile. (1978: 237)

Based upon the evidence introduced above, we argue that imagery and sensorimotor representations constitute basic forms of mental activity which may predominate in certain human activities such as design and production of material artifacts. These systems of information processing constitute distinct forms of conceptual thought and reasoning which may be integrated at various points with linguistic representations, but which are not thereby determined by linguistic structures.

1 Focusing on imagery in productive activity

We will briefly consider evidence from interviews with a blacksmith/ knife-maker in Southern Illinois which allows us to clarify the independence of imagery and sensorimotor representations in productive activity and to demonstrate the potential relationship of representations in these modes to language. Comparable research is available in the literature. For example, Gatewood (1985) demonstrated the place of visual, motor, and emotive representation in the thinking typical of salmon fishermen involved in seining activities or reflecting on these activities. Anthony F. C. Wallace (1978) has similarly addressed the thought of industrial machinists. Ferguson (1977), Hindle & Lubar (1986), and Pye (1978) have illustrated the role of visual spatial thinking in design.

The knife-maker whom we interviewed works alone in his forge when producing his knives. Language is of minimal importance in the productive process as observations and interviews in this case and in previous studies of blacksmithing indicate (Dougherty & Keller 1982, Keller & Keller 1993). In making a knife, the productive process itself is primarily visual and sensorimotor. To cite Wallace again, "In this mode of cognition, language is auxiliary" (1978: 238). In discussing stages preparatory to actually forging a knife blade, the blacksmith says, "I have to get a concrete visualization of the knife going, because I'm going to be out there shaping it with the hammer. I'm dealing with dimensions." He constructs an "umbrella plan" including a design image, prior to initiating production (Keller & Keller 1993). Once production of the blade has begun a dynamic interaction between imagery and material developments guides the production process.

1.1 Making a blade

Our informant makes his knives by forging a piece of steel to an intermediate form which he then grinds to the final shape and dimensions. Forging is used for the initial stages partly because of the predilections of the smith and partly because of the salutary effect it has on the crystalline structure of the steel. Grinding is done in two phases, one before heat-treating the blade to harden and temper it and the second after heat-treatment to achieve the final shape and surface finish. Our discussion here will treat primarily the forging phase, although the requirements of the later phases of production are always constraining factors in the forging process.

The material with which the smith begins the production process is a bar of high carbon steel and in some cases a cardboard or sheet metal template of the desired blade. Since the forging involves either transformation or removal of material from the developing blade, it is important that the original bar have sufficient mass from which to derive the full dimensions of the final blade form. The bar will be thicker by some amount than the desired thickness of the final form, narrower than the final form at its widest point, long enough to provide sufficient mass for the finished length of the forged blade, and perhaps long enough to furnish a convenient handle to use while heating and forging.

The first phase of forging forms the tang of the blade which will ultimately be covered with the handle. Next the length of the finished blade is marked on the anvil with chalk, and if the bar is significantly thicker than the desired thickness of the blade the bar is rough-forged to a closer approximation of the completed knife. Finally the amount of stock required for the blade is estimated in comparison with the chalk mark, the template or "by eye" and the excess steel is cut off the bar.

The smith explains that a blade is a "double wedge." It tapers from ricasso to point and from back to cutting edge. The first of these wedges to be formed is the one which runs from the ricasso to the tip. Beginning at the ricasso, which will be the thickest portion of the blade, the stock is drawn

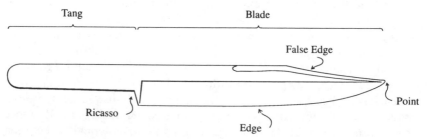

Fig. 5.1   *Knifeblade with significant components indicated*

out. It is gradually reduced in thickness which lengthens the stock while the original width is maintained. A "rudimentary point" is formed by reducing the thickness and width near the tip of the blade. This results in an increase in length to slightly more than the desired finished dimension.

Moving back to the ricasso area, the smith begins to form the second wedge, the taper from the back to what will ultimately be the cutting edge of the knife. Each hammer stroke widens and thins the blade but also stretches the steel a small amount along the blade's length. As a result the incipient cutting edge, which is the area thinned to the greatest degree, is stretched the most and the blade instead of remaining straight begins to curve upward. In order to remove this undesired curve the blade is forged back to straight at the conclusion of each sequence of heating and tapering. A concern in this process is to keep the point in its desired location in relation to the long axis of the blade.

Once the second wedge is completed, the blade straight and the point in the correct position in relation to the midline of the blade, the forging phase is complete and the smith is ready to begin grinding.

1.2 Mental representations for production

Throughout this procedure the smith uses imagery in several different ways: the umbrella plan or design image serves as a mutable standard against which progress in material production is evaluated; abstract referential schemata including representations of a wedge, straightness, perpendicularity and balance, serve in design and evaluation of productions; set-up images provide sequential steps requisite to achieving the ultimately anticipated form such as production of the rudimentary point. These images integrate visual and sensorimotor information in representations which combine a simultaneous visual arrangement with sequentially ordered procedural knowledge. These images are not "enactive representations" (Bruner 1966), fused sensorimotor/perceptual representations predominating in early child-hood. They are, rather, learned, often over long periods of time, and more or less purposefully constructed during the acquisition process. Such visual and/or sensorimotor images may alter over time and are accessible to other representational forms.

The design image, which is a representation of the particular knife being made, involves schematic images of segments, their relative positions and stylistic properties and representation of quantities and qualities of material. As the smith has said, "I'm dealing with *dimensions*" (our emphasis). While he knows how long the finished knife is supposed to be, any material template will be two-dimensional and gives no indication of thickness. So the smith's initial judgment of how much of a bar will be required to make a blade is based on his design image which represents how thick the blade will be and what its stylistic properties are.

With respect to blade thickness, the smith rough-forges to the desired size and when "by eye it looks about right" he refers to the mark on the anvil and cuts off the excess. Here he is referring to a mental image when he decides the rough-forging resulted in the adequate thickness and then to a concrete, perceptual image when he refers to the mark on the anvil.

Another aspect of the design image is the relative position of various segments. This involves, for example, the relationship between the point and the midline of the blade as mentally represented. This image schema is constantly referred to during production.

In addition to the design image the smith also relies on mental images of abstract properties such as wedge, axis, straightness, midline, symmetry, and balance. The blade is constantly evaluated against these representations and corrected if it deviates too far from the mentally held standard. For example, as the blade is tapered from ricasso to tip forging blows must be alternated between the two faces of the blade in order to keep it straight, a process monitored by reference to an abstract image of straightness and sensorimotor representations of balance. The smith focuses on creating an appropriate wedge as he tapers the long axis. He says, "I have to keep in mind...[whether] it is a heavy knife or a light knife." Anticipations based on this kind of imagery are violated when one picks up an object thought to be solid but which is in fact hollow and it "jumps" off the table, or when an object one expects to be balanced feels unequally weighted. For the smith in this case, sensorimotor imagery has to do with how it feels to hold a "heavy" or "light" blade, and how a balanced and symmetrical blade feels as well as how these qualities look. The judgments made while forging the initial taper are based on complex sensorimotor as well as visual images. As Gatewood has argued in discussing the knowledge and practices of fishermen, "one experiences visual imagery and muscular tensions appropriate to certain actions" (1985:206) both in reflecting upon these activities and in anticipating or performing them.

The forging process also involves several discrete images of each stage of production. The tang is forged, blade rough-forged, blade tapered, rudimentary point formed, and the back-to-edge taper established. None of these are precisely in the form they will exhibit in the finished knife. They are intermediate strips which allow the smith to proceed to the final form with the maximum degree of certainty and with minimum effort. These intermediate stages are often called set-ups by blacksmiths. So the smith must carry in his head a repertoire of set-up images against which he can periodically evaluate the work at hand to decide whether it is "done" and he can move to the next stage, or whether more work at the current stage is necessary.

The shape of the blade prior to grinding is one such set-up, albeit a complex one involving a series of prior set-up stages. It is toward the set-up image of the final pregrinding shape that the smith works in forging the blade. He does not aim directly to produce the finished shape, although he also holds an image of the complete blade in mind, but he aims rather to produce a shape which can subsequently be ground to the desired final form.

The images crucially involved in the production of iron artifacts may integrate linguistically represented knowledge with the visual and sensorimotor information. Interviews with smiths and performance of forging tasks lead us to hypothesize that the integrative process is not one of translating visual and sensorimotor formulations into linguistic expression nor vice versa. Neither is the fit between the linguistic and the visual or sensorimotor information such that translation across the representations is a simple process. Rather, different sorts of information are made available through the distinct representational forms. For example, Kosslyn has argued that "The more overlearned a concept is the more likely that a propositional encoding will be primary. Thus imagery is often used to retrieve information learned incidentally such as the number of windows in a room" (Kosslyn 1981: 54). We would add that imagery is often used in the production of novel forms as well where standard linguistic concepts are insufficiently detailed. Sensorimotor representations predominate where performative skills are involved. Kolers & Smythe (1979: 168) have indicated "in perceptuo-motor skills, language by itself rarely, if ever, can aid a performance that must be inculcated by practice." Information from each representational mode, the sensorimotor, the visual, and the linguistic, is functionally appropriate to distinct aspects of production, and therefore predominates at different points in the productive process.

2 The interaction of language and imagery in design

Having made the above claims, we wish to explore integrated cognitive functioning in the process of design. However, in looking at the dynamics of cross-modal information processing we need to focus clearly on the distinctive operations together with their complex interactions. Production, as we have argued, is governed largely by visual and sensorimotor representations. In design, however, for the knife-maker interviewed for this paper, language is important, not as the Sapir–Whorf hypothesis would have us understand it, that is as a structural foundation, but rather as an instrument.

The design process in the case we examined requires verbal interaction, typically over the phone. It is because this communicative dimension is introduced that language is drawn into the design process. Our conversations suggest that in the design stage of his activity, this knife-maker uses language as a tool to retrieve, construct, and manipulate visual images. In this process standard terms arise which are given contextually unique visual interpretations. Such interpretations are not the skeletal image schemata discussed by Lakoff and Johnson. Nor are they culturally normative activity signatures discussed by Hunn although this concept gets closer to their nature. Nor yet are they limited to standard prototype representations. The shared terminology, the specialists' lexicon, allows the knife-maker and his client to select and construct in common potentially novel visual vignettes with inherent design and production implications. What we are documenting here is the relationship between cognitive modes in a convergence zone (Blakeslee 1991) which has been referred to in the literature as the mind's eye or the 3-D image (Jackendoff 1989; Kosslyn 1980; Marr 1982; Ferguson 1977). Linguistic forms and images are reciprocally accessible and in interactive functioning can be mutually constitutive.

When designing a blade by phone in the absence of an immediate way to communicate through drawing, the smith "translates a picture held in his mind" (Ferguson 1977: 828) into words intended to produce "a similar picture in another mind" (p. 828). Rather than the terms or grammatical structures driving the design process, linguistically coded information functions instrumentally to evoke visualizations which provide a basis for interactive product design. Imagery, in the design process, is rich, immediate, and consciously manipulable. The design process is analytical, but the terms of the analysis are primarily visual and sensorimotor. Following is one excerpt from our interview in which the relations of word and image are illustrated.

JK: What if someone calls you and they have a sense of what they want. How do you get to the point where you know what they really want, to the point of actually having a design that you know will satisfy them?

Knife-maker: Pretty easy ... In order to get to the design there are categories of knives ... like *drop points, upswept, trailing point*. These are terms that are used in the conversation that are mutually understood.

JK: Understood in terms of what?

KM: I have in mind what I think a *trailing point* is. It may not be exactly what he thinks it is but there's enough design conformity or uniformity in the term that we have a starting point. For example. [A prospective buyer says] I would like a knife. [I ask] What kind of knife are you interested in? I make a *Bowie*. [The buyer responds] Well, I don't want a Bowie, I want a *boot knife*.

KM: He said not a *bowie* I want a *boot knife* so immediately in my mind I get a picture of a different style of knife.

JK: Do you have in mind a specific design?

KM: No, I don't have a specific design, but I have some ideas in general so how do I go about getting those ideas which are not well formed and he doesn't know how to present them but he'll know it when he sees it? . . . Through the telephone especially, we have to mutually design . . . understand visually . . . that can be tough.

Note the knife-maker's shift in his description of the design process from *easy*, when he is referring to the prototypically defined lexicon, to *tough*, when he begins to deal in the specifics of a particular spatial–visual design.

Following the early stage in his conversation with a client the knife-maker will begin to break the product down into different features and dimensions and he and his client speak of *full tang, half tang, trailing point, drop point, length* . . . all visually represented features. The conversation moves from the general level of generic styles to discussion of the prototypical features to which conventional labels are applied in an attempt to transcend those very prototypes in the process of developing increasing specificity. As the process proceeds, the knife-maker reports that he and a client grapple to find labels for the developing visual segments. The argument that thinking is in language in this process or that language is the medium of conceptual thought is only superficially true. The communicative process prioritizes the linguistic interface, particularly so because of the long-distance nature of the interaction. Words are selected to highlight visual properties central to constructed images. It is the images, which have an essential relationship to the material properties at issue, which are the real subject of this conversation and in terms of which design proceeds. Language is being used as an instrument to facilitate construction and communication of images not as an *a priori* set of limiting possibilities. Language here exemplifies Clark's (this volume) notion of a co-ordinating device. The particular features of a linguistic category relevant in the context of an emerging design may be vague at the outset and negotiated in the design process. It is the contextualized images which give the words of the standard knife lexicon immediate and concrete specifications (F. K. Lehman, Robert Borofsky personal communications) .

As a design becomes increasingly specific, the standard knife lexicon is increasingly inadequate to the process. Key words emerge at this point in the interactive design process to facilitate reference to novel, emergent properties or configurations. In her research on American marriage, Quinn (1985) argues for the central role of "scenario words" in organizing knowledge. She further points out that "one important way in which cultural understanding comes to be shared, and the way in which the knowledge embedded in the scenario words is shared, is through learning to speak a common language." This she argues is an "unabashedly Whorfian claim" (1985: 292). In our conversations with a knife-maker, he himself argues for the importance of words, yet when we look closely at how language functions in blade design, evidence for a Whorfian claim eludes us.

Following is a segment of reported dialogue.

KM: Key words come up in the conversation that tell me how to design the knife. If he [a client] says he wants to *pry* with it, I'll build a knife a little heavier.

JK: What do you mean by the words tell you how?

KM: They tell me a story. [If the fellow says] "I *break* knives." *Break* is the word I hear. It's the word the customer wants me to hear. What he's telling me is: "Don't make me a knife I can break." I know this guy is h . . . on knives so I have to make one that is very thick.

KM: Most of the time a guy will tell me an anecdote. I will see the story that he's telling me . . . I actually visualize what he's telling me. Suppose it's a collector who says "I've got two or three of this other guy's work and they're *sleek*." When the man says *sleek* I think to myself . . . well I do translate it into visual. I actually see an obvious transition. I see that there's going to be a lot of taper beginning in front of the guard going toward the tip. So even though he would use a word like *sleek* which doesn't give you much and it's not a full anecdote which gives you a story. I actually do go over to a visual image.

There are words that trigger in me a visualization. I have a customer in Chicago who over a period of time has told me about several knives. He's a knife-maker. He wanted a big knife and he used the word *massive*. When he said to me "I want the thing massive" then immediately I say "You mean you want this thing 3/8″ thick and he says "Yeah, and maybe 1 3/4″ or 2″ wide." Immediately he started giving the specific information that he had, but if he hadn't said *massive* and I hadn't responded by saying something specific . . . Immediately I went over to the specifics of it . . . because I have to get a concrete visualization of the knife going.

In this interview segment, the knife-maker himself argues for the importance of key words as instruments of interactive design. The words, however, far from structuring the design process, facilitate the construction of shared images by pointing to material properties which are the essence of the conversation. The words do not control or determine the configuration of the images but are themselves configured by reference to the vignettes and their material implications. These terms, which the smith himself refers to as key, are not central to the design process because of their guiding role in thought, but because of their instrumental role in communication. These words are not sufficiently rich in definitional features to guide the design process. Rather, typical or defining features of these terms are selectively highlighted and contextually specified. Participants negotiate their non-linguistic significance. *Sleek*, for example, by reference to exemplars, comes to signify "an obvious transition," "a lot of taper." In this process words are functioning at the interface between cognitive systems and at the interface between minds. The individual (and ultimately the shared) thought constituting the design process both motivates and transcends the instrumental use of language.

3 The mind's eye

We conclude that thinking occurs in diverse modes each of which may function independently in some contexts and all of which may function interactively to at least some degree. We have no evidence to argue for a hierarchical arrangement of these modes. This claim is not new. In *Mind in society* Vygotsky pointed out that even "very small children solve problems using unique mixtures of processes" (1978: 29). Among the scholars cited in this chapter, Wallace, Pye, Ferguson, Jackendoff, Slobin, and Kosslyn have all recognized the existence of independent cognitive processing modes and their differential functionality. What have not been recognized it seems are the implications of diverse cognitive processes for linguistic determinism. Slobin (1979) argued two decades ago that relations between language and cognition more generally required study. He posed two directions for research which are mandated anew by the discussion here. "(1) If we view language as one of many forms of mental representation we must explore the various forms and ask how they are interrelated . . . (2) If we view language as one of the tools of thought, we must examine the ways in which that 'tool' influences cognitive processes."

Clearly, thoughts as linguistically formulated can influence imaging processes. We noted in an earlier paper (Keller & Keller 1993) that a smith will visualize productive strategies differently according to whether he prefers to "think hot" or "think cold." Pylyshyn (1981, 1984) refers to the influence of language on other cognitive modes such as imagery as "cognitive penetrability" documenting the phenomenon extensively. However, what is less often emphasized is that "spatial images and other forms of picturing may operate on our linguistic descriptions to aid our understanding" (Kolers & Smythe 1979: 171); "a good image may in fact help to solve a problem" just as "constructing an inappropriate spatial metaphor can, like adhering to a poor linguistic metaphor, block problem solving" (1979: 171).

We are positing a set of modular information-processing systems (Jackendoff 1989) and convergence zones where information is integrated in conceptualizations which provide the input for action and which are accessible by haptic, visual, linguistic, and sensorimotor modalities. The nature of the code in terms of which distinct forms of information are integrated remains a significant question. However, we find no evidence at this stage to argue that this code is linguistic.

Unless we define thought at the outset as verbal representation and turn the Sapir–Whorf hypothesis into a tautology, it is clear that the presence of independent modes of information processing should direct us to the study of these distinctive mental systems: their representational forms and functionality; and to the study of principles of reciprocal interactions and integrated conceptual representations without any assumption of priority for one mode of thought or another. Whether each cognitive modality – imaging, language processing, sensorimotor representation, might be independently relative – is another question and one which is provocatively addressed by many of the scholars contributing to this volume.

References

Anderson, J. R. 1982. Acquisition of cognitive skill. *Psychological Review*, 89, 369–406.

Blakeslee, S. 1991. Brain yields new clues in its organization for language. *New York Times*, Thursday, 10 September, B5.

Bruner, J. 1966. On cognitive growth. In J. Bruner, R. Oliver, & P. Greenfield (eds.), *Studies in cognitive growth*. New York, John Wiley & Sons.

Dougherty, J. W. D. & Keller, C. 1982. Taskonomy: a practical approach to knowledge structures. *American Ethnologist*, 9(4), 763–74.

Ferguson, E. S. 1977. The mind's eye: nonverbal thought in technology. *Science*, 197(4306), 827–36.

Gatewood, J. 1985. Actions speak louder than words. In J. W. D. Dougherty (ed.), *Directions in cognitive anthropology* (pp. 199–220). Urbana-Champaign: University of Illinois Press.

Greenough, W. T., Black, J. E., & Wallace, C. S. 1987. Experience and brain development. *Child Development*, 58, 539–59.

Hindle, B. & Lubar, S. 1986. *Engines of change: the American Industrial Revolution 1790–1860*. Washington: Smithsonian Institution Press.

Hunn, E. 1985. The utilitarian factor in folk biological classification. In J. W. D. Dougherty (ed.), *Directions in cognitive anthropology* (pp. 117–40). Urbana-Champaign: University of Illinois Press.

Jackendoff, R. 1989. *Consciousness and the computational mind.* Cambridge, MA: MIT Press.

1991. Language as a window into spatial cognition. Lecture presented at the Beckman Institute, University of Illinois, Urbana.

Johnson, M. 1987. *The body in the mind.* University of Chicago Press.

Keller, C. & Keller, J. 1993. Thinking and acting with iron. In S. Chaiklin & J. Lave (eds.), *Understanding practice: perspectives on activity and context* (pp. 125–43). Cambridge University Press.

Kolers, P. A. & Smythe, W. E. 1979. Images, symbols and skills. *Canadian Journal of Psychology*, 33(3), 158–84.

Kosslyn, S. M. 1980. *Image and mind.* Cambridge, MA: Harvard University Press.

1981. The medium and the message in mental imagery: a theory. *Psychological Review*, 88(1), 46–66.

Lakoff, G. 1987. *Women, fire and dangerous things: what categories reveal about the mind.* University of Chicago Press.

Lakoff, G. & Johnson, M. 1980. *Metaphors we live by.* University of Chicago Press.

Lucy, J. 1988. The role of language in the development of representation: a comparison of the views of Piaget and Vygotsky. *Quarterly Newsletter of the Laboratory of Comparative Human Cognition*, 10(4), 99–103.

Marr, D. 1982. *Vision.* San Francisco: W. F. Freeman & Co.

Piaget, J. 1955. *The language and thought of the child.* New York: Meridian Books.

Pinker, S. & Bloom, P. 1990. Natural language and natural selection. *Behavioral and Brain Sciences*, 13, 707–84.

Pye, D. 1978. *The nature and aesthetics of design.* London: Barrie & Jenkins Ltd.

Pylyshyn, Z. 1981 The imagery debate: analogue media versus tacit knowledge. *Psychological Review*, 88, 16–45.

1984. *Computation and cognition.* Cambridge, MA: MIT Press.

Quinn, N. 1985. "Commitment" in American marriage: a cultural analysis. In J. W. D. Dougherty (ed.), *Directions in cognitive anthropology* (pp. 291–320). Urbana-Champaign: University of Illinois Press.

Slobin, D. I. 1979. *Psycholinguistics* (2nd edn.). Glenview, IL: Scott, Foresman, & Co.

Talmy, L. 1983. How language structures space. In H. Pick & L. Acredolo (eds.), *Spatial orientation: theory, research and application* (pp. 225–320). New York: Plenum Press.

Vygotsky, L. S. 1978 [1930–4]. *Mind in society: the development of higher psychological processes.* Cambridge, MA: Harvard University Press.

Wallace, A. F. C. 1978. *Rockdale.* New York: Alfred A. Knopf.

Whorf, B. L. 1956 [1942]. Language, mind, and reality. In: *Language, thought, and reality: selected writings of Benjamin Lee Whorf*, ed. J. B. Carroll. Cambridge, MA: MIT Press.

Wynn, T. 1989. *The evolution of spatial competence.* Urbana-Champaign: University of Illinois Press.

PART II
UNIVERSALS AND VARIATION
IN LANGUAGE AND CULTURE

INTRODUCTION TO PART II

STEPHEN C. LEVINSON

In the introduction to part I we proposed, in connection with the discussion of linguistic determinism, the following sort of syllogism, which represents in its simplest form the hypothesis of linguistic relativity:

(1) languages vary in semantic structure;
(2) semantic categories determine aspects of individual thinking;

therefore

(3) aspects of individuals' thinking differ across linguistic communities according to the language they speak.

In part I we were concerned largely with the evidence for premise (2). In this section we are concerned with the assessment of premise (1).

We noted that, even if there are only slight differences across languages in semantic structure, this together with even the weakest version of (2) will justify (3). Thus some weak conclusion like (3) is almost certainly tenable. Interest now turns to how strong and how systematic such effects on individual thinking might be. Much depends here on how different the semantic structure of languages actually is. The versions of linguistic relativity that have most captured the imagination have been those in which it is supposed that, immanent in the categories of the language, there are semantic parameters or conceptual axes that structure a coherent "world-view," built on different lines from our own (see Hill 1988, Hill & Mannheim 1992 for review).

There is a strong current of thought that goes in the other direction. Thus, it may be claimed, the Kantian categories of space, time, cause, and so on, form the fundamental ground of our reasoning; they cannot be inferred from experience, but are what we bring to the interpretation of experience from our biological endowment. Thus the conceptual architecture, the essential conceptual parameters, are, as Leibniz would have it, "innate ideas." This line of thought dominates current speculations in the cognitive sciences. It is a view reinforced from many quarters: evolutionary biology and neurophysiology stress the closeness of our neurological equipment to that of our mammalian cousins, studies of human development (following Piaget) assume an unfolding of inborn potential, psychological models of processing are often presumed to be models of "hardware" properties rather than models of learned or acquired tendencies or "software,"[1] and so on. In linguistics, the adoption of natural science ideals has led to the search for universals without parallel concern for language differences. Anthropology however remains largely outside this current of thought: viewed from cognitive science it is a reactionary output of empiricist ideas, with an outmoded stress on human ideational difference and the importance of environmental learning.

In this section we collect some dissenting voices. A psychologist and an anthropological linguist point to a large array of empirical problems with the simple assumption of universal, innate conceptual parameters structuring semantic schemata across languages. And an anthropologist quarrels with his own brethren, finding universals where anthropologists are most wont to stress cultural differences in ideas. To appreciate these chapters, it will be helpful to set them in the context of the relevant traditions of research.

1 Language universals and semantic and conceptual structure

There has been an enormous amount of speculation about language universals in the last thirty years or so. The most basic methods of linguistics presume fundamental universals in sound structure, word structure, and syntax. Chomsky (1965: 27ff.) made a distinction between "substantive" universals, or universal inventories of notions like noun and verb, and "formal" universals or underlying universals in rule systems or constraints on them. Of the two main strands of work on universals, the typologists or comparative linguists have tended to concentrate on substantive universals and the generativists on rule systems, or the principles that underlie them.[2] The work on rule systems is necessarily much more abstract, and parallels across languages much harder to ascertain, so despite strong claims of universal properties in this area, it is probably fair to say that the proposals need to be taken with a pinch of salt – they are working hypotheses under constant, often drastic, revision.

One reason for a certain skepticism about proposed universals in rule-systems is that they depend (or ought to depend) on a prior establishment of substantive universals, since rules (or their constraints) are stated over grammatical categories. However, those typologists working on a broad range of languages have found it by no means easy to define satisfactorily across languages even such basic notions as "subject" or "object".[3] Here we come immediately to the heart of the comparative problem. How are we to compare categories across languages without a pre-existing metalanguage which will make all the necessary distinctions in advance? If we start with familiar categories, we may misconstrue or miss altogether the corresponding categories in other less familiar languages. In the case of sound systems, we know in advance that the range of possible speech sounds, and their minimal distinctiveness, is restricted by physiological and acoustic properties. Hence we may utilize a metalanguage (say an ideal version of the International Phonetic Alphabet) that makes all the possible, minimally contrastive, distinctions – a phonetic or "etic" (following Pike 1964) grid on which language-specific phonemes or "emic" distinctions can be mapped. Yet there are no obvious corresponding absolute constraints on syntactic or semantic properties, no self-evident "etic grids." In practice, typologists tend to use loose "family-resemblance" or prototype notions: they know full well that, say, "ergative case" is a kind of case-marking on the agents of transitive verbs which varies substantially across languages, being manifested differently in different grammatical contexts and playing different roles in syntactic processes. Moreover, since relatively few of the over 4,000 languages of the world have been grammatically described (most typologists work with a few hundred at most), typologists are continuously revising and redefining the substantive categories of comparison.

This should make clear that empirical work on language universals is still at an early stage It is even possible that such a comparative science of language will never be able to mature, because of the current high rate of loss of small-scale, traditional speech communities in favor of a few politically dominant written languages which will themselves constitute a biased sample.[4]

In this context, however, we are primarily interested in universals vs. language-specific properties of semantic structure. The discussion of grammatical categories is relevant because, on the Whorfian view, it is the underlying conceptual distinctions built into these categories that may, by virtue of their obligatoriness, repetition, and unconscious nature, be especially inclined to induce distinctive habits of thought. There is just a little recent work that attends directly to this, notably the research by Lucy (this volume, and 1992b) and Slobin (this volume). Here the above cautions are in order: it is important to be clear that even something as straightforward as the notion of "plural" will differ across languages, depending on the presence or absence of oppositions with "dual," "paucal," etc. This of course is the structuralist premise – the content of one term depends on the content of the other terms with which it is in opposition – a premise that relativizes the content of individual terms to systems of oppositions. Such a premise is compatible with substantive universals,[5] but it warns against the presumption of sameness of category across languages. The structuralist approach cautions against both (a) the presumption of an "etic grid" (a language-independent set of distinctions), and (b) the comparison of "traits" or grammatical features (like say "subject" or "ergative case" or "plural") across languages without due regard to the systems into which the isolated traits must fit.

If our knowledge of grammatical universals is still relatively primitive, our knowledge of universals in lexical semantics is still more so. Textbooks often give a contrary impression, because they point to some celebrated achievements in this field, notably the demonstration of universals underlying color terminology, kinship, and ethnobiology. Color terms, it is generally admitted, have a special status, because the peripheral nervous system must here already prestructure the nature of the perception.[6] Thus there may be no general conclusions to draw from this case. Universals of kinship terminology remain somewhat controversial because the analyses rest (for the construction of an "etic grid") on the assumption of a universal set of "kin-types," requiring that, e.g., paternity is a universally recognized concept, whereas in some cultures this notion is at the very least downplayed. In addition, some studies seem to show that the analytical "etic grid" is not the basis of native conceptualization of kinship.[7] Still, the facts remain suggestive of universal conceptual properties in this most basic foundation of human institutions. The universals in ethnobiological classification (made possible by the Linnaean etic grid) are perhaps the best-documented tendency for human conceptualizations of their environment to converge, despite enormous differences in ecology and varieties of focused interest within those ecologies (e.g. according to hunting or pastoral or agricultural ways of life). The convergence is clearest on a notion close to the biological notion of genus (partially overlapping with the notion of species), with superordinate and subordinate layers of taxonomy built around this. There are thus both notional and formal universals of taxonomy in this domain. Western scientific taxonomy can then be seen to be no more than a projection of universal "folk" principles (see Atran 1990).

Beyond these well-documented cases, evidence for substantive conceptual universals in lexical semantics is hard to find: there seem to be universals in pronominal systems, in human body-part designation, and there are a few other such cases.[8] Yet although we may be relieved to find that Whorf's "kaleidoscope flux of impressions" is not segmented arbitrarily, given, for example, natural saliences in the color spectrum or natural kinds in the biological world, none of these findings demonstrate that languages do not segment things *differently*: we must get used to color words that cover 'blue or green,' or even 'dark,' or 'green and succulent,' or 'speckled brown,' and we must get used to kin terms that lump together, for example, grandparents and grandchildren, or father, father's brother, and father's father's brother's son. All the universals proposed in lexical semantics are *constraints on variation*, often quite abstract, not specifications of invariant semantic content. (For inventories of semantic relations or abstract structures perhaps universal in lexical semantics see, for example, Cruse 1986, or Lyons 1977.) Category formation has often been conceived of as a matter of lumping percepts together on the basis of similarity along some parameters, the universality of these parameters being the point at issue. Yet the universal constraints may be much more abstract. Indeed, a current interesting trend is to see categories as projections from abstract, innate causal theories about specific domains of experience, so that the sources of universal patterning may be quite removed from the lexical categorizations themselves (see, for example, Keil 1989, and the chapter in this section by Boyer). Thus universal constraints do not guarantee us a familiar world in other cultures; they merely seem to promise some limits to the strangeness, which has so far been documented in a handful of semantic fields.

Universals of lexical semantics may seem to have little to do with the Whorfian claim that *grammatical* meaning is system-bound, deeply variable, and encapsulates a coherent world-view. Yet relativity claims can be made on the basis of lexical semantics too. True, lexical categories do not have the obligatory, repetitive or out-of-awareness character associated with grammatical categories: ordinary people worry about the meaning of denoting words, but it takes a professional to worry about the meaning of the perfective aspect or the dative case.[9] Yet hidden within the meanings of individual words are the overarching dimensions that lie behind the semantic fields in which those words are systematically opposed. Where those fields have a fundamental importance in both systems of knowledge and daily life, the underlying dimensions come to have precisely the character that interested early proponents of linguistic relativity: they are underlying rather than overt principles, they are repetitively – and whenever the domain needs to be talked of, obligatorily – employed. Such fields are not constituted by words for firewood, or cooking or color or the like,[10] but rather by domains like space, time, cause, epistemic status, modality, and other Kantian categories. These are the sorts of notions that some (but not all) languages require to be coded grammatically: English grammar enforces tense specification, Northwest-coast Amerindian languages enforce spatial or visual specification, many languages require specification of epistemic source (direct vs. indirect knowledge, etc.). They are also the sorts of notions that constitute the very framework for ideas about other notions: we cannot think about matter without implicitly thinking about time and space, we cannot think about events without thinking about time, space, and cause, and so on.

Four of the chapters in different sections of this volume consider the conceptualization of space and its description in language (Bowerman, Levinson, Hanks, and Haviland). Each of these presume commonalities in the underlying domain: terrestrial spatial geometry is a recalcitrant bit of reality. In addition, there appear to be formal or abstract constraints on our understanding of space: both Haviland and Hanks explore universal principles underlying egocentric or deictic coding of spatial locations. Yet all of these chapters also point to significant kinds of variation in the conceptualization and use of spatial notions that can be found in the languages and the cultures of the world. It is worth pointing out that Whorf himself would have been surprised, since he held that unlike time, "probably the apprehension of space is given in substantially the same form by experience irrespective of language" (Whorf 1956: 158).

The two chapters on the language of spatial description in this section are directly concerned with just how much unexpected variation across languages in this domain there in fact appears to be. Thus the Levinson chapter takes one Mayan language and shows how proposed universals of spatial language based in the main on European languages are in many cases falsified by this one language of different stock. The spatial parameters underlying different lexical sets in this language are not familiar distinctions like our 'left,' 'right,' 'front,' 'back,' but rather notions like 'uphill' vs. 'downhill,' or 'ovoid shape in any orientation.' The intriguing fact here is that although notions like 'front,' 'back,' 'left,' 'right' would seem to be inevitable concepts in human visual and bodily experience, they have been bypassed as the basis for systematic linguistic distinctions. This choice of different spatial parameters in this Mayan language can be shown to correlate with distinctive classification of non-linguistic information (Brown & Levinson 1993).

Bowerman approaches the issue of spatial description from the perspective of language acquisition. The idea that spatial categories are prototype "innate ideas," or at least universal by virtue of our common terrestrial experience, is to be widely found in the study of human development. Within studies of language acquisition it has been generally presumed that children first develop non-linguistic ideas about space (as about most other primary domains), and then simply learn the local labels for those ideas. However, where crosslinguistic studies show that the descriptive labels encode quite disparate features, carving up the domain in different ways on fundamentally different parameters, this picture becomes untenable. We have to think of the child as combining non-linguistic knowledge about space with language-specific schematizations of the domain, so that the language actually influences the fundamental conceptualization of the domain.

Thus deep epistemological questions are raised by these studies: the principles of spatial description vary significantly across languages; in order to speak a language one must "buy" the local schematization (at least at the time of speaking, see Slobin, chapter 3 of this volume). There is some much more complex interaction between "innate ideas" and cultural schematizations than most current theory is willing to admit.[11]

2 Cultural relativity and the relativity of ideas

Linguistic relativity can be seen as merely a corollary of a more general attitude to the study of different social and cultural systems, namely cultural relativity.[12] This is not surprising: many students of society are fundamental structuralists – that is, they believe that a social system is a complex interacting whole, where the role of each part, for example each social institution, can only be understood in the context of the whole. Thus it makes no sense to compare, for example, the family across cultures without taking into account that the very notion of 'family' will depend in each culture on the systematic relations it has with other notions concerning kinship, residence, constraints on sex and marriage inheritance, commensality, etc.[13] The corollary is a working maxim: "never assume that institution X in society A is just the same thing as that we call X in society B." We may call this *methodological relativism*, and it would be hard to find an anthropologist who did not at least flirt with such a maxim, even if few manage to consistently live up to it. On the other hand, anthropologists are simultaneously concerned with cross-cultural comparison, using typological categories of a loose, family-resemblance kind. Thus they talk about, say, 'witchcraft' across societies, but at the same time insist that each instantiation is a unique institution.

However, many anthropologists see the parallel between linguistic relativity and cultural relativity as deeper than this. If one thinks of the anthropologist's job as the business of explaining an alien ideational world to our own, then anthropology is essentially a matter of interpretation and translation. Part of the problem is of course quite literally translational – so that linguistic relativity can be seen as close to the heart of cultural relativity. Yet there are also other problems of interpretation. For example, we interpret human activity around us (or at least think we do) on the basis of an assumption of human rationality: we see our neighbours busying themselves and we explain their activities in terms of rational motivations (Bill is planting vegetables, or going off to work). Yet when people ascribe such motivations to trees or thin air, or

think Bill's activities are undirected or preordained, we are up against the
sort of interpretive problem that anthropologists often wrestle with. The
tendency here has been to try to show that, given that the natives believe
such-and-such and do thus-and-thus, firstly (a) such-and-such is not
totally without parallel or foundation in our own belief worlds, and
secondly (b) if one believes such-and-such it would by our own criteria be
rational to do thus-and-thus.[14] The flavor of these accounts is of the
triumph of the interpreter over the forces of cultural and linguistic
relativity.[15]

The chapter by Boyer may seem superficially in line with this tendency,
but has a quite different goal. His goal is not sympathetic interpretation
of alien beliefs, so that we can as it were glimpse their quasi-rationality.
Rather he wants to show that those most alien of belief-systems, other
peoples' religious ideas, are really entirely familiar in basic character. The
domain is well chosen – it is often selected as the *least* likely area to be
constrained by universal principles: thus Kay & Kempton (1984:67)
opine "empirical work on the Sapir–Whorf hypothesis has been restricted
essentially to the domain of colour...There are other areas of human
thought and belief – religion is an obvious example – in which
constraints like those imposed by peripheral neural mechanisms on
possible color classifications seem a priori unlikely to operate."

Boyer starts by questioning some tenets which he believes lie behind
the following "Whorfian" argument: categorization requires grouping by
similarity, this categorization is under-determined by objective reality,
but is suggested by linguistic categories, which therefore play a crucial
role in the transmission of culture across generations. In contrast, Boyer
argues (following Keil 1989 and others) that categorization or conceptual
grouping is really determined by an implicit theory about a particular
domain: for example, animate objects are grouped together by their
teleological behavior (for which there is a pan-human naive theory) and
distinguished by properties of each natural kind (for which, again, there
is a naive theory of essence and reproduction). Such domain-specific
implicit theories are not, he claims, learned, and therefore are
biologically, not culturally, transmitted. Anthropologists, he argues, are
blinded by a few spectacular oddities to the enormous undercurrent of
universal conceptual assumptions, a bit like a novice bird-watcher who,
judging by the outer plumage alone, thinks the brightly coloured male is a
different species from its more sober mate. Applying these ideas to the
comparative study of religion, he suggests that religious ideas have a
reliable crosscultural structure: metaphysical beings are ascribed all the
properties specific to the human domain (with its associated naive theory
of intentional, purposeful behavior) with just a few outlandish properties – e.g. invisibility, omniscience, etc. Drawing on the work of

Sperber,[16] he suggests that even the outlandish elements conform to limited types, which guarantee their memorability and hence their cultural transmission. Cultural transmission then amounts only to the passing on of a few special assumptions, which, taken together with a domain-specific inherent theory, generates a rich local tableau.

Boyer's argument should be compared carefully to Bowerman's. Both focus on the transmission, or acquisition, of ideas across generations as a key area in which to assess universal vs. culture-specific effects. Although clearly very different domains are at stake, Bowerman indeed stresses categorization rather than implicit theory, and emphasizes the importance of the linguistic transmission of ideas, while Boyer downplays the importance of both, drawing on the new ideas about innate causal theories of domains. Both can point to empirical research supportive of their positions. These chapters thus illustrate the strong opposing tensions in current thinking.

Finally, let us remember that universals in no way guarantee uniformity, any more than variation implies the absence of universals. There are no acquired human skills that are not simultaneously supported by universal cognitive predispositions and transformed by specific cultural traditions. Those cognitive abilities have no doubt partly evolved to handle the learning of cultural traditions, which in turn have developed on the foundations of those learning capacities. We are still in need of a sophisticated theory of the co-evolution of mind and culture (see Durham 1991) that will articulate for us how culture is not just a projection of human nature, nor human nature an introjection of culture.

Notes

1 One line of thought goes thus: process may be invariant, while the content processed may (indeed must) be experientially variable. Crosslinguistic psycholinguistic research does not in fact support this: e.g. the nature of the processing involved in speech segmentation is already language-specific in young infants (see Mehler 1988).

2 For discussion of the distinction, which in fact has limited utility, and the two lines of work, see, e.g., Ferguson (1978), Comrie (1981: ch. 1).

3 See, e.g., Comrie (1981: ch. 5). Even grammatical categories like "noun" may be harder to establish universally than is generally presumed – see e.g. Sasse (1993).

4 Some scholars predict that, on current trends, 90 percent of the existing languages will be extinct within a century. See Hale, Krauss, & Watahomigie (1992), and Robins & Uhlenbeck (1991).

5 Universals must then be conceived of as constraints on language-particular systems. For example, one might make the (probably false) claim that all languages make a grammatical opposition between singular and plural, while allowing that the meaning of a plural morpheme in a particular language is system-dependent.

6 As Paul Kay has emphasized on various occasions (see, e.g., Kay & Kempton 1984: 67). The Berlin & Kay study (1969) and its successors have indeed been criticized for confusing the demonstration of such underlying perceptual constraints with a demonstration of universals in lexical semantics (see, e.g., Lucy 1992a).

7 See, e.g., Zeitlyn (1993), Levinson (1977), Danziger (1991).

8 On body-parts see Anderson (1978), on pronouns see Ingram (1978) (although those generalizations do not properly take into account the systems of third-person titles for pronouns employed especially in the S. E. Asian languages). Deixis is an additional field where universals can almost certainly be stated (see Fillmore 1975, Anderson & Keenan 1985). For review over various domains, see Lee (1988).

9 For an important paper on the differential consciousness we have of different aspects of our linguistic system, see Silverstein (1981). Whorf himself, of course, was particularly interested in non-overt grammatical classes, or "cryptotypes," form classes differentiated by their "reactances" (participation in morphosyntactic processes). These same covert classes have intrigued modern students of child language – how do children discern these underlying classes: do they presume them on the basis of innate predispositions (Pinker 1989)?

10 See, e.g., Lehrer (1974).

11 Even the (normally presumed inverse) relationship between range of cultural variation and richness of innate ideas may have been misconceived: as Sperber (1985) points out, one can argue that the more the variation, the richer the innate learning abilities must be to acquire them. Gellner (1985: ch. 3) too makes the point that the presence or absence of a rich set of psychic universals is independent of relativism as a doctrine about ontology. On cultural universals in the history of anthropology, see Brown (1991).

12 Structuralist ideas in linguistics (with Saussure) and sociology (with Durkheim) emerged at about the same time and place (Saussure was in Paris in 1871–81, while Durkheim was there in 1875–82). Explicit relativistic ideas also emerged in parallel in the two disciplines, this time especially in America in the 1940s. For a lively modern discussion of relativism in the social sciences, see Hollis and Lukes (1982). One area, perhaps surprisingly, where discussions of relativism are still "hot" is the history and philosophy of science (see discussion of the "scientific Whorfians" in Devitt & Sterelny 1987: ch. 10)

13 Although the term "structuralist" in anthropology is often used to designate those influenced by recent French thinkers like Lévi-Strauss, as opposed to the immediately preceding British school of "structural functionalists," it is hard to find social theorists who are not structuralist in the sense that societies are conceived of as a system of linked ideas and institutions. Only the typologists like Murdock, who track, e.g., cross-cousin marriage across the globe, can be accused of being non-structuralist in this sense (see Leach 1967). Debates about cultural relativity were strong in just the same era (1940s and 1950s) during which there was most interest in linguistic relativity. A clear statement of cultural relativity is to be found in, e.g., Herskovits (1958), and relativistic ideas about values are embodied in the "statement on Human Rights" presented by the American Anthropological Association to the United Nations Commission on Human Rights in 1947; see, e.g., Tennekes (1971). For a trenchant attack, see Sperber (1985).

14 See, e.g., Evans-Pritchard (1937).
15 Sperber (1985: 60) has criticized this line of reasoning for failing to distinguish various kinds of statement from assertions of belief: "relativism is a sophisticated solution to a problem which...does not even arise...The problem is not one of poor translation..., it is one of poor psychology."
16 See Sperber & Wilson (1986), Sperber (1985).

References

Anderson, E. 1978. Lexical universals of body-part terminology. In J. Greenberg (ed.), *Universals of human language*, vol. III: *Word structure* (pp. 335–8). Stanford University Press.

Anderson, S. & Keenan, E. 1985. Deixis. In T. Shopen (ed.), *Language typology and syntactic description*, vol. III: *Grammatical categories and the lexicon* (pp. 259–307). Cambridge University Press.

Atran, S. 1990. *Cognitive foundations of natural history*. Cambridge University Press.

Berlin, B. &: Kay, P. 1969. *Basic color terms: their universality and evolution*. Berkeley: University of California Press.

Brown, D. E. 1991. *Human universals*. New York: McGraw-Hill.

Brown, P. & Levinson, S. 1993. *Explorations in Mayan cognition*. Working Paper No. 24. Nijmegen: Cognitive Anthropology Research Group.

Chomsky, N. 1965. *Aspects of the theory of syntax*. Cambridge, MA: MIT Press.

Comrie, B. 1981. *Language universals and linguistic typology*. Oxford: Basil Blackwell.

Cruse, D. A. 1986. *Lexical semantics*. Cambridge University Press.

Danziger, E. 1991. Semantics on the edge: language as cultural experience in the acquisition of social identity among the Mopan Maya. Unpublished Ph.D. dissertation, University of Pennsylvania.

Devitt, M. & Sterelny, K. 1987. *Language and reality*. Oxford: Basil Blackwell.

Durham, W. 1991. *Coevolution*. Stanford University Press.

Evans-Pritchard, E. 1937. *Witchcraft, oracles and magic among the Azande*. Oxford: Clarendon Press.

Ferguson, C. A. 1978. Historical background to universals research. In J. Greenberg (ed.), *Universals of human language*, vol. III: *Word structure* (pp. 7–32). Stanford University Press.

Fillmore, C. 1975. *Santa Cruz lectures on deixis*. Bloomington: Indiana University Linguistics Club.

Gellner, E. 1985. *Relativism and the social sciences*. Cambridge University Press.

Hale, K., Krauss, M., Watahomigie, L., Yamamoto, A., Craig, C., Masayesva, J., & England, N. 1992. Endangered languages. *Language*, 68(1), 1–42.

Herskovits, M. H. 1958. Some further comments on cultural relativism. *American Anthropologist*, 60, 266–73.

Hill, J. 1988. Language, culture and world view. In F. Newmeyer (ed.), *Linguistics: the Cambridge Survey*, vol. IV: *Language: the cultural context* (pp. 14–36). Cambridge University Press.

Hill, J. & Mannheim, B. 1992. Language and world view. *Annual Review of Anthropology*, 21, 381–406.

Hollis, M. & Lukes, S. (eds.) 1982. *Rationality and relativism*. Oxford: Basil Blackwell.

Ingram, D. 1978. Typology and universals of personal pronouns. In J. Greenberg (ed.), *Universals of human language*, vol. III: *Word structure* (pp. 213–48). Stanford University Press.

Kay, P. & Kempton, W. 1984. What is the Sapir–Whorf hypothesis? *American Anthropologist*, 86, 65–79.

Keil, F. 1989. *Concepts, kinds and cognitive development*. Cambridge, MA: MIT Press.

Leach, E. 1967. Cross-cultural comparison. *Encyclopedia of the social sciences*. London: Macmillan.

Lee, M. 1988. Language, perception and the world. In J. Hawkins (ed.), *Explaining language universals* (pp. 211–46). Oxford: Basil Blackwell.

Lehrer, A. 1974. *Semantic fields and lexical structure*. Amsterdam: North Holland.

Levinson, S. C. 1977. Social deixis in a Tamil village. Ph.D. dissertation, University of California, Berkeley. Ann Arbor Microfilms.

Lucy, J. 1992a. *Language diversity and thought: a reformulation of the linguistic relativity hypothesis*. Cambridge University Press.

  1992b. *Grammatical categories and cognition: a case study of the linguistic relativity hypothesis*. Cambridge University Press.

Lyons, J. 1977. *Semantics*, 2 vols. Cambridge University Press.

Mehler, J. 1988. Language use and linguistic diversity. In W. Hirst (ed.), *The making of cognitive science* (pp. 153–66). Cambridge University Press.

Pike, K. 1964. Towards a theory of the structure of human behavior. In D. Hymes (ed.), *Language in culture and society: a reader in linguistics and anthropology* (pp. 54–62). New York: Harper & Row.

Pinker, S. 1989. *Learnability and cognition: the acquisition of argument structure*. Cambridge, MA: MIT Press.

Robins, R. & Uhlenbeck, E. (eds.) 1991. *Endangered languages*. Oxford: Berg.

Sasse, H-J. 1993. Das Nomen – eine universale Kategorie? *Sprachtypologie und Universalienforschung*, 46, 187–221.

Silverstein, M. 1981. *The limits of awareness*. Working Papers in Sociolinguistics No. 84. Austin: Southwestern Educational Laboratory.

Sperber, D. 1985. *On anthropological knowledge*. Cambridge University Press.

Sperber, D. & Wilson, D. 1986. *Relevance*. Oxford: Basil Blackwell.

Tennekes, J. 1971. *Anthropology, relativism and method*. Assen: Van Gorcum.

Whorf, B. L. 1956. *Language, thought and reality: selected writings of Benjamin Lee Whorf*, ed. J. B. Carroll. Cambridge, MA: MIT Press.

Zeitlyn, D. 1993. Reconstructing kinship, or the pragmatics of kin talk. *Man*, 28(2), 199–224.

6

THE ORIGINS OF CHILDREN'S SPATIAL SEMANTIC CATEGORIES: COGNITIVE VERSUS LINGUISTIC DETERMINANTS

MELISSA BOWERMAN

When we observe the motion or location of an object in space, we are not aware of imposing categorical distinctions on the scene: "phenomenally, space seems to be completely continuous and homogeneous, stretching without seam in three open-ended dimensions" (Bialystok & Olson 1987: 511). Yet, to talk about motion and location, we must partition space into a discrete number of basic spatial categories. For example, to describe a cookie in contact with the upper surface of a dish, we must decide whether it is 'on' or 'in' the dish. The shape of the dish may be intermediate between a flat plate and a clearcut bowl, but in everyday English we cannot represent the relationship as intermediate between 'on' and 'in.'

Where do the semantic categories associated with words like *on*, *off*, *in*, *out*, *up*, *down*, *over*, and *under* come from? Is non-linguistic spatial perception and conceptualization implicitly categorical, perhaps organized around focal exemplars or perceptual primitives? Or do we divide up space in a particular way because of the language we learn? Obviously no simple appeal to either non-linguistic cognition or the influence of language can provide a complete answer to this complex question. However, in the literature on how children learn locative prepositions non-linguistic spatial development is seen as vastly more important than experience with language. Children are portrayed as acquiring morphemes to express spatial concepts they already have, rather than creating spatial meanings in response to language.

In this chapter I argue that this widespread view of spatial semantic development seriously underestimates the role of language. Languages differ widely in their organization of spatial meanings – for example, in the criteria they use to categorize two situations as instances of "the same" or "different" spatial relations. Although non-linguistic spatial development clearly paves the way for children to acquire spatial morphemes, learners must attend to the linguistic input to discover the particular way space is organized in their language. Little is known about how this language-specific learning takes place, but it begins very early: I present evidence that children's semantic categories for spatial terms may already be profoundly language-specific even before the age of two.

1 The "cognitive" approach to spatial semantic development

Over the last twenty years, many researchers have argued that the process of language acquisition builds critically on children's prelinguistic cognitive achievements. This approach, often called the "cognitive" hypothesis, is embedded in a fundamental change in attitudes towards the relationship between language and cognition.

In the 1950s and 1960s, researchers generally assumed that children construct semantic categories by noticing which properties of referents remain constant across successive uses of a form by fluent speakers. Whorf (1956) claimed that language shapes children's understanding of the world and that learners of different languages end up with different systems of thought. Inspired by Whorf, Roger Brown (1958) described lexical development as "The Original Word Game," a pastime in which the child makes guesses about how to classify referents according to local custom and the adult helps by modeling appropriate lexical usage and correcting the learner.

By the early 1970s, the tide began to turn against the idea that children's categorization of the world is guided by language. Explicit attempts to test the Whorfian hypothesis had yielded mixed or disappointing results. Interest was growing in the work of Piaget (e.g. 1954), who showed that considerable cognitive development takes place in the prelinguistic period. Rosch's work on prototype structure and "basic level categories" (Rosch 1973; Rosch, Mervis, Gray, Johnson, & Boyes-Braem 1976) suggested that natural language categories are less arbitrary than had been thought – more "given" in the correlational structure of reality. This meant that reliable clues to categorization were available to children independently of language. Indeed, as Rosch & Mervis (1977) demonstrated, children can categorize objects at the "basic level" before they learn names for them. At the same time, crosslinguistic research showed that some semantic domains are conceptualized more uniformly across cultures than had previously been supposed (e.g. Berlin & Kay 1969, on color; E. V. Clark 1977, and Allan 1979, on classifiers). For color, there was also evidence linking crosslinguistic similarities to properties of human visual physiology. Infant research demonstrated that babies come "prewired" to perceive changes along certain physical continua in a discontinuous or "categorical" way (see Bornstein 1979, and Quinn & Eimas 1986, for reviews). It began to seem as though the semantic organization of language, far from influencing or determining speakers' categories, was itself simply a reflection of deep-seated properties of human perceptual and cognitive organization.

Among students of language development, this *Zeitgeist* led to a reversal in the way questions about semantic development were formulated: rather than asking how children figure out meanings for the words they hear, researchers began to ask how children find words for meanings they already know (e.g. Nelson 1974, Slobin 1973). Prelinguistic children were pictured as busy building up concepts for understanding and interpreting their experiences. As they begin to want to communicate, they look for linguistic devices – words, inflections, word order patterns, etc. – for expressing their ideas. In this approach, then, the initial stages of language acquisition are seen as a process of learning how to translate from one representational system to another. (See Bowerman 1976, Cromer 1974, Johnston 1985, for general discussions of this position.)

Children's acquisition of locative morphemes is often cited as a paradigm example of how language is mapped onto pre-existing concepts. Three broad lines of evidence are relevant. First, children undeniably learn a great deal about space before they begin to talk (e.g. Gibson & Spelke 1983, Needham & Baillargeon 1993, Piaget & Inhelder 1956; see Van Geert 1985/6, for a useful review). Because of this, R. Brown (1958) in fact excepted space from linguistic shaping in his description of "The Original Word Game": "conceptions of space, time, causality, and of the enduring object . . . , so brilliantly studied by Piaget . . . are the basic referent categories and they are formed with little assistance from language" (p. 195).

Second, there seemed to be a close relationship between the non-linguistic and linguistic structuring of space. In an influential paper H. Clark (1973) argued that the way people perceive and conceptualize the locations of objects ("P-space") is heavily constrained by their biology (e.g. top–bottom and front–back asymmetry, lateral symmetry, upright posture) and their physical environment (e.g. the workings of gravity). He proposed further that the properties of spatial language ("L-space") are conditioned by and isomorphic to those of P-space. This correspondence between the two systems means that "the perceptual features in the child's early cognitive development (his P-space) are reflected directly in the semantics of his language (his L-space)" (p. 30), which in turn allows the child to acquire spatial expressions "by learning how to apply them to his prior knowledge about space" (p. 62).[1]

Third and most important, a variety of studies has shown that the acquisition of spatial words is preceded, guided, and paced by the unfolding of non-linguistic spatial knowledge. It is worthwhile reviewing a few of these, since they support the claim that children's spatial semantic concepts originate in non-linguistic development.

(a) Children often show signs of wanting to communicate about the location of objects before they know spatial morphemes; for instance, they may combine two nouns or a verb and a noun with what seems to be a locative intention, as in "towel bed" for a towel ON a bed and "sit pool" for an event of sitting IN a pool (Bowerman 1973: 242). R. Brown (1973) noted that the prepositions most often called for but usually missing in the speech of his three English-speaking subjects were *in* and *on*. At a later stage, these were the first two prepositions reliably supplied. Citing similar data from a variety of languages, Slobin (1973) proposed that the emergence of a given locative concept sets the lower bound on when the form for expressing that concept will be acquired. After the concept is available, the time the form is actually acquired depends on its formal linguistic properties (its "linguistic complexity" for children). For example, if a locative notion is expressed with a postnominal marker in language-A and a prenominal marker in language B, children learning A will tend to master the marker earlier than those learning B (Slobin 1973: 191).

(b) Within a language, locative forms like the English prepositions are often similar in linguistic complexity, but they do not all come in at once. Rather, they emerge over a long period of time, in an order that is roughly the same across children learning different languages. This order is consistent with the sequence established by Piaget & Inhelder (1956) for the emergence of different kinds of non-linguistic spatial knowledge, which supports the hypothesis that time of acquisition is guided by the maturation of the relevant spatial notions (Johnston 1985, Johnston & Slobin 1979, Slobin 1985). The first locatives to come in express functional and topological notions of containment (*in*), support and contiguity (*on*), and occlusion (*under*), then come notions of proximity (*next to, beside, between, behind, in front of* (in connection with objects with inherent backs and fronts), and finally projective order relationships (*behind, in front of* in connection with nonfeatured objects).

(c) When researchers have compared children's non-linguistic grasp of a spatial concept directly with their knowledge of the word that encodes this meaning, they have invariably found an asymmetry in favor of non-linguistic knowledge. For example, Levine & Carey (1982) tested two- and three-year-old children's non-linguistic grasp of the concepts 'front' and 'back' by having them line up (toy) objects such as a doll, a car, a chair, and a stove in a "parade" and, in a second task, asking them to place these objects so they could have a conversation with a doll held by the experimenter. They then asked the children to point to the 'front' and 'back' of these and other objects. They found that children could distinguish the fronts and backs of objects non-linguistically well before they knew the words *front* and *back*. Similar results have been obtained for the Hebrew equivalents of *in*, *on*, and *under* (Corrigan, Halpern, Aviezer, & Goldblatt 1981; Halpern, Corrigan, & Aviezer 1981), and for the use of *in back of* and *in front of* with featured and nonfeatured objects (Johnston 1979, 1985).

(d) E. Clark (1973) showed that young children often play with objects in ways that show understanding of the spatial notions 'containment' and 'support' before they learn the words *in* and *on* (see also Freeman, Lloyd, & Sinha 1980 for further evidence, but Caron, Caron, & Antell 1988, for some qualifications), and they make systematic use of this knowledge in trying to comply with instructions containing unknown locatives. For example, when told to place object A *in*, *on*, or *under* object B, Clark's youngest subjects typically put A 'in' if B was container-shaped and 'on' if B provided a flat, supporting surface, regardless of the preposition mentioned. This meant that they were almost always correct with *in*, correct with *on* unless B was a container, and never correct with *under*. Clark hypothesized that prepositions whose meanings accord with children's non-linguistic spatial strategies are acquired earlier than prepositions whose meanings do not: hence, *in* is easier than *on*, which in turn is easier than *under*.

To summarize, the hypothesis that children map spatial morphemes onto their non-linguistic concepts of space has rested on three foundations: (i) evidence that prelinguistic children know a lot about space; (ii) arguments for a close correspondence between the perceptual and the linguistic organization of space; and (iii) evidence that spatial morphemes emerge only after the relevant non-linguistic spatial knowledge is in place. All three foundations seem sound: any adequate theory of spatial semantic development will have to take into account both children's non-linguistic spatial cognition and biological or environmental constraints on the meanings of possible spatial morphemes. However, in all the emphasis on what children do NOT have to learn in acquiring spatial morphemes, what they DO have to learn has been neglected. In the next section, let us look at the basic problem presented by differences in the way languages partition space.

2 Crosslinguistic variation in spatial categorization

All languages make categorical distinctions among spatial configurations for the purpose of referring to them with relatively few expressions, such as the spatial prepositions of English.[2] However, they do not all do so in the same way; that is, what "counts" as an instance of a particular spatial relationship varies from one language to another. This is not a problem *per se* for the view that there is a close correspondence between spatial perception and spatial language. "Correspondence" does not mean that all languages have to have identical spatial meanings, but only that their meanings must be "consistent with" hypothesized spatial primitives (H. H. Clark 1973, Miller & Johnson-Laird 1976, Olson & Bialystok 1983). Still, stress on the way perception conditions the semantic organization of space inevitably leads to overestimation of how closely the spatial morphemes of, say, English map onto hypothesized perceptual primitives.[3] This in turn has reconfirmed the assumption that "having a non-linguistic understanding" of spatial relationships is more or less the same as having spatial concepts that are similar in meaning to the English locative prepositions. This assumption needs close examination.

As an exercise, let us investigate the gap between non-linguistic understanding and knowledge of linguistic categories by looking at

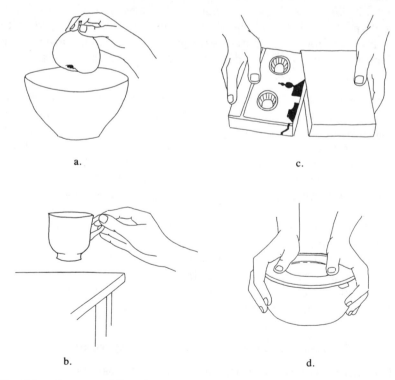

Fig. 6.1 *Four spatial actions*

alternative ways of partitioning topological relationships that all can be described with *in* or *on* in English. Relations of other kinds would serve as well, but 'in' and 'on' relations are especially revealing because investigators have so often assumed that the basic meanings of the words *in* and *on* could be acquired non-linguistically.[4] My argument is consistent with that of cognitively oriented linguists (e.g., Croft 1991, Herskovits 1986, Lakoff 1987, Langacker 1987, and Talmy 1975, 1983, 1985) who have argued that the lexicon and grammar of a language provide conventionalized ways of conceptualizing scenes for given purposes.[5]

Imagine yourself as a child who, like R. Brown's (1973: 327ff.) subject Eve, knows that she can say *in* connection with, for example, putting an apple into a bowl (example [a] in figure 6.1) or *on* for putting a cup on the table (example [b]), and is now faced with deciding which novel situations also qualify as instances of the same spatial relation.

If you associate *in* with 'containment' and *on* with 'support' (see R. Brown 1973: 330), your choice is clear: you will extend *in* from (a) putting an apple in a bowl to (c) putting a video cassette in its case, and *on* from (b) putting a cup on the table to (d) putting a fitted lid on a container. And you would be right – in English. However, if you are learning Korean your reliance on 'containment' and 'support' would lead you astray. In this language, putting a video cassette into its case and a fitted lid on a container are typically distinguished from putting an apple in a bowl and a cup on the table, respectively, and grouped together into the SAME spatial category on the grounds that they both involve bringing an object together with another object in relationship of three-dimensional meshing or fit (Bowerman 1989, Choi & Bowerman 1991). We will return to these differences in the next section; for now the way these events are typically classified in the two languages is simply diagrammed in figures 6.2A and 6.2B.

Now consider figure 6.3, which gives 'apple in bowl' and 'cup on table' as anchor points, along with a set of new spatial configurations, this time static ones rather than motions. In English, *on* applies not only to 'cup on table' but to all the new examples as well: 'handle *on* pan,' 'bandaid *on* leg,' 'ring *on* finger,' 'fly *on* door,' and 'picture *on* wall.' This makes perfect sense to speakers of English: these spatial configurations are all similar to 'cup on table' in that the located object is IN CONTACT with an exterior surface of the reference object and SUPPORTED (but not CONTAINED) by it. (Following Talmy 1975, 1985, I will use the term "figure" for the moving or located object and "ground" for the reference object; these are called "theme" and "relatum" or "trajector" and "landmark" in other treatments.)

Dutch,[6] like English, distinguishes 'apple *in* bowl' from the other configurations shown (using the cognate preposition *in*). However, it

ENGLISH

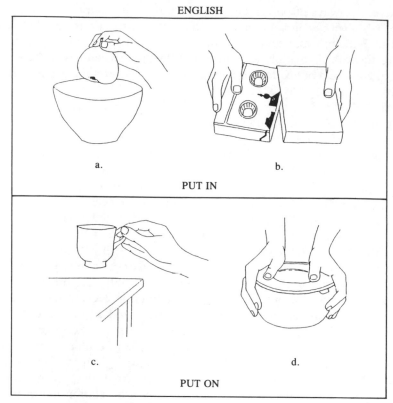

Fig. 6.2A   *Semantic classification of four actions in English*

breaks down the English *on* relations into three different categories, expressed by the prepositions *op*, *aan*, and *om*, as shown in figure 6.4.

Om is like English *around* in specifying a relationship of 'encirclement,' but it is used much more consistently for encirclement than *around* is. English speakers prefer or even insist on *on* for encirclement relations involving contact with and support by the ground object; cf. 'ring *on*/ ??*around* finger,' 'diaper *on*/??*around* baby,' 'pillowcase *on*/??*around* pillow,' while Dutch speakers typically use *om* for these configurations.

Op and *aan*, in many of their uses, divide up one of the basic "use types" described by Herskovits (1986: 140–3) for the English preposition *on*: 'spatial entity supported by physical object.' The difference between them for topological relations like those in figures 6.3/6.4 has to do with how the figure stays in contact with the ground. *Aan* is used when the figure maintains its position – e.g., resists separation from the ground by the pull of gravity or other force, including lateral or upward forces – by being attached, typically hanging or projecting, by one or more fixed

KOREAN

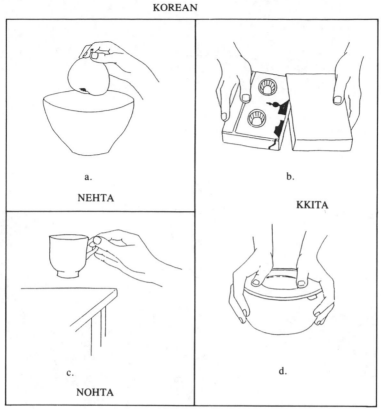

a.

NEHTA

b.

KKITA

c.

NOHTA

d.

Fig. 6.2B   *Semantic classification of four actions in Korean*

points; the ground may, but need not, actually support the figure. Examples include 'clothes on line,' 'picture on wall' (hanging from nail), 'apple on twig,' 'icicles on roof,' 'handle on pan,' 'handle on suitcase,' 'dog on leash,' 'pull-toy on string,' and 'balloon (either helium or ordinary) on string.' *Op* is used for relationships in which the figure is supported by the ground from underneath (e.g. 'cup on table'), or in which a living figure finds support in any orientation ('fly on door,' 'spider on ceiling,' 'snail on wall'), or in which an "adhesive" figure sticks tightly over a broad surface of itself to a ground in any orientation ('bandaid on leg,' 'poster on wall' [glued tight], 'sticker on cupboard,' 'paint on door,' 'raindrops on window'). What seems to unite these seemingly diverse uses of *op* and distinguish them from uses of *aan* is that a figure *op* a ground is perceived as stable, i.e., not in any salient way resisting an underlying force that pulls it away from the ground, while a figure *aan* a ground is seen as being prevented from manifesting a tendency towards separation.[7] It is plausible that underlying "force

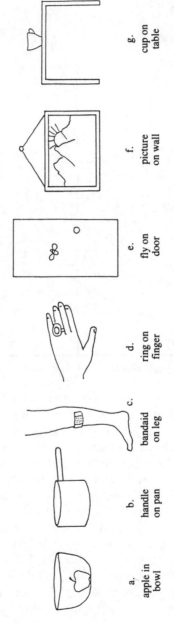

a. apple in bowl b. handle on pan c. bandaid on leg d. ring on finger e. fly on door f. picture on wall g. cup on table

Fig. 6.3 *Some static spatial configurations*

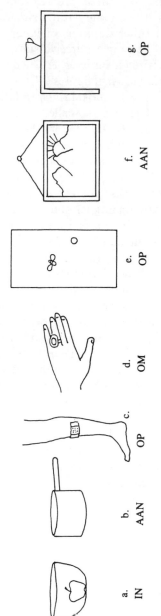

Fig. 6.4 *Semantic classification of static spacial configurations in Dutch*

dynamic" considerations like these are relevant to the semantics of preposition choice even in seemingly static situations, given both their pervasive importance in other domains of language (Talmy 1988) and experimental evidence that people perceive static situations in terms of "forces in equilibrium" (Freyd, Pantzer, & Cheng 1988).

In Finnish the examples shown in figures 6.3/6.4 are broken down in still a different way. Finnish expresses most locative relations with a case ending on the ground nominal. The three so-called "internal" cases are usually translated as *in*, *into*, and *out of*, and the three "external" cases as *on*, *onto*, and *off* (or *from*). These translations are somewhat misleading, however. Only (f) and (g) in figure 6.3 are encoded with the "external" case corresponding to *on* in English, the adessive (-*lla*/-*llä*). All the rest are encoded with the "internal" case corresponding to *in*, the inessive (-*ssa*/ -*ssä*). These differences between English and Finnish are shown in figure 6.5.

To speakers of English, this classification seems strange. Surely the handle is not 'in' the pan, the bandaid 'in' the leg, or the fly 'in' the door! And surely it is the finger that is 'in' the ring, not the ring that is 'in' the finger! In accounting for these differences, it is helpful to invoke a dimension of "relative distance" proposed by Landau & Jackendoff (1993) to explain the difference between locatives such as *in*, *on*, *near*, and *far*. "Relative distance" specifies how close the figure is to the ground: the figure is maximally close when it is located in the interior of the ground (*in*, *inside*), somewhat more distant when it is exterior to the ground but in contact with it (*on*, *against*), still more distant when it is close to the round but not touching it (*near*), and so on. In figures 6.3–6.5, the examples are arranged from left to right roughly in order of increasing "distance," starting with (a) apple in bowl (far left) as the "closest" (located in the interior). A relationship of "exterior to the ground but in contact with it" is represented by several examples, ranging from "fixed attachment" ([b]: handle on pan) through "easily broken attachment" ([c]–[e]: bandaid on leg, ring on finger, fly on door), to "loose contact; no attachment" ([f]–[g]: picture on wall,[8] cup on table).

As figure 6.5 shows, English makes a cut between examples (a) and (b)–(g): it uses *in* for a figure interior to a ground, and *on* for a figure in contact with an outer surface. Finnish, in contrast, puts a cut much further along the continuum, distinguishing (a)–(e) from (f)–(g): -*ssa* (inessive) applies to a figure that is EITHER interior to a ground OR "intimately" in contact with its outside surface (e.g., because it is attached), whereas -*lla* (adessive) is used for a figure "loosely" in contact with the outside surface of a ground.[9] These two partitionings reverse the markedness relations in the two languages. For English, being located in the interior of an object merits special encoding whereas being on the outer surface is undifferentiated (*on* is indifferent to whether the figure is

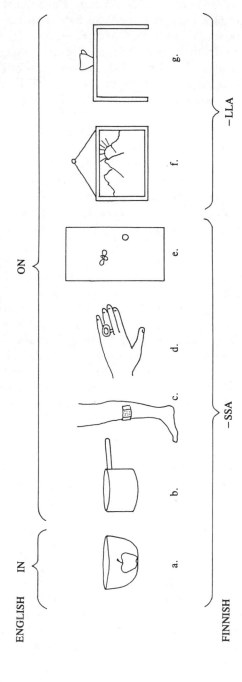

Fig. 6.5   *Semantic classification of static spatial configurations in English and Finnish*

intimately or loosely in contact with a surface). For Finnish, in contrast, being loosely in contact with an outside surface is special, while being "intimately" in contact is undifferentiated (the inessive is indifferent to whether the figure is contained by the ground or "close" to it on its outside surface) (see also Alhoniemi 1979). Independent evidence that the Finnish inessive is unmarked relative to the adessive is that the word *missä*, 'where,' is composed of the morpheme *mi-*, 'what,' suffixed with the inessive case.

These examples show that if you are a child learning Dutch or Finnish you will have to learn to attend to rather different aspects of topological relationships than if you are a child learning English. However, these languages agree with English in one important way: their spatial morphemes are not very sensitive to the shape or identity of figure and ground objects. If you are learning certain other languages, however, you will have to learn to take these properties into account as well in selecting locative forms.

Consider, for example, the spatial configurations shown in figures 6.6A and 6.6B; which all involve a roughly horizontal supporting surface of the kind associated with prototypical uses of *on* in English. For speakers of Mixtec, a language of Mexico, the examples of 6.6A fall into four spatial semantic categories on the basis of the shape of the ground object (Brugman 1984, Brugman & Macaulay 1986, see also Lakoff 1987). Mixtec has no prepositions or other morphemes dedicated to spatial relations. Instead, it expresses locations by metaphorically viewing the ground as an animal or a person and assigning a body part to the region in which the figure is located.[10] Examples (in loose translation): (a) 'the man is-located the house's ANIMAL-BACK'; (b) 'the cat is-located the mat's FACE'; (c) 'the tree is-located the mountain's HEAD'; and (d) 'the man is-located the tree's ARM.' These distinctions do not simply subdivide English *on* relations more finely, but cross-cut them to some extent. For example, the use of English *on* for situations like those in 6.6A requires CONTACT between figure and ground, but many Mixtec locative expressions permit both a contact and an "adjacent space" reading; e.g., 'X is-located the mountain's HEAD' could be said regardless of whether X – a bird, say – is touching the mountain or hovering in the air above it.[11]

Speakers of Tzeltal, a Mayan language, can also use body-part metaphors to locate a figure with respect to a ground if they want to be precise about the region of the ground involved. However, the ground is more typically introduced only with a general preposition *ta* ('at, in, on, to, from,' etc.), and spatial relationships are mostly expressed with closed-class "positional" verbs that subdivide spatial relationships on the basis of the properties of the FIGURE (P. Brown, 1994; Levinson 1990).

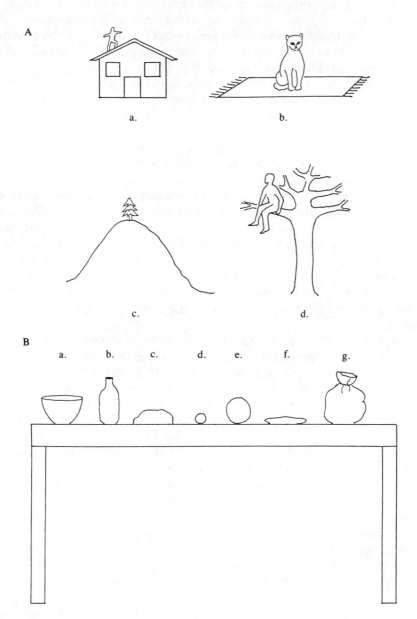

Fig. 6.6 *Some horizontal support relationships*

The objects on a table in figure 6.6B, for example, fall into seven different spatial categories: (a) *pachal* 'to be located' (said of a bowl-shaped figure in upright, canonical position); (b) *waxal* (said of a narrow-mouthed container in upright position); (c) *pakal* (said of an inverted object with flat surface down); (d) *wolol* (said of a small sphere); (e) *k'olol* (said of a large sphere); (f) *lechel* (said of a smallish flat thing); and (g) *chepel* (said of things sitting bulging in a bag). Again, this classification cross-cuts that of English: these descriptions are indifferent to whether a figure is 'on' a table or 'in' some container, as long as it has the relevant shape and orientation.

Let us stop now and take stock of the situation. Languages use surprisingly different criteria to calculate similarities and differences among spatial configurations, and this means that their spatial categories cross-cut and intersect each other in complex ways.[12] When children contemplate spatial configurations like an apple in a bowl or a cup on the table, they may well notice the shape of the figure and the ground, the nature of the contact between the two objects, and so on. However, they cannot know ahead of time which of these properties will be critical for assigning the scene to a spatial category of their language; this is something that can only be learned through attention to how linguistic forms are distributed across referent situations in the speech of fluent speakers.

When does this learning take place? Researchers concerned with cross-linguistic differences have typically assumed that learning from language is a drawn-out process (e.g. Schlesinger 1977, Slobin 1985). This is, of course, consistent with the idea that children initially rely on their own meanings. According to Slobin (1985: 1174), for example, "children discover principles of grammatical marking according to their own categories – categories that are not yet tuned to the distinctions that are grammaticized in the parental language." Later, however, "the language-specific use of particular functors will train the child to conceive of grammaticizable notions in conformity with the speech community." Although this scenario is plausible, I find it sobering that the "non-linguistic spatial concepts" often hypothesized to underlie spatial prepositions – e.g. "containment" and "support" – lend themselves much more readily to shaping into the spatial categories of English than, say, of Tzeltal. In other words, our ideas about plausible "primitives" in the language of thought may themselves be conditioned by the language we have learned.

A different possibility is that children are sensitive virtually from the beginning to the classification patterns displayed in their language. Differences in how languages partition a conceptual domain presumably signal a flexibility in human sensitivity to similarities and differences of various kinds among to-be-classified referents. Children may have fewer options in classification than adults, but there is no reason to assume that they are predisposed to construe things in only one way. To the extent that children are flexible, they may be open from an early age to linguistic guidance (Bowerman 1985, R. Brown 1965: 317, Gentner 1982). Of course, some conceptual domains may be more susceptible to linguistic influence than others; for instance, Gentner (1982) argues that object concepts are cognitively more "given" whereas relational concepts are more imposed by the structure of language. And within a given domain some principles of classification may be easier for children than others – in particular, principles that are used frequently in languages of the world may be cognitively more "natural," hence easier for children to identify, than those that are used infrequently (Bowerman 1993).

One way to compare the roles of cognition and language in structuring children's early spatial semantic categories is to determine how early the meanings of their words are language-specific. If language-specificity is early, then children must have relatively weak language-independent preferences for classifying space and they must pay careful attention to language. Conversely, if there is a period of universal or idiosyncratic meanings followed only later by language-specificity, then children have strong language-independent preferences and less sensitivity to language. In the following section, I describe research Soonja Choi and I have conducted comparing spatial semantic categories in very young children learning English and Korean (Bowerman 1989, Choi & Bowerman 1991).

3 Talking about spatial events in English and Korean

In this research, we have been concerned with spatial events like putting an apple into a bowl or a cap on a pen, taking a cassette out of a case or a hat off the head, and climbing up on a lap or sliding down from a chair. These are the situations in which English-speaking children first use words like *in, out, on, off, up,* and *down,* often still during the one-word period. Several researchers have suggested that these uses reflect previously established dynamic spatial concepts (e.g. Bloom 1973, McCune-Nicolich 1981, Nelson 1974). According to McCune-Nicolich, for example, they encode operative knowledge (knowledge of transformations) attained in the late sensorimotor period (Piaget 1954). She predicts that "since operative intelligence is a universal aspect of cognition, the same categories of meaning would be expected for all children, although various lexical items might be used to encode these" (1981: 18).

English and Korean classify spatial events quite differently. Yet if children learning English use universal sensorimotor concepts to guide their uses of *in*, *down*, etc., they should produce these words in much the same situations in which children learning Korean say some Korean word.

3.1 Adult English and Korean

In adult English, spatial prepositions and particles (e.g. *in*, *out*, *up*, *down*) form a closed-class system for expressing the notion of Path: the location or trajectory of a figure with respect to a ground (Talmy 1975, 1983, 1985). These morphemes are used together with main verbs that express the manner or cause of a motion (or location); e.g., *float/walk/swim/push IN/OUT/UP/DOWN*. Comparable Path-marking systems are found in most Indo-European languages and Chinese.

In a typologically different approach to path-marking, exemplified by Romance and Semitic languages, Path is conflated with motion in the main verb, and manner or cause is expressed optionally as a separate adverbial; for example: (Spanish) *la botella ENTRÓ a /SALIÓ de la cueva (flotando)*, 'the bottle went INTO/OUT OF the cove (floating)/floated into-out of...'; similarly, *subir*, 'go UP,' *bajar*, 'go DOWN,' *meter*, 'put IN,' and *sacar*, 'take OUT.'

Korean presents a mixed picture (Choi & Bowerman 1991). In transitive clauses expressing caused motion, Path is conflated with motion in the main verb, as in Spanish. However, in intransitive clauses expressing spontaneous motion, motion and Path and (optionally) manner or cause are encoded as separate constituents, a pattern not described by Talmy. In both transitive and intransitive clauses, most Path information is expressed with verbs. There are only three locative affixes, -EY, 'at/to,' -LO, 'toward,' and -EYSE, 'from.' These are suffixed to an (optional) nominal specifying the ground, and function like the Spanish prepositions *a*, 'to,' and *de*, 'from,' in the examples above.

Two differences between English and Korean are particularly important for present purposes. First, English Path markers are indifferent to whether a motion is presented as spontaneous or caused; for example, the prepositions are constant in the following sentence pairs: *the mouse went IN the box/John put the mouse IN the box; the mouse went OUT of the box/John took the mouse OUT of the box*. Korean, in contrast, marks most Path meanings with distinct verb roots in intransitive and transitive sentences; for instance, the verbs corresponding to *go IN* and *put IN* these examples are *tule kata*, 'enter go,' (=go in) and *nehta*, 'put-in,' and the verbs corresponding to *go OUT* and *take OUT* are *naylye kata*, 'exit go,' (=go out) and *kkenayta*, 'take-out.'[13]

A second important difference between the two languages is that Korean Path verbs and English prepositions often carve out different categories of Path meanings. For example, there are no transitive Korean verbs directly equivalent to English *put IN* and *take OUT*, or *put ON* and *take OFF*. Instead, there is an extensive set of verbs that specify the joining or separation of figures and grounds as a function of the properties of these objects; some examples are listed under A of table 6.1. Notice that one of these verbs, KKITA, loosely glossable as 'fit,' was responsible for the differences between English and Korean shown earlier in figure 6.2B. A more detailed look at how KKITA cross-cuts the territory of English Path particles is given in figure 6.7. Two more differences in the structure of Path categories are shown in table 6.1: B, where English uses *put ON* for donning clothing of all types, Korean has different verbs for putting clothing on different body parts; C, where English uses *up* and *down* very broadly for motion along the vertical axis,

Table 6.1. *Some Korean Path verbs*

A Join/separate

kkita/ppayta	Cause one 3-dimensional object to 'fit'/'unfit' from another (e.g. Lego pieces, ear plugs–ears, cassette–cassette case, top–pen, ring–finger).
nehta/kkenayta	Put something into/take something out of a loose container (wallet–handbag, ball–box, furniture–room).
pwuthita/tteyta	Join/separate flat surface of an object to/from another flat surface (sticker–book, poster–wall, two table sides).
kkotta	Put a solid object elongated in one dimension into/onto a base. (flower–vase, book–shelf, dart–dartboard, hairpin–hair). Separation: *ppayta* when the base holds the figure tightly, but *kkenayta* when it holds it loosely.
nohta	Put something loosely on a surface (pen–table, chair–floor). Separation: *tulta* when focusing on taking the object into the hand, *cipta* for picking it up.
pwusta/phwuta	Pour liquid or a large quantity of tiny objects into/out of a container (milk–cup, sand–pail).
tamta/kkenayta	Put multiple objects into/take out of container that one can carry (fruits–basket, candies–bowl, toys–box).

B Putting clothing onto one's own body

ipta	Put clothing onto trunk (dress, shirt, pants).
ssuta	Put clothing onto the head (hat, scarf, umbrella)
sinta	Put clothing on the feet (socks, shoes).
chata	Put clothing on the waist or wrist (belt, watch, diaper).

C Motion 'up' and 'down'

naylye kata	'descend go'	go DOWN
ancta	'sit-down'	sit DOWN
nwupta	'lie-down'	lie DOWN
olla kata	'ascend go'	go UP
ileseta	'stand-up'	stand UP

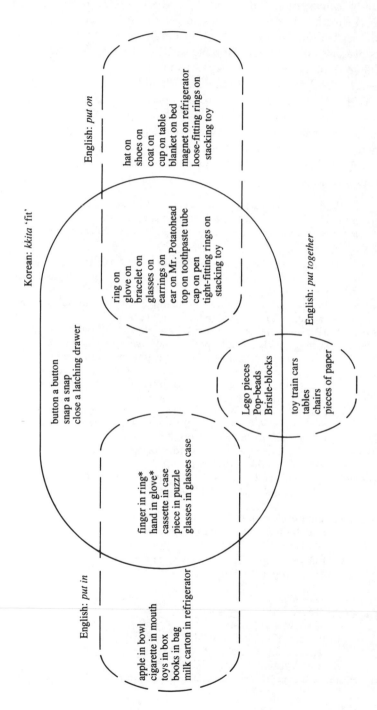

Korean: *kkita* 'fit'

English: *put on*

hat on
shoes on
coat on
cup on table
blanket on bed
magnet on refrigerator
loose-fitting rings on
stacking toy

ring on
glove on
bracelet on
glasses on
earrings on
ear on Mr. Potatohead
top on toothpaste tube
cap on pen
tight-fitting rings on
stacking toy

button a button
snap a snap
close a latching drawer

English: *put together*

Lego pieces
Pop-beads
Bristle-blocks

toy train cars
tables
chairs
pieces of paper

finger in ring*
hand in glove*
cassette in case
piece in puzzle
glasses in glasses case

English: *put in*

apple in bowl
cigarette in mouth
toys in box
books in bag
milk carton in refrigerator

*Canonically, rings are put on fingers and gloves on hands, but envision here a situation in which the ring
or glove is held stable and the finger or hand moves towards it.

Fig. 6.7 *Comparison of the Korean verb* kkita *with English* put in, put on, put together, *and other verbs*

including posture changes, Korean distinguishes "going up/down" from posture changes.

As this sketch should make clear, English- and Korean-speaking children receive different "instructions" about what spatial actions they should regard as similar. For example, English tells them that putting a video cassette IN its case is similar to putting an apple IN a bowl but different from putting a tight-fitting lid ON a container; Korean, however, reverses these judgments. Further, English says that putting a hat ON is in some ways like putting a coat ON, that sitting DOWN on the floor is like climbing DOWN from a chair, and that the trajectory of a ball is the same whether it rolls INTO or is put INTO a box. Korean, however, disagrees.

If children are guided in their early use of spatial morphemes purely by non-linguistic ideas about similarities among events, these linguistic differences should have no effect: children learning the two languages should either associate spatial words with the same underlying concepts, or differ only idiosyncratically. To see whether this is so, Choi and I examined early spontaneous speech data from English- and Korean-speaking children.[14]

3.2 Child English and Korean

In both languages, the children began to produce spatial morphemes at 14–16 months and to use them productively between 16 and 20 months. They also talked about similar events; for example, they commented on their own changes of posture or location, such as sitting down, standing up, and climbing up onto chairs or laps; they appealed to adults for help in changing location or to go outside; they asked to be picked up or carried; and they referred to donning and doffing clothing and to object manipulations of many kinds. These shared preoccupations apparently reflect similarities in the cognitive development and daily activities of children of this age. Underlying the surface look of sameness, however, there were important linguistic differences.

(a) Spontaneous versus caused motion along a Path. By 16–20 months the English-speaking children used words like *up*, *down*, *in*, *out*, *on*, and *off* freely for both spontaneous and caused motions. For example, they said *out* when they climbed out of the bathtub or took something out of a pan, and they said *in* when they climbed into a box or put something into a bag. In contrast, the Korean children made a strict distinction between spontaneous and caused motions: e.g., they said *kkenayta*, 'take out of loose container,' for taking blocks out of a box but not for getting out of the bathtub, and they said *kkita*, 'fit,' while putting plastic shapes into the holes of a shape box but not when they crept into a small space. The

Korean children never violated the distinction between spontaneous and caused motion along a Path throughout the entire period investigated.

(b) Containment and support. For the English-speaking children the distinction between *in* and *on* (and their opposites *out* and *off*) was in place by 18–20 months. Like adults, they used *in* and *out* for Paths into and out of both "tight" and "loose" containers, for example, for putting tiny books into a fitted container and removing them and for putting toys into a pan and taking them out. They used *on* and *off* both for surface attachment (e.g. joining and separating Lego pieces and Pop-beads, caps on pens, lids on jars, magnets and tape stuck on surfaces) and for "looser" surface contact such as climbing on or off a lap or stool and for donning and doffing clothing of all kinds (see also Gopnik 1980, Gopnik & Meltzoff 1986).

The Korean children, in contrast, used no global semantic categories of "containment" and "surface contact and support." They used *kkita*, 'fit,' and its opposite *ppayta*, 'unfit' – their earliest spatial words – both for putting objects INTO/OUT OF tight spaces and for surface-attachment (ON/OFF) manipulations involving caps on pens, lids on jars, Pop-beads, and Lego pieces. By 18–20 months they learned other transitive Path verbs that intersect the domains of English *in/out* and *on/off*, and used them generally appropriately, e.g., *nehta* and *kkenayta*, 'put into/ take out of a loose container,' *nohta*, 'put loosely on a surface,' *pwuthita*, 'put one flat surface to another,' *kkotta*, 'put elongated object to base,' *ipta/ssuta/sinta*, 'put clothing on trunk/head/feet.' These differences between the English- and Korean-speaking children are shown schematically in figure 6.8.

(c) Motion 'up' and 'down.' Like other English-speaking children, our learners of English used *up* and *down* between 16 and 20 months for a wide range of spontaneous and caused motions along the vertical axis (e.g. going up or down stairs, getting up on or climbing down from raised surfaces like chairs, riding toys, and laps, falling, sitting or lying down, standing up, picking up objects off the floor or putting them on raised surfaces, putting objects down on the floor or low surfaces, and as a request to be picked up and held or put down). To account for the early acquisition and broad extension of these words, several investigators have proposed that *up* and *down* are mapped directly to core spatial concepts of "vertical motion" (e.g. Bloom 1973, Gruendel 1977, McCune-Nicholich 1981). If this is so, Korean children – presumably equipped with similar concepts – should seize on Korean words heard often for events involving vertical motion and extend them freely to other such events. For example, they might select *ancta*, 'sit down,' or *naylita*, 'cause to go down,' to mean 'down' in general, or *anta*, 'pick up and carry,' or *ollita*, 'cause to go up,' to mean 'up' in general.

ENGLISH-SPEAKING CHILDREN

	in/out ("containment")	*on/off* ("surface contact, support")
kkita/ppayta ("tight fit and attachment")	piece/puzzle picture/wallet hand/glove book/fitted case	cap/pen lid/jar glove/hand magnet/surface tape/surface Lego pieces together/ apart
other verbs ("loose fit")	toys/bag or box blocks/pan getting in/out of tub going in/out of house, room	clothing on/off (hat, shoe, coat, etc.) getting on/off chair

KOREAN CHILDREN

Read DOWN for English-speakers and ACROSS for Korean-speakers

Fig. 6.8 *Cross-cutting classification of acts of "separation" and "joining" by young English- and Korean-speaking children*

This does not occur. Some of our subjects used *ancta*, 'sit down,' and *anta*, 'pick up and carry,' starting at about 17 months, but they never overextended these words to other situations involving motion 'down' or 'up'. They acquired intransitive and transitive causative forms of *nayl-*, 'descend,' and *oll-*, 'ascend,' very late compared to *up* and *down* in children learning English. The Korean children talked about upward and downward motion just as much as the English-speaking children, but they did so with verbs that classify these events by criteria other than shared vertical motion, e.g. *ancta*, 'sit down,' *nwupta*, 'lie down,' *nohta*, 'put X (down or up) on surface.'

To summarize, children learning English and Korean use the Path morphemes of their language with surprising accuracy well before the age of two. Learners of English extend the same words freely to both spontaneous and caused motions, and they concentrate on notions of containment (*in/out*), support and surface contact, especially attachment (*on/off*), and vertical motion (*up/down*). Korean children use different words for spontaneous and caused motion, they focus on a "tight fit" notion that is orthogonal to containment and support, they distinguish putting clothing onto various parts of the body from other kinds of surface contact, and they distinguish among different kinds of vertical motions.

How significant is this language specificity? Perhaps children simply imitate the words they hear adults use in certain contexts, and have figured out no broader patterns. Yet this is not so. All the children used Path morphemes creatively for novel referents. Their extensions were often quite appropriate; e.g., *on* while holding up yarn against a doll's head (15 months), *down* as the child pushed a cat's head down (17 months), *up* and *down* as the child "walked" her fingers up her body to her neck and back down, *off* while peeling a sticker off a toy bell and while pushing the mother's hand off the page she was drawing on (all 19 months). Some extensions were errors from the adult point of view; e.g., *off* while separating stacked Dixie cups (16 months) (adults would say *[take] apart*), *open* for pulling Pop-beads *apart* (16 months), *in* for putting a pingpong ball *between* the knees (20 months). Errors like these have in the past been interpreted (also by me; cf. Bowerman 1980) as signs that the child is relying on her own non-linguistic concepts instead of being guided by the input. Seen against the backdrop of children acquiring a completely different system, however, it seems that many of these errors are better interpreted as signs of difficulty in working out the details of a system that in broad outline is already quite language-specific (Bowerman 1989, Choi & Bowerman 1991).

4 Discussion

The English and Korean acquisition patterns I have described testify to the contribution of both non-linguistic spatial cognition and the categorization system of the input language to the process of acquiring spatial words. On the one hand, children are not simply mapping morphemes directly onto non-linguistic concepts of containment, support, vertical motion, and the like. From the beginning, they are paying close attention to the way adults use spatial words: across contexts, the word serves as a "lure to cognition," in R. Brown's (1958) felicitous phrase, which draws the learner's attention to properties the referents share. On the other hand, children must be equipped to make sensible guesses about what might be relevant – about what recurrent properties to look for. For example, they do not seem to waste time on the idea that a spatial morpheme could refer only to the location of blue objects, or only to the location of objects in the morning. And some aspects of spatial situations seem to be more salient to them than others – for instance, the distinctions between "containment" and "support" and between "tight fit" and "loose fit" seem to be easy, but other distinctions are not: e.g., children learning English have trouble with "asymmetrical" vs. "symmetrical" joining and separation (e.g., *on/off* vs. *together/apart*), and children learning Korean tend to overextend words for three-dimensional meshing (*kkita*, 'fit'/*ppayta*, 'unfit') to two-dimensional attachments involving magnets and stickers, which require other words.

As Langacker (1987: 148) notes, "our ability to conceive of spatial relationships presupposes some kind of representational space creating the potential for such relationships." However, the representational space children use in judging the properties of spatial referents remains mysterious. One critical question is this: from all the things people can notice about spatial situations, do the spatial morphemes of language draw on a "privileged" subset (Talmy 1983, Landau & Jackendoff 1993)? If so, this would help children enormously in hypothesizing spatial properties of the "right kind" as meanings for the words they hear (Landau & Stecker 1990). Yet it is harder than it first seemed to pin down this privileged subset.

Talmy (1983) and Landau & Jackendoff (1993) proposed that closed-class spatial morphemes encode highly schematic information about topological regions, main axes, and trajectories, but not Euclidean information about angles and distances or about the exact shape or nature of the ground and especially the figural objects. Levinson (1990), however, argues that this is incorrect: the closed-class positional verbs of Tzeltal, for example, pick out a number of Euclidean properties of figures (see also figure 6.6B). Of course, children may give priority to schematic topological information and so find many of Tzeltal's positional verbs difficult to learn, but this remains to be seen. It is troubling for the hypothesized developmental priority of abstract information about topology and trajectory that Choi's and my Korean subjects learned everyday verbs that express schematic Path meanings like 'enter,' 'exit,' 'ascend,' and 'descend' more slowly than verbs with strong restrictions on figure and ground – e.g. clothing and carrying verbs, for which ground objects must be particular body parts (Choi & Bowerman 1991: 117).

In closing, let us raise the Whorfian question: does learning the spatial categories of their language influence the way children conceptualize space non-linguistically? In principle, of course, it need not: the principles of categorization needed for language may be relevant ONLY for language and play no other role (as argued by Slobin 1991, and in this volume). That is, non-linguistic spatial cognition may be uniform across cultures, drawing entirely on language-neutral organizing principles. However, in the research I have presented here, it is striking how quickly and easily children adopted language-specific principles of semantic categorization. There was little evidence that they had strong prelinguistic biases for classifying space differently from the way introduced by their language. This leaves the door open to the possibility that, after all, spatial thought – undeniably one of our most basic cognitive capacities – bears the imprint of language.

Acknowledgments

I am grateful to Herb Clark for helpful comments on an earlier draft.

Notes

1 Related claims about the correspondence between spatial perception and the meanings of spatial morphemes have been made by Bierwisch (1967), Miller & Johnson-Laird (1976), and Olson & Bialystok (1983).

2 Of course, finer distinctions can be made if necessary by combining or modifying these expressions.

3 For example, in arguing that non-linguistic spatial representation is couched in an internal mental vocabulary of spatial "predicates," Olson & Bialystok (1983) propose that "ordinary language yields a relatively full expression of the basic spatial predicates," and that "lexical items express particular spatial predicates and hence have the same structure that mental predicates do" (p. 236).

4 Recall that *in* and *on*, and their counterparts in other languages, are typically among the first spatial morphemes learned by children, often before the age of two. In general, researchers have assumed that morphemes learned very early are especially likely to be mapped to meanings the child has established non-linguistically. Consistent with this, the meanings of *in* and *on* are usually analyzed in terms of functional or topological notions that seem like good candidates for semantic primitives, such as 'containment' or 'inclusion' versus 'support' and 'contact' (see H. H. Clark & Clark 1977, Herskovits 1986, Miller & Johnson-Laird 1976).

5 Languages usually offer alternative ways to encode any given spatial situation, e.g. "the vase is *on* the cupboard" versus "the vase is *on top of* the cupboard." These offer somewhat different perspectives on the scene and are useful for different communicative purposes. In this discussion I will focus on the categories associated with a language's most "neutral" or "pragmatically unmarked" way of describing 'in' and 'on' relations of the kinds considered. I do not attempt to provide a full account of all the ways in which the spatial morphemes at issue can be used, but only to show what kinds of distinctions children have to attend to in order to generalize the morphemes to spatial scenes that are similar in the appropriate way to the ones for which they have heard the forms used.

6 The informal analyses presented here of the way Dutch and Finnish classify spatial configurations like those shown in figure 6.3 are my own. For Dutch I rely on innumerable judgments graciously rendered over the years by native-speaker colleagues and friends (see also Bowerman 1989), and I have also consulted Heestermans (1979), Weijnen (1964), and especially Cuyckens (1991); thanks also to David Wilkins for helpful feedback on my analysis. For

Finnish I am grateful to Riikka Alanen, Olli Nuutinen, Håkan Ringbom, Saskia Stoessel, Jorma Toivainen, and Erling Wande for their judgments and discussion; I have also consulted Alhoniemi (1979) and Leino (1989).

7 For some situations, such as 'glue on scissors,' either *op* or *aan* may be used, reflecting somewhat different construals of the situation.

8 Although the picture hangs from a nail and so might seem to qualify as "attached," its surface is apparently what counts for this calculation, and this is "loosely" in contact with the wall. In Dutch, in contrast, the attached/ hanging relationship of the picture to the nail is critical.

9 The characterization given in figure 6.5 of "what speakers say" for various spatial scenes is inevitably somewhat idealized. In Finnish, as in other languages, some spatial situations are routinely described by a specific spatial morpheme while others allow a choice. Which morpheme is selected in case of a choice is influenced both by overall communicative goals (see note 5) and by how speakers construe the specific situation (cf. note 7) – in this case, by hypothesis, how they construe the "relative distance" between figure and ground. Construal is in turn influenced by factors like the relative size and sometimes the specific identity of the figure and ground entities involved.

10 Body-part spatial systems are widespread among Meso-American and African languages (e.g. Heine 1989, MacLaury 1989). Another language requiring close attention to the properties of ground objects is Atsugewi (Talmy 1975, 1985). This language has about fourteen verb suffixes that are equivalent to English *into* for different kinds of ground objects: e.g. 'into a liquid,' 'into a fire,' 'into an aggregate' (e.g. buses, a crowd), 'down into a gravitic container' (e.g. a basket, a pocket), '(horizontally) into a volume enclosure' (e.g. a house, an oven), 'over the rim into a volume enclosure' (e.g. a gopher hole, a mouth), 'down into or onto an object above the ground.'

11 Indifference to whether a figure above a ground is in contact with it is widespread in spatial semantic systems: e.g., Korean, Chinese, and Japanese all routinely use the same morpheme for situations that English distinguishes as *on* versus *over* or *above*.

12 For other interesting examples of crosslinguistic differences in spatial classification, see Anderson & Keenan (1985), Bavin (1990), Casad (1977), Casad & Langacker (1985), Cienki (1989), Denny (1978), Foster (1969), Friederich (1971), Hill (1978), Talmy (1975, 1983, 1985), Taylor (1988), Zubin & Choi (1984), and Zubin & Svorou (1984).

13 The final *-ta* of these forms marks the citation form of the verb and is not part of the root.

14 Our English data come from detailed diary records of my two daughters from the start of the one-word stage, supplemented by an extensive literature on the early use of English Path particles. Two sets of Korean data were used: (i) from four children whom Choi videotaped every 3–4 weeks from 14 to 24–28 months; (ii) from four additional children taped by Choi, Pat Clancy, and Youngjoo Kim every 2 to 4 weeks from 19–20 months to 25–34 months.

References

Alhoniemi, A. 1979. Suomen kielen 1- ja s-sijojen oppositiosta. *Sanomia; Juhlakirja Eeva Kanasmaa-Minnin 60-vuotispäivaksi*, 14, 89–105. (On the opposition between 1- and s- cases. *Sanomia; Festschrift for E.K.-M.'s 60th birthday*.)

Allan, K. 1979. Classifiers. *Language*, 53, 285–311.

Anderson, S. R. & Keenan, E. L. 1985. Deixis. In T. Shopen (ed.), *Language typology and syntactic description*, vol. III: *Grammatical categories and the lexicon* (pp. 259–308). Cambridge University Press.

Bavin, E. 1990. Locative terms and Warlpiri acquisition. *Journal of Child Language*, 17, 43–66.

Berlin, B. & Kay P. 1969. *Basic color terms: their universality and evolution*. Berkeley: University of California Press.

Bialystok, E. & Olson, D. R. 1987. Spatial categories: the perception and conceptualization of spatial relations. In S. Harnad (ed.), *Categorical perception: the groundwork of cognition* (pp. 511–31). Cambridge University Press.

Bierwisch, M. 1967. Some semantic universals of German adjectivals. *Foundations of Language*, 5, 153–84.

Bloom, L. 1973. *One word at a time*. Amsterdam: Mouton.

Bornstein, M. H. 1979. Perceptual development: stability and change in feature perception. In M. H. Bornstein & W. Kessen (eds.), *Psychological development from infancy* (pp. 37–81). Hillsdale, NJ: Lawrence Erlbaum.

Bowerman, M. 1973. *Early syntactic development: a cross-linguistic study with special reference to Finnish*. Cambridge University Press.

1976. Semantic factors in the acquisition of rules for word use and sentence construction. In D. M. Morehead & A. E. Morehead (eds.), *Normal and deficient child language* (pp. 99–179). Baltimore: University Park Press.

1980. The structure and origin of semantic categories in the language-learning child. In M. L. Foster & S. H. Brandes (eds.), *Symbol as sense: new approaches to the analysis of meaning* (pp. 277–99). New York: Academic Press.

1985. What shapes children's grammars? In D. I. Slobin (ed.), *The crosslinguistic study of language acquisition*, vol. II: *Theoretical issues* (pp. 1257–1319). Hillsdale, NJ: Lawrence Erlbaum.

1989. Learning a semantic system: what role do cognitive predispositions play? In M. L. Rice & R. L. Schiefelbusch (eds.), *The teachability of language* (pp. 133–69). Baltimore: Paul H. Brookes.

1993. Typological perspectives on language acquisition: do crosslinguistic patterns predict development? In E. V. Clark (ed.), *The proceedings of the Twenty-fifth Annual Child Language Research Forum* (pp. 7–15). Stanford: Centre for the Study of Language and Information.

Brown, P. 1994. The INs and ONs of Tzeltal locative expressions: the semantics of static descriptions of location. In "Space in Mayan languages," special issue of *Linguistics*, ed. J. B. Haviland & S. C. Levinson. 32 (4–5), 743–90.

Brown, R. 1958. *Words and things*. New York: The Free Press.

1965. *Social psychology*. New York: The Free Press.

1973. *A first language: the early stages*. Cambridge, MA: Harvard University Press.

Brugman, C. 1984. Metaphor in the elaboration of grammatical categories in Mixtec. Unpublished ms., Linguistics Department, University of California, Berkeley.

Brugman, C. & Macaulay, M. 1986. Interacting semantic systems: Mixtec expressions of location. *Proceedings of the Twelfth Annual Meeting of the Berkeley Linguistics Society*, 12, 315–27.

Caron, A. J., Caron, R. F., & Antell, S. E. 1988. Infant understanding of containment: an affordance perceived or a relationship conceived? *Developmental Psychology*, 24, 620–7.

Casad, E. 1977. Location and direction in Cora discourse. *Anthropological Linguistics*, 19, 216–41.

Casad, E. & Langacker, R. 1985. "Inside" and "outside" in Cora grammar. *International Journal of American Linguistics*, 51, 247–81.

Choi, S. & Bowerman, M . 1991. Learning to express motion events in English and Korean: the influence of language-specific lexicalization patterns. *Cognition*, 41, 83–121.

Cienki, A. J. 1989. *Spatial cognition and the semantics of prepositions in English, Polish, and Russian*. Munich: Verlag Otto Sagner.

Clark, E. V. 1973. Nonlinguistic strategies and the acquisition of word meanings. *Cognition*, 2, 161–82.

    1977. Universal categories: on the semantics of classifiers and children's early word meanings. In A. Juilland (ed.), *Linguistic studies presented to Joseph Greenberg*. Saratoga, CA: Anma Libri. (Reprinted in E. V. Clark, 1979. *The ontogenesis of meaning* (pp. 253–67). Wiesbaden: Akademische Verlagsgesellschaft Athenaion.)

Clark, H. H. 1973. Space, time, semantics, and the child. In T. E Moore (ed.), *Cognitive development and the acquisition of language* (pp. 27–63). New York: Academic Press.

Clark, H. H. & Clark, E. V. 1977. *Psychology and language*. New York: Harcourt, Brace, & Jovanovich.

Corrigan, R., Halpern, E., Aviezer, O., & Goldblatt, A. 1981. The development of three spatial concepts: *in, on, under*. *International Journal of Behavioral Development*, 4, 403–19.

Croft, W. A. 1991. *Syntactic categories and grammatical relations*. University of Chicago Press.

Cromer, R. 1974. The cognitive hypothesis of language acquisition and its implications for child language deficiency. In D. M. Morehead & A. E. Morehead (eds.), *Normal and deficient child language* (pp. 283–333). Baltimore: University Park Press.

Cuyckens, H. 1991. The semantics of spatial prepositions in Dutch: a cognitive–linguistic exercise. Unpublished doctoral dissertation, University of Antwerp.

Denny, J. P. 1978. Locating the universals in lexical systems for spatial deixis. In D. Farkas, W. M. Jacobsen, & K. W. Todrys (eds.), *Papers from the parasession on the lexicon*, Chicago Linguistic Society (pp. 71–84). University of Chicago Press.

Foster, M. L. 1969. *The Tarascan language*. Berkeley: University of California Publications in Linguistics 56.

Freeman, N. H., Lloyd, S., & Sinha, C. G. 1980. Infant search tasks reveal early concepts of containment and canonical usage of objects. *Cognition*, 8, 243–62.

Freyed, J. F., Pantzer, T. M., & Cheng, J. L. 1988. Representing statics as forces in equilibrium. *Journal of Experimental Psychology: General*, 117, 395–407.

Friedrich, P. 1971. *The Tarascan suffixes of locative space: meaning and morphotactics*. Bloomington: Indiana University, and The Hague: Mouton.

Gentner, D. 1982. Why nouns are learned before verbs: linguistic relativity versus natural partitioning. In S. Kuczaj (ed.), *Language development*, vol. II: *Language, thought, and culture* (pp. 301–34). Hillsdale, NJ: Lawrence Erlbaum.

Gibson, E. J. & Spelke, E. S. 1983. The development of perception. In J. H. Flavell & E. M. Markman (eds.), *Mussen handbook of child psychology*, vol. III: *Cognitive development* (pp. 1–76). New York: John Wiley.

Gopnik, A. 1980. The development of non-nominal expressions in 12–24 month old children. Unpublished doctoral dissertation, Oxford University.

Gopnik, A. and Meltzoff, A. N. 1986. Words, plans, things, and locations: interactions between semantic and cognitive development in the one-word stage. In S. A. Kuczaj II and M. D. Barrett (eds.), *The development of word meaning* (pp. 199–223). Berlin: Springer-Verlag.

Gruendel, J. 1977. Locative production in the single word period: study of "up–down," "on–off," and "in–out." Paper presented at the Biennial Meeting of the Society for Research in Child Development, New Orleans.

Halpern, E., Corrigan, R., & Aviezer, O. 1981. Two types of "under"? Implications for the relationship between cognition and language. *International Journal of Psycholinguistics*, 8(4) [24], 36–57.

Heestermans, J. L. A. 1979. *"Naar," "naast," "langs" en "in."* The Hague: Martinus Nijhoff.

Heine, B. 1989. Adpositions in African languages. *Linguistique Africaine*, 2, 77–127.

Herskovits, A. 1986. *Language and spatial cognition: an interdisciplinary study of the prepositions in English*. Cambridge University Press.

Hill, C. A. 1978. Linguistic representation of spatial and temporal orientation. *Proceedings of the Fourth Annual Meeting of the Berkeley Linguistics Society*, 4, 524–38.

Johnston, J. R. 1979. A study of spatial thought and expression: *in back* and *in front*. Unpublished doctoral dissertation, University of California at Berkeley.

 1985. Cognitive prerequisites: the evidence from children learning English. In D. I. Slobin (ed.), *The crosslinguistic study of language acquisition*, vol. II: *Theoretical issues* (pp. 961–1004). Hillsdale, NJ: Lawrence Erlbaum.

Johnston, J. R. & Slobin, D. I. 1979. The development of locative expressions in English, Italian, Serbo-Croatian and Turkish. *Journal of Child Language*, 6, 529–45.

Lakoff, G. 1987. *Women, fire and dangerous things: what categories reveal about the mind*. University of Chicago Press.

Landau, B. & Jackendoff, R. 1993. "What" and "where" in spatial language and spatial cognition. *Behavioral and Brain Sciences*, 16, 217–38.

Landau, B. & Stecker, D. S. 1990. Objects and places: geometric and syntactic representations in early lexical learning. *Cognitive Development*, 5, 287–312.

Langacker, R. W. 1987. *Foundations of cognitive grammar*, vol. I: *Theoretical prerequisites*. Stanford University Press.

Leino, P. 1989. Suomen kielen paikallissijat syntaksin kannalta. *Virittäjä*, 93, 161–219.

Levine, S. C. & Carey, S. 1982. Up front: the acquisition of a concept and a word. *Journal of Child Language*, 9, 645–57.

Levinson, S. 1990. Figure and ground in Mayan spatial description: Tzeltal locative descriptions. Paper presented at the conference on Time, Space and the Lexicon, Max Planck Institute for Psycholinguistics, Nijmegen, November 1990.

MacLaury, R. E. 1989. Zapotec body-part locatives: prototypes and metaphoric extensions. *International Journal of American Linguistics*, 55, 119–54

McCune-Nicolich, L. 1981. The cognitive bases of relational words in the single word period. *Journal of Child Language*, 8, 15–34.

Miller, G. A. & Johnson-Laird, P. N. 1976. *Language and perception*. Cambridge University Press.

Needham, A. & Baillargeon, R. 1993. Intuitions about support in 4.5-month-old infants. *Cognition*, 47, 121–48.

Nelson, K. 1974. Concept, word, and sentence: interrelations in acquisition and development. *Psychological Review*, 81, 267–85.

Olson, D. and Bialystok, E. (eds.) 1983. *Spatial cognition: the structure and development of the mental representation of spatial relations*. Hillsdale, NJ: Lawrence Erlbaum.

Piaget, J. 1954. *The construction of reality in the child*. New York: Basic Books.

Piaget, J. & Inhelder, B. 1956. *The child's conception of space*. London: Routledge & Kegan Paul.

Quinn, P. C. & Eimas, P. D. 1986. On categorization in early infancy. *Merrill-Palmer Quarterly*, 32, 331–63.

Rosch, E. 1973. On the internal structure of perceptual and semantic categories. In T. E. Moore (ed.), *Cognitive development and the acquisition of language* (pp. 111–57). New York: Academic Press.

Rosch, E. & Mervis, C. B. 1977. Children's sorting: a reinterpretation based on the nature of abstraction in natural categories. In R. C. Smart & M. S. Smart (eds.), *Readings in child development and relationships* (2nd edn.). New York: Macmillan.

Rosch, E., Mervis, C., Gray, W., Johnson, D., & Boyes-Braem, P. 1976. Basic objects in natural categories. *Cognitive Psychology*, 8, 382–439.

Schlesinger, I. M. 1977. The role of cognitive development and linguistic input in language acquisition. *Journal of Child Language*, 4, 153–69.

Slobin, D. I. 1973. Cognitive prerequisites for the development of grammar. In C. A: Ferguson & D. I. Slobin (eds.), *Studies of child language development* (pp. 175–208). New York: Holt, Rinehart, & Winston.

  1985. Crosslinguistic evidence for the language-making capacity. In D. I. Slobin (ed.), *The crosslinguistic study of language acquisition*, vol. II: *Theoretical issues* (pp. 1157–256). Hillsdale, NJ: Lawrence Erlbaum.

  1991. Learning to think for speaking: native language, cognition, and rhetorical style. *Pragmatics*, 1, 7–25.

Talmy, L. 1975. Semantics and syntax of motion. In J. P. Kimball (ed.), *Semantics and syntax*, vol. IV (pp. 181–238). New York: Academic Press.

  1983. How language structures space. In H. Pick & L. Acredolo (eds.), *Spatial orientation: theory, research and application* (pp. 225–82). New York: Plenum Press.

  1985. Lexicalization patterns: semantic structure in lexical forms. In T. Shopen (ed.), *Language typology and syntactic description*, vol. III: *Grammatical categories and the lexicon* (pp. 57–149). Cambridge University Press.

  1988. Force dynamics in language and cognition. *Cognitive Science*, 12, 49–100.

Taylor, J. 1988. Contrasting prepositional categories: English and Italian. In B. Rudzka-Ostyn (ed.), *Topics in cognitive linguistics* (pp. 299–326). Amsterdam: John Benjamins.

Van Geert, P. 1985/6. *In, on, under*: an essay on the modularity of infant spatial competence. *First Language*, 6, 7–28.

Weijnen, A. A. 1964. Structuren van Nederlandse voorzetsels. *Tijdschrift voor Nederlandse Taal- en Letterkunde*, 80, 116–32.

Whorf, B. L. 1956. *Language, thought, and reality. selected writings of Benjamin Lee Whorf*, ed. J. B. Carroll. Cambridge, MA: MIT Press.

Zubin, D. A. & Choi, S. 1984. Orientation and gestalt: conceptual organizing principles in the lexicalization of space. *Papers from the parasession on lexical semantics*, Chicago Linguistic Society (pp. 333–45). University of Chicago Press.

Zubin, D. A. & Svorou, S. 1984. Perceptual schemata in the spatial lexicon: a cross-lingual study. *Papers from the parasession on lexical semantics*, Chicago Linguistic Society (pp. 346–58). University of Chicago Press.

7

RELATIVITY IN SPATIAL CONCEPTION AND DESCRIPTION

STEPHEN C. LEVINSON

1 Preamble

The rise of the cognitive sciences has caused a sea-change in our approach to issues concerning the relation between language, culture, and thought. Presuppositions have changed, in epistemology from empiricist to rationalist, in ontology from idealist to realist, and accordingly goals have switched from the description of cultural variation to the search for fundamental underlying universals. In this light, the Sapir–Whorf hypothesis seems uninteresting: it is either (*ex hypothesi*) just plain false, or if (God forbid) true, the weakest and most disappointing of hypotheses one could imagine.[1]

Yet there is surely something wrong about a theory of human cognition that treats that great cultural bulk of human conceptual structure as obfuscating detail: the fact that human cognition is built for culture, and thus built for enculturated variation, is a central fact about it. Like the common juniper, which varies from a three-inch shrub to a twenty-foot tree according to the prevailing conditions, so the important thing about the human mental genotype may be its design for phenotypic variation. From that perspective, a good grasp of the cultural variation is just as important to a science of Mind as it is to a science of Culture. And every plausible universal that fails is actually rather interesting.

In this chapter, we examine a number of plausible cognitive science generalizations about spatial conception and language which seem to be falsified by a couple of errant cultures. It is hard to draw strong conclusions from such failures – different or more abstract universal generalizations may yet be shown to hold. Nevertheless, it is at least tempting to draw the conclusion that a model of universal conceptual constraints ought not to be invariably in the strong Mendelian style (permutations and combinations of a set inventory) favored, for example, by Chomsky, but rather should sometimes be viewed as a set of filters which may radically under-determine the phenotypic cultural variants.[2] This would leave Sapir and Whorf hedged in, but hardly hobbled.

On this view, the filters that constrain how we think about some domain would include at least:

(a) the intrinsic structure of the domain (in relation to our use of it);
(b) our perceptual and cognitive propensities;
(c) intrinsic linguistic structures and communication constraints (including pragmatic constraints).[3]

A set of strong universal filters, however restrictive, may still largely under-determine cultural variation in domain-conceptualization, as illustrated by the following analogy. Consider a map, taken as a conceptual structure B representing terrain A. The intrinsic structure of domain A (mountains, rivers, roads) constrains possible conceptualizations B, B', etc. So does our perceptual apparatus: we can only discern certain sensory or mensurable properties of A (and indeed of B). So does our conceptual apparatus: perhaps we find roads more significant than similar-scale streams. These constraints are detailed, interesting, and important. Still, all these constraints leave the possible structure of B pretty unrestricted (two or three dimensions, colors, scale, projection, co-ordinates, topographical vs. geographical, degree of stylization, etc.), as the history and ethnography of cartography will confirm. It is the last constraint – that B must satisfy the demands of a communication system – that most fully determines the final characteristics of the map: conventions about how to represent features of terrain (semantics), and, equally important, principles about what can be safely omitted as taken-for-granted-for-current-purposes (pragmatics).

Just to amplify the last point: note that part of what is omitted on a map is unreconstructable – the scale may simply be too small to show certain features for example; the symbol for 'church' may fail to give any indication of size. However, other omissions are themselves telling: for example, if the map is of an appropriate scale, where no bridge is shown, there is no bridge; where a building is shown, but is not marked more specifically with the symbol for 'church,' then the building is not a church; where a church is shown, we expect a stereotypical church, not a ruin or a Mormon tabernacle. To some rather interesting extent, such patterns of presumption are independent of the cartographic conventions and the nature of the terrain mapped. They constitute the systematic pragmatics, another kind of systematic filter on arbitrary variation which we shall (somewhat inconclusively) attend to below.

We now turn to examine a particular domain, spatial conception and description, and ask how strongly each of these various kinds of constraints can there be formulated. We contrast a number of proposed universals with the facts from two speech communities of non-Indo-European stock, concentrating on the Mayan language Tzeltal.[4] We focus first on cognitive constraints, then linguistic constraints, and finally (and briefly) on pragmatic constraints.

2 Spatial conception

There are many reasons to think spatial conceptualization central to human cognition: spatial understanding is perhaps the first great intellectual task facing the child, a task which human mobility makes mandatory, but above all spatial thinking invades our conceptualizations of many other domains as diverse as time, social structure, and mathematics.[5]

Spatial conceptualization is also an interesting domain through which to explore issues of cultural relativity, as it is clearly highly constrained by the nature of the physical world as well as by the nature of human psycho-biology. Space has, it would seem, intrinsic physico-mathematical properties, explored in our geometries of two and three dimensions. In addition, our perception, especially our visual system, constrains how we will perceive terrestrial surfaces; while our upright posture, related in turn to the nature of terrestrial gravity, provides one fixed co-ordinate. There is much known, also much unknown, about the physiology, neurology and cognition of vision, motor co-ordination relative to spatial constraints, and spatial conception.[6] Yet there are still, it turns out, quite surprising cultural variations in the conceptualization and linguistic coding of spatial location, some results of which I here briefly report on.[7]

2.1 Under-determination by the cognitive constraints

Obviously, it is not easy to tease apart constraints due to the intrinsic structure of all languages from those due to cognitive constraints of other kinds. However, we describe here a handful of proposed universals that might be attributed directly to cognitive constraints, and briefly describe how they fail, postponing richer linguistic detail to the next section. The proposed universals are:

(a) naive human spatial conception makes no use of fixed "absolute" angles (Miller & Johnson-Laird 1976, Talmy 1983);
(b) it is primarily ego-centric in nature (Piaget & Inhelder 1948, Clark 1973, Miller & Johnson-Laird 1976, Lyons 1977, and many other sources);
(c) it is anthropomorphic: the co-ordinates are established by the verticality and the asymmetry (back/front) of our bodies, with the additional left/right orthogonal. Secondarily, this co-ordinate system may be projected onto an interlocutor or oriented object (Clark 1973, Miller & Johnson-Laird 1976, Lyons 1977: 690–1).

It has been supposed by many psychologists that nearly everything interesting about spatial conception follows from intrinsic perceptual and cognitive constraints: specifically the presumed fact that human perceptual space is ego-centered and relativistic. Miller & Johnson-Laird sum up these ideas as follows:

> The conceptual core of space probably originates, as Cassirer (1923) and others have maintained, with the body concept – with what is at, in, or on our own bodies. The first spatial relatum we learn to use is ego...Piaget & Inhelder (1948) claim that escape from this egocentric space requires considerable cognitive development...The ability to decenter does not displace the egocentric conception of space, but it supplements it...Egocentric use of the space concept places ego at the center of the universe. From this point of origin ego can lay out a three-dimensional co-ordinate system that depends on his own orientation. With respect to this landmark other objects can be located as above or below (ego), in front or in back (of ego), to the left or to the right (of ego).   (1976:394–5)

Using these orthogonals, with ego as the origin of the axes, we can then define search-domains of indefinite extent, radiating out from ego's 'front,' 'back,' 'left,' 'right'; secondarily, we can shift the origin to other objects (*in front of the church*). This then gives the underlying basis for a system of spatial description where objects are located in a projected space relative to another reference object, prototypically the self, which itself provides orientational co-ordinates. In effect, the essential characteristics of human spatial conception are supposed to follow from our being ego-centric, forward-looking and -oriented bipedal primates wandering on a planet with significant gravity.

This view can easily be shown to be wrong by looking cross-culturally at entirely different solutions to spatial conception. Take, for example, the case of the Guugu Yimithirr speakers of N. Queensland, who utilize a system of spatial conception and description which is fundamentally different from that of English-speakers.[8] Instead of concepts of relativistic space, wherein one object is located by reference to demarcated regions projected out from another reference object (ego, or some landmark) according to *its* orientation, Guugu Yimithirr speakers use a system of absolute orientation (similar to cardinal directions) which fixes absolute angles regardless of the orientation of the reference object. Instead of notions like 'in front of,' 'behind,' 'to the left of,' 'opposite,' etc., which concepts are uncoded in the language, Guugu Yimithirr speakers must specify locations as (in rough English gloss) 'to the North of,' 'to the South of,' 'to the East of,' etc. The system is used at every level of scale, from millimeters to miles, for there is (effectively) no other system available in the language; there is simply no analogue of the Indo-European prepositional concepts.[9]

The cognitive prerequisites and consequences of such a linguistic system are fundamental and far-reaching: every speaker must be absolutely oriented at all times, and when moving must dead-reckon all locations that may need to be referred to, or used as reference points. These cognitive processes can be demonstrated independently of language (Levinson 1992b): Guugu Yimithirr speakers can be shown during travel to be able to estimate the directions of other locations with an average error of less than 14°. It can also be demonstrated experimentally that they remember spatial arrays not in terms of egocentric co-ordinates (like in front, behind, to the left or right), but in terms of the cardinal directions in which objects lie. Thus Guugu Yimithirr speakers appear to think about space in a fundamentally different way than we do. That in turn makes available a gestural system (see Haviland 1986 and in this volume), which has further deep interactional and indeed linguistic consequences (e.g. widespread zero-anaphora reinforced by gesture).[10]

Space (of another sort) precludes further details about the Guugu Yimithirr system. We mention it here merely to show how the intrinsic nature of spatial organization, and of our perceptual and cognitive abilities, largely under-determines solutions to the problem of spatial conception and description. There is simply nothing in the world or in the mind that makes a concept like 'in front of' natural or essential.[11]

We turn now to another system of spatial description, that utilized by the Mayan (Tzeltal-speaking) Indians of Tenejapa.[12] This system again makes many contrasts with spatial description in the familiar Indo-European languages. First, there is also, as in Guugu Yimithirr, a use of absolute or fixed angles of orientation, by virtue of reference to a fixed notional 'uphill'/'downhill' inclined plane (corresponding to the overall fall of the terrain along a South/North axis). Thus, even on the flat, two referents can be discriminated by describing the Northerly one as 'downhill' of the other. The system is quite complex and the subject of another paper (Brown & Levinson 1993a). Suffice it to say here that, just as in the Guugu Yimithirr case, we can demonstrate that this system has fundamental cognitive consequences. Spatial arrays are memorized in terms of absolute, fixed directions, not in terms of egocentric co-ordinates. Thus if a Tenejapan is presented with an array like a cup in front of a bottle, and is rotated 180° and asked to make the same array again, he will in nearly all cases arrange the bottle in front of the cup – the egocentric viewpoint is thrown away in order to retain the orientation of the objects on, for example, the 'uphill'/'downhill' axis. Likewise, when required to make non-verbal spatial inferences about locations of objects, the use of a fixed absolute system of directions can be demonstrated.[13]

However, unlike the Guugu Yimithirr system, the Tzeltal system of fixed directions is supplemented by a rich system of spatial description which describes objects as positioned relative to other objects without reference to "absolute" co-ordinates. At first sight such a system looks much more like our own "relative" system of co-ordinates. However, and this is the second point of departure from the Indo-European pattern described in the Miller & Johnson-Laird quote above, the non-absolute system in Tzeltal is not essentially egocentric in character. Instead it makes minimal use of the orientation of the speaker, or the "intrinsic" orientation of other relata: referents are spatially related to other things essentially by being in (near or) *actual contact* with them, not by falling within spaces projected off oriented facets of "landmark" objects (ego or otherwise). Thus the allegedly universal canonical three-coordinate system (up/down, front/back, left/right) does *not* form the core of the Tzeltal spatial reference system: indeed there are no terms for 'to the left' or 'to the right' at all, the terms for 'face' and 'back' refer to body-parts rather than spatial regions, and there is even a possible argument that the vertical dimension is only conceived of as the limiting case of the notional inclined plane mentioned above. That these are more than lexical gaps – i.e., also conceptual gaps – is clear from a series of informal experiments.[14] Tenejapans show an interesting tendency to confuse left–right inversions or mirror-images (i.e., reflections across the apparent vertical axis), even when visually presented simultaneously, which seems related to their absence of 'left' and 'right' terms, and the absence of related asymmetries in their material culture. Indeed, the (at least partial) eclipse of an egocentric co-ordinate system forms an interesting cultural, linguistic, and cognitive complex (see Levinson & Brown 1994).

Tzeltal undermines a third kind of generalization about human spatial conceptualization, namely that naive geometry is topological rather than classically geometrical. Len Talmy (1983) makes this claim in terms that suggest he sees the generalization as a constraint imposed by "natural language schemas," i.e., by coding-constraints rather than conceptual constraints, and we will deal with the issue in those terms below.

Finally, the Tzeltal system arguably undermines the very notion of a naturally delimited conceptual domain concerning spatial location, because spatial locutions in Tzeltal nearly always involve ancillary information (especially shape, position, of the figure but also adhesion, manner in which position was obtained, etc.).[15] English prepositions (and indeed Guugu Yimithirr cardinal point terms) form a contrast set covering a single, coherent, abstract spatial domain, without curious "selectional restrictions" of this sort: we do not, for example, expect an Indo-European language to present us with two locutions for 'in front of,' depending on the texture or other incidental property of the relatum; but in Tzeltal there are many "locative" predicates that distinguish, for example, flexible vs. nonflexible, thick vs. thin, figure-objects.

2.2 Linguistic constraints and Tzeltal locative expressions

We turn now to examine how the following proposed universals of spatial description seem to be falsified by Tzeltal:

(a) motion-description and location-description significantly overlap (utilize the same expressions); the former is primary, the latter often derivative (Talmy 1983);

(b) the geometry of the figure is characterized much more simply than the geometry of the ground (Talmy 1983: 233);[16]

(c) the spatial geometry employed in natural language is topological, not Euclidean (Talmy 1983: 261);

(d) languages make ontological commitment to the notion of *place* as distincts from the notion of *entity* (perhaps attributable to Lyons 1977, W. Klein 1990). (Tzeltal data equivocal.)

We will make the points discursively while introducing the nature of Tzeltal spatial description.

Tzeltal spatial description makes a fundamental cut between motion-description and location-description: the former is coded by a small set (14) of motion verb roots, the latter by a large set (*c.* 300) of stative adjectival predicates, which although derived are never derived from the motion-verb roots. For example, the concepts of 'going up' or 'going down' are lexically unrelated to 'being up' and 'being down' and the motion verb for 'going across' is unrelated to the stative predicate for 'lying across.'[17] There is almost no overlap between locative and motion description, and no evidence for the derivative nature of the former (*contra* Talmy 1983).

We concentrate now just on Tzeltal locative descriptions; even here, though, we shall have to simplify considerably (see P. Brown 1991 for an overall sketch). The basic Tzeltal locative construction consists of a stative adjectival predicate, its nominal subject (the figure to be located), and a prepositional phrase (describing the ground) providing the nominal denoting the *relatum* or landmark-object from whose location the figure-object can be found. Stated thus, the Tzeltal locative construction sounds rather like the basic English prepositional locative construction:

(1) *The cat*   *is*   *on*   *the mat*
    SUBJECT   PREDICATE   PREPOSITION   NP
    [Referent]   [Relation   ][Relatum]
    (figure) (ground   )

The English sentence *The cat is on the mat* states that the cat may be found in a search-domain relative to the relatum (the mat), as further specified by the support-relation encoded by *on* (cf. *above, near,* etc.). Nearly all the semantic load in English is carried by the preposition, and the predicate is nearly vacuous, but in any case what matters is the relation of the figure to the relatum. Hence in English the preposition encodes a great deal about the geometry of the ground, but little or none about the figure. For example, the preposition *opposite* in *The bank is opposite the supermarket* projects a geometrical set-up in which a parallel-edged ribbon or rectangle (e.g. river, road, square) separates referent (bank) and relatum (supermarket) which both fall on a line drawn orthogonal to the ribbon or rectangle.[18] This geometry of the ground is indifferent to the geometrical properties of the figure.

All this makes good sense for conceptual reasons, or so one might suppose: the function of a locative description is to tell us where to find the figure-object, so what we need information about is (a) the ground-object (the relatum), and (b) the geometrical nature of the search-domain projected from the relatum by the relation. On this basis we can construct some very plausible universals about spatial conception, claiming centrally that spatial descriptions specify the geometrical nature of the ground, not the figure (Talmy 1983, see also Miller & Johnson-Laird 1976, Herskovits 1986).

However, Tzeltal locative descriptions don't work this way. Consider the following exemplar of the basic Tzeltal locative construction, here describing the location of a gourd as on a table (glosses very rough):

(2) *pachal*   *ta*   *mexa*   *boch*
    sitting-bowl-like   AT   table   gourd
    PREDICATE-ADJ PREP   NP   SUBJECT NP
    Positional   Relation   Relatum   Referent
    (_____ ground _____) (figure)

'The gourd is on the table'

The predicate adjective *pachal* is derived from one of a set of roots (a core subset of which are called *positional* roots by Mayanists) that describe the disposition of objects in a highly discriminated fashion; for example, other such roots describe of flexible sheets how many times they are folded, or of ropes exactly how they are coiled.[19] Here *pachal* specifies upright location, of a vessel whose greatest diameter is not greater than its mouth. The subject, *boch*, a type of bowl-shaped gourd, meets the specification. For other kinds of vessels, for example, those with upright cylindrical bodies, or narrow necks, other stative predicates will be required. These stative adjectives thus describe in great detail the geometrical nature of the figure rather than that of the ground. Although unlike adjectives without locative uses they collocate with a prepositional phrase which describes the ground, that phrase is optional. Further, the preposition *ta* in Tzeltal is vacuous, because there is only one preposition in the language which has to serve for every spatial and non-spatial (e.g. temporal or manner-adverbial) relation too. The geometrical nature of the ground is almost entirely unspecified in the basic Tzeltal locative construction (but it may be optionally developed by body-part terms, as will be described below).

Thus the "natural" English strategy of presupposing the structure of the figure, but detailing the nature of the ground (i.e. the relation and the relatum) so that the figure may be found within it, is not followed in the Tzeltal case at all. Instead, Tzeltal takes the strategy of specifying in great detail the figure, while presuming the general nature of the ground – the strategy in effect is: "look for something of *exactly this* shape and disposition, which has some unspecified stereotypical relation to the relatum, if a relatum has been provided." A choice of one out of 300 or so detailed predicates is more or less obligatory; one can hardly escape detailing the geometry of the figure, but the ground may be only alluded to or even omitted altogether.[20]

Why does Tzeltal force the speaker into such an arbitrarily detailed geometry of the figure? One answer may be, as just hinted, that the main function of locative expressions is merely to provide a means of successful reference. In that case, Tzeltal emphasizes an alternative strategy for achieving successful reference – English does it by telling you where to look, Tzeltal by telling you what to look for. (The Tzeltal locative construction provides equally good answers to 'Where?' questions and to 'How does it look?' questions.) However, another intriguing suggestion has been made by John Lucy (1992: 73ff.) on the basis of work on the related language Yucatec Maya. Like Tzeltal, Yucatec has a developed set of numeral classifiers. The motivation, Lucy claims, is that nominals in Yucatec fail, by themselves, to individuate entities. It is only by collocation with a numeral classifier or some other shape-discriminating phrase that such nouns can come to designate countable entities. This thesis, carried to its logical extreme, would amount to the claim that all nominals in Yucatec are essentially *mass* nouns and that the language makes no ontological commitment to *entities* as opposed to materials, essence or "stuff" at all. In order to individuate entities, a numeral classifier or some predicate is required to impose individuation on the material, metaphorically in much the way that a cookie-cutter cuts up undifferentiated dough![21]

If the thesis held even partially for Tzeltal, it would help to explain the Tzeltal insistence on specifying the geometrical nature of the figure. Consider, for example, the fact that the Tzeltal nominal *lo'bal* could be glossed 'banana stuff,' because it refers equally to all the parts of the natural kind: to the fruits, to a single fruit, to clusters of fruits, to the trunk of the banana tree, to the leaves of the tree, and so on. Now, given a nominal of such a nature, the kind of geometric and shape information encoded in the stative locative predicates we have examined is not as redundant with the information contained within the subject noun as it first might seem. Consider the examples in (3).

(3) a. *jipil   ta laso   lo'bal*
       hanging AT rope   banana
       'the banana(-fruits) are hanging from the rope'

   b. *k'atal   ta s-ba   s-k'iyojbil kajpej te lo'bale*
      lying-across AT its-top its-drying coffee the banana
      'the banana(-trunks) are situated across the top of the coffee-drying patio'

   c. *palal   lo'bal   ta xujk   na*
      attached-in-bunches banana AT its-side house
      'the banana(-bunches) are against the inside side-wall of the house'

The figure in these three examples is designated by the nominal *lo'bal*. In each case, the 'banana-stuff' to which it refers gets formed up, as it were, by the positional predicate which indicates the nature of the individuated entities involved. Thus, Lucy's conjecture would go rather a long way to explain why it is that Tzeltal and languages like it have such a wealth of locative (and other) predicates, making such fine discriminations between shapes and dispositions of the figure.

Natural languages have finite vocabularies. It follows that lexemes must be semantically general over indefinite exemplary referents (languages are "efficient" as Barwise & Perry 1983 put it). Thus they must "schematize." Are there general principles of schematization? Talmy (1983) claims "yes."[22] One of them, he suggests, is that natural language geometry is *topological*, rather than "Euclidean." Popularly conceived of as "rubber-sheet geometry," topology makes fundamental distinctions between continuous and non-continuous transformations of a geometrical figure (where, informally, continuous transformations ensure that two points that are close together at the start of the transformations are close at the end). Thus a circle and an ellipse, or a straight vs. a curved line, or a square vs. a triangle, are topologically equivalent pairs, though Euclideanly distinct. Talmy's claim is that natural language characterizes spatial relations (and objects generally) "almost solely by more qualitative or 'topological' properties" (1983: 234). The plausibility of the claim can easily be seen by considering Indo-European prepositions like English *in*, which seem to have a topological flexibility of application:[23]

(4) a. The peaches are in the can *[enclosed]*
   b. The peaches are in the bowl *[partially enclosed]*
   c. The dog is in the yard *[bounded in 2 dimensions]*
   d. The shuttle is in outer space *[unbounded??]*

Yet Tzeltal seems much more thoroughly metric and "Euclidean." Consider for example the following stative predicates which distinguish between size and shape (large sphere/small sphere, spherical vs. ovoidal) of the figure. Small deformations, for example of a ball of corn-dough, will cause a category change:

(5) a. *wolol ta mexa* ('sitting-of-small-sphere AT table')
   b. *k'lol ta mexa* ('ditto, of large sphere')
   c. *telel ta mexa* ('ditto, of slightly deformed sphere')

Talmy (1983: 234) claims that "missing from the catalog of geometric types [employed in natural languages], for example, are virtually all properties specific to metric spaces (including the Euclidean) such as particular size, length, distance, angle or contour." Here are some Tzeltal locative/stative predicates as counter-examples that speak for themselves:[24]

(6) The relevance of exact contour (shape)

   a. *t'ikil*   *ta tz'ulja'*   *matz*
      contained$_1$ AT globular-gourd corn-dough
      ('contained, of stuff in vessel with narrow opening')

   b. *pachal*   *ta boch*   *matz*
      contained$_2$ AT hemispherical-gourd corn-dough
      ('contained, of stuff in vessel with wide opening')

   c. *pachal*   *boch*
      located-upright$_1$ hemispherical-gourd
      ('upright, of wide-mouthed vessel')

   d. *waxal*   *p'in*
      located-upright$_2$ necked-vessel
      ('upright, of narrow-mouthed tall container')

   e. *jukul*   *matz*
      located-upright$_3$ corn-dough
      ('upright, of wide-bottomed cone')

(7) The relevance of exact angle/curve

   a. *xik'il*   *si'*
      leaning-0°-to-30°-from-vertical fire-wood

   b. *ta'al*   *si'*
      leaning-30°-to-60°-from-vertical fire-wood

   c. *nitbil*   *laso*
      pulled-into-tight-line the rope

   d. *timil*   *laso*
      pulled-tight-sagging-slightly the rope

   e. *pok'ol*					*laso*
     sagging-deeply-curved the rope

We turn to consider how Tzeltal provides an exception to the egocentric projection of the human frame that Lyons, Clark, Miller, & Johnson-Laird, and others have claimed to be central to natural language spatial description: "Looked at from one point of view, man is merely a middle-sized physical object. But in man's world – the world as man sees it and describes it in everyday language – he is, in the most literal sense, the measure of all things. Anthropocentrism and anthropomorphism are woven into the very fabric of his language" (Lyons 1977: 690). The English system is anthropomorphic in the sense that it takes the essential co-ordinates of up/down, front/back, left/right, from the oriented human frame. It is egocentric in the sense that the primary usage of this system seems to be deictic (*at my side, at my front*, etc.) – i.e., it has ego as relatum; as a secondary usage, we can transfer the center of the co-ordinates onto an object, assign it a *front*, *back*, and *sides*, etc., so that we can use that object as a relatum.[25] The core of this system is the need to *orient* a relatum, because the system makes use of extensive search-domains projected out from these oriented facets (along the co-ordinates up/down, front/back, left/right). For example in English, *I left my bike in front of/at the front of the cathedral*, asserts that the bike could be found in some quadrant-like projection off that face of the cathedral that can be called its *front*. Similarly for *in front of me, at my left, at my right, behind me*, etc., using ego as relatum.

Now the Tzeltal system at first sight does not seem so very different from the English one (setting apart the just described hypertrophy of geometrical detail about the figure encoded in stative predicates). One can find prepositional phrases that gloss rather similarly to English: cf. English *in front of the house* with Tzeltal *ta y-elaw na* 'AT the face of the house.' Yet the Tzeltal pattern is in fact fundamentally different. As mentioned, Tzeltal only has one preposition which cannot therefore achieve discriminations between 'at,' 'in,' 'on,' etc. (we will gloss it arbitrarily as 'AT'); instead, it is possible to build up a complex ground by using possessed body-part terms to designate some part of the ground-object, with literal glosses like 'AT the table's head,' 'AT the house's mouth (= door),' 'AT the house's back,' etc. Compare for example:

(8) a. *waxal   ta mexa te limite*
     standing AT table the bottle
     'the bottle is standing on the table'

   b. *waxal   ta   s-jol   mexa te limite*
     standing AT 3sPOSS-head table the bottle
     'the bottle is standing on the 'head' (end) of the table'

Like many Meso-American languages, Tzeltal analogically maps human and animal body parts onto almost every physical object, ranging in size from a coffee-bean to a mountain, and in ephemerality from a stone to a cloud (cf. e.g. Friedrich 1969 on Tarascan, MacLaury 1989 on Zapotec). The mapping is partially conventional, but largely productive, even open to free invention and can be instantly applied to novel objects. Whether the system is primarily anthropomorphic or animomorphic in origin is perhaps moot: 'tails' and 'horns' figure too, and quadrupedal stance is sometimes the root analogy.[26] In any case, the application of the terms synchronically seems in fact to be governed almost purely by shape (e.g., a small pointed three-dimensional protrusion is called a 'nose'). The mapping requires a partition of the surface of objects, perhaps along similar lines to Marr's theory of visual decomposition of complex objects, a geometric analysis of these segments in terms of major and minor axes, and an analysis of the shapes of the extremities of these axes (see Levinson 1994). The underlying geometry is quite detailed and specific, and is distinctly non-topological in character. Given this geometric basis for the application of body parts to segmented objects, using the possessive construction one can build phrases that have a superficial resemblance to English complex prepositional phrases like *in front of*, *to the side of*, etc.:

(9) Body-part specification of the ground

    a. *jipil   te baj-te' ta   xujk   na*
       hanging   the shelf AT its-side house
       'the shelf is hanging on the side of the house'

    b. *pachal moch   ta xujk   si'*
       sitting the basket AT its-side the firewood
       'The basket is alongside (touching) the firewood'

    c. *palal   lo'bal   ta xujk   na*
       situated-in-bunches banana AT its-side house
       'The banana-bunches are against the (inside) shortwall of the house'

    d. *potzol   lo'bal   ta xujk   p'in*
       wrapped-up bananas AT its-side pot
       'The bananas are in a bag by the side of the pot'

    e. *waxal   kajpej ta   s-ti'   k'ajk'*
       standing coffee AT its-mouth/lips fire
       'The coffee is standing at the edge of the fire'

    f. *xik'il   si'   ta   pat-na*
       leaning-almost-vertically firewood AT back-house
       'The firewood is stacked vertically against the back of the house'
       (in this case the front!)

Yet in fact the underlying *conceptual parallelism* between, say, English *in front of* and the Tzeltal phrase glossing as 'AT the face of' is not there at all. First, the point of the Tzeltal body-part assignment is *not* to establish the orientation of the object: the 'face' of an object is the most salient flat surface in any orientation whatsoever – for example the 'face' of a stone may be upside-down.[27] Thus the 'back' of a log-stool is the sitting surface, on analogy to a quadruped's back, not the side away from one; and the 'head,' 'nose,' 'sides,' 'butt' of any object remain the same when it is inverted in any plane. Secondly, the point of the Tzeltal expressions is *not* to establish a relatum or landmark from which a large search-domain or space can be projected (cf. English *in front of the cathedral*). Instead, all the Tzeltal body-part terminology does is partition objects into their named parts by analogy to the human or animal body. What use is that? It divides the ground-object into smaller named units, and allows one to describe the figure-object as exactly there, in or at one of those smaller units. Thus when one specifies that the figure-object is 'AT the face of' the ground-object, one means exactly that: the figure-object must be located in actual contact (or some close approximation to that) with the flat-facet of any object that can be called its 'face.' There are no extended search-domains. It follows that I cannot refer to the mountain behind me as 'AT my back,' nor to Xpet standing near me on the left as 'AT my side' (there is in any case no word for 'left,' as opposed to the anatomical part 'left hand').[28]

In Tzeltal locative descriptions with body-part expressions, objects are related directly to other objects or their parts. It is as if there were only things, and parts of things, and no such stuff as "space." Indeed, on this evidence alone, one would have to conclude that Tzeltal makes no ontological commitment to any abstract notion of a "space," as conceptually distinct from the objects that fill it.[29] Lyons (1977) has pointed out that, conceptually, places and entities are ontologically of different kinds,[30] yet many languages partially conflate them, for example treating both as common nouns, subjects of equative constructions, etc. In Tzeltal the conflation is extreme because there are no unequivocally locative constructions, the single preposition being used, for example, to introduce temporal and manner adverbials, while the stative verbs that take a locatively interpreted prepositional phrase do so optionally, and are equivocal in their nature.

It is unfashionable to ask what ontological commitments a particular language makes; instead, the question is only asked in a general and abstract way by roving philosophers, while the answer is already universally presumed in formal semantics on the basis of mathematical motivations. Nevertheless, a few stout souls like Lyons (1977: 438ff.) point out that we only identify nouns, verbs, and so on in another language on the basis of a mix of syntactic and ontological critera, and that one can hardly escape the question of language-specific ontology. Consider again Lucy's conjecture about Yucatec nouns as denoting material or essence, not objects (as exemplified above by the remarks on Tzeltal 'banana-stuff'): that would make the ontological prototype for that syntactic category be a property and not an entity. It is not obviously false, it is not obviously unfalsifiable, so it is an interesting idea. It is of course vintage Whorf – see Lucy (1985: 84ff.).

It is worth mentioning that there may well be a connection between the particular nature of these Tzeltal locative descriptions and the cognitive propensity to confuse or conflate mirror-images, as mentioned above. These object-oriented locative descriptions, with their preoccupation with shape and contiguity, contrast with locative descriptions based squarely on abstract spatial predicates, projecting search-domains of indefinite extent from reference objects. As Kant pointed out over two centuries ago, the internal geometry of an object cannot form the basis for distinguishing between an object and its enantiomorph or "mirror-image": to make that distinction one seems to need an overarching system of abstract spatial co-ordinates, like our egocentric system of front, back, left, and right.[31] Tzeltal does offer an overarching system of co-ordinates, namely one that is cardinal-direction-like, but it has the peculiar property that if one is facing North ('downhill'), East and West are designated (at least within that system of grammatical oppositions) by the same term, 'across.' These two facts perhaps conspire to make the distinction between mirror-images like "d" and "b" non-salient to the degree that for most Tenejapans the opposition is conceptually unavailable. For example, given a task of distinguishing various photos, some pairs of which were identical except that they depicted left–right inversions of familiar objects, informants seemed simply unable to tell the inversions apart on repeated trials, despite great success with other distinctions which would have been hard to express in English.[32] Given time and incentive to ruminate on the difference between such a pair of photos, informants pointed to minute asymmetries in arrangement of the objects or in photographic finish. In effect, left–right inversions appeared to be quite literally *invisible* to our informants. Even after training in mirror-image detection, subjects in experiments conflated mirror-images most of the time.[33] The conclusion that I want to draw from the remarks in this and the preceding section is that, although many plausible suggestions have been made about universal constraints on human spatial conception as encoded in language – due to human perceptual and cognitive propensities and the particular schematizing properties of language – most of them fail on just the Guugu Yimithirr and Tzeltal examples, let alone a reasonable cross-cultural sample. There must be some such rich set of intrinsic constraints of course, but whatever they are, they largely under-determine linguistic/cultural solutions to the practical problem of spatial description.[34]

2.3 *Pragmatic constraints*

So far we have seen that neither intrinsic conceptual/perceptual constraints nor constraints on semantic structure seem to severely restrict, or at least determine, the cultural/linguistic conceptualization of a domain like space. However, there are further potential universal constraints on semantic encoding that have to be considered.

The idea of a universal pragmatics is a relatively new ingredient in the relativity debate. Grice and those who have followed him closely, like Atlas, Horn, and myself, have presumed that universal principles of rationality would motivate certain principles of language usage;[35] others, notably Sperber & Wilson (1986), have sought universal usage principles in innate principles of information processing.[36] Pragmaticists of both persuasions argue that much that has been thought of as the semantics of particular lexical items is in fact not part of lexical entries at all, because the information is "read into" the meaning of lexemes by virtue of powerful, general principles of pragmatic interpretation. Consequently, lexical semantics can be much more "sketchy" and schematic than had been thought. Under modern universal theories of syntax and morphology, lexical semantics had alone remained relatively free hunting ground for Whorfians (excluding a handful of domains like color and kinship); now that too is threatened by an unexpected source of universal constraints.

Gricean principles significantly constrain lexicalization possibilities. Horn (1984, 1989), for example, has noted that what is implicated is rarely lexicalized. Thus, given, for example, a contrastive pair of alternates like ⟨*all, some*⟩, where one item is informationally "stronger" than the other, the use of the "weaker" (*some*) will by default implicate 'some but not all' by the first maxim of Quantity (which enjoins the speaker to use the "stronger" description if applicable). It then follows that we do not expect to find a lexical item **nall* meaning 'some but not all' – that would be redundant, its job already done by *some* with its attendant default implicature.

It is worth sketching how such default implicatures may play an important role in the interpretation of English spatial prepositions (especially as there is little such speculation in the literature). In my own version of the Gricean principles, there are three pertinent ones (Levinson 1987). The first (Quantity maxim 1) generates default implicatures as just illustrated, by contrasts of relative informativeness. By this principle the locative prepositions ⟨*at, near*⟩ form a contrast set, such that the use of *near* implicates (rather than entails) 'not at': for example, it would be true but misleading to say *The train is near the station* when it had already reached it; in that case, a co-operative speaker ought to say *The train is at the station.*[37]

The second (Manner) principle derives default implicatures from implicit contrasts between unmarked and (more or less synonymous) marked expressions. By this principle, there is an opposition between {*on, on-top-of*} in at least certain uses (where the relatum has a flat top): *The lamp is on top of the table* suggests some non-canonical relation – perhaps the lamp is normally on the floor, or is not directly supported by the table – all by virtue of the speaker's avoidance of the simpler, unmarked prepositional phrase *on the table*.

The third neo-Gricean principle is derived from Grice's second maxim of Quantity by which, in the interpretation of this principle proposed in Levinson (1987), unmarked expressions will pick out stereotypical interpretations or exemplifications unless the hearer is warned otherwise. It is this last principle which accounts for the divergent interpretations of the preposition in *The coffee is in the cup* vs. *The pencils are in the cup*. Stereotypically, the coffee may be presumed to be in liquid form (or perhaps granules of the instant variety) and thus contained completely within the cup, but one does not expect liquid or granulated pencils, and so presumes that the pencils will lie only partially within the vessel, projecting up and out of a cup of stereotypical size.[38] In this sort of way, as just sketched, it is fairly self-evident how to develop a pragmatic account of the interpretation of English prepositions.

If such principles are indeed universal (and there is a good smattering of evidence for that claim), they might play an important role in constraining the lexicalization of various domains. We expect no English preposition **nat*, meaning 'near but not at,' because of the available contrast ⟨*at, near*⟩. Further we can see that a good deal of pragmatic load can be carried by opposing marked and unmarked synonyms: *on* will pick up stereotypical interpretations readily, *on top of* will stoically resist them. Thus the communicational load of a lexical item is greatly increased by giving it partners in "metalinguistic," pragmatic opposition; the usage of one such item will then always potentially carry information on the basis that its partners have been avoided. This information however can be cancelled by linguistic or non-linguistic context: thus with one lexical item *near* we end up with two interpretations, 'near, but not at' (the default interpretation), 'near and perhaps at' (the possible alternative). Thus we can double the interpretations without doubling the lexicon.

The Tzeltal facts are partially in line and partially out of line with such a theory. The theory stoutly predicts (at least strongly suggests) that no language should have just one preposition. Such a language violates Zipfian first principles.[39] Tzeltal obliges us with a refutation. Why should that be? It is not particularly easy in English to find a function-word with no available oppositions.[40] On the other hand, pragmatic mechanisms of the kind just explicated allow radical under-specification of lexical meaning of just the kind we find in the Tzeltal vacuous preposition, by encouraging rich interpretations of minimal specifications.

In the Tzeltal case, clearly all the interpretive load is handled by the stative/locative predicates. These at least should provide the pragmatic oppositions we have come to expect between saliently contrastive linguistic expressions. For example, the positional adjective *kajal*, glossing as 'lying on,' is unusually weak in specifying no geometrical properties of figure and minimal ones of ground; its use would seem to suggest that a more specific positional would be inappropriate (for example, because the subject is a conjunction of figures with different geometrical properties).

Given the rich lexical content, further enriched by pragmatic oppositions, the interpretation of the preposition can follow the one non-contrastive pragmatic principle sketched above, the interpretation to the stereotype. By providing a superfluity of information about the figure, the addressee is invited to guess the stereotypical disposition of figure to ground. The following examples with identical prepositional phrases but distinct ground-interpretations should suggest how this works:

(10) a. *chawal   koel   ta k'ajk' te chan*
        face-up descending AT fire   the beetle
        'The beetle is lying upside-down (cooking) in the fire'

   b. *lechel   xalten   ta k'ajk'*
        flat-plane-horizontal saucepan AT fire
        'The saucepan is lying horizontally on top of the fire'

   c. *bichil   si'   ta k'ajk'*
        limb-sticking-up firewood AT fire
        'The firewood is in the fire with a fork projecting up out of it'

   d. *p'ekel   ta k'ajk' si'*
        lying-low AT fire   firewood
        'The firewood is lying flat in the fire'

In sum, the universal pragmaticist may be able to hang on to his principles faced with the Tzeltal data, and indeed may point to the semantically vacuous preposition as evidence for the power of contextual inference. Yet such pragmatic constraints clearly enforce no conformity on the lexicalization of a conceptual domain.

3 Conclusions

On the face of it, developments in the cognitive sciences since the 1960s seem to cast doubt on any rampant Whorfianism. Theory, preconception, and, in certain domains at least, substantial evidence emphasize the importance of universal constraints on many levels: the intrinsic structure of the world, the intrinsic structure of our perceptual and cognitive apparatus, the universal structure of our syntactico-semantic system – and even universal constraints on language usage.

Those developments have been coupled with the discovery of some spectacular cross-cultural uniformities in domain conceptualization: arguably in kinship, certainly in color, and in ethnobotany and -zoology. The Berlin & Kay (1969) results almost instantly undermined the empiricist predilections of anthropologists, and gave us a strong model of universal semantic constraints similar to one of universal phonetic constraints: cultural selection from a small, finite inventory of possible percepts/concepts.[41]

Yet the findings reported here do not seem to support such a strong determinism by universal constraints. In an important conceptual domain like space, with its concrete instantiations in the world around us and with our specialized anatomical and neuro-physiological adaptations to that concrete world, such universal constraints seem to under-determine the range of possible conceptual solutions to describing spatial arrangements. There are fundamentally different solutions available, as shown for example by the Guugu Yimithirr use of an "absolute" system of fixed angles in contradistinction to our English "relative" system of search-domains anchored to an ego or viewpoint. Tzeltal introduces a third variant: it has both a system of fixed angles, but of a kind quite different from the Guugu Yimithirr system, and an "intrinsic" system whereby the locations of objects can be specified with regard to other objects without specification of fixed angles. Yet this latter system only serves to show how different such object-oriented systems can be from the kind of system familiar to speakers of European languages: the Tzeltal system de-emphasizes ground (or landmark) objects, does not endow such objects with intrinsic orientations but instead optionally partitions them into named parts on the basis of unoriented shape, eschews extended search-domains projected from them, while simultaneously requiring elaborate non-topological geometrical specifications of the nature of the figure object. In general, Tzeltal does not conform to the "anthropomorphic anthropocentrism" that linguists and psychologists had confidently come to expect.

That universal constraints on so many different levels, which indubitably exist in a field like spatial conception, should fail to produce any kind of cross-cultural conceptual conformity in this domain may certainly be cause for surprise. Good comparative information about the spatial domain is still so thin that we can only expect further surprises from more cross-cultural and crosslinguistic research. Yet even the two cultural systems, the Guugu Yimithirr and the Tzeltal, taken together, give some ground for doubting the likelihood that cultures select (as it were) from a small inventory of possible modes of spatial conception. Taking the Guugu Yimithirr and the English cases alone, one might well argue that the universal inventory offers (a) a system of absolute angles (the Guugu Yimithirr cardinal direction system), (b) a system of search-domains projected from oriented objects, with anthropomorphic and egocentric prototypes, (c) some mix. After all, English-speaking navigators (or dwellers in grid-layout cities) adapt easily to a partial (a)-type system; while all languages do seem to have some spatial deixis, and thus some aspects of a (b) system.[42] However, the core Tzeltal system of locative description is quite different again, with its non-egocentric character, its lack of projected spaces, and its preoccupation with the geometry of the figure. There are not obvious parallels to such a scheme taken as a whole in the other two languages (although analogies may be drawn to specific parts).

Three languages, three largely distinct systems. An inadequate sample of course. Still, this kind of result suggests that a treatment of universal constraints as filters, leaving open indefinite possible cultural variation within outer limits, may in the end not be too weak.[43] There would then be no necessary inconsistency between a rich set of universal constraints and a moderately strong brand of linguistic relativity in at least some domains. The indefinite possible variations within the constraints can then be thought about in two ways. Either the choice is arbitrary: members of the same speech community adopt whatever conceptualization other members use – it mattering little which one is adopted, so long as all settle for it (in the manner of David Lewis's analysis of convention; see Clark, this volume). Or the choice is motivated by other neighbouring conceptualizations, in language or other aspects of culture. Like all good holistic functionalists, and of course like Whorf, one ought to opt for the latter. That would re-legitimize all those Durkheimian speculations about the relation between conceptual structures and social structures.

Notes

1 Presuming of course it's clear enough to be a hypothesis at all! From the point of view of generalizing science, the hypothesis is weak of course, because it seems to make no real predictions about what kinds of linguistic or conceptual variation are to be found.

2 By a "filter" I mean a negative, relatively weak, boundary condition.

3 All the terms here are contentious of course: for example, where constraint A *constrains* cognitive structure B, we might mean that it rules out cognitive structure B', or merely A favours B over B', e.g. makes B "more accessible" than B'. See, e.g., R. Brown & Lenneberg (1954).

4 Since the conference for which this chapter was prepared, parallel work on about fifteen other non-Indo-European languages has been conducted by researchers at the Cognitive Anthropology Research Group at the Max Planck Institute for Psycholinguistics (see Annual Reports for 1992 and 1993). This work confirms the message given by the Tzeltal example here, but the typology of spatial systems in language is now considerably more advanced. See Levinson (in press).

5 Miller & Johnson-Laird (1976) provide a useful synopsis of much relevant literature. See also Levinson (1992a).

6 See, e.g., Stiles-Davis, Kritchevsky, & Bellugi (1988) for summary. As an example of what is still unclear, one may refer, e.g., to the controversy over whether humans have a magnetic sense (see Baker 1989).

7 For more detailed reports, see Bowerman (this volume, and references therein); Levinson (in press).

8 Following initial work by John Haviland, the system has been further explored by Penny Brown, Lourdes de León, and myself, in collaboration with Haviland.

9 See Haviland (1979, 1986, 1993, and this volume) for a description of the linguistic system.

10 See Haviland (1986), Levinson (1986, 1987).

11 The way in which the Guugu Yimithirr system undermines current cognitive science hypotheses should be clear from the following quotations: "Ordinary languages are designed to deal with relativistic space; with space relative to objects that occupy it. Relativistic space provides three orthogonal coordinates, just as Newtonian space does, but *no fixed units of angle or distance* are involved, nor is there any need for coordinates to extend without limit in any direction" (Miller & Johnson-Laird 1976: 380, my italics); "Language's spatial schema...abstracts away from any specificity as to shape (curvature) or magnitude...hence also *from any specificity as to angles*..." (Talmy 1983: 262, my italics and abbreviation).

12 By Penelope Brown and myself in joint work; parallel work by Lourdes de León and John Haviland on the closely related language Tzotzil provides an important control and source of inspiration. We have been able to build on prior grammatical and lexical work on Tzeltal by Berlin, Kaufman, & Maffi (1990).

13 See Brown & Levinson (1993b) for details of the relevant experiments.

14 See Brown & Levinson (1993a).

15 As Wolfgang Klein has put it, we would be loath to consider the verb *drink* a spatial predicate, despite the fact that it describes the motion of stuff into containers. Both the kind of stuff and the kind of container are too specific!

16 We borrow this terminology from Talmy with a slight revision: the *figure* is the **description** of the object (the referent) to be located, the *ground* is the **description** of the **whole complex** of the *relatum* (the landmark-object), the *search-domain* (the space, anchored to the relatum, in which the referent is to be found), and the *relation* (between referent and relatum). See example (1).

17 Although there are occasional uses of motion adverbials in conjunction with locative expressions, these seem to occur in a motivated way: e.g., where a wire is said to hang across the tops of poles, it may also 'move across,' such being the sweep of one's eyes. There are also some marginal uses of the directionals *tal*, 'coming,' and *bel*, 'going,' to describe static alignments. Such usages depend on a close analogy between vector and alignment, and do not extend to static arrays in general.

18 My crude analysis; see Talmy (1983) on *across*.

19 Readers may know Berlin's (1968) description of 545 acutely discriminative Tzeltal numeral classifiers: many of the same roots are involved in locative description.

20 It is an interesting question whether these stative predicates really are locative in character. Functionally there is no doubt. Syntactically however they are one-place predicates, but they optionally subcategorize for a locatively interpreted prepositional phrase, unlike other Tzeltal stative predicates (e.g. color adjectives) – in this regard a bit like English *sit* or *stand* (*John is sitting* vs. *John is sitting on the bench*; cf. *John is tall* vs. **John is tall on the bench*). Semantically, they are even more equivocal, some exhibiting peculiar figure/ground ambiguities and associated switches from one to two semantic arguments. Thus *pachal* can either mean 'sitting-bowl-like' or 'contained within a bowl-like vessel' (see P. Brown 1994: 772ff.). True locatives, one supposes, must be semantically two-place predicates (x is on/in/at y); but as Lyons (1977: 477) warns "locative expressions... have of their very nature a certain syntactic ambivalence."

21 Lucy (1992, this volume) found, for example, that in experimental tasks his Yucatec informants sort entities not primarily according to shape, color or other surface property, but rather according to the stuff out of which things are made.

22 Incidentally, although I quarrel with some details of Talmy's ideas here, his general program is of great interest to the comparative study of semantic systems. Using crosslinguistic evidence as clues, he tries to outline the main components of, e.g., state- or event-descriptions, and to explore the different ways in which such components are fused in single lexicalizations in different language types (see also Talmy 1985).

23 Further thought, though, makes the claim less plausible for English too: consider the non-topological concepts of 'parallel,' 'orthogonal,' etc., encoded in a preposition like *across* or *opposite*. See Herskovits (1986).

24 Such distinctions are not only made in locative/statives but also in descriptive adjectival predicates:

    a. *mak'al*   *si'*
       sliced-at-90°-angle   fire-wood

    b. *p'axal*   *si'*
       sliced-at-oblique-angle fire-wood

25 That this so-called 'intrinsic' usage is secondary may be doubted given the order in acquisition, but, as Clark (1973) points out, the usage often seems to be modelled on how we *confront* things, so that the *left side of the chest of drawers* is defined by the speaker's left, even though it could be said to have an intrinsic front/back, and thus its own right, which we call the left!

26 On the other hand, animal body-part terms are partially based on human ones – e.g. the front limbs of cows are 'arms'! See Hunn (1977). See Levinson (1994) for discussion.

27 There are certain deictic uses of this and a handful of other body-part terms which are exceptions: e.g. the 'face' of a door can mean whichever side is facing the speaker.

28 To invoke such large search-domains, I must use the cardinal direction terms of the 'uphill'/'downhill' system (see the following footnote).

29 In fact, the most fulsome Whorfian position, that Tzeltal makes no ontological commitment to *spaces* as opposed to the objects that fill them, would not be tenable, because there are ancillary ways of indicating search-domains. The central method is similar to the Guugu Yimithirr one, namely to employ fixed angles of a cardinal-point type; in Tenejapan Tzeltal the relevant expressions gloss as 'uphill' and 'downhill,' but the angle is fixed by the prevailing lie of the land (see Brown & Levinson 1993a).

30 Klein (1990) makes the same point by insisting that semantically *The cup is in the cupboard* is a relation between places, which happen to be identified by the objects that occupy them.

31 For discussion of these Kantian themes in the context of Tzeltal, see Levinson & Brown (1994).

32 Our task-replicated one devised by Lourdes de León (1991) and applied to Tzotzil informants, with similar, but not identical, results.

33 See the experiment described in Levinson & Brown (1994).

34 Nothing said here diminishes the plausibility of general, cross-domain, universals of semantic structure, e.g. on the argument structure of predicates. Curiously, though, Tzeltal locative/stative predicates exhibit variable polyadicity at the semantic level while failing ambiguity tests, thus violating one such possible constraint. See Levinson (1991).

35 See, e.g., Atlas & Levinson (1981), Horn (1989).

36 See Levinson (1989) for review.

37 Similarly, in turn, for ⟨on, at⟩: *John is at the table* suggests he is not on it. Notice that these inferences are cancellable without contradiction: one can say *The train is near to, in fact at, the station* (cancelling the 'not at' implicature from *near*); and *John is at, in fact on, the basketball court* (cancelling the 'not on' implicature from *at*).

38 It is clear that such a pragmatic account is in many cases an alternative to a "prototype" theory of the semantic content of expressions. It is preferable in a great range of cases just in the way sketched, because the stereotypical meanings vary with context and collocation.

39 Although Zipf's Force of Unification, or Speaker's Economy, "operating unchecked would result in the evolution of exactly one totally unmarked infinitely ambiguous vocable," it is systematically checked by the antithetical Force of Diversification or Auditor's Economy "leading toward the establishment of as many different expressions as there are messages to communicate" (Horn 1984: 11). Horn identifies these with competing Gricean maxims.

40 The possessive construction comes close: it is semantically very general indeed (*John's books* can be any old books with some connection, causal, resultative, or possessive, to John). Yet even here we have two constructions allowing the Manner opposition *John's picture* vs. *The picture of John*, which at least helps to narrow down the interpretations (only the former could be a picture made by John).

41 It would be useful to have a better hierarchy of "strength" for universal hypotheses, according to their logical types, perhaps (where L is a language and F, G conceivable properties of languages):

  1 Absolute (unconditional: "all Ls are F"):
    1.1 whole set ("all Ls have all properties F & G, etc.")
    1.2 selective ("all Ls have at least one of F or G, etc.")
  2 Conditional ("If an L has F, it has G"):
    2.1 whole set ("G_1 & G_2...," etc.)
    2.2 selective ("G_1 or G_2...")
  3 negative (filters):
    3.1 absolute ("all Ls are not-F")
    3.2 conditional ("If an L has F, it has no G")

and so on. Berlin & Kay's (1969) hypothesis was a heady mix of absolute (at least two basic color terms, at most eleven) and conditional (if blue, then red, etc.). Filters only rule things out, they do not tell you how things will be: "Ravens are non-white" is not as informative as "Ravens are black."

42 Tzeltal has a normal-looking deictic system, with expressions glossing 'here,' 'there,' 'yonder,' 'this,' and 'that.' See Hanks (1990, and this volume).

43 Since this paper was written, work on a dozen more non-Indo-European languages has been conducted in systematic fashion by scholars at the Max Planck Institute for Psycholinguistics. This work suggests that there may indeed after all be just three main spatial systems or frames of reference in language, construed just slightly differently from the three systems as described here. Nevertheless, these three systems are themselves each a broad family of possible solutions, leaving open indefinite variations within them. See Levinson (in press).

References

Atlas, J. & Levinson, S. C. 1981. It-clefts, informativeness and logical form. In P. Cole (ed.), *Radical pragmatics* (pp. 1–61). New York: Academic Press.

Baker, R. R. 1989. *Human navigation and magneto-reception.* Manchester University Press.

Barwise, J. & Perry, J. 1983. *Situation and attitudes.* Cambridge, MA: MIT Press.

Berlin, B. 1968. *Tzeltal numeral classifiers.* Berkeley: University of California Press.

Berlin, B. & Kay P. 1969. *Basic color terms: their universality and evolution.* Berkeley: University of California Press.

Berlin, B., Kaufman, T., & Maffi, L. 1990. *Un diccionario basico del Tzeltal del Tenejapa, Chiapas, Mexico.* Procomith Project, University of California at Berkeley.

Brown, P. 1991. *Spatial conceptualization in Tzeltal.* Working Paper No. 6. Nijmegen: Cognitive Anthropology Research Group.

  1994. The INs and ONs of Tzeltal locative expressions. *Linguistics*, 32(4/5), 743–90.

Brown, P. & Levinson, S. C. 1993a. "Uphill" and "downhill" in Tzeltal. *Journal of Linguistic Anthropology*, 3(1), 46–74.

  1993b. *Linguistic and non-linguistic coding of spatial arrays: explorations in Mayan cognition.* Working Paper No. 24. Nijmegen: Cognitive Anthropology Research Group.

Brown, R. & Lenneberg, E. 1954. A study in language and cognition. *Journal of Abnormal and Social Psychology*, 49, 454–62.

Cassirer, E. 1923. Das Erkenntnisproblem in der Philosophie und Wissenschaft der Neueren Zeit. Berlin: Cassirer.

Clark, H. H. 1973. Space, time, semantics, and the child. In T. E. Moore (ed.), *Cognitive development and the acquisition of language* (pp. 28–64). New York: Academic Press.

de León, L. 1991. *Space games in Tzotzil: creating a context for spatial reference.* Working Paper 4, Cognitive Anthropology Research Group at the Max Planck Institute for Psycholinguistics, Berlin.

Friedrich, P. 1969. "On the meaning of the Tarascan suffixes of space. Memoir 23." Indiana University Publications in Anthropology and Linguistics. Supplement to *IJAL* 35(4).

Hanks, W. 1990. *Referential practice: language and lived space among the Maya.* University of Chicago Press.

Haviland, J. B. 1979. Guugu Yimidhirr. In R. M. W. Dixon & B. Blake (eds.), *Handbook of Australian languages* (pp. 27–180). Canberra: ANU Press.

1986. Complex referential gestures in Guugu Yimithirr. Unpublished ms.

1993. Anchoring, iconicity and orientation in Guugu Yimithirr pointing gestures. *Journal of Linguistic Anthropology*, 3(1), 3–45.

Herskovits, A. 1986. *Language and spatial cognition: an interdisciplinary study of the prepositions in English.* Cambridge University Press.

Horn, L. 1984. Toward a new taxonomy for pragmatic inference: Q-based and R-based implicature. In D. Schiffrin (ed.), *Meaning, form and use in context* (pp. 11–42). Georgetown University Press.

1989. *A natural history of negation.* University of Chicago Press.

Hunn, E. 1977. *Tzeltal folk zoology.* New York: Academic Press.

Klein, W. 1990. Überall und nirgendwo. Subjektive und objektive Momente in der Raum-referenz. *Zeitschrift fur Literaturwissenschaft und Linguistik*, 78, 9–42.

Levinson, S. C. 1986. The semantics/pragmatics of space in Guugu Yimithirr. Unpublished ms.

1987. Pragmatics and the grammar of anaphora. *Journal of Linguistics*, 23, 379–434.

1989. A review of relevance. *Journal of Linguistics*, 25, 455–72.

1991. *Figure and ground in Mayan spatial description: Tzeltal locative descriptions.* Working Paper, MPG Project Group for Cognitive Anthropology, Berlin.

1992a. Primer for the field investigation of spatial description and conception. *Pragmatics*, 2(1), 5–47.

1992b. *Language and cognition: the cognitive consequences of spatial description in Guugu Yimithirr.* Working paper No. 13. Nijmegen: Cognitive Anthropology Research Group.

1994. Vision, shape and linguistic description: Tzeltal body-part terminology and object-description. In "Space in Mayan languages" special issue of *Linguistics*, ed. J. Haviland & S. C. Levinson. 32(4–5), 791–856.

in press. Frames of reference and Molyneaux's question: cross-linguistic evidence. To appear in P. Bloom, M. Peterson, L. Nadel, & M. Garrett (eds.), *Language and space* (pp. 109–69). Cambridge, MA: MIT Press.

Levinson, S. C. and Brown, F. 1994. Immanuel Kant among the Tenejapans: anthropology as empirical philosophy. *Ethos*, 22(1), 3–41.

Lucy, J. 1985. Whorf's view of the linguistic mediation of thought. In E. Mertz & R. Parmentier (eds.), *Semiotic mediation: sociocultural and psychological perspectives* (pp. 73–97). New York: Academic Press.
  1992. *Grammatical categories and cognition: a case study of the linguistic relativity hypothesis.* Cambridge University Press.
Lyons, J. 1977. *Semantics.* 2 vols. Cambridge University Press.
MacLaury, R. E. 1989. Zapotec body-part locatives: prototypes and metaphoric extensions. *International Journal of American Linguistics*, 55(2), 119–54.
Miller, G. A. & Johnson-Laird, P. N. 1976. *Language and perception.* Cambridge University Press.
Piaget, J. & Inhelder, B. 1948. *La représentation de l'espace chez l'enfant.* Paris: Presses Universitaires de France.
Sperber, D. & Wilson, D. 1986. *Relevance.* Oxford: Basil Blackwell.
Stiles-Davis, J., Kritchevsky, M., & Bellugi, U. 1988. *Spatial cognition: brain bases and development.* Hillsdale, NJ: Lawrence Erlbaum.
Talmy, L. 1983. How language structures space. In H. Pick & L. Acredolo (eds.), *Spatial orientation: theory, research and application* (pp. 225–320). New York: Plenum Press.
  1985. Lexicalization patterns: semantic structure in lexical forms. In T. Shopen (ed.), *Language typology and syntactic description*, vol. III: *Grammatical categories and the lexicon* (pp. 56–149). Cambridge University Press.

8

COGNITIVE LIMITS TO CONCEPTUAL RELATIVITY: THE LIMITING-CASE OF RELIGIOUS ONTOLOGIES

PASCAL BOYER

Anthropological discussions of linguistic relativity, and more specifically of the Whorfian hypothesis, generally focus on the possible *extension* of Whorf's ethno-linguistic observations to a more global description of cultural representations. From observed differences in circumscribed domains of experience, the discussion then proceeds to conceptual structure in general. These discussions are generally less than satisfactory, for two main reasons. First, Whorf is presented as the originator or champion of an extreme form of cultural relativism, without much consideration of his original observations and hypotheses. Second, perhaps in a less obvious way, the common anthropological interpretation of Whorf often reduces to an *a fortiori* argument, based on an implicit hierarchy of cognitive capacities. At the bottom of the hierarchy, there are apparently "basic" (natural or experience-driven) domains like spatial orientation or time-reckoning, which are contrasted with apparently more "complex" (speculative or culturally constructed) domains like religious ontologies or social categories. The *a fortiori* argument runs as follows: if one can show that a seemingly "basic" domain like the perception of time is in fact structured by available linguistic resources, then, it is assumed, more complex conceptual constructions should be even more strongly constrained by such linguistic structures. Consequently, they should display even more cultural specificity. As a result of this assumption, discussions of the Whorfian paradigm do not usually include a serious treatment of conceptual relativity at the "complex" end of this spectrum.

After presenting a "reconstructed" version of the Whorfian argument, I will try to show that its implicit assumptions about conceptual structure and conceptual development are not entirely plausible. This implies a departure from ordinary discussions of the Whorfian paradigm, in that I will focus on the cognitive processes involved in cultural transmission, which are often ignored or taken as immaterial. I will try to show that this neglect results in descriptions of linguistic, conceptual, and cultural differences which are less than perfectly plausible. Moreover, if we take into account the cognitive substratum of cultural acquisition, it is possible to show that linguistic differences only provide fragmentary evidence for cognitive differences. Developmental studies tend to show that early conceptual development is constrained by intuitive domain-specific principles, which are not dependent on cultural transmission. I will try to show that these non-cultural principles can be seen to constrain what seems the most "culturally constructed" of all domains of knowledge, namely religious ontologies. These arguments are not meant as a "refutation" of the Whorfian position. Nor do they constitute a counter-example to the fact of linguistic differences, or to the Whorfian hypotheses about their likely cognitive effects. Rather, my aim is to suggest that such linguistic facts and such probable effects cannot be understood with any precision, if we fail to consider the important role played by non-transmitted principles of intuitive knowledge.

1 A reconstructed Whorfian theory

In the following sections I will present some aspects of conceptual structure and cognitive development which are particularly relevant to cultural acquisition. Before engaging in this discussion, however, I must provide a brief outline of the precise claims made by what could be called a "Whorfian paradigm" in the description of linguistic and cultural differences. This Whorfian approach denotes not only Whorf's own formulation, but also a variety of linguistic and anthropological theories, some of them quite remote from Whorf's ethno-linguistic problems. The criticisms presented in the rest of the paper are meant to apply to all such Whorfian approaches, inasmuch as they share a number of premises concerning the differences between natural languages and their consequences for particular styles of thought.

The main insight of the approach is that languages differ in non-trivial ways. That is to say, their differences can be seen to have profound effects on the expression of perceptual and conceptual relations. The ways in which linguistic categories "carve nature," to use the classical phrase, may be different, a fact which is supposed to have direct effects on categorisation and inference, and consequently on the possibility of direct translation. Leaving aside, for the time being, the question of cognitive effects, it may be worthwhile considering what could make such differences possible at all. A constant premise of Whorfian hypotheses is that experience under-determines conceptual structure, that there is no intrinsically "natural" way of describing experiential pattern. If conceptual structure cannot be directly determined by experience, it can be informed on the other hand by structures available in the lexicon and grammar of the language. This is because different languages focus on (and provide rich structures for) different features of experience. What counts as similar and dissimilar in any two experiences cannot be extracted directly from experience, but requires a system of categories to denote relevant similarities. This in turn implies that what makes a concept is the identification of a similarity. What brings together exemplars of lemon, for instance, is what is similar about them that would make them different from, say, exemplars of orange or grapefruit.

To sum up, a Whorfian theory can be described as founded on the following series of assumptions:

(a) concepts are constructed by similarity;
(b) the choice of a similarity metric for any concept is under-determined by experienced reality;
(c) the metric is provided (mainly implicitly) by available linguistic categories;
(d) it is transmitted through linguistic acquisition;
(e) since available linguistic categories differ from one language to another, the corresponding conceptual systems will be different too.

Although the relativity issue is not usually described in those terms in the literature, I believe this interpretation is faithful to the gist of the Whorfian enterprise. Standard arguments for linguistic relativity generally focus on the actual differences observed between natural languages, leaving aside the cognitive underpinnings of these differences. However, we must consider these processes if we want to understand the relevance of Whorfian arguments for broader issues of cultural differences and cultural transmission. In the rest of the chapter, I will try to show why this framework is not entirely satisfactory, notably with regard to conceptual structure and the role in similarity. I will then summarize some findings and hypotheses of developmental psychology, which could help towards a more precise formulation of conceptual development and the role of culturally specific input.

2 Similarity and conceptual structure

It may seem self-evident that concepts are means of putting together singular objects (exemplars) which are similar, in that they share some property or properties. Similarity can be of a perceptual or conceptual nature. The concept CAR brings together objects which share certain observable features, whilst the concept FRIENDSHIP denotes behaviors and mental states which share less directly manifest properties. It therefore seems natural to infer that a conceptual representation consists of some representation of the similarity in question. In this conception, a subject has a certain mental concept if he/she has a representation of what makes the instances of the class similar. Most theories of concept representation are based on some version of the similarity hypothesis.

The approach that is generally called "classical" or "Fregean" in the psychological literature holds that a conceptual representation consists of the representation of a series of features, which are singly necessary and jointly sufficient to characterize the similarity between instances of the concept. For instance, the concept TELEPHONE may be defined as a device that converts sound-waves into modulated electrical current (through a microphone) and vice versa (through a speaker) and can be connected to other similar devices. A device which has all these features is a telephone, a device that lacks any one of them is not. Again, the features may be of very different types. For instance, the definition of NOSEGAY or JACKET may involve perceptual features, as well as functional ones. Whatever these differences, the presence of singly necessary and jointly sufficient features is assumed to define (and exhaust) the mental representation of concepts.

The main arguments against the "classical" approach came from the work of E. Rosch and her colleagues on prototypical effects in categorization (see Rosch 1977, Rosch & Lloyd 1978). The main conclusion of those experimental studies was that membership of a category is not always a yes/no question, as the classical approach would predict. In a number of experimental categorization tasks, subjects seem to make a difference between certain instances, judged to be particularly good examples of the concept, and others which are less representative. For instance, a robin seems a "good" instance of the concept BIRD, but an ostrich seems intuitively less representative. This goes against the very principle of the classical approach: if a series of necessary–sufficient features defines a category, then every object either is or else is not a member of the category. Rosch's solution to this problem was to replace the classical view with an alternative "prototypical" conception, which is based on two premises. First, membership of a category is not a yes/no question; it is a matter of graded judgment, between 0 (non-membership) and 1 (full member- ship). Second, the degree to which any single instance belongs to a concept depends on its similarity to a mentally represented "prototype." Robins for instance are presumably more similar to the prototypical bird than ostriches, which explains that the degree of membership of the category BIRD is higher for the first kind of bird.[1]

Both the classical and the prototypical approaches are based on the idea that having a concept is having some representation of what makes instances of the concept similar. There are, however, many reasons to think that similarity is insufficient; more specifically, in many cases having a concept precisely means having something more than a measure of similarity for a set of objects. To begin with, it is possible to show that people's intuitions of similarity often conflict with intuitions of category membership. If the similarity account was true, a new instance would be considered more likely to be a member of category A than of category B if it is more similar to other members of A than to other members of B. In many cases, however, two instances can be judged similar yet not members of the same category, whilst two instances are judged dissimilar yet members of the same category.[2]

More generally, as many authors have pointed out, the similarity approach is insufficient in the simple sense that any judgment of similarity presupposes certain choices, as to what aspects of the objects considered are taken to be relevant to category membership (McCloskey & Gluckberg 1979; Armstrong, Gleitman, & Gleitman 1983; Murphy & Medin 1985; Medin & Wattenmaker 1987). Any two objects can be judged similar or dissimilar from indefinitely many different points of view. Concepts cannot be based on a pure similarity metric, because such a metric would take all dimensions of similarity as equivalent, which is precisely what people do not do when they categorize objects. They clearly weigh differently the attributes of instances. Size is crucial for 25¢ COIN, relevant for LEMON, and almost irrelevant for PAINTING. It is difficult, however, to introduce such weighing in a similarity-based account without producing models which either are much too vague to account for conceptual coherence (Medin & Wattenmaker 1987: 33) or else break apart the very notion of similarity. If similarity is assumed to be an entirely different type of judgement for coins, lemons, and paintings, then the notion of "similarity" only means that concepts put together things that are supposed to have something in common, which is of course true but trivial.

It is therefore necessary to put forward an alternative account, in which conceptual representation is not based on mere judgments of similarity. Medin's notion of implicit "theories" (Murphy & Medin 1985, Medin & Wattenmaker 1987) is an example of such an alternative. The main assumption here is that the cohesiveness of a category, what holds it together, is constituted by a set of implicit theoretical assumptions. These not only establish the relative relevance of different attributes for categorization, they also provide explanations for the presence of the attributes: "people not only notice feature correlations, but they can deduce reasons for them based on their knowledge of the way the world works" (Medin & Wattenmaker 1987: 36). For instance, one cannot have the concept COIN without having some theoretical assumptions about the production and use of coins that makes certain features (e.g. exact similarity to template, and actual historical origin) more salient than others. As Medin & Wattenmaker put it (1987: 41), the cohesiveness of a category, in this account, "derives both from the internal structure of a conceptual domain and the position of the [category] in the complete knowledge base." Some notion of theoretical assumptions or implicit "micro-theories" is at the foundation of most psychologically realistic models of conceptual structure. Concepts in various domains are described as including inter-related assumptions; these not only describe the entities designated, but also provide a structure which makes relevant certain types of similarities, and make possible certain expectations.[3]

One of the consequences of this approach is to suggest a new conception of the links between conceptual structure and knowledge. In a similarity-based approach, and in fact in commonsense conceptions of categories, concepts are understood as "building bricks" out of which knowledge is constructed. Concepts are seen as elementary units which include some description of the entities they denote. Beyond these elementary descriptions, concepts are linked by theoretical propositions which connect them in more complex structures. Concepts are internally structured by resemblance, and inter-connected by explanatory principles. The concept GIRAFFE for instance is supposed to include some elements which allow users of the term *giraffe* to recognize real giraffes and refer to them. Beyond this, propositions such as "giraffes must eat to survive," "giraffes were born of other giraffes," etc., are conceived as higher-order combinations of simple concepts (GIRAFFE and BIRTH, GIRAFFE and DIET for instance). If the "theory-based" approach is valid, however, this view of knowledge structures is not really tenable. The information about giraffes contained in the above assertions is now seen, not as an association of the concept GIRAFFE with other ones, but as an integral part of that concept itself. The way subjects recognize certain similarities between observed giraffes, and neglect observable differences (or indeed other similarities), seems to be driven by theoretical considerations. If two giraffe-like animals react to a predator in very different ways, this does not seem to cast doubt upon their identification as giraffes. If, however, one of these animals is observed to lay eggs, even unsophisticated observers will assume that it cannot be of the same species as ordinary giraffes. So, again, having the concept means having some way of sorting out which similarities count as relevant and which do not. In a classical picture theories and other forms of complex conceptual structures are seen as combinations of concepts. The "micro-theory" approach suggests that theories are in fact an integral part of conceptual representation, that they are "inside" concepts, to use slightly metaphorical terms.

To conclude, a psychologically realistic theory of concept representation presents a qualified picture of the role of similarity in conceptual structure. Similarity is in most cases insufficient, and in many cases not even necessary for the cohesiveness of concepts. Intuitions of similarity are in most cases not the underlying basis of concepts, but a consequence of their representation.

3 Intuitive principles in conceptual development

Let me now turn to the developmental scenario that is presupposed by what I describe as a "Whorfian" framework. If linguistic differences are supposed to have a direct effect on "world-views," that is, on underlying conceptual organisation, then one must assume that language acquisition is the main process through which conceptual structure develops. This implies that children's pre-verbal conceptual structures are plastic enough to adapt to potentially very different types of conceptual organization. Also, it implies that the children have the conceptual means to identify which types of similarities are relevant to the language they learn. In other words, they should be equipped with some form of general intelligence, which makes it possible to infer the putative reference of potentially diverse concepts.

I will try to show here that this description is not really congruent with the developmental data. Pre-verbal conceptual organization does not seem to have the required plasticity, and the hypothesized general intelligence is simply difficult to trace. On the contrary, developmental data tend to suggest that early conceptual structures impose strong constraints on later development, and that the enrichment of early structures is dependent on *domain-specific principles* rather than general heuristics. These principles correspond to broad ontological categories, e.g. EVENT, PHYSICAL OBJECT, LIVING THING, ANIMATE BEING, PERSON, etc.[4] A number of studies have emphasized the fact that in these different domains, (a) the range of intuitively salient features of categorization may be different, (b) patterns of induction and inference are noticeably different, and (c) conceptual development displays different developmental schedules. Each domain seems to be structured by principles or presumptions which develop early, and seem relatively independent from the structuring principles of other domains. These principles constitute the skeletons of what are often called "intuitive" or "naive" theories (as opposed to scientific ones). They are generally implicit, and seem to play a crucial role in the development of later, partly explicit, representations of the domains concerned. Early cognitive development relies on the construction of a naive theory of physical objects (Spelke 1990), a naive biology (Carey 1985, Keil 1986, 1989), and a naive theory of mental processes (Astington, Harris, & Olson 1988; Wellmann 1990; Perner 1991; Whiten 1991), to mention a few domains explored so far.

A crucial point is that intuitive "theoretical" principles seem to develop spontaneously, in the sense that they are under-determined by direct or implicit tuition or by objective changes in the available information. The development of "essentialist" assumptions in the representation of living kinds, for instance, occurs in children who have very rudimentary notions of biological processes, and therefore make a clear-cut distinction between, for example, members of a living species and members of a class of artifacts, without the conceptual means to explain the distinction. This principle may be interpreted as an enrichment of a deeper principle, which establishes a fundamental difference in expectations concerning animate as opposed to inanimate objects. There is considerable evidence that this distinction is present even in infants (Gelman, Spelke, & Meck 1983; Bullock 1985; Richards & Siegler 1986) and may be grounded in an early sensitivity to the difference between self- and non-self-generated movement in physical objects (Massey & Gelman 1988). In other words, even if essentialist principles develop over time, and are enriched by various "micro-theoretical" assumptions, they require presumptions of differences in causal structure which appear extremely early. Obviously, such presumptions are not taught, and are certainly under-determined by experience. Far from being inferred from experience, "the initial principles of a domain establish the boundary conditions for the stimuli that are candidates for feeding coherent development in that domain" (Gelman 1990: 83).

This point is of course crucial for cultural anthropology. If intuitive principles are not inferred from experience, then they cannot vary as a function of the cultural environment. Indeed, there is a range of evidence to show that important variations in cultural settings do not affect the content of intuitive presumptions on their developmental schedule in a significant way. As regards biological knowledge, the universality of its basic principles is a familiar point (see Berlin, Breedlove, & Raven 1973; Brown 1984; Atran 1985, 1987, 1990). Furthermore, other aspects of conceptual development appear to be similar, even in domains which could give rise to strong cultural influences. For instance, Walker observed that the defining-to-characteristic shift, as described by Keil in American children, occurs in the same form at the same age in Yoruba subjects. Moreover, the shifts display the same domain-specific characteristics. If anything, more variation can be found within the Yoruba sample, between rural and urban subjects, than between the Yoruba average and the American results (Walker 1986, forthcoming a, b). Given the enormous differences in socio-cultural settings, it would require some quasi-miraculous coincidence for such shifts to occur at the same age in the same way in the cultures compared. In the rest of this chapter, I will illustrate some consequences of these developmental facts for a cognitive account of cultural acquisition.

4 Intuitive principles and cultural knowledge

There is no space here to give a full account of the various ways in which culturally transmitted information and intuitive theories combine to produce mature cultural representations. I will only focus on the suggestive domain of religious ontologies, and outline the framework in which it can be treated, a framework that was presented in more detail elsewhere (Boyer 1992, 1993, 1994). Religious categories constitute a limiting-case here, in the sense that they seem to be among the most variable domains of cultural representations, and therefore one of the domains where cognitive constraints would not seem immediately relevant. Religious representations, because they seem culturally specific, also appear to be entirely constrained by cultural input.

This view, however, is not really plausible. Here I will try to show that it is problematic, and that a psychologically realistic alternative can be put forward. I will proceed in several steps. First, on the basis of an ethnographic example, I will show that ethnographic descriptions of religious categories are invariably, and perhaps inevitably, fragmentary. Although they describe explicit cultural input in great detail, they do not provide a full account of the underlying principles people use in the acquisition and representation of that input. Second, I will argue that at least some of these underlying principles, which are indispensable to the acquisition of religious categories, belong to the intuitive domain-specific structures described above, and therefore are not culturally transmitted. Third, I will try to demonstrate that such intuitive principles actually impose constraints on the range of religious ontologies likely to be acquired and transmitted. I will illustrate these theoretical points by taking an example from my own ethnographic work among the Fang of Cameroon, focusing in particular on the notion of *bekong*, 'ghosts' or 'ancestors' (see Boyer 1990: 40ff; 1993). I will first present a very concise account of the assumptions on which this notion is based, and the way they are acquired by Fang subjects. I will then try to show that this apparently simple acquisition process in fact requires intuitive domain-specific assumptions. Although I describe the example in some detail, the conclusions I will draw from this case apply to religious ontologies in general.

The Fang consider that the forest is peopled with wandering shadows, among which are the spirits of the dead, called *bekong*. They dwell in invisible villages (some people see them as underground villages, others as camps in the darkest recesses of the forest) and breed wild animals. A number of general principles are used to describe the ghosts. Everyone characterizes them as invisible and intangible beings. They are also described as able to move extremely fast, although no-one ever supposes that they could be in two places at once. The implications of such principles, and even their entailments, are often surrounded with uncertainty. Although everyone is quite definite that ghosts usually cannot be seen, and that they are never hindered by physical obstacles, no-one ever speculates on the possible implications of such capacities. The way these seemingly non-physical entities eat and drink, the way they domesticate and use wild animals is mysterious, though it constitutes a mystery in which no-one seems to show any interest.

On the other hand, the effects of the ghosts' actions or intentions are of considerable interest, and the subject matter of frequent statements. It is assumed, and explicitly stated on many occasions, that ghosts can send illnesses to people when they are angry with them. The ghosts are likely to interfere in the affairs of the living, whenever the latter violate ritual prohibitions, or deviate from the traditional ways. In the Fang nosology, such situations constitute an explicitly recognized etiological category. There are ritual specialists, and prescribed ritual remedies for such diseases, which of course include many types of misfortune, beyond somatic illnesses.

The above remarks constitute a very concise summary of what most Fang people accept as valid statements concerning the *bekong* and their action. We have here the main elements that would be examined in an anthropological description of this notion. Such a description, however, is essentially fragmentary. This is not just a question of ethnographic detail. Obviously, the account presented above should be completed with a number of precise indications, as regards the ideas, images, and actions which are connected with this notion of *bekong*. I would claim, however, that anthropological descriptions in general are incomplete in a more fundamental sense, because they leave aside certain aspects of conceptual structure without which we cannot understand the phenomenon of cultural transmission. In the following pages I will try and spell out these aspects which are systematically omitted in anthropological descriptions and theories.

Before proceeding any further, I must insist on two general characteristics of the principles mentioned above. First, the explicit assumptions express *counter-intuitive* claims, which are clearly treated as such by everyone. The fact that some beings can go through obstacles, become invisible, or keep wild animals the way humans breed the domesticated species, all these are explicitly treated as out of the ordinary. Second, the transmission of such principles does not seem mysterious at all. Many of them are explicitly stated as valid generalizations, for example "the *bekong* live in the forest," "dead people become *bekong*," and so on. Others can be acquired by generalizing over repeated instances. For instance, one seldom hears the general statement "the *bekong* can provoke misfortune"; its application to singular cases is frequent enough to suggest the generalization even to very lazy inductivists.

5 Background principles

There is no shortage of cultural input, in terms of stated principles, particular anecdotes, and more or less mythical stories concerning the ghosts. From such cultural material, people naturally derive their general notions about the strange physical and causal properties of the ghosts. In order, however, to be able to extract such principles from such material, it is necessary to accept a number of implicit premises. Any inductive generalization requires a background of assumptions, concerning the type of features that can be generalized. This very general point has important consequences for the precise question of cultural acquisition, as we will see below.

Without providing a detailed explanation of Fang notions about ghost-behavior, I must specify those principles which are necessary, in order to produce generalizations in this domain. First and foremost, people can take singular episodes, and ritual statements, as the basis for hypotheses about ghosts in general, because they can understand ghost-behavior in psychological terms. This requires a set of principles, which are both tacit and indispensable. To take the most important of these principles, it is necessary to assume that the ghosts have psychological mechanisms such that they can perceive what people do, form some beliefs on the basis of those perceptions, and keep those beliefs in memory. It seems natural to assume causal arrows from perception to belief to intention to action, not in the opposite direction. It is also assumed, for instance, that the ghosts have mental capacities such that, if they find a certain state of affairs E to be desirable, and know that another state of affairs, C, is necessary to achieve E, then they will desire to achieve C. The ghosts are described as wishing that certain rituals were performed. They are described as expecting that people, if afflicted by misfortune, will eventually oblige. They are said to decide, in consequence, that some illness should be "sent" to the living. When people are making inferences from the explicit cultural material, they necessarily rely on such tacit principles, describing the ghosts' putative psychological mechanisms. These principles are not given in the utterances and other types of explicit information on the ghosts. They are not implicitly transmitted, in the sense that they could be readily deduced from that explicit information. On the contrary, it is because they are assumed to be valid that inferences about the ghosts' behavior can be drawn at all.

These implicit assumptions concerning the ghosts' psychology are themselves based on a further set of assumptions, concerning the stability of their properties as a kind. Obviously, the fact that one can infer general principles from a limited series of examples presupposes that at least some properties of the ghosts are stable. This is especially the case as regards the causal propensities of the ghosts. Subjects spontaneously assume that all or most ghosts have the powers which are exemplified in particular anecdotes or stories. This would not be possible without the prior assumption that ghosts are, precisely, a kind, and that one can safely produce instance-based general principles.

Such tacit assumptions are never mentioned in anthropological descriptions. This is mainly because it seems unnecessary, perhaps even slightly absurd, to insist on such self-evident principles. After all, one would be really surprised if ghosts were described as desiring an effect E, knowing that its condition is C, and not desiring C. However seemingly self-evident, these principles must be mentioned in a description of cultural transmission, because they provide the basis for all inferences about ghosts, and because they are not part of the cultural input.

6 Violation and confirmation of intuitive principles

The Fang ghosts are described in psychological terms, on the basis of a number of tacit premises about mental functioning. These principles of ghost-psychology are not the object of any tuition; nor, in fact, are the corresponding principles of "person-psychology." Ordinary "folk-psychology" is based on a number of intuitive presumptions, which are both "transparent" and theoretically complex. People's commonsense interpretation of other people's behavior is consistently directed by implicit principles concerning motivation, intentions, memory, reasoning, etc. Some of these principles are specific, in that they depend on assumptions which concern only other people's behavior, as opposed to any other kinds of data. Moreover, these assumptions appear early enough to be construed as orienting principles, which structure experience, rather than generalizations inferred from experience by some cross-domain inductive mechanism.[5]

Intuitive principles comprise a number of assumptions about mental objects and their dynamic interaction. Because they are intuitive, self-evident, and make it possible to complexity one's knowledge of other minds, such assumptions are best elucidated by developmental research. Their effect is clearer in subjects who have no explicit vocabulary to express them, and no awareness of their implicit use in particular explanations. To take the most fundamental facts, even small children seem to conceive mental entities (thoughts, feelings, dreams) as non-physical objects; this goes against the classical Piagetian notion of childhood realism, following which children do not distinguish between objects and their representation (Wellmann & Estes 1986). Moreover, children have rudimentary, yet precise, notions concerning causality in mental events. They know that perception causes beliefs, which can cause intentions, and that these causal links are not reversible. This causal schema is a fundamental feature of what D'Andrade called the "folk-model" of the mind (D'Andrade 1987). Cultural variations do not seem to have any significant effect on these phenomena. For example, Avis and Harris made a series of studies on the representation of false belief in Pygmy children. These tests replicate the substance of familiar American experiments, and offer substantially the same results. From an early age (about 4–5) children develop an awareness of false belief, of the fact that other people may store representations of the world which do not correspond to an actual state of affairs, and that they may act on the basis of such a misrepresentation.

In the analysis of a paradigmatic example of a religious notion (the Fang *bekong*), we find that some principles of intuitive, domain-specific conceptual structures can play an important role in shaping and constraining people's beliefs about apparently fantastic religious entities. In this case, the principles in question are notably principles dealing with the explanation of behavior in terms of intentions and beliefs. The common understanding of the notion *bekong* can be paraphrased, roughly, as follows: *bekong* are invisible, intangible sentient beings. This of course constitutes an obvious violation of a commonsense principle, following which intentional beings are physical objects. There is a direct link between intentionality, and other characteristics of sentient beings on the one hand, and "corporeality" on the other. Given such premises, the special characteristics of *bekong* make them a conceptual oddity, a puzzling invention. This is very much the way they are construed by the Fang, and most statements about what *bekong* are, or what they can do, are typically accompanied by remarks concerning the uncertainty that results from this oddity. *Bekong*, however, are also assumed to have many other properties, among which are psychological processes. Those processes, in striking contrast to the assumptions concerning physicality, are intuitive in the sense that they are a straightforward projection of the assumptions made about people's mental processes.

The existence, and importance, of such principles casts doubt on the anthropological notion of "exhaustive cultural transmission." The principles of intuitive mentalistic psychology must be included in our description of the Fang notion *bekong*, if we want to have a plausible psychological description of the way people acquire the notion, build a relatively coherent representation of these entities, and make inferences about their behavior. Now these principles are part of a set of cognitive systems which are not culturally transmitted, and in fact are not transmitted at all.

7 Recurrent violations and a cognitive optimum

Let me now try to show how this type of explanation could be extended further. A natural extension of the Fang example would be to assume that principles of intuitive knowledge may well play a similar part in the construction of religious concepts in general. At this point, obviously, I will have to rely on vastly simplified generalizations to support the speculative claims. I hope this way of proceeding can at least generate a picture of religious ontologies that is at least as plausible as the notion of unbounded cultural construction.

The simplest way to describe these recurrent themes is perhaps to try and construct a list of these ontological assumptions which are the basis of religious systems and violate intuitive expectations. I do not claim that my list is exhaustive, or even precise enough to be of great explanatory power. It should, however, give some indication of the type of explanation the research program is about.

Let me begin with the most obvious and probably the most common way in which religious ideas can be counter-intuitive. This is the postulation of a class (or classes) of beings whose specific properties make them either very strange physical objects, or apparently non-physical ones. The Fang ancestor–ghosts are of course among such entities. Religious systems are almost invariably based on such assumptions, so much so that the idea of non-physical beings has often been taken, from Tylor onwards, as the very definition of religion. The claims concerning the physical properties of such entities typically focus on their intangibility, invisibility, instantaneous changes of location or ubiquity, etc.

Another typical violation concerns the fact that many religious entities are construed as having a particular biological destiny. The entities either do not die, or were not born, or do not grow, etc. Typically, ancestors are biologically "blocked" at the age of death, and gods either are ageless or have a characteristic "age" which does not change with time. In other words, they are explicitly characterized as beings whose existence violates expectations about living beings to do with normal cycles of birth, maturation, reproduction, death, and decay.

A third type of violation concerns the strange mental and communicational characteristics of the supernatural personnel. This is obvious in popular Western Christian conceptions, for instance, which assume that God can detect not only people's actions, but also their thoughts and intentions. As is well known, this explicit assumption can generate many cognitive paradoxes. For example, it is difficult to assume the capacity of intention-reading, and to understand what goes on in a prayer (since God knows one's intentions). However, the assumption is necessary to the type of intention-based morality that is admitted in such groups. Paradoxes can also be generated by other common explicit assumptions, such as the idea that the gods can foresee future events.

How should a cognitive theory of religious ideas approach such seemingly odd principles and assumptions? Anthropologists, being trained both to detect cultural differences and to focus on the counter-intuitive nature of religious claims, tend to provide a distorted view of the cognitive processes involved. Against the grain of received anthropological wisdom, I would therefore argue that (a) violations of intuitive ontologies are far more circumscribed than we usually assume, and (b) the amount of intuitive understanding that is required to acquire religious notions is far greater than the anthropological descriptions lead one to think.

Let me offer a brief illustration of this idea, as concerns the three main types of violations mentioned above. As I said, many creatures such as spirits or ghosts are explicitly described as having counter-intuitive physical properties. I tried to show, on the Fang example, that, in order to acquire ideas about ancestor–ghosts, one must admit implicit intuitive assumptions about belief–desire psychology. In other cases, the distribution of intuitive and counter-intuitive assumptions may be different. The general point, however, is that it would be difficult to acquire and represent ideas about such non-physical beings except against a background of intuitive theories.

The same arguments can be put forward in the description of odd biological properties, or odd mental-communicational capacities. The beings which are explicitly construed as eternal actually have many properties which are directly transferred from intuitive presumptions. Greek gods are eternal and feed on the smell of sacrifices; their common representation, however, included many aspects transferred directly from commonsense understandings, to do for example with their reasonings or feelings. Such beings typically display, again, a form of belief–desire psychology that seems self-evident because it is directly transferred from commonsense intuitive "theories." An omniscient God is nevertheless submitted to intuitive principles of psychology, and produces *modus ponens* inferences or practical syllogisms in much the same self-evident way as ordinary people.

8 Conclusions on relativity

Let me now return to the general question of linguistic relativity, and to the general assumptions mentioned at the beginning of this paper as the implicit structure of the "Whorfian framework." The thrust of the Whorfian paradigm was to show that languages may differ in their implicit metrics for certain categories, and that this difference entails, indeed produces, a corresponding difference in styles of thought.

Against this, I have first argued that similarity-based accounts of conceptual structure are unsatisfactory. Similarity is a vacuous notion unless it is constrained by implicit "micro-theoretical" assumptions. This implies that conceptual relativity, if it exists at all, stems from important differences in these implicit theoretical principles.

This has led me to question another implicit assumption of the framework, following which conceptual structure is mainly constrained by linguistic acquisition. Against this, developmental data tend to show that at least some intuitive, domain-specific conceptual principles appear before language acquisition, and quite independently from cultural input.

Finally, it is possible to show that intuitive domain-specific principles impose constraints on seemingly variable cultural constructions, in at least two important ways. First, culturally transmitted violations of those principles are relevant or attention-demanding only against the background of ordinary, intuitive expectations. Second, the explicit violations cannot be acquired, and cannot be the object of inferences, unless a host of other intuitive principles are implicitly taken as valid.

On the basis of these conclusions, it might be possible to reconsider the "relativity debate" in a more productive way. Discussions of Whorfian hypotheses have often consisted of border disputes, either in the cognitive or the anthropological domains. On the cognitive side, the dispute was whether a series of facts about linguistic differences necessarily entailed "incommensurable" conceptual structures. On the anthropological side, the point was to evaluate to what extent world-views are affected by available linguistic resources. As many authors have pointed out (see for instance Lakoff 1987: 304–37), these debates are often less than satisfactory. "Relativity" is multi-dimensional, and there is no way to understand the effect of linguistic differences if we do not focus on actual cognitive processes. In this chapter I tried to make a case for such a cognitive study, on what is arguably a limiting-case. Religious ontologies are obviously not strongly constrained by the properties of their referents, and display some obvious cultural variation. However, it seems that some aspects of these ontologies can be explained in terms of universal intuitive principles. Some themes constitute "optimal" combinations of violations and confirmations of intuitive domain-specific principles. My claim was that such themes are more likely than others to be memorized and transmitted, and therefore more likely to constitute recurrent features of religious systems. Obviously, the explicit part of these religious assumptions displays a measure of cultural specificity; it is possible to show, however, that even this is limited by intuitive expectations. In other words, we have here a domain of cultural representations where we could expect culturally specific, "incommensurable" constructions. What we find instead are variations around a number of recurrent themes, constrained by a few universal underlying principles. If such is the case, then we should expect cultural variations to be even more constrained in domains which are the direct focus of intuitive principles, and where the properties of the referents contribute additional constraints.

The study of Whorfian linguistic relativity has too often been conducted on the implicit assumption that all relevant features of cultural representations are necessarily the outcome of cultural transmission. Given this assumption, linguistic forms seemed particularly likely to influence culturally transmitted "world-views." This assumption, however, may be simplistic. In the acquisition of cultural representations, cultural input may provide nothing more than specific cues, which by themselves under-determine mature conceptual structures. Those cues trigger spontaneous inferences, the contents of which are strongly constrained by prior intuitive principles, and therefore are likely to be (roughly) convergent within a given cultural community.

Notes

1 This is, obviously, a very concise summary of the similarities and divergence between classical and other accounts of conceptual structure. See Smith & Medin (1981), Neisser (1987) for more detailed accounts.
2 L. Rips's experiments (1989), for instance, provide a striking illustration of this phenomenon. In many circumstances, subjects presented with triads of items (a, b, c) can judge both (i) that a and b are more similar than a and c or b and c, and (ii) that b and c are members of the same category.
3 The use of the term "theory" in this context may be misleading in that it suggests a type of structure that may be too constraining (notably in terms of explicitness, integration, consistency) to accommodate most concepts.
4 Research into the representation of ontological distinctions was initiated by F. Keil (1979). Keil assumed that ordinary concepts and predicates carry implicit ontological categories, which are (a) organized in a hierarchy and (b) made manifest by predicate selection. Not all predicates can be applied to a given term, and the applicability of a given predicate allows one to predict the applicability of others. If it is possible to say that a given X "is breathing," then Xs might also, in certain cases, be "furious," but could certainly not be described as "difficult to make" or "happening tomorrow." Keil's experimental research (1979) showed that even young children make surprisingly fine-grained ontological distinctions, between, e.g., living things and artifacts, and they have precise intuitions on the applicability of predicates.

5 One must distinguish here between implicit assumptions concerning mental contents (the intuitive "theory of mind" or "psychology" proper), and a host of explicit assumptions concerning more complex aspects of mentation (what is often called a "folk-psychology"). To give a simple example, it seems obvious to any human subject, from a very early age, that other people's minds perform practical syllogisms. In other words, a default-value in the intuitive explanation of behavior is that "all else being equal, if people want a state X and know that 'no X without Y,' then they are led to want Y." In all cultural environments, however, intuitive psychology is complemented with a host of specific principles, concerning more complex aspects of human behavior. They focus on such domains as motivation, personality types, the likely psychological effect of certain situations, etc. Many people in the United States for instance produce inferences based on the following principle: "weak-willed people, if they want X and know that 'no X unless Y' but find Y hard to achieve, will give up on X unless they really have a strong desire that X." This type of dynamic explanation is part of a series of hypotheses which are often explicitly represented and used in argument. Here I only consider assumptions of the first type, which are particularly relevant to our problems of religious assumptions. On such theories of the mind, see the various studies in Heelas & Lock (1981).

References

Armstrong, S. L., Gleitman, L. R., & Gleitman, H. 1983. What some concepts might not be. *Cognition*, 13, 263–308.

Astington, J., Harris, P., & Olson, D. (eds.) 1989. *Developing theories of mind.* Cambridge University Press.

Atran, S. 1985. The nature of folk-botanical life-forms. *American Anthropologist*, 87, 298–315.

1987. Ordinary constraints on the semantics of living kinds. A commonsense alternative to recent treatments of natural-object terms. *Mind and Language*, 2, 27–63.

1990. *Cognitive foundations of natural history. towards an anthropology of science.* Cambridge University Press.

Berlin, B., Breedlove, D., & Raven, P. 1973. General principles of classification and nomenclature in folk-biology. *American Anthropologist*, 75, 214–42.

Boyer, P. 1990. *Tradition as truth and communication. A cognitive description of traditional discourse.* Cambridge University Press.

1992. Explaining religious ideas: outline of a cognitive approach. *Numen*, 39, 27–57.

1993. Introduction: cognitive aspects of religious symbolism. In P. Boyer (ed.), *Cognitive aspects of religious symbolism.* Cambridge University Press.

1994. *The naturalness of religious ideas. outline of a cognitive theory of religion.* Los Angeles/Berkeley: University of California Press.

Brown, C. H. 1984. *Language and living things. Uniformities in folk-classification and naming.* New Brunswick, NJ: Rutgers University Press.

Carey, S. 1985 *Conceptual change in childhood.* Cambridge, MA: MIT Press.

D'Andrade, R. 1987. A folk-model of the mind. In D. Holland & N. Quinn (eds.), *Cultural models in language and thought* (pp. 112–48). Cambridge University Press.

Gelman, R. 1990. First principles organize attention to learning about relevant data: number and the animate–inanimate distinction as examples. *Cognitive Science*, 14, 79–106.

Gelman, R., Spelke, E., & Meck, E. 1983. What preschoolers know about animate and inanimate objects. In D. Rogers & J. A. Slobada (eds.), *The acquisition of symbolic skills*. London: Plenum Press.

Heelas, P. & Lock, A. 1981. *Indigenous psychologies. the anthropology of the self*. New York: Academic Press.

Keil, F. C. 1979. *Semantic and conceptual development*. Cambridge, MA: Harvard University Press.

1986. The acquisition of natural kind and artefact terms. In A. Marrar & W. Demopoulos (eds.), *Conceptual change* (pp. 133–53). Norwood, NJ: Ablex.

1989. *Concepts, kinds and conceptual development*. Cambridge, MA: MIT Press.

Lakoff, G. 1987. *Women, fire and other dangerous things*. University of Chicago Press.

McCloskey, M. & Gluckberg, S. 1979. Decision processes in verifying category membership statements: implications for models of semantic memory. *Cognitive Psychology*, 11, 1–37.

Massey, C. & Gelman, R. 1988. Preschoolers' ability to decide whether pictured unfamiliar objects can move themselves. *Developmental Psychology*, 24, 307–17.

Medin, D. L. & Wattenmaker, W. D. 1987. Category cohesiveness, theories and cognitive archaeology. In Neisser (1987): 25–62.

Murphy, G. L. & Medin, D. L. 1985. The role of theories in conceptual coherence. *Psychological Review*, 92, 289–316.

Neisser, U. (ed.) 1987. *Concepts and conceptual development. ecological and intellectual factors in categorization*. Cambridge University Press.

Richards, D. D. & Siegler, R. S. 1986. Children's understanding of the attributes of life. *Journal of Experimental Child Psychology*, 42, 1–22.

Rips, L. J. 1989. Similarity, typicality and categorization. In S. Vosniadou & A. Ortony (eds.), *Similarity and analogical reasoning* (pp. 21–59). Cambridge University Press.

Rosch, E. 1977. Human categorization. In N. Warren (ed.), *Studies in cross-cultural psychology*, vol. I (pp. 3–50). London: Academic Press.

Rosch, E. & Lloyd, B. B. (eds.) 1978. *Cognition and categorization*. Hillsdale, NJ: Lawrence Erlbaum.

Smith, E. E. & Medin, D. L. 1981. *Categories and concepts*. Cambridge, MA: Harvard University Press.

Spelke, E. S. 1990. Principles of object perception. *Cognitive Science*, 14, 29–56.

Walker, S.-J. 1986. *Atimodemo: semantic conceptual development among the Yoruha*. Ph.D. dissertation, Cornell University.

forthcoming (a). Supernatural beliefs, natural kinds and conceptual structure. *Memory and Cognition*.

forthcoming (b). Developmental changes in the representation of word-meaning: cross-cultural findings. *British Journal of Developmental Psychology*.

Wellmann, H. & Estes, D. 1986. Early understanding of mental entities: a re-examination of childhood realism. *Child Development*, 57, 910–23.

PART III
INTERPRETATION IN CULTURAL CONTEXT

INTRODUCTION TO PART III

JOHN J. GUMPERZ AND STEPHEN C. LEVINSON

The chapters in the volume so far have largely focused on the issues central to classical versions of the Sapir–Whorf hypothesis: how much do languages vary in semantic structure, and what are the implications for cognition of varying semantic structures? Those issues arose in the first instance out of structuralist approaches to meaning, where the focus was placed on the role of lexical and grammatical elements inside a system of opposed elements. Theories of meaning have developed far since then, and they are now extensively concerned with the interaction between the content of linguistic expressions and the contexts in which they are used. In the next two sections, the picture therefore broadens: suppose meaning is partially dependent on use, and suppose languages vary systematically in their use – then this suggests a broader dependence of meaning on cultural context, a broader kind of linguistic relativity, along the lines suggested originally by Hymes (1966).

Deixis or indexicality clearly demonstrates that many aspects of meaning depend on use. Consider the sentence *You are now reading this*: what it denotes is *relative* to who reads it where and when – every reading of it will express a distinct proposition. Natural languages are so arranged that nearly all utterances have interpretations only relative to contexts. As mentioned in the introduction, recent developments in the theory of meaning conspire to emphasize this relativity of meaning to context.[1] On the one hand, semanticists are ever increasing the range of expressions that seem to be covertly indexical,[2] while on the other, pragmaticists continue to emphasize the underspecification of semantic content, and the crucial role of pragmatic principles in amalgamating contextual information with semantic content to yield determinate interpretations.[3] These two movements together suggest the view that the abstract meaning of linguistic expressions is quite generally under-specified and indeterminate, and is systematically enriched by contextual parameters and principles of use.

Now if indexicality is rampant through language, and if the interpretation of such indexical items depends on local practices and principles of use, we have to look at the idea of linguistic relativity afresh.

Even if there was complete semantic isomorphism on the level of grammar and lexical meaning (even if, for example, the whole world only spoke English), we could still have linguistic relativity at the level of interpretation! Consider the dense assumptions behind the interpretation of the most banal of linguistic usages, say a postcard received from a friend on holiday with the inscription "It's lovely here." We need to interpret each of the expressions: *is* and *here* are clearly indexicals – the tense restricts the interpretation to the time of writing (look at the postmark? but maybe she didn't post it till later), the *here* restricts the predication to the place of writing (look at the picture: the hotel? the beach? Honolulu?). The pronoun it might be non-referential (cf. *it's raining*), or it might indexically refer to various vague referents, or even something very specific (a shared interest of speaker and addressee – golfing, diving, etc.). We have to do some "transposition" (see below) from the receiving time and place to the writing time and place and the appropriate concerns. *Lovely* is pretty vague – positive evaluation of what and in what respects? Well, the recipient ought to be able to guess (sunshine, the food, the ocean...). Or was perhaps nothing specific intended? Such an item-by-item decoding, if achieved, still leaves the communicative intentions unclear: is it an objective observation, an invitation, a taunt to those left behind, or what? We have to know, by implicit reference to other such texts, that it is just the sort of thing that one writes on a postcard to express the conventional "wish-you-were-here" sentiments. Thus this banal fragment is firmly situated in a host of interpretive expectations, that range from detailed linguistic assumptions (e.g. the likelihood of non-referential *it*) to usage conventions ("postcardese") to non-linguistic assumptions about, for example, the relation between writing postcards and holidays or the temporal relation between writing and mailing and receiving letters.[4] Someone naive about all these expectations should be at an interpretive loss, or come to some alternative conclusion. This is the sort of communicative chasm that can indeed arise between people who share a language but not the relevant interpretive schema (see the chapter by Gumperz in part IV below).

It is a leap in complexity from this trivial example to the interpretation in real time of full-blown interactive discourse in actual settings. This explosion of complexity will become immediately evident on the reading of, for example, the chapter by Haviland below, where it is shown how complex shifts between interpretive frames occur within the shortest utterances. Some of the interpretive dependencies depend on shared knowledge or presumptions about the world, others depend on the very principles organizing the discourse. If interpretations depend on usage-conventions and principles, it makes sense to ask how culturally relative principles of use actually are. Unfortunately, we do not really know.

Although studies in the ethnography of speaking (see, e.g., Gumperz & Hymes 1972, Bauman & Sherzer 1974) have established that there are fundamental variations in the rules governing what, how, and when to speak in even closely comparable speech events across cultures, there are few studies of any depth of the general pragmatic systems of "exotic" languages. Most analysts presume a strong universal basis for principles of language use, but with significant variation in situational application. A case in point would be the expression of linguistic politeness, which can be seen as a close parallel to Boyer's analysis of religious ideas: that which is startling by its cultural specificity may have a strong universal background (see Brown & Levinson 1987, Leech 1983). In the same way, the chapters by Ochs, Levinson, Haviland, Clark, Hanks, and Gumperz, all make strong assumptions about the universality of various principles of use, while also emphasizing the cultural specificity of application. For example, in the next section, the chapters by Gumperz and Ochs both presume that the "framing" of conversational interaction (in terms, for example, of the rhetorical intentions, or the social relationships invoked) is largely achieved by subliminal, covert cues with specific properties that indirectly invoke the relevant frames. In this section, Hanks and Haviland argue that there are both universal and culturally specific factors involved in calculating the denotation of referring expressions, while Clark argues that this is necessarily so. Thus in this section we focus on how contextual factors enter into the determination of reference, starting from the central case of deictic expressions and extending to reference in general.

Hanks argues that deictic systems, although clearly exhibiting similarities across languages, are to a significant extent constructed over time through culturally specific, situated practices. He reports here on one of the most detailed studies of any deictic system (see Hanks 1990), in this case the system of (especially) the spatial deictics in Yucatec Maya. In terms of the kinds of distinction lexically encoded, the system does not look all that "exotic," with terms for 'here,' 'there,' 'this,' 'that,' etc. Less familiar are a set of suffixes ("terminal deictics") which combine with the lexical deictics to indicate modes of access between participants and the deictic referent – e.g. tactual, vs. visual vs. auditory (so *he'el* '*voilà*' combines with *-a* 'direct access' to mean 'Here it is (tactual presentative)'). Hanks argues that the distinction between the lexical deictics and the terminal suffixes mirrors a functional distinction: the suffix indicates what kind of background information the addressee should access in order to interpret the lexical deictic (thus *he'el-a* invokes monitoring of the tactile world, but *he'el-o* directs attention to the visual mode: 'Lo! See it here!'). The suffixes also indicate whether to focus on the speaker, the sociocentric zone of the speaker–addressee, or the addressee's zone.

The suffixes thus serve the general purpose of directing the interpreter's attention to specific search-domains. However, they will not alone suffice to individuate a referent. To find the reference, the addressee must take into account the socially structured distinctions thus invoked. For example, the socio-physical world is structured into domestic spaces of various kinds; e.g. in extended family housing clusters, sub-units will have distinct but unmarked plots of land – such a boundary being, say, immediately pertinent to the interpretation of 'here' vs. 'there.' On top of that, one must take into account that the nature of the boundary will differ according to whether the viewpoint is that of consanguines or affines (for much further detail see Hanks 1990). Thus the interpretation of a deictic item is intrinsically bound up with cultural distinctions and practices, and Hanks draws on Bourdieu's (1977) concept of "habitus" to make the point. Within the field of deictics at least, Hanks makes it seem incontestable that one is dealing with a kind of linguistic relativity at the level of interpretation.

He goes on to argue that rules of use and interpretation become reflected in the structure of the linguistic code. Thus in Maya there is a rule of usage that requires a speaker to express a single consistent 'footing' or mode of access to the referents he is conversing about. This has a systematic reflex in the grammar: only one terminal deictic may appear in each clause, however many referents are referred to. That the constraint is motivated by rules of usage is evident from the fact that speakers can be maneuvered into situations, for example of metalinguistic commentary, in which they will violate the constraint. Thus deictic systems may themselves be grammaticalizations of usage patterns, and thus doubly relative in nature: their interpretation is relative to rules of use, and their very construction relative to those rules from which they are derived.

Haviland's chapter takes some of Hanks's themes further. It has long been noticed (e.g. by Jakobson and Buhler) that deictics are not only context-sensitive in the sense that their referents are picked out relative to a context, but also that the very context can be shifted away from the current context-of-speaking. So in *John wondered what should he say now*, the word *now* does not refer to the speaker's present, but to the present of John's wondering. This phenomenon of "transposition," which has also been studied by Hanks (1990), is the focus of Haviland's chapter. What he shows, through a series of carefully analyzed examples, is how pervasive in natural discourse such transpositions are, and how enormously intricate and multi-layered such switches of interpretive frame can be. For example, consider a story being told by an Aboriginal speaker of Guugu Yimithirr in Cape York. As mentioned in the chapter by Levinson, these people have an "absolute" system of spatial description, involving reference to cardinal directions. Within the story, the teller gestures North, exactly as the protagonists on a particular beach must have done when referring to a boatwreck out at sea; so we are transposed once, away from the context of utterance to the protagonists' context at that moment in the story; then, mentioning a new protagonist, the teller gestures to have the others coming down the beach South towards him, and we are thus transposed to *his* point of view. But then to make sure his listeners have understood the identity of the man, he is identified by a gesture to the work-place of his son of the same name – but this gesture is now in the frame of the *speaking context*. Thus in a few lines and a few transitory gestures we have three 'spaces' of interpretation invoked and slipped between, almost invisibly, but crucially for the interpretation.

Deictic expressions exhibit frequent transpositions, but Haviland argues that once one has grasped the nature of the process, one can find it applying to many expressions that we would not initially think of as deictics or "shifters." We do not just describe situations (as when we report speech), we actively construe them; languages provide various oppositions allowing alternate construals of particular situations; adopting one such construal expresses an attitude of the speaker not only to the event, but also often to the other interlocutors. The complex kind of interpretation required is thus not restricted to deictics, but pervades many aspects of descriptive language. Moreover, particular speech events, for example a curing ceremony, set up specific indexical frames, together with sets of transpositions across them (e.g. into and out of the curing frame). Thus the activity of transposition is intimately tied up with the local expectations governing language use.

Haviland's examples from three cultures leave the distinct impression that one requires long-term socialization in local knowledge and practice if one is to catch such fleeting clues to essential elements of interpretation. Again, this amounts to a *de facto* cultural relativity of interpretation. Yet Haviland is also keen to make the point that there would seem to be universal processes of transposition at work: the sorts of "spaces" shifted between, and the kinds of linguistic and gestural clue to such switches, seem to be of limited kinds.

The idea that linguistic knowledge and practice might be fractionated and differentially distributed through a community, yielding local linguistic relativities, finds perhaps unexpected support from a psychologist. In the chapter included here, Clark argues that the classical picture of linguistic relativity, with us and (say) the Hopi inhabiting different linguistically constructed worlds, fails for the simple reason that it was based on the wrong theory of meaning. Instead of thinking of meaning as inherent in words through arbitrary meaning conventions, one should think of lexical meaning as an outcome of collaboration over a naming or referring practice, with the result that different collaborators may settle on different meanings. An interactionally derived solution to such a referring problem may then provide a precedent for the next occasion – and so we have a "convention" to call an X a "Y," but such a convention is always localized to a network or community (following the analysis of the philosopher David Lewis 1969). Thus the word *murder* may have different stabilized meanings for lawyers, Catholic anti-abortionists, and feminists, who participate in different social networks in the same speech community. And we constantly invent "nonce" terms, knowing that our interlocutors will try to infer the reference that we have in mind, scanning background associations that may be specific to the participants, as in "She's very New York" or "I macintoshed my vita." Furthermore, where we do find stabilized conventions they may not be conventions of meaning so much as conventional ways of conceiving things that run across a series of words: for example we talk of eye-glasses and pants as coming in pairs, the Dutch view them as coming singly – new kinds of pants (Bermudas, hotpants) will always be plural in English but singular in Dutch.

It follows that we cannot think of a "world-view" as inherent in a language, somehow detached from all the practices established for its use. The same point is made in those chapters that focus on indexicals (by Hanks, Haviland, Ochs, and Gumperz), where the meaning is intrinsically connected to use. Yet Clark's argument would make the relativization of meaning to use entirely general. On this account, meaning is also relativized to collections of persons who share the same background of experience and associations. By adopting a theory of the collaborative nature of meaning (itself un-Whorfian), one would seem to end up adopting an extreme form of linguistic relativity. However, this view needs to be taken together with intrinsic psychological constraints on interactive processes of meaning determination, e.g. on what interlocutors will find to be a naturally salient solution to a nonce-concept, and indeed together with universal linguistic constraints on semantic structure.

Thus the papers in this section open up a different perspective by exploring the relativization of meaning to use, and the restriction of shared meanings to communities of use. These ideas are then pursued further in the final section, where they are shown to undermine the idealizations of "language," "culture," and "community," and other such global notions that have played an important role in ideas about linguistic relativity.

Notes

1 They do this, however, in different ways, which is another intriguing variation. English forces temporal specification (our verbs are tensed); other languages force specification of spatial distinctions (e.g. through distal or proximal marking of nouns) or social distinctions (e.g. through marking of honorifics). For an introduction to deixis, see Levinson (1983: ch. 2).

2 For example, most nominals, even proper names, become so under many (diverse) modern treatments; even conditionals and other "logical' connectives are held by some to have inbuilt contextual parameters (see e.g. Barwise & Perry 1983; Davis 1991: section III; Barwise 1986). Another development has been the incorporation of textual dependencies into formal semantics, so that anaphora, definiteness, presuppositional constructions, etc., are seen as formal markings of contextual dependence.

3 Sperber & Wilson (1986), Horn (1989), Atlas (1989), Davis (1991), Levinson (1983).

4 Less banal examples are provided by our uncertainties about the correct reading of texts in our own language, when these were written a generation or more ago (see Steiner 1975: ch. l).

References

Atlas, J. 1989. *Philosophy without ambiguity: a logico-linguistic essay.* Oxford University Press.

Barwise, J. 1986. Conditionals and conditional information. In E. Traugott, A. ter Meulen, J. Reilly, & C. A. Ferguson (eds.), *On conditionals* (pp. 21–54). Cambridge University Press.

Barwise, J. & Perry, J. 1983. *Situations and attitudes.* Cambridge, MA: MIT Press.

Bauman, R. & Sherzer, J. 1974. *Explorations in the ethnography of speaking.* (Reissued with a new introduction and bibliography, 1989.) London: Cambridge University Press.

Bourdieu, P. 1977. *Outline of a theory of practice.* Tr. R. Nice. Cambridge University Press.

Brown, P. & Levinson, S. C. 1987. *Politeness: some universals in language usage.* Studies in International Sociolinguistics, 4. Cambridge University Press.

Davis, S. (ed.) 1991. *Pragmatics: a reader.* Oxford University Press.

Gumperz, J. J. & Hymes, D. (eds.) 1972. *Directions in sociolinguistics: the ethnography of communication.* New York: Holt, Rinehart, & Winston.

Hanks, W. 1990. *Referential practice: language and lived space among the Maya.* University of Chicago Press.

Horn, L. 1989. *A natural history of negation.* University of Chicago Press.

Hymes, D. 1966. Two types of linguistic relativity (with examples from Amerindian ethnography). In W. Bright (ed.), *Sociolinguistics, Proceedings of the UCLA sociolinguistics conference, 1964* (pp. 114–67). The Hague: Mouton.

Leech, G. N. 1983. *Principles of pragmatics.* London: Longman.

Levinson, S. C. 1983. *Pragmatics.* Cambridge University Press.

Lewis, D. 1969. *Convention. a philosophical study.* Cambridge, MA: Harvard University Press.

Sperber, D. & Wilson, D. 1986. *Relevance.* Oxford: Basil Blackwell.

Steiner, G. 1975. *After Babel: aspects of language and translation.* Oxford University Press.

9

LANGUAGE FORM AND COMMUNICATIVE PRACTICES

WILLIAM F. HANKS

1 Linguistic meaning arises only in context

1.1 Partiality and non-uniqueness

It is a truism that the meanings of words sometimes depend upon the circumstances in which they are used. Yet the full extent and consequences of this phenomenon are unclear. The sheer variety of context-dependent factors in language lends itself to an equally various range of theories. Some conversational meanings arise through pragmatic processes, such as Gricean implicature, "contextualized" inference (Gumperz 1982), and illocutionary acts, while others involve indexicals, discourse structure, pragmatic presupposition, and so forth. One common way of describing context dependency is to say that literal meanings, such as would be shown in a dictionary, are overlaid in speech by contextual factors. An utterance can convey much more pragmatically derived information than is literally encoded in its semantic structure, because utterances are made up of semantics *plus* context. In this view, there is a basic difference between those meanings encoded in the language, and those derived from context outside it.[1]

A different tack is represented by those approaches which push context dependency deeper into the language, as it were, and argue that even literal meaning is a product of contextualization. Representative of this are recent works in cognitive linguistics, which incorporate units such as image schemata (Lakoff 1987, Langacker 1984), mental spaces (Fauconnier 1984, 1988), frames (Fillmore 1982), and preference rule systems (Jackendoff 1988). These approaches try to account for aspects of meaning production that go beyond traditional semantics, and they recast the relation between linguistic form and meaning. They start from the premise that properly linguistic meanings are inherently *underspecified* with respect to the propositions that people build up from them.[2] The implication of this research is that meaning – even literal sense – derives from the fusion of language form with context. If this is true, then there is reason to rethink the standard ideas that semantic structure is part of grammar, and grammar is a conventional system organized by its own inner logic.

One of the functions of language in which context-dependency plays a key role is reference. Singular definite reference, as in the italicised portion of "*the man* is at the table" (said of a known individual), is usually associated with the stipulations that the object (the man) must exist and be uniquely identifiable by the speaker (and addressee, to be successful). Searle (1969: 77ff.) treated these as the "axioms of existence and identifiability," and incorporated them into his "rules of reference" (94–6). But how is this identification achieved; how is a referent individuated apart from all other objects? (How do we know which man?) It cannot be the descriptive information encoded in a linguistic expression that fulfills this function, because linguistic meaning is underspecified. Rather, "what secures uniqueness is the user of the expression and the context in which it is used *together* with the expression" (Linsky 1971: 77). Quine (1971: 144, 153) made the related point that individuated reference is impossible apart from the network of terms, predicates, and auxiliary devices that speakers of a language share. Like semantic content more generally, verbal reference arises only through combining a linguistic expression with an interactive context.[3]

A separate but converging line of research seeks to show that basic speech acts, such as referring and describing, are achieved by joint interaction among speakers, and not by mere issuing of words whose meanings are fixed. For example, Clark & Wilkes-Gibbs (1986) treat referring as a collaborative achievement, in which interactants establish reference *together*, by negotiating mutually intelligible terms and monitoring each others' understandings. Similarly, de León (1990) showed that Tzotzil speakers engaged in certain interactive routines when faced with the task of establishing reference to unfamiliar objects. These studies are revealing of the extent to which referring depends upon modes of co-engagement between interactants, showing that "context" must be understood as an ongoing interactive process, not a stable grid. Focusing on spatial reference, Haviland (1989, 1990), Levinson (1990), and Brown (1990) showed the degree to which spatial descriptions can depend upon features of local geography and conventionalized ways in which interactants orient their own bodies in space. Context-dependency, then, implies that verbal forms intersect with contexts defined by more than one interactant.

Although "context" has become a focus in several fields, it is mainly those approaches tied to social theory and ethnography that have made it a central issue (see for instance Duranti and Goodwin 1992). Starting with early Americanist anthropology, and continuing through eth-noscience, the ethnography of speaking, conversation analysis, and contemporary linguistic anthropology, these approaches have consistently challenged the ideal that language form can be analyzed apart from its social and historical context. What are the relations between language structure, habitual ways of speaking, cultural values, and social organization? To what extent are cross-linguistic differences in language form motivated by differences in the social worlds in which the languages exist? How can we conceptualize the mutual structuring of verbal categories, conceptual categories, and ways of experiencing? What is the relationship between the micro-level contexts of utterances directed to one another in a conversation and the larger socio-cultural horizon on which utterances depend for their meanings? What can we learn about verbal meaning by studying silence and the unstated assumptions that speakers bring to bear on talk? Such questions ultimately challenge the very definitions of linguistic form, meaning, and verbal practices (see chapters by Gumperz, Haviland, Kay, and Ochs in this volume).[4]

The notion of linguistic relativity was first formulated by anthropological linguists, and any major rethinking of context necessarily has consequences for this as well. Stated generally, the so-called relativity thesis posits a strong relation between language form, routine patterns of use and habitual modes of thinking. In the strongest versions of the thesis, linguistic categories are claimed to influence or even determine conceptual categories, although such a radical position is not representative of the field. Closer to the spirit of Sapir's and Whorf's early speculations is the idea that language structure, habitual ways of speaking, and thinking are mutually constituting. The key issue is not whether language form and use determine what people CAN think or experience, but rather the extent to which they influence what people usually DO think and experience. Two languages could be virtually identical with respect to a semantic domain, yet if they are used in distinct ways, their categories may have a different weighting and impact on thought (a point made by Paul Kay during the conference at which the content of this chapter was first presented). Similarly, the kinds of indexical structuring studied by Gumperz (1982, this volume), Haviland (this volume), Ochs (this volume) and Hanks (1989, 1990, 1995) provide loci for crosslinguistic variation that may cross-cut otherwise similar semantic organizations. Moreover, if language and culture are mutually-constituting, then neither can be taken to be the cause or simple consequence of the other. The cumulative effect of these shifts towards contextualization is to greatly qualify the notion of relativity. Rather than determine thought, language form and habitual speech patterns enable or tend to foster ways of thinking. Thus as Slobin (this volume) suggests, we need to think of a scale of expressibility, whereby a given linguistic system may make certain ways of expressing relatively easier or more difficult. Put simply, contemporary language studies make it clear that the impact of language form on thought depends crucially on the factors summarized as "context."

Building on the foregoing ideas, this chapter examines the relation between language form and speech practices. The term "practice" is intended to highlight the approach I will take, which can be summarized by a set of working hypotheses and assumptions. The first of these is that, while linguistic systems are governed *in part* by principles unique to language, grammar is neither self-contained nor entirely independent from the social worlds in which the language is used. How people talk has an impact on, and is influenced by, the structure of their language. A corollary of this is the idea that, for two or more people to effectively communicate, it is not sufficient, and perhaps not even necessary, that they "share" the same grammar. What they must share, to a variable degree, is the ability to orient themselves verbally, perceptually, physically to their social world. That is, the basis of linguistic practices is not a common set of categories (whether viewed as verbal or cognitive), but rather a commensurate set of categories, plus commensurate ways of locating oneself in relation to them. There are two points here: (i) that overlapping or merely comparable categories may suffice to enable communication (contrary to the traditional folk wisdom in linguistics that understanding speech presupposes knowing the grammar); and (ii) that how agents situate themselves relative to one another and their context may have real consequences for their ability to communicate. This is partly the phenomenological idea that experience transcends conventional structures, and partly the linguistic observation that many verbal categories incorporate an indexical component. As we will see, pronouns and demonstratives are a case in point, since they can be effectively used only on the condition that speakers orient themselves appropriately to utterance context. Hence it is not that people must share a grammar, but that they must share, to a degree, ways of orienting themselves in social context. This kind of sharing – partial, orientational, and socially distributed – may be attributed to the habitus, or relatively stable schemes of perception to which actors are inculcated.

Part of what I am calling "orientation" consists in agents' predispositions to perceive and act in certain ways. These may be due to universal aspects of human cognition, bodily experience, sociality, and so forth, or they may be due to more local habits or cultural values. More significant than the *universality* of a feature of practice, for our purposes, is its relation to language structure and other aspects of the local context. Certain orientations indicate that an agent is a member of a social group, or is pursuing a determinate course of action, whereas others can be traced to specific features of linguistic structure, or the built environment (in the case of spatial orientations). These are interesting precisely because they give evidence of how social space and language structure are inscribed in habitual action. While some aspects of orientation may consist in ways of thinking, others may be embodied in ways of looking, listening, touching, or in actual physical postures, movements, and other practices of the body. Thus orientations, like habitual practices, cross-cut the line between language and other modes of human engagement with the world.

It follows from the foregoing that the concept of rules plays a much more limited role in a practice approach than in standard linguistic or even sociolinguistic frameworks. It is clear that there exist rules governing the grammatical structure of linguistic forms, as linguists have recognized for millennia. There is no necessary contradiction between the idea of grammar and the idea of practice, since the two focus on different aspects of the total social fact. What is far less clear is that regularities or constitutive aspects of verbal activities can be insightfully described with the metaphor of "rules of use." During the 1960s and 1970s it was widely believed that regularities of speech were motivated by rules of use mapping linguistic forms into types of activity. This belief provided a neat way of extending the notion of grammar from form to use, thus structuring pragmatics in much the same way as semantics. The problem is that rules of use can never give more than the guidelines for verbal action; they cannot describe what actual actors do under real conditions. Further, when actors fail to adhere to putative rules, engaging in creative or *ad hoc* forms of behavior, their actions appear as irregularities, exceptions, and departures from the rules. Thus, from the vantage point of rules, a good deal of the agency that drives actual speech in social contexts appears as exceptional. With a focus on practice comes the goal of describing precisely what an effective player does when engaged in social activities. Rules and codes can describe the playing field and the boundaries beyond which a move will not count, but they cannot explain what goes on in strategizing and actual engagement in actions. For this we need access to the orientations, habitual patterns, and schematic understandings of the agents themselves.

A practice approach therefore leads to an ethnographically dense description of speech, in which language forms are interlinked with other aspects of social context. Unlike standard linguistic accounts, the agents of speech are not assumed to be self-contained individuals whose subjective states and intentions drive linguistic production. Rather, individuals enter into linguistic practices as parties to social relationships, and as actors within fields.[5] In my own work on demonstrative reference and spatial orientation, a practice framework has made it possible to explain aspects of speech and linguistic form that would otherwise remain arbitrary. These include types of mutual orientation between interactants that crucially affect their word choice, relations between language structure and built space, and a variety of corporeal factors not precisely describable in other frameworks (see Hanks 1990, 1995).

In this chapter, we examine context dependency, in which utterance forms combine with social context to yield meanings. The overall framework I will assume is a practice one, although my focus will be linguistic forms and the details of utterance meaning rather than larger-scale social contexts. Basically, I will argue that specific features of the syntax and morphology of Maya demonstratives can be traced to routine patterns of speaking which involve habitual bodily and conceptual orientations. The interplay between verbal form and habitual practice, combined with the underdetermination of meaning by form, together recast the question of linguistic relativity. The issue is not whether grammar somehow constrains what people can think or perceive. Rather, the central question becomes how language serves to sediment routine practices, both constraining and enabling what they habitually do think, perceive, and enact.

1.2 Habituation and typification

Social actors tend to interact in habitual ways and this in turn tends to stabilize their practices, making them repeatable and therefore expectable. This process applies equally well to features of communicative interaction that speakers are aware of and talk about, and to ones they may never even notice. Boas ([1911] 1966: 20–1) observed that in language "the infinitely larger number of ideas has been reduced by classification to a lesser number, which by constant use have established firm associations, and which can be used automatically." In the absence of this reduction, according to Boas, language would require an infinite number of sound vehicles in order to express constantly shifting experiences.

Whorf (1941) significantly developed the Boasian insight that language is a medium of habituation, bringing to it Sapir's attention to the "self-contained system" of classifications in language (Lucy 1985). Whereas Boas examined most closely grammatical categories, rather than syntactic constructions or utterance types, Whorf's analyses encompass whole "patterns of speaking" definable only at the level of phrasal syntax and standard usage (see for instance his analysis of number categories). Following Sapir (1949 [1931]), Whorf saw standard linguistic patterns as providing structures that are formed in relation to certain objective realities, and subsequently extended through analogy to other, objectively dissimilar experiences. For deictic frames, the analogous case would be that referential categories in language are formed in relation to certain habitual phenomenal relations (e.g. Spkr.–Adr.–perceptile object), and only then extended by analogy to other, less transparent cases.

The habituation and automaticity of much of language use was also noted by the Prague School linguists, and used by Havránek ([1932] 1964) as the basis of the functional dimension of foregrounding versus automaticity. Automatized linguistic expressions are those which are typical, expected, routine, and therefore immediately interpretable. Foregrounded uses on the contrary are relatively unexpected, atypical, and may require special interpretation. The distinction can be applied to linguistic forms, or to the conveyed meanings of forms (a routine form can be used in a foregrounded way). Whereas for Boas, conceptual and linguistic categories buffer speakers from the actual unrepeatability of experience, for the Pragueans, relative automaticity and foregrounding is a dimension applicable to both categories and experience. Furthermore, the tension between the two is taken to be a feature of all language use, except for certain socially specific functional dialects, where automaticity is maximized (what Havránek calls "scientific"). Coming from this line of thought, it would be expected that deictic frames, whatever their potential complexities, are to a large degree automatized in any culture, and that foregrounded departures from the routine patterns are both possible and purposeful. Another way of saying this is that routine frames, and the language forms that key into them, make certain ways of speaking highly probable, automatic, or virtually unavoidable. Yet any living language has a range of rhetorical styles and generic modes of speaking, which means that categories that may be "obligatory" from a grammatical perspective may be relatively easy to circumvent in practice. Inversely, categories that are grammatically "optional" may be nearly obligatory due to routine ways of speaking.

Interpretive sociologists have long focused on "typification" in social life, the process whereby actors represent (and therefore understand) themselves and their world through routine patterns of experience and interaction. This too contributes to the production of frames. Schutz (1967: 163ff.; 1970: part II; 1973: 7–27) saw typification as a fundamental feature of the commonsense construction of experience, a prerequisite of intersubjectivity. Following Schutz, Garfinkel ([1964] 1972) focused on the routinization, repeatability, and accountability of experiences, all of which rely on the basic idea that social practice is structured in typical ways. One of the consequences that Garfinkel drew from this was what he called the "specific vagueness" of most of what gets said in everyday interaction, the fact that speakers never make plain precisely what they mean, but rather rely on background expectancies to fill in where their overt expressions leave off (1972: 15). Thus the various discussions of habit in language use can be seen to lead back to the problem of semantic indeterminacy with which we began.

Native actors tend to interact in habitual ways, then, within a commonsense world which is for them typical and repeatable, to anticipate on the basis of past experience, and to fill in unstated meanings on the basis of automatic patterns. While actors surely depart from routines, they do so always against a horizon of prior experience. The inherent partiality of linguistic expression guarantees that this horizon will be in play wherever speech is produced and understood. Insofar as they are schematizations of actional wholes, frames have their ground in the horizon, and tend by routine use to become embodied in interaction. In other words, not only do speakers *actualize* frames in the course of understanding talk, they *reinforce*, potentially *change*, and *produce* them as well. Because schematized aspects of experience derive from more than the language, they can, and ultimately must, be studied on the basis of extra-linguistic data. In my field work on deictic reference among Yucatec Maya speakers, it became clear that some of the frames embodied in their verbal practices are also objectified in such features of context as the boundary divisions between households (which establish the context for inclusion/exclusion frames), local landmarks (which establish the context for near side/far side frames used in giving directions), and ritual altars (which establish relations between directional trajectories, quadrilateral perimeters, and body space). The importance of this is that it adds further elaboration and reinforcement to the frames which make understanding possible.

Through quoted speech, shifts in perspective, and various kinds of creative reference, speakers often use demonstratives in "non-direct" ways. That is, they combine frames so that the actual interactive context of talk is altered or does not serve as the sole ground of reference. Imagine an exchange in which two brothers, Miguel and Feliciano, are talking about their younger brother Pedro and his wife Pilar. They do not like the way Pilar orders Pedro around, and are criticizing her for bossiness. Miguel reports an exchange he witnessed in which she had told Pedro to get out of the kitchen. Miguel quotes Pilar's utterance, saying *šen tuún téʔel oʔ kih e kóʔolel oʔ*, ' "So go over there" that lady says.' Here the quoted demonstrative (*téʔel oʔ*) refers to a place in relation to Pilar at the time she uttered it (outside the kitchen, speaking from inside), but is not intended to refer to any place in relation to Miguel and Feliciano in their deictic field. Transpositions like this one, where the spatial deictic is transposed from its normal ground in the context of utterance (M to F) to the projected ground of the original utterance context (P to P), are typical of quoted discourse. They demonstrate that the actual physical setting of speech is not always the relevant context for understanding deictic reference, and pose a major challenge to frame semantics. What are the principles by which frames are combined in such discourse, and how does language provide resources for tracking reference across frames (see Haviland, this volume)?[6]

There are several factors which tend to anchor deictic reference in the actual physical context of speech, transpositions notwithstanding. Among these are *default assumptions* that speakers make about face-to-face contexts. These reinforce the tendency to schematize the actional wholes of deictic reference at an intermediate level of inclusiveness.[7] (a) Unless indicated or already known otherwise, it is assumed that the person who produces an utterance is the source of the proposition stated, the one who chooses the words, and the one whose position is expressed. That is, it is assumed that what Goffman called animator, author, and principal are identical. (b) If gaze, posture, gesture, and utterance all figure in a communicative act, then either they are reinforcing, or they focus on complementary components of, the frame (e.g. speaker–addressee contact vs. speaker–referent access). Speakers do not routinely direct their interlocutor's attention to several contrasting objects at once. (c) Until further notice, the addressee to whom sound is directed is the target of the utterance, in which case "addressee" and (untargeted) "overhearer" may be adequate categories of reception. Any of these constraints (and others treated in Hanks 1990) can be overridden under proper circumstances, but their routine effect is to reinforce the tendency of interactants to ground reference and address in their current phenomenal sphere. This in turn contributes to the tendency of speakers to produce frames in their own speech, and use them in interpreting the speech of others.

The family of phenomena described in this section combine with the indeterminacy of linguistic meaning to establish a strong link between interactive practices and the linguistic system.[8] On the one hand, such a linkage *relativizes* meaning production in the sense that it makes understanding a function of the relation between language and interactive contexts. If the research cited here is correct, as I believe it is, then this relativity cuts deeply into the semantics of language, and not only into pragmatics. While it is true that demonstrative reference is an extreme instance of such relativity, recent work has shown that indexicality is a general feature of reference and descriptive meaning as well. On the other hand, the same joining of speech with context can have a significant impact on the form of language itself. The cumulative effect of these factors may be to conventionalize in the structure of language basic aspects of interactive context.

2 Grammaticalization in Maya deictics

2.1 Deictic forms and fields

In studying demonstratives and deictics, there is a strong temptation to identify linguistic distinctions with contextual ones and treat the correspondence between the two as transparent. Everyone recognizes that these forms are the prototypical indexicals, whose incompleteness is so clear that the contextual dependency of their semantic content can hardly be overlooked. In order to judge the truth or falsity of "that one was over there," one must obviously know the time, place, and individual involved. Sometimes it even appears that demonstratives lack descriptive content altogether, making them almost entirely dependent upon context in order to have any determinate meaning. The sentence in question could as well describe the momentary arrangement of houseflies on a tabletop as it could the displacement of a large ship by miles after a hurricane. However, this appearance of semantic emptiness is a false one, and natural language deictics are not pure indexicals in the classical sense. They are mixed signs whose conventional meanings do tell us something about their referents, namely how they are to be identified (close, far, visible, nonvisible) (Anderson & Keenan 1985, Hanks 1989, Levinson 1983). Furthermore, systems of deixis commonly encode descriptive information regarding the extent of a referent (regions vs. points), its orientation in space, its gender, animacy or other classificatory features. The importance of these facts is that they indicate that deictic frames are not simply calques of objective placement in space and time, as they are sometimes described. The context which provides for the understanding of a deictic is a socio-cultural one, not a purely natural one. This means it is defined by the values, perspectives, and routine practices of the interactants.

In order to coherently describe the relation of deictics to social context, it is necessary to maintain a distinction between three aspects of referential practices: (i) how the expressions are actually used, and how they contribute to referring as an activity; (ii) how their linguistic structure defines a conventional system whose organization both limits and facilitates certain ways of identifying referents; and (iii) how native speakers commonsensically understand demonstratives and the actional wholes to which they correspond. These three levels or aspects of reference do not line up in any very neat way, nor will an explanation of any one provide the grounds for inferring any of the others, nor is any one more basic than the others. Indeed, one of the main challenges facing any contextual approach to reference is to devise a way of moving systematically between formal structures, actual instances of talk, and socio-cultural contexts.

Following most of the classic studies of the topic, we start from the notion of a deictic field, made up of the combination of several contextual domains that we can call spatial, temporal, participant, discourse, attention focus, and background knowledge. Within each of these domains there are distinguishable modes of access whereby interactants identify individuals and objects of reference. For instance, distinctions such as proximal vs. distal (in space), visible vs. non-visible (perception), simultaneous vs. anterior (temporal), speaker vs. addressee (participant), in focus vs. backgrounded (attention), and known vs. new (background knowledge) are likely to be relevant to the analysis of every deictic system. These modes of access are frequently described as linguistic features or markers, but they are more accurately understood as social relations between participants engaged in reference and the objects that they denote.[9] Being relations, they cannot be understood as attributes inherent in objects (like redness or squareness), describable as one-place predicates. Nor can they be accurately glossed in terms of the coordinates of a map. Rather, they are trajectories leading from agents to objects via different sensory, attentional, and culturally meaningful pathways.

The first point therefore is that deictic systems are not based on sheer physical relations between verbal tokens and things, as might appear, but on relations between actors and significant aspects of their lived space. This gives rise to a second element that comes between the deictic field as a whole and the modes of access into which it is ultimately subdivided. This is what I will call a *zone*. A zone is a portion of the deictic field based on a single participant or configuration of participants, such as the "proximal zone," the "distal zone" or the "addressee zone." Whereas *domains* are characterized by a single class of modes of access (e.g. spatial), a *zone* cuts across various domains (spatial, temporal, attentional), but is unified by a single degree of remove from the ground (proximal, distal). Thus, 'here, there, over there' are members of the same domain, space, but 'this, here, now' are members of the same zone, proximal. As it turns out, deictic forms in Maya actually encode this distinction, with one grammatical class marking differences among *domains*, and another one marking differences among *zones* of relative immediacy crosscutting the domains. The former we will call Initial Deictics, because they occur at the beginning of phrases, and the latter Terminal Deictics, because they occur at the end (see section 2.2 below).[10]

It is commonly asserted in the literature that deictic paradigms are proportionally structured, so that *here* differs from *there* as *this* does from *that*, as *now* does from *then* and so forth, suggesting that a "deictic subsystem" in language could be readily demonstrated. The idea is evidently that deictic zones tend to intersect with domains in a regular, Boolean fashion, so that every domain is subdivided in the same way. This kind of proportionality invites logical reduction, and the literature contains various proposals to reduce all deictics to a single most basic one ("I" for Russell, "this" for Reichenbach). When one examines an actual deictic system in natural language, the evidence for such proportionality is really mixed. My own work on Yucatec Maya deixis indicates that there are indeed a number of parameters on which the entire system is regular, but there are others on which different (subsets of) categories appear idiosyncratic. On the one hand, some deictic expressions are much more marked than others, being more restricted in the contexts in which they can be used. There are also apparent irregularities due to the differences between domains: perceptual deictics may distinguish tactual vs. visible vs. audible in a rank order, whereas spatial categories may dichotomously divide inclusive vs. exclusive and person categories raise still different issues. All of these factors figure in the linguistic organization of demonstrative forms, but do not necessarily correspond to the social organization of modes of access.

A Maya speaker trying to fish a bucket out of a well with a rope and hook has indirect tactual evidence of the bucket whenever the hook clangs on metal and he feels its weight on the rope. I witnessed one such incident, and attested the speaker's reference to the bucket with the utterance *héʔe letiʔ bʼeʔ*, 'There it is [peripheral sensory evidence].' The fit between the word and the scenario seems perfect, but it must be noted that the same linguistic form is used in referring to the smoke of a fire one cannot see and the sound of a bus coming from out of sight. In other words, the actual mode of access (auditory, indirect tactual) was not identical to the deictic feature used (peripheral sensory, which includes all non-visual perceptual evidence). The proper starting point, then, is one in which the language and the socio-cultural context are kept distinct until we have evidence of convergence. It is not just that Maya grammar leaks, but that its deictic system has an organization of its own (Hanks 1990: ch. 10).

Some of the background knowledge that interactants bring to speaking is organized in what have come to be called "frames." Like other schemata, frames are grounded partly in the routine ways in which speakers use their language. Fillmore (1978: 165) defined "frame" as a set of lexical items whose members index portions of some actional or conceptual whole. For instance, *buy* and *sell* correspond to different portions of a single "commercial event," and the names *Monday*, *Tuesday*, *Wednesday*..., correspond to parts in a single calendric cycle called the *week*. The key feature of frames is that the individual items that fit into them, the words, are only intelligible to someone who has access to the entire schema. "What holds such word groups together is the fact of their being motivated by, founded on, and co-structured with, specific unified frameworks of knowledge, or coherent schematizations of experience" (Fillmore 1985: 223). The relation between frames and words is a subtle one, and Fillmore carefully distinguishes "frames" from "lexical fields." The latter are made up of sets of linguistic items organized in paradigmatic opposition to one another – such that it is the relation between the forms that determines the interpretation of any one, and *not* the relation between the forms and some conceptual or actional whole that exists independent of the language.

Frames are not language-internal objects; they are constituents Of the social, cultural, and natural world *in which language is used*. Unavoidably, a semantics based on them is more like an encyclopedia than a dictionary, and incorporates the view that linguistic categories exist in relation to particular "structured understandings of cultural institutions, beliefs about the world" and so forth (Fillmore 1985:231). Rather than supplying a "semantic representation," in the form of an object read off as the interpretation of a sentence, frame semantics takes the internal semantic structure of a sentence as a "blueprint" from which an interpreter constructs a whole understanding. Frames come into play in the extrapolation of this understanding. In this kind of theory, both the acting subject and the background understandings play a role in interpretation. The divide between "properly linguistic meaning" and "speaker's meaning" is maintained in the idea that the former, but not the latter, must figure in all pragmatic contexts.[11] Much as Linsky observed for reference, speaker's meaning is derived from a combination of the words used and the extralinguistic context (Fillmore 1985: 233).[12]

It is very unlikely (if not impossible) that any unified, consistent set of frames could be proposed, for a language, that would suffice to describe all, or even most, of the interpretations that arise in the use of that language. In effect, the idea of embedding acts of reference and predication in frames is directed towards providing a "maximally rich" (Fillmore 1985:234) interpretation, not a neatly bounded one. Still, many questions arise regarding the relative complexity of frames, how they are articulated in speech, how they are produced, and how they change over time. To better approach these questions, consider the example of demonstrative expressions such as *this*, *that*, *now*, *I*, and so forth.[13] These are paradigmatically referring items whose meanings and discourse functions provide a rich case study in the semantics of understanding.

Frames as we have defined them lie on the border between language structure and the schematized understandings that native speakers have of their language and world. Like semantic structures, they are relatively conventionalized, but unlike them, they are not part of language as such. This being so, frames can play a significant role in ethnographic description of context, far beyond questions of language use. In my research in a Maya community, for instance, I found that a limited number of schematic frames helps to organize spatial and temporal orientation across several fields, including deictic reference, people's understandings of local geography, the layout and architecture of domestic space, agricultural practices (especially the swidden cycle of traditional milpa agriculture), and ritual performances (including the building of altars). Frames then range over aspects of social life that are kept distinct in other descriptive approaches, and they help us to understand better the deep-seated continuities between language use and other forms of meaning production.[14]

Demonstrative expressions, and their associated modes of access, are organized according to actional wholes: *I*, *you*, *here*, *this*, and *now* are members of a single set corresponding to some part of "proximal frame." Depending upon how narrowly or broadly one defines deictic frames, *there*, *that*, *then*, and the third-person pronouns may belong to the same one as the proximal forms, since they are all defined in relation to one another, even though they are not all "proximal." In at least some standard uses, the referential function of deixis is linked to presentative (*Here it is, Take it!*) or directive (*There it is, Look!*) illocutionary force, and when so, the communicative whole of which the deictic is part must include these extra-referential effects. It has long been recognized that bodily gestures also – such as pointing, directed gaze, and handing over an object – are a necessary part of (at least some) ostensive reference, and similarly that the current attentional focus of interactants may play a role as well (Bühler 1967, Fillmore 1982, Leonard 1985, Lyons 1977). Thus we should expect the frames of deictic reference to include various extra-referential features. Beyond these quite general indications, we need to work through the details of demonstrative practice in a given cultural setting in order to formulate the relevant frames.

Systems of deictics and demonstratives provide some of the most powerful examples of the grammaticalization of interactive context. One reason for this is that they are in fact systems encompassing several paradigms and representing most or all of the major syntactic categories in a language. Arguments about relativity are always stronger when based on broad-scale patterns in languages, rather than on isolated words or sets of words. This holds whether the relativity is interactive or more broadly cultural in terms of the observations of Whorf and Sapir. In Yucatec Maya, there is what seems a very rich example of grammaticalization in the deictic system. This lies in the distinction between proclitic and enclitic deictic series. In the remainder of this chapter I will spell out some of the grammatical details of these two series, and try to show in what way they are motivated by the routine practices in which Maya speakers make reference. In the following table (taken from Hanks 1990), the two series are labeled Initial Deictics and Terminal Deictics, respectively.

Table 9.1 summarizes the Maya deictic system in matrix form, with Terminal Deictics (TDs) across the top and Initial Deictics (IDs) down the left side. IDs combine with TDs to form complex lexical items, whose standard meanings are more than the sum of the two parts. Often, the complex is discontinuous, with the ID occurring initially in a constituent (Noun Phrase, Adverb Phrase, and so forth, according to the case), and

Table 9.1. Synopsis of Maya deictics

ID base[a]	Terminal Deictics						Gloss
	a?	o?	b'e?	i?	e?	Ø	
OSTEV hé?e(l)	hé?ela?						'Here it is (Tactual Presentative)'
hé?e(l)		hé?elo?					'There it is (Visual Directive)'
hé?e(l)			hé?eb'e?				'There it is (Auditory Directive)'
DMOD hé?e(l)					hé?ele?		'Indeed, for sure'
DLOC té?e(l)	té?ela?						'Right there, here (immediate)'
té?e(l)		té?elo?					'There (non-immediate)'
ti?				ti?i?			'There (anaphoric)'
way					way e?		'(In) here (inclusive)'
to(l)		tol o?					'(Out) there (exclusive)'
DNOM le(l)	lel a?						'This one (immed.)'
le(l)		lel o?					'That one (non-immed.)'
le				le ti?			'This one'
le						le	'The (definite art.)'
PART t-	t-en						'I (1st sg.)'
t-		t-eč					'You (2nd sg.)'
t-	t-ó?on						'We (1st pl.)'
t-		t-é?eš					'You (2nd pl.)'
le				le ti?			'He, she, it, the one (3rd sg.)'
le				le ti?-ó?ob			'They, the ones (3rd pl.)'

DTEMP[b]	walakil	walakil a?		'This time (of day)'
	b'eh?òora	b'eh?òora a?		'Now, presently'
	tolakhéak		tolakhéak o?	'Back then (shared, distant, past)'
	b'ehé?ela			b'ehé?elae? 'Now, today, nowadays'
	taánt			taánte? 'Just (immed. pst)'
	laáyli			laáylie? 'Still, even, now'
DMAN	b'ey	b'ey a?		'Like this'
	b'ey		b'ey o?	'Like that, so'
	b'èey			b'èey 'So, thus, since'

[a] Grammatical categories of IDs: OSTEV (Ostensive Evidential adverb); DMOD (Deictic Modal auxiliary); DLOC (Deictic Locative adverb); DNOM (Deictic Nominal); PART (Participant Deictic); DTEMP (Deictic Temporal adverb); DMAN (Deictic Manner adverb).
[b] Partial display of DTEMPs.

the TD occurring in sentence-final position. Under certain circumstances, a complex occurs in continuous form, for instance when used as a one-word utterance, or in citation form (as in the table). Under the Participant (PART) Deictics, note that the TDs surface in unexpected shapes. Actually, the forms shown are pronominal suffixes which I have aligned with the TDs in order to highlight certain morphosyntactic and semantic parallels to be spelled out in section 2.2 below (for extended discussion see Hanks 1990: Chs. 4 and 10).

Each of the Initial Deictic bases bears a grammatical category feature, and each is associated with a core dimension of the deictic frame. Let us define the core dimension of a linguistic category as that domain in the deictic field that the category subdifferentiates most finely. Perceptual access to referents is almost always a relevant feature of the phenomenal framework of deictic utterances, but no deictics in Maya subdivide the perceptual screen so finely as the ones labeled Ostensive Evidentials (OSTEV). These are sentential adverbs. The Participant (PART) forms are all nouns and their core dimension is the participant roles in speech events. The Deictic Locatives (DLOC) are all circumstantial adverbs and their core dimension is space. Like perception, spatial relations are virtually always part of the actional context of deictic reference, but it is the DLOCs alone that distinguish five kinds. And so on for the other categories. The IDs, then, encode two crucial kinds of information: (i) the *grammatical features* which govern how the deictic referent will be integrated into a linguistic message, and (ii) the *metapragmatic features* which govern how the referent is to be localized within the indexical and referential frames projected in deixis (i.e., via perception, relative spatial contiguity, participant role).[15] It is obvious from table 9.1 that one can infer from the occurrence of *way*, 'here,' that an egocentric regional spatial reference is being made, and from the utterance of *héʔe*, '(t)here it is,' it follows that an act of ostensive reference is being made. All ostensive acts, so defined, rely on a perceptual cue. Notice that although the IDs give information regarding the *domain* of deictic reference, most do not specify the *modes of access* within the domains (*héʔe* does not specify which perceptual mode is in play).[16]

The Terminal Deictics work differently, and this is the first clue that the split is motivated. Speaking grossly, TDs indicate the relative proximity of the referent to the ground, with *aʔ* being the most proximal and *iʔ* the least. By my analysis, *eʔ* is semantically empty. TDs have no grammatical category features apart from the TD category itself. While there are co-occurrence restrictions between TDs and IDs, for the most part the TDs combine with every category of ID (holding aside the PART category). Similarly, there are some associations between given TDs and specific domains of the deictic field (such as the fact that *bʼeʔ* is invariantly

Peripheral Perceptual), but for the most part the TDs *cut across* the domains rather than coinciding with them. What they differentiate instead are *modes of access within the domains*, such as relative Immediacy in Space, relative fullness of Perceptual access (Tactual, Visual, Peripheral) and relative role within the Participation framework (Spkr., Adr., Other). These are what I have called Relational Values, which are *metapragmatic features* at a lower, finer level of definition than the dimensions. In some cases, IDs are specific to Relational Values, such as the Exclusive (*tol*) and Inclusive (*way*) DLOCs, but for the most part, it is the TDs which distinguish values at this level.

Not all TDs combine with all IDs, and this means that there are implicational relations holding between the two series.[17] Complexes such as **héʔel iʔ*, **tol aʔ*, **téʔel eʔ*, **way iʔ*,... simply do not occur and are uniformly rejected by native speakers in elicitation. In some cases, there is apparently a functional motivation for the gap, such as *tol aʔ*, where the ID and TD are intuitively incompatible, the former indicating maximal distance from ground, and the latter indicating maximal proximity. For the most part however, the formal gaps are best treated as arbitrary facts of Maya language, since it is virtually always possible to create a distinction for an additional form, or to associate it functionally with some already existing distinction(s). The TDs *aʔ* and *oʔ* are the most fully implemented, since they figure in all categories except PART. *b'eʔ* and *iʔ* are on the opposite extreme, since the former occurs only in the OSTEVs (and, marginally, in Nominal Deictics [DNOM]) and the latter occurs only in the DLOCs.[18] *eʔ* figures only in the Deictic Modal (DMOD), Deictic Locative (DLOC), and Temporal (DTEMP) categories.

There are therefore significant differences among the TDs in terms of their privileges of combination with IDs. Whatever the motivation, this means that, within the deictic system, the features encoded in TDs do not combine freely with those encoded in the IDs. To the extent that the former distinguish *modes of access* while the latter distinguish *domains*, this indicates that the deictic field is not a uniform grid in which all coordinates are subdivided to the same degree of delicacy. In other words, despite the impressive regularity of the system, as evident in the matrix, still the categories are not arrayed in neat proportional oppositions.

2.2 A functional hierarchy

Each TD is consistently associated with certain ranges of relational features and bodily gestures, corresponding to certain modes of access in the deictic field. This consistency anchors the linguistic forms into a single, repeated pattern, and contributes to the regularity of the system as a whole.

All *aʔ* forms are associated with high-focus gestures, such as extending the referent in hand, touching or pointing to it with directed gaze, all of which imply that the Spkr. is in a relation of contiguity with the object. These are the preferred deictics for segmenting the Spkr.'s corporeal schema, current performance or immediate region, and all of them tend to be indexically asymmetric. That is, they focalize the Spkr.'s zone as opposed to the shared ground, new information in discourse as opposed to what is already known, and anticipated objects rather than the ones already passed by.

All *oʔ* forms are associated with relatively less focal gestures, such as a vague toss of the hand or a less ostentatiously directed point. In many cases, there is no gesture at all. These are the forms used to make reference to objects in the Adr.'s zone or in the common ground. They are relatively symmetric in our terms, and are used for reference to prior discourse, or coreference with it, as well as for resumptive closing of discourse or actional units (as in English *So that's that.*). Thus, we can say that the formal similarities between categories correspond to functional ones as well, *héʔel aʔ : héʔel óʔ :: téʔel aʔ : téʔel oʔ :: lel aʔ : lel oʔ : b'ey aʔ : b'ey oʔ*.

The remaining TDs are more specialized but can be regularly graded in terms of the richness of information they convey. *b'eʔ* is by far the most specific TD in the language, since it invariantly conveys presence of Peripheral and absence of Tactual or Visual evidence of a referent. It tends to be used in symmetric indexical frames in which both participants can perceive the referent, although it is also used when only the Spkr. has access. *iʔ* and *eʔ* are both non-Concrete, indifferent to relative perceptual or spatial immediacy.[19] The former is used to convey unique individuation of a referent (individual or place) in the symmetric frame of background knowledge or prior discourse. The latter is an empty place holder with a variety of syntactic functions. It adds no sensory evidentiality to *héʔ e(l)* in the modal DMOD, and apparently adds no information to the already specific DLOC *way*, 'here.' There is a contrast in the DLOCs between simple focus *tiʔ . . . iʔ* and split focus *tiʔ . . . LOCeʔ*, where the former is anaphoric and the latter is not. We can phrase this as follows: when the locative reference is identified solely by the DLOC, the interpretation is anaphoric and the TD is *iʔ*; when the referent is identified by a lexical description, the description overrides any potential anaphoric interpretation, and the TD is *eʔ*. I take this to be a neutralization of the privative opposition *iʔ* [+Specified] vs. *eʔ* [Ø Specified], with the unmarked term occurring in the neutralizing context.

The relative ordering which emerges from these observations is *aʔ* > *oʔ* > *b'eʔ* > *iʔ* > *eʔ*. This hierarchy is based on the relative immediacy of access to the referent conveyed by the TDs, with more immediate preceding less immediate. It is *prima facie* evidence that their referential import is in fact defined relative to the modes of access. There is a stronger bit of evidence for such motivation, however, which has to do with the syntactic relation between IDs and TDs. In order to see this, we need to briefly review constraints on the distribution of Terminal Deictics.

2.3 Two constraints

There are two major constraints on the normal syntactic distribution of TDs:

Constraint 1–TDs occur only at the final boundary of a topic phrase or sentence;

Constraint 2–Only one TD occurs at any boundary.

This means that sentences containing a plurality of ID bases nonetheless have only a single TD associated with them, ruling out examples like the following.[20]

(1) *héʔel eʔ   ubʹin lel oʔ   maák
    DMOD TD VC DNOM TD N
    surely will go that man
    'That man will surely go'

(2) *tíʔ iʔ   an lel oʔ   šíʔipal tinwiknal
    DLOC TD V DNOM TD N   RN
    there is that boy at my place
    'There('s where) that boy is, at my house'

(3) *way eʔ   yaàn lel aʔ   ʔinsukúʔun
    DLOC TD VC DNOM TD NP
    here is this my brother
    'Here ('s where) this brother of mine is'

(4) *téʔel oʔ   ʔič   kʔíʔiš
    DLOC TD PREP N
    'There in (the) thorns'

The correct forms for these sentences are (5–8), in which the TDs have all been shifted to S-final position, and only one TD appears in each S.

(5) héʔel ubʹin le maák oʔ   'That man will surely go'

(6) tíʔ an le šíʔipal tinwiknal oʔ   'There('s where) that boy is, at my house'

(7) way yaàn le ʔinsukúʔun aʔ   'Here('s where) this brother of mine is'

(8) téʔ ʔič kʹíʔiš oʔ   'There in (the) thorns'   (F.137.A.115)

The first constraint that TDs occur only at the final boundary of an S or topic will properly rule out medial TDs as in (1–4), and the second constraint that only one occur per boundary rules out (9–11).

(9) *héʔel ubʹin le   maák oʔ eʔ
    DMOD VC DNOM N   TD TD
    'That man will surely go' (cf. 1, 5)

(10) *tí? an le ší?ipal tinwiknal e? o?
  DLOC VB DNOM N RN   TD TD
  'There('s where) that boy is, at my house' (cf. 2, 6)

(11) *tí? kub'in le hé?el a? a? i?
  DLOC VC DNOM OSTEV TD TD TD
  'That's (where) this one is going'

When a sentence contains an embedded clause, the TDs occur at the final S boundary, and not at the internal clause boundary. In (12), the complement clause 'to work' is separated from the matrix verb 'I went' by the DLOC base *té?*, indicating that the DLOC is part of the matrix clause (cf. *té? h b'inen meyah a?*, 'there (is where) I went to work'). This fact notwithstanding, the TD obligatorily follows the subordinate clause.

(12) *tulaá? ?àaño ká hb'inen té? meyah a?*
  RN N Comp VC DLOC VC TD
  'The next year, when I went there to work, ...'   (BB.4.76)
  (cf. **tulaá? ?àaño ká hb'ine té? ela? meyah*)

Similarly, in (13), the ID base separates the verb of going from its complement, but the TD must follow the complement, not precede it.

(13) *kó?oš té? šiimb'al o?*
  VC DLOC VC TD
  'Let's go there walking'   (F.137.A.1 15)
  (cf. **kó?oš té?elo? šiimb'al*)

Given only the two syntactic constraints on TDs, it is impossible to predict which from a potential *n*-tuple will appear in final position in the sentence or topic. The constraints operate uniformly on all TDs, regardless of their identity, or the identity or syntactic placement of an ID with which they are cointerpreted. Yet it is clear that the selection of one or another from a possible set of TDs is not random. This is where the functional hierarchy comes into play. The correct generalization appears to be that in any potential *n*-tuple of TDs, the one which is highest (leftmost) in the hierarchy is the one that will appear on the surface. Alternatively stated, any member in the ordering $a? > o? > b'e? > i? > e?$ is automatically overridden by all those to its left.

This is equivalent to saying that the most immediate deictic subframe projected in any act of reference takes precedence over all others. The relatively arbitrary syntactic constraints on these deictics force Maya speakers to choose, and the normal expectation is that they will choose the highest values available. This reflects the basic tendency in the system for the immediate, more concrete zone to take precedence over the remote, less concrete.

In the following routine examples, the (simplified) lexical version of the sentence is on the left and the actual attested forms, conforming to syntactic constraints, are on the right. The precedence relations at play in the example are shown in parentheses after the English gloss. For instance, in (14), we know that the ID *tol* always co-occurs with the TD *o²*, and that the *a²* which appears in final position in the attested surface form must originate as part of the DNOM.

SEMANTIC: [ID__]   SYNTACTIC: [ID X___##]

(14) *tol   o² tinkaštah lel   a² b'a²al → tol tinkaštah le b'á²al a̲²*
      DLOC T̄D VC   DNOM T̄D N
      'Out there (is where) I found this thing' (*a² > o²*)

(15) *hé²e   b'e² kub'in lel   o² maàk → hé² kub'in le maák o̲²*
      OSTEV T̄D VC   DNOM T̄D N
      'There goes the guy (listen!)' (*o² > b'e²*)

(16) *tí²   i² kab'in lel   o² maàk → tí² kub'in le maàk o̲²*
      DLOC T̄D VC   DNOM T̄D N
      'There (is where) the guy goes' (*o² > i²*)

(17) *b'ey   o² lel   o² biida tó²on   way e² →*
      DLOC T̄D DNOM T̄D N   PART DLOC TD
                                              b'ey le biida tó²on way o̲²
      'That's how life (is) for us (around) here' (*o² > e²*)   (BB.4.12)

(18) *má² i²   way   e² kutàal   →   ma² way kutaal i̲²*
      Neg TD DLOC TD VC
      'Here (is) not (where) he comes' (*i² > e²*)

These simple generalizations will account for the selection and placement of the vast majority of TDs in routine Maya, but there are complications. If an ID base occurs in S-final position, as they often do when not foregrounded, then the constraints on *continuous* combinations of this base with TDs may override the hierarchy. In other words, the lexical gaps in the paradigm of canonical citation deictics reassert themselves, ruling out superficial forms like **tol a²*, **hé²el i²*, **way b'e²*, and **way i²*, regardless of the syntactic environment in which they might be expected to occur. Thus, the non-focused version of (14) is *tinkaštah le b'á²al tol o̲²*, not **tinkaštah le b'á²al tol a²*; the non-focused version of (18) is *má² kutàal way e̲²*, not **má² kutàal way i²*. There is a further snag however, since, in some cases, the syntactic constraints on TD selection override the citation forms nonetheless, as (17) shows: *way o²* is not a valid citation form and does not arise unless the TD has a lexical source elsewhere in the sentence, but it is the standard form in cases like this one. The best I can say of these facts is that they are either irregularities in the system, or points on which my understanding is inadequate.

2.4 Grammaticalization

To what extent are these "design features" of Maya deictics motivated by
the referential practices in which the forms are used? Or, to ask a slightly
different but related question, to what extent are they grammaticalizations of routine practices? In each major category in table 9.1, there is a
split between two formal series, the IDs and the TDs. With very few
exceptions, canonical lexical forms are composed of a pairing of one ID
with one TD, always in the same order. Given that both series have stable
ranges of encoded meanings, the fact of grammatical composition invites
one to ask:

To what extent do the functional segmentations in the language
correspond to socio-cultural segmentations of the deictic field?

One need not look outside the language to expect that the deictics
would be composed of more than one morpheme, or that the enclitic
series would be of the shape (C)VC. Maya is a language with a relatively
rich morphology, most of which is suffixal; tense/aspect distinctions and
most kinds of derivation are marked by suffixes, whose canonical shape is
VC.[21] It is also a language with a relatively rich inventory of particles
(non-derivable, usually non-inflectable, words), which fall into different
sets defined by their distribution as proclitics or enclitics, and which very
often compound. If anything, it would be noteworthy were the deictics
not polymorphemic. The more interesting question is why the TDs
appear to encode systematically different information than that encoded
in the IDs.

TDs signal the mode of access between participants and referents, that
is, how an interlocutor experiences the referent at the moment of
utterance. So *héʔel aʔ* usually conveys tactual access, *héʔel oʔ* visible or
peripheral, and *héʔe bʔeʔ* always conveys peripheral. In space, *téʔel aʔ* is
immediate and anticipatory, *téʔel oʔ* non-immediate and common
background knowledge. All forms with the same TD signal the same
relative immediacy to (or remove from) the participants in the deictic
field. At the same time, TDs distinguish kinds of participant structures, as
in the egocentric zone of the speaker marked by *aʔ*, the sociocentric zone
of Speaker–Addressee (*oʔ*, *bʔeʔ*, *iʔ*), and the altercentric zone of the
addressee (*oʔ*). Thus they are the main signal of what I have called
the relative symmetry (sharedness, mutuality) of indexical context. IDs,
as we said, signal domains in the deictic field, that is, the general
dimension in which the referent is accessible, such as Perception, Space,
Discourse, and so forth (see table 9.1). They also encode grammatical
information regarding the role of the referent in the proposition, and they
distinguish predicative, referential, and non-referential uses.[22] An ID–TD
pair therefore conveys information sufficient for an interlocutor to

identify a referent in the interactive context, by orienting his or her attention and drawing selectively on available information (including prior discourse). Part of the interpretation (s)he constructs is an evaluation of the speaker's stance or footing relative to the referent and to the addressee – is this common knowledge, new and high focus, available on the periphery of our perceptual field? Speakers monitor these social relations continuously in talk, and their ability to engage in referential practices rests on their ability to situate themselves and their referents relative to other, co-participating actors. Much like what Gumperz (this volume) has dubbed "contextualization cues," the TDs thus play a crucial role in framing the referential content of an utterance within the interactive context of its occurrence. Unlike contextualization cues, which tend to be prosodic and whose pragmatic values vary across contexts, the TDs are morphemes in a regular paradigm, whose meanings remain relatively constant across contexts. By their frequency in discourse and widespread distribution in the deictic system, TDs are the primary indicators of these aspects of utterance context. There is therefore a *de facto* correspondence between the linguistic meanings of these forms, and the organization of the deictic field into domains, modes, and zones.

When integrated into a phrase or a sentence, the two parts of a deictic are typically discontinuous, with the ID in initial position in the phrase and the TD at the end of the sentence (or topic phrase). Since IDs represent all the major syntactic phrase types in Maya, a sentence very often contains several of them. TDs form a single set of mutually exclusive sentence enclitics; just one TD may occur per sentence and it must be in final position. This raises another question regarding grammaticalization:

Is the one-only constraint on TDs motivated by referential practices?

In sentences containing several IDs, the one-only constraint forces speakers to select a single TD out of several possible ones. This selection appears to be highly systematic, and to follow the functional hierarchy of information encoded in the TDs. The rule is that the more specific and immediate the mode of access indicated by the TD, the more likely it is to appear as the sentence enclitic. This implies a kind of neutralization, such that the form associated with the most referentially specific, high-focus information in a sentence takes precedence over any less specific ones. Although I have not discussed pronouns in this chapter, for the sake of brevity, they offer a compelling analog to the information hierarchy in TDs.

There are two series of bound pronouns in Maya, prefixal and suffixal. The suffixes mark transitive objects, equational subjects, and plurality of agent, intransitive subject or possessor. When, for whatever reason, a verb complex contains two suffixal pronouns, their linear order always conforms to the rule that first person precedes second, and second precedes third. This rule is exceptionless to my knowledge, and applies regardless of the grammatical roles of the two pronouns. Thus, *ʔa-sukúʔun-éʔš- óʔob*, 'they are your elder brothers,' *ʔu-sukúʔun-éʔš-óʔob*, 'you are their elder brothers,' where the underscored suffixes mark 2nd pl. possessor plus 3rd pl. equational subject in the first case, and 2nd pl. equational subject plus 3rd pl. possessor in the second case. Despite the reversal of grammatical roles (indicated by the prefixal forms, 2nd-person and 3rd-person, respectively), the order of suffixes is fixed. In other words, the familiar person hierarchy operates on the inflection of Maya verbs and nouns by determining sequential order of morphemes.

It is easy enough to see the parallel between the first person and asymmetric *aʔ*, specializing in high-focus, often egocentric, information; between the second person and symmetric *oʔ*, specializing in mid- to low-focus, typically shared, information; and the third person and the remaining TDs, which are more peripheral or abstract. It is intuitively clear, if not always strictly accurate, that the neutralized TDs tend to encode information that is common knowledge and recoverable. To this extent, the choice of TD conforms to a very well-known and evidently universal principle that recoverable information can be elided. Yet what motivates the one-only constraint in the first place?

The implication of the one-only constraint is that sentences tend to be anchored in just one zone and just one mode of access.[23] That is, a single utterance tends to be contextualized relative to a particular participant relation (say, egocentric or sociocentric), and a particular experience (say vision, touch or memory). In theory, a speaker could adopt a different footing relative to each of the objects to which he refers in an utterance, by selecting deictics that incorporate different features for modes of access and zone. In fact, just a single footing is signalled in the lone terminal deictic. This suggests that the semantic structure of deictic expressions is fixed at the level of the sentence, and not its individual constituents. An interlocutor attempting to understand the utterance in (19) or (20) must in effect take account of the entire sentence in order to have the "blueprint" from which to construct an understanding of the very first word (*téʔe* and *héʔe*, respectively). It is only at the end that he would get the TD, which is what determines which lexical deictic is in sentence-initial position.

(19) *téʔe   kumaán le   bùus kawáʔalik aʔ*
     DLOC VC   DNOM N   VC   TD
     there passes that bus you're talking about
     'That's where the bus you're talking about goes'

(20) *hé?*   *le*   *ti?*   *e*   *nohoč* *maák* *be?*
    OSTEV DNOM TD DNOM ADJ   N   TD
    There's the one the great person audible
    'There's that old guy (listen!)'

The one-only constraint is a case of grammaticalization in which a routine feature of referential practice is encoded in the grammar – namely the strong tendency of speakers to adopt a single footing in the deictic field per utterance.[24] I take this as an indication that deictic frames in this language are selectively weighted towards the most focal modes of access, so that only the most immediate one gets signalled, in accordance with the hierarchy presented above (*a?* to *e?*). One way to see this is to consider non-routine, atypical examples in which the constraint is violated. Examples in the next section will show that violations occur precisely when speakers are foregrounding their own footing relative to the discourse. We know from the occurrence of deictic transpositions that speakers can manipulate these forms in order to alter the perspectival framework of interaction. The occurrence of bundles of TDs in Maya speech is a case in point.

3 Foregrounded forms for foregrounded practices

Foregrounding is a pervasive feature of Maya discourse and accounts for numerous departures from the standard patterns described above. As with the foregrounding possibilities for IDs (Hanks 1990: ch. 10), the ones for TDs involve something akin to copying or reduplication, as well as combinations of non-identical forms. These constructions are fairly common in talk, and are clearly intelligible and purposeful for native Maya speakers. At the same time, they are obviously non-canonical, and are usually rejected as "not Maya" by speakers in elicitation settings.

3.1 TD foregrounding

There are two main kinds of construction in which the functions of TDs are foregrounded, those involving the expansion of a single TD by way of stretching or reduplication, and those involving the combination of two non-identical TDs in a continuous bundle. For heuristic purposes, I will call the former *TD stretching*, and the latter *TD1–TD2 couplets*. Both of these entail departures from the one-only constraint, but it is likely that they require different explanations. I prefer "stretching" to "reduplication," because in the few cases of foregrounded *b'e?* that I have attested, it was ... *b'e?e?* that was said, and never *b'e? b'e?*. For all of the *V?* terminals, a reduplication analysis would be possible and may be preferable, although I will not address the question directly. To my knowledge, there are never more than two TDs (or one stretched one, as the case may be) at the end of a single S, a constraint as arbitrary as the one limiting pronoun suffixes to a maximum of two (see Hanks 1990: ch. 4). The constraint that TDs occur at the final boundary of topic or sentence is evidently not violated for communicative purposes.[25] TD stretching is by far the more common of the two kinds of foregrounding, and the functional motivations for it are quite diverse. We take these up first, before proceeding to the more exotic TD1–TD2 couplets.

3.1.1 TD stretching

TD stretching is illustrated by sentences such as the following. (21) was produced by a monolingual Maya man during work on an irrigation canal in a field. He was explaining the lie of the land to a co-worker, recommending placement of a new canal. The remaining examples were uttered by a bilingual man who was describing the local geography to me.

(21) *hé?*   *yaálka? le*   *ha? b'ey*   *a?a?*
    DMOD VC   DNOM N   DMAN TD TD
    Surely will run the water like this
    'The water will surely run (off) this way'   (BB.5.60)

(22) *lel*   *a? č'é?en→...yan keš dyèes   mekàates i?→*
    DNOM TD N   VC NUM N   TD
    'This (is the) well...There's about 10 mecates there.'

    tí?an   lel   *a꜒ a? ↓ le*   *k   b'èel o?*
    DLOC DNOM   TD TD DNOM PRO N   TD
    'There's this one. Our path'   (F.4.B.292)

(23) *lel*   *a? nah dón alpòonso→̂ lel*   *a? a?→̂   č'é?em↓*
    DNOM TD N   NAME   DNOM TD TD N
    'This is Don Alfonso's place. This (pause) is (the) well.'   (F.4.B.203)

If my analysis of the constraints on TDs is correct, then these forms are foregrounded, but *what* is being pushed to the fore? My data include three distinguishable sorts of case: *expressive stretching*, where the Spkr. conveys an intense involvement in the utterance, or special emphasis on some aspect of it (21); *stretching as a staging device*, marking a topicalized element, member of an ongoing list, or utterance fraction otherwise preparatory to some further statement (22); and *stretching as a pause-filler*, or hesitation device that may build some dramatic tension or merely hold an interlocutor's attention in preparation for some imminent continuation (23). The latter two are obviously related and may be the same, while the former seems distinct from both.

What I am calling expressive stretching commonly arises in discourse contexts in which the expressive utterance responds to a previous question or to some other aspect of the interactive framework. In (21) DP (a 65-year-old *nohoč maák*, 'big man,' used to laying down the law) was looking at the lay of the land in his field, and the question of how the rain-water would run was already established; he was answering it. In other cases an explicit question is voiced, as in (24)–(27), in which he and another speaker were correcting my Maya.

(24) DP   *má² klàaro i²↓*   'It's not clear'
     WH   *má² klàaro i²↑*   'It's not clear?'
     DP   *má² klàaro i²istak o̧ᴖo²→*   'Of course it's not clear!'   (F.1.A.895)

(25) DB   *kuȼonik č'iíč ⁻͢ b'ey→(laughter) má²a tub'éel i̧ᴖ i²*
          VC   N   DMAN   NEG ADV TD TD
     ' "He shoots birds, like so." (laughter) It's not correct.'   (F.92.A.280)

(26) *b'eéyli   e² ↑ ken   teč→   kinká²ak'aátik teč   e²→*
     DMAN TD QUOT PART VC   PART TD
     ' "It's still so?" I say to you. I ask you again.
     kawáak   e²   b'aáyli   o̧ᴖ o²→
     VC   TD   DMAN TD TD
     You say, "It's *still* so." '   (F.92.B.478)

(27) *má²   sùuk   utàal e   wiíl↑ tch! ti²ili   sùuk   ukutal e² e²→*
     NEG ADV VC   TD NAME   DLOC ADV VC   TD TD
     ' "Doesn't he customarily come, Will?" "Tch! (Of course)
          there'(s where) he customarily sits." '   (F.1.A.804)

In (24) DP asserts his authoritative judgment that a previous example utterance by me was poorly constructed. When I ask for confirmation, he makes the judgment definitive, marking it formally with the emphatic enclitic *i²istak o²*. This form is functionally specialized in two ways; it signals forceful assertion, but only in response position. That is, it answers some previous utterance with an assertion – as opposed, for instance, to another question, a directive, a mitigated suggestion, or a hypothetical statement. The fact of its occurring in response position is indexed by the TD *o²* (which as we have seen is the one for anaphoric and pre-established, symmetrically accessible referents), and it is noteworthy that this is the only TD that normally co-occurs with *i²istak*. The emphasis already inherent in the enclitic is then bumped up another notch of intensity by the stretched TD; there was no need to seek a second confirmation after this one.

Example (25) also occurred during metalinguistic discussion, this time with Balim, a mainly monolingual man in his mid forties. In the first portion of his utterance, he is attempting to repeat an example I had presented to him for glossing, namely *kuȼ'onik b'ey č'iíč' le maák o²* 'the man shoots like birds.' He found it so garbled and laughably bad that he was unable to repeat it accurately. By stretching out the TD he foregrounds the certitude of his opinion.

Balim was the speaker of (26) also, in which the stretched TD is again in response position, this time in a hypothetical exchange. Note that the TD from the target utterance *b'eéyli e?* has been shifted to *o?*, in the answer, a conventional index of its status as response. The stretching indexes the emphasis of the assertion.[26]

Example (27) is another hypothetical exchange created by DP showing the same configuration of emphatic assertion in response position. The ingressive click, *tch!*, is a conventional expressive type used in other kinds of foregrounding, and reinforces the emphasis of the TDs.

Another class of TD stretchings is associated with topicalization and what Brown & Yule (1983:134), following Grimes and others, called "staging." As used here, the notion of staging is loose and heuristic, and meant to be more inclusive than "thematization," but still focuses on the function of some utterance fractions in foregrounding one portion of a scene as the point of departure for what follows it. Although these examples often occur in response position, staging is rather the function of the utterance to anticipate and set up the conditions for further commentary. In my metalinguistic discussions with Maya speakers, the hypothetical forms I offered them for glossing prepared the ground for their comments, and were commonly repeated by them at the outset of their response. This is the case in (28–30).

(28) WH *čeén té? le hé?el o?*↓
 Prt DLOC DNOM OSTEV TD
 'Just "*te? le hé?el o?*"' ('"There that one" what does it mean?')

 DP *čeén té? le hé?el o? o?*↑ *miš b'á?ah kyáaik*
 Prt DLOC DNOM OSTEV $\overline{\text{TD}}$ TD NEG N VC
 '"Just *té? le hé?el o?*"? It means nothing' (F.1.A.354)

(29) B *tumèen bey* → *bey kub'in e maák saánsamal*
 RN DMAN DMAN VC DNOM N ADV
  o⫯o?↑ *kyere desir e?*...
  $\overline{\text{TD}}$ TD
 'Because "So, So goes that man every day," it means...'
  (F.92.A.460)

(30) WH *tí? atàal i?* → *b'á?aš uk'aát yá?ale*
 DLOC VC TD N VC VC
 '"There (is where) you come from." What does it mean?'

 DP *pwes uk'aát yá?al tí? atàal e? e?* → *pór ehemplo*...
 Prt VC VC DLOC VC $\overline{\text{TD}}$ TD PREP N
 'Well, "There is where you come from", it means, for example...'
  (F.1.A.774)

Note in (30) that the TD of the target form I had offered DP has been switched in his response from *i?* to *e?*. The motivation for this is the shift in status of the phrase from an isolated utterance in the mention mode to a topical element on which DP is beginning a commentary. In his response, it is still "mentioned" rather than directly used, but it has been partially integrated into the direct discourse of his gloss.

In (31) the utterance fraction mentioned initially is part of a list of alternative utterances that DP was making to illustrate the form *ti²ili e²*. Observe that immediately afterwards, as he launches into a gloss, he shifts the TDs from the citation form to the *o²* form. This is a standard index of the anaphoric relation holding between the form he is glossing and the one mentioned in the immediately preceding discourse. The flanking *le...o²* is a direct, fully referential DNOM whose indexical ground is the corporeal frame that DP and I were occupying.

(31) DP   *ti²ili*   *sùuk*   *uhàanl*   *e*ꟼ *e²*→   *le*   *ti²ili*   *oo²*↑
        DLOC   ADV   VC   TD   TD   DNOM   DLOC   TD   TD
        ' "There('s where) he customarily eats." That '*ti²ili*,

        ²éskeh tut'àam pero...
        Comp   VC   CONJ
        it's that it speaks (is meaningful), but...'   (F.1.A.735)

What do these examples indicate about the one-only constraint? Obviously, it can be over-ridden for the right reasons; when it is, as in (21–31), the resulting utterance is to that extent foregrounded. Yet if the one-only constraint is the grammaticalized reflex of a communicative practice, then it should be possible to make more specific predictions about foregrounded forms. What exactly gets foregrounded? In (21–31), where a single TD is reduplicated, or stretched, it appears that what is brought to the fore is the relation between Spkr. and the proposition asserted, or Spkr. and Adr. In the former case what is conveyed is an increased expression of the Spkr.'s sense that the assertion is obvious, beyond question. In the latter cases, it serves as a pause filler or other staging device which maintains the Adr.'s attention focus in anticipation of an immediately following utterance. Rather than a lamination of two or more frames, what we have here is the special highlighting of one or another indexical zone within a single frame – the asymmetric zone of Spkr. expressivity or the symmetric one of the common Spkr.–Adr. ground. It is interesting that, in discourse, any TD can be stretched, to foreground either symmetric or asymmetric zones, yet at the level of the lexical values of individual TDs, some are inherently symmetric and others inherently asymmetric. In (23), the TD *a²* is lexically asymmetric, being the preferred form for introducing new information (the point being made by the speaker was, in fact, a new one), yet the stretching added an overlay of symmetric attention to the utterance, by foregrounding our phatic contact. The implication of such facts is that the syntactic resources for foregrounding provide speakers with means of altering and combining different values for deictic zones and modes of access. The most dramatic examples of foregrounding turn on the pairing of two different TDs in a single utterance.

3.1.2 TD1–TD2 couplets

It is noticeable that most of the foregoing examples of TD stretching are taken from metalinguistic commentary by three adult male Maya speakers. This is an accidental feature of my recorded data and does not reflect the limitations of the phenomenon in Maya speech. In my experience, all kinds of speakers use stretched TD forms under a wide variety of everyday circumstances. The same cannot be said for the next set of examples, which involve TD1–TD2 bundles. These forms are highly specialized functionally, and are not encountered in routine Maya to my knowledge. I found in working with them that they are rejected straightaway as ungrammatical by DP, the very speaker who produced the most florid examples. A senior head of household and monolingual Maya speaker known for his verbal skills, DP produces these forms repeatedly and purposefully. Furthermore, they are not simply garbled utterances without sense, but follow the functional patterns of the language, while casting into sharp relief the capacity of a Maya speaker to adapt the system to uncommon circumstances.

We were discussing the meanings of deictic expressions, and DP was producing glosses that combined mention with direct use, as well as what appear to be semi-direct shadings between the two. In (32) he has repeated verbatim the citation form I offered for commentary, while simultaneously marking it as a topical item in the current utterance. The shift in footing from mention to direct is an indexical transposition signalled by the pairing of TDs. Note that the superficial order of TDs preserves the integrity of the cited form, as it does also in (33). I had offered the citation form *hé²el eč e²* in order to see whether the DMOD could be directly inflected for person, and DP assured me that it cannot (a judgment corroborated by my observations of direct use). His utterance preserves the boundary between the two footings, and embeds the citation within the DNOM *le...o²* 'that,' itself the standard way of signalling anaphoric identity.

(32) WH *b'd²aš uk'aát yá²al tí²ili   o²→*
　　　　　Q   VC   VC   DLOC TD
　　　　　'What does '*tí²ili o²*' mean?'

　　　DP *pwes [...] čeén tí²ili   o² e² → mišbá²ah kut'anik→*
　　　　　Conj   Prt DLOC T̄D TD Neg N   VC
　　　　　'Well, [...] just '*tí²ili o²*,' it means nothing.'   (F.1.A.788)

(33) DP   *le   héʔel   eč   eʔ oʔ* →   *mišbʼáʔah kiyáaik* →
          DNOM DMOD Pro TD TD NEG N   VC
          'That *héʔel eč eʔ* (that you've said), it means nothing.'   (F.1.B.168)

Example (34) is parallel to the preceding two in that a citation form (underlined) is reproduced intact, and embedded within a direct utterance. DP was listing alternative ways of saying what he took to be my intended meaning, marking off the hypothetical status of these utterances with the indefinite particle plus TD *wáʔ. . . eʔ*. The circumfixing particles are part of the direct discourse, and the circumfixed is part of the citation.

(34) DP . . .*ʔáwra tíʔili   eʔ*→ *tíʔili   e   sùuk   e   maák óʔabʼ oʔ*→
         ADV DLOC TD DLOC TD ADV DNOM N   PC   TD
         '. . . now (if you say) "there customarily," "there('s where) those guys customarily (are),"

         wá   tíʔili   sùuk   ubʼin   iʔ eʔ →
         Comp DLOC ADV VC   TD TD
         or "there('s where) they customarily go,"

         wá   tíʔ   sùuk   umaán   iʔ→ . . .
         Comp DLOC ADV VC   TD
         or "there('s where) he customarily passes," . . .'   (F.1.A.733)

Thus in these examples, the one-only constraint is violated in order to signal that two frames are laminated in a single utterance, corresponding to the imagined world in which the hypothetical target form is actually used, and the real world in which DP and I are sitting together discussing his language. The former is presented as speech mentioned but not actually said, hence I as interlocutor draw no inferences about our current deictic field from these utterance fractions. On the other hand, DP's and Balim's assertions about the correctness or implausibility of hypothetical utterances belong directly to our deictic field, and I draw the relevant inferences about how my interlocutor(s) would understand the utterances were they to receive them (cf. Haviland, this volume, for other cases of lamination).

The next example is more complex, because the boundary between the citation and the direct commentary is partly effaced. Note that the citation form ends in the TD *eʔ*, whereas in DP's utterance this has been replaced by the couplet *aʔ oʔ*. By my analysis, both of these TDs are indexically grounded in the basic corporeal frame of my interaction with DP. The *eʔ* terminal of the citation has been treated as part of the direct speech, and overridden by the other two hierarchically superordinate forms, just as would be expected under normal circumstances.

(35) WH   *tíʔili   eʔ*↑ *bʼáʔaš   ukʼaát iyáʔaleh* →
          DLOC TD WH Q VC   VC
          ' "*tíʔili eʔ*" What does it mean?'

DP   *pwes   uk'áat iyá?al le   tí?ili   a? o?* →
      Comp VC   VC   DNOM DLOC TD TD
      'Well, this "*tí?ili*" (that you've said),

      ?óli   ká k?á?al   ump'eé b'á?a sùuk →
      ADV Comp VC NUM   N   ADJ
      it's sort of like if we were to say a customary thing'   (F.1.A.685)

The *o?* terminal in this utterance is motivated by the anaphoric relation to
my utterance, since DP is repeating what I have just said. The motivation
for the *a?* is more elusive. There appear to be two factors at work: (i) the
target form had just been introduced into our interaction by DP, as I was
in the course of asking about a different series of citation forms, and he
suggested this one on his own; this contrastive asymmetry is consistent
with the TD *a?*; (ii) there is an overtone of anticipatory reference in that
DP, having introduced his new form, then goes on to explain to me how it
is used. Although the form is too rare to make secure generalizations, it is
also noteworthy that the two TDs are in the linear order that would be
predicted by the hierarchy, $a? > o?$.

Example (36) occurred during elicited metalinguistic discussion, but
does not involve decentered discourse. Once again, the linear order of the
forms is consistent with the hierarchical ordering. DP had explained that
the underlined expression required a pointing gesture in order to be used
appropriately, and I double-checked this by repeating his judgment. His
response was the emphatic assertion that, obviously, what he was saying
was so. The *o?* TD is once again an index of the relation to what precedes,
reinforcing the response-position *i?istak*. The *e?*, by my reckoning, is
added in order to index that this assertion of DP's is not the last word,
but will be followed by another illustration. In other words, it is a staging
device, combined with an anaphoric one.

(36) WH   *?àah   ?eske   k'ab'eét awé?esik ti?* →
            COMP ADV   VC   PREP
            'Oh, so (you're telling me), you've got to show it to him'

      DP   *klàaro pwos   b'ey i?istak o e?* → *ti?   atàal té?el   a?   ?oómeŋ↓*
           ADV   CONJ DMAN   TD TD DLOC   VC   DLOC TD N
           'Clearly, well of course that's how it is, "Come right here, man!"'
                                                                        (F.1.A.82)

Unlike the cases of TD stretching in (21-31), utterances which contain
two non-identical TDs in final position do involve the lamination of more
than one discourse frame. This is the reason that metalinguistic discourse,
in which mention and direct speech combine, is one of the prime contexts
for TD doublets. Each TD signals the speaker's footing in a frame, and
the formal contrast is a direct mirror of the functional dichotomy
between hypothetical frames and actual ones.

4 Conclusion

The basic argument of this chapter has been that certain aspects of linguistic form can be best understood as grammatiealizations of routine communicative practices. This is not a novel idea, but it is a difficult one to spell out carefully. It does not mean that context causes the language to have the grammar it does, nor that there need be an unqualified homology between grammatical structure and conversational practices. It does mean however that habitual practices can become embedded in the conventional semantic system of a language. In Maya referential practice, we find evidence for this in both routine and non-routine uses. The former embody a habitual limitation of the deictic zone to a single footing, signalled by the most highly focused TD in the sentence. The one-only constraint combines with the lexical hierarchy to produce utterance forms in which symmetrically given information is elided and the most high-focus, new information is signalled. TD doubling provides speakers with the resources to signal more than one footing in a single utterance. Our analysis of the lexical values of the TDs predicts that the frame laminations signalled by doubled TDs will conform roughly to expectations based on routine usage. This is borne out in (32–36).

Starting from the underspecification of meaning in sentences, which is recognized by a variety of current semantic frameworks, I suggested that even literal content is the product of encoded sense in combination with the circumstances of utterance. Independent trends in eontemporary research support the claim that descriptive and referential content are both derived from context. If frame theories have any descriptive validity, then languages are designed so as to provide instructions to speakers on how to build up understandings out of this combination. "Context" is not the purely ephemeral situation of an act, but is also embodied in schemata based on routine experience. It is wrapped up in native actors' self-descriptions. The idea of habituation, which has figured prominently in social theories of language throughout this century, can provide a ground for schematization, and thus frames. Schemata are not simply given to all people by human nature, but are socially produced, manipulated, and subject to change. We see this in the contrast between routine and foregrounded deictic frames in Maya, as signalled by deictic enclitics. To the extent that literality is a contextual production, it is wrapped up not only in the structure of givcn languages, but in the habitual ways that speakers interact. Semantic indeterminacy requires habituation, and this leads to a profound linkage between what people say and how they expand on what is said to interpret what is really meant. Reinforced by these things, linguistic form can come to grammaticalize routine verbal practice, and therefore provide speakers with formal resources for non-routine acts of reference.

As I pointed out at the beginning of this paper, the grounding of pro-positional content in interactive practices recasts questions of linguistic relativity. It is no longer possible to ask straight away how language structure affects or reflects thought, because the relevant aspects of language are underspecified, and the mental representations people derive from utterances always depend on the socio-cultural context. It is of course clear that cultures, no less than languages, have universal features, and an argument towards eontextualization is *not* necessarily an argument towards cultural relativity. It *is* an argument about language and thought, however, namely that the fit between them is loose and mediated by practice. Deixis is a good case in which to consider such a question, because it appears so directly mapped into context, and yet so clearly universal at the same time. What could be more natural than hereness? Both appearances are half-truths, the first because deicties encode more information than commonly recognized, and the second because the deictie field is not an objective grid, but a social experimental one. Until we transpose our frame of reference from Western scientific "objectivity" to human experience, debates over relativism will continue to be mired in the blunt certainties of commonsense and belief. Before asking if the Maya live in a different world because their language makes a different distinction than ours, we should consider the extent to which linguistic systems derive from the grammatiealization of habitual practice. Rather than asking what speakers of a given language *can* think because of the categories of their language, the real question is what they routinely *do* think, because of the contours of their practices.

Notes

1 This chapter was originally prepared for the Wenner-Gren-sponsored Conference on Rethinking Linguistic Relativity in Ocho Rios, Jamaica, May 1991. I wish to thank all of the participants of the conference for their excellent contributions and critical reflections; in particular, thanks to Steve Levinson and John Gumperz, the organizers, Melissa Bowerman, Elsa Gomez-Imbert, John Haviland, Paul Kay, Jean Lave, Elinor Ochs and Dan Slobin.

2 Notwithstanding basic differences between cognitive and formalist approaches, many of the latter share with cognitivists the premise that propositional content depends crucially on the increment of context. Thus consider the distinction between character and content in Kaplan's indexical semantics, and the role of context in situation semantics (Barwise 1988). There are of course major differences in what different approaches take "context" to be, but for our purposes the key point is the widespread recognition that meaning arises out of the interaction between language and circumstances, rather than being encapsulated in the language itself.

3 Often, though not always, this frame will include antecedent discourse in which the object has been identified already. Thus, Donnellan (1979) distinguishes two kinds of referential use of definite descriptions, (i) those that occur in an "anaphoric chain," and (ii) those that do not. The former individuate a referent through a relation of *coreference* with preceding words in the discourse. The latter usually rely on presupposed background knowledge shared by participants; a kind of tacit anaphoric relation in which prior experience secures uniqueness of reference.

4 For the purpose of introduction I am alluding here to an extensive body of literature of which Duranti and Goodwin (1992) provide an excellent synthesis and set of examples.

5 Although we will not explore it in this chapter, the concept of a field is a key one in practice theory (see Bourdieu 1991, Hanks 1990).

6 This question is one of the main foci of Hanks (1990).

7 The question here is how general or specific, concrete or abstract are the features of utterance context that become schematized, as opposed to others which may never enter into frames directly. Part of the answer to this lies in the related concepts of prototypicality and basic level categorization. For the sake of brevity these will not be treated here.

8 Unless otherwise stated, the term "practice" includes within its reference both actions and native schematizations of them.

9 This is a heuristic simplification: transposed uses such as quoted discourse may involve computing reference relative to an indexical center that does not include the current participants in an interaction, as in " 'Just put it right over there', he said to her." The temporal, spatial, and second-person reference in the quoted speech do not refer to aspects of the context in which the quote is reported, as they would if the same utterance were issued in direct discourse I have investigated transpositions in some detail in Hanks (1990) and will not address them in this chapter. The important point is that the modes of access are socially established relations between referents and (some) context.

10 I take advantage of this sequential fact to label the two classes, but assume it to be more or less arbitrary in relation to the domain vs. zone distinction.

11 Note that this is distinct from Donnellan's definition of "semantic meaning" which is what the speaker's words mean *on a particular occasion of use.*

12 Fillmore's position here appears to be most closely in line with Grice's (1967, 1975, 1978) distinction between what is *said* (encoded, conventionalized) and what is *conveyed* (encoded plus implicated) in an utterance. One important difference is that Fillmore's interpretations are built directly on the conventional meanings of linguistic forms uttered, not on the logical semantics of the proposition (fragment) corresponding to the forms (Fillmore 1985: 234). Langacker (1984: 172) starts from the more radical, and problematic, assumptions that semantics and pragmatics are *not* distinct, and nor are linguistic and non-linguistic knowledge. Fillmore's position is more consistent with the one adopted here.

13 The class of expressions I will discuss encompasses most of what Jakobson (1957) called "shifters," following Jespersen. I will use the term "deictic" interchangeably with "demonstrative." For more careful distinctions see Hanks (1989, 1990), Levinson (1983, 1987).

14 In Hanks (1990) I argue for the distinction between frames and what I call frameworks. The former are schematic resources that speakers bring to the task of speech production and interpretation, while the latter are the emergent

processes in which speech actually takes place, and frames. are concretized, combined, and potentially produced.

15 These features are metapragmatic in the sense that they encode a categorization of the pragmatic contexts in which reference is accomplished.

16 Exceptions are *way*, *tol*, and several of the Temporal Deictics, in which the ID base conveys both kinds of information.

17 The following generalizations bear on *continuous* deictic constructions, and particularly canonical citation forms. Cases of the two series combined in discourse, where they may be discontinuous, are taken up in the following section.

18 At this point, I hold aside other functions of the TD *i* when it is without accompanying ID, such as partitive anaphoric (e.g., give me some *of it*), negative (*má . . . i?*), and anaphoric locative (*kub'in i?*, 'he goes there').

19 Where there is a minimal contrast between one of these and the other TDs, such as *hé?el e?*, the *e?* form conveys absence of immediacy. This is expectable if *e?* is unmarked for immediacy, as I am suggesting.

20 Examples are glossed according to the following: interlinear morpheme breakdowns (see list of abbreviations), literal gloss, loose gloss.

21 Tense, aspect, mode may also be encoded in preverbal auxiliaries.

22 For instance, the OSTEVs are predicative while DNOMs and DLOCs are referential. The DMOD is a non-referential marker of speaker certainty; plain *bey* (DMAN) signals comparison or approximation.

23 This inference is hedged in the case of IDs like *way* and *tol* which already encode features for deictic modes and zones.

24 This is close to a definition of the utterance, offered by Levinson (1987), as the unit of speech over which a speaker maintains a single footing. The main difference is that, in this chapter, I allow that a single utterance can have more than one footing. I state the generalization in terms of utterance and not sentence because the same constraints apply to sentence fragments.

25 I have attested a few possible examples of medial *o?*, but it is unclear to me whether it is actually the TD, or the residuum of another morpheme, such as plural *ó?ob'* that has been phonologically reduced. Alternatively, a slight pause at the TD may indicate that these examples actually involve a hesitation or boundary, which is absent in a subsequent recycling.

26 The shift from *b'eéyli* to *b'aáyli* is an independent variable, the conditioning factors for which are unclear to me.

References

Anderson, S. & Keenan, E. 1985. Deixis. In T. Shopen (ed.), *Language typology and syntactic description*, vol. III: *Grammatical categories and the lexicon* (pp. 259–308). Cambridge University Press.

Barwise, J. 1988. On the circumstantial relation between meaning and context. In U. Eco et al. (eds.), *Meaning and mental representation* (pp. 23–39). Bloomington: Indiana University Press.

Boas, F. 1966 [1911]. *Introduction to the Handbook of American Indian languages* (reprint edited by P. Holder) (pp.1–79). Washington, DC: Georgetown University Press.

Bourdieu, P. 1991. *Language and symbolic power*, ed. intro . J. B . Thompson. Trans. G. Raymond, M. Adamson. Cambridge, MA.: Harvard University Press.

Brown, G. & Yule, G 1983. *Discourse analysis*. Cambridge University Press.
Brown, P. 1990. Spatial discrimination in Tzeltal. Paper presented at the seminar on Spatial Conceptualization in Mayan Language and Action, Max Planck Institute for Cognitive Anthropology, Berlin.
Brown, P. & Levinson, S. C. 1993. Uphill and downhill in Tzeltal. *Journal of Linguistic Anthropology*, 3(1), 46–74.
Bühler, K. 1967. *Teoría del lenguaje*. Madrid: Revista de Occidente. (Originally published in German as *Sprachtheorie: die Darstellungsfunktion der Sprache*. Stuttgart: Gustav Fischer Verlag. 1982.)
Clark, H. & Wilkes-Gibbs, D. 1986. Referring as a collaborative process. *Cognition*, 22(1), 1–39.
Donnellan, K. S. 1979. Speaker reference, description and anaphora. In P. French (ed.), *Contemporary perspectives in the philosophy of language* (pp. 28–44). Minneapolis: University of Minnesota Press.
Duranti, A. & Goodwin, C. 1992. *Rethinking context*. Cambridge University Press.
Fauconnier, G. 1984. *Espaces mentaux: aspects de la construction du sens dans les langues naturelles*. Paris: Les Editions de Minuit.
  1988. Quantification, roles, and domains. In U. Eco, et al. (eds.), *Meaning and mental representation* (pp. 61–80). Bloomington: Indiana University Press.
Fillmore, C. 1978. The organization of semantic information in the lexicon. In D. Farkas, W. M. Jacobsen, & K. W. Todrys (eds.), *Papers from the parasession on the lexicon* (pp. 1–11). Chicago Linguistic Society.
  1982. Towards a descriptive framework for spatial deixis. In R. Jarvella & W. Klein (eds.), *Speech, place, and action: studies in deixis and related topics* (pp. 31–59). New York: John Wiley & Sons.
  1985. Frames and the semantics of understanding. *Quaderni di Semantica*, 6(2), 222–53.
Garfinkel, H. 1972 [1962]. Studies of the routine grounds of everyday activities. In D. Sudnow (ed.), *Studies in social interaction* (pp. 1–30). New York: Free Press.
Grice, H. P. 1967. Logic and conversation. William James Lectures, Harvard University.
  1975. Logic and conversation. In P. Cole & J. Morgan (eds.), *Syntax and semantics*, vol. III: *Speech acts* (pp. 41–59). New York: Academic Press.
  1978. Further notes on logic and conversation. In P. Cole (ed.), *Syntax and semantics*, vol. IX: *Pragmatics* (pp. 113–28). New York: Academic Press.
Gumperz, J. J. 1982. *Discourse strategies*. Cambridge University Press.
Hanks, W. F. 1989. The indexical ground of deictic reference. In B. Music, R. Graczyk, & C. Wiltshire (eds.), *Papers from the Twenty-Fifth Annual Regional Meeting of the Chicago Linguistic Society, Part Two. Parasession on Language in Context* (pp. 104–22). Chicago Linguistic Society.
  1990. *Referential practice: language and lived space among the Maya*. University of Chicago Press.
  1995. *Language and communicative practices*. Boulder, CO: Westview Press. (In the monograph series: Critical Essays in Anthropology, series eds. J. L. Comaroff, P. Bourdieu, & M. Bloch).
Haviland, J. B. 1989. Complex referential gestures. Unpublished ms., 52 pp.
  1990. Space in Tzotzil morphology. Paper presented at the seminar on Spatial Conceptualization in Mayan Language and Action, Max Planck Institute for Cognitive Anthropology, Berlin.

Havránek, F. 1964 [1932]. The functional differentiation of the standard language. In P. Garvin (ed. and tr.), *A Prague School reader in esthetics, literary structure, and style* (pp. 3–16). Washington, DC: Georgetown University Press.

Jackendoff, R. 1988. Conceptual semantics. In U. Eco et al. (eds.), *Meaning and mental representation* (pp. 81–97). Bloomington: Indiana University Press.

Jakobson, R. 1957 [1911]. Shifters, verbal categories, and the Russian verb. In *Selected writings of Roman Jakobson*, vol. II (pp. 130–47). The Hague: Mouton.

Lakoff, G. 1987. *Women, fire and dangerous things. what categories reveal about the mind.* University of Chicago Press.

Langacker, R. W. 1984. Active zones. In C. Brugman & M. Macaulay (eds.), *Proceedings of the Tenth Annual Meeting of the Berkeley Linguistics Society* (pp. 172–88). Berkeley Linguistics Society.

de León, L. 1990. An experiment in Tzotzil spatial reference. Paper presented at the seminar on Spatial Conceptualization in Mayan Language and Action, Max Planck Institute for Cognitive Anthropology, Berlin.

Leonard, R. A. 1985. Swahili demonstratives: evaluating the validity of competing semantic hypotheses. *Studies in African Linguistics*, 16(3), 281–95.

Levinson, S. C. 1983. *Pragmatics.* Cambridge University Press.

1987. Putting linguistics on a proper footing: explorations in Goffmans's concepts of participation. In P. Drew & A. Wootton (eds.), *Erving Goffman: exploring the interaction order* (pp. 161–227). Oxford: Polity Press.

Linsky, L. 1971 [1967]. Reference and referents. In D. Steinberg & L. Jacobovits (eds.), *Semantics: an interdisciplinary reader in philosophy, linguistics and psychology* (pp. 76–85). Cambridge University Press.

Lucy, J. 1985. Whorf's view of the linguistic mediation of thought. In E. Mertz & R. Parmentier (eds.), *Semiotic mediation: sociocultural and psychological perspectives* (pp. 73–97). New York: Academic Press.

Lyons, J. 1977. *Semantics.* 2 vols. Cambridge University Press.

Quine, W. 1971. The inscrutability of reference. In D. Steinberg & L. Jacobovits (eds.), *Semantics: an interdisciplinary reader in philosophy, linguistics and psychology* (pp. 142–54). Cambridge University Press.

Sapir E. 1949 [1931]. Communication. In *The selected writings of Edward Sapir in language, culture, and personality*, ed. D. G. Mandelbaum (pp. 104–9). Berkeley and Los Angeles: University of California Press.

Schutz, A. 1967. *The phenomenology of the social world.* Tr. G. Walsh & Lehnert. Evanston: Northwestern University Press.

1970. *On phenomenology and social relations*, ed. H. R. Wagner. University of Chicago Press.

1973. *Collected papers, vol. I: The problem of social reality*, ed. M. Natanson. The Hague: Mouton.

Searle, J. 1969. *Speech acts: an essay in the philosophy of language.* Cambridge University Press.

Whorf, B. L. 1956 [1941]. The relation of habitual thought and behavior to language. In *Language, thought and reality: selected writings of Benjamin Lee Whorf*, ed. J. B. Carroll (pp. 134–59). Cambridge, MA: MIT Press.

PROJECTIONS, TRANSPOSITIONS, AND RELATIVITY[1]

JOHN B. HAVILAND

1 Arriving

There is a Tzotzil verb, *yul*, which means 'arrive.' Suppose that you tell your friend Paxku` about your trip to San Cristóbal from the village of Nabenchauk, where you are now having the conversation. She asks you:

(1*)[2] *Jayib   ora   l-a-yul?*[3]
       how-many hour CP-2A-arrive[4]
       'What time did you arrive?'

and, remembering that you got to San Cristóbal about noon, you reply:

(2*) *ta ol k'ak'al*
       'At noon.'

You will be misunderstood (or, rather, you *have* misunderstood), for the question asks not when you arrived there (in San Cristóbal), but rather when you returned home, i.e., arrived *here*, where you and your friend are now speaking. If Paxku` had wanted the answer you gave, she would have used the verb *k'ot*.

(3*) *Jayib ora l-a-k'ot*
       'What time did you arrive?'

Here the language records, in verbs of arriving, the same deictic contrast built into, say, Spanish *ir* and *venir*: the choice of verb depends on direction seen from the perspective of where the speaker (and usually also her face-to-face interlocutor) are. Thus *yul* means 'arrive here' and *k'ot* 'arrive somewhere else.' Moreover, this perspective can be shifted or *transposed*.

2 Transpositions

Conversational exchanges, and indeed virtually all uses of languages, are characterized by transpositions between, among other things, perspectives, deictic origos, participation frameworks, and activity types. In practice, such transpositions – as, for example, prosaic discursive shifts between pronouns, tenses or demonstratives, or between different spatial-deictic centers in narrative – are rapid, transitory, and evanescent. They are managed by linguistic and gestural devices both grammaticalized and roundabout, both conventional and *ad hoc*. They rely heavily on participants' knowledge – not only schematic socio-cultural knowledge, but also contingent facts of biography. Being sparsely coded, and rhetorically potent, they are the natural province of inference. For the same reasons, they are fraught with possibilities for misunderstanding.

A privileged status is usually accorded to a given "here and now" as the context of utterance against which the denotata of indexical elements within utterances are understood. Hanks (1990) develops the referential foundations of such a context – what he calls "the actual corporeal field" (1990: 217) – and its central "participant frames." He then brings together what have often been treated as disparate phenomena under the single rubric of "decentered participant frames," phenomena that "rest on displacement or alteration of the indexical ground of utterance" (1990: 197). In direct quotation, for example, not only personal pronouns but all shifters (Jespersen as cited in Jakobson [1957] 1971), including indices of place and time, must be understood not in relation to the "here and now" of the quoting utterance, but to the "then and there" of the quoted utterance, real or imaginary. Direct quotation thus requires "recentering." Hanks assimilates into the same model various types of what Bühler ([1934] 1965): 210ff.) originally called transposition: devices, often conceived of as stylistic, which involve no *explicit* decentering but in which an utterance is cast *as though* indexically grounded in a context different from the immediate one. A canonical example is the use of the "dramatic present tense" (Jespersen [1924] 1965: 290), in which a narrator recounts past events with "present tense" forms, thus "recentering" current speech by projecting himself back to the narrated moment. Hanks extends his model to "complex frames" in several Yucatec Maya interactive routines, showing that a simple model of demonstrative reference, juxtaposed against a more or less complex layering[5] of participant structures, can resolve pronominal reference in such activities as divination and prayer.

As Hanks notes, a mechanism like "recentering" is required to resolve the reference of all deictics, not just pronouns (1990: 252). I have widened Buhler's term *transposition* precisely to extend the range and scope of the phenomena in question, and to highlight features of transposition relevant to the present discussion of "linguistic relativity."

First, I concentrate on the nature of *projection*, from utterances to contexts, a relationship which complicates considerably the "givenness" of an unmarked physical "here and now." Hanks concludes his presentation of decentered frames recognizing that "[t]he current 'here-now' of any utterance is itself a space of possibilities, not a concrete object immediately given to observation" (1990: 254). What is the nature of a projectable and, hence, transposable "space of possibilities"? The importance of projection to the discussion of relativity in the present volume is that a projected contextual space is precisely the arena of substantive differences between communicative traditions which have often inspired relativistic rhetoric.

Second, what sorts of transpositions occur? I extend the discussion beyond shifts in the *referents* of indexical elements, to include non-referential aspects of indexical projections, as well as issues of *perspective* (Talmy 1978) and *construal* (Langacker 1987, 1990), whether indexically signaled or not. Exactly the same logical mechanism is required to "calculate" the meanings of linguistic elements that project, for example, social relations between interlocutors, or points of view on a scene, as of those whose job is (at least in part) to pick out referents. Transposition can in general force recalculation of all projectable elements.

Further, the emphasis on transposition in the present chapter focuses attention on *shifts* in projected grounds. I am therefore especially concerned with "triggers" – formal elements that signal a shift in projected context. What mechanisms signal transpositions, and allow interlocutors to recover them? Direct quotation, as in Hanks's analysis, will be a prototypical transpositional trigger, signaling that recalculation of indexical projections is in order. Similarly, we must consider the problem of recoverability: techniques by which interlocutors keep transpositions straight, and interpret them, if not "correctly," at least coherently.

3 Deictic transpositions

The unmarked sort of deictic origo is presumed to derive from a canonical speech situation in which (eliminating many details elaborated by Hanks) interlocutors (canonically a single speaker and addressee) are face to face and more or less in the same "here and now." This "here and now" anchors among other things the directionality encoded in the Tzotzil "setting out" or inceptive roots *bat*, 'go,' and *tal*, 'come,' and the "arriving" or achievement roots *yul*, 'arrive here,' and *k'ot*, 'arrive there.' Motion towards the place where interlocutors are conversing is encoded with *tal* or *yul* whereas motion towards any other place is encoded with *bat* or *k'ot*.

In conversational practice, however, things are rarely so neat, and the anchoring point may be transposed in a variety of schematic ways. It may move from the speaker's perspective to that of her addressee (now seen as distinct); or, through quoted or reported speech, it may move to the perspective of a quoted or reported speaker, or again to *her* addressee. Such transpositions are familiar and widely discussed in linguistic literature (e.g. Fillmore 1975).

Manvel is recounting your first conversation with Paxku` to Antun, another Zinacantec, as they work in their cornfield in the lowlands. They are far from both San Cristóbal and Nabenchauk. Manvel tells what Paxku` asked you, and he decides to report your answer.

(4*) *Chal ti Xune [ti iyul/ik'ot ta ol k'ak'al]*
      'John says [that he arrived at noon].'

Which does he choose – *yul* or *k'ot*? Or does it make any difference?

Of course, he might be more likely to use "direct quotation" in the first place, a favored Zinacantec narrative device.

(5*) *[Liyul ta ol k'ak'al] xi.*
      '["I arrived at noon,"] he said.'

Here, in the pronominal markers, we have a classic case of transposition through quotation. Manvel's 'I' is embedded in the pronominal prefix of the quoted verb *l-i-yul*, ⟨CP-1A-arrive⟩, 'I arrived.' It refers, of course, not to Manvel but to the quoted speaker, Xun. The ground with respect to which the referents of pronouns are calculated has shifted from the current speech situation, with Manvel speaking to Antun, to a reported speech situation in which Xun speaks to Paxku`. However, not only the pronouns have to be recalculated under transposition: the "here" lexicalized in the verb is also transposed, moving, as it were, from Hot Country where Manvel is speaking back up the mountains to Nabenchauk, where Xun was speaking.

Or perhaps Manvel will report Xun's speech with an evidential embellishment, making the appropriate conversion of person. He inserts the particle *la* which signals that he, Manvel, is reporting hearsay – that is, that he knows only by report that Xun arrived at noon. But what does he say? Will he use *yul* or *k'ot*?

(6*) *I-O-yul/i-O-k'ot   la   ta   ol   k'ak'al*
       CP-3A-arrive/arrive QUOT PREP half day
       'He arrived, it is said (he says), at noon.'

Worse, when interlocutors communicate from widely separated locations, neither the speaker's nor the hearer's "here and now" can be jointly taken for granted. How is the "here" indexed by *yul* to be construed? When people talk on the telephone, for example, they must decide whether to share a deictic origo (defined on a variety of possible scales), or whether each is to maintain her own. Lacking conventional solutions to the problem, certain negotiations may be necessary for communication to proceed.

You are now talking to Paxku ` by telephone. She is in San Cristóbal, and you are in Nabenchauk. Again, the subject is your trip to town, and she again asks

(7*) *Jayib ora l-a-yul?*
      'What time did you arrive?'

Now you face a new interpretive problem. You know her verb means
'arrive-here' – but whose "here"? Distinctions between verbs like *come*
and *go* are slippery in such circumstances (Fillmore 1982). What does
Paxku` mean? When the origo has suddenly slipped away from a point
shared by you and your interlocutor, it needs to be fixed. How do
Zinacantecs establish the relevant "here"? Let me leave the reader in the
dark about this for the moment (since the answer is not necessarily
obvious). Instead I will provide a non-invented conversational example of
multiple transposition, involving, among other things, these same Tzotzil
verbs of motion.

In fragment (8), C is a Zinacantec who has gone illegally to work in the
United States. He is instructing X, the ethnographer who is about to visit
his village, what to have his parents back home say, should anyone ask
about his whereabouts. There are various spaces available in which to
anchor the "here and now" that the deictic motion verbs project. First,
there is the shared perspective of C and X as they speak (in Oregon, in
June 1988). Second, there is the "then and there" of C's parents in
Nabenchauk, engaged in a hypothetical future conversation with
inquisitive neighbors. There is also the perspective of the parents
reporting their supposed conversation with X, the ethnographer who
will have taken news of C back to the village. (Hidden in the background
is another space and time: the moment, presupposed in the last two
mentioned spaces, when X arrives in Nabenchauk and tells the parents
about C and his instructions to them.)

Now consider the transpositions between these spaces, primarily as
signaled by the deictically anchored verbs in the passage itself (which are
underlined). Line 1 conjures a supposed future "here and now" when
prying neighbors interrogate C's parents about C's whereabouts. At this
future time, X will have 'arrived here' (the verb is *yul*, at line 2) in
Nabenchauk, armed with news of C in faraway Oregon. This *yul*,
referring to X's arrival "here" in Nabenchauk, and the verb *bat* (line 3),
referring to the 'departure from here' of C and his companions, are
buried inside a piece of imagined discourse, in the mouths of the nosy
neighbors who have, from the perspective of C's parents, *chtal yal*, 'come
to say' (line 6) such things once they hear that X has reached the village.

(8) akuyal (88.08B, 21 June 1988, Portland)
     1 C: *ak'o ak'o timi o much'u sjak'e*
            'Suppose someone should ask'
     2   *bweno . mi: lavi iyul xa li Xune*
            ' "Well, now that Xun has arrived here," '

3   *k'u x`elan ti Chepe k'u x`elan ti kremotik* <u>*bateme*</u> =
      ' "How is <u>Chepe</u>? How are those boys that <u>have gone</u> there?" '
4   = *m:*
      'If-'
5 X: <u>*bweno*</u>
      '‚Okay.'
6 C: *mi much'u xi mi oy much'u* <u>*chtal*</u> *yal un*
      'If someone <u>comes here</u> to say that'
7 X: *ji*
      'Yes.'
8 C: *ak'u yalik*
      'Then let them say (to such a person)'
9   *bweno este:*
      ' "Well, uh," '
10   *lek la este ch`ab-*
      ' "They are alright [according to what (John) says.] They-" '
11   *ch`abtejik xi ika`i li Xune*
      ' " 'They are working,' I heard John say." '
12   *mu- muk' bu- mu to bu ijak'bekotik lek*
      ' "But we haven't asked him properly yet." '

There is a further layer of speech, which involves no motion roots, in lines
(10)–(11), where the parents hypothetically report hypothetical speech by
X, who is portrayed as saying that C and his companions in Oregon 'are
working' (i.e., have found jobs).

Here, the perspectives adopted are clearly different from the immediate
surround of X and C as they speak in Oregon: they are *transposed*
perspectives, centered on the village. This transposition is necessarily
reflected in the choice of directional verbs, whose very use always indexes
some deictic origo.

A few diagrams may make the example clearer. Hanks (1990) adapts
notational conventions of Jakobson ([1957] 1971) to represent indexical
projections and their transpositions in decentered frames. Jakobson
distinguishes between a speech event (E^S) and a narrated event (E^N).
Many referential indexes in speech involve calculating a referent in the
latter from a contextual element in the former. A canonical deictic is
represented in figure 10.1.

Notice what one means here by "indexical projection." When you say
liyul 'I arrive (here)' we could represent the relational structure as a
projection from the locus of the speech event to the target locus (the place
of arrival) in the narrated event, as in figure 10.2. (The letters S, A, and O
stand for "Speaker," "Addressee," and "Other" throughout.) An
alternative representation is to laminate the arrival scene onto the

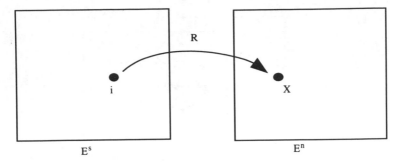

R is the relational feature of the shifter.
i is the indexical ground (in the current speech event).
X is the referential object (in the narrated event frame).
    (After Hanks 1990: 204.)

Fig. 10.1   *Relational structure of deixis as a complex frame*

space of the speech situation so that the arrival point referred to coincides with the deictic "here." This alternative, shown in figure 10.3, suggests that the context of the speech event and the circumstances being narrated are being brought together, or calibrated (Silverstein 1992), by the verb *yul*, around the anchor of a shared locus. In principle, *both* spaces may be adjusted (their presuppositions shifted, or their structures internally rearranged) so as to bring about this calibration. There is much to recommend the lamination view, notably the fact that a good deal of what is represented about a narrated event is literally played out on the scene of the narrating (speech) event.

Consider what I have called distinct perspectives in (8) represented as transposed (or perhaps superimposed) "spaces." The original speech event (E^s) has C(hep) talking to X(un), in Portland, in June 1988. They

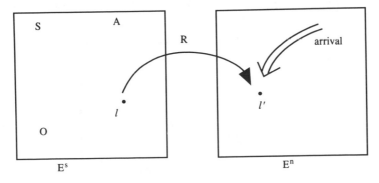

Fig. 10.2   Yul, *'arrive here,'* as a projected index

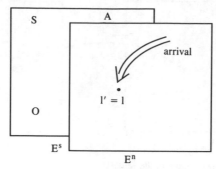

Fig. 10.3 Yul, *'arrive here,' as lamination*

imagine a visitor talking to C's parents in the village. Thus the narrated event is, in turn, a speech event – in fact, two such narrated speech events (E^{NS}), since the hypothetical visitors say two things: (1) "now that Xun has *arrived here*" (line 2); and (2) "how is Chep who has *gone*?" (line 3). Since the verbs in these narrated speech events have a deictic component, both involve a projection from the event of the launching speech event. In line 6, both of these narrated speech events are in turn characterized as something that 'someone *comes* to say,' framing them again with an indexical motion verb. Whereas the earlier verbs involve an indexical projection, the verb *tal*, 'come,' in line 6 involves a transposition, since it talks about the stranger's coming to talk to C's parents *as if* they were coming to "here," to the locus of the outermost speech event E^S – that is, Portland. The current interaction has thus been transposed to the village of Nabenchauk. The projections (shown with a solid arrow) and transposition (shown with a dotted arrow) are diagrammed in figure 10.4.

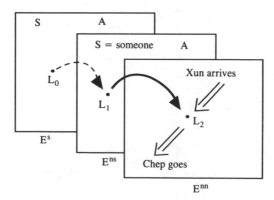

Fig. 10.4 *'Xun has arrived; Chep has gone'*

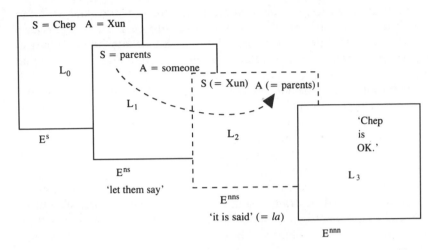

Fig. 10.5 *'Let them say: "Chep is (reportedly) all right"'*

A similarly multilayered projection is involved in the parents' hypothetical declaration, in line 10, that Chep *lek la*, 'is all right (reportedly).' The quotative particle *la* projects a shadowy secondary narrated speech event, shown as a laminated layer with a dotted edge in figure 10.5, in which someone (presumably Xun) tells the parents that Chep is all right.

Conversational transpositions are not limited to shifts of spatio-temporal location and speech participants. I have in mind a much wider family of phenomena studied under the rubrics not only of "transposition" (Bühler [1934] 1965), but also of "metalanguage" and "reported speech" (Voloshinov 1986), "voice" (Bakhtin 1986), "(re/de)centering" (Bauman 1986, Hanks 1990, and others), "layering" and "demonstration" (Clark & Gerrig 1990), "empathy" (Kuno 1987), "contextualization" (Gumperz 1982), "calibration" (Silverstein 1992), "participation roles" (Levinson 1988), and even "alternative schematizations" (Talmy 1985). Perhaps the most thorough treatment – and certainly a leading inspiration for the present chapter – is the elaborate analytic machinery, already employed above, which Hanks (1990) develops to present Maya deictic usage.

4 Projection

Familiar deictic transpositions depend on a deictic "origo," minimally a set of coordinates including speech participants, more globally a centered and detailed "point of view." In fact there is already an equivocation here between an origo located, as it were, in the "real" world, and an origo understood as a constructed schematic (necessarily partial) *representation* of the world. Interlocutors speak and gesticulate in a physical environment, but their signs refer in a universe populated by conceptual entities.

Radiating from a deictic origo is a structured "space" within whose surround deictics "point." In the locational case, this radiating space is literally three-dimensional space, or a schematic view of it. In the general case, however, what I call "space" is merely a mathematical *space of relations* which extends from a single elemental point to other elements, and the relations between them.[6] Thus, the first element of potential variation and difference (between situations, languages, cultures, or what-have-you) exposed by transposition is the very nature of a structured space. Around what is it centered (what is its origo)? How much (how wide an area? what "objects"? how structured a perspective?) does it encompass?

On standard formulations, the deictic origo is typically the "here and now" that includes "the spatiotemporal context created and sustained by the act of utterance and the participation in it, typically, of a single speaker and at least one addressee" (Lyons 1977: 637). The "here and now" can be more fully fleshed out, to include "the appearance, bearing and attitude of the various participants in the language-event...; preceding, concomitant and subsequent activity; other events taking place in the vicinity; and so on" (Lyons 1977: 571).

However, an indexical origo is by itself exceedingly austere, amounting to nothing more than what is "projected" by a single indexical sign.

Any indexical sign form, in occurring... hovers between two contractible relationships to its "contextual" surround: the signal form as occurring either PRESUPPOSES (hence, indexes) something about its context-of-occurrence, or ENTAILS ["CREATES"] (and hence indexes) something about its context-of-occurrence, these *co-present* dimensions of indexicality being sometimes seen as essential properties of the signs themselves, "appropriateness-to-context-of-occurrence" and "effectiveness-in-context-of-occurrence."

Seen this way, every indexical sign, or, to be more precise, every sign insofar as it signals indexically (whatever other semiotic modalities it may be involved in) serves as the point-from-which, or semiotic origin of, a presuppositional/entailing projection of whatever is to be understood as context. There is no necessary connection between, nor even necessary coherence of, the various indexical projections-of-context logically implied by the semiotic fact of indexicality associable with any collection of signal forms: each occurrent signal form indexes its own context-of-occurrence, and that is all that we know by purely indexical (pragmatic) semiosis.   (Silverstein 1992: 36)

Each indexical sign projects a corresponding element of context, an elemental origo from which – by a further projection – an entire space may be seen to radiate. The additional task of interpreting a collection of indexical signs as a *coherent sequence* (of meanings, actions, events, or interactional moves – for Silverstein, "interactional text") requires that these discrete projectable spaces be co-ordinated and interrelated, a process Silverstein calls *metapragmatic regimentation*. Sometimes this co-ordination may be achieved through lamination, much as one overlays transparencies. Extending the notion of minimal projected context to composite, more fully fleshed-out, laminations of such partial contexts inspires my metaphor of "space." The laminations may not be complete, of course, as indexical signs in natural language schematically project (parts of) rather different sorts of context-of-occurrence. Nonetheless, to laminate at all projected spaces must **fit**: they must be commensurable with respect to certain properties, such as orientation and what I call below grain or resolution. Moreover, the current (though moving) "here and now" is never very far away: any proposed laminate will be partially played out on the stage given by the context of utterance.

Silverstein's formulation (see also Silverstein 1976) suggests how to understand the relation of "projection" which, in my loose usage, obtains between a sign and a contextual space. It will be a relation somewhere along Silverstein's continuum from presupposing to creative (entailing) indexicality: from being appropriate to only a certain sort of context (thus projecting a space of the appropriate sort), to creating a certain sort of context (thus projecting such an altered space). The fact that individual projected origos **radiate** wider spaces complicates the continuum. There may be truly creative indexical signs, which bring something totally new to a projected context; there may also be creative indexes which merely make explicit some implicit but presupposa**ble** facet of an otherwise available space.[7] Moreover, default assumptions about what all spaces contain will structure all projected contexts and will only be suspended when explicitly questioned.

Of course, since signs take their life from interactive use, the business of constructing coherence across projected indexical surrounds is typically a multi-party affair. It is something that interactants do together, with and for one another, though perhaps only implicitly. There must be mechanisms to help interlocutors get this co-ordination right (or to fight it off), mechanisms both to regiment the construction and co-ordination of transposed spaces, and to make it plain when things have come out wrong.[8] Hanks (1990) emphasizes that a socio-cultural structure of possibilities constrains projections before they ever happen. Culturally codified participant-frames instantiate parts of a space of possibilities; thus, for example, Maya discourse genres are preestablished, culturally routinized, "frame spaces."[9] Clearly, only bodies of knowledge and tradition (cultural and otherwise) allow projection from given signs to specific "values" or entities. It is the link between utterance form, situated activity, and local knowledge, that puts linguistic pragmatics at the heart of ethnography (and vice versa).

5 A formalization

To schematize the notion of transposition, we must represent spaces of relations, and laminations of them. As we have seen, diagrams of the sort employed by Hanks represent an indexical projection as a relation $\{i,R,X\}$ between an indexical ground i (in the speech event), a relational feature R of the deictic element (in the expression uttered), and a referent X (in the denotational space of the narrated event). A transposition, on this account, involves first transposing from an element of the primary indexical ground i in the actual speech context, to an element i^* in some other indexical ground, for example, a narrated speech event, or a distant scene. Figure 10.6 (where the notation E^T stands for "transposed event") illustrates Hanks's analysis.

In situation semantics (Barwise & Perry 1983) – which provides a formalism for picking apart separable referential strands in interpreting utterances – the "meaning" of a sentence (φ is taken to be a relation $u|\varphi|e$ "between situations u in which φ is uttered and situations e described by such utterances" (1983: 120). As Barwise & Perry remark, the utterance φ constrains both the u and the e situations. The meaning relation can be dissected, in part, by describing a relation $d,c|\varphi|\sigma,e$. Here d is a "discourse situation" (with, among other things, a speaker, an addressee, a discourse location,[10] and an expression α); c is the *speaker's connections*, "a partial function from referring words α to their referents $c(\alpha)$" (1983: 125) as intended by the speaker; and σ is a *setting*, a collection of

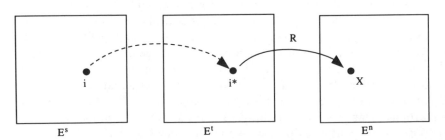

Transposition of the indexical ground. The referent
(X) is identified relative to a new indexical ground (i*).
(After Hanks 1990: 208.)

Fig. 10.6 *Transposition of the indexical ground*

situational elements, other than the discursive ones, provided by the utterance situation – typically, elements derived from other expressions contiguous to φ in a wider time-slice.

We could (very roughly) represent the denotational meaning of a linguistic element like the Tzotzil verb *YUL* as a relation $d,c|YUL|\sigma,e$ just in case the following is true:

(9)
in *e*: at *l*: is_located, **a**, yes
      at *l'*: is located, **a**; no
      (*l'* temporally precedes but spatially coincides with *l*)
where $l \subseteq l_d$

That is, for some indeterminate individual (represented as **a**, a variable which ranges over possible logical subjects of *yul*), the situation *e* includes a location *l* and a temporally prior but spatially identical location *l'* such that **a** is located at *l* but not at *l'* (i.e., has 'arrived at' *l*); and, crucially, that *l* coincides (spatially) with the *discourse-location*, l_d. In this representation, the final clause shows how the described situation *e* is *anchored* in *d* the discourse situation (part of the overall utterance situation *u*). The projection involved in the use of a word like *yul* is captured in the equation $l \subseteq l_d$ which bridges two distinct situations, *d* and *e*.

On this account, we could posit a function, invoked by the verb *yul*, that aligns a discourse situation *d* (in which *yul* is uttered) with an "arrival situation" *e* (described by that utterance) by mapping ("projecting") *l* onto l_d, or by calibrating *d* with *e* with respect to their locations, as follows:

$$d = \{ \ldots \ldots \ldots l_d \ldots \ldots \ldots \}$$
$$|$$
$$e = \quad \{ \ldots \ldots l \ldots \ldots \ldots \ldots \}$$

In Hanks's terminology, such a projection is "centered" because it connects a narrated event with a privileged *center*, the here and now or "actual corporeal field" of the speech event *d* (and more generally *u*, the whole situation of utterance).

Decentered frames, including Bühler's transpositions, involve replacement, in such formulas, of elements of *u* with elements of some *other* situation *u'*. Situation *u'* will be at least partly of the same type as *u* (it may include a discourse situation, for example), but it will not be the actual situation of the utterance in question. In quotation, for example, the whole of the anchoring situation in a formula like (9) must be transposed away from the actual uttering situation to the described or presupposed utterance of the quoted speech. In other cases, only subparts of *u* may require transposition, typically only the elements of *d*, the schematic discourse situation that includes speech-act participants, their location, and an expression. When the salesman at the door – in what has been called "altero-centric address" – asks the child "Is Mommy here?" he has transposed Speaker and Addressee roles, without necessarily shifting other parts of the situation of utterance. Transpositions involving speaker's connections c and a setting σ are also possible, as we shall see in what follows. Using this notation, "projection" can be generalized from a relation between an element of context, a deictic sign, and a referent (as in Hanks's model $\{i, R, X\}$) to a relation between entire situations or settings, mediated by a complex expression φ, thus $\{\sigma, \varphi, \sigma'\}$. Non-indexical signs can, on this view, also "project" and thus give rise to transpositions.

Indeed, the interesting transpositions will not be wholesale replacements of σ by σ' but *operations* on σ to produce σ', by means of additions, deletions, collapsings, perspective shifts, zooming, and the like. Moreover, even if it has been transposed away from, the privileged original u, corresponding to the actual here and now of the speech situation, will presumably remain as a potential background or default laminate for all transposed spaces – even as it is revised and updated over the course of an interaction. Indeed, a kind of "bleaching" seems to apply to deeper and deeper layers of transposed "spaces": the farther they get from the fully fleshed "here and now" the more schematic they become. Constraints on spaces lessen with each transpositional remove.[11]

The projection involved in normally centered discourse may often be hard to perceive. Indeed, the embedding of speech in an unmarked here and now is often nearly invisible, cued largely implicitly, without formal, segmentable marking in the utterances involved (Silverstein 1981, Gumperz 1982). Insofar as the perspectives, reference points, or partial situations which figure in projective relations are differently structured – from one speaker, language, or communicative tradition to the next – these differences of structure are suddenly brought into analytical focus in the context of transpositions. The possibility of a shift highlights the existence of something that *can be shifted*. Thus, if the mechanism of transposition (signaled by varied formal means) is a linguistic universal, transposition provides a universal window on substantive (linguistic, cultural, or situational) differences in *what there is to transpose*, that is, in what aspects of situations are projected by utterances. This, indeed, will be my slender contribution to the present discussion of linguistic relativity: first, that the phenomenon of transposition is non-trivially ubiquitous in human interaction (and hence in the linguistic practices that centrally comprise interaction); and second, that transposition exposes to view substantive differences between human groups in the raw material of interaction: what can and must be transposed. This one example may help show a level of analysis appropriate to discussions of what is shared and what is not in human language and social life.

My discussion will proceed through various apparent differences in the nature of linguistically projectable partial situations, exposed to view by transposition, to some devices which "trigger" transpositions in the first place. I will return to the bearing of the discussion on the relativity issue when I finally trudge to a conclusion.

5.1 The structure of physical space

Considerable classic work analyzes the nature of the deictic field, and recent detailed attention has been paid to demonstratives (Hanks 1990) and personal pronouns (Irvine 1987, Levinson 1988, and Hanks 1990). The Tzotzil verbs with which I began illustrate the lexicalization of a standard spatial "deictic *origo*," the "here" with respect to which a lexical contrast like *yul/k'ot* must be understood. The Tzotzil verb pair exploits a familiar deictic distinction roughly present in both Tzotzil *tal/bat* and English *come/go*; in place of *yul/k'ot*, however, English has just a single verb *arrive* that neutralizes the distinction.

The "location" in three dimensions of a point in projected space is of course only one example of what can be projected. The "here and now" is both socially and spatially constituted in rather complex ways, even if we limit attention to indexical projections explicitly coded in language. Let me assemble a rather patchy inventory of elements in such projections.

First, what is the nature of "here"? Physical space itself may have a complexity not always obvious. One likely locus of cultural variation is precisely what a projected physical space can or must contain. The idealized location *l* of situation semantic notation is highly schematic, and different languages may insist on different degrees of detail.

A striking example is the "absolute" orientation of locations and vectors of motion as represented in the speech of many native Australians. Speakers of Guugu Yimithirr (GY), from the area around Cooktown in northeast Queensland, use a conceptual and linguistic system of orientation based on cardinal points – or more accurately, cardinal edges – of roughly the North/South/East/West variety. These directions provide an orientational anchor to all spaces which can be described and with relation to which, for example, gestures may be performed – see Haviland (1986), also Evans (1995).

In GY speech, rarely a sentence will pass without some morphologically specific form of a cardinal direction root, and virtually **all** location is described in such terms.[12] Moreover, using GY gesture one can distinguish, at varying levels of spatial resolution (from fish-eye to zoom, so to speak) those spaces that are necessarily oriented, with respect to the system of cardinal edges, from those spaces that are at least partly *emancipated* from this system. These latter "free" spaces are primarily constrained by the immediate interactive configuration – the speaker and his or her interlocutors, as they share a space to speak in – rather than, as it were, by the earth itself (Haviland 1989, 1992). However, talk and gestures relating to landmarks, for example, must always be "correctly" oriented by the compass, although sometimes in complicated ways.

If for GY speakers any space is potentially oriented with respect to the system of cardinal edges, for most English speakers spaces are **not inherently** so oriented. They can be turned any old way – a fact that GY speakers have long ago discovered in conversation with non-Aboriginal interlocutors.

The oriented nature of physical space in GY has a singular consequence for an indexical (or indeed any) sign which, in GY discourse, projects a locational space, referentially or otherwise. This space will, by default, have to be anchored with respect to the cardinal edges: it will have a North/South/East/West, and not just incidentally, but exploitably. Thus, the fact that orientation is attached to projected locations may both require explicit calculation, in transposition, and also be relied upon to energize inferential processes.

Consider the transpositions in the following (slightly simplified) passage from one of the late Jack Bambi's marvellous stories. While sitting at the Hopevale Aboriginal community, he is recounting how he and a companion had to swim three and a half miles through stormy seas to shore after a shipwreck. The events themselves took place some thirty years before and some thirty kilometers away, to the northeast. The transcript at (10) includes both Jack's words and also the rough extent of his gestures, which turn out to be important inferential triggers. At this point in the narrative, Jack's companion, exhausted and terrified after the long swim, has knelt on the beach to pray. Jack, unconcerned, stands beside him to survey the horizon, and he leans down to summon the older man's attention.

(10) Boat: 1st level transposition[13]
          138 *ngayu nhangu bagay, eh...*
                'I poked him (and said), "Hey..."'

                . . . .!. . . . .
          140 *yarra gunggaarr nhaawaa*
                '"Look yonder there to the North!"'
                                                      Left hand from down beside body left
                                                      side, flips up pointing North.
          141 *ngaana thadaara*
                '"What's that going along?"'
          (Several lines omitted...)

```
............!...........................
```
150 *You could see that gulnguy just horizonbi=*
   'You could just see that boat on the horizon.'
             Right hand tracing horizontal back and forth motion,
                "horizon?"; performed in front of face (= West).
151 *= gunggaalu black spot*
   'Like a black spot to the North.'

The first transposition here is launched by the "quotation" at lines 138–140. Jack acts out – as Clark & Gerrig (1990) would have it, *demonstrates*, complete with poke – what he said to the other man: "Look yonder there to the North" (where Jack had spied a shark swimming). Thus, Jack invites his interlocutors to imagine themselves with him on the beach; once so transported (transposed) he can point North (and say a word for 'North'), meaning "North *from there*." (See figure 10.7, where Jack's right arm is extended due North as he "points" to the shark.) The projected space within which Jack points is itself oriented. The anchor is the orientation of the "here and now," upon which the transposed space – including the gesture – can be understood to be laminated.

By contrast, Jack's second gesture at lines 150–151 is more abstract. His words describe looking North to see the wrecked boat on the horizon. As before, he thus verbally invites a transposition: the boat

Fig. 10.7 *'Look north'*

Fig. 10.8   *'The boat on the horizon*

could be spied on the horizon "North" from the narrated site, and not from the spot where Jack is now telling the story. However, Jack's gestural demonstration (sighting along the horizon) seems to pick out only the boat's bobbing motion, and *not* its direction, since the gesture is performed in front of where he sits, to the *West*. His gesture is here emancipated from orientational anchors and seems, instead, to be constrained by the immediate interactive surround of Jack and his interlocutors. It was close attention to the different character of the spaces projected by gesture that first alerted me to the seeming consistent difference between GY speakers' spaces and my own.

There are doubtless further variable properties of physical space and location that figure in transposition: the nature of places and their associations (e.g., with people, social groups, history); conventionalized knowledge about regions and directions (for example, that in a certain direction lies Hot Country, or the place where one works or performs other marked sorts of activity, or an area considered dangerous, and so forth). I merely note without further elaboration such potentially projectable features of space.

5.2 Objects and configurations

Another variable aspect of a projected space is the inventory of entities it can comprise. Jack Bambi's shipwreck story invokes some local conceptual representation of a well-known stretch of territory with several discrete components: named places, a coral reef, particular sand dunes, and later specific trees and the houses of important protagonists in the story. How much of the potential population of a space is invoked in a given projection can vary. Moreover, subtle transpositions can involve shifting the *resolution* or *grain* of a projected space: zooming, as it were, from the beach as an undifferentiated whole, to the contours of its surface, or to its local details. An indexical sign can project a space in rough outline, or in great detail; and a transposition can move from one resolution to the other.

Tzotzil, for example, provides a contrast between two definite articles, *li* and *ti*. *Ti* is the relatively more marked of the two, indicating not only definiteness but also remoteness in time or space. That is, using *ti* as opposed to *li* projects the referent of the noun phrase as relatively distant from the here and now. It thus invites the construction of a remote space – a "then-and-there" – which the referent inhabits. A discursive stretch, however, can transpose that referent space, bringing it closer or pushing it away. In (11) P is telling how the muleteers whom he used to accompany as a boy would go to sell corn. This was long ago, and he first presents the *moletik*, 'old people,' with the remote article *ti* at line 290.

(11) t9006al
  289 P: *ti vo`ne un te =*
      'long ago'
  290   *= chk'ot ixim. te- **ti moletik** une*
      'the old people would take their corn,'
  291   *te chk'ot ixim taj yo` ch'ivit chkal une*
      'take their corn there to the old market'
  ... (several lines omitted)
  392 P: *la: j yuch'ik talel*
      'They would drink all (the liquor) up coming home.'

He continues to use the remote article in reference to the old people until line 393. He now describes how the men, after selling their corn, would stop off to buy cane liquor on their way home, getting progressively drunker and drunker. He switches suddenly to the proximate article *li*, bringing the space of his protagonists into closer (perhaps affective) proximity to the moment of telling.

  393   *puta xyakubik xa **li** pentejo **moletik** kavro: n*
      'Damn! Those old bastards already got drunk!'

P may be projecting himself back to his youth – Bühler's "Muhammed goes to the mountain" type of transposition (see Hanks 1990: 217).

He may, alternatively, be bringing the old men metaphorically close, shifting himself back to his youthful consciousness – "The mountain comes to Muhammed." He performs (quotes) his own inner thoughts of the time: "Damn, those old bastards are already (= *now*) getting drunk!"

In the terminology introduced above, the shift of articles involves projection across transposed sets of "speaker's connections" *c* (the speaker's intended referents) and "setting" σ (the situation built up from surrounding utterance context, which has previously placed these referents in a remote space).

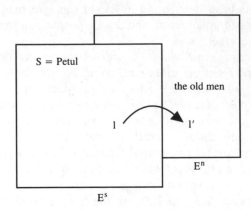

Fig. 10.9   *P transposes himself to his youth*

Furthermore, even with a fixed inventory of contents, and a constant level of detail, a space can be projected with what Talmy (1983) calls "alternative schematizations." First, objects can participate simultaneously in different spatial configurations. Second, a single spatial configuration may be presented with attention to different features. Here is one of Talmy's examples:

If we say that the man went *across* the wheatfield, then we are abstracting forth one aspect of the wheatfield complex, the fact that it has a horizontal bounded land parcel, and are disregarding the fact that there is wheat growing atop this

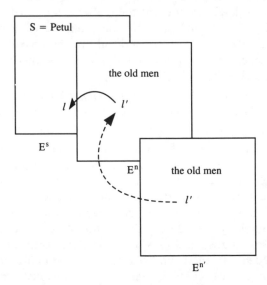

Fig. 10.10   *P brings his youthful thoughts closer*

land. If... we say that the man went *through* the wheatfield, then the wheatstalks, conceived together as constituting a medium are abstracted forth from the whole physical complex, and now the presence of a land surface underneath, horizontal and bounded, is irrelevant. (1983: 265)

Talmy offers further examples of alternative schematization invoked by count vs. mass nouns ("the cabbage in the bin" vs. "the cabbages in the bin") and the deictic contrast between *this* and *that* ("Get this [vs. that] bicycle out of the driveway" – both versions being possible without changing the relative *spatial positions* of speaker, bicycle, and addressee). Here, different descriptions of "objectively" identical situations involve choices between different projected relationships between entities, both within the described situation *e* and in the relationship between setting σ or discourse situation *d*, and the described situation *e*. It is thus possible to shift subtly between the sets of relations so defined.

Languages like Tzotzil are richly endowed with lexical items which are highly schematizing, in Talmy's sense. Positional roots predicated of objects regiment their referents in detail. They not only describe position, shape, arrangement, etc., but they also project wider schematizations: the configuration of the referent, and so on. The choice of a particular root to describe an object requires a particular "take" on the configuration of that object in space.

Consider the root *pat*, which Laughlin (1975) glosses in its stative adjective form as follows:

patal = sitting bowed over, lying face down, setting (hen), standing (lizard, turtle, rabbit, frog, mouse), lying down (dog, tiger)

Here is an odd sort of a word, it would seem, which can mean sitting, standing, or lying down. In fact, the word's meaning combines position (belly down, flat to the ground) with virtual anatomy (limbs somehow outstretched, and supporting the body in close proximity to the surface below). Predicating the root of an object, then, invokes varying configurations of figure and ground depending on the nature of the object. To *patan* (place in a *patal* position) a hen would be to set it down in the fluffed-out way that hens favor when setting. To *patan* a child would be to lay it belly down, but, for example, leaning forward on its elbows. Yet to *patan* a trussed pig, as in the following short fragment from a pig-butchering session, involves a schematization in which the pig is arranged belly down, but with its limbs outstretched fore and aft.

(12) Pig1: putting it face down, hauling it by the legs
    4 C: *la jpatantik ali. jpatantik Antun*
        'Let's lay it down – let's lay it down, Anthony.'
      [

5 A: *a bweno*
       'Ah, okay.'
       1. . . . .
6 C: *malao ali ja`. xi toe Xun*
   'Wait, uh . . . this way, John.'
       1: grabbing one of the legs and pulling it.
       [
7 X: *bweno*
       'Okay.'
    2. . . . .
8 C: *ja` li` xtal ya`ele*
   'It should come like this, it seems.'
       2: continuing to pull the leg towards speaker,
        so that the whole pig rotates face down.
9 X: *eso*
   'Right.'
10 C: *ja` chk le une*
   'Just like that.'

The deictics, supplemented by gestures in lines 6 and 8, give schematic hints about how to arrange the pig in the *patal* manner that C (who is directing the butchering) has in mind. (Note, also, that X, the ethnographer, has misunderstood; thinking that *patal* means simply lying face down, he has missed the schematic element that involves the pig's legs.) The schematization imposed on a space, through the application of a positional predicate, thus involves focusing (e.g., on a particular aspect of an object's anatomy and the consequent de-emphasis of other such potential aspects). Schematizing one space can thus prime subsequent spaces, by leaving the focused elements available for future focus, much as a figure/ground selection, once made, tends to persist as the scene develops, as one space is laminated onto another, or as a single space is gradually assembled from a sequence of projecting signs.

The schematization imposed by positional descriptions can also involve relationships of markedness and differential specificity, invoking processes of inference familiar in other pragmatic realms. Thus, a given descriptive predicate may implicate a prototype, features of which can be canceled by subsequent descriptors. For example, in the following fragment, P is describing a photograph of a wooden figurine. He first characterizes its position as *puch'ul,* 'prone.' Zinacantecs, however, normally lie down on their backs or sides. This figure's position, therefore, appears to call for a revised schema: he is not lying down "properly" but *nujul,* 'face down.'

(13) Wooden man
    24 P: *puch'ul* {...}
       'It's lying down'
    25   *pero . pero ma`uk lek puch'ul*
       'But it's not lying down properly.'
    26   *pero nujul yilel*
       'It seems to be face-down.'
(several lines omitted...)
    32   *pero lok'eb k'ak'al bat sjol*
       'Its head is going towards where the sun rises.'

P also laminates the space of the photograph onto the immediate physical here and now, as is shown by his appeal to absolute orientation in line 32. It is only because he has so oriented it that the figure in the photo is heading East, and his interlocutor (who is trying to pick the matching photograph out of a larger group[14]) must make the transposition and orient the laminates accordingly.

These schematic projections involve not only shifters, but grammatical elements like prepositions and full lexical predicates. The objects and actions[15] of a situation are not unproblematically given. They, too, are selectively invoked by the component signs of the utterance. I may be holding the dead pig, but I focus on its splayed legs only when the positional *pat* instructs me to do so.

5.3 Participation frames

A parallel aspect of the immediate physical "here and now" – that it, too, must be projected and assembled to be available to speech – has been long recognized in connection with participation frames. The deictic origo is ordinarily understood to center on the participants in the speech event, taken as typically copresent, individual, embodied carriers of biography. Hanks devotes considerable attention to the nature of participation frames around which indexical spaces are organized, to the social constitution of the participant "space," and to the crucial features of symmetry and asymmetry within it. The participant spaces projected by different constellations of linguistic signs can also differ to the extent that the social constitution of identity differs between different traditions. Once again, transpositions may be expected to make plain what elements are available for shifting.

In Australia, where language is an especially delicate instrument for managing social relationships, identity and kinship are a constant background to speech. The so-called "Mother-in-law" or "Brother-in-law" vocabularies (Dixon 1971, Haviland 1979) – special lexically marked registers that must be used in the presence of certain affines – are a well known symptom of the phenomenon.

There are less dramatic instances. On a trip to the bush north of Hopevale, George, a man of about fifty, calls out in Guugu Yimithirr to Bob, an obviously much older man.

(14) Wakooka
    GR: *Sonny! nganhthaan yiway dagu yii nhaathi buurraay*
           dudaariga =
        'Sonny! We're here...well, did you see the water running?'

Why does George call Bob "Sonny"? Several generations of complex social history and biography are built into – evoked, indexed, and projected by- this single vocative. The short answer is that George is Bob's classificatory *biiba*, 'father,' and hence can consider the older man to be "like a son." That he uses an *English* diminutive form, and that he chooses to index this particular kin relationship at all under the circumstances (they are visiting a piece of country to which Bob can lay a legitimate claim of ownership – see Haviland 1982), speak to details of the men's relationship and of recent political history in their community too complex to relate here. Note, though, that these details are present in the social space projected implicitly by the talk.

As is to be expected, in a society with such a salient kinship system, even now that the former custom of using special "brother-in-law" words with one's affines has faded, there are verbal ways of projecting a more highly regimented social space on top of the normal, everyday (and, to many older GY speakers, "crooked") sets of social relations of the modern Hopevale Mission. GR's use of the vocative *Sonny* is one. In the following passage, BF and JJ are repairing spears – an activity already associated, in an era of Landcruisers and nylon fishing nets, with the past. In place of their normal usage, they adopt mutual terms of address (shown in boldface) which suddenly shift their relationship towards another, more traditional context.

(15) Spears
    81 JJ: *dagu yii nguba =*
           'Well, this perhaps,,,'
    82 *= yigaar-amal **yurra*** (1.0)
           'is going to crack, you.'
    83 BF: *ngaanii* (.5)
           'Why?'
    84 JJ: *yii ba* (3.8)
           'This part.'
    85 BF: *nhaathi **yambala*** (.8)
           'Do you see, **yambala**?'

JJ and BF stand in what would traditionally have been an avoidance relationship, since BF married a woman who would have been JJ's classificatory daughter. The two men have grown up under a Mission regimen that nonetheless made them close friends and frequent associates. JJ's use of *yurra* – in ordinary GY, a 3rd person **plural** pronoun – in line 82 invites BF to re-establish, as it were, the formal, respectful nature of their traditional relationship. This proposal BF clearly accepts, responding in line 85 with a vocative form derived from the now all-but-forgotten word *yambaal*, 'man,' from the "Brother-in-law" respect vocabulary.

Note further that sometimes, in GY conversation, people explicitly insert kinship relations into talk. Upon mention of a protagonist, participants will often add a comment linking themselves to that protagonist with the appropriate kin term. In (16), B recounts a trip he took, years before, with a man known as Rob. His two interlocutors, in turn, evidently as part of working out who this Rob was, insert their relationship to him into the discourse, at lines 29 and 30. Several social spaces are thereby projected and mutually adjusted: the inhabitants of the current participation frame align themselves to the protagonists of the narrated participant frame, consequently also realigning themselves – or reinforcing their current alignment – with respect to each other.

(16) Cape Melville
```
10  B:  = mm.ngaliinh Rob gurra
          'Rob and I'
(...several lines later)
25  B:      i: ...dinggii-thirr bada ngaliinh- =
            'We set out (a long way) in a dinghy.'
26      = nganhthaan   (.5)
          'all of us'
27  T:  Rob?  (.5)
28  B:  thaday bada =
          'We went down.'
29  T:                  = ngathu warra ngathi   (2.3)
                          'My old grandfather.'
30  R:  juway ngathu
          'My nephew.'
```

If we try to formalize these transpositions, deficiencies in the notation adapted from situation semantics become painfully apparent. For here the spaces of relations involved cannot be captured by, for example, shifts in "speaker's connections" – functions from referring expressions to speakers' intended referents. Instead the transpositions involve, roughly, kinship alignments, presupposed in the context, between the three interlocutors – something not projectable onto the plane of reference at all. Each interlocutor, in turn, triangulates his preferred kinship relationship with the third person referent, Rob, thereby forcing readjustments in the kinship network that links them all together.

5.4 Texts and co-texts

Part of the space projected by language is itself linguistic. The context of speech represented by the setting σ in the formulas above, as a rule includes speech. Perhaps the clearest example of how speech itself forms part of a projected space is the intratextuality of conversation: my words now recall (presuppose, or creatively cast in a new light) words just uttered. Indeed, the whole point of some talk is to get straight other episodes of talk. To do so may require that interlocutors rehearse a textual stretch several times, each time adding a new layer of indexicality.

Consider the following fragments from a Mexico City argument.[16] The two speakers were fighting over an incident which took place when P's new boyfriend had come to call for the first time at the apartment L and P shared. L received him with some suspicion, and the resulting repercussions are now being hammered out between the two roommates. In the course of the increasingly vituperative discussion, the scene at the door of the apartment is repeatedly replayed. Here is the first version:

(17) Pilar
      187 L: *te juro.*
               'I swear to you'
      188   *que llegó y me dijo aquí vive Pilar Gonzalez.*
               'that he arrived and he said "Pilar Gonzalez lives here?"'
      189 P: *pues sí*
               'why of course'
      190 L: *aquí vive Pilar Gonzalez?*
               '"Pilar Gonzalez lives here?"'
               [   ]
      191 P: *es obvio*
               'it's obvious'
      192 L: *así me lo preguntó*
               'that's how he asked me'
      193 P: *a pues sí*
               'ah, of course'

The issue here is whether L was justified in what she claims was her suspicion that the man at the door was not a boyfriend but an undercover policeman. Everything rests on how the man greeted her, and how he asked for P(ilar). By performing his question, with no courteous preamble, and in police-like tones, at line 190, L projects herself back to the relevant moment, and builds into it the character she seeks to depict in the interaction.

Notice that P doggedly refuses to "hear" more than the literal words the visitor uttered. He was asking for her, "obviously." She ignores the depicted tone, and with it the full transposed scene that L is offering. Here is a case where the interactive uptake of transposition is subject to negotiation. Since the two interactants are fighting, they do not actively collaborate.

On the second replay, after many harsh words have been exchanged, L tries again to project the original event. Here she even "quotes" what the boyfriend **didn't** say, projecting a kind of negative space from which certain events are missing.

(18) Pilar2

> 107 *abrí la puerta y no-*
> 'I opened the door and he didn't-'
>
> 108 *él no dijo buenas no: ches*
> 'He didn't even say "Good Evening."''
>
> 109 *el no-*
> 'He didn't'
>
> 110 *dijo. Aquí vive Pilar Gonzalez?*
> 'he said, "Pilar Gonzalez lives here?"''
>
> 111 *eso fue lo gue dijo*
> 'That is what he said'

Again the issue is what the text was in the then-and-there.

Finally, L tries one last time, making the visitor's abrupt tone even more explicit.

(19) Pilar3

> 122 *te juro que no dijo buenas noches dijo*
> 'I swear to you that he didn't say "Good Evening," he said'
>
> 123 *Aquí. vive. Pilar. Gonzalez?..*
> '"Pilar-Gonzalez-lives-here?"''
>
> 124 *dije..*
> 'I said'
>
> 125 *quién la busca ¿no?*
> '"Who's looking for her?" No?'

In line 125 L demonstrates her protective, defensive "Who wants to know?" in response to the boyfriend/policeman's query. She tries explicitly to solicit responsive agreement from P (with the tag *¿no?*), as if to say, "Wouldn't you have reacted the same way?" Thus even affective tone can project onto the space which signs presuppose and create; and the result is interactively negotiable.

5.5 Perspective, the point of view "centered" on an origo

Let me retrace my steps so far. I began with a set of familiar circumstances in which interpreting speech requires that one adjust or recalculate the values of certain indexical signs, which are ordinarily calculated in relation to the "here and now" of the speech situation. In such cases the "here and now" is apparently *transposed* to some other reconstructible then-and-there. Taking such transpositions as evidence for the nature of a "here and now" – a space projected from the signs themselves – I have sketched an inventory of a few elements that seem to be transposable: spatial, schematic, and social. But a transposable space is not only populated; it is structured. In particular it has an origo, a center, a vantage point from which it is presented. Transpositions can involve movement not from one space (situation) to another, but between points within the "same" space. Where and how utterances (and utterers) are *positioned* relates to standard discussions of "point of view" or "empathy" (e.g. Kuno 1987).

The issue is again easy to grasp in connection with spatial deixis. Recall that the Tzotzil verb *tal* means 'come'; it describes a vector towards the "here," typically, of the current speaker. In a transposed space, for example in narrative, the point towards which the motion denoted by *tal* is directed can thus be construed as a transposed origo, the vantage point from which a protagonist surveys the scene. This allows what would be, in non-transposed space, a Tzotzil oxymoron: the combination of *tal*, 'set out to here,' with the general, but highly presupposing, spatio-temporal locative *te* 'there [and then] (i.e., some explicit location *other than* here [and now]).' In the following conversation, a Zinacanteco X is describing what happened to him in a distant city, as he and a companion stood on a streetcorner.

(20) Z8808B26

    383   *te jtzob jbatikotike*
             'We had met each other there.'
             [
    364 J: *aa*
             'Oh.'
    365   *bweno*
             'Okay.'
    366 X: **te tal** *jun. tzeb*
             'A girl came there.'
    367 J: *bweno*
             'Okay.'
             [
    368 X: *este lisk'opon vo`one*
             'Uh, she spoke to me.'

Clearly, X projects himself into a transposed space, centered on the streetcorner (*te*, 'there'), with the girl coming towards him. The projection is not total, however, as the use of the locative *te* shows that X still has one foot, as it were, in his current speech situation: the two spaces coexist, pinned together around X's own position in both.

Projected vantage point, however, can also be social, psychological, and even epistemological. Consider verbal mood in Japanese. Kuroda (1973) was among the first to point out that grammar can accord special treatment to those events or states, many of them psychological, which at least in Japanese one can only reliably predicate of oneself – 'being sad,' for example. Grammatically, only the experiencer (or an imagined omniscient narrator) is entitled to use what Kuroda calls a nonreportive description of such states and events, as in (21a).

(21) (Kuroda 1973)
 a. *Yamadera no kane o kiite, Mary wa kanasikatta*
     'Hearing the bell of the mountain temple, Mary was sad.'
     /nonreportive/
 b. *Yamadera no kane o kiite, Mary wa kanasigatta.*
     'Hearing the bell of the mountain temple, Mary was sad.'
     /reportive with *gat*/

By contrast, the *gat* form of (21b), appropriate to an evidentially less secure report of someone *else's* state of mind, "has definite referential force directed toward the 'judger' " (Kuroda 1973: 388). That is, the form "points semantically to the existence of a subject of consciousness whose judgement the sentence is understood to represent" (p. 388) and who must be distinguished from the experiencer of the state described. The outsider's lack of *access* to someone else's inner facts is here morphologically encoded, and so, thereby, is his existence as a separate participant (with a separate viewpoint) projected by the grammar. Moving between such morphological forms thus allows speakers to index a transposition of vantage points: inside and outside someone's head, as we might put it.

The vantage point of different protagonists in narrative can be interactively positioned, as well. In (22), R is recalling his arrival at Cape Bedford Mission when he was locked in a building (see Haviland 1991a). T, his interlocutor, lived at the Mission at the time and tried to peek at the new arrival through the slats of the wall. R then tried to poke T in the eye with a stick. His presentation of his thoughts at the time in "quotation" (at line 219) establishes a transposed space in which both T and R, participants in the current speech event, are also present in their childhood incarnations.

(22) Roger
    218 R: *nha-gala bama ngayu nha-gala. gaday*
             'Then I just came.'
    219   *bama nyulu nganhi yii nhaamaalma*
             '"Man, that one, he's looking at me."'
    220   *yuguunh ngaanaarru. miil bagaalgay nhangu*
             'So with a stick I was – uh – poking him in the eye.'
             [
    221 T: ((ha ha ha))
    222   *dagu I wasn't a schoolboy I was just a little boy*
             'Well, I wasn't a schoolboy, I was just a little boy.'

T explicitly touches up the psycho-social details of R's transposed space, by inserting a comment at line 222: he, T, was only a tiny child at the time in question. (He implies that he did not really understand what was going on, so that his peering through the slats of the building where R was imprisoned was wholly innocent.)

5.6 The nature of transposition: types and triggers

What we have seen so far suggests a range of projectable material, different relations between the spaces created by the discourse event *d*, and various construals of the described event *e*. Such different "projectables" in turn suggest a typology of transpositions that range from full shifts from one space to another, to changes in resolution of representation of a "single" space (zooming in and out, clipping, reorienting), to altered perspective (metaphorical movement) within a space. Clearly considerable delicacy is possible when, for one reason or another, one indexical projection is "cast," as one says in C (Kernighan & Ritchie 1988: 205), onto another.

    Working outward from the necessary, putatively universal, categories of the originating "utterance situation," we can imagine a series of expectable transposition types, to be encountered in all linguistic traditions. Thus, we may expect (a) transpositions of participant frames, as in standard pronominal shifts; (b) transpositions of relationships, between interlocutors and protagonists, as in social deictic pronominal shifts; (c) transpositions of (oriented) locations/spaces (including temporal frames), as in the GY gesture case cited – a subtype of (a) above with participant-frames extended to spatio-temporal locations; (d) changes in resolution, from wide to zoom: how close? how far? how much detail or schematization?; (e) transpositions of perspective or vantage point, involving not only physical positioning,[17] but also "empathy" and access. Finally, we imagine that speech routinely, perhaps universally, facilitates (f) transpositions of activity type: "what we are doing now." No utterance is separable from its (il- or per-)locutionary character, and shifts between genres and registers pull interlocutors into and out of one activity or another, as examples to come of Zinacantec prayer will illustrate.[18]

Let me now turn to some of the mechanisms that trigger (or perhaps depend upon) different sorts of transpositions, gradually working my way back to the deictically anchored Tzotzil motion verbs with which I began.

5.7 Quotation

Almost the paradigm case of a transpositional trigger, as many authors have observed, is "quotation." Hanks (1990: 206), for example, treats direct quotation as "decentered, meaning that the indexical ground is displaced from the current corporeal frame of the Spkr making the quote." Once again, the classic observation relates to pronominal and deictic shifts. The first person pronouns in the quoted speech of (8) refer not to the speaker, but to his parents talking to an imagined neighbor. The second person addressee of the command "Look yonder there to the North" at line 140 of (10) is not Jack Bambi's addressee of the narrating moment, but his addressee of the narrated moment when he stood on the beach. (In both cases, a certain lamination occurs, to the extent that the co-present addressee must be tempted, and is in effect interactively invited, to project him or herself onto the narrated context.)

"Quotation" is, of course, something of a misnomer, since nothing need literally be quoted. Thus "quotation" occurs in hypothetical, invented, and fantasized frames, in deliberately contrafactual, if not scurrilous, gossip, and so on. Clark & Gerrig (1990) (hereafter C&G) propose a useful theory in which quotation, unlike canonical description which operates with reference and predication, involves a distinct semiotic modality they call demonstration, which in turn involves depicting rather than describing what it "refers" to. Thus Jack Bambi, in "quoting himself" in (10), is demonstrating (aspects of) what he did (and, indeed, how he felt) that day on the beach: his words, his bodily attitudes, his gestures, all can contribute to the demonstration. C&G also distinguish a third modality they call "indicating" which involves pointing directly to an intended referent. Whether or not the three modalities can be rendered autonomous (since depictions can clearly depend upon descriptions and indications, and vice versa), seeing quotation as demonstration makes plain the indexical shift that triggers a transposition. When a speaker "quotes" she does not simply speak but invites her interlocutor to inspect her speech as performance; and the

performance carries its own space – the space created by the performance – onto which the words and the illocutionary effects of the
quotation must be transposed.[19]

C&G argue that "[d]emonstrations usually depict their referents from a
vantage point" (p. 767); and that they are "selective in what they depict of
their referents" (p. 768). Correspondingly, I have claimed that indexically
projected transposed spaces are centered or oriented around a certain
perspective, variously established; and that they are schematic, only
partially populated.

C&G also espouse a "principle of markedness" which I think can
help with the problem of recoverability in transposition. Jack Bambi,
sitting at Hopevale, has established a transposed space (the beach near
the shipwreck one stormy afternoon in the past). When he points, or
uses a pronoun, how do we know whether he is pointing or referring
in the "here and now" or the then-and-there? The problem for
quotation is similar: I may quote what you said, but I do it with *my*
body and *my* voice (even if I try to imitate yours). If I have a cough
or a gringo accent when I quote you, is that part of what I am trying
to depict? Clearly, it depends; and how will my interlocutors know?
C&G's principle of markedness states: "Whenever speakers mark an
aspect of a quotation, they intend their addressees to identify that aspect
as nonincidental – that is, as depictive, supportive, or annotative"
(p. 774).

Consider the transposition involved in the quoted parts of the
following account, by a GY speaker, of how a famous fight between
some Aboriginal stockmen and their white employers began. Several
men had run out of tobacco, and the narrator and his friend wanted
to ask the boss if they could have their tobacco ration a day early.
Their quoted dialogue at lines 66–68, as well as the commentary at
line 70, is in GY.

(23) Dougie
    66 D: *nyundu thaabangala*
          ' "You ask him!" '
    67   *gaari ngayu yinil*
          ' "No, I'm afraid." '
    68   *gaariga ngayu galmba yinil*
          ' "I'm also afraid." '
    69   ha ha ha
    70   *ngalgal thaabangathi*
          'So I asked for tobacco.'

Yet when the narrator performs the request to the white stockman, he
switches to English.

71   "Heey, Roy
72   "these fellows run out of smokes."
73 J: aa
74 D: "any chance –"
75   ration day tomorrow, see

Following the markedness principle, the shift to a **marked** language variety at line 71 must be non-incidental to the depiction. If we can operationalize the notion of markedness (and to do so will clearly require a rather powerful inferential engine[20]), this seems a promising approach. Still, what does the shift of languages mean, after all? It clearly does not necessarily mean that the narrator and his friend *actually* spoke to each other in GY and that D then used English with the boss, Roy (who was, in fact, a part-Aboriginal GY speaker himself). This *may* have been what happened. However, the marked switch of varieties clearly fosters a further subtle transposition in the projected context of utterance. D has already moved from the discursive moment, sitting under a Hopevale mango tree telling the story to a group of friends, to the narrated moment: the stockmen in their bush camp. (The time is also transposed: observe that "ration day" was "tomorrow" [line 75].) The register shift at line 71 amounts to a further change of footing: a "cast" in which the focus in transposed space moves from the Aboriginal friends talking *sotto voce* with each other to the more public confrontation between workers and bosses.

C&G's markedness principle can help us to see how interlocutors know what to transpose and what to calculate from the vantage point of the unmarked "here and now."[21] However, the subtleties of transposed spaces show that "demonstrations" are themselves complex semiotic processes which can exhibit all the familiar indexical properties.

Evidential devices may be more frequent in discourse than direct quotation, and their greater degree of grammaticalization may render them somewhat less available to "metapragmatic awareness" (Silverstein 1981) than explicit quotation, where the implied transposition is especially plain. On a localist view, evidential embellishment to speech can be seen as a kind of metaphorical movement. One distances oneself from an utterance by suggesting that it comes from another's mouth; or one embraces the vantage point of another, taking it as one's own.[22]

Evidentials can be morphologically implicit transposers. For example, the quotative clitic *la*, which we met in example (8), accompanies declarative sentences in Tzotzil to mark them as not directly attested by the speaker. The clitic is, for example, particularly appropriate to myths.[23] The indexicality of such a word is particularly obvious when it appears in an interrogative sentence, as in the following question about a volcanic eruption:

(24) Chichonal

> A: *Mi li`oxuk `ox **la** k'alal iyal tane,*
> 'Were you here when the ashes fell **la**?'

The quotative effect here must be understood to fall on the illocutionary force of the utterance, rather than on its propositional content. The quotative clitic must be understood, that is, to point implicitly to a questioner other than the speaker himself: "Were you here when the ashes fell? (X [that is, someone else] wants to know; or X asked me to ask you.)" The use of such evidential devices invites the interlocutor to construct a space onto which the question (and its original author) can be transposed.[24] The resulting transposition formally resembles that signaled by direct quotation, but the more highly grammaticalized signaling device masks the lamination of spaces.

5.8 Narration

Narrative in general canonically triggers transpositions. As a narrator sketches the actions of his protagonists, the ground upon which they act is a necessary backdrop to the narration. As in all transposition, however, there remains a tension between the narrated space and the narrating space: between the spot where a protagonist was and the spot where the narrator is. This is especially true when narrator and protagonist are one (or at least different phases of the same "self"), as in the following passage when L is telling J about his former life working on road gangs.

(25) LOL1

> 622 L: *pero mu xkuch ku`un li `abtele*
> 'But I couldn't survive the work.'
> 623 *toj ch'aj lilok'*
> 'I turned out very lazy.'
> 624 J: *k'u ma yu`un?*
> 'Why?'
> 625 L: *chiti`olaj*
> 'I would get restless.'
> 626 *ta jna' **tal** li jnae*
> 'I would miss my home.'

The tension between "here" and "there" in this passage is apparent in the deictically anchored directional *tal* in line 626. L has described the arduous work building roads and bridges in the Chiapas lowlands. He tells the story sitting in his highland home. At line 626 he presents the perspective of his former self suffering in the lowland heat. He uses an incompletive verbal aspect with the verb *jna`*, 'I miss/would miss [my home],' suggesting that his perspective is transposed to that place and time. Simultaneously, he exhibits the currently embodied "here and now" with the directional *tal*, 'towards here,' suggesting that the home he missed is the home where he actually **is** at the moment of speaking.

Skilled narrators can also exploit the availability of different inter-transposable spaces, switching rapidly between them. Gesture is particularly potent in this regard. In (26), Petul is describing a rural *cantina* where the men used to stop to drink on the way back to Nabenchauk from San Cristóbal. He has set up a transposed space in which his gestures point at an imaginary fence and gate: the *tey*, 'there,' to which he points with the gesture shown as [8] is in line 7, and the *ti`be*, 'gate,' which he represents with gesture [10] in line 8.

(26) Tzan-tzan
        . . . . 8 . . . . 9 . . .
      7 *oy tey nakal krixchano un*
        'There were indeed people living there.'

8: cupped hand palm down, arm still extended, taps once up and down out [N]. *{living there}*

9: right hand points down quickly, then curls back in →SW to position in front of face. *{people}*

Fig. 10.11   *'A gate by the path'*

        10
      8 *ta ti`be*
        'beside the path.'

10: hand flat, vertical
     down and up
     motion (gaze to
     hand). {*gate*}

   11a   11b

9 *yech smuk'ul chk i na chk li `e*
   '(It) was the same size as
   this house here.'

   11a: right hand
       crosses to SW,
       and gaze also,
   11b: and points to
       kitchen house,
       before returning
       to rest. {*size*}

This house
right here.

Fig. 10.12   *'Same size as this house'*

Swiftly, however, he brings his gesture back to the current "here and now," in order to point, at [11], line 9, directly at the kitchen house where he and his interlocutor are seated. " *That* house [whose gate I can point to in transposed narrative space] was the same size as *this house* [which I can point to here]."

5.9 Generic brackets

Some speakers utilize paralinguistic "quotation marks" (not unlike "writing" them in the air beside one's head while speaking) to mark a stretch of talk as what C&G call "non-serious." Such bracketing devices can be gestural, as when a skilled narrator like Jack Bambi shifts posture and gaze to act out the different roles in a performed/narrated conversation. The brackets in turn signal a transposition.

A much studied bracketing device is the shift between registers or entire speech genres. Not unlike the GY man's switch to English in (23) above, or the aping of funny accents, marked genres can conjure indexical spaces rather different from the ordinary "here and now." Hanks (1990: 236ff.) illustrates two varieties of Maya shamanic performance which "systematically produce complex frames in which transpositions and decenterings play a basic role." These transpositions are "governed by relatively specific conventions" and are "highly constrained." Indeed, Hanks's example suggests that the structure of transpositions can itself be a conventionalized cultural product.

Zinacantec curing, too, is characterized by specially marked speech, usually structured in parallel couplets (Haviland 1987, 1994). As in the Yucatec case, Zinacantec shamans construct a partially transposed indexical surround for prayer. Their apparent addressees – all referents of second-person forms – are saints and ancestral deities whose good auspices are sought for their healing virtues. The agents of verbs of curing and efficacy, in such prayers, are also invariably in the second person. Here are some isolated illustrative lines from a bonesetting prayer.

(27) 2nd-person and vocative forms in curing prayer[25]
ch'ul nichimal me` || nichimal kaxayil
'holy flowery (= beautiful) mother, flowery lady'
smajbenal avok || yikal ak'ob
'the beating of your foot, the wind of your hand (i.e., the disease)'
komun-ch'ul k'opan || komun-ch'ul ti`an
'speak in common, talk in common (i.e., intercede)'

The patient, face-to-face with the shaman, appears in prayer only as a shadowy third person, frequently encoded as the *possession* of a second-person deity, or with the remote definite article *ti*.

(28) 3rd-person references to the patient
ti yut spate || ti yut xokone
'the inside of his back, the inside of his side (i.e., his body)'
(s)k'uxel || yavanel
'his hurt, his pain (i.e., his affliction)'
tz'ul ti yoke || tz'ul ti sk'obe
'his foot slipped, his hand slipped (i.e., he was injured in an accident)'

(29) References to patient mediated by 2nd-person possession
tamanbil vinike || tatojbil vinike
'your bought man, your paid-for man'
alok'ol || ajelol
your copy, your replacement (i.e., made in your image)'
tavalab || lanich'nab
'your child, your offspring'

The shaman herself appears as first person, but normally in non-active roles (as beneficiary or recipient).

(30) 1st-person references to shaman
chayambekon || chayochbekon
'you will ease for me, you will loosen for me (i.e., the disease)'
k'elbekon || ilbekon
'watch for me, see for me'
xach'ul-tambekon || (xa)lekil-tambekon
'lift for me sacredly, lift for me well'

The arrangement in which a passive 1st-person shaman asks for the intercession of powerful 2nd-person deities, for the benefit of a backgrounded 3rd-person patient, is thus a standard, culturally pre-fabricated indexical space, for Hanks a "p-frame." Such a space is invoked, automatically as it were, by the opening lines of a curing prayer, uttered in the appropriate voice, and structured in the rhythmic parallel constructions of ritual Tzotzil. Similarly, as in the following extract from the same bonesetter's prayer, the reverse transposition can be instantly effected when the curer switches out of parallel speech. Ordinary pronominal values are, temporarily, restored by the frame-break.

(31) bonesetting prayer
      385 *tach'ul pom xa tal // tach'ul ch'ail xa tal kajval*
          'may your holy incense come, may your holy smoke, come,
             my Lord'   ("you" = ancestors)
          ((blows incense))
          ((switches from prayer voice to normal speech))
      388 *nupo ta ak'ob*
          'Put your hands together'   ("you" = patient)
          ((pours liquor into patient's hands))
      389 *ak'o me ta ajole*
          'Put it on your head.'
          ((Then returns to prayer))

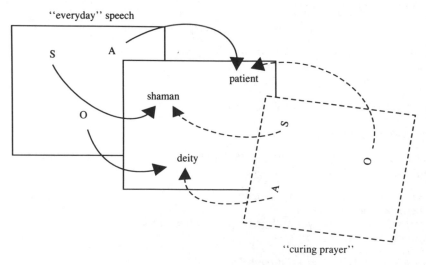

Fig. 10.13   *Transposition from prayer*

Here a generic bracketing forces a switch between transposed spaces. The curer returns briefly to the ordinary "here and now" to give direct instructions to the patient.

The discursive progress of an interaction creates its own kind of activity space: what is this event all about? What are we doing ("here and now")? What is there to do? Generic features of a register can project a range of such activity spaces. Thus, in Tzotzil, one can move from prayer to instruction, or from formal denunciation to mere complaint, simply by switching from parallel constructions to ordinary, non-parallel speech. Note that such shifts can transpose space, time, personae, and activity, perhaps all at once.

The signaling devices that function as what I have called transpositional triggers may frequently have the implicit, unmarked character of what Gumperz (1982) has called "contextualization cues." Even to begin to calculate referents for the plainest of deictics, interlocutors must participate in immanent wholesale patterns of local knowledge about how reference is to be achieved. The catalog I have offered lists as triggers only the most codified, formally marked sorts of transposition, making the process seem more mechanical than it doubtless is.

Transitions from one space to another may proceed in tiny steps. Similarly, the "here and now" does not stand still, so that as a sequence of utterances (or even a single utterance) unfolds, the contextual facts may change. Len Talmy has remarked[26] that "spaces" can be in motion. "Real" motion presents the canonical case: a train is "whizzing past." In such circumstances, a transposition might simply **freeze** the frame, to portray motion as stasis. Indeed, linguistic coding itself produces certain "moving" effects by casting non-linear spaces onto the linear stream of speech. Gesture and other communicative modalities thus present especially notable alternative possibilities for signaling transposition, a topic that cannot be pursued in the present chapter.

5.10 Calibrating and centering transposed spaces

As Silverstein's formulation, quoted earlier, points out, a single indexical sign projects only an atomic, schematic context; only interlocutors' interpretive (in Silverstein's terms, *metapragmatic*) skills expand these origos to full spaces, or coordinate/laminate spaces projected by a collection of distinct signs, creating coherent sequences. Yet, if speakers routinely project and transpose the indexical grounds upon which their talk stands, there must be means by which interlocutors flesh out spaces, find coherence between them, and locate indexical centers within them.

My two final examples illustrate the problem and indicate where further attention is required.

First, let me return to the GY orientation system. I have claimed that physical spaces as projected in GY are typically absolutely oriented, anchored by the compass points. The default assumption is that North is always North, and that what can vary is where one is centered. We saw above in (10) that a GY narrator could transpose between the narrating space and the narrated space, keeping his directions straight all the while. In the following fragments from later in the same narrative, Jack establishes a transposed space, centered on another man who watched the two men who had swum to shore as they walked South along the beach. First, at line 156, he shows with his gesture that the storm clouds moved off to the West, an orientation that is potentially equivocal as to its center. (That is, the storm presumably blew westwards both from the points of view of the beach, and of the Mission where Jack is now telling the story.)

(32) Boat2[27]

         ....!........
156 *mathi*   *past-manaathi*
     rain + ABS past-become-Past
     'The rain had passed over.'

                  right hand: palm out, pulled towards E then
                             push out W, slight drop.

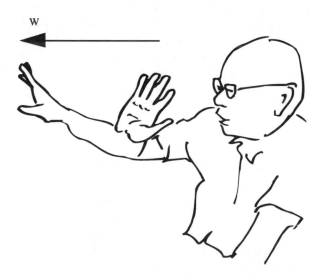

Fig. 10.14   *'The rain passed'*

...!..................................
157 *and yuwalin   nguumbaarr   guthiirra   nhaathi*
       beach-LOC shadow + ABS two + ABS see-PAST
                                              gadaariga
                                     come + RED-PAST-SUB
    'and (he) could see two shadows coming along the beach.'
                       right-hand: pointing with straight arm W,
                                moving S to rapid drop to lap.

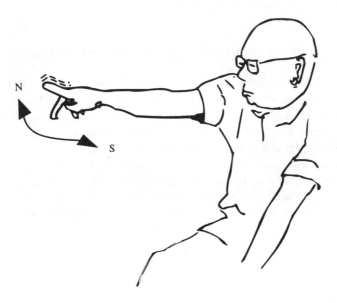

Fig. 10.15   *'He saw two shadows coming along the beach'*

In line 157, he describes the shadows of the two men seen from afar as they
walked along the beach. The vector of their motion is again shown by
gesture: they walked North to South. The gesture would be appropriate
precisely to the new protagonist, Woibo, watching them progress down
the beach *from where he stood at the time.* That is, combining the gestures
with what they know of the (past) geography of the area, Jack's audience
can fix the act of seeing squarely on Woibo, who goes on in "quoted"
thoughts at line 160, to speculate on what had happened.

              1: . . . . . .   2: . . . . ! . . . .
158 *nyulu   thawuunh   Woibongun   yarrba   nhaathi*
      3sNOM friend + ABS Woibo-ERG this way see-PAST

'He, (my) friend, Old Woibo saw that,'
> 1: right hand: up in "baby O," points W, then N and up.
> 2: right hand: curls back to SE point, with gaze and head
> nod, ends in E over L shoulder, 2nd nod as hand
> retracts to lap.

159 *nyulu-*
 3sNOM
 'he-'

160 *nyuluugu*   *gurray*   *bula*   *nhayun*   *nguba*
 3sgNOM-EMPH say-PAST 3duNOM that + ABS perhaps
                                    guwa-janji
                                    sink + PAST
 'He thought to himself, "perhaps those two sank the boat."'

There remains a puzzle, namely Jack's pointing gesture over his left shoulder to the Southeast as he mentions Woibo in line 158 (see figure 10.16). If my interpretation of this gesture is right, it exemplifies both the potential rapidity of transpositions, and the difficulty posed by their recoverability: the fact that interlocutors can keep them straight. For here, apparently, Jack is pointing over his shoulder to a place (the Hopevale store) where the protagonist's eldest son (also called Woibo) works and is normally to be seen. That is, with his gestures, this narrator has leapt from a secondary transposed narrated space back to the

Fig. 10.16   *'My friend Woibo'*

immediate "here and now" (although schematized: it is not certain that
the son is *actually* visible at this moment). His pointing indexes both
spaces in quick succession. How to calibrate different projected spaces,
how interlocutors can decide when to expand, laminate, or simply switch
between transposed "spaces," are questions for further investigation.

Now let me return to the riddle which I posed at the beginning of this
chapter. Sometimes interlocutors find themselves interacting in abnormal
conditions; for example, they may not be face-to-face, or they may have
to interact at great distance, back-to-back (de León 1990), or in a variety
of other circumstances that Hanks characterizes as asymmetric.
Managing transpositions under such circumstances involves crucial
indexical dilemmas that admit of both conventional and *ad hoc*
solutions. In example (7) I invented a scenario in which you talk to a
Zinacantec by telephone. In example (33), we see a complex series of
transpositions that illustrate one attested Zinacantec solution to this
telephone-call problem.

Here there are three conversants: M, a man who has run away from the
village of Nabenchauk with crushing debts; C, a young unmarried man
also from Nabenchauk who accompanied M for the adventure of it; and
J, M's *compadre*. The conversation takes place in Mexico City, and M is
recounting a telephone conversation with his daughter Josefa. He spoke
to her from Mexico City, although she was in the village. The dance of
directionals and auxiliaries fixes M's perspective, in this reported
conversation, firmly "at home" in Nabenchauk.

(33) Chepa
    1 M: *ali ijk'opon li Chepa une*
        'Uh, I spoke with Josefa.'
    2 J: *aa*
        'Oh.'
        [
    3 M: *k'u xa'elan xiyut lek ya'el xkut un*
        ' "How are you?" she said to me. "Alright, it seems,"
        I told her.'
    4 J: *mjm*
        'Mmm hmm.'
        [
    5 M: *aa xi*
        ' "Oh," she said.'

At line [6], M's daughter asks, centering herself deictically on
Nabenchauk, "When are you coming?" M replies, evidently transposing
his deictic center to their shared *socio-centric* origo, Nabenchauk. He also
employs the anchored verb *tal*, 'set out to *here*.'

6   *k'u to ora chatal xi ch'abal to bu chital xkut =*
      ' "When will you be coming?" she said. "I'm not coming yet,"
      I told her.'
7 J: *= ch'abal to*
      'Not yet-'
8 C: *mu xital*
      ' "I'm not coming." '
            [
9 M: *k'usi tal jpas ch'abal xkut*
            ' "What will I come to do? Nothing," I said.'

At line [8] notice that C, M's companion, echoes these reported words.
C's *mu xital*, 'I'm not coming,' represents (at least) a double
transposition, since C first must transpose himself into M's shoes, as it
were, and thereafter into the transposed perspective of the village (to
which M can 'come').[28] M ends his conversation with the rhetorical
question of a man in exile, wishing he were home (and indexically
transposing himself there): "What will I come [home to Nabenchauk]
to do?" Remembering his debts, he provides his own forlorn answer:
"[I have] nothing [to come home to]." (See Fig. 10.17.)

5.11 Transpositions and relativity

Mexico city apartment dwellers, Zinacantec corn-farmers, and Guugu-
Yimithirr-speaking storytellers are not like Wittgenstein's lion. They

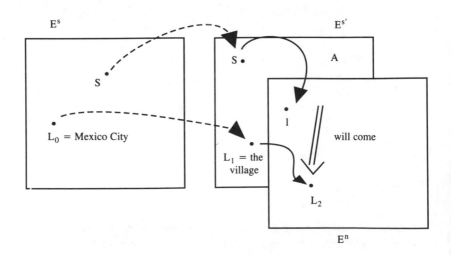

Fig. 10.17   *'What will I come to do?'*

can speak, and we **can** (more or less) understand them. I suggest that the phenomenon of transposition can direct us to the proper level of analysis to locate discussions of linguistic relativity and universality.

Suppose that we take as the simplest model of transposition a single quotation, as in line 6 of the last example, (33). M utters the words *k'u to ora chatal xi?* " 'When will you be coming?' she said." There are several familiar deictic elements in the morphology here. Ignoring tense/aspect and a certain perspective issue built into the clitic *to*, 'still,' there are at least the 2nd-person pronominal subject of the verb *ch-a-tal*, and the deictically anchored directionality of the verb stem itself. Both of these deictics project a skeletal context. The 2nd-person prefix wants an "addressee" as referent; the verb wants a "here" as a goal. There is also the 3rd-person subject of the verb *xi*, '[he/she/they] said,' which requires a non-speaker non-addressee as referent. But as M utters the words, his addressees are C and J, and his "here" is Mexico City. The values of the deictics must, therefore, be recomputed on the basis of an indexical surround different from that of the immediate "here and now." The "she" becomes Josefa, M's daughter; the addressee becomes M himself, in the transposed space in which Josefa speaks to him. Finally, "here," in an understandably plaintive socio-centric alignment, becomes the village of Nabenchauk from which M has fled with no prospects of returning. The formal fact of deictic projection, a commonplace of every human language, is here given a local, Zinacantec substance. The interpretive problems posed by the universal formal dilemma of projection under transposition are solved in a local, perhaps extemporaneous, maximally situated manner.

Many deictic elements in language require referents, whose values must be computed in (projected onto) a transposed space. Other, non-referential indexes may require or impose upon their projected spaces different sorts of configurations and elements, some of which may likewise require projection onto a transposed space. Further non-indexical signs may denote, more or less explicitly, parallel configurations which must also be projected across spaces of relations. My examples have first been intended to illustrate the range of projectable (and in principle transposable) elements.

It would be comforting to suppose that, to test linguistic relativity, we need only catalog those transposable elements explicitly coded in linguistic form. Clearly these are not only the most tractable objects of study but also the most likely vehicles for allegedly habitual or conventionalized patterns of communicative action. Discussions of linguistic relativity often start (and, too often, also end) with catalogs of encoded distinctions that vary from one language to another. Mere categorial variation, at the level of *projectables*, is probably neither significant (for human cognition) nor interesting (for social or linguistic theory). However, insofar as they demarcate the boundaries of the first term in the traditional language/thought/reality triad, linguistically encoded projectables, and the accompanying details of language form, provide an unavoidable, if not irresistible, starting point.

Indexicals in language are central to understanding the triad as well. In conference discussion, Stephen Levinson coined the slogan: "indexicality is the chink [in the armor of referential language, presumably] through which context flows into meaning." One could also reverse the priority, finding in the linguistically facilitated abstraction of reference and predication the characteristic leakage (or seepage) out of otherwise insistently situated communicative action. In either case, "context" *is* reality, and "meaning" is, minimally, the denotative substance regimented by linguistic form, for purposes of the triad.

Insofar as transpositional cues (or "triggers") are built into language itself, the linguistic code partly predetermines the available transposable spaces. The availability of respectful "Brother-in-law" words, for example, pulls the realm of social relations it indexes into a position ever hovering in the background of Guugu Yimithirr interaction.

Transposition is like demonstration, however. Clark & Gerrig argue that since "demonstrations can depict anything recognizable – whether linguistic or not – quotations [which, as has been argued, involve canonical transpositions] should be able to too" (1990: 781). Thus, one assumes that transposed spaces can contain anything ordinary (i.e., immediate, untransposed) spaces can. Moreover, even these "immediate" or untransposed spaces are themselves never "given" but always projected.[29] One good reason for detailed scrutiny of situated examples is to find evidence for the transpositions implied in talk, and to try to discover those elements – "whether linguistic or not" – which signal them.

Once we have cataloged the potentially exotic inventory of projectable relations, transposition gives us a special purchase on specific, perhaps highly local and variable, linguistic practices. For it is precisely when indexical signs project a space that differs from the immediate, unmarked, and taken-for-granted contextual surround – when they require transposition – that the transposed features spring to attention. A static scene may seem easier to perceive than a moving picture. Nonetheless, it is a commonplace of nature that something still is easier to *overlook* than something in motion. So it is with the entities projected by linguistic forms. They may remain invisible because they are routinely presupposed precisely until, through transposition, they must be re-projected, adjusted, or calculated anew. Transposition thus illustrates a characteristic tension between what might be called the necessary and the variable. The universal fact of transposition, a logical consequence of the universal employment in human language of certain semiotic modalities, itself provides a particularly acute lens with which to focus on substantive differences, between communicative traditions, in the universe of projectable entities and the relations between them: differences in "the world" as it can be talked about.

The presumed cognitive operations involved in transposition, in turn, bring us unavoidably to the missing term of the triad: thought. Keeping track of storytellers' referents and pointing fingers alike presumably requires certain mental gymnastics. Indeed, the dizzying complexities of the conversational examples cited point directly to the need for a theory of conversational reasoning, with an inferential engine powerful enough to show how transpositions are, at least sometimes, successfully brought off between interlocutors.[30] Projected "spaces" are a necessary mediating link between static and processual modes of thought, since one cannot get from utterance to interpretation except via such schematic representations; the universal process of transposition brings a complicating dynamic into the process. Being located in interaction, transpositions are also prime exemplars of a further Levinson slogan: that interaction is, "in effect, displayed cognition." (Indeed, the gestures of a gifted storyteller like Jack Bambi literally display his presumed cognitive representations on interactively defined physical space.)

The nature of the limiting mechanisms there may be on the projection and transposition of the indexical spaces we call "context" remain to be explored, then. Such limits may be both substantive and formal.[31] The default orientational anchoring of any projected space in GY talk is a possible example of the former. The requirement that transpositions must be interactively recoverable – by means that still remain largely a mystery to me – is an example of the latter.

Notes

1 The original version of this chapter was prepared for the Wenner-Gren Conference on Rethinking Linguistic Relativity, organized by John Gumperz and Stephen Levinson, 3–11 May 1991, Ocho Rios, Jamaica. I am indebted to Lourdes de León for her patient comments on the first draft, and to discussion by other participants, anonymous comments, and especially written comments by Gumperz and Levinson, that have been shamelessly exploited for this revision.

2 Examples marked with asterisks are invented, others are transcribed from conversational recordings.

3 I write Tzotzil, a Mayan language of Mexico, in a Spanish-based practical orthography in use in Chiapas.

4 In Tzotzil morpheme-by-morpheme glosses the following abbreviations
   appear:

1A	1st person Absolutive affix
2A	2nd person Absolutive affix
3A	3rd person Absolutive affix
CP	completive aspect
PREP	general preposition
QUOT	quotative evidential clitic

5 Herb Clark, in recent work on quotation, has used the term "layering" – which I
   borrow here – to describe something comparable to Hanks's complex frames.
6 During conference discussion, John Lucy criticized the metaphor of "space"
   as inviting confusion and suggesting equivocation. Does the metaphor suggest
   that any "space" has a full set of coordinates, or a continuous extent? "Real"
   physical space is, of course, a leading example of what can be projected and
   then transposed; the deictic origo, as normally (minimally) populated, is only
   a special case of such projection. Physical space is often, then, taken as a
   prototype for many, if not all, linguistically coded relations. See Lyons (1977),
   Langacker (1990), Fauconnier (1984).
7 This observation is due to comments by John Lucy.
8 People can interpret wrongly, be thought to have transposed when they
   haven't meant to, and so forth. All of this, as Herb Clark (this volume and
   elsewhere) is at pains to point out, is collaborative from the start.
9 Ochs (this volume) suggests that phenomena like those I treat as transpositions
   are examples of constitutive activities, which necessarily display issues of
   membership: who is who to whom within a communicative tradition.
10 "Location" is understood as some spatio-temporal extent.
11 I am indebted to Ed Robinson for this observation.
12 In fact, there are nearly no other devices available for specifying location or
   direction: none of the familiar sorts of ego- or object-relative locatives like *left*
   and *right* or even *front* and *back*.
13 The timing of gestures, including stroke phases (shown as !) and their full
   extent (shown with...), is represented above each verbal transcript line.
   Written descriptions that follow such lines are sometimes keyed to numbered
   points on the gesture line itself.
      Many gestures are characterized by a putative English gloss (shown in
   italics enclosed within curly brackets following a verbal description of the
   gestural form). The compass directions associated with the gestures are
   sometimes also shown. The following abbreviations occur in gestural
   descriptions:

   "baby O" = a hand shape resembling the ASL finger-spelling shape of the
   same name, composed of a "ring" made by thumb and index finger, with
   the remaining fingers folded into the palm of the hand

E = East
L = left hand
N = North
R = right hand
S = South
SW = Southwest
W = West

14 The design of the experiment is due to Lourdes de León (1990).

15 As Melissa Bowerman remarked in comments at the conference, the familiar competitive recasting of events by interlocutors, often for quite strategic ends, has the formal character of transposition even if it involves no explicit shifters. Thus, in Melissa's example, a child defends herself against another's accusation: "You broke it." "No, I just pushed it and it broke." Here the retort relies on a transitivity "transposition" that invites construction of a different described scenano *e*, in which the thing *breaks* without *somebody's breaking* it. Such transpositions are, as it were, wholly denotational. For treatment of a similar rhetorical use of Spanish reflexive, see Berk-Seligson (1983).

16 The material presented here derives from a joint study with Lourdes de León. See Haviland & de León (1988).

17 Consider Talmy's (1985) distinction between static and moving frames: do we see the moving train from the outside or, as it were, from the train itself?

18 The catalog of transpositional types could doubtless be extended. For example, various entities suggested by Langacker as aspects of "construal" – for example, things vs. relations, setting vs. participants, "search domains" – can presumably give rise, by a shift in utterance form, to alternative or transposed construals.

19 This is, incidentally, part of the difficulty with maintaining that "indications" – in ordinary parlance, indexes – work by inducing interlocutors to perceive their referents "by direct experience" (Clark &: Gerrig 1990: 765). As should be evident, one can point in a *transposed* space, so that an interlocutor can "perceive" the object of a pointing gesture only by imagining that space.

20 See Sperber & Wilson (1986) for one attempt.

21 Parallel kinesic marks – major body shifts, changes in gestural tension or "effort," shifts in gaze – also accompany shifts in other sorts of interaction. See Kendon (1972), Goodwin (1981), Haviland (1991b). It seems plausible, as suggested by Len Talmy in the conference, that certain sorts of cues may allow interlocutors to distinguish what's in the "here and now" from what must be understood in a transposed space. Features of gestural morphology may have this character. Another possibility might be found in changes in the synchrony between word and gesture. It has been argued (Kendon 1980, 1981, Schegloff 1984, McNeill 1985, 1992) that gesture routinely coincides with or slightly precedes the verbal material it is meant to illustrate. However, there is some evidence that this strict pattern of synchrony may not obtain in, for example, quoted "demonstrations."

22 Evidentials also implicate a complex social system in which authority is circumscribable and personhood or voice problematic – an important arena for comparative investigation that I cannot pursue here. See Chafe & Nichols (1986), and especially Lucy (1993).

23 But see Laughlin's description of one storyteller. "Quite deliberately he neglected to add the particle la which indicates that the story was only hearsay, for he wants you to know that he was there at the time of the creation" (1977: 94).

24 Levinson (1988), in a kind of *reductio* argument based on Goffman (1979), builds an elaborate theory of finely discriminated participant roles to account precisely for the existence of such shadowy participants as are encoded in grammatical devices like the Tzotzil evidential *la*. Contrast Irvine (1987) and Hanks (1990: ch. 4).

25 Double slashes are used to separate matching elements of parallel constructions.
26 In discussion at the conference.
27 The following abbreviations are used in morpheme-by-morpheme glosses of Guugu Yimithirr:

3du = 3rd person dual pronoun
3s, 3sg = 3rd person singular pronoun
ABS = absolutive case (usually realized as zero)
EMPH = emphatic nominal suffix
ERG = ergative case
LOC = locative case
NOM = nominative pronominal form
PAST = past tense suffix
PREP = preposition
RED = reduplicated verbal form (continuative aspect)
SUB = subordinating verbal suffix

28 I am indebted to Bill Hanks for noticing this echoed line on the transcript, and pointing out its transpositional complexity.
29 See Hanks (1990: 516): " 'Here-now' is never a sheer physical reality to which we can meaningfully apply objective measures. As the ground and by-product of communicative practices, it is inevitably **lived space** made up of perspective subspaces, costructured with the corporeal fields of human actors, and located within a broader sociocultural frame space."
30 The literature on mutual knowledge (for example Clark & Marshall 1981, Sperber & Wilson 1982) and "relevance theory" (Sperber & Wilson 1986) makes the problem, though hardly the solution, explicit.
31 Herb Clark, playing a psychologist's role in discussion, pointed out that there may be cognitive limits on what can be required in a transposition. Mentally producing a mirror image, for example, may be hard for human beings; perhaps 180° rotations are impossible. What is already known about "thought" may suggest where transpositional devices are likely to succeed, and where they will not venture.

References

Bakhtin, M. M. 1986. *Speech genres and other late essays*. Austin: University of Texas Press.
Barwise, J. & Perry, J. 1983. *Situations and attitudes. Cambridge*, MA: MIT Press.
Bauman, R. 1986. *Story, performance and event: contextual studies of oral narrative*. Cambridge University Press.
Berk-Seligson, S. 1983. Sources of variation in Spanish verb construction usage: the active, the dative, and the reflexive passive. *Journal of Pragmatics*, 7(2), 145–68.
Bühler, K. 1965 [1934]. *Sprachtheorie: die Darstellungsfunktion der Sprache*. Jena: Gustav Fischer. (Reprinted 1982. Stuttgart: Gustav Fisher Verlag.)
Chafe, W. & Nichols, J. (eds.) 1986. *Evidentiality: the linguistic coding of epistemology*. Advances in Discourse Processes. Norwood, NJ: Ablex.
Clark, H. H. & Gerrig, R. J. 1990. Quotations as demonstrations. *Language*, 66(4), 764–805.

Clark, H. H. & Marshall, C. R. 1981. Definite reference and mutual knowledge. In A. K. Joshi, B. Webber, & I. A. Sag (eds.), *Elements of discourse understanding* (pp. 10–63). Cambridge University Press.

de León, L. 1991. *Space games in Tzotzil: creating a context for spatial reference.* Working Paper 4. Berlin: Research Group of the Max Planck Institute for Psycholinguistics.

Dixon, R. M. W. 1971. A method of semantic description. In D. D. Steinberg & L. A. Jakobovits (eds.), *Semantics* (pp.436–71). Cambridge University Press.

Evans, N. 1995. *A Grammar of Kayardild*. Berlin: Mouton de Gruyter.

Fauconnier, G. 1984. *Espaces mentaux: aspects de la construction du sens dans les langues naturelles*. Paris: Les Editions de Minuit.

Fillmore, C. 1975. *Santa Cruz lectures on deixis*. Bloomington: Indiana University Linguistics Club.

1982. Towards a descriptive framework for spatial deixis. In R. Jarvella & W. Klein (eds.), *Speech, place, and action: studies in deixis and related topics* (pp. 31–59). New York: John Wiley & Sons.

Goffman, E. 1979. Footing. *Semiotica*, 25(1/2), 1–29.

Goodwin, C. 1981. *Conversational organization: interaction between speakers and hearers*. New York: Academic Press.

Gumperz, J. J. 1982. *Discourse strategies*. Cambridge University Press.

Hanks, W. F. 1990. *Referential practice: language and lived space among the Maya*. University of Chicago Press.

Haviland, J. B. 1979. Guugu Yimidhirr. In R. Dixon & B. Blake (eds.), *Handbook of Australian languages* (pp. 27–181). Canberra: ANU Press.

1982. Kin and country at Wakooka outstation: an exercise in rich interpretation. *International Journal of the Sociology of Language*, 36, 53–70.

1986. Complex referential gestures. Ms. Center for Advanced Study in the Behavioral Sciences, Palo Alto, CA.

1987. Tzotzil ritual language without ritual. Ms. Austin Discourse Conference.

1989. Complex referential gestures revisited: the "iconicity" of pointing in Guugu Yimidhirr. Paper and videotape presented at the University of Chicago, Oct. 1989, and at the invited session, "The interactive organization of talk: analyses of video tape from five cultures," organized by C. Goodwin and A. Kendon, Annual Meetings of the American Anthropological Association, Washington DC, Nov. 1989.

1991a. "That was the last time I seen them, and no more": voices through time in Australian Aboriginal autobiography. *American Ethnologist*, 18(2), 331–61.

1991b. Xi chbat ta lok'eb k'ak'al "It goes towards the sunrise": sculpting space with the body. Ms. Cognitive Anthropology Research Group, Max Planck Institute for Psycholinguistics, Nijmegen, Oct. 1991.

1993 Anchoring, iconicity, and orientation in Guugu Yimithirr pointing gestures. *Journal of Linguistic Anthropology*, 3(1), 3–45.

1994 [1992]. Lenguaje ritual sin ritual. *Estudios de Cultura Maya*, 19, 427–42.

Haviland, J. B. & de León, L. 1988. "Me tengo que tragar mis broncas (I have to swallow my problems)." Paper presented to the invited session "Restructuring interactive narrative: tellings and retellings in a cross-cultural perspective," organized by A. Duranti and C. Goodwin, Annual Meetings of the American Anthropological Association, Phoenix, Nov. 1988.

Irvine, J. 1987. The implicated dialog: structures of participation in discourse. Paper presented to the Annual Meetings of the American Anthropological Association, Chicago, Nov. 1987.

Jakobson, R. 1971 [1957]. Shifters, verbal categories, and the Russian verb. In *Selected writings of Roman Jakobson*, vol. II (pp. 130–47). The Hague: Mouton.

Jespersen, O. 1965 [1924]. *The philosophy of grammar*. New York: W. W. Norton.

Kendon, A. 1972. Some relationships between body motion and speech. In A. W. Seigman & B. Pope (eds.), *Studies in dyadic communication*. Elmsford, NY: Pergamon Press.

 1980. Gesticulation and speech: two aspects of the process of utterance. In M. R. Key (ed.), *Relationship between verbal and nonverbal communication* (pp. 207–27). The Hague: Mouton.

 1981. Geography of gesture. *Semiotica*, 37, 129–63.

Kernighan, B. W. & Ritchie, D. M. 1988. *The C programming language, second edition*. Englewood Cliffs, NJ: Prentice Hall.

Kuno, S. 1987. *Functional syntax: anaphora, discourse and empathy*. University of Chicago Press.

Kuroda, S.-Y. 1973. Where epistemology, style, and grammar meet: a case study from Japanese. In S. Anderson & P. Kiparsky (eds.), *A festschrift for Morris Halle* (pp. 377–91). New York: Holt, Rinehart, & Winston.

Langacker, R. W. 1987. *Foundations of cognitive grammar*, vol. I: *Theoretical prerequisites*. Stanford University Press.

 1990. *Foundations of cognitive grammar*, vol. I: *Concept, image & symbol: the cognitive basis of grammar*. Washington, DC: Smithsonian Institution Press.

Laughlin, R. 1975. *The great Tzotzil dictionary of San Lorenzo Zinacantán*. Washington, DC: Smithsonian Institution Press.

 1977. *Of cabbages and kings: tales from Zinacantán*. Washington, DC: Smithsonian Institution Press.

Levinson, S. C. 1988. Putting linguistics on a proper footing: explorations in Goffman's concepts of participation. In P. Drew & A. Wootton (eds.), *Erving Goffman: exploring the interaction order* (pp. 161–227). Cambridge University Press.

Lucy, J. (ed.) 1993. *Reflexive language: reported speech and metapragmatics*. Cambridge University Press.

Lyons, J. 1977. *Semantics*. 2 vols. Cambridge University Press.

McNeill, D. 1985. So you think gestures are nonverbal? *Psychology Review*, 92(3), 350–71.

 1992. *Hand and mind: what gestures reveal about thought*. University of Chicago Press.

Schegloff, E. 1984. On some gestures' relation to talk. In J. M. Atkinson & J. Heritage (eds.), *Structures of social action: studies in conversation analysis* (pp. 266–96). Cambridge University Press.

Silverstein, M. 1976. Shifters, linguistic categories, and cultural description. In K. Basso & H. Selby (eds.), *Meanings in anthropology* (pp. 11–55). Albuquerque: University of New Mexico Press.

 1981. *The limits of awareness*. Working Papers in Linguistics No. 84. Austin: Southwestern Educational Laboratory.

 1992. Metapragmatic discourse and metapragmatic function. In J. Lucy (ed.) *Reflexive language* (pp. 33–58). Cambridge University Press.

Sperber, D. & Wilson, D. 1982. Mutual knowledge and relevance in theories of comprehension. In N. Smith (ed.), *Mutual knowledge* (pp. 61–131). London: Academic Press.

1986. *Relevance*. Cambridge, MA: Harvard University Press.

Talmy, L. 1978. Figure and ground in complex sentences. In J. Greenberg (ed.), *Universals of human language*, vol. IV (pp. 625–54). Stanford University Press.

1983. How language structures space. In H. Pick & L. Acredolo (eds.), *Spatial orientation: theory, research and application* (pp. 225–320). New York: Plenum Press.

1985. Lexicalization patterns: semantic structure in lexical forms. In T. Shopen (ed.), *Language typology and syntactic description*, vol. III: *Grammatical categories and the lexicon* (pp. 56–149). Cambridge University Press.

Voloshinov, V. N. 1986. *Marxism and the philosophy of language*. Tr. L. Matejka, I. R. Titinuk. Cambridge, MA: Harvard University Press.

COMMUNITIES, COMMONALITIES, AND COMMUNICATION

HERBERT H. CLARK

What is the link between the thoughts we have and the language we speak? Benjamin Lee Whorf argued for two proposals. One was *linguistic relativity*: as languages differ, so do the thoughts of the people who use them. Whorf suggested, for example, that English and Hopi encode different points of view – different perspectives or representations – of the physical and social world, and when people use the two languages, they buy into these differences. The other, more radical, proposal was *linguistic determinism*: the language people speak helps determine the very way they think about their physical and social world. As an example, Whorf compared English and Hopi nouns for physical quantity. English has both count and mass nouns, as in *many dogs* and *much sand*, so for speakers of English, according to Whorf, "the philosophic 'substance' and 'matter' [of mass nouns] are the naive idea; they are instantly acceptable, 'common sense.'" Hopi, on the other hand, has only count nouns, so for speakers of Hopi, he claimed, the notions of substance and matter are not common sense – though he offered no evidence for this. Linguistic determinism is clearly the stronger doctrine. It is one thing to say that English and Hopi encode different points of view. It is quite another to say that English and Hopi speakers are forced to think in ways dictated by these differences.

Yet how do languages differ in their representations of the world, and how might these representations help determine the way we think? Surely, the answers depend on what we take to be language, or thought. Whorf himself concentrated on the lexicon and the grammar. He was readiest to compare two languages in how their words categorized the world, and in how their grammatical features might influence people's conceptions of time, space, number, and other abstract objects. But what about other aspects of language and language use, such as conversational practice, literacy, politeness, native fluency? What about other aspects of thought, such as mental imagery, social skills, technical know-how, and memory for music, poetry, places, or faces? About these Whorf had nothing to say. So the doctrines of linguistic relativity and linguistic determinism are not two monolithic theories, but rather two families of hypotheses about particular aspects of language and thought. It is not the doctrines *per se* that are true or false, but only the member hypotheses, some of which may be true and others false without contradiction.

In proposing these doctrines, Whorf seemed to take for granted that language is primarily an instrument of thought. Yet this premise is false. Language is first and foremost an instrument of communication – the "*exchange* of thoughts," as one dictionary puts it – and it is only derivatively an instrument of thought. If language has an influence on thought, as Whorf believed, that influence must be mediated by the way language is used for communication. The alliteration in my title is not accidental, for communication, as its Latin root suggests, is itself built on commonalities of thought between people, especially those taken for granted in the communities in which each language is used. Once this is made explicit, I suggest, we will find it difficult to distinguish many potential influences of language on thought from the influences of other commonalities of mental life, especially the beliefs, practices, and norms of the communities to which we belong.

I will apply this argument to the lexicon. One reason for choosing the lexicon is that it was one of Whorf's main test laboratories for linguistic relativity and linguistic determinism. Another reason is that it presents us with examples *par excellence* of how language is an instrument of communication. That will enable us to go beyond Whorf's simple doctrines to a more perspicuous view of the relation between language and thought.

1 Co-ordination in language use

People use language to do things together. In conversation – the primordial form of language – they talk face-to-face, interactively, as they plan, transact business, gossip, and accomplish other goals with each other. A hallmark of these activities is that they are joint activities. They are like shaking hands or playing a piano duet: they cannot be accomplished by the participants acting autonomously. They need co-ordination, and when co-ordination fails, they break down. At one level, there must be co-ordination between the speaker's issuing an utterance and the addressees' paying attention, listening, and trying to understand it. At a higher level, there must be co-ordination between what speakers mean and what addressees take them to mean. Speakers and addressees cannot achieve that co-ordination without establishing commonalities of thought between them. Let us see how.

1.1 Schelling games

Suppose Anne points to a clump of trees and asks Burton, "What do you think of that tree?" Anne is using "that tree" to refer to a particular tree that she intends Burton to identify. They are faced with a co-ordination problem: to get Anne's meaning and Burton's construal of her meaning to match. In 1969, David Lewis offered a general analysis of co-ordination problems like this. He argued, in effect, that Anne and Burton must come to the mutual belief about which tree Anne is using "that tree" to refer to. To do that, they need a *co-ordination device*, a notion he drew from the work of Thomas Schelling (1960).

Schelling's approach is best illustrated in a form of co-ordination problem I will call a *Schelling game*. Suppose I approach two students named June and Ken individually, show them each a picture of three balls – a basketball, a tennis ball, and a squash ball – and tell them:

Select one of these three balls. I am giving the same picture and instructions to another student in the next room, someone you don't know. You will both get a prize if the two of you select the same ball, but nothing if you don't.

As Schelling argued about such a game:

Most situations – perhaps every situation for people who are practiced at this kind of game – provide some clue for coordinating behavior, some focal point for each person's expectation of what the other expects him to expect to be expected to do. Finding the key, or rather *a* key – any key that is mutually recognized as the key becomes *the* key – may depend on imagination more than on logic; it may depend on analogy, precedent, accidental arrangement, symmetry, aesthetic or geometric configuration, casuistic reasoning, and who the parties are and what they know about each other.   (1960: 57).

June might assume, for example, that she and Ken will both see the basketball's large size as the clue, focal point, or key that would allow them to co-ordinate their expectations and would therefore choose the basketball. I will call her choice of the basketball her *Schelling choice*. If Ken made the same assumption, he would make the same Schelling choice, and they would co-ordinate. They would have treated this assumed commonality of thought – the large size of the basketball – as a co-ordination device.

Schelling's insight was that almost any commonality of thought can serve as a co-ordination device – in the right circumstances. He mentioned a variety of rationales. One is precedent. If June is playing a second time with the same student, and they won the first time by picking out the basketball, she can use that precedent as the rationale for picking out the basketball again. Another co-ordination device, as Lewis noted, is convention. If, for some reason, it happened to be conventional among students to pick out basketballs in Schelling games like this, June could assume she and the student in the next room would see this as a co-ordinating device, and they could choose the basketball. In the lexicon, convention is of paramount importance because word meanings are thought to be conventional. However, as we shall see, other co-ordination devices are also important in co-ordinating on word meaning, and these include precedence.

1.2 Joint salience

The problem is that there is always an overabundance of available co-ordination devices. In the Schelling game with Ken, June could have appealed to the small size of the squash ball, the unique color of the squash ball, the uniqueness of the tennis ball as part of an outdoor game, or any of an infinity of other rationales. Which should she appeal to? The answer, I argue, is this:[1]

Principle of joint salience: For the participants in a co-ordination problem, the optimal co-ordination device is the one that is most salient in the participants' current common ground.

The idea is straightforward. For June to succeed in the Schelling game, she must think about the rationale her partner will rely on, and he must think about her rationale. Obviously, she cannot base her rationale on information she alone is privy to. How could Ken come up with the same rationale? The same logic applies to him. The only information they can base it on is information they fully share at that moment. This is their *common ground*, the sum of their mutual knowledge, mutual beliefs, and mutual suppositions at the moment. Then, of all the rationales available in their common ground, they must pick the most obvious, most conspicuous, most salient one, because that is the only one they can count on being a unique key – *the* key.

To see the force of this principle, suppose I tell June I am giving the same picture and instructions not just to "another student in the next room, someone you don't know," but to "your friend Ken, who knows you are his partner." Since she and Ken play squash regularly, that is a salient part of their common ground, and if she thinks it is more salient than the basketball's size, she will choose the squash ball. Suppose, instead, that I tell her that her partner is Ken, but that he does not know she is his partner. Once again, she should choose the basketball. She should realize that for Ken this version of the game is indistinguishable from the original version, and the squash ball is no longer the most salient co-ordination device in the common ground Ken would assume he held with the student in the next room.

For Schelling and Lewis, Schelling games are always third-party Schelling games. I am a third party when I pose the ball game to June and

Ken. Schelling games can also be *first-party Schelling games*. As a first party, I could present the game to June in this form:

Select one of these three balls. I have already selected one myself. You and T will both get a prize if you select the ball I have selected, but nothing if we don't select the same one.

As before, June should try to find the most salient co-ordination device in her and her partner's common ground. However, now she can take advantage of the fact that I am her partner. She can assume that I devised the game so she and I would be sure to win. The optimal solution should be so salient, so accessible, in our common ground that she cannot help but see it. It is as if I had worded the problem this way:

Select one of these three balls. I have already selected one myself. I have good reason to think you can readily and uniquely select that ball on the basis of our current common ground. You and I will both get a prize if you select the ball I have selected, but nothing if we don't select the same one

1.3 Optimal design

Co-ordination in language use is, in effect, a first-party Schelling game. Let us return to Anne pointing to the clump of trees and asking Burton, "What do you think of that tree?" It is as if Anne had presented Burton with this first-party Schelling game:[2]

Select a referent for "that tree." I have already selected a referent myself. I have good reason to think you can readily and uniquely select that referent on the basis of my utterance "What did you think of that tree?" taken against the rest of our common ground. You and I will both get a prize if you select the referent I have selected, but nothing if we don't select the same one.

The referent Burton selects is equivalent to his Schelling choice in this game. The general principle reflected here is this (E. V. Clark & Clark 1979; H. H. Clark 1983; Clark, Schreuder, & Buttrick 1983; H. H. Clark & Gerrig 1983):

Principle of optimal design: Speakers try to design their utterances in such a way that they have good reason to believe that the addressees can readily and uniquely compute what they mean on the basis of the utterance along with the rest of their common ground.

First-party Schelling games are simply a combination of the principles of optimal design and joint salience.

Some years ago two colleagues and I (Clark, Schreuder, & Buttrick 1983) tested this hypothesis in detail. In four experiments, we gave some students utterances like "What do you think of that tree?" along with a picture of many trees and asked them to make referential choices for "that tree." We gave other students the equivalent Schelling games and asked them to make Schelling choices. Our findings were clear. First, referential choices closely matched Schelling choices. Second, both choices reflected what the students took to be the most salient object in the speaker's and their common ground. In the situations we tested, these choices were based on the students' assumed mutual beliefs about perceptual salience, the speaker's goals, the speaker's explicit presuppositions and assertions, and cultural beliefs. Finally, students were more confident in their referential choices for some utterances than for others. Players in the Schelling games were more confident in their Schelling choices for the corresponding games. Put differently, the more confident you are that you have understood my reference, the more confident you would be that you and I had won the corresponding Schelling game. There is a tight fit, then, between the foundations of reference and the foundations of first-party Schelling games.

The principles of optimal design and joint salience are not limited to reference. They apply any time speakers mean something by what they do. That includes direct and indirect illocutionary acts as performed by means of full, elliptical, or phrasal utterances. It includes conventional and novel words and constructions. And it includes much more. Co-ordination *à la* Schelling is fundamental to language use.

1.4 Collaboration

In practice, however, co-ordination in language use is rarely achieved in one-shot episodes. Conversation is not a sequence of Schelling games, but a process in which Schelling co-ordination plays just one part. People in conversation have to co-ordinate not only on the *content* of what they say – the essence of Schelling co-ordination – but also on the *processes* by which they establish that content. In language use, co-ordination of content and co-ordination of process are interdependent: people cannot co-ordinate on one without co-ordinating on the other.

The basic idea is that contributing to a conversation takes the collaboration of both speaker and addressees. Consider this actual example:

> Anne: that wasn't the guy I met was it -
> Burton: *u:m*.
> Anne: *when we* saw the building -
> Burton: saw it where -
> Anne: when I went over to Chet*wynd Road*
> Burton: *yes -*[3]

When Anne produced "that wasn't the guy I met was it" she was presenting an utterance for Burton to consider. Both of them realized that presentation was not enough by itself to establish what she meant. Burton indicated as much by hesitating and saying "um" instead of giving an answer. That led Anne to expand on her reference with "when we saw the building." When Burton indicated that he still did not understand, by asking "saw it where," Anne expanded once more with "when I went over to Chetwynd Road." Only then did Burton believe he had understood, as he implied by going on to answer her original question "yes."

As this example illustrates, contributing to a discourse is ordinarily achieved in two phases: presentation and acceptance.[4] If A is the person trying to contribute to the conversation (e.g., Anne), and B is her partner (e.g., Burton), then the two phases take this form:

Presentation phase: A presents an utterance for B to consider. She does so on the assumption that, if B gives strong enough evidence, she can believe that he understands what she means by it.

Acceptance phase: B accepts A's utterance by giving evidence that he believes he understands what A means by it. He does so on the assumption that, once A registers the evidence, she will also believe that he understands.

Anne, for example, presented Burton with the utterance "that wasn't the guy I met was it" in order to ask him about a man's identity. However, since Burton could not accept the utterance as having been understood, he initiated an extended acceptance phase. That phase ended only when Burton went on to answer her question "yes," which was evidence that he believed he had understood what she meant by her utterance. In the simplest acceptance phase, he would have provided that evidence straight off. A and B's goal in the entire process is to reach the *grounding criterion*: the mutual belief that B has understood A well enough for current purposes.

When Anne uttered "that wasn't the guy I met was it," what she did, in effect, was present Burton with a first-party Schelling game. She may have thought it would succeed – that Burton could compute the referent of "the guy I met" against their current common ground – but it did not. To get it to succeed, she had to reformulate it first as "the guy I met when we saw the building" and then as "the guy I met when we saw the building when I went over to Chetwynd Road." The point is that participants in conversation realize that it is never enough merely to present a first-party Schelling game, regardless of how simple or obvious its solution is. Speakers have to get their addressees to register the game in the first place, and they may mis-hear, or become distracted. Speakers may also misjudge what their addressees assume to be in their common ground. Both speakers and addressees must take the extra step and *ground* what is said: establish the mutual belief that the addressees have understood, well enough for current purposes, what the speakers meant.

Many actions are guided by conservation of effort, but *joint* actions are guided by conservation of *joint* effort. Grounding is no exception: people try to reach the grounding criterion with the *least collaborative effort*. Take Anne's first reference to the guy she met. She could have expressed it any of these ways:

(a) him
(b) the guy
(c) the guy I met
(d) the guy I met when we saw the building
(e) the guy I met when we saw the building when I went over to Chetwynd Road.

If she had chosen (a) ("that wasn't him was it"), she and Burton would be required many more turns, extra collaborative effort, to reach the grounding criterion. If she had chosen (e) ("that wasn't the guy I met when we saw the building when I went over to Chetwynd Road was it"), they would have needed no extra turns – but the initial effort would have been great. She chose (c), we can assume, precisely because she judged it was probably specific enough to succeed without extra turns, with the least collaborative effort. Sometimes, indeed, the most efficient strategy is to force extra turns. If Anne can not think of a name on the fly, it may take less collaborative effort for her to forge ahead with "Did you happen to see what's-his-name yesterday?" and let Burton offer the name to complete the process.

Although this is just one example of the collaborative process, it brings out three properties characteristic of spontaneous language use. First, meaning is established not in one shot, but over time. Second, meaning is created jointly by the participants establishing commonalities of thought between them. The process is opportunistic in that the participants may have no idea beforehand of the commonalities they will actually establish. Third, what speakers mean is narrower than what they say. The man Anne was referring to was not uniquely specified by the phrase "the guy I met." She depended on Burton narrowing in on the right man partly in the very process of grounding.

In ordinary discourse, then, speakers do not merely design optimal utterances – first-party Schelling games they believe will succeed. They demand evidence of success, the mutual belief that the addressees have understood what they mean. That relieves them of a heavy burden. It doesn't force them to design the optimal utterance every time, because what they mean is always open to repair and adjustment. They can even start with nothing – "what's-his-name" – and establish what they mean entirely by collaboration.

2 Common ground

If co-ordination devices are fundamental to language use, where do they come from? By the principles of joint salience and optimal design, they should be based on the common ground of the participants at any moment in a discourse. How you and I co-ordinate, with or without collaboration, depends on the information we believe we share at that moment. But how? For that, we need to understand what two people's common ground consists of (H. H. Clark & Marshall 1981).

The common ground between two people – our Anne and Burton, say – can be divided conceptually into two main parts. Anne and Burton's *communal common ground* represents all the knowledge, beliefs, and assumptions they take to be universally held in the communities to which they mutually believe they both belong. Their *personal common ground* represents all the mutual knowledge, beliefs, and assumptions they have inferred from personal experience with each other.

2.1 Communal common ground

Anne and Burton belong to a diverse set of cultural groups, systems, or networks that I will call cultural communities. We might say of Anne, for example, that she is a San Franciscan, an educated American adult, a physician, a pediatrician, a speaker of American English, a baseball fan, a Yalie. With each of these attributions we are saying, in effect, that she is a member of an identifiable cultural community – the community of all San Franciscans, physicians, pediatricians, speakers of American English, baseball fans, or Yalies. Within each community, there are facts, beliefs, and assumptions that every member believes that almost everyone in that community takes for granted. So if two people mutually believe they both belong to that community, this is information they can take to be communal common ground.

What sort of information is this? As two speakers of American English, Anne and Burton take for granted a vast amount of knowledge about syntax, semantics, phonology, word meanings, idioms, and politeness formulas. As two educated American adults, they take for granted a certain acquaintance with American and English literature, world history and geography, and recent news events – disasters, election results, military coups, films. They also take for granted such broad concepts as the nature of causality, religious beliefs, and expected behavior in standing in lines, paying for food at supermarkets, and making telephone calls. As two physicians, they take for granted facts about basic human anatomy, major diseases and cures, and the technical nomenclature taught in medical school.

Regardless of the information Anne and Burton share as English speakers, San Franciscans, and physicians, that information does not become part of their common ground until they have established the mutual belief that they both belong to these communities. They can establish this in many ways – by assertion ("I'm a pediatrician," "Ah, so am I"), by showing (they recognize each other speaking American English), and by many other means (Isaacs & Clark 1986, Krauss & Glucksberg 1977, Schegloff 1972). The more communities they establish joint membership in, the broader and richer is their communal common ground.

2.2 Communities

The notion of cultural community I am appealing to here[5] is itself built on the common ground of its members. Physicians, for example, do not all live in one place and know each other. Yet when Anne and Burton establish that they are both physicians, they assume they share an expertise about medicine and its practice that makes them part of the same community – members of a set of people who share the same system or network of beliefs, practices, conventions, values, skills, know-how. The shared expertise may show up in a variety of characteristics:

(a) *language*: American English, Dutch, Japanese
(b) *nationality*: American, German, Australian
(c) *education*: university, high school, grade school
(d) *place of residence*: San Francisco, Edinburgh, Amsterdam
(e) *occupation*: physician, plumber, lawyer, psychologist
(f) *religion*: Baptist, Buddhist, Muslim
(g) *hobby*: classical piano, baseball, philately
(h) *subculture*: rock musicians, drug users, teenage gangs
(i) *ethnic origin*: Black, Hispanic, Japanese American

The idea is that when Anne becomes a physician, she believes she has done more than gain expertise in medicine. She believes she has become a member of a select group of people – those who are expert in medicine and have a common set of beliefs, practices, conventions, values, skills, and know-how. Membership in these communities, indeed, is reflected in such English nominals as *American, student, university graduate, San Franciscan, physician, Baptist, classical pianist, rock fan,* and *Latino.*

It is easy to underestimate the network of communities Anne and Burton may belong to. Place of residence, for example, really defines a set of nested communities. Anne may be a resident of Sacramento Street, Pacific Heights, San Francisco, the San Francisco Bay area, Northern California, California, the Western United States, the United States, and English-speaking North America. Each of these communities has associated with it distinguishable beliefs, practices, and assumptions that Anne can appeal to when she needs to. Suppose, for example, Anne and Burton establish they are both residents of Pacific Heights. They can take for granted a great body of information, universal to residents of Pacific Heights, that they could not take for granted if they were only joint residents of San Francisco. Think of all the detailed perceptions, experiences, geographical knowledge, and social beliefs you can take for granted with others in your neighborhood but not with others in the rest of your city, region, or state.

Just as place of residence can be differentiated into a nesting of communities, so can other characteristics listed earlier. For nationality, the nesting goes from local neighborhoods to nations; for language, from local dialects (San Francisco Bay area) to mutually intelligible languages (English); for occupation, from specialties (psychiatric pediatrician) to occupational classes (white-collar professional); for religion, from sects (Baptist, Missouri Synod) to general (Christian); and so on. Some of these nestings are correlated – like language and place of residence – but they are nevertheless distinct. The communities defined by education probably partition not just by amount of education, but by type (e.g., sciences vs. humanities), place (Ivy League vs. Big Ten Universities), and other features. People belong to an immense number of distinguishable communities, and each has its own universal set of beliefs, perspectives, practices, and understandings.

Communal common ground is obviously akin to the everyday notion of culture, so my characterization of it is hardly definitive or complete. All I have tried to do is bring out three properties. First, cultural beliefs, practices, conventions, values, skills, and know-how are not uniformly distributed in the population. Second, most of them are identified with experts or authorities within the population, people who are defined by their special training or background and who are identified as belonging to particular communities. Third, when two people meet, they identify each other as members of such communities and use that membership to infer which features they can and cannot take to be common ground. My analysis is intended only as a beginning for the issues I take up later.

2.3 Personal common ground

Once Anne and Burton meet, they begin openly to share experiences, and these form the basis for their personal common ground. Most joint experiences originate in one of two sources – *joint conversational experiences* or *joint perceptual experiences*. Whenever Anne and Burton participate in the same conversation, they are responsible for ensuring that everyone understands what has been said, and everything they succeed on they assume to be part of their common ground. That is the outcome of the process of grounding. For example, when Anne asked "that wasn't the guy I met was it?" she and Burton worked collaboratively to establish the mutual belief that he had understood what she meant. So what she meant became part of their personal common ground. Likewise, whenever Anne and Burton attend to the same perceptual events, such as a shot in a basketball game, and realize they are both doing so, they can ordinarily assume that everything they are jointly attending to is also common ground (Schiffer 1972, H. H. Clark & Marshall 1981). Even if at first they didn't know they were at the same basketball game, once that becomes mutually known, they can assume that its salient public parts are common ground.

An important difference between personal and communal common ground is in the way people keep track of them. For communal common ground, they need encyclopedias for each of the communities they belong to. Once Anne and Burton establish the mutual belief that they are both physicians, they can immediately add their physician encyclopedias to their common ground. For personal common ground, on the other hand, they need to keep diaries of their personal experiences; but not personal experiences alone. Anne's diary, to be useful, must record for each personal experience who else was involved in it – who else was openly co-present with her. Anne can count as personal common ground with Burton only those diary entries for which the two of them were openly co-present. The more entries there are, the richer their personal common ground.

In fact, it is not the personal experiences themselves that Anne and Burton share as personal common ground, but their interpretations. These interpretations are always shaped by their assumed communal common ground. Suppose Anne and Burton view a skin ailment together, and Anne, a physician, interprets it as eczema. If she believes Burton is not a physician, she will not assume that he interprets it as eczema. Yet because she believes he is an educated American adult, she will assume he does see it as a rash. In the end, everything we believe we share relies for its justification on our communal common ground.

The common ground that Anne and Burton can establish, therefore, may be vast, but every piece they do establish needs a basis. The basis may be the communities they believe they both belong to, which leads to what I have called their communal common ground; or it may be their openly shared experiences, which leads to their personal common ground.

3 Convention

With co-ordination and common ground as background, we can return to the best known of all co-ordination devices – convention. What is so important about convention? My argument is simple. Whorf's doctrines of linguistic relativity and linguistic determinism are about languages like English and Hopi, and these languages are systems of conventions. The problem is that Whorf took the notion of convention for granted. He appeared to consider it self-evident and therefore of no consequence to his doctrines. That, indeed, has been the attitude of most linguists, psychologists, and anthropologists since. The notion of convention, however, is anything but self-evident, and it bears directly on how we interpret and test Whorf's two doctrines. To see this, let us turn to the analysis by David Lewis (1969).

Languages like English, Japanese, and Lakota, according to Lewis, are really conventional signalling systems. English, for example, is a system of signalling conventions such as these: *dog* can be used to denote the domesticated carnivorous mammal, *Canis familiaris*; the morpheme -*z* on nouns can be used to denote plural number; a sentence can be composed of a noun phrase followed by a verb phrase in that order. Conventions are what is represented in the rules of phonology, morphology, syntax, semantics, and pragmatics.

Yet what is a convention? Lewis based his answer on Schelling's analysis of co-ordination problems and argued that it is a community-wide solution, a co-ordination device, for a recurrent co-ordination problem. In brief:

a convention:
(a) is a regularity in behavior;
(b) is partly arbitrary;
(c) is in common ground;
(d) applies in a given community;
(e) is (used as) a co-ordination device;
(f) tackles a recurrent co-ordination problem.[6]

Take greeting. When any two old friends meet, they have a recurrent co-ordination problem of how to greet. In some American communities, the co-ordination device that has evolved is for two men to shake hands and for a man and woman, or two women, to kiss each other once on the cheek. These actions, then, constitute a regularity in behavior. They are a co-ordination device that solves the recurrent co-ordination problem of how to greet. The regularity is common ground for the members of those communities. It is also partly arbitrary, for it could have been different; in other communities, two men hug; in still others, two people kiss two, or three, times instead of just once. Hence this regularity is a convention for these communities.

Words in the lexicon have the same six properties. The recurrent problem is how to co-ordinate the speakers' specification of types of entities with the addressees' recognition of these types. How, for example, can speakers and addressees co-ordinate on the speakers' use of a term to denote a domesticated carnivorous mammal, *Canis familiaris*, and their addressees' recognition of the type they are denoting? In the community of English speakers, one solution is to use the word *dog*. Among German, French, and Spanish speakers, a like solution is to use *Hund*, *chien*, and *perro*. So the use of *dog* is a regularity in behavior, partly arbitrary, that is common ground among English speakers as a co-ordination device for the recurrent problem of denoting members of the type *Canus familiaris*. All conventional words are subject to a similar analysis.

Lewis's analysis raises two points that are especially relevant to Whorf's two doctrines. The first is that conventions do not hold for people in general. They each hold only for members of particular communities. If so, it is essential to specify for every convention the communities in which it holds. The second point is that conventions are, at their foundations, ways of solving recurrent co-ordination problems. However, conventions are not the only way of solving co-ordination problems, even recurrent ones. So it is essential to distinguish conventions from other co-ordination devices. These two points, I will argue, raise havoc with linguistic determinism.

4 Whorf and conventions

For Whorf, the lexicon offered compelling evidence for linguistic relativity and linguistic determinism. When a language has words for some categories and not others, he argued, speakers of that language habitually see the world divided into those categories and not others. As he put it:

> We cut nature up, organize it into concepts, and ascribe significances as we do, largely because we are parties to an agreement to organize it in this way – an agreement that holds throughout our speech community and is codified in the patterns of our language. The agreement is, of course, an implicit and unstated one, but *its terms are absolutely obligatory*; we cannot talk at all except by subscribing to the organization and classification of data which the agreement decrees.   (Whorf 1956: 213–14, Whorf's emphasis)

Whorf's "implicit and unstated" agreement that "holds throughout our speech community and is codified in the patterns of our language" is, of course, Lewis's conventional signalling system, a system of conventions. So Whorf's claims were, first, that we cannot talk without subscribing to these conventions (linguistic relativity) and, second, that even when we are not talking, we "cut nature up, organize it into concepts, and ascribe significances as we do" in accordance with these conventions (linguistic determinism).

Whorf was at his rhetorical best in this quotation. His versions of the two doctrines are strong and uncompromising. The doctrines can, of course, be formulated in other terms – stronger or weaker. Still, for many lay readers, Whorf's statement captures what his position was really about. When we can, it is worth taking Whorf at his word.

However, once we view language use as a joint activity, we discover that the two doctrines, in either their strong or their weak form, are not as clear and testable as they appeared to be. I will first take up four problems that come from a close analysis of conventions: communal lexicons, origins of conventions, historical change, and conceptual conventions.

4.1 Problem 1: communal lexicons

What is the lexicon for English? It is common to gather up all the words available to any English speaker from Alaska to Bombay, throw them into a single hopper, and call that the English lexicon. That, of course, is nonsense. Every conventional word meaning, in Lewis's account, holds not for the word *simpliciter*, but for the word *in a particular community*. You cannot talk about conventional word meaning without saying what community it is conventional in.

Word knowledge is properly viewed, then, as dividing into *communal lexicons*, by which I mean sets of word conventions that are taken for granted in individual communities. When I meet June at a party, she and I must establish as common ground which communities we both belong to simply in order to know what English words we can use with each other with what meaning. Can I use *fermata*? Not without establishing that we are both music enthusiasts. Can I use *rbi*? Not without establishing that she and I are both baseball fans. What about *murder*, surely a word that every English speaker knows and agrees on? Even here, I must establish which communal lexicon I am drawing on.

Every community has a specialized lexicon. We recognize the existence of these lexicons in the terms we have for them in English:

for places: regional or local dialect, patois, provincialisms, localisms, regionalisms, colloquialisms, idiom, Americanisms, Californiaisms, etc.;

for occupations or hobbies: jargon, shoptalk, parlance, nomenclature, terminology, academese, legalese, medicalese, Wall Streetese, etc.;

for subcultures: slang, argot, lingo, cant, vernacular, code, etc.

Probably every identifiable region has a distinctive dialect, patois, or idiom with distinctive terms for everything from food to geographical features. Every occupation and hobby, from physics to philately, has its own technical jargon or terminology. And so does every subculture, from drug addicts to high-school cliques.

When we think of jargon, slang, or regionalisms, we tend to focus on the words that are unique to a communal lexicon. *Meson, pion*, and *quark* are terms that only a physicist could love. Yet most common word-forms belong to many communal lexicons – though with different conventional meanings. Examples are common. In Britain, what are called *biscuits* can be sweet or savory, but in America, they are always savory. In common parlance, *fruit* denotes a class of edible, sweet, fleshy agricultural products; among botanists, it denotes the ripened ovary or ovaries of seed-bearing plants, whether or not they are edible, sweet, and fleshy, and that includes tomatoes, pumpkins, and nuts. Two botanists in conversation would have to establish which lexicon they were drawing on. You and I would be forced to stay with common parlance.

Other examples are less obvious. Take the word-form *murder*. The conventional meaning associated with it varies in subtle ways as we go from one communal lexicon to the next. It has slightly different meanings for American, British, and New Zealand lawyers, for example, and for pro-choice advocates, anti-abortionists, army officers, animal rights activists, pacifists, vegetarians, and primary school children. The complication is that most of us belong to more than one community at once and, depending on who we are talking to, appeal to a different conventional meaning. Two lawyers talking about legal matters will take for granted a legal definition, but in talking to an anti-abortionist, pacifist, or army sergeant they will have to negotiate how the word is to be interpreted on that occasion. The collaborative process of grounding I described earlier is designed to handle just this sort of discrepancy.

The conventional meanings for *murder* in all these communal lexicons are related, but they hardly "cut nature up, organize it into concepts, and ascribe significances" in the same way. What is more, the very ways they differ seem part of the fabric of the distinctive beliefs, assumptions, practices, and traditions of these communities. If you and I are both lieutenants in the US army, we subscribe to a vast system of beliefs, assumptions, practices, and traditions that are common ground for everyone in the army. (Even if we do not subscribe to the system, we know the system.) When you and I meet in uniform for the first time, that is the salient common ground against which we expect to co-ordinate. I can only assume that your use of *murder* is consonant with that system – that, for example, killing the enemy in combat is not murder. Change "US army" to "Salvation Army," and not only will our common ground change, but so will the conventional denotation of *murder*. So the conventional use of *murder* in each community reflects its particular system of beliefs, and not vice versa. That violates at least the spirit of linguistic determinism; and examples like *murder* can be multiplied indefinitely.

When Whorf formulated his two doctrines, he was thinking of broad languages and not communal lexicons – of English, Hopi, and Nootka, and not legalese, baseball jargon, or chemical nomenclatures. We may speak loosely of doctors, lawyers, acid rockers, and baseball players as "speaking different languages," but for Whorf this is surely only a figure of speech. To test Whorf's version of linguistic determinism, we would need to identify a specifically English-language lexicon – a lexicon for the community of English speakers that is separate from all other communal lexicons. Is there such a lexicon? Do we ever classify our interlocutors merely as English speakers? I suggest that we do not. We see them at least as adults or children, as educated or uneducated, as speakers of American or Filipino English, as members of other communities. If so, it will be difficult to distinguish entries in the English language lexicon from those in other communal lexicons. It may ultimately be impossible.

4.2 Problem 2: origins of conventions

Conventions do not come out of the blue. They evolve and become entrenched within a community, in Lewis's view, precisely because they are effective co-ordination devices for the people they serve. A co-ordination device is effective in a community only if it is both useful and usable in that community. To be *useful*, it must be a solution to a recurrent co-ordination problem that is important for a broad segment of the community. Driving on the right solves a widely applicable co-ordination problem; driving with one's hat on does not. To be *usable*, the co-ordination device must have two properties. Members of the community must find the regularity in behavior easy to represent and reproduce; how to shake hands is probably easier to remember and reproduce than how to perform a complicated pattern of finger touchings. Also, they must be able to recognize and represent the recurrent co-ordination problem for which it is a solution; it is probably easier to recognize when to use *dog* than when to use *dalmatian*. In a lexicon, a word is more usable to a community (a) the simpler its form given the other words in that lexicon, and (b) the more applicable its meaning for the community.

The content of communal lexicons, then, is no accident. There is a good reason why *dog*, *potato*, and *tree* evolved in the greater community of English speakers, but *embolism*, *thrombosis*, and *rhinitis* evolved only among physicians, *fly out*, *infield*, and *rbi* only among baseball aficionados, and *staccato*, *fugue*, and *fermata* only among musicians. *Dog*, *potato*, and *tree* were both useful and usable to most English speakers, whereas *embolism*, *rbi*, and *fermata* were useful and usable only in the more specialized communities. Words evolve in a community in direct response to their usefulness and usability in that community, and not vice versa.

What, then, about differences between languages? According to Berlin & Kay (1969), the Dugum Dani of New Guinea have only two basic color terms (for light and dark), whereas Mandarin speakers have six (for black, white, red, green, yellow, and blue) and English speakers eleven (also, brown, purple, pink, orange, grey). Now, by linguistic determinism, English speakers should have eleven "thoughts" when they contemplate colors, whereas Mandarin speakers should have only six and the Dani two. Yet if conventions evolve in response to their usefulness and usability in a community, all that these differences show is that the Dani have not found color terms useful or usable enough for co-ordination in talk in their culture to have evolved more than the two. The communities in which Mandarin and English are spoken have. Otherwise, Dani, Mandarin, and English speakers should see colors in the same way. Indeed, two colors that are similar for English speakers are just as similar for the Dani (Heider 1972, Heider & Olivier 1972; see also Kay & Kempton 1984).

The idea that terminology evolves to reflect the culture is hardly new. Berlin & Kay argued that the greater the "general cultural complexity (and/or level of technological development)," the more elaborate the color lexicon. Brown (1977, 1979) argued much the same thing in accounting for the number of so-called life forms found in a language's botanical lexicon (tree, grass, bush, vine, herbs) and zoological lexicon (bird, fish, snake, worm, bug, mammal).

4.3 Problem 3: historical change

If conventions arise only when they are useful and usable in a community, they should also disappear when they are not. That has been demonstrated again and again in studies of historical change: as a culture changes, lexical conventions change to reflect it.

Take an example of Berlin's (1972). When the Spanish arrived in Mexico in the sixteenth century, they brought along sheep, chickens, and pigs, animals unknown to the Tenejapa Tzeltal in Chiapas. However, the Tzeltal knew about deer, or *čih*, for example, so they called sheep *tunim čih*, literally 'cotton deer.' Over the centuries, as sheep became an important livestock for the Tzeltals, it was for sheep, not deer, that they needed the briefest co-ordination device. As a result, the bare term *čih* came to denote sheep, and deer were referred to with the marked term *te?tikil čih*, or 'wild sheep.' So as the relative importance of sheep and deer changed, *čih* changed from meaning 'deer' to meaning 'sheep';

likewise, the pre-Conquest words for bird and wild pig changed to mean 'chicken' and 'pig.' Analogous historical changes happened in other native American languages (Witkowski & Brown 1983) . In various communities, the word for tapir changed to 'horse,' peccary to 'pig,' opossum to 'pig,' dog to 'horse,' caribou to 'horse,' bison to 'cattle,' arrowhead to 'bullet,' and bow to 'gun.' Closer to home, British English *carriage*, which once meant 'large horse-drawn vehicle' and contrasted with *horseless carriage*, now means 'railway car' and contrasts with *horse-drawn carriage*.

Modern languages are filled with words whose lexical conventions moved out from under them. *Lady* once meant 'kneader of bread,' and *buxom*, 'obedient, yielding.' Books on historical linguistics are full of examples (e.g. Waldron 1967). Modern languages are also filled with words invented to handle new cultural phenomena – from *boycott* and *sabotage* to *radio* and *stereo* – just as are more specialized communal lexicons. Most changes in word meaning have been in response to cultural changes – new commodities (sheep, automobiles), an invading language (as with the Norman invasion of Britain), spreading expertise (terms like *ego* from psychoanalytic theory), and so on. Few modern word-forms have the same conventional meanings they did 500, or even 100, years ago.

Often, the brute morphological analysis of a word tells us more about its history than what it means now. At one time, whales were thought to be a type of fish, and that is reflected in Dutch and German, where they were called 'whalefish' – *walvis* and *Walfisch*. Over time, beliefs about whales changed, and the terms *walvis* and *Walfisch* now denote a type of mammal despite their morphological insistence to the contrary. In medieval physiology, people's character was thought to be determined by a dominant humor, and that led to such terms as *humorous, sanguine, phlegmatic, choleric, melancholy, in a good humor*, and *in a bad humor*. In modern times, we retain the terms, but without subscribing to, or even knowing about, the theories that gave rise to them. Examples of this type can be multiplied indefinitely.

The generalization, then, is that, as a community's beliefs, assumptions, concepts, and practices change, so its lexicon changes to reflect them. Whorf's strong form of linguistic determinism does not sit well with this generalization. If "we cut nature up, organize it into concepts, and ascribe significances as we do" because of the conventions of language, and if "its terms are absolutely obligatory," then a language should not change in response to a change in a community's system of beliefs. It should continue to dictate the way that community cuts nature up. This version of linguistic determinism is obviously untenable. But the generalization weakens any version of linguistic determinism. If linguistic determinism has any force historically, we should find examples of beliefs *failing* to change over time because of the conventions that exist in the language. Such examples do not come readily to mind.

4.4 Problem 4: conceptual conventions

Some of the most compelling arguments for linguistic relativity and determinism are made by comparing two languages for words of the same conceptual domain. Take English *trousers* and the equivalent Dutch *broek*. In English, *trousers* and its near relatives are plural: *pants, trousers, breeches, shorts, panties, longjohns, dungarees*, and so on. In Dutch, *broek* and its near relatives are singular. The same plural–singular contrast is found in the terms related to English *glasses* vs. Dutch *bril*, and those related to English *scissors* vs. Dutch *schaar*.[7] If language determines thought, these differences should *cause* English and Dutch speakers to think differently about trousers, glasses, and scissors. Indeed, there is good evidence that English and Dutch speakers do think differently about these objects – at least for purposes of communication.

(a) *Pairs*. Not only do English speakers use *pants, glasses*, and *scissors* in the plural, but they speak of *pairs* of pants, glasses, and scissors. They think of these objects as coming in pairs – a conception I will call "pairings." Dutch speakers. in contrast, use *broek, bril*, and *schaar* in the singular and never talk about *pairs* of pants, glasses, or scissors. Their conception I will call a "singleton."

(b) *Demonstrative pronouns*. When English speakers refer to a single pair of pants, glasses, or scissors, they can use the bare *those*. In the same situation, Dutch speakers use the bare *that*. This is consistent with English speakers' thoughts of pairings, and Dutch speakers' thoughts of singletons.

(c) *Coinages*. When new terms for these objects are introduced into English and Dutch, they are made to conform to the contrasting concepts of these objects. When *jeans, Levis*, and *tights* came into English, they were treated as plural, and their referents were conceived of as coming in pairs. In contrast, when the English word *hotpants* was introduced into Dutch, it was treated as singular despite its plural use in English to denote pairs.

(d) *Entrenchment*. These concepts are deeply entrenched in the culture. US clothing merchants have occasionally tried to slip *a pant*, *a slack*, and *a jean* into clothing advertisements, but to no avail. Here is a letter to Lands' End about their clothing catalogue: "As a somewhat loyal Lands' End customer, I must protest your use of the singular form of the word for denim casual pants. There is no such word as 'jean.' When you get up in the morning, do you put on your pant? Or slack? And under that, do you wear your brief? Or short? Do you cut with a scissor? Do you sing the blue? No – and you don't wear a jean either. The word is jeans – plural – even if you're referring to only one. (Signed)"

Here, then, is a compelling case for linguistic determinism – as compelling as one finds. English and Dutch words for pants, glasses, and scissors contrast in number, and English and Dutch speakers' conceptions for these objects seem to differ in response. Even this case, however, is open to a competing account.

Conventions cover many types of regularities in behavior. Some govern the co-ordination of *practices* such as placing silverware on tables and locating hot and cold water faucets in sinks. Others govern the co-ordination of *actions* such as shaking hands and passing through doors; and so on. In communication, we must distinguish between conventions that govern the co-ordination of word use *per se* (lexical conventions) and conventions that govern the co-ordination of our conceptions of things (conceptual conventions). The distinction is important because conceptual conventions can determine language use without being conventions of language *per se*.

Consider the numbering of floors in buildings. In most of Europe, the floor at ground level is the ground floor, and the floor above that is the first floor. In the US and Canada, the floor at ground level is the first floor. The floors above the first floor are numbered the same way in both systems. It is tempting to say that *first*, *floor*, or *first floor* therefore differ in meaning between British and American English, but that is surely not the right description. Floor numbering is a property not of languages (e.g. American or British English, French, or Polish), but of communities (e.g. North Americans and Europeans).

Floor numbering is what I will call a *conceptual convention*. It is the convention people in a community subscribe to in counting floors. It is a convention because it is a co-ordination device, partly arbitrary, for solving the recurrent co-ordination problem of how to number floors. It also happens to be a convention that does not depend on the language spoken. Travelers take the European system for granted when they are in Europe, and the North American system when they are in the US, no matter what language they are speaking. These two systems provide people with highly salient co-ordination devices for talking about floor numbers. They determine how we talk about floors without being part of the languages *per se*.

Conceptual conventions are ubiquitous. Many are linked to cultural practices. In Britain, small businesses are named for the person running them – the butcher's shop, the grocer's, the greengrocer's, the ironmonger's, etc. In North America, they tend to be named for the product sold – the meat market, the grocery store, the fruit market, the fish market, etc. Same language, but different conceptual conventions for thinking about such businesses. In Britain vs. the rest of Europe (and America), differences in the way cars are manufactured and driven lead to different conceptual conventions of "passenger seat," "driver's side," "across the traffic," etc. In some English-speaking communities, boats above a certain size are conventionally viewed as female and are referred to as *she*. In other communities, the same goes for cars.

The problem is that many lexical conventions are difficult, if not impossible, to distinguish from conceptual conventions. Consider two accounts for trousers, glasses, and scissors. First, a *lexical* account claims that there is a lexical convention in English that *trousers*, *glasses*, and *scissors* denote pairings, and in Dutch that *broek*, *bril*, and *schaar* denote singletons. Second, a *conceptual* account claims that there is a conceptual convention in most English-speaking communities that trousers, glasses, and scissors are pairings, and in most Dutch-speaking communities that they are singletons. Which account is to be preferred, or do the two accounts come to the same thing?

The lexical account comes in at least two versions. In the first version I will consider, the word forms for pants, glasses, and scissors are specified morphologically as [+pl] in English and [+sg] in Dutch, just as the words for sun and moon are [+masc] and [+fem] in French, but the reverse in German. That is, the contrast between English and Dutch is in the *morphological* feature of number, and otherwise the assignment is arbitrary, unmotivated, accidental. This version of the lexical account, however, fails to explain several essential phenomena.

Uniformity of treatment. In German, clothing terms may be [+masc], [+fem], or [+neut]; for example, the words for pants and shirt, *die Hose* and *das Hemd*, are [+fem] and [+neut]. In French, these terms vary not only in morphological gender (*le pantalon* is [+masc] and *la chemise* [+fem]), but also in morphological number (*le pantalon* is [+sg] and *les blue-jeans* [+pl]). In contrast, the terms for pants, glasses, and scissors in English are all [+pl] and in Dutch they are all [+sg]. Moreover, when new words are coined in these domains – such as *briefs*, *shades*, and *nippers* – in English they are always [+pl] and in Dutch [+sg]. Nothing in this version of the lexical account explains this uniformity.

Pairings. Nor does anything in this version require *pants, glasses,* or *scissors* and their close relatives to denote pairings.

Pronoun morphology. In German and French, anaphoric and demonstrative pronouns ordinarily take the morphological gender and number of the nouns that would be used for their referents. In German, you would point at a pair of pants and say *die* [+fem], to agree with *die*

Hose, and in French, *celui-là* [+ masc], to agree with *le pantalon*. Point at a shirt instead, and you would say *das* [+neut], to agree with *das Hemd*, and *celle-là* [+fem], to agree with *la chemise*. Or point at a pair of jeans, and you would say *die* [+pl], to agree with *Jeans*, and *ceux-là* [+pl +masc], to agree with *les blue-jeans*.

Yet whenever an object has a natural gender that conflicts with its name's morphological gender, speakers generally engineer utterances to get the morphology to agree with natural gender. So in German, one might say *Das Mädchen hat sein Geld verloren, und darüber ist sie sehr böse* – that is, 'The girl [+neut] lost *its* money, and *she* is very angry about it.' Although *sein* ('its') agrees with *Mädchen* in morphological gender, *sie* ('she') matches the referent in natural gender. Indeed, you could point at a pair of pants and say *das* [+neut], to agree with the natural gender of the pants. In French, one might say *Le professeur, elle est excellente* – that is, 'The professor [+masc], she [+fem] is excellent [+fem].' If you point at the same professor, you could say *Celle-là est excellente* – that is, 'That one [+fem] is excellent [+fem].' The crucial evidence here is that in English, the number associated with pants, glasses, and scissors behaves like natural and not morphological plural. Speakers use *they*, *these*, and *those* in referring to a single pair of pants, glasses, or scissors both anaphorically and deictically. The plurality associated with *pants*, *glasses*, and *scissors* is not morphological. The first version of the lexical account is not enough.

In the second version, the lexical conventions specify, instead, that *pants*, *glasses*, and *scissors* denote pairings, and that *broek*, *bril*, and *schaar* denote singletons. This version solves several problems. It says that *pants*, *glasses*, and *scissors* are plural because their referents are plural objects – pairings – and that *broek*, *bril*, and *schaar* are singular because their referents are singletons. The version also accounts for agreement with natural number in the pronouns of English and Dutch. At first glance, it seems to solve all the problems.

However, there is still the issue of uniformity: why should all the nouns in the domains of pants, glasses, and scissors denote pairings? In principle, *jeans*, *spectacles*, and *shears* could denote pairings at the same time that *brief*, *goggle*, and *plier* denoted singletons. Yet that isn't how it works. The convention we need must capture more than the concepts of single words. It must apply to entire domains. What is most telling is that it must apply even to objects that do not yet have names. "What are those called?" I would ask a welder of something that looked like goggles, not "What is that called?" Conceptual conventions have precisely these properties. They offer a natural way of accounting for all these phenomena.

Most conventions are deeply entrenched because they are part of a larger system of conventions. That is why Lewis's conventional signalling systems (e.g. English or Dutch) are so stable. Their constituent conventions – for example, their lexical conventions – are so tightly interlinked that a community cannot change one without changing many others. Conceptual conventions are no different. Indeed, the conceptual convention of pairing in the domains of trousers, glasses, and scissors is maintained in part by its link to the consistent use of the plural and to the word *pair*. However, ultimately it is maintained by our need to co-ordinate in talking about these objects and others like them.

The argument, then, is this. Among most English speakers, there is a conceptual convention that trousers-, glasses-, and scissors-like objects are to be viewed as pairings. That, in turn, leads English speakers (a) to denote them with plural nouns; (b) to speak of *pairs* of trousers, glasses, and scissors; (c) to coin new words also as denoting pairings; (d) to use the pronouns, *they*, *these*, and *those* in referring to a single pair – even when they have no names for them. The conceptual convention is needed to account for their uniformity of treatment beyond the specific words already in the domain.

Conceptual conventions seem to be part and parcel of the expertise of specialized communities. In every medical community, there is a body of unwritten conventions about how to view diseases, cures, the human body, and medical practice. These conventions differ across the communities of standard physicians, chiropractors, holistic physicians, faith healers, and shamans and help determine the uses of a vast family of medical terms such as *disease*, *pain*, *sick*, and *cure*. It is the acquisition of these conventions, in part, that makes a person a member of these communities. With conceptual conventions, we have come full circle to the primacy of communities and their common ground.

5 Whorf and nonconventional co-ordination

Almost anything can serve as a co-ordination device – conventions are only one type. Yet when students of language investigate language use, they tend to focus on the conventional and ignore the nonconventional. Whorf was a good example. For him, the conventions of a language constituted "an implicit and unstated" agreement: "*its terms are absolutely obligatory*; we cannot talk at all except by subscribing to the organization and classification of data which the agreement decrees." Yet nonconventional devices are also essential to language use. Their use is absolutely obligatory. We cannot talk at all except by subscribing to the organization and classification of data that they decree. The problem for Whorf's two doctrines is that nonconventional devices are not part of language as a system – part of Whorf's agreement – precisely because they are not conventional.

Nonconventional co-ordination in language use raises further problems for the interpretation and application of linguistic relativity and iinguistic determinism. Here I will consider three interrelated problems: nonconventional co-ordination devices, semantic indeterminacy, and conceptual creativity.

5.1 Problem 5: nonconventional co-ordination devices

Nonconventional co-ordination devices have regularities of use too. That makes them easy to confuse with conventional devices – especially linguistic conventions. However, these regularities do not fall under the jurisdiction of linguistic relativity or linguistic determinism. They cannot be appealed to as evidence for or against these doctrines.

Suppose I tell a friend, "In the drugstore today I noticed another interesting Gumperz phenomenon." What did I mean by *Gumperz phenomenon*? It is a novel compound, so I cannot be relying on a convention. I expect my friend to consult our common ground and, as in any first-party Schelling game, find the most salient interpretation. What interpretation that is depends on the Gumperzes we know in common, the information we share about them, the drugstore I was referring to, and on and on. Suppose I actually meant "the phenomenon of misunderstanding between people of different social groups, as described by John Gumperz." This interpretation might possibly be classified as an instance of the general pattern "phenomenon *from* Gumperz" or "noun2 from noun1." If we look at enough of these compounds, we might conclude, as Lees (1960), Levi (1978), and Li (1971) all have done, that they form a small number of patterns that cover all possible English noun compounds. In Levi's analysis, there are exactly twelve such patterns. The rules of compound formation allow these and no others. For her, the pattern "noun2 from noun1" is a convention of English noun compounds.

Yet there *are* no such conventions of English. First, the relations in noun compounds such as *Gumperz phenomenon* can in principle be anything people can think of (Downing 1977, Gerrig & Murphy 1992, Gleitman & Gleitman 1970, Jespersen 1942), and that is true for many other so-called contextual constructions as well (E. V. Clark & Clark 1979, H. H. Clark 1983, Kay & Zimmer 1976). Second, the relation "noun2 from noun1" is a regularity at only one level of abstraction. Levi could just as well have abstracted over a more specific set of relations and arrived at "noun2 described by noun1" or "noun2 of language use described by noun1." Levi's twelve types are at an arbitrary level of abstraction. There are an infinity of levels she could have chosen. Third, it is easy to find novel noun compounds that do not fit Levi's categories.

In one study (Coolen, Van Jaarsveld, & Schreuder 1991), trained judges disagreed about 40 percent of the time in trying to fit novel compounds into Levi's categories.[8]

What are Levi's regularities regularities of? I suggest they are really regularities in what people have used noun compounds to talk about. They give a statistical picture of the relations people (a) can think of and (b) want to denote in typical communicative circumstances. They inventory the relations people tend to find salient in common ground as they talk, where these are conceptual relations independent of language *per se*. When we think about the relations that might hold between a dog and a sled, we may think first of dogs pulling sleds (the relation that arises in *sleddog* and *dogsled*). Yet in the right circumstances, we may also think of dogs chewing on, riding on, running after, being transported by, being obsessed by, or being transmogrified into sleds. The last few relations may be rare, but they are perfectly usable in the right circumstances.

If Levi's categories are really a statistical inventory of common regularities, they ought to hold in other areas of language where these relations might appear, and they do. Her relations are also the ones E. V. Clark & Clark (1979) found commonest in a large sample of conventional and novel denominal verbs. So in *They milked the cow*, the abstract relation between cow and milk is "noun2 from noun1," the Levi category I appealed to earlier. We took these to be statistically common regularities, not conventional relations, and gave many arguments for thinking so. Many of these relations are also common in denominal adjectives (like *milky*) and denominal nouns (like *dogger*).

Compounds like *Gumperz phenomenon* are hardly the only constructions that depend on nonconventional co-ordination devices. Here is just a partial list of such constructions with an example of each:

1. Indirect nouns: "He plays jazz *piano*?"
2. Compound nouns: "I noticed another *Gumperz phenomenon*."
3. Possessives: "Here comes *my* bus."
4. Denominal nouns: "He's a *dogger*."
5. Denominal verbs: "He managed to *porch* the newspaper today."
6. Eponymous nominals: "The photographer asked me to do a *Napoleon* for the camera."
7. Pro-act verb *do*: "Alice *did* the lawn."
8. Denominal adjectives: "He held a *Churchillian* pose."
9. Non-predicating adjectives: "I have an *electric* knife."
10. Eponymous adjectives: "She's very *San Francisco*."   (H. H. Clark 1983)

Nonconventional co-ordination devices, I suspect, play a much greater role in everyday language use than standard models of semantics would lead us to think.

The lesson is that many regularities in language use are only statistical regularities associated with people in communities. They are a combination of (a) possible human conceptions, (b) possible salient conceptions for use in Schelling games, and (c) recurrent community interests. Although (a) may be universal, (b) and (c) vary with personal and communal common ground. These factors determine aspects of language use without being part of language *per se*. There are many aspects of word use that lexicographers, linguists, psychologists, anthropologists, and others assume are conventional. It is an open question how many of these aspects will turn out to be mere statistical regularities. The argument has to be made word by word.

5.2 Problem 6: semantic indeterminacy

Even if conventional words cut nature up into categories, as Whorf claimed, many of these categories are semantically indeterminate. Take the adjective *muddy*. The dictionary defines it as "covered, full of, or spattered with mud." Yet when I use it on a particular occasion, I always mean something much more specific. If I tell you "My shoes are muddy," I don't just mean they are "covered, full of, or spattered with mud." Depending on the situation, I may mean there is mud on the soles, or on the leather surface; I am unlikely to mean they are "full of mud." There is an entirely different range of salient occasion meanings for *muddy* in *muddy water* (e.g., water with mud dissolved in it), *muddy road* (e.g., road with a surface of mud), *muddy windshield* (e.g., windshield with mud on the outside surface), and *muddy floor* (e.g., floor with mud patches on it). The category we cut the world into when I tell you "My shoes are muddy" is particular and only indeterminately specified by the conventional meaning of *muddy*.

What words like *muddy* mean on each occasion is really a combination of (a) conventional meaning and (b) nonconventional co-ordination devices. With "My shoes are muddy," I am presenting you with a first-person Schelling game about the specific category of muddiness I intend. I expect you to see the salient way in which mud could be "had" by shoes, and that is to be adhering to their soles. It is related to shoes in the way we would mutually expect it to be on this occasion.

Examples like this pose two problems for the two Whorfian doctrines. One is that it is difficult, empirically, to separate lexical conventions from systematic but nonconventional co-ordination devices. We are tempted to give *muddy* different conventional meanings corresponding to the ways in which it modifies *shoes*, *water*, *road*, *windshield*, and *floor*. Indeed, the dictionary definition ("covered, full of, or spattered with mud") is better viewed as a list of the most common occasion meanings, typical exemplars, than as a list of conventional senses. If I am right, *muddy* has only a general conventional meaning, which gets particularized on each occasion through a first-party Schelling game and through collaboration. How many of Whorf's lexical concepts are nonconventional particularizations instead of true conventional meanings? That is hard to know without looking at the vocabulary word by word.

The second problem is that if words like *muddy* have such a nonspecific conventional meaning, the categories they cut nature into, the concepts and significances they determine, are broad and diffuse. For these words, linguistic relativity and linguistic determinism are of little consequence. The more pervasive semantic indeterminacy is, the less consequence they have.

5.3 Problem 7: conceptual creativity

One standard view of cognition holds that, by the time we are adults, we have a large stock of ready-made concepts, like "apple" and "gun" and "crawling," and that we draw on these in interpreting the world around us. It also holds that the most basic of these concepts correspond to the words in our language, words like *apple*, *gun*, and *crawl*. This seems to have been Whorf's view, as it seems to be required both for linguistic relativism and linguistic determinism. Yet this view has many problems. The most important for us here is its lack of imagination – its incapacity for conceptual creativity.

We are deft at creating new concepts on the fly. We do that every time we interpret complex expressions such as *things that could fall on your head* or *ways to make friends* or *things to inventory in a department store*. Although we may never have thought of the categories denoted by these phrases before, we have no trouble creating the right concepts on the spot. These are what Lawrence Barsalou (1983) called *ad hoc categories*, and they pop up everywhere in daily life, both in and out of language use. What is remarkable, as Barsalou showed, is that they have many of the same properties as ready-made categories like "fruit" and "furniture." In particular, they have the same graded structures. For "fruit," we consider apples and oranges to be typical instances, and raisins and pomegranates atypical. Likewise, for "things that could fall on your head," we take apples and flower pots to be typical instances, and dogs and radios atypical. And there are other properties correlated with this graded structure.

In language use, I suggest, we create concepts for *ad hoc* categories for almost every predication we meet, whether the predication is made with a phrase like *things that could fall on your head* or a single word like *fruit*. Suppose I tell you, "Down at the beach the other day, I saw a great number of birds." Just what am I predicating I saw a great number of?

Certainly not birds pure and simple. The prototypical instances of that category are robins and sparrows (see, e.g., Rosch, Gray, Johnson, & Boyes-Braem 1976), whereas the prototypical instances of the category of thing you would infer I saw were gulls and sandpipers – and even that would depend on which beach you understood me to be referring to. I used the bare noun *bird*, and yet I intended you to create a concept for an *ad hoc* category something like "bird I would be likely to see at that beach." You would be mistaken in thinking that the prototypical entities I had in mind were robins and sparrows. I presented you with a first-party Schelling game, and the category I denoted with *bird* was that *ad hoc* category that was most salient given our current common ground. Change "down at the beach" to "up in the mountains" and the category I denoted by *bird* would change enormously.

So the way "we cut nature up, organize it into concepts, and ascribe significances" for the bare noun *bird* changes from one use to the next – sometimes radically. The conventional meaning for *bird* plays only one part in the process. This poses a problem for linguistic relativity and linguistic determinism. In Whorf's view, my use of *bird* leads you to call forth, in an "absolutely obligatory" process, a ready-made concept of birds, pure and simple. Yet if it leads you each time to create a novel concept for an *ad hoc* category, the absolutely obligatory link between language and thought is broken, and much of the potential influence of language on thought is thrown into doubt.

6 Conclusions

The argument I have presented has taken many steps. Language use between two people, Anne and Burton, depends fundamentally on them co-ordinating what Anne means with what Burton takes her to mean. They co-ordinate by means of co-ordination devices, and these devices must be part of their common ground – communal or personal. More than that, they collaborate moment by moment, making opportunistic use of that common ground. Now the Whorfian doctrines of linguistic relativity and linguistic determinism are really claims about the conventional parts of a language. The first problem is that in the lexicon it is difficult to know which conventional aspects belong to the language as such and which do not. The second is that conventions are only one means by which Anne and Burton co-ordinate.

The first problem is inherent in the notion of convention. Conventions are co-ordination devices that hold only for particular communities. For any word meaning, we must ask "In which community is this a convention?" Many word meanings, perhaps most, hold not for all speakers of a language *per se*, but only for communities defined by other cultural characteristics – and there are many of these. And the word meanings that evolve in a community evolve in response to their usefulness and usability in that particular community – in line with its members' common beliefs, assumptions, practices, and traditions.

The second problem is that many regularities of language use are easy to mistake for conventions of language. Some regularities, like the numbering of floors, are conventions, not of language, but of a community's way of conceiving things. Other regularities, like the relations in noun compounds, are statistical summaries of the community interests that typically arise when people talk. Many conventional meanings, like *muddy*, are also highly indeterminate, and what they are actually taken to denote is created *ad hoc* on the fly. Many regularities in word use come not from conventional meanings, but from the momentary non-linguistic co-ordination devices that are exploited in their use.

What about linguistic relativity and linguistic determinism? The arguments here suggest a greatly expanded and more detailed version of linguistic relativity. Language use varies not merely by major language communities – English vs. Hopi – but by any cultural community that corresponds to people's social identities – from plumber or San Franciscan to university graduate or baseball aficionado. At the same time, the arguments here weaken or limit linguistic determinism. Yes, people who speak differently think differently, but much of the correspondence comes from the common beliefs, assumptions, practices, and traditions in the communities to which they belong. There can be no communication without commonalities of thought. But there can be thought, even commonalities of thought, without communication.

Notes

1 The argument here is drawn from E. V. Clark & H. H. Clark (1979), H. H. Clark (1983), H. H. Clark & Gerrig (1983), but most directly from H. H. Clark, Schreuder, & Buttrick (1983).
2 Levinson (1990) has independently proposed a similar analysis.
3 From the London–Lund corpus of English conversation (Svartvik & Quirk 1980). I retain the following symbols from the London–Lund notation: "." for a brief pause (of one light syllable); "-" for a unit pause (of one stress unit or foot); ":" for a lengthened vowel; and asterisks for paired instances of simultaneous talk (e.g., *yes*).
4 See H. H. Clark & Wilkes-Gibbs (1986), H. H. Clark & Schaefer (1989), and H. H. Clark & Brennan (1991).
5 You can substitute the term *cultural group*, *cultural network*, or *cultural system* if you don't like the term *cultural community*, but it should be defined as I am defining it here.
6 This simplifies Lewis's formulation and terminology but retains the heart of his account. See Lewis for the full story.

7 Here is a partial list of trouser words in English: *trousers, pants, breeches, slacks, jeans, levis, blue jeans, denims, dungarees, jodhpurs, overalls, pyjamas, pedal-pushers, plus-fours, trunks, shorts, bermuda shorts, hotpants, tights, longjohns, boxer shorts, briefs, panties, knickers, bloomers.* A partial list of glasses words: *glasses, eyeglasses, spectacles, goggles, binoculars, readers, bifocals, sunglasses, shades.* And a partial list of scissor words: *scissors, shears, snippers, secateurs, tweezers, dividers, calipers, forceps, clippers, nippers, pliers, snips, wirecutters.*

8 In fact, *Gumperz phenomenon* does not fit at all comfortably into Levi's "noun2 from noun1" (the closest of her categories), which she illustrates with such compounds as *olive oil*, i.e., "oil from olives."

References

Barsalou, L. W. 1983. Ad hoc categories. *Memory and Cognition*, 11, 211–27.

Berlin, B. 1972. Speculations on the growth of ethnobotanical nomenclature. *Language in Society*, 1, 51–86.

Berlin, B. & Kay, P. 1969. *Basic color terms: their universality and evolution*. Berkeley & Los Angeles: University of California Press.

Brown, C. H. 1977. Folk botanical life-forms: their universality and growth. *American Anthropologist*, 79, 317–42.

1979. Folk zoological life-forms: their universality and growth. *American Anthropologist*, 81, 791–817.

Clark, E. V. & Clark, H. H. 1979. When nouns surface as verbs. *Language*, 55, 797–811.

Clark, H. H. 1983. Making sense of nonce sense. In G. B. Flores d'Arcais & R. J. Jarvella (eds.), *The process of language understanding* (pp. 297–332). Wiley: New York.

Clark, H. H. & Brennan, S. E. 1991. Grounding in communication. In L. B. Resnick, J. M. Levine, & S. D. Teasley (eds.), *Perspectives on socially shared cognition* (pp. 127–49). Washington, DC: American Psychological Association.

Clark, H. H. & Gerrig, R. J. 1983. Understanding old words with new meanings. *Journal of Verbal Learning and Verbal Behavior*, 22, 591–608.

Clark, H. H. & Marshall, C. R. 1981. Definite reference and mutual knowledge. In A. K. Joshi, B. Webber, & I. A. Sag (eds.), *Elements of discourse understanding* (pp. 10–63). Cambridge University Press.

Clark, H. H. & Schaefer, E. R. 1989. Contributing to discourse. *Cognitive Science*, 13, 259–94.

Clark, H. H. & Wilkes-Gibbs, D. 1986. Referring as a collaborative process. *Cognition*, 22(1), 1–39.

Clark, H. H., Schreuder, R. & Buttrick, S. 1983. Common ground and the understanding of demonstratives. *Journal of Verbal Learning and Verbal Behavior*, 22, 245–58.

Coolen, R., van Jaarsveld, H. J., & Schreuder, R. 1991. The interpretation of isolated novel nominal compounds. *Memory and Cognition*, 19, 341–52.

Downing, P. A. 1977. On the creation and use of English compound nouns. *Language*, 53, 810–42.

Gerrig, R. J. & Murphy, G. L. 1992. Contextual influences on the comprehension of complex concepts. *Language and Cognitive Processes*, 7(3/4), 205–30.

Gleitman, L. R. & Gleitman, H. 1970. *Phrase and paraphrase some innovative users of language*. New York: W. W. Norton.

Heider, E. R. 1972. Universals of color naming and memory. *Journal of Experimental Psychology*, 93, 10–20.

Heider, E. R. & Olivier, D. 1972. The structure of the color space in naming and memory for two languages. *Cognitive Psychology*, 3, 337–54.

Isaacs, E. A. & Clark, H. H. 1987. References in conversation between experts and novices. *Journal of Experimental Psychology: General*, 16, 26–37.

Jespersen, O. 1942. *A modern English grammar on historical principles*, vol VII: *Morphology*. Copenhagen: Ejnar Munksgaard.

Kay, P. & Kempton, W. 1984. What is the Sapir–Whorf hypothesis? *American Anthropologist*, 86, 65–79.

Kay, P. & Zimmer, K. 1976. On the semantics of compounds and genitives in English. Paper presented at the Sixth Annual Meeting of the California Linguistics Association, San Diego, California, May 1976.

Krauss, R. M. & Glucksberg, S. 1977. Social and non-social speech. *Scientific American*, 236, 100–5.

Lees, R. B. 1960. The grammar of English nominalizations. *International Journal of American Linguistics*, 26, Publication 12.

Levi, J. N. 1978. *The syntax and semantics of complex nominals*. New York: Academic Press.

Levinson, S. C. 1995. Interactional biases in human thinking. In E. Goody (ed.), *Social intelligence and interaction* (pp. 221–59). Cambridge University Press.

Lewis, D. 1969. *Convention: a philosophical study*. Cambridge, MA: Harvard University Press.

Li, C. N. 1971. Semantics and the structure of compounds in Chinese. Unpublished doctoral dissertation. Berkeley: University of California.

Rosch, E., Mervis, C., Gray, W., Johnson, D., & Boyes-Braem, P. 1976. Basic objects in natural categories. *Cognitive Psychology*, 8, 382–439.

Schegloff, E. A. 1972. Notes on a conversational practice: formulating place. In D. Sudnow (ed.), *Studies in social interaction* (pp. 75–119). New York: Free Press.

Schelling, T. 1960. *The strategy of conflict*. Cambridge, MA: MIT Press.

Schiffer, S. R. 1972. *Meaning*. Oxford: Basil Blackwell.

Svartvik, J., & Quirk, R. 1980. *A corpus of English conversation*. Lund, Sweden: Gleerup.

Waldron, R. A. 1967. *Sense and sense development* (2nd. edn.). London: Deutsch.

Whorf, B. L. 1956. *Language, thought, and reality: selected writings of Benjamin Lee Whorf*, ed. J. B. Carroll. Cambridge, MA: MIT Press.

Witkowski, S. R. & Brown, C. H. 1983. Marking-reversals and cultural importance. *Language*, 59, 569–82.

PART IV

THE SOCIAL MATRIX: CULTURE, PRAXIS, AND DISCOURSE

INTRODUCTION TO PART IV

JOHN J. GUMPERZ

The chapters in the preceding section explore the idea that meaning and reference are relativized to context, in large part through the mechanism of deixis. Thus we may say the same words but refer to different states of affairs. Understanding what someone says depends on construing the context in the same way and applying the same complex interpretive principles that link context and interpretation. If indexicality were a marginal feature of language, this relativity of interpretation would hardly shake the core of common understandings; but as the preceding chapters make clear, the phenomenon is rampant and moreover the principles are complex enough to be variably applied in many different ways. The chapter by Clark in the preceding section is an important bridge to the issues in the present section: he claims that the phenomena are not restricted to indexicals or deictic expressions, but hold for any expressions whatsoever: we have to agree on what we will mean by the use of specific words, and we do this by building (or building on) a tradition of use in our social networks.

So far then, these views seem to establish in a straightforward way a relativity of meaning broadly construed: meanings are relative to contexts, and context and principles of interpretation (or at least applications of them) are relative to shared networks (or communities, in Clark's sense). To put the matter in another way: differences in the use of language imply differences in meaning or interpretation. However, terms like use and function are construed in many different ways by different theorists. Lucy (this volume) covers one line of work that builds on Roman Jakobson's (1960) typology of semiotic functions. The chapters in this section are more directly concerned with function thought of in terms of on-line interpretations. They take a somewhat eclectic approach that combines elements of the conversational analysts' approach to the sequential organization of speech exchanges (Atkinson & Heritage 1986) with the linguistic philosophers' notion of implicature (Grice 1990) and the more recent semiotic functional approaches to metapragmatics (Silverstein 1976, 1992, 1993, Urban 1991, and Lucy 1993).

The phrase "linguistic relativity" usually invokes more than just issues of difference in meaning or interpretation; it suggests a principled incommensurability, and potential gulfs in understanding. The chapters by Ochs and Gumperz illustrate how this incommensurability can arise through shared history and through socialization into specific indexical practices and how this affects understanding, even within what we take to be a single language. As Gumperz argues, incommensurability can exist when individuals who do not share "common ground" are, in some situations, unable to achieve shared interpretations, even though every effort to communicate is being made through a shared language. Naturally, this makes problematic the very notions of a shared language and speech community. The chapter by Gomez-Imbert examines an especially problematic and celebrated case, exploring the long-term effects of communicative practices in multilingual family interaction in Amazonia. Thus the focus of this section is the way in which interpretive strategies are embedded in networks and communities, and passed on as shared communicative traditions, in which social knowledge and interpersonal relations are as critical as linguistic knowledge.

The relation between community and interpretive strategies, or language use and function, can be approached from a number of directions. One direction, not further developed here, was adopted in earlier (and at the time quite influential) work by Basil Bernstein (1971, 1972) who saw a precise parallel between the full Sapir–Whorf hypothesis and the relativity introduced by variation in language use. Compare for example our "Whorfian" syllogism in the introduction to part I, and the following interpretation of Bernstein's ideas about restricted and elaborated codes and their mental effects:

(1′) there are systematic differences in language use;
(2′) if one uses language in a systematically different way, one learns to think differently;
therefore
(3′) differences in language use are correlated with differences in cognitive style.

Bernstein's ideas were attacked (perhaps unjustly) on the basis that, *inter alia*, they confused dialect differences with differential patterns of use. A more serious criticism is that he was unable to establish a systematic relationship between thought and language. An interesting interpretation of Bernstein's ideas that did try to tie a range of grammatical patterns to ranges of use or function was developed by Kay (1977). The idea was that some kinds of language use, and some kinds of linguistic constructions, have relatively context-independent interpretations (Bernstein's elaborated code), and these are the kinds favored in communication across subgroups and networks in complex societies. The differential reliance on context in interpretation is perhaps correlated with levels of societal complexity. These ideas have in fact been independently much discussed in other disciplines, such as the history and philosophy of science or sociology. Bertrand Russell, for example, was much interested in the possibility of the elimination of indexicality, precisely because without this elimination a context-independent discourse for science cannot be achieved. Juergen Habermas's concept of a "public sphere," which presupposes "communicative rationality" that rests on free access to truth through "undistorted" and presumably context-free communication (Habermas 1984, 1987), and which has received a great deal of attention in recent years, rests on similar notions.

However, the chapters in this section tend in another direction. They seek to establish that there are a complex set of inter-relations and causal strands that link meaning, context, culture, and society together. They thus address another part of the Sapir–Whorf hypothesis, the link between meaning and social life. The circle of interactions is, in a nutshell, as follows: differential use of language yields different interpretive strategies, partly via the now familiar indexical mechanisms, partly by further processes spelled out in the chapters by Gumperz and Ochs, whereby specific linguistic features invoke the very context of interpretation to be employed (see immediately below). Since sharing this context of interpretation, and sharing knowledge of the signs by which it is invoked, is dependent on cultural transmission and a history of co-operation in shared networks, and is the prime guarantor of intersubjectivity, it can be argued that in some sense, as both Ochs and Gumperz propose in different ways, socialization into this system constitutes socialization into the society itself. Different social networks in the same society, city or street are likely to yield (in the way Clark sketched) different meaning systems, provided they persist over time and become "institutionalized." Thus complex social systems breed communicational subsystems with communicative barriers and different evaluations of verbal performances (see Cohn 1987 and also Luhrman 1989 for vivid illustrations of how such contextual barriers come about and work). The simple association of one tribe, one culture, one language, which was implicit in the older Humboldtian and Sapir–Whorfian traditions, then breaks down. We can have speakers of the same language fractionated by interpretive subsystems associated with distinct social networks in complex societies, and conversely, we can have social networks that transcend cultural and grammatical systems to create shared interpretive systems beneath linguistic diversity (Gumperz 1971).

1 Community, network, and language differentiation

The Humboldtian idealization of one language: one society: one culture had its origins in the romanticism of the period which coincided with the consolidation of the European nation states, and which in fact created large multilingual, differentiated speech communities, with a consequent yearning for the lost, allegedly simple, linguistic identities of the past. When Whorf worked with his bilingual Hopi collaborator, he could look at this bilingualism as an accident of recent history. And much bilingualism in the world today does indeed token a transitory stage on the way to monolingualism. However, this is not the only source of linguistic differentiation. For in fact many traditional communities have had elaborate internal differentiation from time immemorial. A South Indian village may have as many as four languages, along with distinct caste dialects, and differing varieties related to educational level and regional experience (Gumperz & Wilson 1971; see also the discussion in Leach [1954] 1964: 44f.). Gomez-Imbert (this volume) describes a dramatic case of such intra-community diversity in the Vaupés basin of Amazonian Latin America, a region that has long been cited as a key example of inter-community linguistic and cultural variability.

Modern sociolinguistics had its beginning with the recognition that anyone seeking to relate linguistic to social and political forces must take the speech community, seen as a group of communicating individuals, as the analytical starting-point rather than focusing on languages or dialects as such. Speech communities, broadly conceived, can be regarded as collectivities of social networks. Networks come in different types. Of crucial importance for linguistic and cultural transmission is the primary network of socialization, into which one is recruited by kinship, and from which are recruited friends and often neighbors and co-workers. Yet as they enter adult society individuals are socialized into additional occupational, educational, and other networks.

This network structure can be viewed in terms of a Durkheimian division of labor, which in one form or other is characteristic of all human collectivities. As Irvine (1989) (following Hilary Putnam) has argued, it also implies a linguistic division of labor. Long-time interpersonal co-operation in network-specific pursuits favors the institutionalization of practices, such that members talk more and more intensively to each other about specific matters than they do to others. As a result certain communicative practices or genres may become conventionalized through habituation, typification, and ultimately grammaticalization (Hanks, this volume). In this way the details of indexicality reflect network-specific practices. They constitute discourses that serve to facilitate communication within the group, while at the same time limiting access to participation by non-members.

Thus speech communities, because of the ways they are constituted from diverse networks, tend towards diversification and this restricts the extent to which linguistic forms, conceptual structures, and culture are shared. These centrifugal forces tend to be counter-balanced by centripetal ones. For example, nation states incorporate local communities through commerce, industrialization, conquest, and consolidation. These forces create national elites who then, through their own power and action and through the community's public institutions, impose their linguistic ideologies and their own "superposed varieties" (Gumperz 1962, 1971). Linguistic variability thus becomes valorized, and constitutes cultural or symbolic capital that, much like price differentials in the economic sphere, can be competitively employed to advance economic or political interests (Bourdieu 1991).

We use the term linguistic ideology to refer to the beliefs, values, and attitudes to language, in part socially transmitted but also in part overtly propagated, that affect the evaluation of talk in everyday life. It is well known, for example, that in many regions of the world, continuous chains of local dialects are crossed by national boundaries, and one and the same variety can be thought of as, for instance, Dutch or German. On the other hand major linguistic divergences (as between the different spoken Arabics) can be thought of as mere local varieties. Ideology thus has a significant effect on how we categorize linguistic forms. Yet, beneath such ideological constructions, networks of interacting individuals continue to bring about linguistic change. Where these networks cross language boundaries and even language families, we obtain the striking convergences across linguistic phyla in what Emeneau (1964, 1980) dubbed "linguistic areas." Whorf, in talking of Standard Average European, presumed such a European linguistic area. The chapter by Gomez-Imbert in this section, which describes how speakers of many distinct and in part historically unrelated languages share a common regional rhetorical system as well as norms of interpersonal relations and ritual practices, suggests that the Vaupés basin has similar areal characteristics .

To summarize: distinct communicative practices arise through communicative co-operation in different networks of relationship. Social networks are of different kinds. On the one hand, "multiplex" networks of socialization (where kinship, education, and local community overlap) are the primary sites within which the greatest range of language functions are handled, and within which reliance on background-specific context-bound interpretations is therefore most deeply entrenched. This is primary support for the dialect or natal variety. On the other hand, networks that span such primary networks, that have limited functions, and support varieties with specialist uses, can cut right across language boundaries, encouraging convergence phenomena, the formation and maintenance of creoles and lingua franca, etc. The ideologies of nation states hide these underlying realities, which are the source of constant regeneration of diversity.

2 Language function and invocation of context

So far we have argued that patterns of language use and interpretation are linked to social networks which are in turn structured by larger social forces. However, we need more refined concepts of language use and function than have been traditional in sociolinguistics, and in particular we need to build a perspective on language function that bridges the gap between language and social worlds. The general sociolinguistic literature of the sixties and seventies tended to deal with function in terms of "rules of alternation" (Ervin-Tripp 1972), basically descriptive statements specifying: "who speaks what, why and under what circumstances" (Fishman 1970), where the "whats" are largely folk categories of language, dialect or style, and the "circumstances" situations defined by the community's social norms. Hymes (1966: 114) argued that "linguistic relativity is a notion associated, via Whorf (1940), with the structure of language . . . Less studied, but I think, theoretically prior, is a linguistic relativity that has to do with the use of language." Hymes's (1962, 1974; Gumperz & Hymes 1964, 1972) writings on ethnography of communication set out an initial program for comparative research on language use and function. The early ethnographers of communication adopted Roman Jakobson's notion of the "speech event" as an intermediate level of analysis, rather than the speech community as such. Events are, on the one hand, units of interaction in terms of which talk can be examined, and, on the other hand, they are also named and valorized entities that enter into everyday talk. Thus social information on relevant norms and constraints can more readily and more reliably be obtained from the study of speech events than if one had to rely on general information about the communities' values.

Hymes's writings stimulated a wide variety of empirical studies.[1] At first, analyses concentrated largely on such named and bounded entities as public performances: ceremonies, rites, rituals, political oratory, and the like. Language function was described in terms of locally collected ethnographic data on relevant norms or "rules" of appropriateness governing conduct in the event and their relation to choice of speech style (Bauman & Sherzer 1974). Yet, as Brown & Levinson (1979) demonstrate, structuralist rules of language use are bad predictors of what actually happens. They cannot account for the many often unforeseeable contingencies that govern everyday behavior (see also Bourdieu's (1977, 1991) well-known critique). Furthermore when detailed discourse analyses of actual performances became available, the notion of event as the extra-linguistically defined context determining language usage also became untenable. Anthropologists and folklorists concentrating on performance discovered that more often than not events were not clearly bounded. Rather, the participants' definition of what the relevant context is "emerged" in and through the performance itself (Bauman 1988, Bauman & Briggs 1990, Hymes 1981). In such cases, as Hanks puts it in his article on genre: "The idea of objectivist rules is replaced by schemes and strategies, leading one to view genre as a set of focal and prototypical elements, which actors use variously and which never become fixed in a unitary structure" (1987: 681, quoted in Bauman & Briggs 1992).

These lines of investigation converge to suggest that contexts are themselves evoked as part of the sequential ordering of talk. At first there is a puzzling self-reflexivity here: how can language carry with itself the key to its own interpretation? In fact the discussion of deixis and transpositions in the previous section has already introduced us to one solution: a strong presumption that speaker and addressee can find the common ground within which to interpret an utterance provides an effective search heuristic for so finding it. Context-invoking meta-messages provide a powerful, but subliminal, system governing the inferences that constitute language understanding. The analytical issue therefore shifts from language choice or style as traditionally conceived within sociolinguistics, to the question of how and by what signalling devices language functions to evoke context. The role of deixis has been discussed in the prior section. Here we will turn to a second set of signs that participants employ to construe social worlds via interactive frames.

Initial insights into the relevant cognitive processes came from studies of code-switching. The term code-switching is commonly used to refer to alternation among different speech varieties within the same event. Such alternations are employed throughout the world, particularly in local networks, and are frequently described via rules of alternation that specify the "determining" situational factors (e.g. in the old Catholic church service Latin was appropriate for prayer, while for sermons the native language was used). Yet if we examine switching as it enters into the communicative practices that constitute the event it soon becomes apparent that just as with the folk performances referred to above, it is not the situation that determines language use, but rather the choice of language and topical content that evoke the shift in context. In other words code-switching functions as an indexical signalling strategy which is employed to suggest the presuppositions in terms of which constituent messages are to be understood.

In more general terms code-switching can be seen as one of a set of indexical/metapragmatic signs, "contextualization cues" which, when processed in co-occurrence with other grammatical and lexical signs, serve to construct the contextual ground for situated interpretation (Gumperz 1982). As metapragmatic signs, contextualization cues represent speakers' ways of signalling and providing information to interlocutors and audiences about how language is being used at any one point in the ongoing stream of talk. What sets prosodic contextualization cues apart from lexicalized meta-discursive signs is that they are of course intrinsically oral forms.[2] Since no utterance can be pronounced without supersegmentals, contextualization cues are ever-present in the talk and, to the extent to which they can be shown to affect interpretation, they provide direct evidence for the necessary role that indexicality plays in talk (Ochs, this volume). Furthermore contextualization strategies signal largely by cueing indirect inferences. Since in conversation we could not possibly express all the information that interlocutors must have to plan their own contributions and attune their talk to that of their interlocutors, it is easy to see the reason for this indirectness. But finally and perhaps most importantly, indirect (not overtly lexicalized) signalling mechanisms are for the most part culturally or subculturally specific. For example prosody and "accent" (in the sense of phonetically marked features of pronunciation) are among the principal means by which we identify where people are from and "who" they are – that is, assess their social identity. As Ochs argues, we are socialized into society via indexical communication, and through indexical signs we indicate our "stance" vis-à-vis what is happening.

Analyses of contextualization processes, and of the way in which they are mapped on grammatical and lexical form in ongoing talk exchanges, provide empirical methods for recovering the often unverbalized premises that underlie interpretation. These premises are demonstrably related to the ethic of interpersonal relations in specific cultural traditions and to the cultural ideologies on which the relevant values are based (Gumperz 1992). Because of its intrinsic cultural specificity, contextualized talk is of special significance for what, following Sherzer (1987), has come to be called a "discourse-centered approach to culture." As Urban (1991) argues in the introduction to his book by that title: "culture is localized in concrete, publicly accessible signs, the most important of which are actually occurring instances of discourse." Many of the performance features Urban examines are in fact contextualization cues in our terms.

So far, studies in the above tradition have concentrated on bounded ceremonial performances. By incorporating the notion of contextualization into analyses of everyday discursive practice, we can extend the discourse-centered approach to examine the workings of context-bound interpretive processes in general. Moreover analyses need not remain confined to specific encounter types. It becomes possible to expand the analytical scope and show how verbal actions, produced and interpreted in a specific context, are recontextualized and differently assessed with respect to other contextual and ideological presuppositions, so as to provide a more dynamic picture of the relation between linguistic and social.forces. Cross-contextual analysis yields some significant insights into the issues of communicative incommensurability (as illustrated in the chapter by Gumperz, this volume) and indicates the subtle bases of the relativity of linguistic interpretations.

Finally since contextualization analysis reveals sharing of interpretive practices and does not depend on *a priori* assumptions about the language and group identity, the population units it reflects are empirically isolable regional units marked by overlapping networks of interaction. For tribal regions, such units look much like the system Gomez-Imbert describes for the Vaupés area. In complex nation states the relevant analytical units take the form of dynamic systems or fields in Bourdieu's (1991) sense, where local diversity is balanced by shared rhetorical practices and controlled by power relationships and ideological forces. Thus it is interaction channelled and constrained by the interplay of local and supra-local forces that ultimately determines the nature of linguistic and cultural distinctions.

3 The chapters

Elinor Ochs takes the position that culture is learned through its embodiment in practice, but especially, she argues, in linguistic practices. She outlines an ambitious theory of socialization through the medium of language. The claim is that many linguistic elements are Janus-faced, performing the task of contributing to propositional statements on the one hand, but simultaneously through inherent indexicality constituting moves on the level of discourse and social interaction on the other. Ochs tries then to formulate some general constraints or patterns that characterize these socially laden indexicals. One of her more interesting ideas is that most such indexicals work indirectly, by virtue of indicating the speaker's *stance*, or attitude (modal or affective), towards the proposition expressed. Then, at second remove, the assumption of a particular stance may suggest a specific social action or relationship. For example, the English modal hedge *maybe* might index speaker's epistemic uncertainty, and then indirectly, deference to addressee, or it might index speaker's deontic indecisiveness ("Candy after supper, maybe!") and thus indirectly signal authority over addressee; and so on, for a wide range of particles, grammatical elements, prosodic features, etc. Ochs tries to generalize over the kinds of markers thus employed and their social effects, and claims that one may detect strong universal patterns underlying culture-specific tendencies to exploit these patterns to different degrees. She suggests that the human ability to acquire and transmit culture might quite largely depend on this shared universal complex of associations between stance-markers on the one hand and social actions and relationships on the other. Human inbuilt implicit understanding of these indexical relations between stance and social life provides children with a means to construct the learning environment in which the rest of culture can be acquired. Linguistic relativity in this regard would then be closely circumscribed by universal tendencies.

Ochs's position on the social valence of language can perhaps be placed as intermediate between two earlier kinds of tradition. The one, associated with Bateson, early paralanguage investigators (Birdwhistell and others), and later social psychologists, attempts to find distinct channels for social information in human communication. Thus one hopes to isolate social markers or indexes. The other tradition, eloquently argued by Edmund Leach, is that such "ritual" information is not carried by any particular acts or events, but by the manner in which all acts are conducted (much sociolinguistic theory belongs here, e.g. research on politeness). Thus one cannot isolate social markers or indexes, since the social information lies in the modulation of every action throughout its course. Ochs's intermediate position here would seem to be very close to Gumperz's but, whereas she emphasizes individual linguistic indexes, Gumperz emphasizes how a constellation of "contextualization cues" index a whole social frame of interpretation, which, depending on circumstances, may then in turn lead to inferences about individual participants' states of mind.

John Gumperz further pursues the theme of how frameworks essential to interpretation can be invoked by the communication itself. He outlines his notion of "contextualization cues," cues that indicate how an utterance is to be understood and what its rhetorical role in a sequential discourse is. Like Haviland, he shows how subtle and fleeting such cues are, and how bound they are into local discourse practices, by analyzing, for example, a collaborative storytelling episode. However, he concentrates on the analysis of what was introduced above as a hypothetical case, the situation where speakers of the same grammatical/lexical system (e.g. English) have distinct systems of indexical interpretation. On the basis of long-term studies, he argues that many speakers of English from the Indian subcontinent utilize distinct sets of contextualization cues from those employed by native-born English speakers in England, where both reside. Concentrating on interview situations with bureaucratic "gatekeepers," Gumperz discerns two ways in which contextualization cues can be culturally relative. First, the signalling media, the linguistic triggers, may themselves be different across cultures, and even across speakers of the same language. For example, speakers of Indian English highlight parts of an utterance in a different way using pitch register and/ or loudness shifts that extend over an entire phrase to indicate a rhetorical point, while standard British English speakers use syllable accent. Secondly, the content that is signalled – whether the global framework of the activity or the more local turn-by-turn rhetorical point – may significantly vary. For example, the Indian English speakers tend also to have a quite different concept of a "gatekeeping" interview, assuming that this should be conducted more in the manner of a petition to a benevolent superior (compared to the British expectation that one should make a case for one's rights under the rules).

Gumperz argues that such interpretive differences significantly affect ability to sustain conversational collaboration, which may have direct consequences for how individual participants fare in an interaction and for cultural transmission. Contextualization cues invoke the very framework of interpretation, much as Ochs's stance-markers are held to constitute the social matrix for culture-learning, so that small "misfires" at this level create massive misunderstandings at other levels, whether referential or social. Gumperz claims that the mastering of such cues and their meanings is dependent on direct participation in network-specific practices and in social relationships of the "friendship" type. Psychologists might question whether there might not be a "critical period" for the acquisition of such cues, drawing attention to the difficulty of adult second-language acquisition in just such subtle areas, but that would not be inconsistent with the requirement also for a special kind of social interaction experience. Social anthropologists might wonder whether such interviews are partly in the nature of a test of real or adopted ethnicity. However, Gumperz argues that it is in the nature of complex social structures to engender diverse social networks, which then acquire linguistic specializations that breed interpretive barriers. He thus views the fundamental linguistic relativity at this level as a universal by-product of (a) complex social organization, and (b) universal principles of contextualization cueing.

Clark and Gumperz emphasize how practices which determine linguistic interpretation are differentially distributed in a community. The point is also made with extraordinary ethnographic material by Elsa Gomez-Imbert on the basis of her fieldwork in the Vaupés basin of

Northwest Amazonia. The area is well known for its linguistic exogamy,
where a man must find a wife who speaks a different language. These
facts challenge presumptions about the whole conception of linguistic
relativity as based in the association of "one tribe, one culture, one
language." However, Gomez-Imbert draws attention to a number of
misconceptions in the sociolinguistic literature. Some corrections for the
record: a few language groups are divided into exogamic sub-units;
women continue to speak their native language throughout their lives to
everybody; their children are raised speaking the mother's language, then
switch to their father's language from about the age of six, and thus are
raised bilingually; the preferential marriage exchange system makes it
likely that a boy will marry a girl from his mother's language group, who
speaks his own developmentally first language, although his socially first
language is his father's. This helps to explain how linguistic exogamy is
possible across major language boundaries.

What happens to languages in such intimate contact? Could one have
linguistic relativity, i.e. semantic non-isomorphism, under such conditions; if so, is linguistic determinism of conceptual categorization possible
even amongst systematic bilinguals? Gomez-Imbert focuses on the
relation between the genetically unrelated Arawakan and Tukanoan
families of languages in the domain of animal classification. It seems that
the animal taxonomies across such languages are at least nearly
isomorphic, despite very few cognates. However, the grammatical
systems generally, and in particular the systems of classification encoded
in numeral/nominal classifiers, are extremely different. The Tukanoan
languages use nominal shape-based classifiers only with inanimate nouns
but in many grammatical contexts; the Arawakan languages use shape-
classifiers with both animate and inanimate nouns in more restricted
grammatical contexts. The shape distinctions made are also different in
part. Underlying the application or non-application of classifiers, there
seems to be a different semantics for nominals. Nouns that take classifiers
L seem to be viewed as mass-nouns or collectives, the classifiers serving to
individuate them (compare Lucy's 1992 interpretation of Mayan). The
evidence for this is that, for example, in Baniwa (an Arawakan language)
a species of pig that roams in bands requires a classifier, but a bigger
species that wanders solo requires no classifiers (as with other salient
individual animals). There are thus conceptual underpinnings to the
classification system.

What happens historically over long periods of contact? Gomez-Imbert
looked in detail at one language, Kubeo, that seems intermediate: it is a
Tukanoan language but has Arawakan-like nominal-classifiers on
animate nouns. Investigations reveal that Kubeo has a peculiar history:
it is spoken by the descendants of Arawakan-speakers, who moved into

Tukanoan territory and adopted a Tukanoan language. They now practice linguistic exogamy with Arawakan speakers of the language (Baniwa) their ancestors probably originally spoke, as well as with other Tukanoan language-groups. Their nominal classification system is grammatically Tukanoan, except that, in addition, it carries an overlay of the Arawakan system squeezed into novel grammatical interstices. Above all Kubeo speakers classify animals, except the very salient individuals, although the system is not quite isomorphic with Arawakan languages like Baniwa. Gomez-Imbert concludes that what we have here is the preservation of a conceptual scheme, carried across from an Arawakan into a Tukanoan language, where it is regrammaticalized. The conclusion would be that even in such intensely multilingual communities, it is possible to maintain distinct conceptualizations of domains attached to specific languages. This conclusion contrasts, for example, with work by Gumperz & Wilson (1971) in India that has suggested that in such circumstances languages tend to acquire grammatical and semantic isomorphism, with "token" surface differentiation. Kay (this volume) has argued that the conceptual perspectives encoded in language must be relatively trivial, because speakers of one language hold inconsistent perspectives; Gomez-Imbert's data would suggest that even when distinct conceptualizations are in the same (multilingual) "head," they can be powerful enough to force the restructuring of an adopted language. The Vaupés situation dramatically illustrates Hanks's argument that both conceptual distinctions and communicative practice play a role in the maintenance of linguistic distinctness as well as the Gumperz and Clark point that one cannot think about linguistic relativity as semantic diversity simply across localized tribes or nations; rather one has linguistic relativity across geographical as well as social space.

Notes

1 See Baumann & Sherzer 1974, reissued in 1989 with a new introduction and an extensive bibliography of more recent work.
2 Although punctuation and document design work in some ways like contextualization, their role in writing is basically much more limited and their effect on interpretation differs from that of contextualization cues in talk.

References

Atkinson, P. & Heritage, M. 1986. *Structures of social action.* Cambridge University Press.
Bauman, R. (ed.) 1988. *Story, performance, and event: contextual studies of oral narrative.* Cambridge Studies in Oral and Literate Culture, 10. Cambridge University Press.

Bauman, R. & Briggs, C. 1990. Poetics and performance as critical perspectives on language and social life. *Annual Review of Anthropology*, 19, 59–88.

Bauman, R. & Sherzer, J. 1974. *Explorations in the ethnography of speaking.* (Reissued with a new introduction and bibliography, 1989.) London: Cambridge University Press.

Bernstein, B. 1971. *Class codes and control.* London: Routledge & Kegan Paul.

1972. A sociolinguistic approach to socialization: with some reference to educability. In Gumperz & Hymes (1964): 465–97.

Bourdieu, P. 1977. *Outline of a theory of practice.* Tr. R. Nice. Cambridge University Press.

1991. *Language and symbolic power.* Cambridge, MA: Polity Press.

Briggs, C. L. & Bauman, R. 1992. Genre, intertextuality and social power. *Journal of Linguistic Anthropology*, 2(2), 131–72.

Brown, P. & Levinson, S. C. 1979. Social structure, groups, and interaction. In H. Giles & K. Scherer (eds.), *Social markers in speech* (pp. 291–341). Cambridge University Press.

Cohn, C. 1987. Sex and death in the rational world of defense intellectuals. *Signs*, 12, 687–718.

Emeneau, M. 1964. India as a Linguistic Area. In D. Hymes (ed.), *Language culture and society.* New York: Harper & Row.

1980. *Language and linguistic area. Essays by Murray B. Emeneau*, ed. A. S. Dil. Stanford University Press.

Ervin-Tripp, S. 1972. On sociolinguistic rules: alternation and co-occurrence. In Gumperz & Hymes (1964): 213–50.

Fishman, J. 1970. *Sociolinguistics.* Rowley, MA: Newbury House.

Grice, P. 1990. *Studies in the ways of words.* Cambridge, MA: Harvard University Press.

Gumperz, J. J. 1962. Types of linguistic communities. *Anthropological Linguistics*, 4(1), 28–40.

1971. *Language in social groups.* Stanford University Press.

1982. *Discourse strategies.* Cambridge University Press.

1992. Interviewing in intercultural settings. In P. Drew & J. Heritage (eds.), *Talk at work* (pp. 302–30). Cambridge University Press.

Gumperz, J. J. & Hymes, D. 1964. "The ethnography of communication," special issue of *American Anthropologist.* 66(6), part 2.

(eds.) 1972. *Directions in sociolinguistics. the ethnography of communication.* New York: Holt, Rinehart, & Winston.

Gumperz, J. & Wilson, R. 1971. Convergence and creolization: a case from the Indo-Aryan/Dravidian border. In D. Hymes (ed.), *Pidginization and creolization of languages* (pp. 151–67). Cambridge University Press.

Habermas, J. 1984. *The structural transformation of the public sphere.* Boston: Beacon.

(ed.) 1987. *Lifeworld and system: a critique of functionalist reasoning.* Boston: Beacon.

Hanks, W. F. 1987. Discourse genres in a theory of practice. *American Ethnologist*, 14(4): 668–92.

Hymes, D. 1962. The ethnography of speaking. In *Anthropology and human behavior.* Washington, DC: Anthropological Society of Washington.

1966. Two types of linguistic relativity (with examples from Amerindian ethnography). In W. Bright (ed.), *Sociolinguistics. Proceedings of the UCLA sociolinguistics conference, 1964* (pp. 114–67). The Hague: Mouton.

(ed.) 1974. *Studies in the history of linguistics. traditions and paradigms.* Bloomington: Indiana University Press.

1981. *"In vain I tried to tell you." Essays in native American ethnopoetics.* Philadelphia: University of Pennsylvania Press.

Irvine, J. 1989. When talk isn't cheap: language and political economy. *American Ethnologist*, 16, 248–67.

Jakobson, R. 1960. Concluding statement: linguistics and poetics. In T. A. Sebeok (ed.), *Style in language* (pp. 350–77). Cambridge, MA: MIT Press.

Kay, P. 1977. Language evolution and speech style. In B. G. Blount & M. Sanches (eds.), *Sociocultural dimensions of language change.* New York: Academic Press.

Leach, E. R. 1964 [1954]. *Political systems of highland Burma.* 2nd edn. London School of Economics & Political Science.

Lucy, J. 1992. *Grammatical categories and cognition: a case study of the linguistic relativity hypothesis.* Cambridge University Press.

(ed.) 1993. *Reflexive language. reported speech and metapragmatics.* Cambridge University Press.

Luhrman, T. 1989. *Persuasions of the witches craft.* Cambridge, MA: Harvard University Press.

Shener, J. 1987. A discourse-centered approach to language and culture. *American Anthropologist*, 89, 295–309.

Silverstein, M. 1976. Shifters, linguistic categories, and cultural description. In K. Basso & H. Selby (eds.), *Meaning in anthropology* (pp. 11–55). Albuquerque: University of New Mexico Press.

1992. The indeterminacy of contextualization. In P. Auer & A. Di Luzio (eds.), *The contextualization of language* (pp. 55–76). Amsterdam: John Benjamins.

1993. Metapragmatic discourse and metapragmatic function. In Lucy (1993) 33–58.

Urban, G. 1991. *A discourse-centered approach to culture: native South American myths and rituals.* Austin: University of Texas Press.

THE LINGUISTIC AND CULTURAL RELATIVITY OF CONVERSATIONAL INFERENCE

JOHN J. GUMPERZ

Research on verbal communication since the 1960s has made fundamental contributions to our understanding of how language works in everyday encounters. It is by now generally accepted that discourse and conversation have their own forms of organization, distinguishing them from mere strings of sentences or clauses, forms that need to be analyzed in their own terms. We also have good evidence to show that situated understanding is to a large extent a matter of context-bound indirect inferences. Propositional content and grammar are thus not the sole determinants of meaning assessments. Among other factors, discourse-level characteristics of verbal signs and culturally specific background knowledge, along with generalized world knowledge, also play a significant role. Yet, while discourse focused perspectives have by now become quite important in the literature on communication, their import for basic issues of linguistic and cultural relativity has so far received comparatively little systematic attention.

As attention shifts from structural analysis of clause-level grammar and lexical semantics to situated discursive practice, can we continue to rely on notions of culture as abstract systems of meanings shared by members of socially bounded populations, speaking a single grammatically homogeneous language? In the earlier chapters of this volume such context-free approaches to relativity have been questioned from a number of perspectives. In particular the chapters in part III argue that reference must be analyzed in terms of how it is grounded in everyday discourse. They provide empirical evidence revealing the frequently unnoticed grammatical and interpretive complexities that context-bound meaning assessments involve. In the present chapter I intend to raise yet another set of questions: to what extent are the discursive processes, by which interpretive frames are invoked and shared interpretations negotiated, themselves linguistically and culturally variable? How is this variability distributed among human populations and how does it affect the way we view the relativity debate?

The perspective here is on discursive practice as an interactive and basically social process, involving co-operation on the part of more than one individual. Although, as Grice has argued (1989), all understanding presupposes conversational co-operation, this collaborative activity must be actively initiated and maintained, for the most part through talk. Therefore not everything that is said in an encounter is equally important in conveying substantive information. Talk always has a variety of communicative goals. Among other things it also serves to initiate and terminate encounters, to enlist conversational co-operation, assess the import of what is said in relation to preceding and following talk and the like. Meaning and function are always closely intertwined. Therefore the initial objects of study cannot be abstract lexical or grammatical meanings as such, but on-line interpretive assessments made in the course of a sequence of moves and counter-moves that constitutes a speech exchange. We are always faced with an array of potentially situated interpretations such that the significance of what happens at any one point can only be understood in relation to what precedes and what is expected to follow.

The discussion in this chapter will be based on illustrative analyses of extracts from a corpus of transcripts prepared in connection with comparative analyses of discursive practices in formal and informal intra- and interethnic encounters in European and North American urban settings. Methods employed combine elements of the conversational analysts' approach to sequential ordering of talk (Atkinson & Heritage 1986) with interactional sociolinguistic study of indexically grounded interpretations of communicative intent (Gumperz 1981, 1992). I will focus on what I call conversational inference, defined as the situated and presupposition-bound interpretive processes by which interlocutors assess what they perceive at any one point in a verbal encounter and on which they base their responses.

How do such context-bound and, by their very nature, transitory phenomena relate to what is traditionally understood by linguistic and cultural relativity? Consider the following excerpt from Edward Sapir's writings:

Communication processes do not merely apply to society; they are indefinitely varied as to form and meaning for the various types of personal relationships into which society resolves itself. Thus a fixed type of conduct or a linguistic symbol has by no means necessarily the same communicative significance within the confines of the family, among the members of an economic group, and in the nation at large. Generally speaking, the smaller the circle and the more complex the understandings already arrived at within it, the more economical can the act of communication afford to become. A single word passed between members of an intimate group, in spite of its apparent vagueness and ambiguity, may constitute far more precise communication than volumes of carefully prepared correspondence exchanged between two governments.

(Sapir [1931] 1951)

In this much-quoted passage Sapir suggests – among other things – that certain aspects of linguistic variability directly reflect the history and the quality of social relationships among interactants. Intensive communication among individuals, bound by ties of mutual trust and support (such as we associate with peer groups and family life) and by co-operation in the pursuit of occupational goals, are likely to produce locally specific interpretive and communicative conventions. Over time, as shared modes of understanding and ways of speaking, such practices act to increase the ease and depth of interaction within the communicating group. One could go on to argue that once established shared communicative conventions foster a sense of group identity and belonging and that social groupings are largely constituted and sustained by communicative practices.

However, Sapir's discussion of communication is largely programmatic. Where language structure and change are concerned he continued to hold to the structuralist view for which he is famous. The article on communication is reprinted in his *Selected writings* (1951) following the chapter on "Language and environment," an early statement of his views on language, which argues that linguistic structure is relatively impervious to historical and social influences. It is this structural perspective on grammar and culture that forms the basis for his foundational comparative studies of language typology and change, and has continued to be the basis for most work on language and culture since. The remarks on communication were meant to apply to lexical and other non-structural aspects of linguistic variability such as one finds within a larger structurally bounded population unit. However, note that, in contrast to others who tend to speak of variability below the level of structure as a matter of individual psychology or expressive behavior, or see it as analyzable only at the quantitative level of groups, Sapir takes a distinctly social view of variability as interactionally based. Thus his remarks can be interpreted as providing at least the outlines of an approach that may enable us to show how individual action might, under certain conditions, bring about systematic linguistic and socio-cultural distinctions.

By now, more than fifty years since Sapir's work, the assumption that our social world comes segmented into discrete internally homogeneous language/culture areas has become increasingly problematic. Cultures are no longer homogeneous and language divisions have become more and more permeable. In today's nation states, tied as they are into a global economy, with its rapidly changing modes of production and its ever-increasing pace of population movements, diversity is a fact of everyday life. Previously isolated peoples, including many of those described in the classical ethnographic studies on which our theories of culture rest, have come to live and work as one among several minority groups, in the nation states of their former colonial masters, where they participate to varying degrees in a common political economy either adapting to or resisting the hegemonic pressures of the dominant ideology.

They tend to settle alongside others who share their background, maintaining the accustomed family and peer relations. Yet they can hardly be regarded as social isolates. No matter how much they seek to preserve their heritage, the situation in which they find themselves inevitably brings them into close communication with the surrounding world. In advanced industrial culturally diverse societies cultural identity must, as Turner (1994), in a recent discussion of multiculturalism, points out, be asserted and defended within a supralocal arena. To make themselves heard minority group members are forced to enter into or react to the debates of a Habermasian public sphere and, as Urban (1993) has recently argued, this sphere has a supralocal culture of its own. I would add that it also has its own distinct rhetorical conventions, separate from those of the local cultures.

The resultant new modes of interaction cannot but affect communicative practices. Multilingualism and code-switching strategies become common. Linguistic diffusion begins to level pre-existing grammatical and lexical differences. While the old language names are maintained, new speaking genres develop which may range from Creole-like formations to ways of speaking that differ to varying degrees from the pre-existing languages. As grammatical and semantic distinctions attenuate, linguistic and cultural boundaries within the communicating region become blurred. Moreover, since the changes in question diffuse at different rates, speakers of the same languages may find themselves separated by deep cultural gaps, while others who speak grammatically distinct languages share the same culture (Gumperz 1982, Scollon & Scollon 1981). At the same time group boundaries are rapidly changing and less sharply marked. We can thus no longer assume that language and culture are co-extensive and shared understandings cannot be taken for granted. The assumption of a one to one relationship between language and cultural variability must now be seen as an oversimplification.

It is under these conditions of multiculturalism, where traditional macro-social categories no longer account for everyday human action, that Sapir's remarks take on new significance. A similar argument has been developed in some detail by Bergman and Luckmann (1994) as the foundation for their own constructivist approach to social institutions. Based on extensive long-term studies of talk in family groupings, medical and other public situations, Bergman and Luckmann argue that communication within the context of institutionalized environments leads to the creation of linguistically distinct modes of talk. Over time and depending on historical forces, such linguistic markers become conventionalized in the form of genres via Schutzian processes of habituation and typifications like those described by Hanks (this volume).

The English-speaking South Asians in Britain whose discursive practices I will be examining are typical of the above minority popula-tions. Most of them emigrated at a time of economic expansion – frequently in family groups – and found work in factories and service establishments. In Britain they have set up religious institutions and voluntary organizations of their own. Both at home and at work individuals spend most of their time in contact with others of similar background, and rely on them for economic survival. This means that for most South Asian immigrants, opportunities for direct interaction with native speakers of English are relatively limited. Except for service encounters or relatively formal, and therefore hierarchical, situations like interviews and contacts with local authorities, there are few opportunities for in-depth conversational involvement in the conditions of equality that are most conducive to learning. This is the sort of situation that favors the formation of group-specific communicative convention and the creation or maintenance of cultural distinctions. Under the veneer of a common grammar and lexicon the discursive practices of the urban minority groups have many of the earmarks of what has traditionally been seen as linguistic and cultural distinctness. How can these practices be analyzed to reveal the interaction of language and culture?

1 Contextlalization-based conversational inference

In discursive practice two or more individuals actively collaborate in the production of talk, alternately speaking, listening, and producing signs of recipiency through gaze, body posture or verbal back-channel signals. The collaboration that this involves is not automatic, it is in large part achieved as part of the interaction. Typically collaboration is initiated with a set of opening turns, greetings or other largely formulaic phrases, in which interpersonal relations are attuned and something of the flavor of what is to come is conveyed. Once involved in an exchange, participants take on obligations towards each other that require them to do more than simply put information into words. While current speakers expect to be given a chance to complete, speaking-turns need to be timed in such a way as to allow for regular speaker change. Regardless of whether interlocutors agree or are actively disputing, some topical and thematic continuity has to be maintained. Whatever is said must somehow fit into, or be relatable to, themes established as part of the preceding talk. Communicating is therefore not just a question of individuals translating their ideas into lexically and grammatically meaningful utterances. Interlocutors must plan, that is think – in a sense similar to what Slobin and Clark (this volume) call thinking for speaking/communicating – about what to say as well as about how and when to say it.

Conversational analysts seek to account for the workings of speech exchanges through turn-by-turn examination of their sequential ordering (Schegloff 1986). Yet while interpretation always depends on how acts are positioned within the stream of talk, positioning alone is not enough. Even with relatively simple utterances, propositional content can only be assessed, as Clark (part III) has shown, with reference to shared frames or common ground. To account for the semantic complexities and constantly changing frames and functions of talk in multi-turn exchanges we must assume that participants rely on additional signs produced as part of the talk. *Contextualization cues* (Gumperz 1992),[1] verbal and non-verbal metalinguistic signs that serve to retrieve the context-bound presuppositions in terms of which component messages are interpreted, play an important role here. A contextualization cue is one of a cluster of indexical signs (Lucy, this volume) produced in the act of speaking that jointly index, that is invoke, a frame of interpretation for the rest of the linguistic content of the utterance. Such frames are subject to change as the interaction progresses and have different scopes, from individual speech acts to sets of turns and responses, to entire social encounters.

As verbal signaling mechanisms, contextualization cues typically operate at the following level of language: (a) prosody, including accent and intonation; (b) rhythm, tempo, and such related phenomena as pausing, overlap, and latching, between either utterances or turns at speaking; (c) shifts (i.e., lowering or raising) in pitch register; (d) selection among the code options within a linguistic repertoire (Gumperz 1971), as in language, dialect or style switching and selection among phonetic or morphological variables – part of what is commonly regarded as a single language, dialect or style (Gumperz 1992). From the perspective of utterance-level linguistics these types of cues are formally quite distinct – at least, they tend to be treated as such in the existing literature and are not ordinarily grouped together. Yet at the level of discourse they have similar functions and are processed together to produce communicative effects. They serve to foreground and set off segments of the stream of talk (be it one or more syllables or words, phrases or clauses, or strings of utterances or a set of speech exchanges) from the surrounding strings. Co-participants who perceive and respond to the shift are then led to resort to their background knowledge and, by an inferential process akin to Gricean implicature, to retrieve contextual presuppositions in terms of which the signs can be understood.

Since contextualization cues are automatically produced and interpreted, they need to be analyzed by indirect means. The starting point of my analysis in the examples below is segmentation of the raw transcript into speech events, temporally organized sequences of verbal acts, separable from the surrounding talk by empirically identifiable beginnings and ends or outcomes, which provide evidence with which to validate the analysis of constituent interpretive processes. Events, as ethnographers of communication have pointed out (Hymes 1972, Bauman & Sherzer 1974), can be seen as miniature social units, in the sense that action is governed by principles of conduct reflecting those of the surrounding social world. Events are also goal-oriented and interpretations of what the communicative goals are serve to filter or frame the body of potentially applicable knowledge, in such a way as to yield presuppositions of what is to be done and how it is to be interpreted. The filtering or shifting of world knowledge makes it available to the inferential process in the form of presuppositions on which inferencing depends.

Understanding in everyday encounters always rests on indirect inferences that simultaneously provide several types of information. Apart from assessments of speakers' communicative intent, information on stance (Ochs, this volume), and on what is expected by way of a response is also conveyed. Moreover inferences are made at every point in the speech exchange so that any one interpretation is in some ways the cumulative outcome of a series of prior assessments and of the history of previous interpretations. Initial interpretive assessments can thus be confirmed or disconfirmed by examining how they are received in the moves and countermoves of the event.

Contextualization affects the interpretive process in two ways. To begin with, it plays an important role in the construction of an exchange. Turn-taking requires that participants be able to identify what conversational analysis calls possible turn-construction units. Interlocutors rely on rhythm, tempo and pausing, pitch register and volume shift as well as sequential placement of final intonational contours to chunk the stream of talk into intonation units, idea units, or information units as I prefer to call them. Grouping items into a single information unit acts as an instruction both to set them off from other similar strings and to process them as units vis-à-vis surrounding elements. To be sure, most information units also constitute syntactic wholes. Yet, while syntax constrains the chunking process, it does not always uniquely determine it. Prosody and paralinguistic signs also carry additional information not usually conveyed through syntax. In turn 2 of example 3 for instance, "y'wanna tell em where we went" would count as a single unit from a purely syntactic perspective. In this instance the speaker foregrounds the "tell 'em" as a separate information unit, and thereby – along with the stress on *tell* – calls attention to the fact that there is something special about this particular act of telling, i.e. the telling is being given some special meaning which we should then expect to be clarified later on in the exchange.

2 Contextualization and interpretation

The following brief examples provide some preliminary illustration of the aspect of contextualization that is most relevant for the present discussion: its effect on interpretation.

2.1 Example 1

The first two extracts come from a recording of a public address by an African American political leader in the 1970s at the time of the Vietnam war (see appendix for details of transcription conventions):

(a) We will not fight and kill other people of color, in the world, who like black people, are victims of US imperialism.
(b) *F... that motherf... *ma:n. we will *ki:ll *Richard **Nixon. we will *ki:ll every *motherf who *sta:nds in our way.

(Gumperz 1981: 200)

Consider the two uses of "kill." In the first utterance the verb is part of the phrase "fight and kill" and prosodically and rhythmically in no way different from the preceding and following talk. Given the context in which it occurs, it is clearly used in its commonly known sense of 'take a life.' In the second extract, however, the verb is embedded in a sequence where the speaker has switched from a relatively standard style of speaking to a style that is set off from the preceding talk by such typical African American features as: (a) considerably slower tempo; (b) markedly contoured rhythm; (c) a shift to higher volume; and (d) marked vowel lengthening in words like *kill*, *man*, and *stands*. Now it is well known that in African American rhetorical tradition death and illness are commonly referred to through euphemisms such as *waste* or *off* for 'taking a life,' while, on the other hand, words like *sick* and *kill* are more commonly employed hyperbolically in utterances such as *that killed him around here* (i.e., destroyed his influence) or *they killed that bottle* (finished off the contents). Those who are familiar with this tradition can therefore reasonably infer that, given the way it was contextualized, and that the speaker was giving a political address he intended to use "We will kill Richard Nixon" in the sense of 'destroy his influence.' Contextualization through code-switching here is a major determinant of the referential assessment.

2.2 Example 2

The following example is anecdotal, but it illustrates important aspects of the inferential process. While driving to the office some time ago, my radio was tuned to a classical music station. At the end of the program the announcer, a replacement for the regular host who was returning the next day, signed off with the following words:

I've enjoyed being with *you these last two weeks.

I had not been listening very carefully but the extra strong accent on "you" in a syntactic position where I would have expected an unaccented pronoun caught my attention. It sounded as if the speaker were producing the first part of a formulaic exchange of compliments. Yet, since there was no one else with him on the program, I inferred that by the way he contextualized his talk the announcer was indirectly – without putting it "on record" – implicating the second part: "I hope you have enjoyed listening to me."

The first example typifies what is commonly understood by context-bound interpretation: the meaning of a word shifts with context. It is also true that contextualization there works like grammar and lexicon in Haviland's (this volume) transpositions, to evoke context. However, note that, unlike grammar, knowledge of contextualization conventions is not shared by all "speakers of the language." Only those who through socialization have become familiar with African American discursive practices – and that does not include all African Americans, nor does it depend on race – are likely to draw the relevant inferences. It is in this relatively restricted sense that interpretation is culturally specific.

In the second example, the inferential processes are more complex. When looked at in isolation interpretations are far from unambiguous. To begin with, the interpretation rests on listeners' ability to perceive that "you" is being foregrounded. Although, as our data will show, this presents no problem for speakers who have native-like control of either American or British English, listeners who have been socialized in the South Asian rhetorical tradition frequently have difficulty in hearing the accent. Secondly, we arrive at the specific interpretation via an implicature-like process by virtue of which the foregrounding strategy indexically invokes the memories of what Bakhtin has called previously heard texts, suggesting likely interpretations.

While it is clear that contextualization cues cannot be assigned context-independent, stable meanings, it is also true that contextualization cues cannot be dismissed as merely conveying transitory non-referential, expressive, emotive or attitudinal effects as some sociolinguists' as well as phoneticians' studies of decontextualized prosodic and paralinguistic signs tend to suggest. As relational signs – not readily amenable to decontextualized treatment – contextualization cues signal by making salient certain lexical strings within the context of grammatical rules. Foregrounding, moreover, does not rest on any one single cue. Rather assessments build on co-occurrence judgments that simultaneously evaluate clusters of cues to generate hypothesis-like tentative – i.e., valid for the moment – assessments that draw on typified knowledge and are subject to constant change as the interaction progresses. Unlike better-known indexes such as Hanks's 'here,' 'there,' or 'this' and 'that' (1990), which tend to index contexts that are either visually available or directly referred to in preceding talk, in the case of contextualization cues context is not overtly specified. It is this that suggests the parallel with Gricean implicature, where inferring also involves a two-step process in which the contextual ground, in terms of which an assessment of what is perceived is made, must first be retrieved and related to stored memories before an interpretation is arrived at. Contextualization cues channel the inferential processes that make available for interpretation knowledge of social and physical worlds.

Finally, it is important to note that, because of the complexity of the inferential processes involved and their inherent ambiguity, contextualization cues are not readily learned, and certainly not through direct instruction, so that, as the following examples will show, second-language speakers may have good functional control of the grammar and lexicon of their new language but may contextualize their talk by relying on the rhetorical strategies of their first language. Contextualization conventions are acquired through primary socialization in family or friendship circles or intensive communicative co-operation in a finite range of institutionalized environments. A precondition for learning is that the novice be given the benefit of the doubt and allowed to make mistakes, as for instance in the family settings that Ochs (this volume) describes. Yet, whereas acquisition of a first language is largely complete at the age of five or at least before the child enters into contact with the surrounding world, the learning of contextualization conventions continues throughout the life-cycle as a function of the network-specific practices into which a speaker enters.

3 Comparative studies of discursive practices

In the following analyses of discursive practices in longer encounters, I will begin by illustrating the extent to which interpretation rests on contextualization and then go on to show how contextualization practices and other rhetorical strategies vary cross-culturally and will finally discuss the interactive, as well as long-term, consequences of culturally based communication failures.

3.1 Example 3: Excursion to San Francisco

The example below comes from an informal conversation in California. Two teachers of English as a Second Language (R and J) have taken a group of their students on a sight-seeing trip to San Francisco and are talking about the events of the day with several colleagues (M, P, and G).[2] The recording sets in shortly after the encounter has begun. In response to a question about the trip J asks R to tell the others what happened. In his opening turn R talks about the fog. When one of the audience remarks that it doesn't sound as if he enjoyed it, R and J jointly rejoin that it was a very good trip. Then J takes over the principal narrator's role and proceeds to give an account of where they went and of what they saw. R collaborates by supplying elaborative detail and occasional corrections.

1 P: yeah, {[hi] where'd you *go/} where'd you all *go/
2 J: well, y'wanna *tell 'em, where we went?
3 R: we went uh.., almost **everywhere/ except that it was *foggy/
  for {[lo]*half} the time we were over there/
4 M: {[hi] yeah,} you don't seem too enthusiastic about it/
5 R: {[hi] oh} it =was a good *trip/ {[hi] yeah,
  it *was/ *yeah//=}
6 J: ={[ac] [hi] well, it was a great *trip/ except=that/
  {[dc] it was a *foggy *day//
  and we started out by going to Twin Peaks,
  at nine thirty in the morning/
  on a *foggy *day// you know what we *saw?
  we saw **fog, {[lo] up to*here//}
7 R: ==we saw *fire down the *hill//
8 J: {[lo] a *fire down the *hill,=that's right//=
9 R: =there was a (f--) was on*fire//=
10 P: {[hi] that was {[lo] good}=(--)//}=
11 J: =and then= after the *fog,
  and it was *windy, we.., decided to go to the beach//
  we went to the beach, and it *was-, we saw some sea lions, though//
12 R: ==there were about *three//
13 J: ==then we had a ho-..*hot dogs on a *stick//
14 M: ==uh-huh/
15 R: **some of them/ **some of them,
  had *hot dogs on *stick//

16 M: ( ) hi G/
17   : [enters]
18 J: hi G/ ..and uh, we uh ..,
      talked ( ) about *tourists there, and we {[lo] left},
      and went to the *Palace,.. of the Legion of Honor/ right?
19 R: ==again, for a view of the Golden *Gate//
20 J: ==for a *view, of the {[lo] Golden} Gate *Bridge
      {[ac] and there was /] {[lo] no} view//
21 G: ah::

At first glance the exchange seems like a typical personal narrative. From the way he phrases his opening question, P sounds as if he is quite interested in hearing about the trip. And when R begins by emphasizing how foggy it was, M questions whether the two really did enjoy themselves. He is evidently expecting a straight narrative account. The two story tellers hasten to reply by jointly and emphatically reiterating that the trip was indeed "good"; but then they follow up by once more dwelling on the fog and the lack of visibility, giving no further specifics about what actually happened. The remainder of their account is organized around a list of tourist locations such as Twin Peaks and the Beach, and other mentionables of interest to foreigners: a fire, sea lions, hot dogs on a stick. The list sounds strangely uninformative. Presented as they are without elaborative detail, these are not topics a local audience is likely to find especially interesting. Yet, apart from M's observation, none of the listeners query the account. On the contrary in turn 10, P, the initiator of the encounter, interjects "that was good," with apparent approval, and subsequent audience reactions give no indication that they find anything odd.

It is only in line 15, when R repairs J's "we" in the phrase "we had hot dogs on a stick" – which could have been taken to refer to the group as a whole – with the more specific non-inclusive "some of them," that we begin to suspect what is happening. Apparently, without ever making it explicit, the two narrators have been talking about the students all along. What is more, they have been quoting and, by imitating their foreign accent, in fact parodying the students' speech. They seem to have been employing a metapragmatic strategy – common on American college campuses – of using quotations as a way of expressing one's opinion about a speaker's actions. So that, although the students are nowhere explicitly referred to, the story centers about *their* reactions, not those of the narrators. In the course of the talk, what started out as a personal narrative has gradually been transformed into another sub-genre, an ironic tale or seemingly sarcastic allusion to what it is like to have to spend one's time with people who by their stereotypical reaction show that they are unable to appreciate the real charm of the city.

How are these interpretive effects achieved? Choice of stylistic grammatical and lexical options clearly plays an important role. In turns 1, 5, 6, 13, 15, 19 and 20, repetition is employed for communicative effect. Another common rhetorical strategy is the repeated use of stylistic devices designed to raise the listener's expectation such as "we went almost everywhere" (turn 3); "it was a great trip," "you know what we saw?" (turn 6); "we saw some sea lions, though" (turn 11). These expectations are then regularly violated in the immediately following talk. Yet, in co-occurrence with such lexicalized strategies, contextualization through prosodic and paralinguistic signs clearly plays a key role in conveying what is intended.

Note the way accent and shifts in tempo and pitch register (i.e. raising or lowering of tone over a phrase) are deployed. P's initial question in turn I has raised pitch register, and in the second phrase "go" is repeated with stress. J responds by stressing "tell" and R then comes in with an extra high stress on "everywhere." This leads us to infer that the audience is looking forward to hearing an interesting story and that the narrators most probably have something interesting to report. However, in R's next phrase, "foggy" is accented and following that there is a sharp drop to low pitch on "half the time." Given what has just been said this shift in prosodic treatment is unexpected. Hence the comment "you don't seem too enthusiastic." Yet R and J, speaking in overlapping turns and using high pitch and accent on "trip," implicate that is not what they intended to say. Had J, who then launches into the main part of the actual narrative, continued in the same vein, we would have had no reason to suspect that they were not giving a straight account. However, after seemingly denying M's inference, he once more picks up R's fog theme repeating "foggy day" twice with the same stress. There follows a rhetorical question: "you know what we saw," which serves to highlight the third reference to fog after which the pitch shifts to low on "up to here."

The prosodic treatment in the remaining part of the narrative merits special attention. Beginning with R's "it was a good trip," to the end of the narrative, the performance is marked by an intermittent rhythmic patterning that has all the characteristics of what Couper-Kuhlen & Auer (1992), redefining Kenneth Pike's original notion, have called isochrony: repetitive regular spacing of accented rhythmic beats across more than two turns of speaking. Let me illustrate this. R's turn 5 overlaps J's comment "it was a great trip, except that," which is spoken in fast tempo, but then J's next phrase "it was a foggy day" picks up the rhythmic patterning of R's "it was a good trip." There follow two lines in unmarked colloquial rhythm but "on a foggy day" and "up to here" in the next two lines are isochronous with the foggy day phrase in turn 6.

The same is true for "fire down the hill," "a (f--) was on fire," "that was good" in turns 7, 8, 5 and 10. The pattern is once more picked up with "hot dogs on a stick" in 13 and 15. The isochrony again recurs with "of the Golden Gate Bridge" in turn 20. It is also once more repeated in turn 20, which ends the narrative. The "ah" in the concluding turn 21 is in a slot where we would ordinarily expect an acknowledgment, but it is also pronounced in "foreigner" talk style. Although G, the speaker, has only just joined the group, he has obviously caught on to what is happening.

The two principal speakers and the audience have been co-operating in producing what we could call a verbal game that involves collaboration at every stage in the proceedings. Note how closely the two narrators work together in producing their account. Each speaker is in tune with what the other is saying, frequently completing the other's message and even anticipating what he is going to say. It is R who initiates the rhythmic pattern which J then turns into the isochronous sequence and which the audience later picks up on. The performance relies on shared knowledge that goes beyond what is ordinarily understood by narrative strategies abstractly conceived. Context-specific eontextualization plays a key role. Some of these strategies such as the tone grouping that chunks the stream of talk and suggests semantic ties among phrases, use of accenting to signal distinctions between given and new information, as well as shifts in rhythm and tempo, are common among speakers of English in the United States and Britain. However, other types of cue are more situation- and group-specific. From the way the narrators and the audience work together it seems quite likely that this is not the first time that they have engaged in this kind of game. They seem to be making use of communicative conventions learned while working together as second-language instructors and generalized and internalized in the ways discussed earlier in this chapter.

As a performance the narrative resembles the ritual performances described in some of the recent anthropological literature on small, highly localized, and relatively isolated populations in the Amazonian jungle (Urban 1991, Basso 1992). In both types of situation culturally specific rhythmic and grammatical parallelisms conventionalized through past communicative experience are deployed for communicative effect. Urban, arguing in favor of a discourse-centered approach to culture, maintains that: "culture is located in concrete, publicly accessible signs, the most important of which are actually occurring instances of discourse" (1991: 1). I agree, but I would go on to argue that culture is most clearly revealed in the way we react to what we hear and otherwise perceive in particular situations.

In what follows I will provide more specific examples to show how conversational inferences vary with cultural background and how they affect interpretation, by examining extracts from recordings made as part of a comparative study of encounters involving native speakers of English born in England and native speakers of South Asian languages. The latter have learned English as a second language in India and, having lived and worked in Britain for a number of years, have acquired a functionally adequate instrumental control of English grammar and vocabulary. Yet, as I hope to show, they rely on the rhetorical and contextualization practices of their native language. When their talk is interpreted by European or North American native English speakers in terms of the English system, communication difficulties arise.

3.2 Example 4: argument

A heated and at times highly argumentative discussion occurs between L, an instructor at a British adult education center, and D, a native South Asian adult student. L has co-operated with colleagues at a neighboring college in designing a new course on intercultural communication. The course is to be offered at the *college* (not the center). L will be one of the lecturers. D had expressed interest in taking the course and L had promised to send him a copy of the announcement when it became available. When D did not receive it and found that copies were already available at the college office, he went to see L to ask for an explanation. The recording sets in as D has just accused L of intentionally withholding information from him. The argument is beginning to heat up.

1 D: this is not a-
2 L: ==of *course, {[ac] it is not a secret.}
3 D: =that it is *a secret*..=
4 L: =I haven't *said= it was a secret,
    {[ac] I didn't say it was a secret.}
    what I *said was, ..that it was *not a suitable course,
    ...for you to *apply for, because it is (--)
    ..{[lo] now if you *want to apply for it,} ..{[hi] of *course,}
    you can do what you *want.
    but, {[hi] if you are doing the twilight course at the *moment,}
    ..{[lo] it was not something which-}
    ..Mrs. N and Mr. G *thought, *originally,
    that it was a course to carry *on, *with the *twilight course
    {[hi] but this is **not the case.}
5 D: no. what you- you take *one thing at a time*.
    this case. that whatever {[f] *they know*.}
    I get that even .. hmm. for a D ..*me*.{[lo] and I am *student in E college//*}
    and Mr. W *know me/* he-. I am student in the *same school*.

{[f] he knows *my qualifications*.
and what- whether I'm suitable *or not.* =but.=
6 L: =this= has nothing to =* do with qualifications. =
7 D: ={[f] but you can't know.}=

After angrily denying that she has been trying to keep the information from him, L goes on to point out that, in any case, since he is currently enrolled in a remedial communication course, the new course is not really what he needs. She realizes that his instructors at the center had announced the course as something that might be of interest but points out that is wrong. The prosodic contextualization strategies she employs to organize her argument are much like those of the Americans in example 3. She relies on a selection of final pitch contours (",," and ".",), as well as on shifts in rhythm, tempo or pitch register to chunk her talk into intonational phrases and her choice among these options has communicative import. In line 2, for example, "of course," which on purely syntactic grounds could count as part of the following phrase, is made into a separate intonational phrase. This serves to foreground the next phrase: "it is not a secret," which then becomes the main theme of the following three lines. Similarly in the seventh line of turn 4 "but" is chunked into a separate phrase by a "," terminal contour and a rise in pitch register, thus highlighting the twilight course theme. There follows a three-line side sequence cued by a lowering of pitch, whereupon in line 12 a rise in pitch marks the return to the main argument. Accent placement within an intonational phrase marks pragmatic focus and suggests semantic (or rather interpretive) ties across units. Note how accenting works to lend special interpretive import to the frequent repetitions. Contrastive accent on "said" in line 1 of turn 4 is followed by unmarked "say" in line 2 and a third, this time accented, "said" in line 3. In foregrounding the verb in this way L is indirectly accusing D of not paying attention to her words. In the remaining part of her turn she makes another attempt to clarify what she had wanted to convey, and in this she once more relies heavily on prosodic cues to highlight her point that, since he did not have the prerequisites for the course, she did not think he would profit from it.

In his reply D fails to react to L's argument about the new course. Instead he acts as if she were questioning his personal abilities. It may be that, for whatever reason, he simply did not believe her and chose to ignore what she said. Yet the fact is, his contextualization strategies are systematically different from hers. He uses different prosodic cues and different strategies for signaling sequential level relationships. His phrases end mostly in period falling contours, almost never in comma or "?" boundaries. Moreover, he does not employ syllable accents to mark pragmatic focus. He tends to contrast or set off either a part of a phrase or an entire phrase from what precedes or follows by a combination of shifts in tempo, staccato enunciation, and sometimes increased loudness. I have used italics to mark the relevant contrasts.

These strategies are subconsciously internalized and used automatically without overt reflection. As the discussion will show they are widely shared among other South Asian English speakers of similar communicative background. Consider the following excerpt from a radio interview with a successful engineer of North Indian background who has just joined a new firm. Although the interviewee's English syntax is almost native-like, he uses pitch level and volume contrasts to chunk his intonational phrase into two contrasting parts and does not employ syllable accent and distinguish between comma and period final contours.

> 1 A: how do you like your job?
> 2 B: I may tell you that *since joining the firm.*
>   I have been *very happy.*

Although more detailed work is required to determine what the relevant contextualization system is, how it relates to that of the native language, and how it works, I believe there is enough evidence to argue that we are dealing with cognitively significant systematic differences in contextualization conventions, acquired over time in the course of informal interaction under conditions similar to those referred to above (see Gumperz 1982: 120–2 for more detailed discussion). It would of course be difficult to argue that differences in contextualization conventions are the immediate cause of the misunderstandings in example 4. However, subsequent examples will show that this is at least a likely explanation.

3.3 Example 5: selection interview

Two native English speaking interviewers, R and C, are questioning a native Pakistani applicant, who is seeking admission to a paid training course. They begin by going over the written answers on his application form.

> 1 R: ... and you've put here that you want to apply for that course,
>   because there are more jobs in:, {[dc] the *trade.}
> 2 A: {[lo] yeah}
> 3 R: so perhaps you could explain to Mr. C,
>   ahmm ... a*part from that reason,
>   *why else you want to, apply for e*lectrical work.
> 4 A: I think I like *..this job* ..in my-
>   *as a* profession//

5 C: ..{[lo] and *why do you think you'll *like it.}
6 A: ...why?
7 C: could you explain to me *why?
8 A: < 1 sec > why do I like it? well,
    I think is ..ah more job *prospect/*

The questioning and indirect probing strategies in this exchange are much like those found in other placement interviews I have examined. With native English speakers they are successful in eliciting additional specifics on past work experiences, and we can assume that this is what the interviewers are looking for. However, in the present case, the mode of questioning merely serves to confuse the applicant. In turn 1 R is treating the expression "the trade" as a separate information unit and then in turn 3 "apart," "why," and "electrical" are accented. Native speakers would infer here that they are being asked to give a different reason for wanting to apply. A, however, simply gives a lexical alternate for "trade." His answer is punctuated with pauses. In turn 6 he queries the second interviewer's "why," as if to say "I don't understand what you mean." When C, who by now sounds a bit annoyed, continues R's accenting strategy, A hesitates for a full second, repeats the question once more and then comes up with an answer that is essentially identical to his earlier ones. He seems to be interpreting what he hears in terms of his own native language contextualization system and as a result he does not perceive that accenting is being used contrastively to suggest that the interviewers are less interested in his personal "likes" than in his previous work experience. Not knowing what is expected of him, he is by now quite unsure of himself.

Interviews like the above are intrinsically hierarchical situations marked by a sharp differential in power, between professional experts and lay clients, and the interviewers are just not willing to be more explicit. Perhaps they are prejudiced against the applicant and are taking advantage of his limited English in order to justify his eventual rejection. The situation could thus be seen as a typical instance of symbolic domination (Thompson 1991), where those in power, whose practices are more authoritative, apply their own standards in evaluating the actions of the less powerful. Yet, in other parts of the same recording, not analyzed here, the interviewers do turn to direct questioning, and in response the applicant does give evidence that he has a serious interest in electrical work. Moreover, since similar questions are asked of all applicants, there are no direct indications that the present applicant is being singled out for special treatment. The fact remains that, whatever the participants' motives are, we are dealing with differences in the interpretation of specific utterances, that are directly related to knowledge of linguistic resources. For the present discussion it is important that, in each of the two preceding examples, native and non-native speakers of English, relying on different perceptions of what the relevant utterance-level contextualization cues are and different presuppositions of what their signalling import is, interpret the same stretch of talk differently. So the variability in contextualization convention is culturally significant.

3.4 Example 6: argument 2

Now consider the following example from a later part of the argument in example 4, involving additional kinds of interpretive issues.

1 L: I was one of the members of the committee,
2 D: ==yes.
3 L: who de*signed the course at E College.
   but I have nothing to do with the appli*cations or anything,
   because I'm *here.
   it's a *college course/ not a *center course.
   =and ok center=
4 D: =no it's center=
5 L: Mr. D I know **more about this course, than *you do.
   I **designed=it=.
6 D:=yes=
7 L: at E *College, but I am **telling you.
   I'm not involved in the appli*cations.
   I'm =telling you.=
8 D: =but you have=
9 L: Mr. D I **know whether or not-.
10 D: you have an equal say even.
11 L: I **don't have an equal say actually. it's-..
12 D: yes.
13 L: I'm telling you. .. I**know.
   #several turns later#
14 L: but nobody is going to, *ask me for my opinion.
15 D: ( ) I think so *for the admission.*
16 L: {[hi] Mr. D *stop telling me, that I am a **liar.}
   {[hi] I'm telling you the *truth. oh *yes you are.}
   =you're-=
17 D: =I'm not= *telling you..*

When L points out that, although she participated in planning the new course at E College, her appointment is at the Center and she has no say in admissions, D breaks in with an overlapped response. L interprets this as an attempt to contradict her. She accuses him of refusing to believe her on matters that only she can know and at times becomes quite emotional.

D on the other hand does not raise his voice. In fact in turn 17 he explicitly denies he is accusing her of not telling the truth. Although the differences in the use of prosodic contextualization cues are also evident here, it is L's interpretation of what D has been saying, both here and in other parts of the encounter, that is mainly responsible for the communicative failure. Is D really being as hostile as L seems to think he is?

Note that L has the initiative throughout this fragment. D's contributions are limited to an occasional yes or no, and short comments. Other previous studies have shown that *yes* and *no* back-channel responses function differently in English and Asian English (Gumperz, Aulakh, & Kaltman 1982). In this exchange D makes no overt "on record' accusations. His comments are very brief. Twice they overlap L's talk. At other times there are indications he is being cut off before he has a chance to explain further. Once, when L says: "I don't understand why you are so insulted with me," he replies: "I am not insulting you." When I interviewed D in his home sometime after the encounter and showed him the transcript, he said: "I was trying to ask her to help me." If that was what he was trying to achieve, how do we explain his seeming unresponsiveness and refusal to accept what L is saying? Could it be that his idea of what the encounter is about differs from hers? Now consider the following recording of a native Pakistani house-owner being interviewed by a native English-speaking counselor of Sikh background.

3.5 Example 7: advice center

1 A: #name# Arundel Street//

2 B: Arundel Street//

3 A: ==yes// I got walls/ *tumble down*//
 ...friday...eh/ *Saturday night yeah*//

4 B: the walls tumble down/ you mean they fell down//

5 A: fell down yeah/ *..fell down*//
 but could you tell me/ *which*//
 [pointing to a small map he has with him]
 ...that's my wall/ ya somebody else's wall//

6 B: hm well is your wall here? [pointing]

7 A: both sides/ *..and the front of that*//

8 B: here here and here//

9 A: hm yes//

10 B: aha um there would be/
 ...it would be a party wall between you and your next
 door neighbor here// this guy and this guy here//

11 A: yes but see next door/ *I think is your house*/
 Calmore Center's//

12 B: Calmore Center//
13 A: yes/ .. forty one/..*and thirty nine mine*//
14 B: hm/
15 A: but that up there/ *Lisit-Lisit's garden*/
this/ ..Cambridge Street here// *and eh I want to know-*
16 B: you want to know who is responsible to put them back up//
17 A: up for this front one/
18 B: I see/ .. so if you want that/
..so if you want that, ..uh that wall to be put up/
19 A: only here//
20 B: this one here//
21 A: uh up there yes//
22 B: you want to know if you are the only one who is liable
to pay for it//
23 A: pay for it/ that's what I want to know//

Someone reading this transcript without special background knowledge might have difficulty at first in determining what the talk is about. It appears from what happens later down the line that A has come to make an inquiry. Yet he never explicitly states what he really wants. Without any preliminaries he begins by directly launching into a factual account of the events that brought about the circumstances in which he finds himself, stating that his wall has fallen down. Then he proceeds to refer to a map, asking the interviewer to tell him where *his*, i.e. A's, own wall is – as if he himself did not know that.

A's account is purely fact-oriented throughout. He makes no attempt to assess or evaluate the import of the information he is giving. Yet the interviewer never asks for verbal clarification. He regularly repeats what he has heard, as if to confirm that he understands what is at issue. Occasionally he rephrases A's statements, sometimes supplying information that he assumes the client wants to convey but has not put into words. In turns 10, 18, and 22, it is he, the counselor, who formulates the client's requests. The client, on his part, consciously as it seems from the extensive pausing and hesitation that mark his talk, refrains from giving his own opinion. He relies on the counselor to evaluate the import of the facts he provides, much as in our cultural tradition patients are not encouraged to tell the doctor what they think their illness is. They are expected to present their symptoms which the doctor then proceeds to assess.

What is of interest here is that the two interactants understand each other. Like the language instructors above they are in tune and co-operate well in the encounter. The client seems to be mapping strategies acquired in his native language environment onto his English-language performance. The interviewer whose rhetorical strategies are basically

English is sufficiently familiar with North Indian discursive practices to be able to respond in accordance with the client's expectations. Although the account may seem odd to English-speaking outsiders, both participants demonstrably agree on what the activity is and how it is to be contextualized.

3.6 Example 8. sickness benefit

The above example is not an isolated case. Similar strategies are employed in a number of other counseling and interview situations. For example, in a second Asian-run advice center in the Birmingham area (Gumperz and Roberts 1991),[3] the client, a newcomer to the center, speaks in Urdu which for the purpose of this example is rendered in a literal English translation that preserves the prosodic and rhythmic organization of the original. He is asking for help in sorting out difficulties with his sickness benefits payments, and opens as follows:

```
 1  B: ah: =tell=
 2  A: ={[hi] two times-}=
 3  B: me/
 4  A: {[hi] two time} I came here/
 5  B: [nods]
 6  A: {[hi] but you} weren't available/
 7  B: [nods]
 8  A: [{hi] much trouble} is befalling me/ ("I have great problems.")
 9  B: what is the matter.
10  A: [turns towards his 8- or 9-year-old son who hands him a document,
        which A puts on the table between himself and B]
11  B: [follows A's movements with his gaze and nods]
12  A: {[hi] this} is a calendar/ [displaying the document]
13  B: [nods]
14  A: [unfolds the calendar and points to a particular spot]
15  B: [holds down one corner of the paper and directs his gaze to the
        marked spot]
16  A: {on the twenty five I}.. signed/
17  B: {you signed} twenty five/
18  A: {[hi] hm/}...{[hi]on June eight,} is my signing time/
        {[hi] On the seventh I went to the hospital.}
        #several turns omitted#
19  A: ah {[hi]my.. money,} wasn't given/
20  B: no money/
21  A: they didn't send any/
22  B: {[hi] from signing place, hospital,} no money
23  A: [nods]
```

The client's initial moves seem designed to underline the gravity of his situation and in his statement in turn 8 he represents himself as a victim of circumstances. But then, like the house-owner in the preceding exchange, he does not explain his problem nor does he say what he wants. Yet the counselor, who, like the counselor in the previous example, is able to operate in both the South Asian English and British communicative traditions, once more, makes no effort to question him on these matters. Instead he proceeds to elicit background information on the facts that led to the problem. After another long series of fact-centered exchanges, like those reproduced above, the counselor himself assesses the problem in turn 21: "from the time you signed in at the hospital you received no money."

One could of course argue that he was forced to do this since the interviewee had only rudimentary knowledge of English. The pattern is repeated, however, in a subsequent exchange with a second new client, a young South Asian woman who speaks English with a native speaker's accent and has come accompanied by several family members and a house guest, to seek a visa extension for the guest who is threatened with deportation. She begins as follows: "They're going to send him back to (xxxx)." When the counselor asks her to tell the story from the beginning, when he first arrived, she goes on with: "He came here on the twenty eighth of May," without giving any further detail. Then he once more initiates a series of fact-centered exchanges, after which he proceeds to explain the difficulties they will face in obtaining a visa extension. In a third encounter, a South Asian woman who apparently wants to change apartments is talking to a housing officer. She begins with a statement: "My children out in the street, they beat them." When the officer asks what she means, she repeats: "My children in the street, they beat them." Then after a second clarification question, she goes on: "When they are in the hallway they shout at them." Finally the interviewer asks: "Do you have a housing problem?" He is evidently expecting the client to formulate a problem before he proceeds to help her. The ethnographic data on such situations show that interviewers are expected to be careful not to put words into the client's mouth, but from the way he responds it is evident he is not sure what the client wants.

The South Asians' practices differ systematically from those which native English speakers would expect in similar situations. Yet the relevant inferential processes, while they are grounded in contextualization conventions, are not entirely identical with the localized utterance-level processes described in the earlier examples. More general metapragmatic assessments are involved, on such matters as: what is to be expected in the exchange, what should be lexically expressed, what can be conveyed only indirectly, how moves are to be positioned within an exchange, what interpersonal relations are involved, and what rights to speaking apply. I will use the term activity-level inferences to refer to such assessments.

It is clear from the existing literature on discourse that, to enter into an encounter, participants always need some advance extra-textual knowledge about what is expected to be accomplished and how it is to be conveyed. Yet such initial presuppositions are always attuned and realigned in interaction. It is the ability to make these adaptations that tends to breaks down in intercultural encounters of the kind described here. The South Asian clients are aware that they are engaged in an interview where they must provide information. Yet they differ from native English-speaking counselors in their notions of what actions this entails.

Let me return to example 3 to illustrate this point. Recall that at first listeners were under the impression that they were hearing a personal narrative told from the speaker's perspective. However, the inconsistencies at the level of content, the violations of expectations raised in the earlier moves, the repetitive dwelling on information of no special interest, and the seemingly peculiar use of rhythm and stress all worked together to touch off a memory search for other more likely explanations. In this search participants rely on previous communicative experiences and their ability to establish intertextuality by remembering specific ways of talking and the situations and activities indexically associated with their use. People who share common background experiences are of course more likely to succeed in negotiating shared interpretation than those who do not.

The following final example will illustrate the communicative problems that can arise in this connection.

3.7 Example 9: introductions

A Pakistani-born maths teacher (A), who had his secondary-school and teacher education in England and who, after a year or so of probationary teaching, has been unable to secure a permanent post, was told to seek more training in communication skills. He has gone to see a specialist in an adult education center to find a suitable course. After a few preliminary exchanges the counselor (B) turns to the interview proper and the following ensues:

1 B: ye:s/ tell me what =it is— you want//
2 A: =hmm=
   hmm, may I first of all request for the introduction
   please//
3 B: oh yes/ sorry/
4 A: ==I am sorry// < 1 sec >

  5 B: I am B//
  6 A: oh yes// ={[breathy] I see ..oh yes .. very nice//} =
  7 B: = and I am a teacher here in the Center/=
  8 A: very nice//
  9 B: ==and we run-
10 A: ==pleased to meet you// < laughs >
11 B: ==different =courses= yes, and you are Mr. A?
12 A: = < laughs > =
    N.A.//
13 B: N.A.// yes, yes, I see < laughs >// okay,
    that's the introduction// < laughs >
14 A: would it be enough introduction?

B is interpreting A's request for an introduction in Western terms, as basically a social move. Her efforts to get what she sees as the preliminaries over with and start the interview proper are not successful. Not only does A fail to follow her lead but the response he gives sounds odd to say the least. At issue here are not simply different interpretations of what the term "introduction" means. The misunderstanding feeds back into the interaction and seriously affects both the outcome of the encounter and the ability of the participants to sustain conversational involvement. When B complies with A's request by giving her name and attempting to say a few words about herself and the Center, his overlaps and latchings interrupt her several times. There is much stumbling and awkward-sounding laughter, and in response to A's "very nice" B reacts with embarrassment. It seems that the fact that the two do not share sequential-level contextualization strategies keeps them from being able to repair the differences in activity-level inferences. One might suspect that A is purposely being disruptive, but that seems unlikely since he is asking for B's help with his course program. Neither participant seems to be quite clear about what the other is doing. The recurrent violations of preference expectations and the seemingly unmotivated responses suggest that, although both participants agree that they are engaged in a counseling interview, they do not agree on what this involves. The counselor who is assessing the encounter in terms of her own linguistic ideology is quite likely to conclude that A is acting irrationally and her conclusions are readily defensible in the public sphere where similar ideological principles apply. If, however, we admit the possibility that the question is one of semantic interference, we come to different conclusions.

Exactly what the South Asians' activity-level expectations are is difficult to determine from the relatively limited data available here. In what follows I list some preliminary hypotheses derived from re-analyses of topical organization in a wide range of examples, in co-operation with native South-Asian-language-speaking research assistants.[4] It is interesting to note that at first all three of us had difficulties in explaining what was happening in encounters such as the above. It was only when we began to reexamine the argument example, looking both at the content and at the way talk was contextualized and positioned within the exchange, that we hit upon a possible explanation. One of the research assistants remarked that the interviewee's expressions "sounded" as if he were "pleading" with the interviewer. When she quoted a few typical formulaic Hindi pleading phrases, I began to recall similar expressions I had heard in North India, in cases where students came to ask for recommendations. When I felt I did not know enough about the students' work and that there was nothing I could do, they countered with phrases like "oh no, you can do anything." At the time I was puzzled, but I believe that now, after these analyses, I have a better appreciation of what may have been involved.

After reviewing our data with the above in mind, we came up with the following general hypothesis: South Asian interviewees are treating the interviews as relatively formal hierarchical situations of pleading, marked by a sharp division between the interviewer, who is treated as the expert, and the clients, who act as petitioners, dependent on the interviewer's help. From this basic principle a number of expectations follow. For example, clients are expected to avoid expressions of personal opinions, feelings, and beliefs. They commonly background their own accomplishments and try not to present information that they have reason to believe the interviewer already knows, while building up or sometimes even exaggerating what the interviewer can do. Note for instance the way in which the client in the advice center points to a street-map, and goes about step by step securing agreement on the boundaries of his property, until the counselor identifies the boundary wall that needs to be rebuilt and later volunteers the information that the Center may be expected to share in the rebuilding cost. In the sickness benefits example, the client states that he went to the center twice and that the counselor was not there, as if circumstances had conspired against him, rather than saying outright: "I came to see you." He then constructs his case through a series of factual statements, which the counselor then assesses in formulating his own summary statement of what is at issue. The interviewer, on the other hand, is treated as someone who has the knowledge and power to assess the import of what the clients say and formulate what is at issue. The two South Asian interviewers in our examples are in fact quite ready to offer interpretations, acting in some ways like physicians would in giving their diagnoses on the basis of patients' factual reports of symptoms. Native English speakers not familiar with South Asian activity-level presuppositions on the other hand clearly have difficulty in coming up to the clients' expectations.[5]

Although it may not be immediately evident, the argument example can also be understood in the above terms. In reacting to L's efforts to explain the workings of the admission process, D most probably did not intend to contradict her. Responses like D's "but you have an equal say" or "if you feel somebody is not suitable you can say no," that sound just like the Hindi expressions I recall hearing from students in India, can be interpreted as generalized or formulaic assertions that indexically suggest "I am asking for your help," which is exactly what D told me when I interviewed him. Similarly in asking for introductions in example 9, A was most probably trying to find out what B's "status" in the institution was, so that he could judge how best to present his case. Although B was a teacher, she was also the center's program officer. Thus his question "Is that enough introduction?" was in fact meaningful. He sensed that he had not been given the response that he felt he needed. B on the other hand was both set back by A's inability or refusal to engage in the kind of discussion of his "problems" that she was looking for. Her impatience led her to try to cut him short, but, because of her inability to tune into his sequential-level strategies, she repeatedly cut him off in mid argument. He in turn was frustrated by her failure to deal with or evaluate his presentation of the relevant facts, so that in the end he went away with the impression that she was not interested in what he had to say and had failed to do her job.

The differences in notions of activity reflected here are not unlike what we found in example 3. In that case, however, the apparent oddities of content and style led to new implicature-like inferences which made sense of the account so that the initial misunderstandings were readily repaired. What distinguishes the intercultural situations is that (leaving aside for the moment other matters of background experience and power relations that also affect interpretation), because of the interaction of activity-level and sequential-level inferences, the workings of contextualization conventions, and the universal tendency to interpret in terms of one's own presuppositions, attempts at repair misfire, so that miscommunication is likely to be compounded rather than resolved by further talk and may turn into pejorative evaluation. Let me emphasize that what I am talking about here are not individuals' feelings, beliefs or values, but indexical ties between verbal form and context that function metapragmatically to create interpretive effects. The interviewers and interviewees may express approval or anger in reaction to what transpires in the encounter, but they do not necessarily assume that other participants are inferior or superior. Language use when seen in these terms evokes situated reactions, it does not directly reflect generalized beliefs or attitudes.

4 Concluding remarks

I began this chapter by arguing that the move to situated discourse as the principal object of analysis calls attention to new dimensions of variability that have so far not been sufficiently addressed. If we essentialize languages, cultures, and communities as self-contained and internally coherent abstract "structures," we cannot, as several of the authors in this volume have shown, account for the empirical facts of referential practice. Yet this does not mean that such notions ought to be dropped. They need to be recognized for what they are: ideological formations, based in history and in more or less stable conventionalized discursive practices, that are subject to change in response to changes in the surrounding worlds.

The argument applies as much to the relatively small isolated groups that students of language and culture have tended to study in the past as to the South Asians, the language teachers, and the social service professionals described in this chapter. In each case individuals rely on typified practices, acquired through communicative collaboration in institutionalized networks of relationships and that have become conventionalized through habituation, typification, and grammaticalization (Hanks, this volume). Linguistic and cultural relativity ultimately has its origin in such processes. What distinguishes the small communities from the urban minority populations is the way variability is distributed. Until quite recently, in the former groups, networks of relationships overlapped so that there was much justification for treating them as isolates. However, as we have learned during the last few years, this isolation is rapidly disappearing. Formerly highly localized peoples have now become integrated into modern nation states, and to preserve their lands and their rights they must compete in the public sphere much as other groups do. Bi- and multi-lingualism is increasing with the result that the communicative conditions under which they carry on their affairs have more and more come to resemble those of the urban minorities. This is to say that cultural differences are becoming increasingly functional and less and less structural. These conditions lend relevance to an approach to variability that focuses on how language and culture work either to create shared understanding or to set up and maintain distinctions and on the effect of these processes in everyday life.

I have therefore concentrated on comparative analyses contrasting encounters among individuals who share communicative backgrounds with ones among those who do not, rather than relying on established macro-categories of cultural or ethnic identity. The view of interpretation as a complex inferential process, in which grammar and lexicon are only two among a number of other factors, led me to reexamine both the linguistic and cultural factors in communication. Following Silverstein and his students it has become common to draw distinctions between two types of linguistic signalling processes: symbolic signs that convey information via grammatical and semantic rules, and indexical signs that signal by virtue of conventionalized associations between signs and context.

The focus on contextualization cues as a subclass of indexical signs calls attention to the fact that, as the analysis of South Asian discursive practices shows, knowledge of indexical signs and particularly contextualization conventions on the one hand, and grammatical signs on the other, is differentially distributed in human populations. Contextualization practices diffuse in accordance with institutionalized networks of relationship and their acquisition is constrained by the economic, political, and ideological forces that serve to minoritize large sectors of the population. This mismatch becomes particularly important as formerly isolated populations become absorbed into modern nation states, so that intercultural distinctions become matters of function. This is of course also true for some of the most frequently cited examples of Whorfian effects, such as, for example, the frequently cited case of the "empty" gasoline drums (Whorf 1956: 135ff.). Seen from the perspective of structure such phenomena could be dismissed as "mere" matters of usage. Contextualization analysis of the kind illustrated here suggests ways of showing how discourse-centered cultural knowledge is acquired and how it works either to maintain or blur existing distinctions.

I have used the term *culture* to refer to locally specific, taken-for-granted, knowledge of background information and verbal forms, acquired through communicative collaboration with others in and outside of home environments. Perhaps Bourdieu's *habitus*,[6] dispositions to act and react in certain ways, more adequately accounts for what I want to convey. While I accept the gist of Bourdieu's argument, my position differs from his in several ways. I argue that in discourse the relevant actions and reactions are cued by isolable signalling mechanisms emitted through practice and are inculcated through communication in institutionalized collaborative relationships. As a result the signs come both to index and to evoke the memory of activities specific to these relationships. *Habitus* thus does not directly mirror macro-social categories like class or ethnicity as Bourdieu would have it. Although relationships with macro-categories clearly exist, they are always mediated by institutionally specific practices and it is via these practices that they need to be studied. Secondly, I argue that *habitus*, when seen in interactive terms, does not just involve abstract dispositions to action, it also constitutes practices in which actions are embedded. The relationship between *habitus* and action is always a reflexive one.

In view of the many uses that the term *culture* has been put to in recent times, the perspective on culture emerging from the analyses is clearly limited. Like Slobin and Clark (this volume), I am concerned with culture and cognition as they enter into communication. I have only alluded to the clearly pervasive effect that linguistic ideologies have on how action is interpreted[7] in multicultural settings. Moreover, discursive practices always operate within what Bourdieu calls a field (Thompson 1991). It is the power relations in this field that ultimately determine access to participation in the institutionalized networks of relationships that lead to learning. In this sense, discursive practices relate to macro-social forces.

Since all interpretation is always context-bound and rooted in collaborative exchanges that rest on shifting contextual presuppositions, contextualization must be a universal of human communication. It has its origin in a social universal, the division of labor, which in one form or another is characteristic of all human collectivities. The division of labor leads to differential access to knowledge of the material world and creates experts whose word on certain matters comes to be vested with the authority of direct experience. As ethnographers, we can interpret this as implying that the division of labor brings about specialization in certain ranges of activities. Yet participation in such activities is not a matter of individual inclination; it takes the form of interpersonal co-operation in institutionalized networks of relationship, such that members talk more to each other about certain matters and certain types of action than they do to non-members. Therefore, while the particular practices that I have compared are situation-specific, the cultural distinctions they reflect have their root in human action, in the way it is constrained by power relations, and in its relation to the distribution of knowledge.

Appendix: transcription system

Symbol	Significance
*// *	Final fall
/	Slight fall indicating "more is to come"
?	Final rise
,	Slight rise as in listing intonation
-	Truncation (e.g. "what ti- what time is it/")
..	Pauses of less than 0.5 second
...	Pauses greater than 0.5 second (unless precisely timed)
<2>	Precise units of time (=2-second pause)

=	To indicate overlap and latching of speakers' utterances e.g.

R: so you understand =the requirements=
       B: =yeah, i under = stand them/
       R: so you understand the requirements?
       B: ==yeah, i understand them/
       R: ==and the schedule?
       B: yeah/

	with spacing and single "=" before and after the appropriate portions of the text indicating overlap, and turn-initial double "=" indicating latching of the utterance to the preceding one.
::	Lengthened segments (e.g. "wha::t")
~	Fluctuating intonation over one word
*	Accent; normal prominence
**	Accent; extra prominence
CAPS	Extra prominence
{[ ]}	Non-lexical phenomena, both vocal and nonvocal, which overlay the lexical stretch e.g. {[lo] text//}
[ ]	non-lexical phenomena, both vocal and nonvocal, which interrupt the lexical stretch e.g. text [laugh] text//
( )	Unintelligible speech
di(d)	A good guess at an unclear segment
(did)	A good guess at an unclear word
(xxx)	Unclear word for which a good guess can be made as to how many syllables were uttered with "x"=one syllable
(" ")	Regularization (e.g. "i'm gonna ("going to") come soon"
# #	Use hatchmarks when extratextual information needs to be included within the text e.g.

R: did you ask M#surname#to come?

Notes

1 The notion of contextualization cues was first proposed by Cook-Gumperz and Gumperz (1978). It has since been more systematically developed and applied to a variety of interactive situations (Gumperz 1981, 1982, 1992, Auer & Di Luzio 1992).

2 From Falk (1979). The analysis is largely my own.

3 In the original A speaks in Hindi; his talk has been translated into English for the purposes of this discussion. B, the counselor, answers in English. The applicant has a passive command of English and the two clearly understand each other. The fact that this is possible is evidence to suggest that South Asian English speakers are mapping their native rhetorical strategies onto their English.

4 I am grateful to Dr. Arpita Misra and Mr. Gurinder Aulakh for key analytical insights.

5 See Becker (1979) for a vivid description of similar cross-cultural differences in activity-level presuppositions. Young (1994), in a study similar to the present one, shows how native speakers of Mandarin often tend to map

presuppositions based in Chinese cultural ideology onto their English and argues that this has had a significant effect on the Western view of the Chinese.
6 The best explanation of what this term entails is found in Thompson (1991). Thompson's words are worth quoting here: "The habitus is a set of dispositions which incline agents to act and react in certain ways. The dispositions generate practices, perceptions and attitudes which are 'regular' without being consciously coordinated or governed by any 'rule'... Dispositions are acquired through a gradual process of inculcation in which early childhood experiences are particularly important. Through a myriad of mundane processes of training and learning, such as those involved in the inculcation of table manners... the individual acquires a set of dispositions which literally mold the body and become second nature. The dispositions produced thereby are also structured in the sense that they unavoidably reflect the social conditions within which they were acquired."
7 See the recent special issue of *Pragmatics* (Kroskritty et al. 1992) for detailed discussion on these matters.

References

Atkinson, M. & Heritage, J. (eds.) 1986. *Structures of social action*. New York: Cambridge University Press.

Auer, P. & Di Luzio, A. (eds.) 1992. *The contextualization of language.* Amsterdam/Philadelphia: John Benjamins.

Basso, E. B. 1992. Contextualization in Kapalo narratives. In A. Duranti & C. Goodwin (eds.), *Rethinking context*. Studies in the Social and Cultural Foundations of Language 11 (pp. 253–70). Cambridge University Press.

Bauman, R. & Sherzer, J. 1974. *Explorations in the ethnography of speaking*. New York: Cambridge University Press.

Becker, A. L. 1979. Text-building, epistemology and esthetics in Javanese Shadow Theater. In A. L. Becker & A. Yengoyan (eds.), *The imagination of reality* (pp. 211–43). Norwood, NJ: Ablex.

Bergman, J . R. & Luckmann, T. 1994. Reconstructive genres of everyday communication. In U. Quasthoff (ed.), *Aspects of oral communications*. Berlin: Mouton de Gruyter.

Cook-Gumperz, J. & Gumperz, J. 1978. Context in children's speech. In N. Waterson & C. Snow (eds.), *The development of communication* (pp. 3–23). Chichester: Wiley.

Couper-Kuhlen, E. & Auer, P. 1991. On the contextualizing function of speech rhythm in conversation. In J. Verschueren (ed.), *Levels of linguistic adaptation* (pp. 1–18). Amsterdam: John Benjamins.

Falk, J. 1979. *The duet as conversational process*. Ph.D. dissertation, Princeton University.

Grice, H. P. 1989. *Studies in the way of words*. Cambridge, MA: Harvard University Press.

Gumperz, J. J. 1971. *Language in social groups*. Stanford University Press.
   1981. *Language and social identity*. Cambridge University Press.
   1982. *Discourse strategies*. Cambridge University Press.
   1992. Contextualization and understanding. In A. Duranti & C. Goodwin (eds.), *Rethinking context: Language as an interactive phenomenon* (pp. 229–52). New York: Cambridge University Press.

Gumperz, J. J., Aulakh, G., & Kaltman, H. 1982. Thematic structure and progression in discourse: ethnic style and the transition to literacy. In D. Tannen (ed.), *Coherence in spoken and written discourse* (pp. 3–20). Norwood, NJ: Ablex.

Gumperz, J. J. & Roberts, C. 1991. Understanding in intercultural encounters. In J. Blommaert & J. Verschueren (eds.), *The pragmatics of intercultural communication* (pp. 51–90). Amsterdam: John Benjamins.

Hanks, W. F. 1990. *Referential practice: language and lived space among the Maya.* University of Chicago Press.

Hymes, D. 1972. Models of the interaction of language and social life. In J. J. Gumperz & D. Hymes (eds.), *Directions in sociolinguistics: the ethnography of communication* (pp. 35–71). New York: Holt, Rinehart & Winston.

Kroskritty et al. (eds.) 1992. Special issue on Language Ideologies, *Pragmatics.*

Sapir, E. 1951 [1931] Communication. In *The selected writings of Edward Sapir in language, culture, and personality*, ed. D. G. Mandelbaum (pp. 104–9). Berkeley and Los Angeles: University of California Press.

Schegloff, E. A. 1986. On the organization of sequences as a source of "coherence" in talk-in-interaction. Prepared for discussion at SRCD conference on Development of Conversational Coherence, University of New Orleans, May 1986.

Scollon, R. & Scollon S. B. K. 1981. *Narrative literacy and face in interethnic communication.* Norwood, NJ: Ablex.

Thompson, J. 1991. *Language and symbolic power.* New York: Polity Press.

Turner, T. 1994. Anthropology and multiculturalism: what is anthropology that multiculturalists should be mindful of it? *Cultural Anthropology*, 8(4), 411–29.

Urban, G. 1991. *A discourse-centered approach to culture: native South American myths and rituals.* Austin: University of Texas Press.

1993. Culture's public face. *Public Culture*, 15 (Oct.), 213–38.

Whorf, B. L. 1956. The relation of habitual thought and behavior to language. In *Selected writings of Benjamin Lee Whorf*, ed. J. B. Carroll (pp. 134–59). Cambridge, MA: MIT Press.

Young, L. W. L. 1994. *Cross talk and culture in Sino-American communication.* New York: Cambridge University Press.

13

LINGUISTIC RESOURCES FOR SOCIALIZING HUMANITY[1]

ELINOR OCHS

1 Language socialization

Using language and participating in society are closely related activities in that using language is integral to social life and participating in society is integral to the process of making sense of linguistic constructions. It is difficult to imagine, on the one hand, how one might assign meanings to lexical, grammatical, phonological, and discursive structures without an understanding of the social situations which those structures depict. On the other hand, it is difficult to imagine how one might engage in social interactions, social institutions, social relationships, and other societal phenomena without the use of language. For better or for worse, language is our human medium for constructing a social order and a philosophy of taste, causality, knowledge, and experience. For those reasons, language can be viewed as a system of symbolic resources designed for the production and interpretation of social and intellectual activities. From this perspective, the acquisition of language and the acquisition of social and cultural competence are not developmentally independent processes, nor is one process a developmental prerequisite of the other. Rather, the two processes are intertwined from the moment a human being enters society (at birth, in the womb, or at whatever point local philosophy defines as "entering society"). Each process facilitates the other, as children and other novices come to a perspective on social life in part through signs and come to understand signs in part through social experience. In this sense, students of language acquisition need to reckon with the system of social and cultural structures that inform speaking and understanding in communities just as students of socialization need to reckon with the system of lexical, grammatical, phonological, and discursive structures that give meaning to facilitate social conduct and intellectual expertise in communities (see Bernstein 1964, Heath 1983, Hymes 1972, Ochs & Schieffelin 1984, Sapir [1927] 1963, for further discussion of this point).

A number of scholars have begun to examine language acquisition and socialization as an integrated process called *language socialization*.

Language socialization is the process whereby children and other novices are socialized through language, part of such socialization being a socialization to use language meaningfully, appropriately, and effectively (Schieffelin & Ochs 1986a, b). An important premise of language socialization research is that language socializes not only through its symbolic content but also through its *use*, i.e., through *speaking* as a socially and culturally situated activity. The emphasis in language socialization studies is not on how languages as symbolic systems encode local world-views (e.g. as lexical paradigms) and, as such, how acquisition of language (e.g. acquisition of lexical paradigms) entails acquisition of a world-view, in the vein of many ethnosemantic studies of linguistic relativity (e.g. Boas 1911, Conklin 1955, Whorf 1941). Rather the emphasis is on language *praxis*, what Sapir called "fashions of speaking" (Sapir 1963). A prevailing perspective in language socialization research is that language practices are socially organized and that, as novices recurrently engage in these practices with more expert members of society, they develop an understanding of social actions, events, emotions, esthetics, knowledgeability, statuses, relationships, and other socio-cultural phenomena. For example, I am socialized to understand and recognize who I am and who you are and what you and I are doing at any one moment in time in part because our linguistic practices characterize us and our actions in certain ways (i.e., give us and our actions meaning). In this sense, language praxis is a hand-maiden to culture, a medium for the passing of cultural knowledge from one generation to the next. Language socialization research reports this version of linguistic relativity, one that emphasizes the socializing power of *parole* (utterances).

This focus on language practices as resources for socializing social and cultural competence links language socialization research to post-structural sociological paradigms that portray *social structures as outcomes of social practices* (see Practice Theory [Bourdieu 1977], Structuration Theory [Giddens 1979]) and to psychological paradigms that portray *cognitive structures as outcomes of speaking* (see Slobin, this volume, for a discussion of "thinking for speaking") *and of social interaction* (see Cicourel 1973, 1980, 1989; Cole 1990; Cole & Griffin 1987: Engeström 1987, 1990; Lave & Wenger 1991; Leont'ev 1981a, b; Rogoff 1990; Rogoff & Gardner 1984; Scribner & Cole 1981; Vygotsky 1978, among others).

A basic challenge of language socialization research has been to articulate the role of language praxis in the process of becoming a member of society. This challenge has been addressed largely by detailed studies of language socialization in particular communities and settings (see for example Bernstein 1964; Briggs 1984, 1986; Cook-Gumperz 1973,

1981, 1986; Crago 1988; Eisenberg 1986; Goodwin 1990; Heath 1983; Kulick 1990; Miller 1982; Miller & Sperry 1988; Ochs 1988; Ochs, Taylor, Rudolf, & Smith 1992; Platt 1986; Schieffelin 1990; Scollon 1982, among others). The present chapter draws upon these studies to address two critical dilemmas.

The first dilemma concerns *how language practices encode and socialize information about society and culture.*[2] Since, typically, information about social identities, actions, stances, and the like is not made explicit (e.g. "This woman is an honoured guest," "We are telling a story," "This is a scientific fact"), how is such information otherwise conveyed? To say simply that the meaning of utterances is indeterminate is not itself illuminating vis-à-vis understanding the relation of linguistic form to the socialization of culture. We need to delve into the notion of indeterminacy to see if there is an architecture therein, much like other researchers seek order within chaos (Prigogine & Stengers 1984, Briggs & Peat 1989). In the discussion to follow, the process of language socialization will be related to the capacity of language practices to *index* socio-cultural information.

A second dilemma is the relation of language socialization not just to local culture but to *human culture* as a species phenomenon. We have for so long pigeon-holed culture as antithetical to universals of human nature that we have scarcely attended to culture as a singularly human enterprise. "Cultural universal" is not an oxymoron. A universal of human behavior is not necessarily an outcome of innate mechanisms; it may be an outcome of pan-species commonalties in the human accommodation to, and structuring of, social life. Without diminishing the importance of differences, it is important to recognize these commonalties as facilitating social co-ordination across social groups. What does this imply about language socialization? One implication is that human beings across societies may be using language in similar ways to both structure their environment and socialize novices. One challenge of language socialization research is to present candidate universals in the relation of language to socialization and the structuring of culture.

To this end, in this chapter I draw on diverse studies in pragmatics, sociolinguistics, conversation analysis, and linguistic anthropology to formulate three principles (the principles of indexicality, universal culture, and local culture) concerning the indexing and socializing of culturally relevant information through language practices and the scope of these processes across human societies. For purposes of this discussion, culture is here conceptualized as a set of socially recognized and organized practices and theories for acting, feeling, and knowing, along with their material and institutional products, associated with membership in a social group.

2 The Indexicality Principle

The fields of pragmatics, linguistic anthropology, sociolinguistics, conversation analysis, and ethnomethodology all articulate ways in which the meaning of cultural forms, including language, is a function of how members engage these forms in the course of their social conduct. By now it is generally appreciated that members use cultural forms, including linguistic forms within their code repertoires, variably according to their conceptualization of the social situation at hand. In the social sciences "situation" is usually broadly conceived and includes socio-cultural dimensions a member activates to be part of the situation at hand such as the *temporal and spatial locus* of the communicative situation, the *social identities* of participants, the *social acts* and *activities* taking place, and participants' *affective and epistemic stance*. For purposes of this discussion, situational dimensions other than space and time are preliminarily defined as follows:

> *social identity* encompasses all dimensions of social personae, including roles (e.g. speaker, overhearer, master of ceremonies, doctor, teacher, coach), relationships (e.g. kinship, occupational, friendship, recreational relations), group identity (e.g. gender, generation, class, ethnic, religious, educational group membership), and rank (e.g. titled and untitled persons, employer and employee), among other properties;

> *social act* refers to a socially recognized goal-directed behavior, e.g. a request, an offer, a compliment;

> *activity* refers to a sequence of at least two social acts, e.g. disputing, storytelling, interviewing, giving advice;

> *affective stance* refers to a mood, attitude, feeling, and disposition, as well as degrees of emotional intensity vis-à-vis some focus of concern (Ochs & Schieffelin 1984, Labov 1984, Levy 1984);

> *epistemic stance* refers to knowledge or belief vis-à-vis some focus of concern, including degrees of certainty of knowledge, degrees of commitment to truth of propositions, and sources of knowledge, among other epistemic qualities (Chafe & Nichols 1986).

Every novice enters a fluid, sometimes volatile, social world that varies in certain conventional, non-random ways. Membership is accrued as novices begin to move easily in and out of linguistically configured situations. As they do so, novices build up associations between particular forms and particular identities, relationships, actions, stances, and the like. A basic tenet of language socialization research is that *socialization is in part a process of assigning situational, i.e., indexical, meanings* (e.g. temporal, spatial, social identity, social act, social activity, affective or epistemic meanings) to particular forms (e.g. interrogative forms, diminutive affixes, raised pitch and the like). I will refer to this tenet as the Indexicality Principle. To index is to point to the presence of some entity in the immediate situation-at-hand. In language, an index is considered to be a linguistic form that performs this function (Lyons 1977, Peirce 1955). Peirce, for example, defines index as follows:

> [An index is] a sign, or representation, which refers to its object not so much because of any similarity or analogy with it, nor because it is associated with general characters which that object happens to possess, as because it is in dynamical (including spatial) connection both with the individual object, on the one hand, and with sense or memory of the person for whom it serves as a sign, on the other hand.   (Peirce 1955: 107).

A linguistic index is usually a structure (e.g. sentential voice, emphatic stress, diminutive affix) that is used variably from one situation to another and becomes conventionally associated with particular situational dimensions such that when that structure is used, the form invokes those situational dimensions.[3]

An example of linguistic indexing of *affective stance* is provided in (1) below. Affect is richly indexed in all languages of the world (see Ochs & Schieffelin 1984). In addition to indexing particular kinds of affect (e.g. positive affect, negative affect), languages also index degrees of affective intensity. "Intensity operates on a scale centered about the zero, or unmarked expression, with both positive (aggravated or intensified) and negative (mitigated or minimized) poles" (Labov 1984: 44). In (1), a stance of heightened affect is indexed in the immediate situation through the use of the following structures in English: quantifiers ("all over," "a lot") as well as emphatic stress (e.g. "a lot," "that long"), phonological lengthening (e.g. "s::-so," "jus::t"), interjections ("Go:d"), laughter, and repetition (e.g. "I didn't eat one bit I didn't take one bite").[4]

> (1) Mother approaches her two children (Jimmy and Janet), who are eating dinner. Jimmy has just commented that Janet has drowned her meat in A1 sauce and compares this with how he used to drown his pancakes in syrup:

→	Jimmy	when I had pancakes one- pancakes (that) one time?
→		I like syrup? I put syrup? - <u>all over</u> my pancakes
→		and a <u>lot</u> - an - I didn't eat one bit I didn't take one
→		bite - I took some bites but =
	Mother:	= when was that?
	Jimmy:	a long time ago? - bout ((tosses head)) ten? - ten years old? - a:nd - the: [(Ja)
→	Mother:	[(that wasn't <u>that</u> long
→	Jimmy:	(well who knows) - but um th- the <u>pancake</u>- it was
→		s::-so soft (you) could - like (break) it with your -

→   - ju::st (pull it off) - <u>Go:d</u> hh
                     ((pause))
       Jimmy: (I) tried to scrape some of it <u>off</u> but hchehe
                     ((pause)) ((TV going))
       Mother: just sinks in

A second example of indexicality focuses on the indexing of *social identity*. This example is taken from interaction between two siblings in a Western Samoan household. Western Samoan society is elaborately hierarchical, with ranking on the basis of title, generation, and age among the variables. Traditional expectations assume that higher-ranking parties to an interaction will be less physically active than lower-ranking parties. Hence directives using the deictic verbs *sau*, 'come,' and *alu*, 'go,' are appropriately addressed to those of lower rank (Platt 1986). Within the analytic framework of the present chapter, we consider these verbs to index not only spatial dimensions but social relational dimensions of the social situation as well. In particular, the verbs *sau* and *alu* index that the speaker is of a higher rank than the addressee. In example (2), Mauga addresses her younger sibling Matu'u (2 years 2 months), with each instance of the deictic verbs indicating the asymmetrical nature of their relationship:

(2) Matu'u's older sister, Mauga, is sitting at the front edge of the house. Matu'u is at the back of the house:

→   Mauga: *Matu' u sau*
                   Matu'u, come here.'

→   *Matu'u sau*
                   Matu'u, come here.'
                   ((Matu'u goes to Mauga))

→   *alu mai sau 'ie*
                   'Go get a piece of clothes (for you).'

→   *Alu amai le mea solo ai lou isu*
                   'Go get it to wipe your nose.'

→   *kamo' e, alu e amai le solosolo 'ua e loa 'ua e loa*
                   'Hurry, go get the handkerchief, you know, you know.'

When we examine the situational meanings linguistic structures index, certain situational dimensions appear to be grammaticized more than other dimensions across language communities. Pragmatic studies attest to rich indexical systems referring to *time* and *space* (Fillmore 1982, Hanks 1990, Lyons 1982, Talmy 1983). Less recognized is the fact that, in many languages, *affective* and *epistemic stance* is encoded at many levels of linguistic structure. For example, degrees of certainty are indexed through sentential adverbs, hedges, presuppositional structures (e.g. cleft constructions, determiners), and sentential mood (e.g. interrogative mood indexing uncertainty/unknowing state), among other structures. As example (1) attests, affective stance is also elaborately indexed through grammatical structures such as diminutives, augmentatives, quantifiers, verb voice, sentential adverbs, and intonation (see Labov 1984, Ochs & Schieffelin 1989). While *social identity* is indexed across the world's language communities through pronominal systems and honorific morphology among the structures, social identity does not appear to be grammaticized through a wide diversity of grammatical structures, in comparison to grammatical resources for indexing time, space, and affective/epistemic stance.

Furthermore, other situational dimensions such as *social acts* and *social activities* are even less widely grammaticized. Thus while *act* meanings may be indexed through sentential mode, e.g. interrogatives (which might, in certain circumstances, for example, index that one is performing the act of asking a question), imperatives (which might, in certain circumstances, for example, index that one is performing the acts of commanding or reprimanding), and declaratives (which might, in certain circumstances, index that one is performing the act of asserting); relatively few grammatical structures directly index act meanings. Indeed a case could be made that interrogative, imperative, and declarative modes are not indexing act meanings but instead epistemic stance meanings, e.g. interrogative foregrounding relative uncertainty. (The relation between stance and social act meanings will be discussed in section 2.2.)

Similarly, while the use of specialized lexicons, e.g. legalese, may index particular social activities, e.g. a trial, it is difficult to locate grammatical structures that directly index activity meanings. Are there grammatical structures that directly index that one is having an argument, making a decision, giving directions, coaching, or attempting to solve a problem at hand? As will be discussed below, the indexing of social activities may be accomplished through the indexing of other situational dimensions, e.g. the indexing of narrative activity may be accomplished through the indexing of historical present time.

It is important to stress at this point that the assignment of situational meanings is a complex, interactionally accomplished process. Interlocutors have available to them a reserve of linguistic structures – some grammatical, others discursive – that are conventionally associated with particular situational dimensions. Interlocutors may use these structures to index a particular identity, affect, or other situational meaning; however, others co-present may not necessarily assign the same meaning. This circumstance is captured by Searle's distinction between illocutionary act

(act meaning intended by performer) and perlocutionary act (act meaning interpreted by others) where illocutionary and perlocutionary act meanings are not the same (Searle 1970). Cases of indexical breakdown have also been central to Gumperz's study of "crosstalk" wherein interlocutors project different contexts of situation from linguistic "contextualization cues" (Gumperz 1982). In some cases of crosstalk, the discrepancy in interpretation goes by unnoticed as interlocutors strive to interact as if they do understand one another. In other cases, mutual understanding may be sought and sometimes jointly achieved through conversational devices such as repair structures (Schegloff, Jefferson, & Sacks 1977) or other types of negotiation.

It is also important to note before going on that assignment of indexical meaning involves more than perception of a single linguistic form alone. Rather, the situational interpretation of any one linguistic form is an outcome of its relation to co-occurring linguistic forms in the prior and present discourse structure, to subjective understandings of the propositional content of the utterances thus far and of the activity those utterances are constituting as well as subjective understandings of gestures and other dimensions of the non-vocal setting (see Brown & Levinson 1979, Ochs 1988, 1990, 1992, Silverstein 1987).

Indexical knowledge is at the core of linguistic and cultural competence and is the locus where language acquisition and socialization interface (Ochs 1990). A novice's understanding of linguistic forms entails an understanding of their indexical potential (i.e. the situational constellations of by whom, for what, when, where and to what ends forms are conventionally employed) in co-ordination with co-occurring linguistic forms and other symbolic dimensions of the situation at hand. A novice's understanding of social order similarly crucially relies on an understanding of how that order is linguistically realized moment by moment over interactional time.

As early as the first year of life, infants begin to be attuned to the indexical meanings of particular structures. For example, infants confronting novel objects will monitor the voice quality and intonation of significant others (along with facial gestures) as indexes of their stances towards that object, an activity developmentalists call "social referencing" (Campos & Stenberg 1981: Klinnert, Campos, Sorce, Emde & Svejda 1983). This observation is supported by developmental phonologists, who note that children at the single-word stage can discern and respond appropriately to culturally relevant emotional stances indexed by diverse intonational contours (Cruttenden 1986, Halliday 1973, Peters 1977). Young children also grasp indexical meanings of morphological structures. For example, Platt's observations of children at the single-word and two-word stage in Western Samoa suggest that they have considerable understanding of the social rank indexed by specific verbs (Platt 1986). In particular, Samoan children grasp that the deictic verbs *sau*, 'come,' and *alu*, 'go,' can be used in directives only to inferiors, but that *aumai*, 'give,' in the imperative (begging) can be directed to kin regardless of status. As a consequence, Samoan children produce the semantically more complex form 'give' earlier and more often than the less complex forms 'come' and 'go.' Children at this stage of life appropriately address 'come' to animals, the only appropriate lower-status creatures. At this same period of development, Samoan children are able to appropriately switch between two different phonological registers and use competently the affect-marked (sympathy stance) pronoun *ta' ita*, 'poor me,' to index stance (Ochs 1988). Similarly, Kaluli children in Papua New Guinea master the affect-marked (appeal stance) pronoun *nel*, 'to me (appeal),' by two years of age (Schieffelin 1990).

Researchers have also observed that two- to four-year-old English-speaking children understand so-called indirect act meanings (e.g. indirect requests) indexed by co-occurring grammatical structures (e.g. indirect word order, pronouns) (Shatz 1983), and children as young as four vary linguistic structures according to social status of addressee (Shatz & Gelman 1973). By the age of five, English-speaking children understand and use productively linguistic forms that index social relationships such as doctor–patient, teacher–student, parent–child, and native–foreigner (Andersen 1977).

2.1 Indexical property of constitutiveness

The Sapir–Whorf hypothesis promotes the notion that language does not merely mirror "reality," it also shapes it. While deterministic interpretations of this generalization have been refuted, there lingers among anthropologists and sociologists of language the notion that nonetheless language does structure the phenomenological world. This notion is foregrounded in Austin's notion of performatives as verbal predicates that bring about social actions through their utterance (Austin 1962), in conversation analyses of how turn organization structures future interactional moves (Goodwin & Goodwin 1987; Sacks, Schegloff, & Jefferson 1974; Schegloff 1987), and in studies of how situationally bound linguistic forms bring into being particular social situations (Brown & Levinson 1979, Goodwin & Duranti 1992, Hanks 1990, Ochs 1988, 1990, 1992, Silverstein 1993). In some cases the linguistic forms may bring about the same situational definition for all participants but, in other cases, participants may use the linguistic forms to construct divergent situations (Gumperz 1982).

This property of language means that, when interlocutors use indexical forms, they may *constitute* some social structure in the immediate situation at hand. For example, in (2), Mauga uses the deictic verbs not only to indicate that she is of higher rank than her younger sibling, Matu'u, but also to bring that ranking into the situation at the moment. In using the deictic verbs, Mauga is both attempting to define her relationship with Matu'u and socializing Matu'u into the social indexical scope of these grammatical forms. When Matu'u complies with Mauga's directives to 'come' and 'go,' she ratifies Matu'u's definition of the relationship for that moment. This is not to say that all socialization is characterized by compliance and ratification on the part of the children and other novices. In some cases, novices (including children) struggle to redefine, i.e., to reconstitute, their relationship to more knowing members of the community. The important point is that interlocutors, including experts and novices, build up definitions of situations turn-by-turn, moment-by-moment, in the course of their interaction.

In this perspective, members of societies are agents of culture rather than merely bearers of a culture that has been handed down to them and encoded in grammatical form. The constitutive perspective on indexicality incorporates the post-structural view that the relation between person and society is dynamic and mediated by language. In an intellectual era that has brought paradigms such as practice theory and cultural psychology into academic parlance, we have come to entertain the notion that, while person and society are distinguishable, they are integral. Person and society enter into a dialectical relation in that they act on each other, draw upon each other, and transform each other. In such paradigms, while society helps define a person, a person also helps to (re)define society.

Socialization in this constitutive view is not a uni-directional transaction from member to novice but rather a *synthetic, interactional achievement* where novice is an active contributor. In this view as well, while language is a socio-historical product, language is also an instrument for forming and transforming social order. Interlocutors actively use language as a semiotic tool (Vygotsky 1978) to either reproduce social forms and meanings or produce novel ones. In reproducing historically accomplished structures, interlocutors may use conventional forms in conventional ways to constitute the local social situation. For example, they may use a conventional form in a conventional way to call into play a particular gender identity. In other cases, interlocutors may bring novel forms to this end or use existing forms in innovative ways. In both cases, interlocutors wield language to (re)constitute their interlocutory environment. Every social interaction in this sense has the potential for both cultural persistence and change, and past and future are manifest in the interactional present.

2.2 Indexical valences

Many pragmatic and anthropological linguistic studies of indexicality tend to focus on only *one* situational dimension associated with *one* set of linguistic forms. For example, several decades ago, Whorfian-inspired research tended to analyze a single ethno-semantic situational domain, such as time (Whorf 1956). Pragmatic studies within linguistics and philosophy also analyze lexical and grammatical systems that appear to index a single situational dimension, e.g. pragmatic studies of honorific systems that index social identity (Comrie 1976, Kuno 1973), evidential systems that index epistemic stance (Chafe & Nichols 1986), or performative predicates that index social acts (e.g. Austin 1962, Searle 1970). The situational dimension chosen for analysis is usually grammaticized or lexically expressed in complex and interesting ways. Further, that situational dimension seems to be the foreground semantic field – i.e., the conventional, recognized meaning – that is associated with those particular linguistic forms.

In all societies, however, members have knowledge of norms, preferences and expectations that relate particular indexical dimensions to one another. That is, in all societies, members have tacit under-standings of norms, preferences, and expectations concerning how situational dimensions such as time, space, affective stance, epistemic stance, social identity, social acts, and social activities cluster together. For example, the Rundi as described by Albert (1972: 82) expect high-ranking men in public settings to exhibit a detached stance:

Caste stereotypes represent those in the upper strata of society as never raising their voices or allowing anger or other emotions to show...That total, glacial silence of a perfectly immobile Mututsi who has chosen not to speak has to be experienced to be appreciated. To all appearances, the silence can be maintained indefinitely and in the face of every known technique of provocation, domestic or imported.

To consider another example, in middle-class American families, the role of mother is associated with the acts of eliciting and initiating family stories during family dinnertime (Ochs & Taylor 1992). Performing these acts is part of what is expected of a middle-class mother. Other acts associated with mothers of this social group include praising children and verbally guessing at their unintelligible utterances (Ochs 1988). One way of considering such cultural associations is to think of particular situational dimensions as linked to other situational dimensions through socially and culturally constructed *valences*. Somewhat like elements in a chemical compound, these valences show how a particular situational dimension is linked to other situational dimensions (e.g. among the Rundi, the situational display of detachment has valences that link it to high status). Fundamental to membership in a community is knowledge of the valences that link one situational circumstance to another.[5]

Because particular situational dimensions (e.g. particular stances, acts, statuses etc.) are linked through socio-cultural valences, the realization of any one situational dimension (e.g. the linguistic indexing of a particular stance) may invoke or *entail* (for members of particular communities) other culturally relevant situational dimensions (Ochs 1990, Ochs 1992, Silverstein 1993). While a number of studies of language use dwell on the relation of linguistic forms to only one situational dimension and ignore situational dimensions socio-culturally linked to that dimension, other studies – predominantly linguistic anthropological studies – consider a range of situational dimensions socio-culturally entailed by a set of linguistic forms (see Brown & Levinson 1979, 1987, Duranti 1984, 1990 Gumperz 1982, Hanks 1990, Haviland 1989, Ochs 1988, 1992, Sehieffelin 1981, 1990, Silverstein 1993). From a current linguistic anthropological perspective, indexicality does not stop at one situational domain. For example, for members of Rundi society, the linguistic forms that index an affective stance of detachment also index (because of socio-cultural valences that link situational dimensions) a particular social status. In other communities, reported speech forms (e.g. "they say") index more than an epistemic stance (indirect knowledge). Depending on community and circumstance within the community, reported speech forms may also index a range of situational dimensions including the act of reporting and/ or some degree of authoritative status of the speaker vis-à-vis the expressed proposition. Relations of entailment among situational dimensions may vary across social groups even within the same language community. For example, for certain patients in the United States, knowledge that some party is a medical doctor may entail the stances of being knowledgeable, objective, and caring, and a set of actions and activities (medical procedures). On the other hand, for the community of medical personnel, such entailments do not necessarily hold. Indeed medical personnel assume medical doctors will display a range of knowledgeability, acts, and activities, and, in certain contexts (e.g. in grand rounds), will scrutinize one another's stance and practices (Cicourel 1989).

It is important to distinguish the range of situational dimensions that a form (set of forms) *potentially* indexes from the range of situational dimensions that a form (set of forms) *actually* indexes in a particular instance of use (in the mind of any participating interlocutor – speaker, addressee, overhearer, etc). The indexical potential of a form derives from a history of usage and cultural expectations surrounding that form. When a form is put to use in dialog, the range of situational dimensions that particular form indirectly helps to constitute and index is configured in a particular way. Not all situational meanings are necessarily entailed.

Indexical valences and entailed indexicality are useful constructs in understanding linguistic relativity, for they are powerful linguistic vehicles for socializing novices into the cultural structuring of everyday life. Knowledge of entailed situated meanings of particular indexical forms offers a wedge into how members construe their local worlds. Language acquisition and language socialization can be seen as unfolding understanding of the indexical potential of particular linguistic forms and the skill to apply that understanding to construct situations with other interlocutors.

2.3 The centrality of stance

Section 2.2 stresses the point that situational dimensions are linked by socio-cultural valences (i.e. expectations, preferences, norms) such that the calling into consciousness of one particular dimension may culturally entail other relevant dimensions. A way of recouching relations of entailment that obtain among situational dimensions (for members of a social group) is to view situational dimensions entailed by some other situational dimension as components that help to constitute the meaning of that situational dimension. Thus, in the case of the Rundi, a component of the meaning of upper caste (social identity) is impassivity (affective stance) in public. Or the converse: a component of the meaning of impassivity (affective stance) is the social identity of upper caste (as well as any other social identity to which those stances are linked). Similarly, as noted earlier, in the minds of many patients in the United States part of the meaning of medical doctor (social identity) is the set of stances of being knowledgeable, objective, and caring, as well as the activity of diagnosis (Cicourel 1989). Or the converse: part of the meaning of the cluster of stances "knowledgeable, objective, and caring" is the social identity of medical doctor (as well as any other social identity to which those stances are linked). Likewise, particular temporal dimensions are socio-culturally linked to affective stances (Hanks 1990) and as such can help to constitute the meaning of particular affective stances. For example, for many speakers of English, the temporal dimension of the present moment, "now," may help to constitute a stance of affective intensity (as in the utterance "Now look at what you have done"). And as well, for many speakers of English, the stance of affectivity/intensity is part of the meaning of "now."

Any situational dimension (any temporal/spatial dimension, affective/ epistemic stance, social act, social activity, social identity) can in theory help to constitute the meaning of any other situational meaning. In this section, I focus on affective and epistemic stance and propose that these stances are central meaning components of social acts and social

identities and that linguistic structures that index epistemic and affective
stances are the basic linguistic resources for constructing/realizing social
acts and social identities. Epistemic and affective stance has, then, an
especially privileged role in the constitution of social life. This role may
account in part for why stance is elaborately encoded in the grammars of
many languages.

2.3.1 Stance as a component of social acts
2.3.1.1 Affective stance

In all communities, affective stances are socio-culturally linked to social
acts, in the minds of speakers (illocutionary acts), of hearers
(perlocutionary acts), or of both speakers and hearers. For example,
sadness may be conventionally linked to condolences, negative affect to
complaints, positive affect to praises, and so on. We can think of these
relations constitutively in the sense that particular affects help to constitute the meaning of particular acts. Where these affects are indexed by
a linguistic form, that form may also constitutively index associated
social acts. Example (3) illustrates an interaction between a Samoan
mother and child in which the selection of a particular variant of the
Samoan first person pronoun *ta 'ita* conventionally indexes the affective
stance of sympathy or love for the referent ('poor me'). This affective
stance, however, helps to constitute the meaning of the act performed in
(3), namely begging. In (3), the use of *ta 'ita* then not only indexes
sympathy/love, it also constitutes and indexes the social act of begging:[6]

> (3)   K (1 year 7 months) with mother, who holds food
>
> | K | Mother |
> |-----|----------|
> | ((crying)) *//mai /* | *//(leai) leai/* |
> | 'give (it)' | '(no) no' |
> | ((calls name of mother)) | |
> | | *'o le a* |
> | | 'what is it?' |
> | →   *(i)ta/* | |
> | '(for) dear me' | |

In Samoan, there are two alternate forms (*a'u*, 'I' and *ta 'ita* 'dear me')
for referring to the first person. Only *ta 'ita* indexes a sympathetic
affective stance. *Ta 'ita* is conventionally used by Samoan speakers to
both give and elicit sympathy. It is used to console and to appeal. In this
segment of interaction, K first uses the verb *mai*, 'give,' with a crying tone
of voice. These structures help to constitutively index a demand, which

the mother rejects. K then elicits his mother's attention again and utters the sympathy-marked pronoun *ita* (a form of *ta 'ita*). While foregrounding the affect of sympathy for self, this form in this context (i.e. following the expression of *mai*, 'give') transforms the demand into begging. If the child had used the more affect-neutral pronoun *a' u*, 'I', the act might not be necessarily interpreted as begging despite the child's use of crying. *Ita* alters the meaning of the utterance sequence to cumulatively mean something like 'Have pity and give it to this wretched soul.' A similar pronoun in Kaluli (Papua New Guinea), *nel* 'to me (appeal),' not only indexes sympathetic affect but is central to defining acts of appeal, and is frequently used by two-year-olds in appealing for the breast (Schieffelin 1990).

In much the same way as the affect markers *ta 'ita* in Samoan and *nel* in Kaluli are central to constituting the acts of begging/appeal, so the use of respect vocabulary in Samoan and many other languages may be a central affective component of requests. The potential range of act meanings entailed by respect vocabulary, as with other affective forms, is large. Depending upon other co-occurring structures and circumstances, interlocutors hearing a switch from everyday to respect vocabulary try to interpret the nature of the social act being constituted through this display of deferential affect. In the course of fieldwork, our research group was often visited by members of the Samoan community who knew us well and spoke to us informally. Occasionally these same folks approached using respect vocabulary. During these occasions, we came to understand that these expressions of deference (e.g. *maalie lou finangalo*, 'please your wish') were helping to constitute a request for an item of some magnitude such as a loan or a ride into town.

Linguistic structures that index affective **intensity** also help to define acts. In the examples below taken from American family interactions, intensity markers such as emphatic stress, loudness, syllable lengthening, intensifying adverbs ("freezing cold"), interjections ("BU::::RR"), as well as repetition, index not only affect but also the act of **complaining**:

    (4) Mother, Father, and Grandfather, and three children [Heddi, Sharon, and Kit] are eating dinner:

→	Heddi:	the PEAS are <u>CO:::LD</u>!
	Mother:	what ((*to Heddi*))
	Sharon:	((*while tapping plate with fork*)) [( )
	Kit	[mu mu mu mu mum
→	Heddi:	[these peas are cold!
	Mother:	(it won't hurt/okay) -
		((*to Father*)) were- were <u>your</u> peas [cold when you ate 'em?
	Kit:	((*Kit continues to struggle and whimper*))

Father:	I didn't eat 'em - I (haven't had/didn't have) any yet ((*pause*))
Mother	((*to Kit*)) just a <u>minu</u>te I'll get you some mo:re
→ Sharon:	BU:::[:RR!
?:	(what's a matter Sharon)
→ Sharon	bur[r these peas are cold!
Heddi:	[they're f- ((*as she looks into pan for more food*))
Mother:	oh=
→ Heddi:	=they're <u>freezing</u> co::ld!

Other examples, from this same family dinner, of affect intensifiers (e.g. emphatic stress) that help constitute complaints include:

(5) Heddi's complaint about the spare rib she is eating:

Heddi:	this huge thing, I <u>can't</u> even <u>chew</u> it ((*throws down bone on plate*))

(6) Father's complaint about the way in which Heddi is choosing a slice of cantaloupe from the serving bowl:

Heddi:	((*Heddi is searching bowl for a slice and looks several times to compare sizes with Sharon's slice*))
→ Father:	((*annoyed*)) <u>Pick</u> one Heddi and <u>stop</u> (this) diggin' around.

2.3.1.2 Epistemic stance

As noted earlier, epistemic stance includes qualities of one's knowledge, such as degrees of certainty as to the truth of a proposition and sources of knowledge, including perceptual knowledge, hearsay knowledge, commonsense knowledge, and scientific knowledge, among other phenomena. These stances in turn may be constitutive of social acts. For example, in example (7) below, the use of the epistemic indexical term "maybe" as a postscript to the earlier utterance "finish chewing and then you may talk" constitutively indexes not only relative uncertainty but also an act meaning something on the order of an implied threat or perhaps a warning:

(7) Mother, Father, and two children (Susan and Artie) are eating dinner. Susan talks with food in her mouth:

Mother:	((*deliberately, to Susan*)) finish chewing. and then you may talk
Artie:	((*takes a noisy gasp for air*))
→ Mother:	((*continuing in same tone of voice to Susan*)) <u>may</u>be

Samoan has a sentence-final particle e which functions in a similar way to this post-completion use of "maybe" in English, as illustrated in (8):[7]

(8) In a Samoan house, a mother is talking with one of her three
children who is acting selfishly towards his siblings.

Mother: *e*   *le*   *koe*   *fa'akau aa*   *mai*
          TA NEG again buy   EMPH DEICT.PRT
          aa   *sau*   *fagu e:!*
→   EMPH ANY.YOUR GUN EMPH

'she won't buy again any water pistol for you (unless you shape up)!'

Here the Samoan particle *e* marks a future world that might come true if
certain behaviors continue that the speaker does not condone. As with
the use of "maybe" in example (7), the particle helps to constitute the
utterance as a conditional threat or a warning. In both examples (7) and
(8), the speaker is threatening to possibly withdraw something the
addressee desires: in (7), to talk, in (8), to have a water pistol.

The recent monograph by M. H. Goodwin (Goodwin 1990) about the
discourse of pre-adolescent Black children vividly displays how these
speakers lace their utterances with epistemic forms that lend definition to
the act meanings in play. In (9) below, Ruby uses the epistemic verb
"know" both to constitutively index her certain knowledge about the
proposition "it's a free world" and to construct a **challenge** to Stacey's
possible assumption that "it's a free world" is news to Ruby:

(9)   Stacey: Fight yourself.
     Ruby: Well you **make** me fight myself.
     Stacey: I can't **make** you. Cuz it's a free world.
→   Ruby: I **know** it's a free world.   (Goodwin 1990: 154)

Similarly, the children used modal verbs such as "can" and "could" to
constitutively index not only the epistemic stance of possible or uncertain
worlds but also the act of **suggesting**, as displayed in the following
utterances:

(10)a.
→   Bea: We could go around looking for more bottles.

   b.

              ((*Discussing where to break bottle rims*))
→   Martha: We **could** use a sewer.
              ((*Discussing keeping the activity secret from boys*))
→   Kerry: We can *l*imp back so nobody know where we
              gettin' them from.   (Goodwin 1990: 111)

2.3.2 Stance as a component of social identity

As noted earlier, "social identity" encompasses participant roles, positions, relationships, reputations, and other dimensions of social personae. In all societies, these identities are conventionally linked to affective and epistemic stances. One way of considering affective and epistemic stances is to see them as perspectives independent of social identities, which members expect of those who hold those identities. For example, we might consider the stances of being knowledgeable, objective, and caring as perspectives independent of the social identity of medical doctor in the United States. Similarly, we might consider the stances of hesitancy and delicacy as independent of female gender identity in Japanese society (Cook 1988). On the other hand, another way of considering stances is to view them as not outside the category of social identity. They do not merely point to a social identity but rather *help to constitute* that identity. In the case of medical doctor, one may display the stances of knowledgeability, objectivity, and care to build a certain kind of medical professional identity. In radically different circumstances, a Japanese woman may display hesitancy and delicacy to create a female gender identity for the situation at hand.

In all societies, members may vary which stances they display and in so doing build different sorts of social identities. In Japanese society, females do not necessarily display hesitancy and delicacy in every situation but rather select when to display these stances. Women the world over may play up or play down their female gender identity. They build their social personae using stance displays variably within and across social interactions (Cook 1988, Ohta in press). In West & Zimmerman's language (1987), a woman may choose to "do gender" or "do being female" to varying degrees and in different ways. In like manner, one may opt for "doing being mother," "doing being son-in-law," "doing being grandparent," or even "doing being baby" (as when two-year-old "reverts" to a baby identity when an infant sibling arrives home from the hospital).

Fluidity in stance and social identity is characteristic of institutional interactions as well. For example, a medical doctor may vary his or her stances within the same interaction with a patient or with a medical peer to create different professional identities at the moment, e.g. shifting between stances of greater or lesser certainty to create more or less authoritarian professional identities (Cicourel 1989, Fisher 1991). Similarly, Jacoby & Gonzales (1991) document how the director of a physics laboratory in the United States and the graduate students within the laboratory fluctuate between the role of expert and that of novice by modulating their displays of epistemic stance from certainty to uncertainty even while on the same topic in the same laboratory meeting. Even in highly prescribed, formal interactions, participants have some fluidity in the social identities they enact. In highly formal decision-making councils (*fono*) in Western Samoa, for example, all the participants have the title of orator or high chief and each of these titles is ranked with respect to another tradition. Yet in any one meeting or even at any one point in the meeting, the participants may constitutively index themselves in a different, usually lower, status through the stances they linguistically and non-linguistically display (Duranti 1981).

3 The Universal Culture Principle

Section 2 of this chapter addressed "The display dilemma" (i.e., how does language display and socialize cultural knowledge?) by articulating ways in which linguistic practices index, constitute, and entail socio-cultural dimensions of situations. But what about "The scope dilemma" (i.e., what are the cultural boundaries of language socialization?)? Do these principles preclude the possibility of non-absolutive universals in the linguistic structuring of human culture? I think not. Culture is not only tied to the local and unique, it is also a property of our humanity and as such expected to assume some culturally universal characteristics across communities, codes, and users. Principle 2, the Universal Culture Principle, proposes that there are certain commonalties across the world's language communities and communities of practice in the linguistic means used to constitute certain situational meanings. This principle suggests that human interlocutors use certain similar linguistic means to achieve certain similar social ends. In this sense, the Universal Culture Principle is a limited (linguistic) means–ends principle. The principle is limited in the sense that it applies to some but not all indexical practices, in the sense that the common indexical practices may characterize many but not all communities, and in the sense that the indexical practices may give rise to unpredictable consequences; that is, linguistic means/social ends relations are inherently non-linear. Given these limitations, what is the basis for the Universal Culture Principle?

First, in all societies, linguistic forms are exploited to constitutively index the *general situational dimensions* of time and space, epistemic and affective stance, acts, activities, and identities (e.g. roles, relationships).

Second, within the dimensions of stance and social act, there are certain comparable categories of *stance and act meaning* across communities of speakers. For example, within the dimension of stance, epistemic categories such as relative certainty/uncertainty and experiential vs. reported knowledge are distinguished in many communities. Similarly, affective categories such as intensity/mitigation, surprise, positive and negative affect are indexed universally. Within the dimension of social act meanings, acts such as greeting, asserting, prompting, thanking, agreeing, disagreeing, accepting, rejecting, refusing, approving, disapproving, reporting, announcing, prompting, asking questions, and requesting goods and services appear across the world's communities. Furthermore, there are common valences linking stance and act meanings across communities. Certain stance meanings are common critical meaning components of social acts that characterize culture universally; for example, uncertainty is an epistemic stance component of questioning, negative affect is an affective stance component of rejecting; positive affect is an affective stance component of thanking.

As noted earlier, these commonalties do not necessarily imply that the full social meanings of particular acts or particular stances are shared across communities. Indeed in all likelihood the rich network of valences and entailments will not be shared (Gumperz 1982, this volume). The valences and entailments that link stances and acts to, for example, social identities and activities may or may not span local community boundaries, may characterize universal culture or may characterize local culture. Candidate universal entailments may include the following.

In the realm of *social identities*, relatively low rank may be universally linked to stances and acts of accommodation. Interlocutors may universally display lower rank through displays of attention and willingness to take the point of view of a higher-ranking party or otherwise meet that party's wants or needs. By implication, these same stances and acts of accommodation universally mark the other party's higher rank. Higher rank as well may be universally linked to rights to direct others through such acts as ordering and summoning. In the realm of *activity* entailments, disputes probably universally entail at least one act of disagreement and a display of negative affect (not necessarily reflecting an interlocutor's psychological state); clarifications probably universally entail the stance of relative uncertainty and either a request to restate a proposition, an assertion of noncomprehension, or a request to confirm/disconfirm a guess; planning activities entail at least some act (e.g. a suggestion, a directive, an assertion) that presents a method for responding to a present or future problem; and story narratives entail at least one assertion about a past event that is understood as part of a temporally ordered sequence of events.

A third dimension of the linguistic structuring of universal culture is that certain *linguistic forms* are used across a wide spectrum of communities to constitutively index comparable stance and act meanings. For example, in the domain of *epistemic stance*, indirect knowledge is widely indexed through reported speech predicates and particles (e.g. "says," "reports"); uncertainty is widely indexed through modals (e.g. "can," "could," "may," "might"), rising intonation, and interrogative structures; and certainty through factive predicates (e.g. "know," "realize"), determiners (e.g. "the"), cleft constructions and iteratives ("He's smoking again") (Levinson 1983). Candidate universals for the linguistic structuring of *affective stance* include the indexing of heightened affective intensity through the use of vowel lengthening ("It's co::ld"), modulating volume (as in shouting or whispering), modulating the pace of delivery (by speeding up or slowing down), switching to a marked form (e.g. using plural marking for a single referent, using demonstrative pronoun to refer to a person [in Italian, *quello*, 'that one,' instead of *lui*, 'him': Duranti 1984]), and code-switching between registers. Brown & Levinson's (1987) study of politeness indicates that numerous communities use similar linguistic forms to index affects of deference and sympathy. For example, sympathetic affect is widely indexed through diminutives (e.g. in Italian *orsettino*, 'cute little chubby bear,' versus *orso piccolo* / *piccolo orso*, 'little bear'), in-group address terms, and switching to a local variety.

Candidate universals in the linguistic structuring of *social acts* include the use of interrogative pronouns and syntax and rising intonation to constitutively index requests for information and requests for goods and services, the use of tag questions and particles to constitutively index requests for confirmations, and the use of imperatives and address terms to constitute summons (e.g. "Young man!") and orders. Further, probably all societies have affirmative and negative particles to constitutively index the acts of agreement and disagreement.

We will find candidate universals in the linguistic structuring of *social identities* and *activities* much less commonly than in the case of stances and acts. Universals in the linguistic indexing of social identities and activities are conditional in part on the extent to which identities and activities share similar stance and act components across communities and the extent to which these stances and acts are constitutively indexed through the same grammatical, lexical, and phonological forms across communities. A candidate universal may be the linguistic structuring of dispute activities to the extent that disputes entail a stance of negative affect and acts of disagreement and to the extent that negative affect and disagreement are constitutively indexed through such linguistic forms as negative particles and increased or decreased loudness. Another candidate universal may be the linguistic structuring of relatively low/ high rank to the extent that rank entails receiving or projecting a stance and acts of accommodation, particularly deferential stance and acts, and to the extent that deferential stances and acts are constitutively indexed through similar linguistic structures across societies, for example respect vocabularies, honorific marking, hedges, modals.

These suggested universals in the linguistic structuring of social life have implications for the scope of language socialization and for communication across community lines. I am convinced that children and other novices around the world enjoy a common ground of socialization experiences. With respect to language as a socialization tool, I am convinced that experienced and novice members of most societies use language in certain similar ways to co-ordinate their interactions and to index and structure their social environments. That is, children and other novices may well be acquiring common linguistic strategies for structuring social life regardless of the society in which they seek membership.

These commonalties characterize our humanity, our human culture. They afford, i.e. allow for the possibility of (Gibson 1979), a singularly human conversation in which some ways of displaying stances, some ways of acting, and some ways of meaning are recognizable as we traverse local borders. As each of us treads on "foreign" territory, we discern some common indexical threads that link us to one another as members of one human cultural fabric. The challenge to all cultural travellers is to go beyond these commonalities to recognize distinctly local ways of indexing and constituting social situations and cultural meanings.

4 The Local Culture Principle

The Local Culture Principle proposes that local culture is constituted in part by the myriad of situationally specific valences that link time, space, stances, acts, activities, and identities. (I am not trying to reduce the texture of local culture to these variables.) Culturally distinct patterns in stance–act–activity–identity relations lie in cultural expectations regarding (a) the *scope* of stances and acts associated with particular activities and identities, (b) the *preferences* for particular stances and acts within particular activities and for particular social identities, and (c) the *extent* of particular stance and act displays within particular activities and for particular identities.

4.1 Local scope

Local cultures may differ in expectations concerning the kinds of stances and social acts to be displayed in a particular activity or by a person of a particular status and/or in a particular social relationship among interlocutors. Thus while certain stances and acts associated with relatively low and high rank may be universal (i.e. accommodating stances and acts), others may be quite particular to a local group. For example, while the social identity of high chief in traditional communities in Western Samoa entails certain of the same stances and social acts of high-ranking persons across societies (e.g. receiving deference, rights to direct certain other parties to gain access to desired goods and services), other stances and acts are particular to Samoan chiefs. For example, in decision-making activities, chiefs have the right, and are expected, to express opinions to lower-ranking persons (in this case, orators), whereas lower-ranking persons are expected to make suggestions when invited to do so (Duranti 1981). For members of the Samoan community, the social identity of chief (and orator) has distinctly local act entailments. Another way of looking at this relation is to say that in this community, the act of giving an opinion in decision-making councils constitutively indexes the social identity of high chief. The act of giving an opinion in decision-making councils in other communities does not necessarily index and constitute such an identity or even high rank more generally. This particular constellation of act–identity valences/entailments is constitutive of local cultural knowledge that Samoan children eventually come to grasp and some may even come to challenge in light of their experiences in New-Zealand- and Australian-style school classrooms.

4.2 Local preference

In addition to differences in which stances and acts are linked to particular identities and activities, there are local differences in the stances and acts preferred by particular identities and for certain activities. For example, in the sequence of acts comprising the activity of clarification, language communities and communities of practice will differ in their preferences for one or another act strategy for achieving clarification of an unintelligible or partially intelligible message. These preferences may be across the board for all speakers and settings or may be tuned to specific situational conditions. In traditional communities of Western Samoa, speakers have available in their pragmatic repertoire all the clarification strategies listed earlier as possible universals. Certain of these strategies, however, are highly preferred and others highly dispreferred. In particular, in most circumstances, Samoan interlocutors overwhelmingly prefer either the act strategy of directing the party producing the unintelligible utterance to repeat or simply asserting non-comprehension and overwhelmingly disprefer the act strategy of verbally guessing the nature of the message (Ochs 1988). The dispreference for making an explicit guess is strongest in the condition where the party producing the unintelligible utterance is a young child. Of all the possible clarification strategies, explicit guessing requires the most cognitive accommodation in that the guesser presumably tries to assume the perspective of what the other may be thinking/intending, whereas simply stating that one does not understand or directing the other to repeat does not demand the same degree of accommodation. As noted earlier, accommodation is a stance/act that constitutively indexes actors of lower rank. In the case where the child produces the troublesome utterance, others co-present are higher rank than the child, rendering inappropriate acts of explicit guessing.

4.3 Local extent

Communities are particular not only in their preferences for one act or stance strategy over another vis-à-vis particular identities and particular activities but also in the *extensiveness* of those stance and act displays by those identities and in those activities. For example, members of communities the world over engage in prompting activities constituted by discrete acts of prompting. These same communities, however, may differ quite dramatically in the extensiveness of the prompting activities, i.e., how long and complex the prompting is in general and in particular situational conditions (Ochs 1990, Schieffelin & Ochs 1988). It is certainly one of the more frustrating experiences for language socialization researchers to report on the cultural import of prompting activities among the Kaluli or Kwara'ae or White working-class Baltimore families only to hear from a member of the audience that prompting goes on among mainstream American families as well. Yes it does. Indeed it goes on in all communities as far as we can see. What gives prompting a cultural importance among Kaluli (Schieffelin 1990) or Kwara'ae (Watson-Gegeo & Gegeo 1986) or White working-class Baltimore (Miller 1982) families, among other things, is its complexity and duration. In these communities, prompting talk covers pages of transcript and is used in triadic (A prompts B to tell C) as well as dyadic (A prompts B to tell A) interactions across a wide range of interlocutory relationships to elicit a vast range of stance, act, and activity displays. The use of prompts in mainstream American families pales in comparison: prompting activities tend to boil down to a two-turn prompt sequence between an adult and a child to display politeness ("Say 'thank you'") or in routines such as labeling objects ("say 'bird'"), or occasional prompts in dyadic or triadic interactions to facilitate a child's storytelling.

Scope, preference, and duration are three dimensions that characterize how "locals" choreograph language distinctly to index and constitute what people are feeling, knowing, and acting and how they are defining themselves as social identities. The steps of this choreography are particularly important for children and other novices to acquire and they do so by participating centrally and peripherally (Lave & Wenger 1991) in locally choreographed interactional "performances" from birth on. Through these interactions, children come to understand the locally entailed indexical meanings surrounding linguistic forms. It is this area of knowledge that seems so elusive to the culture-travellers, those who find themselves by accident, by choice, or by necessity living a multi-cultured life, perhaps without even moving outside their homes or neighborhoods. Cross-cultural communication tends to break down not because interlocutors do not understand one another at all, but rather because, from the perspective of one or another interlocutor, the stance or act display was not expected (a breakdown in the domain of "scope") or was unusual (a breakdown in the domain of "preference") or went on too long or not long enough for the particular social identity or activity underway (a breakdown in the domain of "extent"). Some understanding is shared but not all, and that difference between some and all makes a difference, generating the bases for culture shock and negative stereotyping.

5 Socializing humanity

The three principles of indexicality, universal culture, and local culture together suggest that indexicality is at the heart of language socialization. Even more strongly, the principles suggest that a theory of indexicality is a theory of socialization and that a theory of socialization is only as strong as the theory of indexicality that underlies it.

Additionally, the three principles indicate that language socialization is a more potent and more pervasive process than the reader might have imagined at the start of this essay. Language socialization is potent in the sense that, once novices understand that language has a constitutive potential, they have a semiotic tool not only for constructing a world that abides by historically achieved conventions but also for transcending that world to create alternative worlds for other interlocutors to ratify or challenge. We have only to look at the language of working women in management positions to see how their language practices constitute alternative conceptions of leadership in the workplace (e.g. decision-making as consensual versus authoritarian); or take a look at minority and female lawyers whose insistence on the use of personal narrative in legal argumentation challenges status quo expectations. Language socialization is potent in that it is our human medium for cultural continuity and change.

Language socialization is also pervasive. It is everywhere. All communities rely on language socialization to persist. All persons experience language socialization. What is more, language socialization is a lifelong enterprise. I have come to think of language socialization as a perspective on social interaction, rather than as a kind of social interaction. By this I mean that any social interaction can be examined for what transpires between a less and a more knowing party in terms of constituting knowledge and/or skills. In all of our interactions, we sometimes act as the knowing party (expert) and sometimes as the unknowing party. Or, as my research colleague phrased it, like yin and yang, there is an expert and a novice in all of us (Taylor 1991). Depending on topic and circumstance, we linguistically index/constitute ourselves as either one or the other. I might add, as a final note, that the socialization of a humane world depends on a continual human willingness to assume the status of novice as parents, as teachers, and as culture-travelers.

Notes

1 I am grateful to the following institutions for their support of this study: The National Institute of Child Health and Development (1986–90), The National Science Foundation (1986–90), and The Spencer Foundation (1990–3). This essay has also benefited from the careful reading of earlier drafts by Alessandro Duranti, Patrick Gonzales, Sally Jacoby, Carolyn Taylor, and the editors of this volume.
2 In posing the dilemma in this fashion, I do not wish to suggest that language socialization is exclusively a unidirectional process in which the language practices of competent members inculcate knowledge among novices. In the broader view of socialization held in this chapter, socialization is bidirectional in that the language practices of novices may socialize so-called "experts" as well as the reverse (see Ochs 1988, 1990, Jacoby & Gonzales 1991). Indeed it is the interaction of expert and novice language practices that generates knowledge and perspective among members of a social group at any one point in developmental or historical time.
3 A number of social scientists have examined different dimensions of indexicality and have created distinct terms in their analyses. The reader is referred to the essays of Bühler on "shifters" and "pointing words" (1934), Goffman on "keys," "frames" (1974), and "footing" (1981), Gumperz on "contextualization cues" (1981, 1982, this volume), Hanks on "deictic fields" and "deictic zones" (1990), Rommetveit on "co-ordinates" of the act of speech (1974), and Silverstein on presuppositional and creative indexicality (1987, 1992).
4 The transcription notation uses the following symbols.
Square brackets denote the onset of simultaneous and/or overlapping utterances, for example:

> Jimmy: a long time ago? - bout ((*tosses head*)) ten? - ten
> years old? - a:nd - the: [(Ja)
> Mother: [(that) wasn't <u>that</u> long

Equals signs indicate contiguous utterances, in which the second is latched onto the first; or an utterance that continues beyond an overlapping utterance:

> Mother: oh=
> → Heddi: =they're freezing co::ld!

One or more colons represent an extension of the sound syllable it follows ("co::ld"); underlining indicates emphasis ("<u>freezing</u>"); capital letters indicate loudness ("BU::::RR"); audible aspirations (hhh) and inhalations (.hhh) are inserted where they occur ("Go:d hh"); pauses and details of the conversational scene or various characterizations of the talk are inserted in double parentheses (((*pause*)) ((*TV going*))); items enclosed within single parentheses indicate transcriptionist doubt ("jus::t (pull it off)").

5 In cognitive science paradigms, these valences might be seen as structuring situational schemata (cf. Johnson 1987).

6 In Samoan child language transcripts using parallel columns to represent speakers' turns, the notation '/' marks the end of an utterance and '//' marks a point of overlap across turns.

7 TA marks tense/aspect; DEICT.PRT marks deixis: EMPH. marks emphasis: NEG marks negation.

References

Albert, E. 1972. Cultural patterning of speech behaviour in Burundi. In J. J. Gumperz & D. Hymes (eds.), *Directions in sociolinguistics: the ethnography of communication* (pp. 72–105). New York: Holt, Rinehart, & Winston.

Anderson, E. S. 1977. Learning to speak with style: a study of the sociolinguistic skills of children. Ph.D. dissertation, Stanford University, Palo Alto, CA.

Austin, J. L. 1962. *How to do things with words*. Oxford University Press.

Bernstein, B. 1964. Elaborated and restricted codes: their social origins and some consequences. In J. J. Gumperz & D. Hymes (eds.), *The Ethnography of Communication*. American Anthropologist, 66, 6, pt. II, 55–69.

Boas, F. 1911. Introduction. In F. Boas (ed.), *Handbook of American Indian languages*. Washington, DC: Smithsonian Institution.

Bourdieu, P. 1977. *Outline of a theory of practice*. Tr. R. Nice. Cambridge University Press.

Briggs, C. 1984. Learning how to ask: native metacommunicative competence and the incompetence of fieldworkers. *Language in Society*, 13(1), 1–28.

1986. *Learning how to ask: a sociolinguistic appraisal of the role of the interview in social science research*. Cambridge University Press.

Briggs, J. & Peat, F. D. 1989. *Turbulent mirror*. New York: Harper & Row.

Brown, P. & Levinson, S. C. 1979. Social structure, groups, and interaction. In H. Giles & K. Scherer (eds.), *Social markers in speech* (pp. 291–341). Cambridge University Press.

1987. *Politeness: some universals in language usage*. Studies in Interactional Sociolinguistics, 4. Cambridge University Press.

Bühler, K. 1934. *Sprachtheorie: die Darstellungsfunktion der Sprache*. Jena: Gustav Fischer.

Campos, J. & Stenberg, C. 1981. Perception, appraisal, and emotion: the onset of social referencing. In M. E. Lamb & L. R. Sherrod (eds.), *Infant social cognition*. Hillsdale, NJ: Lawrence Erlbaum.

Chafe, W. & Nichols J. (eds.) 1986. *Evidentiality: the linguistic coding of epistemology*. Advances in Discourse Processes. Norwood, NJ: Ablex.

Cicourel, A. 1973. *Cognitive sociology*. Harmondsworth: Penguin.

1980. Three models of discourse analysis: the role of social structure. *Discourse Processes*, 3, 101–32.

1989. Medical speech events as resources for getting at differences in expert–novice diagnostic reasoning. Paper prepared for the American Anthropological Association Meetings. Washington, DC, November 1989.

Cole, M. 1990. Cultural psychology: some general principles and a concrete example. Paper presented at the 2nd International Congress for Research on Activity Theory, Lahti, Finland, May 1990.

Cole, M. & Griffin, P. 1987. *Contextual factors in education: improving science and mathematics education for minorities and women.* Wisconsin Center for Education Research, School of Education, University of Wisconsin–Madison.

Comrie, B. 1976. Linguistic politeness axes: speaker–addressee, speaker–reference, speaker–bystander. *Pragmatics Microfiche,* 1(7), A3–B1.

Conklin, H. 1955. Hanunóo color categories. *Southwestern Journal of Anthropology,* 11, 339–44.

Cook, K. W. 1988. A cognitive analysis of grammatical relations, case and transitivity in Samoan. PhD. dissertation, San Diego: University California.

Cook-Gumperz, J. 1973. *Social control and socialization.* London: Routledge & Kegan Paul.

1981. Persuasive talk – the social organization of children's talk. In J. L. Green & C. Wallat (eds.), *Ethnography and language in educational settings* (pp. 25–50). Norwood, NJ: Ablex.

1986. Keeping it together: text and context in children's language socialization. In D. Tamen & J. E. Alatis (eds.), *Georgetown University Round Table on Languages and Linguistics 1985: The interdependence of theory, data, and application* (pp. 337–56). Washington DC: Georgetown University Press.

Crago, M. B. 1988. Cultural context in communicative interaction of Inuit children. Unpublished Ph.D. dissertation. McGill University, Montreal.

Cruttenden, A. 1986. *Intonation.* Cambridge University Press.

Duranti, A. 1981. *The Samoan fono: a sociolinguistic study.* Pacific Linguistics Monographs, series B, 80. Canberra: Australian National University, Department of Linguistics.

1984. The social meaning of subject pronouns in Italian conversation. *Text,* 4(4), 277–311.

1990. Politics and grammar: agency in Samoan political discourse. *American Ethnologist,* 17(4), 646–66.

Eisenberg, A. 1986. Teasing: verbal play in two Mexican homes. In Schieffelin & Ochs (1986b).

Engeström, Y. 1987. *Learning by expanding. an activity–theoretical approach to developmental research.* Helsinki: Orienta–Konsultit Oy.

1990. Activity theory and individual and social transformation. Paper presented at the 2nd International Congress for Research on Activity Theory, Lahti, Finland, May 1990.

Fillmore, C. 1982. Towards a descriptive framework for spatial deixis. In R. Jarvella & W. Klein (eds.), *Speech, place and action: studies in dexis and other related topics* (pp. 31–59). New York: John Wiley & Sons.

Fisher, S. 1991. A discourse of the social: medical talk/power talk/oppositional talk. *Discourse & Society,* 2(2), 157–82.

Gibson, J. J. 1979. *The ecological approach to visual perception.* Boston, MA: Houghton Mifflin.

Giddens, A. 1979. *Central problems in social theory: action, structure and contradiction in social analysis.* Berkeley: University of California Press.

Goffman, E. 1974. *Frame analysis. an essay on the organization of experience.* New York: Harper & Row.

1981. *Forms of talk.* Philadelphia: University of Pennsylvania Press.

Goodwin, C. & Duranti. A. 1992. Rethinking context: an introduction. In A. Duranti & C. Goodwin (eds.), *Rethinking context: language as an interactive phenomenon* (pp. 1–42). Cambridge University Press.

Goodwin, M. H. 1990. *He-said-she-said: talk as social organization among black children.* Bloomington: Indiana University Press.

Goodwin, M. H. & Goodwin, C. 1987. Children's arguing. In S. Philips, S. Steele, & C. Tanz (eds.), *Language, gender, and sex in comparative perspective* (pp. 200–48). Cambridge University Press.

Gumperz, J. J. 1981. *Language and social identity.* Cambridge University Press.

1982. *Discourse strategies.* Cambridge University Press.

Halliday, M. 1973. *Explorations in the functions of language.* London: Arnold.

Hanks, W. 1990. *Referential practice: language and lived space among the Maya.* University of Chicago Press.

Haviland, J. B. 1989. "Sure sure": evidence and affect. *Text,* 9(1), 27–68.

Heath, S. 1983. *Ways with words: language, life and work in communities and classrooms.* Cambridge University Press.

Hymes, D. 1972. On communicative competence. In J. B. Pride & J. Holmes (eds.), *Sociolinguistics* (pp. 269–85). Harmondsworth: Penguin.

Jacoby, S. & Gonzales, P. 1991. The constitution of expert-novice in scientific discourse. *Issues in Applied Linguistics,* 2(2), 149–82.

Johnson, M. 1987. *The body in the mind: the bodily basis of meaning, imagination, and reason.* University of Chicago Press.

Klinnert, M., Campos J. J., Sorce, J. F., Emde, R. N., & Svejda, M. 1983. Emotions as behavior regulators: social referencing in infancy. In R. Plutchik & M. Kellerman (eds.), *Emotion: theory, research, and experience* (pp. 257–85). New York: Academic Press.

Kulick, D. 1990. *Having head and showing knowledge: language shift, Christianity, and notions of self in a Papua New Guinean village.* Department of Anthropology, Stockholm University.

Kuno, S. 1973. *The structure of the Japanese language.* Cambridge, MA: Harvard University Press.

Labov, W. 1984. Intensity. In D. Schiffrin (ed.), *Meaning, form, and use in context: linguistic applications, GURT '84* (pp. 43–70). Washington, DC: Georgetown University Press.

Lave, J. & Wenger, E. 1991. *Situated learning: legitimate peripheral participation.* Cambridge University Press.

Leont'ev, A. N. 1981a. The problem of activity in psychology. In J. Wertsch (ed.), *The concept of activity in Soviet psychology* (pp. 37–71). Armonk, NY: M. E. Sharpe.

1981b. *Problems of the development of the mind.* Moscow: Progress Publishers.

Levinson, S. C. 1983. *Pragmatics.* Cambridge University Press.

Levy, R. 1984. Emotion, knowing and culture. In R. Shweder & R. Levine (eds.), *Culture theory: essays on mind, self, and emotion* (pp. 214–37). Cambridge University Press.

Lyons, J. 1977. *Semantics.* 2 vols. Cambridge University Press.

1982. Deixis and subjectivity: Loquor, ergo sum? In R. Jarvella & W. Klein (eds.), *Speech, place, and action: studies in deixis and other related topics* (pp. 101–25). New York: John Wiley & Sons.

Miller, P. 1982. *Amy, Wendy, and Beth learning language in South Baltimore*. Austin: University of Texas Press.

Miller, P. & Sperry, L. 1988. Early talk about the past: the origins of conversational stories of personal experience. *Journal of Child Language*, 15, 293–315.

Ochs, E. 1988. *Culture and language development: language acquisition and language socialization in a Samoan village*. Cambridge University Press.

1989. Language has a heart. *Text*, 9(1), 7–25.

1990. Indexicality and socialization. In J. W. Stigler, R. Shweder, & G. Herdt (eds.), *Cultural psychology: essays on comparative human development* (pp. 287–308). Cambridge University Press.

1992. Indexing gender. In A. Duranti & C. Goodwin (eds.), *Rethinking context: language as an interactive phenomenon* (pp. 335–58). Cambridge University Press.

Ochs, E. & Schieffelin, B. 1984. Language acquisition and socialization: three developmental stories and their implications. In R. Shweder & R. Levine (eds.), *Culture theory: essays on mind, self, and emotion* (pp. 276–320). Cambridge University Press.

Ochs, E. & Taylor, C. 1992. Family narrative as political activity. *Discourse and society*, 3(3), 301–44.

Ochs, E., Taylor, C., Rudolf, D., & Smith, R. 1992. Story-telling as a theory-building activity. *Discourse Processes*, 15(1), 301–40.

Ohta, A. in press. Evidentiality and politeness in Japanese. Los Angeles, CA.

Peirce, C. 1955. *Philosophical writings of Peirce*. New York: Dover Publishers.

Peters, A. 1977. Language learning strategies. *Language*, 53, 560–73.

Platt, M. 1986. Social norms and lexical acquisition: a study of deictic verbs in Samoan child language. In Schieffelin & Ochs (1986b), pp. 127–51.

Prigogine, I. & Stengers, I. 1984. *Order out of chaos*. New York: Bantam.

Rogoff, B. 1990. *Apprenticeship in thinking*. New York: Oxford University Press.

Rogoff, B. & Gardner, W. 1984. Adult guidance of cognitive development. In B. Rogoff & J. Lave (eds.), *Everyday cognition. its development in social context* (pp. 95–116). Cambridge, MA: Harvard University Press.

Rommetveit, R. 1974. *On message structure: a framework for the study of language and communication*. New York: John Wiley & Sons.

Sacks, H., Schegloff, E. A., & Jefferson, G. 1974. A simplest systematics for the organization of turn-taking for conversation. *Language*, 50, 696–735.

Sapir, E. 1963 [1927]. The unconscious patterning of behavior in society. In *Selected writings of Edward Sapir in language, culture and society* (pp. 544–59). Berkeley: University of California Press.

Schegloff, E. A. 1987. The routine as achievement. *Human Studies*, 9, 111–51.

Schegloff, E. A., Jefferson, G., & Sacks, H. 1977. The preference for self-correction in the organization of repair in conversation. *Language*, 53, 361–82.

Schieffelin, B. 1981. Talking like birds: sound play in a cultural perspective. In J. Ley (ed.), *The paradoxes of play* (pp. 177–84). New York: Leisure Press.

1990. *The give and take of everyday life: language socialization of Kaluli children*. Cambridge University Press.

Schieffelin, B. & Ochs, E. 1986a. Language socialization. *Annual Review of Anthropology*, 15, 163–246.

1986b. *Language socialization across cultures*. Cambridge University Press.

1988. Micro–macro interfaces: methodology in language socialization research. Paper presented at the American Anthropological Association Meetings, Symposium on Methodology in Psychological Anthropology. Phoenix, AZ, Nov. 1988.

Scollon, S. 1982. Reality set, socialization and linguistic convergence. Unpublished Ph.D. dissertation. Honolulu, University of Hawaii.

Scribner, S. & Cole, M. 1981. *Psychology of literacy.* Cambridge, MA: Harvard University Press.

Searle, J. 1969. *Speech acts. an essay in the philosophy of language.* Cambridge University Press.

Shatz, M. 1983. Communication. In *Handbook of child psychology (fourth edition)*, vol. III: *Cognitive development* (pp. 841–90). New York: John Wiley & Sons.

Shatz, M. & Gelman, R. 1973. *The development of communication skills: modifications in the speech of young children as a function of listener.* Monographs of the Society for Research in Child Development, 38, no. 152.

Silverstein, M. 1987. The three faces of "function": preliminaries to a psychology of language. In M. Hickmann (ed.), *Social and functional approaches to language and thought* (pp. 17–38). New York: Academic Press.

1993. Metapragmatic discourse and metapragmatic function. In J. Lucy (ed.), *Reflexive language* (pp. 3–58). New York: Cambridge University Press.

Talmy, L. 1983. How language structures space. In H. Pick & L Acredolo (eds.), *Spatial orientation: theory, research and application* (pp. 225–82). New York: Plenum Press.

Taylor, C. 1991. Socializing a belief system about language and self. Los Angeles, Department of Linguistics, University of Southern California.

Vygotsky, L. S. 1978. *Mind in society: the development of higher psychological processes*, ed. and trs. M. Cole, V. John-Steiner, S. Scribner, & E. Souberman. Cambridge, MA: Harvard University Press.

West, C. & Zimmerman, D. H.1987. Doing gender. *Gender & Society*, 1(2),125–51.

Whorf, B. L. 1941. The relation of habitual thought and behavior to language. *Language, culture, and personality: essays in honor of Edward Sapir.* Menasha, Wi, Banta.

1956. *Language, thought and reality: selected writings of Benjamin Lee Whorf*, ed. J. B. Carroll. Cambridge, MA: MIT Press.

14

WHEN ANIMALS BECOME "ROUNDED" AND "FEMININE": CONCEPTUAL CATEGORIES AND LINGUISTIC CLASSIFICATION IN A MULTILINGUAL SETTING

ELSA GOMEZ-IMBERT

1 Introduction

In this chapter I will describe a sociolinguistic situation existing in the Vaupés area of Northwest Amazonia and discuss its relevance for the issue of linguistic relativism.[1]

Linguistic exogamy is the name given to the unique marriage system of Eastern Tukanoan groups whereby some fifteen genetically related Eastern Tukanoan languages are brought into contact. This complex of Tukanoan-speaking groups is surrounded by Arawakan-speaking groups. Although linguistic exogamy and multilingualism are Tukanoan characteristics, some Arawakan groups on the border of this area also participate in linguistic exogamy by intermarrying with some Tukanoan groups. Linguistically speaking, the Eastern Tukanoan languages form a closely related group: systematic correspondences exist at all levels of linguistic analysis. However, they are typologically very different from Arawakan languages, with no systematic correspondences. It is a well-known fact about this area that Tukanoans and Arawakans have attained a high degree of cultural homogeneity through mutual influence and interchange (by trade, marriage, ritual, and verbal communication). As I will show, one major consequence of linguistic exogamy in the Vaupés is systematic, generalized multilingualism. This creates an unusual and potentially interesting contact situation between languages which can be either closely related (i.e. between Tukanoan languages) or radically unrelated (i.e. between Tukanoan and Arawakan languages), but whose speakers all share the same culture. This situation raises interesting questions for linguistic relativism. I will examine one linguistic aspect of the relation between language and culture, nominal classifier systems, in terms of the distance between the languages in contact.

2 The Vaupés groups

The traditional territory of the Eastern Tukanoan groups is the basin of the Rio Negro and its affluents – the main one being the Vaupés – together with the Piraparaná, a small affluent of the Apaporis river along the frontier between Colombia and Brazil. On the Colombian side, the population is estimated at some 20,000 inhabitants, 95 percent of whom are Indians. The Tukanoan groups live along the rivers in the central part of the territory and are surrounded by Arawakan groups, who also live along the rivers to the North and South of this area. This river people share this territory with forest people, traditionally nomads, known as Makú.

The languages spoken in the area are the following (see Fig. 14.1):

(a) TUKANOAN family: Bará, Barasana, Desana, Karapana, Kubeo, Makuna, Piratapuyo, Pisamira, Siriano, Tanimuka-Retuama, Tatuyo, Tukano, Tuyuka, Wanano, Yuriti;
(b) ARAWAKAN family: Baniwa-Kurripako, Kawiyari, Yukuna, and Tariana[2];
(c) PUINAVE-MAKU family: Kakua, Hupda.

Unlike the Arawakan groups, the Makú groups do not participate in linguistic exogamy because they are not considered as equals by the Tukanoans. Thus, in their case, there is both a linguistic and a social barrier between the groups.

2.1 Linguistic exogamy

Students of linguistic exogamy in the Vaupés have usually had a limited knowledge of the language involved, and this has given rise to a certain number of misleading ideas. Here is an example:

There are two crucial facts to be remembered about this community. First, each tribe speaks a different language – sufficiently different to be mutually incomprehensible and, in some cases, genetically unrelated ... Indeed, the *only* criterion by which tribes can be distinguished from each other is by their language. The second fact is that the five phratries (and thus all twenty-odd tribes) are exogamous (i.e. a man must not marry a woman from the same phratry or tribe). Putting these two facts together, it is easy to see the main linguistic consequence: a man's wife *must* speak a different language from him ... a third fact: marriage is patrilocal ..., and there is a rule that the wife should not only live where the husband was brought up, but should also use his language in speaking to their children (a custom that might be called "patrilingual" marriage). The linguistic consequence of this rule is that a child's mother does not teach her own language to the child, but rather a language that she speaks only as a foreigner ... The reports of this community do not mention any widespread disruption in language learning or general "deterioration" of the languages concerned, so we can assume that a language can be transmitted efficiently and

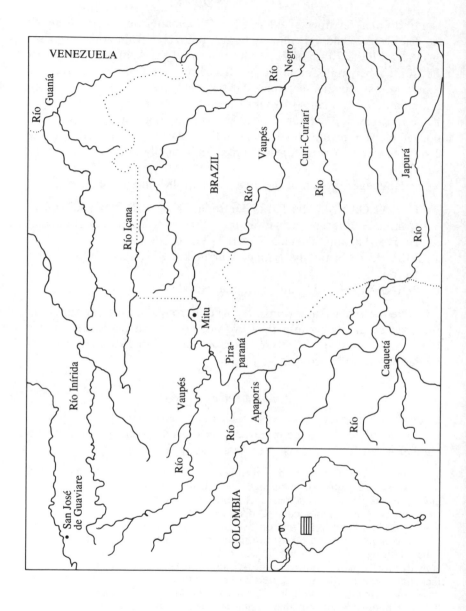

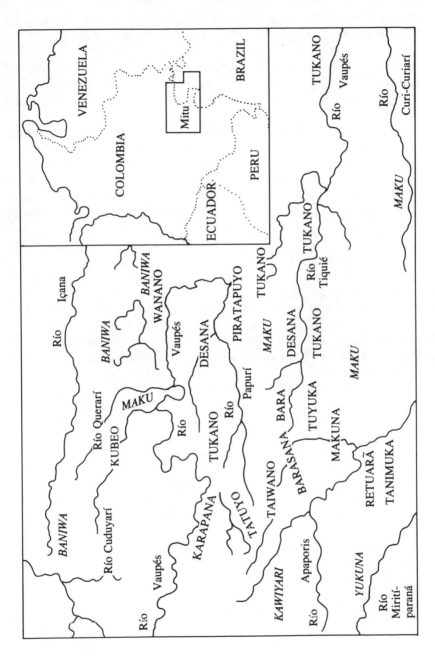

Fig. 14.1 *The Vaupés languages*

accurately even under these apparently adverse circumstances, through the influence of the father, the rest of the father's relatives and the older children.

(Hudson 1980: 8–9)

Anthropologists working in the Vaupés avoid the term "tribe" and prefer "sib," "language group," "exogamous group," and "phratry."[3] "Exogamous group" and "language group" both refer to the exogamic Tukanoan units, emphasizing their identity with respect to language or exogamy. Although there is an ideal correspondence between exogamic group and language group, there are exceptions. The Kubeo, Makuna, and Taiwano situations are among these. Kubeo speakers belong to three exogamous phratries, each composed of various sibs, that intermarry mostly among themselves but also with non-Kubeo speakers. Thus most Kubeo speakers also marry Kubeo speakers. The Makuna are made up of twelve sibs split up into two distinct intermarrying phratric categories, I and II.[4] Five out of the six sibs in category II are identified as Barasana sibs who speak Makuna.[5] Consequently, for category II sibs the Barasana are "brothers," while for category I sibs the Barasana are "brothers-in-law."[6] Thus the Makuna speakers in category I will marry both other Makuna speakers (category II) and Barasana speakers. Finally the Taiwano are an exogamous group who today speak Barasana, the language of their Barasana affines, but who claim that they speak a Taiwano language, different from Barasana. Taiwano is, in fact, a dialect of Barasana.[7]

These patrilineally defined exogamic/linguistic groups are units composed of a variable number of sibs or clans – ideally five, but usually more – arranged hierarchically according to a mythical birth sequence. Both linguistic/exogamic groups and sibs are named units, while the highest level of social organization relevant for exogamy rules, the phratry, is unnamed. Linguistic groups in the same phratry cannot intermarry, even if they speak different languages, because an agnatic relationship exists between them. Although there is agreement on the existence of phratries, nobody knows what their number is. However, a kinship term marking this relationship and its consequences for marriage rules makes it a real unit of Vaupés social structure. This organization, with phratries and exogamic sibs, is shared by the Arawakan Baniwa-Kurripako.

From the above it follows that ideally, though not strictly in practice, each exogamic group is identified by its language. People belonging to the same linguistic and/or exogamic group are patrilineally related; they are classificatory brothers and sisters and cannot marry within their own group. The basic rule is that one does not marry someone who speaks one's own language. The use of the father's language marks one's social identity and, furthermore, language is seen as the manifestation of an individual's essence. Thus, the communities in the Piraparaná river distinguish carefully between 'speaking' and 'imitating' a language: one can speak one's own (i.e. father's) language, but one can only 'imitate' other languages.

Linguistically, the degree of difference between the "languages" of these different exogamic groups covers a wide spectrum, ranging from mutual incomprehensibility – Barasana and Kubeo, for instance – to mere dialectal variations – Taiwano and Barasana, for instance. The Barasana and Kubeo live far away from each other and do not normally interact; the Barasana and Taiwano are close neighbors and affines engaged in intense exchange, and this situation has apparently led the Taiwano to abandon their own language for Barasana. Geographical subsystems, such as the one in the Paraparaná area, each involving fields of more intense exchange and interaction, are consolidated in this way, and the global tendency for languages of affinal groups within such systems is to become more and more alike.

The "deterioration" of languages in this intense contact situation is basically due to interference from the mother's language and affects the father's language. This "deterioration" is noticeable from one generation to another and adults strive to resist it. It is a consequence of the fact that the mother's language is the first language to be learned by children. In principle, women and men use their father's language throughout their life, and women speak their own language with their children during the first years of childhood – one of the main conditions for the persistence of multilingualism. Children use their mother's language until the age of five, approximately, and switch over to their father's language between five and six. However, I have observed some cases of reluctant children, who resisted switching to their father's language (even as late as the age of eight), in spite of the general pressure for them to conform. Socialization and a general agreement between the father's group and the mother is the key to success; these are the factors that lead the child to abandon progressively his mother's language and adopt exclusively his father's language, the mark of his or her identity.

Since marriage is patrilocal, the dominant language in a local community – traditionally a longhouse – tends to be the father's language; but each in-married woman has her own language and must use it throughout her life in all situations, particularly with her husband and children. Only under exceptional conditions do people switch to another language: either momentarily (for instance when quoting someone else, or in order to make oneself clearly understood, or perhaps for reasons of secrecy[8]), or definitely (for instance if someone grows up in a different linguistic community, or if a married man or woman finds him/herself linguistically isolated from his/her group – the man because he has chosen to reside with his affines, the woman because her own language, unknown to her in-laws, is a barrier to communication). These switches are evaluated in relation to the ideal situation where "each one speaks his/her father's language."[9] C. Hugh-Jones observed roughly the same patterns in code-switching (1979: 17), while Jackson's observations do not fit my own: "In the Vaupés, the rules which determine the selection of language do take into consideration situational constraints such as location, etc., but these rules always operate in conjunction with the particular father-language identities of the participants (as well as, of course, with other components of their individual identities, such as sex and age)" (1974: 58).

The marriage system is based on the exchange of real or classificatory sisters and involves preferential exchange relations between two groups – more precisely between sibs of equivalent rank from two exogamic groups. As a result, a man's wife's language is often his mother's language, and a woman's husband's language is often her mother's language.[10] In fact, through marriage, people often renew and reinvigorate their knowledge of their mother's language. This is the situation which prevails among the people I have been working with, Tatuyo and Barasana on the one hand and Kubeo and Baniwa on the other: for this very reason, they have been precious informants for comparative studies.

The mother's language is of particular importance, especially in a situation like that of the Kubeo and Baniwa. These languages are genetically unrelated, and typologically too far apart to be readily learned by adults (in general, it is a rather straightforward matter for a native speaker of a given Tukanoan language to learn another Tukanoan language). Thus I have seen Kubeo–Baniwa couples communicate in Spanish because they did not have a common language – a common mother's/father's language. Yet there are also couples who maintain both the Kubeo and Baniwa languages – even though a major family barrier separates them.

2.2 *The contact situation*

Linguistic exogamy creates a situation in which languages are permanently in contact. However, the intensity of contact is variable. Regional subgroups emerge on a geographical basis, and preferential relations develop between the linguistic/exogamic groups, reinforced by ceremonial, economical, and marriage exchanges. Thus, the Kubeo maintain close ties with their Tukano, Wanano and Baniwa neighbours, but only episodical contact with the Tatuyo or the Barasana. Roughly speaking, groups living in the same river basin are in closer contact than those who live in different basins: the Tatuyo and the Barasana maintain close ties among themselves and with the other groups from the

Piraparaná river; the same holds for the groups on the Vaupés river and its affluents, i.e. the Kubeo, Piratapuyo, Yurutí etc. (see fig. 14.1). In fact, contact is best seen as a chain of proximity.[11]

Linguistic exogamy, and the manifestation of patrilineal affiliation through the exclusive use of the father's language, entails that everyday verbal interactions are typically bilingual or multilingual. This multilingual setting raises the question of what defines a linguistic community. In the Vaupés, linguistic homogeneity is obviously not a definitional element; nor is the number of languages involved, because it varies according to the participants. It is a large shared background that warrants the success of verbal and cultural exchange: the culture is basically the same, and the languages are largely isomorphic.

There seems to be a requirement for the stability of the multilingualism associated with linguistic exogamy: the languages involved must be genetically related. Some facts seem to support this idea. First, I have been able to observe isolated cases of marriages between a (Tukanoan) Barasana or Tatuyo and an (Arawakan) Kawiyari. In this peculiar, and exceptional, situation, the in-married spouse, regardless of sex, ends up adopting the language of the host community. Second, there do exist cases of linguistic exogamy between groups speaking genetically unrelated languages. These have not been studied carefully, but in the case of the (Tukanoan) Tanimuka-Retuama and the (Arawakan) Yukuna, the evidence I have been able to gather suggests a "deterioration" of Tanimuka under the influence of Yukuna (e.g. loss of vowel /ɨ/[12] and a drastic simplification of the nominal classifier system). Thus, in these two examples, linguistic exogamy, which entails the persistence of multilingualism, does not seem to function.

There is, however, another case of contact between Arawakans and Tukanoans, in which linguistic exogamy does seem to work, contradicting apparently the requirement we stated above. This is the Kubeo–Baniwa situation.[13] I will use it as a case study of linguistic exogamy across genetically unrelated languages, in order to determine what linguistic conditions have made it possible. Although descriptions of these two languages are not sufficiently reliable and complete to allow systematic investigation, it will nevertheless be possible to make some relevant observations (see section 5).

2.3 The Kubeo and Baniwa relation

Today, the Kubeo intermarry with other Kubeo speakers, with other Tukanoan-speaking groups (such as the Wanano, Desana, Siriano, Yurutí, and Tukano), and with speakers of Baniwa. The intermarrying Kubeo sibs live on the Vaupés and Cuduyarí rivers; Kubeo sibs marrying

Baniwa people live on the Querarí river, an affluent of the Vaupés that constitutes the northern border of the Tukanoan area (see fig. 14.1). The Kubeo themselves claim that their relations of linguistic exogamy with other Tukanoan groups are recent and that their traditional alliances involved three exogamic Kubeo phratries, each made up of a series of sibs. According to their own oral tradition, the Kubeo-speaking sibs from the Querarí[14] came from the Isana and Rio Negro areas (the present-day territory of the Baniwa-Kurripako) some 200 years ago: chased from their territory by warrior groups of Baniwa-Kurripako and Ñekatú (Tupian family), they invaded the Querarí. The Kubeo groups already living on the Querarí were also warriors. To avoid fighting, they established relations of alliance based on the exchange of women with some of them, and with others, relations of "brotherhood" within a common phratry. Eventually, the invaders – who spoke an Arawakan language they call Inkaʃa[15] – abandoned their language and switched to Kubeo. Some of those communities still preserve ceremonial chants and spells in their ancient language. More generally, Arawakan influence on the whole Tukanoan area is clearly visible in the Tukanoans' use of ritual dance songs that are in Arawakan.

The first records we have on the Tukanoans and Arawakans emphasize the rapidity of cultural interchange and give examples of observed fast linguistic acculturation between these two families.[16] Cultural interchange among the Indian groups in the Northwest Amazon has been, and is still, viewed as an old and intricate process, not very well known, but whose result is a high degree of cultural homogeneity. This is particularly true of the cultural relations between Tukanoans and Arawakans, which have been described in the following terms:

Of more recent date and a more striking example of acculturation...is the Arawakan influence. In the relationships between Arawakan-speaking tribes and Tucanoans there has been the opportunity for massive interchange of cultural features, for apart from the ordinary modes of cultural influence, of trading, visiting, and intermarrying, entire social segments, usually sibs, it would seem, have been accepted as entities into one another's tribal organization. Since sib relations in the region are founded upon intensive reciprocal ceremonial participation, it is inevitable that entire ceremonial complexes will be exchanged once a foreign group has been drawn into the social structure. That the social structures will also become mutually compatible may be taken for granted. The student of Cubeo is almost instantly aware of the Arawakan influence, in vocabulary and in religious concepts. The Cubeo culture hero Kúwai is the Arawakan Kówai. The term for shaman and for jaguar, *yaví*, is shared by Tukanoans and Arawakans. As Koch-Grünberg was the first to observe (1909, I, 199ff.) the complex mourning ceremonies among Cubeo and among Arawakan-speaking tribes are also remarkably similar.[17]

Although there are no reliable statistics concerning the Vaupés population, it is clear that today only a small part of both the Kubeo and Baniwa speakers are involved in linguistic exogamy.[18] In spite of this reduced contact, I think that past intensive Arawakan influence on Kubeo, together with linguistic acculturation, could explain one remarkable morphological difference between Kubeo and the other Tukanoan languages. I will concentrate on this morphological difference in the following section.

3 Nominal classification

According to the relativistic hypothesis, language determines thought: the way we perceive the surrounding world and think about it depends on the language we speak. The Vaupés contact situation – where children learn at least two languages and two or more languages are normally used in communication – could offer a testing-ground for linguistic relativism. If the languages involved are semantically isomorphic, then multilingual speakers could simply be encoding in different languages a single way of thinking. But what if the languages involved are radically different? Will the people see reality under a different angle depending on the language they use? As already mentioned, some degree of linguistic isomorphism seems necessary for the persistence of multilingualism – and yet, linguistic differences pertaining to perceivable features of things in the world can exist in closely related languages, languages spoken by people who share the same physical and cultural environment, without apparent effects on communication. One wonders whether such differences influence the way people see the world.

We will concentrate in the rest of this chapter on a difference in nominal classification systems. Nominal classification is a prime example of a grammatical category assumed to strongly reflect human categorization. In Eastern Tukanoan languages, nominal classification has the following basic pattern:

(1) (a) there is a basic, grammaticalized distinction between "animate" and "inanimate" nouns;
   (b) the animate feminine classifier appears on faunal designations only when reference is intended to female members of the species;
   (c) shape classifiers appear systematically and exclusively on "inanimate" nouns.

While studying the faunal taxonomy of Kubeo, I discovered a striking morphological feature which violates the above Tukanoan pattern of nominal classification: it appears that in Kubeo most generic faunal designations can bear one of two markings: the feminine classifier or a shape classifier. For instance, the generic terms for 'deer' and 'armadillo,' which are inherently masculine and bear no classifier in the other Tukanoan languages, each have a different marking in Kubeo: 'deer' is 'feminine,' like women, and 'armadillo' 'round,' like fruit. In Kubeo, the morphology of faunal nouns seems to be a generalization of the standard Tukanoan morphology for "inanimate" nouns.

Because of the particular relation between the Kubeo and Baniwa groups, it is tempting to interpret this generalization as an Arawakan influence. Indeed, several facts do lend support to this hypothesis. First, Kubeo is the only Tukanoan language with this characteristic. Second, contact between Kubeo and Baniwa has a long history. Third, in Baniwa, animals are classified by shape. All of this makes the idea of "influence through contact" an appealing one.

However, the two classifier systems as they exist today are not isomorphic. One can also think of other hypotheses: the origin of this particular feature of Kubeo could be internal to the Tukanoan family – perhaps the remains of an old Tukanoan feature, or a spontaneous generalization of the system, yielding a new categorization. However, since nominal classification exists in both the Eastern and the Western Tukanoan branches (which are no longer in contact), it is possible to check whether Kubeo is the only Tukanoan language with this characteristic. If shape classification for animates were an old Tukanoan feature, other languages could exhibit it systematically; this is not the case. The explanation of origin by Arawakan influence is more plausible, since the Baniwa system of classifiers categorizes both animals and objects in terms of shape.[19] Considering the long contact history between these groups, my hypothesis is that because of the Baniwa (or Arawakan) influence, the original (Tukanoan) system of categorization in Kubeo for this particular semantic domain has been overlaid by a system which involves additional semantic distinctions which are morphologically marked in Baniwa. This will be my central hypothesis, since classification systems seem quite vulnerable in contact situations. Finally, I will try to conceive some internal dynamism responsible for that change, in relation to "affective" uses of classifiers observed in Yurutí, another Tukanoan language.

3.1 The basic distinction: animate vs. inanimate

Nominal classification is a fundamental Tukanoan[20] grammatical category. Categorization of entities in the world is indicated via morphological marking which is equivalent in all languages.[21] Basically, the system establishes a partition between animate and inanimate entities, with a single marker for the animate plural class (2a) as well as for the inanimate class (2b), in nominals such as the deictics. This is shown by the Tatuyo and Kubeo corresponding forms in (2) (classifiers are underlined):

(2) Deictics   a. animate   b. inanimate
                 proximal   distal   proximal   distal
   Tat.   áti-~bahá   i-~bahá[22]   áti-e   i-hé
   Kub.   i-dá   ~adí-dá   i-jé   ~adí-e

The deictics in (2) apply exclusively to non-individuated referents: (2a) may refer to any group of animate entities, while (2b) may refer to any collection or mass of inanimate entities.[23]

At the sentence level the same basic distinction is marked by agreement in predicates with third person subject: -~**ba** when animate (3a); -**bu** when inanimate (3b). Note that the deictics in (2) appear in the subject phrases in (3):

(3) Kubeo: subject   predicate
    (a)   i-dá   ~kodé-ßa   ~beá-da-~ba
               'these   woodpeckers   are good/nice'

    (b)   i-jé   ~idé   ~beá-bu
               'these   pupuña-fruit   are good/nice'

3.2 The feminine classifier

Animates are specified as either masculine or feminine when singular. This appears at the sentence level by subject agreement of the predicate, which distinguishes a masculine (4a–d) from a feminine (4e–h) subject in both Tatuyo (4a–b, e–f) and Kubeo (4c–d, g–h). The agreement is different when the subject has plural reference (4i–l), giving a concordial system of three elements for animates:

(4) Sentence: subject   predicate
    masculine
    Tat.   a. wekí   atí-~bí   'a tapir comes'
                  b. ká-~bahó-ki   atí-~bí   'a male-person comes'

    Kub.   c. ßekí   da-kí-be   'a tapir comes'
                  d. ~poé-ki   da-kí-be   'a male-person comes'

    feminine
    Tat.   e. wekí-ó   atí-~bó   'a female-tapir comes'
                  f. ká-~bahó-ko   atí-~bó   'a female-person comes'

    Kub.   g. ßekí-ko   da-kó-be   'a female-tapir comes'
                  h. ~poé-ko   da-kó-be   'a female-person comes'

    plural
    Tat.   i. wekí-á   atí-~bá   'tapirs come'
                  j. ká-~buhá   atí-~bá   'people come'

    Kub.   k. ßekí-ßa   da-dá-~ba   'tapirs come'
                  l. ~poé-ßa   da-dá-~ba   'people come'

(4) gives sentences with animal and human subjects for each case. The morphology of nominals in subject position illustrates some general

principles of the Tukanoan languages. Usually, common nouns with human reference exhibit a classifier in both masculine *-ki* (4b, d) and feminine *-ko* (4f, h) forms.[24] Nouns with animal reference have an unmarked generic and implicitly masculine form (4a, c), the feminine classifier *-o, -ko* appearing when reference is intended to the female of the species (4e, g). Because of an independent morphological constraint, faunal nouns exhibit classifiers only when they are nominalizations, as in the Tatuyo nouns in (5) where the classifier acts as a nominalizer of the verbal root *botí-*, 'to be white'.[25] Yet even in cases like (5) the masculine form (5a) is the generic term:[26]

(5) Derived faunal nouns:
    Tatuyo:
    (a) masc.   ∼*áá-bó-kí*   'cockerel'
    (b) fem.   ∼*áá-bó-kó*   'hen'
    (c) pl.   ∼*áá-∼bó-∼dá*   'cockerels/hens'
                 /*Tinamus* sp.-white-CL/

A first difference between Kubeo and Tatuyo concerns the use of faunal name marked for feminine as the generic term. In response to a question like "How do you say 'deer'?", a Kubeo will give the noun marked as feminine ∼*jabá-ko*, while a Tatuyo will give the unmarked form ∼*jaba*. Sentence (6a), where the subject noun is marked as feminine and the predicate shows feminine agreement *-ko*, would be used in Kubeo to refer to any 'deer,' even when it appears to be a male individual, i.e., it has horns. The equivalent sentence in Tatuyo is (6b), where the noun is unmarked and inherently masculine, as shown by the corresponding agreement marks on the predicate:

(6) Generic faunal nouns:
    Kub.   (a) ∼*jabá-ko da-kó-be*   'a deer comes'
    Tat.   (b) ∼*jabá atí-∼bí*   'a deer comes'

Thus, nouns marked feminine in Kubeo may have one of two different interpretations: in the case of nouns like 'tapir' (see 4) – which follow the general Tukanoan pattern – the feminine refers solely to the female of the species (4g), whereas in the case of nouns like 'deer' (6a) the feminine refers generically to the species 'deer.' This difference reveals another characteristic of the Kubeo system: some faunal names remain unaffected by this supplementary categorization.

3.3 Shape classifiers

We have shown the unity of the animate domain marked in plural deictics by a single classifier *-da* in Kubeo (2a). Singular forms exhibit a masculine

-*ki* and feminine -*ko* classifier on nominals with agreement on the predicate (4). Predicates with an animate subject exhibit the final morphemes -*be* and -~*ba* for singular and plural respectively. A single final morpheme -*bu* is found in the same paradigm when the subject is inanimate, with both collective (7d–e) or singularized (7f–g) reference. (7) shows the contrast between -*be*, 'animate,' (7a–c) and -*bu*, 'inanimate' (7d–g)

(7) Kub.:   subject   predicate

    (a)   ~*a-jí* ~*poé-ki*   *hoéßé-ki-be*
          'that   male-person   is a Tukano'

    (b)   ~*a-jó* ~*poé-ko*   *hoéßé-ko-be*
          'that   female-person is a Tukano'

    (c)   ~*kúú-ki*   ~*jebí-ki-be*
          'the earthworm   is black'

    (d)   *i-jé*   ~*idé-bu*
          'this   is pupuña *Guilielma gasipaes*'

    (e)   *i-jé*   *hi-ßeá-bu*
          'this   is my corn'

    (f)   *i-kí*   *hoé-ki*   ~*beá-ki-bu*
          'this   axe   is good'

    (g)   ~*bedé-*~*be*   ~*kihí-*~*bé-bu*
          'the *Inga* fruit   is small'

Other original Kubeo features are illustrated by the preceding sentences. First, a noun may function as the stem of a predicative word and bear the same inflection as a verbal stem: in 7(a–b) the nominal stem *hoéßé*, 'toucan' and in 4(c–d, g–h) the verbal stem *da-*, 'come,' exhibit the same suffixes; (7d–e) are also built up on nominal stems. Second, shape classifiers appear inside the predicative word: -*ki*, 'cylindrical' (7f) and -~*be*, 'thin filiform' in (7g). In Tatuyo, a copula is needed in forms equivalent to (7a, b, d, e, g), to support the verbal inflection, and shape classifiers are restricted to nominal constructions. Contrasting with the Tukanoan pattern, shape classifiers appear also in the predicate in Baniwa, as we will see.

The unity of the inanimate domain is marked on words like deictics (2b) and on the predicate (7d–g). In most nominal constructions, an important paradigm of classifiers appear whenever entities are singularized. These classifiers categorize entities mainly according to their shape and compactness: rounded, oblong/concave, cylindrical, tubular, flat, filiform, circular, reticular, etc.[27] The following are the most characteristic shape classifiers:

(8)

	Kubeo	Tatuyo	Barasana	gloss
(a)	-di	-a/-ka	-a/-ga/-ka	'rounded'[28]
(b)	-bo	—	—	'rounded bigger'[29]
(c)	-ka	-ro	-ro	'oblong/concave'
(d)	-ki	-i/-ki	-i/-gi/-ki	'cylindrical'
(e)	-jo	—	—	'cylindrical small'
(f)	-~ji	-wi	-bi	'tubular'
(g)	-~be	-~we	-~ba	'filiform'[30]
(h)	-~bu	—	—	'filiform thick'
(i)	-ße	-~pai	-~hai	'flat'
(j)	-~ku	-~toó	-~too	'bunch'

As can be seen in (8), the equivalences between Tatuyo and Barasana are almost perfect.[31] However, Kubeo differs in two ways: first, it introduces the feature "size" and distinguishes two kinds of rounded (8a–b), cylindrical (8d–e), and filiform (g–h) shapes. This distinction is found in Baniwa too. Second, the detail of the entities covered by each Kubeo classifier differs: for instance (8c) does not include concave/convex forms like in Tatuyo and Barasana; these are put in with 'bunches' (8j); in Kubeo (8f) classifies palm-trees together with tubular objects, while in Tatuyo and Barasana palm-trees have a specific classifier. In spite of these kinds of differences, correspondences between different Tukanoan languages are easily established by their speakers.

The three animate classifiers and the inanimate classifiers constitute a single paradigm which shows up in nominal constructions like deictics, quantifiers, and nominalizations.[32] The absence of definite and indefinite articles is to be related to the omnipresence of classifiers. The only nominal words where classifiers do not overtly appear in a systematic way are nouns.

While the presence of classifiers in the various nominal constructions is concordial most of the time, specific qualitative and quantitative operations accompany their appearance on nouns. Shape classifiers on nouns constitute a major lexicogenic device in all Tukanoan languages. A lexical stem may receive different classifiers which determine different agreement patterns. (9) shows a case from plant taxonomy:

(9)

	Kubeo	Tatuyo	gloss
(a)	~idé	ide	'pupuña *Guilielma gasipaes*'
(b)	~idé-~ji	~ide-~jo	'palm of G.'
(c)	~idé-di	~ide-a	'fruit of G.'
(d)	~idé-~ku	~ide-~toó	'bunch of G.'
(e)	~idé-ßi	?	'field of G.'
(f)	~idé-bóhi	~ide-kée	'leaf of G.'
(g)	~idé-jabé	~ide-ape	'grain of G.'

(9a) without classifier is the generic term for the species and has indefinite use.[33] The introduction of classifiers in (9b–g) is referential: it singularizes different manifestations of the species by assigning them a specific shape. Mass nouns are morphologically like (9a): they have no classifier and trigger agreement with "general classifier" *-je/-e* (2b). The derivational system yields nouns denoting natural entities as well as artifacts in the same derivational series, as shown by (10f):[34]

(10) Noun derivation in Tatuyo:

(a)	~*uju*	'avocado sp.'	(d)	~*bidó*	'tobacco sp., snuff'
(b)	~*uju-i*	'avocado plant'	(e)	~*bidó-i*	'tobacco plant'
(c)	~*uju-a*	'avocado pear	(f)	~*bidó-á*	'snuffbox (rounded)'

3.4 Shaping animals

Before examining shape classifiers on animal names in Kubeo, let us summarize the use of classifiers on nouns in a language like Tatuyo. The contrast is clear in the two sets of floral and faunal nouns, which are inanimate and animate respectively. In the case of floral nouns, a bare noun stem (10a, d) denotes the species, a homogeneous substance or a collection of individual entities produced by the species; it has a generic and non-singular interpretation. The name for the plant (10b, e) or the fruit (10c) is obtained by suffixing the appropriate shape classifier that singularizes an entity of the species. Thus, shape classifiers qualify 'rounded' and quantify 'unit' in words like (10c).

Faunal nouns without a classifier are inherently singular and masculine, as shown by the agreement pattern in (4a). A bare noun stem (11a below) is generic and has an indefinite use;[35] it also has singular referential value.[36] The feminine classifier *-o* is added only to refer to a single female animal, never for the species (11b). Female designations are usually used only for mammals. Thus masculine is the unmarked and feminine the marked class. Plurality is indicated by adding suffix *-a* (11c). Only in the case of nouns denoting small gregarious animals does the inflectional system change: the basic form is a noun stem that has plural meaning[37] (11e); to indicate a single representative of the species, a singulative suffix that is not a classifier is added: *-~bi* (11d):

(11) Tatuyo

	singular		plural
	masc.	fem.	
(a)	*weki*	(b) *weki-ó*	(c) *weki-á*
	'tapir'	'tapir-female'	'tapirs'
(d)	~*beká-~bi*	—	(e) ~*beká*
	'one-ant'		'ants'

The singulative Tukanoan suffix *-~bi* has no equivalent in Kubeo. Shape classifiers on faunal nouns in Kubeo operate singularization in the same way as that singulative suffix: the Kubeo emphasize the fact that when a classifier appears on a faunal noun the use of the numeral 'one' sounds odd, because it is redundant. Classifiers also introduce qualitative specifications for animals: most of them become -*di*, 'small rounded,' -*bo*, 'big rounded,' or -*ki*, 'cylindrical'[38]; some become -*jo*, 'small cylindrical,' -~*be*, 'thin filiform' or -*βe*, 'thin flat.' The feminine classifier -*ko* is also one of the frequent specifications acquired by faunal nouns, as illustrated in (6). This acquisition of classifiers by nouns is not exhaustive: some faunal names remain unclassified. Thus in Kubeo, faunal names split up into two groups: a morphologically unmarked group – like in all Tukanoan languages – and a classifier-bearing group, like natural objects and artifacts – contrary to the other Tukanoan languages.

Fish taxonomy gives an idea of the relative frequency of this procedure: for more than thirty-four fish names – including the life-form name – we counted ten -*ko*, ten -*di*, six -*bo*, three -*ki*, one -*jo*, one -~*be*, one -*βe*, and two unshaped. This rich classification fits well with the importance of fish in Indian life and diet: the Vaupés groups are essentially river people, fishermen and fish-eaters; hunting is a subsidiary activity.[39] This is true of all Tukanoan groups.

We will first examine the semantic motivation for assigning feminine and shape classifiers to faunal nouns; we will then consider the possible origin of this almost exhaustive shape and feminine categorization.

4 Semantic motivation for assigning shape to animals

4.1 'Feminine' animals

The search for semantic motivation of faunal classification calls for a brief remark on Tukanoan lexical categorization. In general terms, two parameters, based on the experience principle, distinguish all fauna as being either edible or non-edible, and as being harmless or dangerous. The designations for the main edible creatures are grouped under hypernyms, the two major ones being 'fish' and 'game' (literally 'mature fish').[40] Game are subdivided into 'flying creatures,' 'creatures that go from tree to tree,' and 'creatures that walk on the ground.' 'Flying creatures' includes the larger, edible birds; 'creatures that go from tree to tree' includes monkeys and other arboreal animals such as sloths, porcupines, and squirrels; 'creatures that walk on the ground' includes both small and large mammals. There is also a hypernym 'bird' which covers both small, inedible birds and pets, which are very important in Indian life.[41] Fish, game, and smaller edible creatures such as frogs and ants are all grouped together under a hypernym 'edible creatures' which contrasts with 'inedible and unpleasant creatures.' Although felines, or 'creatures that eat people,' are recognized as being similar to game, they are not normally included in that category.

I relied mainly on the answers given by Kubeo speakers concerning the semantic motivation for assigning feminine and shape classifiers to animals. As might be expected, informers sometimes give straightforward explanations but sometimes have no explanation to offer. The most interesting cases to understand semantic motivation are those of species classified as feminine. By assigning "femininity" to certain animals, some further connotative meaning, rather than sex specification, is added. (12) gives a sample of 'feminine' species:[42]

(12) classifier-ko:'feminine'	Kubeo		Baniwa
(a) 'deer *Mazama* sp.'	~jabá	-ko	(-na)
(b) 'fish (*yacundá*) *Crenicichla* sp.'	~deí.dókí	-ko	(-da/-apa)
(c) 'woodpecker *Picidae* sp.'	~kodé	-ko	(-da)
(d) 'bird (*pava*) *Penelope* sp.'	~bíó	-ko	(-apa)
(e) 'fish sp. (*mojarra*)'	~wadí	-ko	(-da)
(f) 'fish (*yacaco*) *Loricariid* sp.'	jaká	-ko	(-da)
(g) 'fish (*calochito cañero*) *Gimnotid* sp.'	bikóé	-ko	(-da/-kha)
(h) 'fish sp. (*caloche*) *Gimnotid* sp.'	húhi	-ko	(da/-kha)
(i) 'fish sp. (*caloche largo*) *Gimnotid* sp.'	~dudíta	-ko	(-kha)
(j) 'shrimp'	~dahó	-ko	
(k) frogs and toads (all species)		-ko	
(l) 'rodent (*tintín*) *Myoprocta acouchy*'	hibíka	-ko/-kí	(-apa)
(m) 'monkey (*waicoco*) *Callicebus* sp.'	waó	-ko/-ɵ	(-ita)

The only 'feminine' big mammal is the 'deer' (12a). In the Tukanoan languages 'deer' appears as prototypical of anything thin and spindly. Thus 'deer' is used metaphorically for (a) a thin wooden frame used in the preparation of manioc, itself a quintessentially female task, and (b) for the spindly praying mantis, a creature known for eating its male partner. The fish *yacundá* (12b) is used by the Kubeo (and Baniwa) god Kúβai to create his wife's sex; this fish is said to be particularly viscous because a couple made love lying on it in a canoe.[43] Again, in the mythology of the region, the *yacundá* fish communicates specifically with women using its salient mouth, an attitude which the myths link metaphorically to both lips and vulva.[44] Throughout the whole region, terms for 'woodpecker' (12c) are also applied metaphorically to the clitoris, establishing a clear relation between 'woodpecker' and "femininity." Woodpeckers are also employed by the god Kúβai to make his wife's body from a tree trunk. Animals and fish in this class are said to be thin and delicate. Note that varieties of the same species (12g–i) usually receive the same classifier. Thus, in addition to some specific cultural associations, woman-like behavior and appearance motivate this classification.

The *tintín* (12l) and *waicoco* (12m) cases are critical because different attitudes towards those species are marked by the use of classifiers: a woman may present them as feminine, while a man uses -*kí*, 'cylindrical,' in the former and no classifier in the latter, explaining that a woman may think of them as pets and talk emotionally about them (Indian women particularly affectionate [121] as a pet). We found similar occasional uses of classifiers to express emotional attitudes in the Yurutí language. Thus, a Yurutí speaker reported that classifying animals by shape is a strategy for modalizing purposes in speech, in situations like the following: (a) if, when fishing, a fisher brings up a turtle instead of the expected fish, he could call the turtle a *kúu-pe* (*-pe*, 'rounded thing') instead of the normal *kúu*; (b) if a deer startles someone by appearing suddenly, the person could call it ~*yábá-doto*, 'deer-bundle,' instead of the normal ~*yábá*. Returning to Kubeo, a woman with very thin legs may be called a ~*yábá-todi*, 'deer-trunk.'

These individual uses of classifiers to express human attitudes with respect to animals indicate that human perspective is a cue to understanding the system. We will examine the split between shaped and unshaped animals from this angle.

4.2 'Unshaped' animals

Some animals are 'closer' to human beings than others. This closeness makes them perceptually salient, and this is reflected at the linguistic level by unmarked forms. Salient properties should be related with physical appearance, behavior, or the sort of relation humans entertain with animals in everyday experience. According to this hypothesis, animals that remain 'unshaped' by a classifier would already be individuated because of their saliency, whereas animals 'shaped' by a classifier would need to be individualized by reference to some specific property. Thus, saliency would determine a straight individualized perception that locates some animals on a perceptive foreground, while others may remain on a perceptive background. This fits the general pattern of Tukanoan languages, where nouns referring to non-gregarious (salient) vs. gregarious (non-salient) animals are morphologically different (see 11). A representative sample of unmarked nouns is given in (13).

(13) Unshaped animals in Kubeo: Baniwa

    (a) 'jaguar *Felis onça*'   (*-na*)
    (b) 'tapir *Tapirus terrestris*'   (*-da*)/(*-na*)
    (c) 'peccary (*cerrillo*) *Tayassu tajacu*'   (*-da*)
    (d) 'anteater *Myrmecophagida tridactyla*'   (*-na*)
    (e) 'big rodent (*guara*) *Dasyprocta aguti*'   (*-na*)
    (f) 'opossum *Didelphis marsupialis*'
    (g) 'fish (*tarira*/*dormilón*) *Hoplias malabaricus*'   (*-apa*)
    (h) 'fish sp. (*pintadillo*)'   (*-kha*)
    (i) 'parrot *Amazona* sp.'   (*-da*)
    (j) 'toucan *Ramphastidae* sp. '   (*-apa*)
    (k) 'small toucan *Pteroglossus* sp.'   (*-apa*)
    (l) 'macaw (*guacamayo*) *Ara* sp.'   (*-apa*)

(m) 'parrot (*quinaquina*) *Pyrrhura picta*'	(-*apa*)
(n) 'howler monkey *Alouatta seniculus*'	(-*ita*)
(o) 'monkey (*maicero*) *Cebus apella*'	(-*ita*)
(p) 'sloth *Bradypus* sp.'	(-*ita*)
(q) 'monkey (*ulamán/mico-león*) *Eira barbara*'	(-*ita*)
(r) 'monkey (*churuco*) *Lagothrix lagotricha*'	(-*ita*)
(s) 'monkey (*chucuto*) *Cacajau* sp.'	(-*ita*)
(t) 'generic snake'	(-*kha*)

Size, as well as behavior, seems to be a property giving saliency; (13a–d) are all big mammals. The jaguar (13a) is the most impressive and powerful animal, very important in Indian life (a powerful shaman is called 'jaguar'). The tapir (13b) is the biggest mammal of the South American forest. The non-gregarious pig *Tayassu tajacu* (13c) remains unshaped, while the other peccary species (*Tayassu pecari*), which is gregarious, receives a classifier (-*ki*); thus behavior wins over size in this case as far as saliency is concerned. Size seems to be a relative criterion, as shown by the difference established between the two anteater species: the big anteater enters into the unmarked class (13d), while the small arboreal one (*Tamandua tetradactyla*) enters into the marked class (cl. -*ki*). The two fish in this group are the biggest ones in that area (13g–h); other fish are all shaped. Most small creatures are treated as non-salient, their names receiving a classifier: ants, termites, wasps, lice, fleas, harvest ticks, worms, palm-worms (cl. -*ki*); frogs, toads, grillons, lizards, shrimps (cl. -*ko*); spiders and mice (cl. -*bo*); bats, honey bees, *cigales*, crabs (cl. -*di*); sardines, *mandí* fish, humming birds, the small squirrel monkey species (cl. -*jo*). Two exceptions have been found to the equation small = non salient: fireflies and scorpions; but they are salient because of other properties. Some birds are also salient (13i–m), maybe because of their bright color – toucan, macaw – or because of their behavior: the *quinaquina* is an imitator.

The 'creatures that go from tree to tree' are all unshaped (13n–s) except the porcupine (-*di*), the squirrel (-*di*), and squirrel-like monkey species, the smallest monkeys (-*jo*). Monkeys are seen as having human-like behavior: Indians do not really enjoy killing them, and they are amongst the most dangerous game.

The preceding interpretation in terms of saliency is consistent with the idea that this additional faunal categorization is a generalization from a linguistically marked category with inanimate referents (natural objects and artifacts) to a category of animate non-human referents. Most animals become closer to inanimates in some respect, as if they were submitted to a perceptive rank demotion. The individual uses of shape classifiers for derogatory purposes strongly support this idea. The cultural selection observed may basically obey universal constraints intrinsic to the structure of the world and perception. Our interpretation supports Levinson's view (this volume) of "strong universal constraints and a moderately strong brand of linguistic relativity." Two aspects should be emphasized in relation to the relativistic hypothesis: first, the various categorizations expressed in Kubeo do not in any way determine on the part of Kubeo speakers a different attitude than the rest of the Tukanoans with respect to animals; second, other Tukanoans have no difficulty in mastering the Kubeo system when they learn the language.

5 'Shaped' animals in Kubeo and Baniwa

As we already suggested, some internal dynamism could be responsible for the extension of shape categorization to faunal names. Nevertheless, some aspects common to Kubeo and Baniwa point to a possible substratum in Kubeo of the Baniwa way of categorizing animals. We wish to argue now for a possible Baniwa origin of the Kubeo faunal shaping. In the preceding section we mentioned two common points between Kubeo and Baniwa: first, the appearance of shape classifiers on predicates; second, the use of the feature "size" to distinguish pairs of classifiers.

In Baniwa, classifier suffixes appear with numerals and in adjectival constructions equivalent to those introduced in (7f–g).[45] Semantically, the Baniwa system differs from the Tukanoan in that the distinction between animate and inanimate is not a basic parameter so that, for example, the same classifier may be applied to certain fruit and animals and also human beings. Baniwa combines gender and classifier markers: gender markers *-ri* (masculine) and *-zu* (feminine) combine with *-da*, the classifier for human beings or with *-apa*, the classifier for most birds. Compare the Baniwa predicates in (14) with the Kubeo ones in (7):

(14)

(a)	*matsi-da-ri*			'nice masculine (person)'
(b)	*matsia-da-zu*			'nice feminine (person)'
(c)	*apa-apa*	*dzaatte*	*matsia-apa-ri*	'one nice toucan bird'
	/one-cl.	toucan	nice-cl.-gender/	
(d)	*apa-apa*	*karaka*	*keeφe-apa-zu*	'a hen who is a good layer'
	/one-cl.	hen	lay-cl.-fem./	

The solution adopted by Kubeo seems to combine the basic Tukanoan semantic classification frame – i.e., a gender system – with the basic Baniwa system of shape classifiers.

Although there are no systematic correspondences between shape classifications in the two languages, another similarity exists between the two that makes Kubeo still more different from the other Tukanoan systems: for the rounded, cylindrical, and filiform shapes a distinction is made along a dimension parameter: small/big for rounded and cylindrical, and thin/thick for filiform (see 8). In Baniwa, there is a distinction between two kinds of rounded shapes: *-da/-apa*; trees are classified either by *-apu* (not in our list, denoting medium size) or by *-na* (denoting both age and large size) if the tree is bigger; and for some species the classifier changes as the animal grows (that is, changes in shape).

In order to allow a comparison of the two sets, we present the five Baniwa classifiers which categorize fauna:[46]

(15) Main Baniwa classifiers:
  (a) classifier *-da*: 'short-rounded'[47] includes human beings, some fish, some birds, and some mammals: the tapir when young, peccaries, paca, sloth, porcupine (*Coendu prehensilis*), armadillo, the *tintín* when young; turtle; rounded fruits: lime, pineapple; rounded body parts: head, testicle, eye, egg; stones;
  (b) classifier *-apa*: 'longer-rounded' includes all birds (except the few ones in *-da*); some fish; the *tintín* when adult; longer-rounded fruits: banana, cacao, *guama* (*Inga dulcis*), tubers like manioc (*Manihot sp.*)
  (c) classifier *-ita*: 'longer-flat' includes all monkeys[48]; generic fish; flat-shaped fish, shrimps, crabs; insects; knives, machettes, axes, paddles;
  (d) classifier *-kha*: 'thin-longer' includes all snakes and anacondas, long-shaped fish; caiman; vines; paths and rivers; cables, chains, thread;
  (e) classifier *-na*: 'thick-longer and old': the tapir when adult, anteater, deer, jaguar, *guara*, old trees.

Baniwa and Kubeo classifier correspondences are presented in (12) and (13) and in the samples below. Faunal classification in Baniwa seems much simpler than in Kubeo: all monkeys in the same class, all snakes and anacondas thin and long. The rounded shape classifiers in Kubeo are most frequently found on fish and bird names, as shown by the samples (16) and (17).[49] They correspond most of the time to the two Baniwa classifiers defined as rounded: *-da* (15a) and *-apa* (15b):

(16) classifier *-di*: 'rounded small'[50]	Kubeo	Baniwa
(a) 'fish (*jaco*) *Myleus sp.*'	*-di*	(*-da*)
(b) 'fish (*misingo*) catfish sp.'	*-di*	(*-da*)
(c) 'fish (*cuyucuyú*) *Doras sp.*'	*-di*	(*-da*)
(d) 'fish sp. (*aguadulce*)'	*-di*	(*-apa*)
(e) 'bird (*tente*) *Psophia crepitans*'	*-di*	(*-da*)/(*-apa*)
(f) 'parakeet (*patilico*) *Pionites melanocephala*'	*-di*	(*-apa*)
(g) 'parrot *Touit sp.*'	*-di*	(*-apa*)
(h) 'parakeet sp.'	*-di*	(*-apa*)
(i) 'bird swift'	*-di*	(*-apa*)
(j) 'bird sandpiper *Calidris sp.*'	*-di*	(*-apa*)
(k) 'fish (*mandí*) *Pimelodus sp.*'	*-di*	(*-ita*)
(l) 'fish sp. (*colarrojo*)'	*-di*	(*-ita*)
(m) 'armadillo *Dasypus sp.*'	*-di*	(*-da*)

Also: porcupine, squirrel, bat, owl, bee, crab.

(17) classifier -*bo*: 'rounded bigger'[51]
    (a) 'fish (*puño*) *Serrasalmo* sp.'   -*bo*   (-*da*)
    (b) 'fish sp. (*capaz*)'   -*bo*   (-*da*)
    (c) 'bird (*gallineta*) *Tinamus* sp.'   -*bo*   (-*da*)
    (d) 'rodent (*paca*) *Cuniculus paca*'   -*bo*   (-*da*)
    (e) 'mouse'   -*bo*   (-*da*)
    (f) 'turtle'   -*bo*   (-*da*)
    (g) 'bird (*paujil*) *Crax* sp.'   -*bo*   (-*apa*)
    (h) 'fish (*tucunaré*) *Cichla ocellaris*'   -*bo*   (-*ita*)
    (i) 'fish (generic *tucunaré*)'   -*bo*   (-*ita*)

The distinction between small and big birds is particularly clear in the preceding Kubeo samples. For fish, some dialectal variation exists in Baniwa.[52] The reason for the categorization of the generic terms 'fish' and 'bird' as cylindrical (18b–c), 'like a piece of wood' say the Kubeo, remains unclear; perhaps this is the ideal, standard shape for them. (18) shows a sample for cylindrical (small, thin and flat) shape:

(18) classifier -*ki*: 'cylindrical'	Kubeo	Baniwa
(a) 'fish sp. *guaracú*'	-*ki*	(-*apa*)
(b) 'generic bird'	-*ki*	(-*apa*)
(c) 'generic fish'	-*ki*	(-*ita*)
(d) 'snake (*cuatronarices*) *Bothrops atrox*'	-*ki*	(-*kha*)
(e) Also: generic terms for ants and insects.	-*ki*	

           -*jo*: 'small cylindrical'[53]

(f) 'monkey sp. (*tití*)'	-*jo*	(-*ita*)
(g) 'fish sp. *guaracú colarrojo*'	-*jo*	(-*apa*)

           -~*be*: 'filiform thin'[54]

(h) 'fish sp. (*mandí*)'	-~*be*	(-*ita*)

           -*ße*: 'flat small'[55]

(i) 'fish sp. sardine'	-~*ße*	(-*ita*)

The most frequent correspondence concerns rounded shape. The Kubeo 'rounded' classifiers -*di* (16) and -*bo* (17) correspond most of the time to Baniwa 'rounded' classifiers -*da* and -*apa*, occasionally to 'longer-flat,' -*ita*, but not to -*kha* nor -*na*. Seen from a Baniwa perspective, -*da* and -*apa* may correspond to -*di* and -*bo*, or have no corresponding classifier in Kubeo (see 13), the latter applying also to -*ita*, -*kha* or -*na*. For the Kubeo classifiers in (14) nothing significant can be said on the base of the Baniwa equivalences.

Two problems arise for our interpretation concerning the source of the Kubeo assignment of shape properties to animals. It cannot be considered a mere mapping of the Baniwa-like system for two reasons: the Kubeo assignation of shape classifiers is not a semantic copy of

Baniwa, as the preceding samples show; moreover, in Kubeo the shape classifier appears on nouns while in Baniwa it appears on numerals and adjectives.

A comparison of faunal designations in Kubeo and Baniwa shows term-to-term correspondences even if the number of lexical cognates is not very high: some 10 items out of 100.[56] In the following sample, the comparison with Tatuyo shows some of the Kubeo and Baniwa cognates (19a–d), and also cognates for the three languages (19e, f); in one case cognates are found for Baniwa and Tatuyo but not for Kubeo (19g). In contrast, the comparison with (20) below shows most frequent correspondences between Tatuyo and Kubeo.

(19)	Kubeo	Baniwa	Tatuyo	
(a)	*kadídí*	*kúrizi*	*wai.pɨ̈*	'fish (*pintadillo*) *Pseudoplatystoma* sp.'
(b)	*βaáβi-ko*	*wáaβi*	∼*biká*	'fish (*yacundá*) *Crenicichla* sp.'
(c)	*kúti*	*kútθiu*	∼*búpu*	'monkey sp.'
(d)	*kapáro*	*káapazu*	*héii*	'monkey (*churuco*) *Lagothrix* sp.'
(e)	*jaβí*	*jáaβi*	*jai*	'jaguar (*tigre*) *Felis onça*'
(f)	*jupádi-di*	*dúpari*	*dupári*	'fish sp. (*colarrojo*)'
(g)	*hoéβe*	*jáatθe*	*rahé*	'toucan bird (*chajoco*) *Ramphastus* sp.'

We must keep in mind that the Kubeo-speaking sibs who now marry the Baniwa were once Arawakan speakers. We may suppose that this fact, together with that of linguistic exogamy, has resulted in a set of Kubeo faunal designations which are morphologically different from those in the other Tukanoan languages. They also differ morphologically from the Baniwa designations but they share with them a semantic feature, namely that animals are specified by shape properties. The following list of Tatuyo, Kubeo, and Baniwa nouns shows how different the Kubeo nouns appear from both Tukanoan and Arawakan, because of the classifying suffixes:

(20)	Tatuyo	Kubeo	Baniwa	
(a)	∼*wádí*	∼*βadí-ko*	*jáβiza*	'fish (*mojarra*) *Cichlid* sp.'
(b)	*bóhó*	∼*hibíka-ko*	*púútθu*	'rodent (*tintín*) *Myoprocta acouchy*'
(c)	∼*kode*	∼*kodé-ko*	*kuφé*	'bird (*carpintero*) *Picidae* sp.'
(d)	∼*újú*	∼*ujú-di*	*púze*	'fish sp. (*aguadulce*)'
(e)	∼*tiíti*	∼*taití-di*	*máajari*	'bird (*tente*) *Psophia crepitans*'
(f)	∼*pabo*	∼*pabó-di*	*aarídari*	'armadillo *Dasypus* sp.'
(g)	∼*áá*	∼*aká-bo*	*máámi*	'bird (*gallıneta*) *Tinamus* sp.'
(h)	∼*hebe*	∼*hebé-bo*	*dáápa*	'rodent (*paca*) *Cuniculus paca*'
(i)	*bótéká*	*bodíka-ki*	*táári*	'fish (*guaracú*) *Leporinus* sp.'

In the first lists of Kubeo lexical items collected by Koch-Grünberg in 1904, shape classifiers already appear on faunal designations,[57] thus providing evidence that, if there was an influence of Baniwa on Kubeo, it is not very recent. The oral tradition of the Kubeo people who once spoke Arawakan says the contact and acculturation happened some two centuries ago, as we reported in 2.3. The comparison of faunal designations in Kubeo and Baniwa shows term-for-term correspondences, with the same genus and species categorization as the other Tukanoan languages, even if the stems are not cognates.[58]

A rough comparison of the two languages yields the following picture. Phonologically, Kubeo and Baniwa are totally different and no correspondence rules can be established between them. However, there exist in the lexicon lexeme-to-lexeme relations, at least in some semantic domains. These are domains classically studied in ethnolinguistic research, such as social categorization. When we say that there is an isomorphic relation between terms in both languages, we are well aware of the fact that although an isomorphic relation seems to hold between denotative meanings, connotative or metaphorical extensions may diverge.

For instance, in the case of social space, the same distinctions between categories of people are lexically marked. This applies in the case of:

(21) (a) people in a relation governed by marriage rules where distinctions are made between kin, affines, and affines of affines;
 (b) 'non people,' i.e., those on the fringes of, or beyond, the social space of the group concerned. Examples are: Makú groups who are classed as 'servants' and to whom both Kubeo and Baniwa refer as 'cigar lighters,' and White men.

Baniwa and Kubeo kinship terms systems share the same basic organization. They distinguish between parallel kins (which they frequently assimilate with patrilineal kins) and affines, amongst which bilateral cross-cousins are preferential marriage partners. The following terminological identifications are made:[59]

(22) (a) in the first ascending generation: father's brother = mother's sister's husband; father's sister = mother's brother's wife; mother's brother = father's sister's husband; mother's sister = ather's brother's wife;
 (b) in ego's generation: father's sister's son = mother's brother's son; father's sister's daughter = mother's brother's daughter;
 (c) in the second ascending and descending generation, no distinction between kin and affines etc.

The above examples of social categorization, kinship terminology, and faunal classification thus indicate rough lexical semantic equivalence, at least in domains where the cultural and ecological environment are highly relevant for the configuration of reference.

In the case of grammatical relations between Kubeo and Baniwa one cannot simply map features, units, or constructions straight from one language onto the other, as is the case for languages of the Tukanoan complex. When studying grammatical structures, a search for construction-to-construction correspondence is not a fruitful strategy. Some general characteristics are shared by both languages, like the distinction between absolute and dependent nouns – kinship and body-part terminology behaving in both languages as dependent nouns – and the existence of nominal classification.[60] Yet, as the exploration of classifiers shows, there exists a marked typological difference between them. Thus we have to decide on the basis of this partial comparison how commensurable the two systems are.

6 Summary

I have argued for an interpretation of the Kubeo "shape" and "feminine" classification of faunal taxonomy in terms of Arawakan influence. Given the multilingual setting I described, it is the most attractive hypothesis, when seen from the Tukanoan side. The fact that the regular Tukanoan pattern of nominal classification breaks down in those places where Tukanoans are in contact with Arawakans is probably not a coincidence. Nominal classification systems seem to be vulnerable in contact situations. In the classic Dyirbal case a four-class system with an intricate semantic motivation has changed into a semantically transparent three-class system, resembling an ideal gender system. The fact that young Dyirbal grow up speaking English primarily could account for that change.[61] As mentioned earlier, a similar situation exists between Tanimuka-Retuama (Tukanoan) and Yukuna (Arawakan), where the Tanimuka-Retuama inanimate shape classifiers have broken down into a minimally simple distinction between rounded/cylindrical/oblong/trees. Not unexpectedly, Yukuna also has a reduced system of numeral classifiers.

However, in the Kubeo–Baniwa contact situation the result has been a complication instead of a simplification. The crucial difference between the two cases might be the relation described by the descendants of the Arawakan warriors who arrived in Kubeo territory two centuries ago: these ancestors, belonging to the most prestigious culture in the area,[62] invaded the Kubeo territory; they established affinal or kin alliances with the Kubeo sibs. Children from the Baniwa–Kubeo marriages grew up with Kubeo mothers in Kubeo territory: their mother's language was Kubeo and their father's Baniwa. In such a context, it is not surprising that they ended up adopting Kubeo as their identity language.[63] Those bilingual children found themselves confronted with two different conceptual categorizations of the world around them – different, but not different enough to produce a breakdown of the system. In a certain way they continued 'thinking'

Arawakan when speaking Kubeo. Baniwa categorization in terms of animal shape would remain as a cognitive frame; and the pre-existing Tukanoan categorization of inanimate entities in terms of their shape would simply be generalized to animate entities.

The Kubeo–Baniwa example would demonstrate the indirect reproduction in one system of certain cognitive patterns from the other, in harmony with already existing patterns. This linguistic acculturation process would leave a substratum: a classificatory pattern imported into the Kubeo language by former Arawakan speakers; by diffusion, shape classification on faunal taxonomy has become a feature of the Kubeo grammar. The result is a similarity between Kubeo and Baniwa that is not shared by the other Tukanoan languages. This codability by extension, based on the Tukanoan system, seems to be at work when other Tukanoan people learn Kubeo: the Kubeo maintain that other Tukanoans show no difficulty in mastering Kubeo animal shape classification.

If my interpretation is correct, it lends support to a form of linguistic relativity at work: cognitive categories expressed in one language would be available in the speaker's mind to be matched in the language he adopts, provided that the same categories already have some expression in that language. A completely new category would probably enter the language through morphological borrowing. Direct borrowing of the Baniwa pattern would have meant a radical break and rearrangement of a basic semantic grammatical pattern in Kubeo. The adjunction of classifiers to noun stems could well be the only alternative way to combine the two different categorizations. According to this interpretation of the data, classifiers reproducing the Baniwa cognitive frame have been added in Kubeo to the only nominal construction which has no explicit and systematic marking in the Tukanoan languages: the nouns. We have seen that in Baniwa both gender and classification markers appear in the adjectival construction; this combination exists also in Kubeo. And the size distinction between rounded, cylindrical, and filiform shapes, which exists in Kubeo but not in the other Tukanoan systems, could also be of Baniwa origin.

When only Tukanoan languages are involved, their semantic isomorphism would make it possible for multilingual speakers to encode a single underlying categorization across the board in different languages. In the Tukanoan–Arawakan situation, however, the languages would be too different for this option to be available: to each language would correspond different underlying categorizations of the same reality; and it is tempting to interpret the Kubeo–Baniwa facts as a situation where multilingual speakers have continued 'thinking' in

Arawakan after having switched to Tukanoan. If my interpretation is correct, then some form of linguistic relativism seems to be correct. Nevertheless, the choices for animal shaping presented in 4.2 indicate that – whatever the origin of the Kubeo feature may be – strong universal perceptive/conceptual constraints are at work in the process of recategorization.

Notes

1 Parts of the research and writing of this paper were done in collaboration with Dr. Stephen Hugh-Jones (King's College, Cambridge) whose help and assistance is gratefully acknowledged. The maps I use are computerized versions of those in C. Hugh-Jones (1979) and S. Hugh-Jones (1979), elaborated by Tulio E. Rojas.
2 The Tariana live mainly in Brazil; although most of them are linguistically acculturated and now speak the Tukano language, some may have kept their language.
3 See for instance Jackson (1983: ch. 5), C. Hugh-Jones (1979: ch.2), Journet (1995: ch. 1).
4 Århem (1981: ch.5, table 3).
5 By C. Hugh-Jones (1979: 283).
6 Århem (1981: ch.5, tables 5–6).
7 The main difference between the language spoken by the Taiwano and the Barasana resides in the pitch-accent system.
8 For instance, a Kubeo whose mother's language is Baniwa reports that when visiting their Baniwa affinals who did not understand Kubeo, his mother switched to Kubeo when she needed to warn her children about something, and they resorted to Kubeo when they wished to exchange news about their relatives without being understood by others.
9 This idea is so strongly felt that the Kubeo who marry Kubeo women justify themselves by claiming that, even though they speak the same language, they are not, in fact, their sisters.
10 This does not mean that languages always go in pairs; for instance, the Tatuyo marry the Bará, the Barasana, the Taiwano, the Karapana, the Tuyuka, the Tukano, the Makuna, and the Yurutí.
11 Only exceptionally will a Tatuyo man marry a Kubeo woman because the two groups are too far from each other; nevertheless it is possible to meet Tatuyo who speak Kubeo fluently.
12 A high, back, unrounded vowel.
13 This language, which exhibits dialectal variations, is known as Baniwa in Brazil and Kurripako in Colombia. We use Baniwa-Kurripako or Baniwa alone, to distinguish it from another Arawakan language spoken in Venezuela and known simply as Kurripako.
14 Three Kubeo-speaking sibs are said to be of Arawakan origin: the Juré.~baβa, the Tarábíáβɨ, and the Jokákiβei.
15 It is not clear whether Inkaʃa was a Baniwa dialect or a separate language, but we can reasonably imagine that it was quite close to Baniwa.
16 These observations were made by Koch-Grünberg, who travelled in the Kubeo area in 1904.
17 Goldman ([1963] 1979: 14).

18 The estimations found in the literature for the Kubeo population in Colombia vary between 2,000 and 4,600 speakers. According to Simón Valencia, a Kubeo from the Querarí river, my collaborator on this work, only about 5 percent of the marriages on the Querarí river involve Kubeo and Baniwa speakers, for a total population of some 1,500 inhabitants on that river.

19 This is true for other Arawakan languages like Achagua, where, for instance, 'fish' are classified as 'oblong' (Meléndez 1989: 38).

20 Tukanoan is used hereafter for the Eastern Tukanoan branch. I will use Tatuyo and Barasana examples to illustrate the Eastern Tukanoan patterns.

21 My reference languages are mainly Tatuyo and Barasana. For the languages I have not studied systematically, I was able to check these points in teaching sessions with Indian teachers from the different Vaupés groups. My sources for Kubeo are mainly S. Valencia (1989) and personal work with this author and his sister; their father's language is Kubeo and their mother's language Baniwa.

22 In these two deictics, the noun 'people' acts as classifier in Tatuyo; but in most contexts, a cognate of the Kubeo classifier is found: $-\sim ra/-\sim da$. The symbol $/\sim/$ marks nasal morphemes; nasality is a phonological property of morphemes.

23 The sun, the moon, the stars, thunder, and rainbows – all living beings in the mythology – belong to the animate class along with human beings and animals. Inanimate covers the rest, including abstract notions.

24 The two exceptions I found in Tatuyo are 'shaman,' *kubu*, and 'baby,' $\sim cuá$.

25 A regular phonological process deletes the final syllable of *botí-*.

26 The expression equivalent to 'a hen's egg' has the generic masculine 'cockerel's egg.'

27 This is a very schematic presentation of the paradigm, which also includes, for instance, special classifiers for entities like pots, rivers, paths; quantitative classifiers grouping entities into rows, piles . . . , or dividing homogeneous substances into bags, tins . . . , and a number of lexical units that function as classifiers, like 'house' and 'garden.'

28 And 'small' in Kubeo.

29 "Compactness" is often associated with this classifier.

30 And 'thin' in Kubeo.

31 For instance, in Tatuyo, paths are not classified with filiform objects (classifiers $-\sim wa$ and $-\sim we$ respectively), while in Barasana they are grouped along with them (classifier $-\sim ba$).

32 Adjectival functions are expressed by nominalizations. Classifiers also appear suffixed to nominal stems indicating locative linking, possessive linking, and derogatory meaning. For a detailed description see Gomez-Imbert (1982).

33 It appears in sentences like: "I'm going to collect G," "Give me G.," "There is G," "It is G." See also (7d). It is also the form given in answer to the question: "How do you say: 'pupuña'?"

34 For details on plant taxonomy see Gomez-Imbert (1985).

35 It appears in sentences like: "How do you say: 'tapir'?," "I'm going to hunt tapir."

36 "I saw a tapir," "I killed the tapir," "The tapir ran away."

37 All these nouns end by an -a vowel, certainly the plural marker in (11c) that can no longer be segmented.

38 The 'masculine' and the 'cylindrical' classifier are homophonous in many contexts; they are nevertheless distinguished by agreement: thus, sentences like (7a, c) with the masculine classifier, and (7f) with the cylindrical classifier, exhibit different agreements. On faunal nouns, we first identified -*ki* as 'masculine,' but Kubeo speakers identify it quite systematically as 'cylindrical.' In a few cases they say it is not clear whether it is masculine or cylindrical. This ambiguity is common to the Tukanoan languages.

39 The importance of experience for folk taxonomy is now generally recognised. Hunn (1979, quoted in Hunn 1985: 121) reports that "Sahaptin speakers, who depend heavily on fish as a staple food, recognize 60 percent of the native fish species nomenclaturally but only 25 percent of the native bird species."

40 The Kubeo term is different, literally 'eaters' sons' (Spanish: 'hijos de los que comen'). The generic term for the anaconda is 'the eater.'

41 By extension, any pet is called 'my bird.'

42 I indicate the Baniwa classifier appearing on numerals in parenthesis, for further comparative purposes. The local Spanish name is given in parenthesis too. My Baniwa transcription is roughly phonetic, while it is phonological for Kubeo and Tatuyo. For Kubeo we follow the phonological analysis of Valencia (1989).

43 Its real name should be ~*doé.dokí* /vulva-viscous/.

44 See S. Hugh-Jones (1979: 265).

45 My sources for Baniwa are my own work with Luis E. Rojas, a Baniwa speaking the Isana dialect whose mother is Kubeo, S. Valencia, and Taylor (1991).

46 This list is not exhaustive; we enumerate the most characteristic entities included in each group.

47 I keep the glosses given by Baniwa speakers.

48 My informant explained the inclusion of monkeys by saying that their bodies are 'flattish and at an angle to the surface.' This classifier is identified as "animate masculine" by Taylor (1991).

49 Of twenty-four 'flying creatures' and 'bird' names, eight are -*di*, four are -*bo*, four are -*ko*, and eight receive no classifier; the generic 'bird' receives the cylindrical classifier.

50 Classifies rounded body parts: liver, heart, eye, testicle, penis, egg; all rounded small fruits; small stones, etc.

51 Classifies body parts: liver, testicle; big rounded fruits; big stones.

52 For example, the Gimnotid species (12g–i) were -*kha* for one informant but -*da* for another.

53 Classifies body parts: tooth, finger, bone, leg; objects: small flute, arrow, pencil.

54 Classifies thin vines, thread, veins, hair.

55 Classifies flat objects: paddle, knife, machette, arm, nail.

56 This is not a statistical account, for our sample is not an exhaustive list of the hundreds of faunal designations, but mainly those referring to small species, the most numerous in Amazonia. Nevertheless, it is representative of the shape classification system.

57 Koch-Grünberg (1913–16: 114–58).

58 Only incidentally did we detect differences like the following: while Kubeo (and Tatuyo and Barasana) marks lexically a difference between two species of the fish *yacundá*, it is not marked in one of the Baniwa dialects; but in another dialect the difference exists; besides, the former Baniwa dialect introduces a

new difference for another species of *yacundá*, nonexistent in Kubeo (see items 12g–i):

	Kubeo	Baniwa 1	Baniwa 2
'red *yacundá*'	βaáβi-ko	βáaβi	βáaβi
'*yacundá*'	~déí.dókí-ko	βáaβi	ketθínari
'green *yacundá*'	βaáβi-ko ~hibé-ko		júutari βáaβi

In the latter case, Kubeo adds a supplementary lexical specification: 'green one.'

59 This kinship terms system is characterized as "Dravidian type" (C. Hugh-Jones (1979:76), N. Journet (1995:152)). For a comparison, see C. Hugh-Jones (1979: ch. 4) and N. Journet (1995: ch.3).
60 These are widespread features in this lowland area.
61 This situation, described by A. Smith, is synthesized in Lakoff (1986).
62 This is said even in the Piraparaná stories: the Baniwa people brought for the first time weapons/clubs with iron ends; and even today they are the owners of, i.e., they make, the manioc graters, one of the most important tools in manioc processing.
63 The history of the Black Karib group, with Karib warriors invading the Caribbean islands, killing Arawakan men and marrying Arawakan women but eventually losing their language, is a parallel case. Linguistically, the result is an Arawakan language with Karib substratum (see Queixalos & Auroux 1984).

References

Århem, K. 1981. *Makuna social organization*. Stockholm: Almqvist E. Wiksell International Eds.

Goldman, I. 1979 [1963]. *The Cubeo. Indians of the northwest Amazon*. University of Illinois Press.

Gomez-Imbert, E. 1982. *De la forme et du sens dans la classification nominale en Tatuyo (langue Tukano orientale d'Amazonie colombienne)*. TDM 19. Paris: Université Sorbonne, Ed. ORSTOM.

  1985. Les classificateurs nominaux et la dénomination des espèces végétales en Tatuyo (Colombie). *Linguistique, ethnologie, ethnolinguistique: actes du Colloque International du CNRS (Sèvres, 1981)* (pp. 159–68). Paris: SELAF.

Hudson, R. A. 1980. *Sociolinguistics*. Cambridge University Press.

Hugh-Jones, C. 1979. *From the Milk River. Spatial and temporal processes in Northwest Amazonia*. Cambridge University Press.

Hugh-Jones, S. 1979. *The palm and the Pleiades: ritual and cosmology in Northwest Amazonia*. Cambridge University Press.

Hunn, E. 1985. The utilitarian factor in folk biological classification. In J. W. D. Dougherty (ed.), *Directions in cognitive anthropology* (pp. 117–40). Urbana and Chicago: University of Illinois Press.

Jackson, J. 1974. Language identity of the Colombian Vaupés indians. In R. Bauman & J. Sherzer (eds.), *Explorations in the ethnography of speaking* (pp. 50–65). Cambridge University Press.

  1983. *The fish people. Linguistic exogamy and Tukanoan identity in Northwest Amazonia*. Cambridge University Press.

Journet, J. 1995. *La paix des jardins. Structures sociales des Indiens curripaco du haut Rio Negro (Colombie)*. Paris: Institut d'Ethnologie, Musée de l'Homme.

Koch-Grünberg, T. 1913–16. Die Betoya-sprache Nordwestbrasiliens und der angrenzenden gebiete. *Anthropos*, 8, 944–77; 9, 151–95, 569–89, 812–32; 10/11, 114 58, 421–9.

Lakoff, G. 1986. Classifiers as a reflection of mind. In C. Craig (ed.), *Noun classes and categorization* (pp. 13–51). Amsterdam: John Benjamins.

Meléndez, M. A. 1989. El nominal en achagua. In *Orinoquía. Lenguas aborígenes de Colombia. Descripciones* (pp. 3–66). Bogotá: CCELA.

Queixalos, F. & Auroux, S. 1984. La geste caraïbe: langue et métalangue. In S. Auroux & F. Queixalos (eds.), *Pour une histoire de la linguistique amérindienne en France* (pp. 127–44). Paris: AEA.

Taylor, G. 1991. *Introdução à língua Baniwa do Içana*. Campinas: Ed. da UNICAMP.

Valencia, S. 1989. Fonología y clasificación nominal en Kubeo. Bogotá: Universidad de los Andes.

INDEX

Note: *Page references in italics indicate tables and figures*